T0235105

Lecture Notes in Computer Science 9863

Commenced Publication in 1973
Founding and Former Series Editors:
Gerhard Goos, Juris Hartmanis, and Jan van Leeuwen

More information about this series at http://www.springer.com/series/7407

Samira El Yacoubi · Jarosław Wąs
Stefania Bandini (Eds.)

Cellular Automata

12th International Conference on Cellular Automata
for Research and Industry, ACRI 2016
Fez, Morocco, September 5–8, 2016
Proceedings

 Springer

Editors
Samira El Yacoubi
University of Perpignan
Perpignan
France

Jarosław Wąs
AGH University of Science and Technology
Krakow
Poland

Stefania Bandini
Department of Computer Science
University of Milano-Bicocca
Milan
Italy

ISSN 0302-9743   ISSN 1611-3349   (electronic)
Lecture Notes in Computer Science
ISBN 978-3-319-44364-5   ISBN 978-3-319-44365-2   (eBook)
DOI 10.1007/978-3-319-44365-2

Library of Congress Control Number: 2016947928

LNCS Sublibrary: SL1 – Theoretical Computer Science and General Issues

Printed on acid-free paper

This Springer imprint is published by Springer Nature
The registered company is Springer International Publishing AG Switzerland

Preface

This volume contains a collection of original papers covering a variety of theoretical results and applications of cellular automata, that were selected for presentation at the 12th International Conference on Cellular Automata for Research and Industry - ACRI 2016, held in Fez, Morocco, September 5–8, 2016. The conference was organized by the University of Perpignan, IMAGES_Espace-Dev, the UMR 228 IRD UM UG UR "Espace pour le Développement", and the AGH University of Science and Technology of Kraków, Poland, in association with the International Systems Theory Network located in Morocco and represented by the University Moulay Ismail of Méknès. Its primary goal was to bring together researchers from a large variety of scientific fields in order to enforce international collaborations on cellular automata research as well as spread knowledge between experts in several scientific areas: pure and applied mathematics, computer science, physics, biology, and mathematical systems theory.

Cellular automata represent a very powerful approach to the study of spatio-temporal systems where complex phenomena are built up out of many simple local interactions. They are discrete, abstract computational systems that have proved useful both as general models of complexity and as simplified representations of non-linear dynamics in a wide range of scientific areas. In the last few decades, cellular automata have generated a great deal of interest both in academia and industry as they are attracting an increasing community of researchers working in different fields and dealing with theoretical aspects as well as practical applications.

The ACRI conference series was first organized in Italy, namely, ACRI 1994 in Rende, ACRI 1996 in Milan, ACRI 1998 in Trieste and followed by ACRI 2000 in Karlsruhe (Germany), ACRI 2002 in Geneva (Switzerland), ACRI 2004 in Amsterdam (The Netherlands), ACRI 2006 in Perpignan (France), ACRI 2008 in Yokohama (Japan), ACRI 2010 in Ascoli Piceno (Italy), ACRI 2012 on Santorini Island (Greece), and ACRI 2016 in Kraków (Poland).

From the start, ACRI conferences have constituted interesting biennial scientific meetings for researchers and innovation managers in academia and industry. They are dedicated to the expression and discussion of viewpoints on current and future trends, challenges, and state-of-the-art solutions to various problems in the fields of physics, biology, chemistry, communication, theoretical computer science, ecology, economy, geology, engineering, medicine, sociology, traffic control, etc.

This 12th ACRI conference aimed at widening the classical topics to include other areas related to or extending cellular automata. This offered a larger community the opportunity to discuss their work in various related fields such as: complex networks, lattice gas and lattice Boltzmann models, bio-inspired computing, agent-based models, etc.

This volume contains invited contributions and accepted papers from the main track and from the three organized workshops. We would like first to take this opportunity to express our sincere thanks to the invited speakers who kindly accepted our invitation to give plenary lectures at ACRI 2016: Anna Lawniczak from Ghelph University, Canada; Bastien Chopard from the University of Geneva, Switzerland; Bernard De Baets from Ghent University, Belgium; and Laurent Lefèvre from INP Grenoble, ESISAR, France. We regret that Raul Rechtman, from the National Autonomous University of Mexico, had to cancel his talk.

The submission and refereeing process was supported by the EasyChair conference management system. Each submission was reviewed by at least three referees and finally 45 articles were selected for oral presentation at the conference, from a total of 60 submissions. We express our gratitude to the Program Committee members for their excellent work in making this selection. We also thank the additional external reviewers for their careful evaluation. All these efforts were the basis for the success of ACRI 2016.

The whole book is divided into two parts. The first part deals with theoretical and computational aspects and the second one with applications derived from physical, biological, environmental, and other systems. Each part is partitioned into sections containing a number of papers arranged in alphabetical order. The first part is organized according to three topics: (1) Cellular Automata Theory and Implementation (2) Cellular Automata Dynamics and Synchronization (3) Asynchronous Cellular Automata and Asynchronous Discrete Models - ACA. The second part of the volume contains three topics: (4) Modelling and Simulation with Cellular Automata (5) Crowds, Traffic, and Cellular Automata – CT&CA (6) Agent-Based Simulation and Cellular Automata – ABS&CA.

The contributions from topics (3), (5), and (6) were selected within the organized workshops ACA, CT&CA, and ABS&CA respectively. On this occasion, we would like to express our sincere thanks to the workshop chairs for their very good and valuable work, specifically Stefania Bandini, Andreas Schadschneider, and Katsuhiro Nishinari for the workshop on Traffic, Crowds, and CA; Alberto Dennunzio, Nazim Fates, and Enrico Formenti for the workshop on Asynchronous Cellular Automata and Asynchronous Discrete Models; and Andreas Pyka, Giuseppe Vizzari, and Jarosław Wąs for the workshop on Agent-Based Simulation and CA.

It should be stressed that the realization of this conference would have been impossible without the help and continuous encouragement of a number of people, especially the members of Steering Committee who strongly supported the organization of ACRI 2016 in Fez, Morocco.

Many people contributed to the success of ACRI 2016 and to the accomplishment of this volume. Our first acknowledgement is to all the scientists that submitted their work, and to all Program Committee members and reviewers for their precious collaboration.

In particular, we would like to express our gratitude to the International Organizing Committee for their excellent work, as well as to the Local Organizing Committee from Morocco for their help with local logistics. A special mention goes to Franco Bagnoli, Abdelhaq El Jai, and Yves Maurissen for their strong involvement during the organization of this conference.

Finally, the organization of ACRI 2016 was made possible thanks to the financial support of the international Systems Theory Network, the Academy of Science and Technology in Morocco, the laboratory "ESPACE pour le Développement", UMR 228 IRD UM UG UR, the Institute of Research and Development-IRD, specifically the "Département Dynamiques Internes et de Surface des Continents" - DISCO, the University Moulay Ismal and the Science Faculty of Méknès, and other institutions and local authorities.

July 2016   Samira El Yacoubi
                                                             Jarosław Wąs
                                                             Stefania Bandini

Organization

ACRI 2016 was organized by the University of Perpignan and the UMR ESPACE-DEV associated with the Systems Theory Network, in Fez, Morocco.

Conference Chairs

Samira El Yacoubi	University of Perpignan, France
Jarosław Wąs	AGH University of Science and Technology, Poland

Workshops Chair

Stefania Bandini	University of Milano-Bicocca, Italy

Asynchronous CA

Alberto Dennunzio	University of Milano-Bicocca, Italy
Nazim Fatès	Inria Nancy-Grand Est, France
Enrico Formenti	Nice Sophia Antipolis University, France

Crowds Traffic and CA

Stefania Bandini	University of Milano-Bicocca, Italy
Katsuhiro Nishinari	University of Tokyo, Japan
Andreas Schadschneider	University of Cologne, Germany

Agent-Based Simulation and CA

Andreas Pyka	University of Hohenheim, Germany
Giuzeppe Vizzari	University of Milano-Bicocca, Italy
Jarosław Wąs	AGH University of Science and Technology

International Organizing Committee

Franco Bagnoli	University of Florence, Italy
Abdelhaq El Jai	University of Perpignan, France
Samira El Yacoubi	University of Perpignan, France
Thérèse Libourel	UMR Espace-Dev, UM, France
Maud Loireau	UMR Espace-Dev, IRD, France
Morgan Mangeas	UMR Espace-Dev, IRD, France
Yves Maurissen	UPVD, France
Frédérique Seyler	UMR Espace-Dev, IRD, France
Marie-Claude Simon	University of Perpignan, France

Local Organizing Committee

Larbi Afifi	University of Casablanca, Morocco
Abdelaaziz Belfekih	Faculty of Science and Technology of Tanger, Morocco
Abdes Samed Bernoussi	Faculty of Science and Technology of Tanger, Morocco
Ali Boutoulout	University of Meknes, Morocco
El Hassan Zerrik	University of Meknes, Morocco

International Steering Committee

Stefania Bandini	University of Milano-Bicocca, Italy
Bastien Chopard	University of Geneva, Switzerland
Samira El Yacoubi	University of Perpignan, France
Giancarlo Mauri	University of Milano-Bicocca, Italy
Katsuhiro Nishinari	University of Tokyo, Japan
Georgios Sirakoulis	Democritus University of Thrace, Greece
Hiroshi Umeo	University of Osaka, Japan
Thomas Worsch	University of Karlsruhe, Germany

Program Committee

Andrew Adamatzky	University of the West of England, UK
Ioannis Andreadis	Democritus University of Thrace, Greece
Jan Baetens	Ghent University, Belgium
Franco Bagnoli	University of Florence, Italy
Stefania Bandini	University of Milano-Bicocca, Italy
Olga Bandman	Siberian Branch of Russian Academy of Science, Russia
Abdes Samed Bernoussi	Faculty of Sciences and Technology, Tanger, Morocco
Bastien Chopard	University of Geneva, Switzerland
Alberto Dennunzio	University of Milano-Bicocca, Italy
Andreas Deutsch	Dresden University of Technology, Germany
Salvatore Di Gregorio	University of Calabria, Italy
Bernard De Baets	Ghent University, Belgium
Alexandre Dupuis	University of Geneva, Switzerland
Pedro de Oliveira	Universidade Presbiteriana Mackenzie, Brazil
Michel Droz	University of Geneva, Switzerland
Witold Dzwinel	AGH University of Science and Technology, Poland
Abdelhaq El Jai	University of Perpignan, France
Samira El Yacoubi	University of Perpignan, France
Nazim Fatès	Inria Nancy, Grand Est, France
Enrico Formenti	University of Nice, France
Ioakeim Georgoudas	Democritus University of Thrace, Greece

Sebastien Gourbiere	University of Perpignan, France
Rolf Hoffmann	University of Darmstadt, Germany
Francisco Jiménez Morales	University of Santa Clara, Spain
Jaap Kaandorp	University of Amsterdam, The Netherlands
Toshihiko Komatsuzaki	Kanazawa University, Japan
Krzysztof Kułakowski	AGH University of Science and Technology, Poland
Martin Kutrib	Universität Gießen, Germany
Anna Lawniczak	Guelph University, Canada
Laurent Lefevre	University of Grenoble, France
Sara Manzoni	University of Milano-Bicocca, Italy
Genaro J. Martínez	National Polytechnic Institute, Mexico
Morgan Mangeas	IRD, France
Giancarlo Mauri	University of Milano-Bicocca, Italy
Angelo Mingarelli	Carleton University, Canada
Shin Morishita	Yokohama National University, Japan
Katsuhiro Nishinari	University of Tokyo, Japan
Abdennebi Omrane	University of Guyane, Guyane
Paola Rizzi	University of Sassari, Italy
Emmanuel Roux	IRD, France
Dipanwita Roy Chowdhury	Indian Institute of Technology, India
Roberto Serra	University of Modena and Reggio Emilia, Italy
Biplab K. Sikdar	Bengal Engineering and Science University, India
Marie-Claude Simon	University of Perpignan, France
Georgios Ch. Sirakoulis	Democritus University of Thrace, Greece
Domenico Talia	University of Calabria, Italy
Marco Tomassini	University of Lausanne, Switzerland
Paweł Topa	AGH University of Science and Technology, Poland
Leen Torenvliet	University of Amsterdam, The Netherlands
Abdessamad Tridane	University of Arab Emirates, UAE
Hiroshi Umeo	University of Osaka Electro-Communication, Japan
Giuseppe Vizzari	University of Milano-Bicocca, Italy
Gabriel Wainer	Carleton University, Canada
Jarosław Wąs	AGH University of Science and Technology, Poland
Thomas Worsch	University of Karlsruhe, Germany
Radouane Yafia	University Ibn Zohr, Morocco

Workshop Program Committees

Asynchronous CA – Program Committee

Luís Correia	Lisbon University, Portugal
Alberto Dennunzio	University of Milano-Bicocca, Italy
Nazim Fatès	Inria Nancy, France
Enrico Formenti	Nice Sophia Antipolis University, France
Henryk Fukś	Brock University, Canada
Maximilien Gaudouleau	University of Durham, UK

Eric Goles	Universidad Adolfo Ibáñez, Chile
Adrien Richard	CNRS and Nice Sophia Antipolis University, France
Thomas Worsch	University of Karlsruhe, Germany

Crowds, Traffic, and CA – Program Committee

Andrew Adamatzky	University of the West of England, UK
Cecile Appert-Rolland	Orsay, France
Dietmar Bauer	Arsenal Research Vienna
Henryk Fukś	Brock University, Canada
Rui Jiang	University of Science and Technology of China, China
Makoto Kikuchi	Osaka University, Japan
Franziska Klügl	Örebro University, Sweden
Gerta Köster	Munich University of Applied Sciences, Germany
Tobias Kretz	PTV AG, Germany
Sven Maerivoet	Transport and Mobility Leuven, Belgium
Shin Morishita	Yokohama National University, Japan
Michael Schreckenberg	Duisburg University, Germany
Armin Seyfried	Jülich Supercomputing Centre, Germany
Georgios Sirakoulis	Democritus University of Thrace, Greece
WeiGuo Song	University of Science and Technology of China, China
Shin-ichi Tadaki	Saga University, Japan
Tetsuji Tokihiro	The University of Tokyo, Japan
Giuseppe Vizzari	University of Milano-Bicocca, Italy
Daichi Yanagisawa	The University of Tokyo, Japan
Peter Wagner	DLR Berlin, Germany
Jarosław Wąs	AGH University of Science and Technology, Poland

Agent-Based Simulation and CA – Program Committee

Vincent Chevrier	Université de Lorraine, France
Jan Dijkstra	Eindhoven University of Technology, The Netherlands
Alexis Drogoul	IRD, France
Guy Engelen	Flemish Institute for Technological Research (VITO), Belgium
Nazim Fatès	LORIA – Inria Nancy, France
Rolf Hoffmann	University of Darmstadt, Germany
Andrea Roli	Alma Mater Studiorum, Università di Bologna, Italy
Leigh Tesfatsion	Iowa State University, USA
Paul Torrens	University of Maryland, USA
Mirko Viroli	Alma Mater Studiorum, Università di Bologna, Italy
Roger White	Memorial University of Newfoundland, Canada

Invited Talks

Discrete Numerical Methods
for Biomedical Applications

Bastien Chopard

Scientific and Parallel Computing Group, CUI
University of Geneva, 7 route de Drize, 1227 Carouge, Switzerland
Bastien.Chopard@unige.ch

Abstract. Numerical modeling and simulations are becoming a central approach to better understand physiological processes involving several scales and the interaction of different physical, biological or chemical phenomena. Numerical models such as lattice Boltzmann models coupled with discrete/continuous a Lagrangian descriptions of particles offer a powerful and flexible method to describe and simulate such processes. In this presentation, we will present such an approach for the case of thrombosis in cerebral aneurysms and for the description of platelet adhesion and aggregations.

New Directions in the Classification and Identification of Cellular Automata

Bernard De Baets

KERMIT, Department of Mathematical Modelling, Statistics and Bioinformatics
Ghent University, Coupure links 653, 9000 Gent, Belgium
Bernard.DeBaets@UGent.be

Abstract. Catalyzed by the emergence of modern computers, cellular automata (CAs) became a full-fledged research domain in the eighties of the previous century. The relevant literature is of a dichotomous nature in the sense that studies either focus on the spatio-temporal dynamics that is evolved by CAs, while others merely use the CA paradigm to build a model for a given biological, natural or physical process. It goes without saying that a profound understanding of CA dynamics is a prerequisite for building realistic, identifiable CA-based models, though this is not straightforward due the fact that a CA is discrete in all its senses.

In an attempt to quantify CA behaviour in a meaningful and reproducible way, several so-called behavioural measures have been proposed during the last two decades. Here, we show how Lyapunov exponents and Boolean derivatives can be used to get a complete picture of CA dynamics in the sense that they not only make it possible to unravel the nature of a given CA, but also allow for assessing the effect of changing model design parameters on the CA behavior. Finally, we introduce the so-called Lyapunov profile of a CA, which may be understood as the counterpart of the Lyapunov spectrum of a smooth dynamical system. These profiles capture the spreading properties of a set of defects, as well as the exponential accumulation rates of defects within this set.

In a second part, we focus on 1D CAs and the space-time diagrams they evolve. We present a novel approach to the automated classification of 1D CAs according to Wolfram's classification scheme by relying on texture features grasping the diagrams' nature, followed by nearest neighbor classification. Finally, we consider the identification of 1D CAs in the context of spatially and/ or temporally incomplete space-time diagrams. We formulate the identification problem as an optimization problem and present a genetic algorithm variant with individuals of variable length, corresponding to different neighborhood radii. Connections between the dynamical properties of CAs and the performance of the algorithm are explored.

Cognitive Agents Learning to Cross a Cellular Automaton Based Highway

Anna Lawniczak

Department of Mathematics and Statistics
University of Guelph, Guelph, Canada
alawnicz@uoguelph.ca

Abstract. Research in swarm robotics has shown that, for carrying out some tasks (e.g., target or source search, task allocation, exploration, mapping, cooperative transportation, unmanned aerial vehicle (UAV) controlling, post-disaster relief), it may be more efficient, reliable and economical to employ a large number (hundreds or thousands) of very simple robots than to employ a small number of sophisticated ones. For the development of swarms of autonomous robots, which may require them to learn how to accomplish some tasks in unknown dynamically changing environments, it is important to study the process of learning through observation and repetition.

Since individual robots in a swarm are usually architecturally minimal with limited computational capabilities, it is important that, in a swarm of robots, the implemented learning algorithms are not computationally demanding. In the microscopic modeling of swarm of robots, individual robots may be identified as cognitive agents capable of performing cognitive acts; i.e. a sequence of the following activities: (1) Perceiving information in both the environment and that which is provided by other agents (2) Reasoning about this information using existing knowledge; (3) Judging the obtained information using existing knowledge; (4) Responding to other cognitive agents or to the external environment, as it may be required; (5) Learning; i.e. changing (and hopefully augmenting) the existing knowledge if the newly acquired information allows it.

In this talk a simple example of a minimal cognitive agent that could be used as a virtual experimental platform to explore agent ability to learn will be identified and discussed. We will discuss the model of cognitive agents learning to cross a CA based highway. As the emphasis is on minimal storage and logical primitives, the formal methods of computational intelligence and established algorithms such as reinforcement learning algorithms are not used in this example. Instead, inspired by biomimicry, simple learning algorithm based on an observational social learning principle, i.e. each agent learns from observing the outcomes of the behaviours of other agents, is designed and its performance is investigated. We discuss the effects of the agents different decision-making cognitive processes, the effects of the agents knowledge base accumulation through observation and repetition and the effects of other model parameters on the agents success of learning to cross a CA based highway.

Some Control Problems for Distributed Parameter Systems

Laurent Lefèvre

Laboratory of Conception and Integration of Systems - LCIS
ESISAR - Valence, France
`laurent.lefevre@lcis.grenoble-inp.fr`

Abstract. Modern control theory emerged in the late 50s and since then successfully addressed many theoretical and application problems related with the online observation and control of finite dimensional dynamical systems. Later on, from the late 60s, some system theorist (mainly applied mathematicians) were getting involved in the analysis and control of spatially distributed dynamical systems, also termed as distributed parameters or infinite dimensional systems, whose dynamics is usually described with sets state partial differential equations. From then, many problems were solved, especially those related to classical control problems for linear distributed parameter systems. However very challenging questions arise specifically for spatially distributed systems.

In this talk we will review briefly the traditional settings for distributed parameters control systems and some important questions related to the control and observation of these systems. Then we will present some control problems related to the spatial distribution of these systems for which cellular automata like approaches could be relevant.

Contents

Asynchronous Cellular Automata and Asynchronous Discrete Models-ACA

Cellular Automata Modelling and Simulation

Cellular Automata Theory
and Implementation

Pseudorandom Pattern Generation
Using 3-State Cellular Automata

Kamalika Bhattacharjee[✉], Dipanjyoti Paul, and Sukanta Das

Department of Information Technology,
Indian Institute of Engineering Science and Technology,
Shibpur 711103, West Bengal, India
kamalika.it@gmail.com, dipanjyotipaul@gmail.com, sukanta@it.iiests.ac.in

Abstract. This paper investigates the potentiality of pseudo-random pattern generation of 1-dimensional 3-state cellular automata (CAs). Here, a pattern represents configuration of a CA of length n. We have identified 805 CAs which have great potentiality to act as pseudorandom pattern generator (PRPG).

Keywords: Pseudo-random pattern generator (PRPG) · 3-state Cellular Automata(CAs) · Fixed-Point Graph (FPG) · Diehard · TestU01

1 Introduction

This paper investigates the (pseudo) randomness behaviour of 1-dimensional 3-neighborhood (that is, nearest neighbor) CAs having 3 states per cell with periodic boundary condition. A list of works already exists in literature using binary (2-state) 3-neighborhood CAs as source of randomness [2,3,8]. However, the randomness of binary CAs with increased neighborhood dependency is not known, but it is well-known after Smith that, a CA with higher neighborhood dependency can always be emulated by another CA with lesser, say 3-neighborhood dependency [7]. In this paper, we have selected 1-D 3-neighborhood finite 3-state CAs, and checked the randomness of the patterns which are configurations of the CAs.

As the rule space of 3-state CAs is huge, we have developed greedy strategies (Sect. 3) and some theories to filter out the potential CAs (Sect. 4.1). These CAs are, however, further tested for randomness using *Diehard* battery of tests [5] as the testbed (Sect. 4.2). Finally, we have got 805 CAs which are verified and claimed to be excellent source of randomness (Sect. 5). We have also tested some existing PRPGs on the same testbed Diehard with same specifications as our PRPGs and compared the result. It is seen that, our PRPGs beat the existing CAs based PRPGs for $n = 15$ (Sect. 5.3).

This research is partially supported by Innovation in Science Pursuit for Inspired Research (INSPIRE) under Dept. of Science and Technology, Govt. of India.

S. El Yacoubi et al. (Eds.): ACRI 2016, LNCS 9863, pp. 3–13, 2016.
DOI: 10.1007/978-3-319-44365-2_1

2 Background

Here, we have considered 1-D 3-neighborhood 3-state CAs, where each cell can take any of the states $S = \{0, 1, 2\}$. The local rules are expressed by a tabular form (see Table 1), where the table contains entries for the combinations of left (x), self (y) and right (z) neighbors of a cell. Each of these combinations with respect to the value $R(x, y, z)$, where R is the local rule, is termed as *Rule Min Term (RMT)(r)* and is generally represented by its decimal equivalent. In this paper, $R(x, y, z) \equiv R[r]$. The number of RMTs of a 3-state CA rule is $3^3 = 27$. We represent R by the values of $R[r]$ with $R[0]$ as the right most digit.

Table 1. Rules of 3-state CAs. Here, PS is present state and NS is next state

P.S.	222	221	220	212	211	210	202	201	200	122	121	120	112	111	110	102	101	100	022	021	020	012	011	010	002	001	000
RMT	(26)	(25)	(24)	(23)	(22)	(21)	(20)	(19)	(18)	(17)	(16)	(15)	(14)	(13)	(12)	(11)	(10)	(9)	(8)	(7)	(6)	(5)	(4)	(3)	(2)	(1)	(0)
N.S.	2	1	1	2	1	1	2	0	2	0	0	0	0	0	2	0	1	0	2	1	2	1	2	0	1	2	1
	1	0	2	0	1	2	1	0	2	0	1	2	1	0	2	1	0	2	0	2	1	0	1	2	0	0	2
	1	1	2	2	2	1	0	1	0	1	1	2	2	2	1	0	0	0	1	1	2	2	2	1	0	0	0

Definition 1. *An RMT r of a rule R is said to be self-replicating, if $R[r] = y$, where $r = x \times 3^2 + y \times 3 + z$ and $x, y, z \in \{0, 1, 2\}$.*

For example, for the CA 102012102012102102021021012 (4th row of Table 1), the self-replicating RMTs are RMTs $2(002), 3(010), 7(021), 10(101), 14(112), 15(120), 19(201), 22(211)$ and $24(220)$. Moreover, a rule is called *balanced* if it contains equal number of RMTs for each of the three possible states for that CA [1]. In Table 1, the rule of 5th row is unbalanced, whereas the rest rules are balanced.

A configuration of a CA can also be represented as a sequence of RMTs, called *RMT sequence*. For example, let 0120 be a configuration of a 4-cell CA. Then the RMT sequence corresponding this configuration is $\langle 1, 5, 15, 18 \rangle$. To get a RMT sequence, we consider an imaginary window of length 3 which slides over the configuration, one cell right at a time. The decimal value corresponding to this 3-cell window is i^{th} RMT in the sequence. Note that, in a RMT sequence, only a specific set of RMTs can be selected after a RMT. For example, after RMT $1(001)$, either of the RMTs $3(010), 4(011)$ or $5(012)$ can be present in a RMT Sequence. For any RMT, the set of 3 RMTs from which the next RMT for the RMT sequence is selected, are named as *sibling* RMTs. Similarly, a set of 3 RMTs always results in creating the same sibling RMT set, which are termed as *equivalent* RMTs.

There are $3^2 = 9$ sets of equivalent RMTs and 9 sets of sibling RMTs. We represent $Equi_i$ as a set of RMTs that contains RMT i and all of its equivalent RMTs. That is, $Equi_i = \{i, 9 + i, 18 + i\}$, where $0 \le i \le 8$. Similarly, $Sibl_j$ represents a set of sibling RMTs where $Sibl_j = \{3j, 3j + 1, 3j + 2\}$ $(0 \le j \le 8)$. Table 2 shows the relationship among the RMTs of 3-state CAs [1]. If in a RMT sequence, a RMT is chosen from $Equi_i$, then the next RMT in the sequence must be chosen from $Sibl_i$.

Table 2. Relations among the RMTs for 3-State CA

	Equivalent set			Sibling set	
#Set	Equivalent RMTs	Decimal equivalent	#Set	Sibling RMTs	Decimal equivalent
$Equi_0$	000, 100, 200	0, 9, 18	$Sibl_0$	000, 001, 002	0, 1, 2
$Equi_1$	001, 101, 201	1, 10, 19	$Sibl_1$	010, 011, 012	3, 4, 5
$Equi_2$	002, 102, 202	2, 11, 20	$Sibl_2$	020, 021, 022	6, 7, 8
$Equi_3$	010, 110, 210	3, 12, 21	$Sibl_3$	100, 101, 102	9, 10, 11
$Equi_4$	011, 111, 211	4, 13, 22	$Sibl_4$	110, 111, 112	12, 13, 14
$Equi_5$	012, 112, 212	5, 14, 23	$Sibl_5$	120, 121, 122	15, 16, 17
$Equi_6$	020, 120, 220	6, 15, 24	$Sibl_6$	200, 201, 202	18, 19, 20
$Equi_7$	021, 121, 221	7, 16, 25	$Sibl_7$	210, 211, 212	21, 22, 23
$Equi_8$	022, 122, 222	8, 17, 26	$Sibl_8$	220, 221, 222	24, 25, 26

Definition 2. *A fixed-point attractor is a configuration of CA, for which the next configuration is the configuration itself. That means, if a CA reaches to a fixed-point attractor, then it remains at that particular configuration forever.*

For example, 0^n is a fixed point attractor of the CA 112221010112221010112221000 with n cells, $n \geq 3$. Generally, one state x is called a quiescent state, when $R(x, x, x) = x$, where R is the rule of the CA. If a CA has a quiescent state at x, then there exists a fixed point attractor at x^n, for any cell length n.

3 Cellular Automata as PRPG

CAs are considered to be a good source of randomness. However, for 3-state CAs, total number of rules is $3^{3^3} = 7.625597485 \times 10^{12}$, which is a huge number for exhaustive testing. So, we concentrate on finding some properties of a CA, which make it a candidate to have good randomness quality. Following is the first property:

Property 1: The randomness of balanced rules, in general, are better than that of unbalanced rule.

If a CA rule is unbalanced, then at least one of the states 0/1/2 has more presence in the rule than the other state(s). Therefore, during evolution from an arbitrary configuration, the CA will be biased towards the state(s) having more presence in the unbalanced rule. The number of balanced 3-state CA rules is $\frac{3^3!}{(3^2!)^3} = 227873431500$, which is also a big number. However, in a random system, information on a localized change eventually flows through the whole system. In a CA based random system, a small change at a local cell by a local rule eventually propagates throughout it, effecting globally. Hence, to have good randomness, the CA must have a sufficient rate of information transmission, so that it does not become stable in a finite time. But, only balancedness does not ensure the flow of information on left or right side in CA. Therefore, we take a greedy approach to choose the balanced rules which have a constant rate of information transmission on at least right direction. Success of this scheme, however, remains on how efficiently we are choosing the balanced rules.

Please recall that, the set $\{xy0, xy1, xy2\}$ represents the set of sibling RMTs, where $x, y \in \{0, 1, 2\}$ (see Table 2). So, our strategy is to choose the CA rules, where the sibling RMTs have different next state values, which implies that, there is a constant rate of information transmission towards the right side.

STRATEGY: *Pick up the balanced rules in which the RMTs of a sibling set have the different next state values, that is, no two RMTs of $Sibl_i$ $(0 \leq i \leq 8)$ have same next state value* [1].

There are $(3!)^{3^2} = 10077696$ balanced rules that can be selected as candidates following this strategy. These CAs are potential nominees to be good PRPGs. Moreover, we also want to consider the flow of information to the left direction for these rules. This implies the RMTs of $Equi_i$, $0 \leq i \leq 8$, should have different states. We define an index, termed as *equiRMTCount*, which measures the amount of information flow towards left direction by observing the equivalent RMT sets.

Definition 3. *The* equiRMTCount *is the cumulative sum of the number of RMTs in $Equi_i$ $(0 \leq i \leq 8)$, which have the same next state value. That means,* equiRMTCount *is increased by 1 if $R[r_1] = R[r_2] \neq R[r_3]$ (or $R[r_1] \neq R[r_2] = R[r_3]$, or $R[r_1] = R[r_3] \neq R[r_2]$) and it is increased by 2 if $R[r_1] = R[r_2] = R[r_3]$, where $r_1, r_2, r_3 \in Equi_i$, $\forall i$ and R is the rule of the CA.*

Table 3 shows an example of finding *equiRMTCount* of a rule R. First column notes the set number, whereas, next 3 pairs of columns shows the RMTs and corresponding next state values. RMTs $0, 9$ and 18 of the rule have same next state values, so, *equiRMTCount* is 2 for $Equi_0$. Similarly, RMTs 10 and 19 of the rule have same state value, so $Equi_1$ gives 1 increment to *equiRMTCount*.

This index gives idea about the information flow in the left direction. For example, for a CA 012012021012012021012012021, *equiRMTCount*= 18, that is, no information flow at the left direction. However, for the rule of Table 3, *equiRMTCount* = 8, that means, there is at maximum $\frac{18-8}{18} = 55.56\%$ chance of information travel in the left direction.

Note that, our requirement is to select the rules which have a constant information transmission in the right direction, as well as, at least a certain rate of information transmission in the left side. This is to ensure that, a small ripple in a local cell propagate in both sides. To validate our argument, an experiment is constructed, where some rules are arbitrarily chosen and tested on Diehard testbed; *equiRMTCount* for these rules is also calculated. Figure 1 shows the plot of these rules. In this figure, X-axis represents *equiRMTCount*, Y-axis the number of randomness tests passed and the count of rules with any particular *equiRMTCount* value that passes any number of tests is shown in Z-axis.

This figure clearly shows that, if *equiRMTCount* value is high (≥ 15), then practically there are insignificant number of rules that passes any randomness tests. So, in our work, we have chosen the rules following STRATEGY which

Table 3. Calculation of *equiRMTCount* for the CA 1020121020121021020021021012(*R*)

#Set	RMT i	$R[i]$	RMT i	$R[i]$	RMT i	$R[i]$	Match count
			Equivalent RMTs				
$Equi_0$	0	2	9	2	18	2	2
$Equi_1$	1	1	10	0	19	0	1
$Equi_2$	2	0	11	1	20	1	1
$Equi_3$	3	1	12	2	21	2	1
$Equi_4$	4	2	13	0	22	1	0
$Equi_5$	5	0	14	1	23	0	1
$Equi_6$	6	1	15	2	24	2	1
$Equi_7$	7	2	16	1	25	0	0
$Equi_8$	8	0	17	0	26	1	1
			equiRMTCount =				8

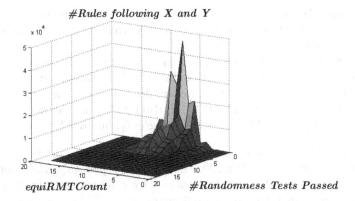

Fig. 1. Test Result of 61249 arbitrarily selected CAs

have *equiRMTCount* $\leq$ 14. There are 10067760 rules that pass this condition. In the next section we define some filtering criteria on these rules based on the inherent structure of the CAs and experiment to select the potential PRPGs.

4   Two-Step Filtering

In this section, the set of 10067760 rules are first filtered based on some theories developed in the following subsection and then, on these rules randomness tests are applied repeatedly for different seeds.

4.1   Theoritical Filtering

Here, we have worked with the CAs, which have at least one quiescent state. Recall that, for a quiescent state, a fixed-point attractor in generated in the CA.

Now, in the configuration transition diagram of CAs, one can observe that, a fixed-point attractor [9] may be associated with long chains of configurations, or small chains, or it may be isolated and most of the configurations are part of a long cycle. Moreover, a CA with long cycle length (or very long chains) have better randomness property than that of the CAs with small cycles (or, small chains). This is because, longer the cycle length, lesser the number of times any state in the cycle get repeated - implying better randomness. Note here that, max-length CAs [2] has maximum possible cycle length; but for classical CAs, there is no known existence of max-length CA. However, a classical CA can have long cycle only when it does not have a tendency to converge to the fixed-point attractor. Therefore, identifying the fixed-point attractor and its connection to other configurations is important for selecting the CAs having good randomness property. We now define a graph, termed as fixed-Point graph (FPG) which helps to identify any fixed-point attractor and its nature in the CA. This graph was introduced in [6] for asynchronous CAs.

Fixed-Point Graph: The fixed-point graph (FPG) is a directed graph, where the nodes represents the self-replicating RMTs. To draw the FPG for a CA, first a forest is formed with the self-replicating RMTs of the CA as the individual nodes. Now, there is a directed edge from vertex u to vertex v, if $u \in Equi_k \Rightarrow v \in Sibl_k$, $0 \leq k \leq 8$, for any u, v (see Table 2). For example, if RMTs 1, 3 and 9 are self-replicating for a CA, then we can draw directed edges from RMT 1 to RMT 3, RMT 3 to RMT 9 and RMT 9 to RMT 1. But we can not draw directed edge from RMT 1 to RMT 9, as RMT $1 \in Equi_1$, but RMT $9 \notin Sibl_1$.

Example 1. This example illustrates the procedure of drawing the FPG for the CA 102012210120021021012102120. First, the self-replicating RMTs for this CA, i.e. the RMTs $0, 5, 6, 11, 12, 16, 18, 22$ and 24 are drawn as individual vertices. Now, we start from vertex 0, the minimum of the RMTs, as the first vertex. RMT $0 \in Equi_0$ and the sibling RMTs from RMT 0 are $Sibl_0 = \{0, 1, 2\}$. However, only RMT 0 is a vertex in this graph, so, a self loop is drawn to vertex 0. The next vertex is vertex 5. Now, RMT $5 \in Equi_5$, and from RMT 5, the next RMTs are $Sibl_5 = \{15, 16, 17\}$. Among these RMT 16 is a vertex, so, a directed edge is drawn from vertex 5 to vertex 16. Similarly, from vertex 16, we draw an edge to vertex 22, from vertex 22 to vertex 12, vertex 12 to vertex 11, vertex 11 to vertex 6, vertex 6 to vertex 18 and vertex 18 to vertex 0. Finally, from vertex 24, directed edge is drawn to vertex 18 completing the graph. Figure 2a shows the fixed-point graph for this CA.

Every fixed-point attractor in a CA can be identified easily by using this graph. To identify a fixed-point, we start with any vertex in the graph. Now, if this vertex can be reached again by traversing a sequence of vertices in the graph, then the RMT sequence corresponding to this traversal represents a fixed-point attractor. That means, if there is a loop of length l in the FPG, then the RMT sequence corresponding to this loop portrays a fixed-point attractor for the CA when cell length is equal to multiples of l.

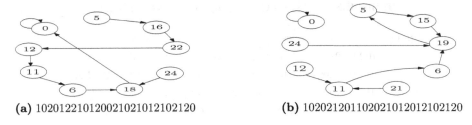

(a) 102012210120021021012102120   **(b)** 102021201102021012012102120

Fig. 2. Fixed-point graphs (FPGs) for CAs

Example 2. Figure 2b shows the fixed-point graph for the CA 102021201102021012012102120. In this graph, vertex 0 has self-loop. So, the configuration 0^n represents a fixed-point attractor for any values of n. Apart from that, starting with vertex 5, this vertex can be reached by traversing the edges connecting vertices 5 to 15, 15 to 19 and 19 to 5. Therefore, the RMT sequence $\langle 5, 15, 19 \rangle$ represents the fixed-point attractor $(120)^n$ or $120120 \cdots 120$ for the CA, when n is multiple of 3. However, for the CA of Fig. 2a, there is no other loop in the graph, except the self-loop at vertex 0. Therefore, 0^n is the only fixed-point attractor for the CA 102012210120021021012102120 for any values of n.

Note that, for the CAs following this strategy, there are 9 vertices in the FPGs and one RMT from each of $Sibl_i$, $0 \le i \le 8$ forms a vertex in the graph. However, our target is to get the CAs which have long cycles. Nevertheless, we define some conditions for filtering these CAs.

Filtering Conditions: We select those CAs as our candidates for experiment with battery of randomness tests, which have one and only one fixed-point attractor. To achieve this, the following two conditions are applied on the CAs–

(a) Only 1 quiescent state: Here, we consider the CAs, which have only one quiescent state. For this quiescent state, a fixed-point attractor is created in the CA. For 3-state CAs, the RMTs for quiescent state are RMT 0(000) for 0 as the quiescent state, RMT 13(111) for 1 as the quiescent state and RMT 26(222) for 2 as the quiescent state. So, we select the CAs which have 0 at $R[0]$, and 0/2 at $R[13]$ & 0/1 at $R[26]$, for providing the quiescent state 0. Similarly, the condition for only quiescent state at 1 (respectively, 2) is $R[13] = 1$ (respectively, $R[26] = 2$) and $R[0] \ne 0$ & $R[26] \ne 2$ (respectively $R[0] \ne 0$ & $R[13] \ne 1$), where $R[i]$ implies the RMT i of rule R. The following Table 4 gives some examples.

(b) No other fixed-point attractor: To ensure that the fixed-point attractor due to the quiescent state is the only fixed-point attractor in the CA, the fixed-point graph (FPG) for that CA is used. Recall that, any loop in this graph represents a fixed-point attractor for the CA. However, as the CAs fulfill the above condition, so, the fixed-point graphs have a self-loop at either of RMT 0, RMT 13 or RMT 26. If apart from this self loop, there is any other loop in the

Table 4. Some 3-state CAs having only one fixed-point

Fixed-point	Rules	Condition
0	102012210120021021012102120	$R[0] = 0$, $R[13] = 2$, $R[26] = 1$
0	012012120012021012012012210	$R[0] = 0$, $R[13] = 2$, $R[26] = 0$
1	012012102201012210012012102	$R[0] = 2$, $R[13] = 1$, $R[26] = 0$
2	201210021102102201210012012	$R[0] = 2$, $R[13] = 0$, $R[26] = 2$

FPG, then it implies a RMT sequence, that is a valid configuration depicting another fixed-point attractor. In this case, we reject the CA. For example, in the FPG for the CA 012012120012021012012012210 (Fig. 2a), there is only one fixed-point at 0^n for the quiescent state 0. So, this CA satisfies the filtering conditions. However, the FPG for the CA 102012201102021012012102120 (Fig. 2b) has another fixed-point attractor apart from the same for the quiescent state. So, this CA is rejected.

Among the 10067760 CA rules from the strategy, we get 1117008 rules which satisfy these theoretical filtering conditions. Now, there is greater chance of getting long cycle, if the fixed-point is isolated and not reachable from any other state. In the next subsection, we assure this through experiment and apply randomness tests on the selected rules.

4.2   Experimental Filtering

Some more rules can be screened out, if the possibility of reaching the trivial configurations from other configuration is considered, that is, if the trivial configurations are isolated and not connected with other non-trivial configurations.

Non-reachable Trivial Configuration: If any of the trivial configuration (0^n, 1^n or 2^n) is reachable from other non-trivial configuration, and the trivial configuration is associated with a fixed-point attractor, then there is a tendency to converge to that fixed-point attractor from any non-trivial configuration. In this case, the fixed-point attractor is not isolated and there is a chance of getting small cycles. This is an undesirable situation which weakens randomness property of the corresponding CA. Note that, this behavior is cell dependent, and relates with the length of the loop in the fixed-point graph for the CA. So, to avoid those rules, an experiment is conducted, where for each rule, it is checked whether the trivial configuration is reachable from the standard non-trivial configuration (all cells are 0, except the middle cell which is 2, i.e. $0^k 2 0^k$, $k = \lfloor \frac{n}{2} \rfloor$), similar to [8]. If the trivial configurations are reachable and has a fixed-point attractor, then the rule is discarded. This experiment is repeated on each of the 1117008 rules for the cell length n, $5 \leq n \leq 15$. We have found 637406 rules which have reachable trivial configuration. Therefore, the working rule set is of size 479602 on which the randomness tests are performed. We have used Diehard battery of tests as the initial testbed.

Filtering with Diehard Battery of Tests: Although from the theoretical development, 479602 rules are selected as the working set of candidates for PRPG with 3-state CA using the strategy, but, all of these rules may not be good for every circumstances demanding randomness. Therefore, rigorous and exhaustive randomness testing is applied on these rules to get the set of best rules. Note that, a rule is part of this best set only when it passes a minimum number of tests on every initial condition.

Wolfram in [8] showed that the binary CA with rule 30(00011110) is a good source of randomness. However, in that paper, he considered the randomness of the vertical sequence generated by the middle cell for a certain number of time stamps. But, for our CA, we have considered the randomness of the pattern generated in the configuration of a n-cell CA, where each cell can take any of the states $\{0, 1, 2\}$. Therefore, for our CA based PRPGs, finding n as minimum as possible is very important.

All the 479602 rules are tested with Diehard for arbitrary initial configuration as well as fixed initial configuration (i.e. $0^k 20^k$, $k = \lfloor \frac{n}{2} \rfloor$). By experimentation, we have got the minimum cell length for which the PRPG beats other existing CA based PRPGs is $n = 15$. So, for testing each CA, n is taken as 15 uniformly.

At each time, the CAs are tested with Diehard with random initial configuration and only the good CAs are put to test again. Here, a CA is considered *good*, when it passes at least 7 tests out of the 15 tests of Diehard. We have repeated this experiment several times. The rules, which have passed the minimum tests (that is, at least 7 tests) in all these runs, are selected to be potential PRPGs for any seed or initial condition. We have got 805 such 3-state CA rules. Table 5 gives some of these rules.

5 Verification of Result

In this section, we verify our final set of rules of size 805 to confirm their competency as excellent PRPGs. To reaffirm that, we have tested these CAs again with Diehard battery of tests for 5 different arbitrary initial seeds and fixed initial seed (i.e. $0^k 20^k$, $k = \lfloor \frac{n}{2} \rfloor$) and with more stringent TestU01 library.

5.1 Test with TestU01 Library

As TestU01 library [4] offers many more stringent battery of tests, we test our final rule set with TestU01 library. Among the different battery tests, we have selected the battery *rabbit* (bbattery_RabbitFile()) which takes a binary file as input and contains 39 stringent tests. Each of the 805 rules, when tested with the battery rabbit, passes $12 - 15$ tests for any arbitrary initial configuration. Some of the results of the 805 rules with TestU01 library for fixed initial configuration is shown in Table 5.

Table 5. Sample of good PRPGs. The test results are for fixed initial configuration

3-state CA Rules	#Tests passed in Diehard ($n = 15$)	#Tests passed in TestU01 ($n = 20$)	3-state CA Rules	#Tests passed in Diehard ($n = 15$)	#Tests passed in TestU01 ($n = 20$)
012012120021021021201021210	9	13	210120201201021210120021021	8	12
210201102210102012201102201	8	10	210201021210120201120102021	8	11
012012120012012102120210012	7	15	012012021120012210021120012	9	15
210120021210201021021120021	7	14	102201102012210120102210201	9	10
210102102210201012210102012	8	13	120210021012210012021210012	8	14
210201201210201102021120201	8	13	120012120201210120120021012	9	10
210210021201120012021021201	8	8	012012120102012102210012102	8	14
012012102102012201012012021	9	14	012012120012012102210012102	7	14
012012102021012021102102021	7	14	012120201012201210210021210	9	12
210201021201201021201021021	7	14	102210012021210201120210012	9	14
012012210102210120120210102	9	13	210102102210102012210102201	7	15
012012201120012102210012102	9	12	012012021201012012021012012	7	13
210210102201102102120102102	7	14	012012201201012201102012102	7	14
201102102210102210201102201	9	12	210201012021012010221102102	8	14
201102102210201012210120021	9	13	012021012210012210210021210	8	14
210201102210120201021210102	8	11	210210210210021012201021021	8	7
012210012210012201120210012	8	11	012021021021201201021210021	8	11
012021120012102012021210210	8	12	012021120012120210120021210	8	12
012021120120120120120201120	8	11	012021210012021021012210120	8	12
012102210210102012102102210	8	10	012120120012120021120021120	8	11
012120201012201120021201120	8	12	012201012210210102012210201	8	9
012201102012012210210210021	8	9	012102210201012120210012102	8	9
012201201021201210012201210	8	12	012201210120102102201102120	8	12
012102201201210120201210201	8	8	012210012002101210212012102	8	8
012210120210120120012210012	8	11	012210201012210120012210012	8	12
021012012021012012201012102	8	12	021012012210012102201012201	8	11
201102102102201120201210012	7	9	102210120120210021120210012	7	12
102210120012120120102102120	7	9	102210120102102120102210210	7	11
201021201201021021210210102	7	12	012021201201201210202021012201	7	12

5.2   Cycle Length Test

We have conducted an experiment to find out the cycle lengths of these 805 rules for different values of n. Table 6 gives cycle lengths for a sample run on different values of n for some rules of Table 5. Note that, although, for some CAs, cycle length varies with cell length, but, we can observe that, the 805 CAs selected as possible PRPGs, have sufficiently long cycle length for most values of n, especially for $n = 15$ and thus strengthens our selection process.

Table 6. Cycle lengths from a sample run for some 3-state CAs of Table 5

Rule	$n = 5$	$n = 6$	$n = 7$	$n = 8$	$n = 9$	$n = 10$	$n = 11$	$n = 12$	$n = 13$	$n = 14$	$n = 15$
012021120021202012012021210	104	65	22	55	1043	104	4630	5210	28456	22	123824
012021120120120120120201120	4	5	139	2	77	4	170	6575	20643	13005	96764
012021210012021021012210120	4	13	244	47	140	739	4421	1015	7201	7944	116924
012102202012102120201210201	94	95	258	1	1214	223	274	89	2846	8987	49094
012102210210102012102102210	54	17	42	231	2114	144	2309	17	19980	3156	91184
012120201012201120021201120	34	8	27	51	368	34	527	10475	11998	29553	36224
012201012210210102021210201	34	23	146	271	22	34	208	911	4731	2461	84284
012210012210012201120210012	94	17	167	143	188	339	2375	2639	378	9561	74234
012210120012120120102210012	19	5	167	3	143	39	21	357	17146	293	88364
021012012021012012201012102	36	5	251	3	134	2999	10262	8	24556	11570	151214
021012012210012102201012201	109	62	153	687	152	189	1033	9239	8878	8735	137534
201102102210120201210120021	49	8	31	2	458	49	2826	3563	6759	11129	54554

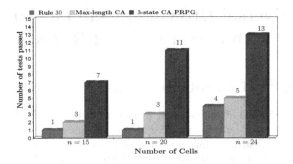

Fig. 3. Comparison of rule 30, max-length CA and 3-state CAs as potential PRPGs

5.3   Comparison

We have selected most popular binary CA with rule 30 [8] and a max-length CA [2] with rules 150 and 90 and tested on Diehard testbed for different values of n, such as $15, 20,$ & 24 with fixed initial seed, i.e., all zero except the middle bit as one $(0^k 10^k$, $k = \lfloor \frac{n}{2} \rfloor)$. Figure 3 shows the comparison result. In this figure, among the 805 3-state CAs, a CA is arbitrary selected as our PRPG, which is the rule 012012102012012102120210012 in this case. It can be observed that, our PRPG beats the PRPG based on rule 30 as well as the max-length CA for the minimum cell length $n = 15$.

References

1. Bhattacharjee, K., Das, S.: Reversibility of d-state finite cellular automata. J. Cell. Automata **11**(2–3), 213–245 (2016)
2. Chaudhuri, P.P., Chowdhury, D.R., Nandi, S., Chatterjee, S.: Additive Cellular Automata Theory and Applications. IEEE Computer Society Press, New York (1997). ISBN 0-8186-7717-1
3. Das, S., Sikdar, B.K.: A scalable test structure for multicore chip. IEEE Trans. CAD Integr. Circ. Syst. **29**(1), 127–137 (2010)
4. L'Ecuyer, P., Simard, R.: TestU01: A C library for empirical testing of random number generators. ACM Trans. Math. Softw. **33**(4), 22 (2007)
5. Marsaglia, G.: DIEHARD: a battery of tests of randomness (1996). http://stat.fsu.edu/geo/diehard.html
6. Sethi, B., Roy, S., Das, S.: Asynchronous cellular automata and pattern classification. Complexity (2016). doi:10.1002/cplx.21749
7. Smith III, A.R.: Cellular automata complexity trade-offs. Inf. Control **18**, 466–482 (1971)
8. Wolfram, S.: Random sequence generation by cellular automata. Adv. Appl. Math. **7**(2), 123–169 (1986)
9. Wuensche, A.: Complex and chaotic dynamics, basins of attraction, and memory in discrete networks. Acta Phys. Pol. B-Proc. Suppl **3**, 463–478 (2010)

On a Universal Brownian Cellular Automata with 3 States and 2 Rules

Teijiro Isokawa[1][(✉)], Ferdinand Peper[2], Koji Ono[1], and Nobuyuki Matsui[1]

[1] Graduate School of Engineering, University of Hyogo, Hyogo, Japan
isokawa@eng.u-hyogo.ac.jp
[2] Center for Information and Neural Networks,
National Institute of Information and Communications Technology,
Osaka University, Osaka, Japan

Abstract. This paper presents a 3-state asynchronous CA that requires merely two transition rules to achieve computational universality. This universality is achieved by embedding Priese's delay-insensitive circuit elements, called the E-element and the K-element, on the cell space of a so-called Brownian CA, which is an asynchronous CA containing local configurations that conduct a random walk in the circuit topology.

1 Introduction

Cellular Automata (CA) attract increasing attention as architectures for computers with nanometer-scale devices (nano-computers), because their regular structures and local connectivity offer much potential for manufacturing based on molecular self-assembly [1–4]. An obstacle to the realization of nanocomputers is the effect of noise and fluctuations in operating nanometer-scale devices, in which amplitudes of circuit signals could be comparable to those of noise and fluctuations. Assuring the normal operation of circuits will be difficult in the framework of traditional techniques, such as the suppression of noise or the correction of errors caused by noise.

For this reason, alternative approaches to circuit operations need consideration. One possible approach is to make use of noise as information carrier or—more indirectly—for the operations of circuits [5,6], in a way that is sometimes found in biological systems [7]. When realized in terms of CA, noise-driven computation is described by the term *Brownian Cellular Automata (BCA)* [8]. BCA are a type of asynchronous CA, where certain local configurations propagate randomly in the cellular space, resembling Brownian motion. The BCA in [8] is proven computational universal, by embedding so-called Brownian circuits [9] on the cell space. The number of states in a cell is 3 in this model and the number of transition rules is 3, which is much less than comparable models in asynchronous CA with computational universality. The resulting decrease in the complexity of a cell is very useful for the efficient implementation of nanometer-scale devices.

K. Ono has been with Glory Limited, Japan, since 2011.

S. El Yacoubi et al. (Eds.): ACRI 2016, LNCS 9863, pp. 14–23, 2016.
DOI: 10.1007/978-3-319-44365-2_2

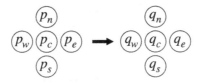

Fig. 1. Transition on BCA

This paper presents a computational universal BCA, in which the number of cells' state is 3, like in [8], but in which the number of transition rules is decreased to 2. Computational universality in the proposed BCA is shown by embedding a set of previously known delay-insensitive circuit elements, called K-element and E-element [10], on the cell space.

2 Preliminaries

2.1 Brownian Cellular Automaton

A BCA [8] is a two-dimensional asynchronous CA of identical cells, each of which can assume one of a finite number of states at a time. Cells undergo transitions in accordance with transition rules that operate on each cell and its direct four neighbors, shown in Fig. 1. The rules are of a type called Von Neumann neighborhood aggregate rules. In a BCA, transitions of the cells occur at random times, independent of each other. Furthermore, it is assumed that neighboring cells of the cells being in transition never undergo transitions at the same time to prevent a situation in which such cells simultaneously write different states into the same location.

We assume that the transition rules are rotational symmetric, i.e., one transition rule has four rotated analogues. Consequently, when we represent the transition in Fig. 1 as

$$(p_c, p_n, p_e, p_s, p_w) \rightarrow (q_c, q_n, q_e, q_s, q_w), \tag{1}$$

the following three rules also exist:

$$(p_c, p_e, p_s, p_w, p_n) \rightarrow (q_c, q_e, q_s, q_w, q_n)$$
$$(p_c, p_s, p_w, p_n, p_e) \rightarrow (q_c, q_s, q_w, q_n, q_e)$$
$$(p_c, p_w, p_n, p_e, p_s) \rightarrow (q_c, q_w, q_n, q_e, q_s)$$

2.2 Computational Elements

A few decades ago Priese [10] proposed circuit elements from which arbitrary delay-insensitive circuits can be constructed. Called the E-element and

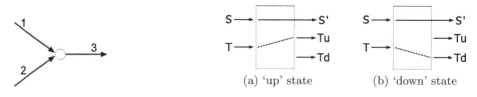

Fig. 2. K-element

Fig. 3. E-element in (a) 'up' state and (b) 'down' state

K-element [10], these elements—schematically shown in Figs. 2 and 3—are universal, forming a base for the construction of a sequential automaton. The circuits constructed from E-elements and K-elements have in common that they employ only one signal at a time. Though inefficient, this is sufficient to guarantee universality.

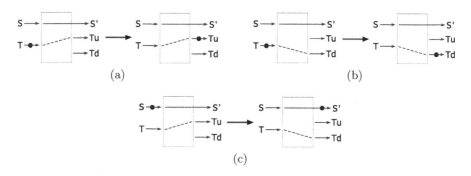

Fig. 4. Operations of an E-element: (a) when in the 'up' state, (b) when in the 'down' state, and (c) changing state upon receiving an input signal on wire S. A token (blob) on a wire denotes a signal.

The K-element has two input wires and one output wire and it accepts a signal coming from either input wire and outputs it to the output wire.

The E-element is an element with two input wires (S and T) and three output wires (S', T_u, and T_d), as well as two internal states ('up' or 'down'). Input from wire T will be redirected to either of the output wires T_u or T_d, depending on the internal state of the element: when this state is 'up' (resp. 'down'), a signal on the input wire T flows to the output wire T_u (resp. T_d) as in Fig. 4(a) (resp. Fig. 4(b)). By accepting a signal from input wire S, an E-element changes its internal state from 'up' to 'down' or from 'down' to 'up', after which it outputs a signal to output wire S', as shown in Fig. 4(c).

3 Implementing Computational Elements on Brownian Cellular Automaton

3.1 Basic Elements

A cell in the proposed BCA can be in one of the 3 states, as shown in Fig. 5. Figure 6 shows two transition rules used in the proposed CA. To construct the delay-insensitive circuit elements, we first define the basic elements on the above-mentioned BCA, called *signal, signal line, terminator, hub, crossover,* and *switch*.

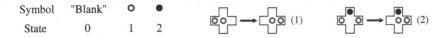

Fig. 5. The symbols used to represent the states of a cell

Fig. 6. Transition rules

The most basic elements are the *signal* and the *signal line*. A signal can travel bidirectionally along a signal line (Fig. 7(a)). This is implemented on the BCA by appropriate placements of state 1, as shown in Fig. 7(b). The transition rule #1 is used for moving a signal to and fro on a signal line, whereby the direction of the signal is determined by which cell first undergoes a transition. In the example in Fig. 7(b), both ends of a signal line are terminated by *terminators*, thus a signal travels between terminators.

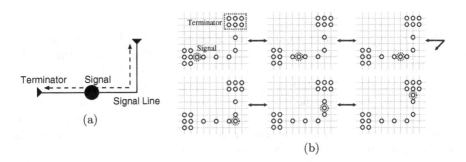

Fig. 7. (a) Signal, Signal line, and Terminators, (b) Their implementations on BCA, where a cell with a dotted circle will undergo the transition.

A *hub* is used for branching a signal line (Fig. 8(a)). The signal on the port a goes out from a, b or c. A configuration of a hub on BCA is shown in Fig. 8(b). The transition rule #1 is also used for this element.

A *crossover* element (Fig. 9(a)) accepts a signal at port N (or S) and produces an output signal from port S (or N, resp.). In a similar way, the ports W and E are connected to each other. Figure 9(b) shows a configuration of a crossover on BCA.

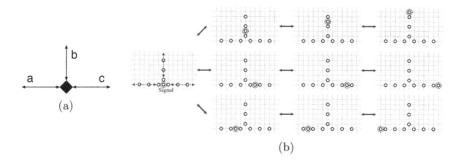

Fig. 8. (a) a Hub and (b) its implementation on BCA

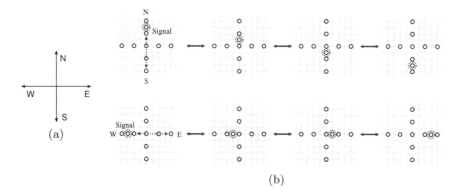

Fig. 9. (a) a Crossover and (b) its implementation on BCA

The next circuit element requires some kind of switching behavior, for which the basic mechanism works like in Fig. 10. Using transition rule #1, this mechanism drags the right end of a signal line on which no terminator exists in the right direction. Dragging of the right end continues until the signal arrives at the other signal line, somewhere to the right, resulting in the line end to become attached to the left end of this line. This effect of dragging the end of a line towards another line can also be used in combination with curves of a line, in which a signal turns to the left or to the right. It is used in an element called *switch* (Fig. 11). A switch element has two ports, both of which can be used for input or output, and it takes one of two states, the R-state and the L-state. An arrow in a switch represents the direction of a signal that can be passed: in the R-state (Fig. 11(a)), a signal at port W can go out from port E but a signal at port E never passes through the element. Similarly, a signal at port E can go out from port W in the L-state (Fig. 11(b)). On acceptance of a signal, the switch element changes its state from L to R (or R to L, resp.) (see Fig. 11(c)). A configuration of a switch and its switching behavior is shown in Fig. 12.

There is another switching element, called a *line selector* and shown in Fig. 13. This element has six input/output ports and takes one of two states, the U-state

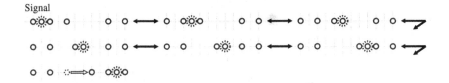

Fig. 10. Dragging state 1 from one signal line to a signal line right of it.

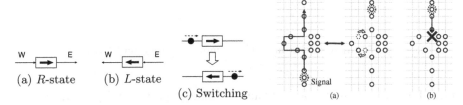

(a) *R*-state   (b) *L*-state

(c) Switching

Fig. 11. A Switch element (a) *R*-state, (b) *L*-state, and (c) switching from *L* to *R*.

Fig. 12. A BCA implementation for switch element

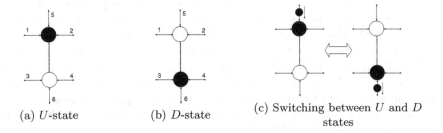

(a) *U*-state   (b) *D*-state   (c) Switching between *U* and *D* states

Fig. 13. A line selector element (a) *U*-state, (b) *D*-state, and (c) switching by a signal.

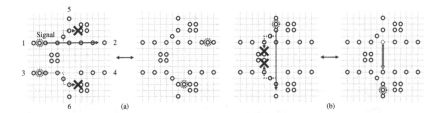

Fig. 14. A line selector element implemented on BCA

and the *D*-state. A line selector in the *U*-state (Fig. 13(a)) connects the port 1 and the port 2 by a signal line, thus allowing a signal on port 1 (or 2) to move to port 2 (or 1). In this state, ports 3 and 4 are not connected, i.e., a signal on port 3 never goes out from 4 and vice versa. When this element is in the

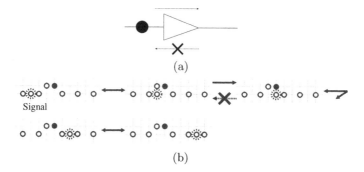

Fig. 15. (a) A ratchet and (b) its implementation on BCA

D-state (Fig. 13(b)), on the other hand, it connects port 3 and port 4, but it does not connect port 1 and port 2. The switching of the state of a line selector is conducted by a signal traveling from port 5 to port 6. When a line selector is in state U, it accepts a signal from port 5, then produces a signal at port 6, and finally changes its state to D (Fig. 13(c)). Similarly, a line selector in state D changes its state to U when it accepts a signal at port 6.

The behavior of a line selector can be realized on the proposed BCA by utilizing the dragging behavior in Fig. 10 on an appropriate configuration of state 1s. Figure 14 shows a line selector implemented on BCA.

The last of the basic elements is called a *ratchet*. Figure 15 shows a ratchet and its configuration on BCA. This element has one input port and one output port. A signal on the input port will go out from the output port, but this signal cannot return to the input port from the output port. For realizing this mechanism, an additional state (i.e. state 2) and an additional transition rule (rule #2) are used (see Fig. 15(b)).

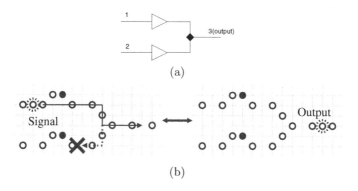

Fig. 16. (a) A K-element by basic elements and (b) its implementation on BCA

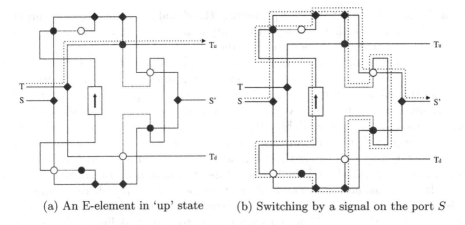

(a) An E-element in 'up' state   (b) Switching by a signal on the port S

Fig. 17. An E-element constructed by basic elements, where it is in the state 'up'. (a) Trajectory of a signal on the port T. This results in the signal going out from T_u. (b) Trajectory of a signal on the port S. The state of the element changes to 'down' and the signal goes out from the port S'.

3.2   Constructing Computational Elements

To ensure the computational universality on the proposed BCA, we implement two elements—the E-element and the K-element—as configurations on BCA. Implementing a K-element is straightforward. Figure 16(a) shows a construction of a K-element in terms of the basic elements. It uses one hub for combining two

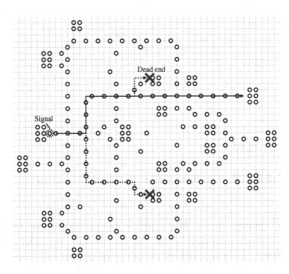

Fig. 18. An implementation of an E-element on BCA. A solid line with an arrow represents a trajectory of a signal.

input lines, and two ratchets for preventing the signal going out from the input ports. A signal on either 1 or 2 will be output to port 3. A configuration of a K-element on the BCA is shown in Fig. 16(b).

A construction of the E-element is shown in Fig. 17(a), where it is in the 'up' state. The states of four line selectors and a switch in the element determine the state of this E-element: in the case of the 'up' state, a signal at the port T will eventually move to port T_u. A trajectory of a signal on port T is shown as a dashed line in Fig. 17(a). Switching the state of an E-element is accomplished by a signal on port S, resulting in this signal going out from port S'. Figure 17(b) shows a trajectory of a signal that is input to port S and goes out from S'. All the states of the switch and the line selectors are changed by this signal.

A BCA implementation of an E-element is shown in Fig. 18, where the state of this element is 'up'. A solid line with an arrow in this figure shows a trajectory of a signal on the port T, which corresponds to a dashed line in Fig. 17(a). Transitions of switching from the state 'up' to 'down' are shown in Fig. 19.

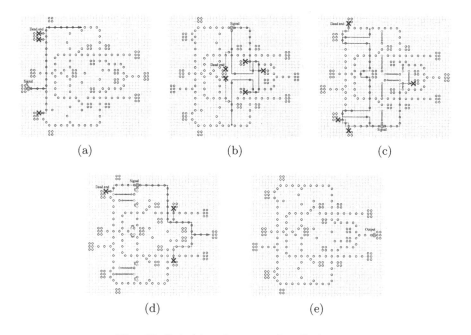

(a)   (b)   (c)

(d)   (e)

Fig. 19. Switching the state of an E-element

By arranging E-elements and K-elements and connections between them in appropriate ways on the proposed BCA, we can realize any circuit consisting of these elements. Thus, the proposed BCA is computationally universal.

4   Conclusion

This paper presents a 3-state computationally universal Brownian CA, in which the number of transition rules is two. This is one rule less than in the Brownian CA model in [8].

There is some limited room for further reduction of the number of states and the number of rules. Obviously, the limit is two states and one rule. Interestingly, the E-element, which is the most complicated of the two circuit elements, requires exactly this number of states and rules for its implementation. It is for two reasons that a third state and a second rule are necessary. The first reason is that a ratchet appears to require such an addition of one state and one rule. Rule #1 is symmetric in itself, and it is likely unable to provide for the asymmetry of the ratchet. Regarding the need for an additional state, it is unclear at this stage whether a ratchet can be implemented without relying on it, so further research is needed to provide more clarity. The second reason why two states and one rule appear insufficient is that a 1-cell shift is caused by a turn left or right of a line, and this shift makes it impossible to line up certain input and output lines. The construction of the ratchet provides for this shift in a signal line, but, as stated above, an additional state and rule are necessary for this.

Acknowledgment. This work was supported by a Grant-in-Aid for Scientific Research on Innovative Areas "Molecular Robotics" (No. 15H00825) of The Ministry of Education, Culture, Sports, Science, and Technology, Japan.

References

1. Biafore, M.: Cellular automata for nanometer-scale computation. Physica D **70**, 415–433 (1994)
2. Durbeck, L.J.K., Macias, N.J.: The cell matrix: an architecture for nanocomputing. Nanotechnology **12**, 217–230 (2001)
3. Peper, F., Lee, J., Adachi, S., Mashiko, S.: Laying out circuits on asynchronous cellular arrays: a step towards feasible nanocomputers? Nanotechnology **14**, 469–485 (2003)
4. Peper, F., Lee, J., Isokawa, T.: Cellular nanocomputers: a focused review. Int. J. Nanotechnol. Mol. Comput. **1**, 33–49 (2009)
5. Kish, L.B.: Thermal noise driven computing. Appl. Phys. Lett. **89**(14), 144104 (2006)
6. Dasmahapatra, S., Werner, J., Zauner, K.P.: Noise as a computational resource. Int. J. Unconventional Comput. **2**(4), 305–319 (2006)
7. Yanagida, T., Ueda, M., Murata, T., Esaki, S., Ishii, Y.: Brownian motion, fluctuation and life. Biosystems **88**(3), 228–242 (2007)
8. Lee, J., Peper, F.: Efficient computation in brownian cellular automata. In: Peper, F., Umeo, H., Matsui, N., Isokawa, T. (eds.) Proceedings of 4th International Workshop on Natural Computing, vol. 2, pp. 47–56. Springer, Tokyo (2009)
9. Peper, F., Lee, J., Carmona, J., Cortadella, J., Morita, K.: Brownian circuits: fundamentals. ACM J. Emerg. Technol. Comput. Syst. **9**(1), 1–24 (2013). Article no. 3
10. Priese, L.: Automata and concurrency. Theoret. Comput. Sci. **25**(3), 221–265 (1983)

FResCA: A Fault-Resistant Cellular Automata Based Stream Cipher

Jimmy Jose[1,2(✉)] and Dipanwita Roy Chowdhury[1]

[1] Crypto Research Laboratory, Department of Computer Science and Engineering,
Indian Institute of Technology Kharagpur, Kharagpur, India
{jimmy,drc}@cse.iitkgp.ernet.in
[2] Department of Computer Science and Engineering,
National Institute of Technology Calicut, Calicut, India
jimmy@nitc.ac.in

Abstract. Grain is a stream cipher suitable for restricted hardware environments. The cipher is particularly vulnerable to fault attacks. It has been shown that fault injection in either the linear or nonlinear block of Grain can break the cipher. Fault attacks generally exploit the linear behaviour and the reversibility of the cipher states. Using Cellular Automata (CA), we propose a Grain-like cipher which is shown to be strong particularly against fault attacks.

Keywords: Fault analysis · Grain cipher · Stream cipher · Cellular automata

1 Introduction

Encryption techniques in general can be broadly classified into two, namely symmetric-key encryption (secret-key encryption) and asymmetric-key encryption (public-key encryption). Stream ciphers fall under symmetric-key encryption where the sender and the receiver share the same secret key. Stream ciphers may be classified into synchronous where the keystream depends only on the key and asynchronous where the keystream depends on both the key and the ciphertext.

The importance of stream ciphers stems from the fact that they are suitable for resource-constrained environments where computing power, memory, etc. are at a premium. Stream ciphers may be efficient in software meaning they need fewer instructions to execute or may be hardware efficient meaning they need less hardware circuitry.

eSTREAM [1], the ECRYPT Stream Cipher Project, was conceptualised to promote the design of efficient stream ciphers. The shortlisted ciphers under the the project falls into two categories. One set of ciphers are more suitable for software applications with high throughput requirements and the other set of ciphers are suitable for restricted hardware environments. Grain cipher falls under the second category and our interest is on 128-bit version of Grain known as Grain-128 which is described in detail in Subsect. 2.1. In this paper, reference to Grain implies Grain-128 version of the cipher unless otherwise stated.

S. El Yacoubi et al. (Eds.): ACRI 2016, LNCS 9863, pp. 24–33, 2016.
DOI: 10.1007/978-3-319-44365-2_3

Side channel attacks (SCA) are attacks that target the limitations in the physical implementation of the cryptosystem. They can be either active or passive. Fault attacks are active side channel attacks and in particular, they find relevance against stream ciphers [9]. Faults are injected into unknown bit positions in the cipher state and by tracking these faults, the state of the cipher is found. These attacks are suitable when the cryptosystem is not vulnerable to direct attacks. Some of the fault attacks that were proposed against Grain are fault injection in LFSR [4], fault injection in NFSR [12], and the attack which is applicable to Grain family of ciphers [3].

The immunity of a CA based Trivium-like stream cipher against fault attacks was shown [10] in ACRI 2014. In [7], a scalable stream cipher based on CA was proposed. In this paper, we propose a CA based Grain-like stream cipher FResCA which is resistant to fault attack. Analysis of its cryptographic strength is provided with a special emphasis on fault attacks.

The paper is organised as follows. In Sect. 2, we give a brief description of Grain and suitability of CA as better cryptographic primitive against fault attacks. The proposed cipher FResCA is described in Sect. 3. Section 4 discusses the security of the proposed cipher and Sect. 5 describes the cipher's strength against fault attacks. We conclude with Sect. 6.

2 Preliminaries

Boolean functions should have certain desirable cryptoproperties so that they can be employed in practical cryptosystems. A detailed discussion on Boolean functions and their cryptoproperties can be found in [14]. In this section, a brief description of Grain is provided followed by a discussion on CA's suitability as cryptographic primitive against fault attacks.

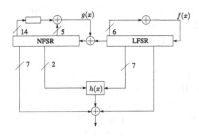

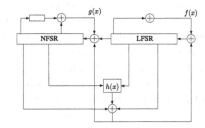

Fig. 1. Grain block diagram   **Fig. 2.** Grain Initialisation

2.1 Grain-128 Description

Grain [8] has three blocks namely an LFSR, an NFSR, and an output function as shown in Fig. 1. The contents of the LFSR and NFSR are denoted by $(s_i, s_{i+1}, \cdots, s_{i+127})$ and $(b_i, b_{i+1}, \cdots, b_{i+127})$ respectively at clock i and together determine the 256-bit state of the cipher. The LFSR feedback polynomial $f(x)$ updates the LFSR as

$s_{i+128} = s_i \oplus s_{i+7} \oplus s_{i+38} \oplus s_{i+70} \oplus s_{i+81} \oplus s_{i+96}$.

The NFSR feedback polynomial $g(x)$ together with s_i from LFSR updates the NFSR as

$$b_{i+128} = s_i \oplus b_i \oplus b_{i+26} \oplus b_{i+56} \oplus b_{i+91} \oplus b_{i+96} \oplus b_{i+3}b_{i+67} \oplus b_{i+11}b_{i+13}$$
$$\oplus\, b_{i+17}b_{i+18} \oplus b_{i+27}b_{i+59} \oplus b_{i+40}b_{i+48} \oplus b_{i+61}b_{i+65} \oplus b_{i+68}b_{i+84}.$$

The nonlinear function h is defined as

$h = b_{i+12}s_{i+8} \oplus s_{i+13}s_{i+20} \oplus b_{i+95}s_{i+42} \oplus s_{i+60}s_{i+79} \oplus b_{i+12}b_{i+95}s_{i+95}$.

The output bit z_i is given as

$z_i = b_{i+2} \oplus b_{i+15} \oplus b_{i+36} \oplus b_{i+45} \oplus b_{i+64} \oplus b_{i+73} \oplus b_{i+89} \oplus h \oplus s_{i+93}$.

In the initialisation phase, the key $(k_0, \cdots, k_{127})$ and IV $(v_0, \cdots, v_{95})$ are loaded into the NFSR and LFSR as

$(b_0, \cdots, b_{127}) \leftarrow (k_0, \cdots, k_{127})$

$(s_0, \cdots, s_{127}) \leftarrow (v_0, \cdots, v_{95}, 1, \cdots, 1)$.

Then the cipher is iterated 256 times without producing the keystream in the initialisation phase as shown in Fig. 2. Instead, the keystream bits are fed back and XORed with the input of both the LFSR and NFSR. After the initialisation phase, these feedback paths are removed and keystream bits are available through the output line.

2.2 CA as Better Cryptographic Primitive Against Fault Attacks

CA can provide fast evolution and high nonlinearity if appropriate CA rules are employed. CA diffuse the state bits very fast and in a single cycle, every bit undergoes transformation. This parallel transformation forces the introduced fault to spread quickly and dissipate. So fault tracking becomes very difficult.

Most of the stream ciphers that are vulnerable to fault attacks use a reversible algorithm. That is, if we know the state of the cipher at any instant, the cipher can be run backwards until it reaches the initial state revealing the key which was used for the cipher initialisation. CA can be effectively employed in such a way that it is practically infeasible to reverse the cipher.

Since nonlinearity of CA based stream ciphers is quite high if appropriate CA rules are employed, it is very difficult to generate linear equations which can be solved to extract state bits of the cipher as done in a general fault attack. Thus, a CA based stream cipher can be designed such that it prevents fault attack.

Other than these, CA prevent correlation attacks too. CA based stream ciphers can provide fast initialisation as they achieve desirable values of cryptographic properties in less rounds. They can be designed in such a way that they are suitable in hardware as well as software.

3 FResCA Description

Our cipher model is Grain-like and has three blocks, namely nonlinear, linear, and a mixing function as shown in Fig. 3. Nonlinear block uses highly nonlinear

4-neighbourhood CA rule whereas linear block uses 3-neighbourhood maximum length CA and both are of 128-bit length. Third block performs nonlinear mixing and produces the output stream.

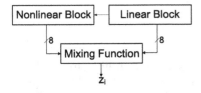

Fig. 3. FResCA block diagram

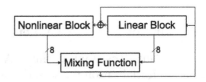

Fig. 4. FResCA Initialisation

3.1 Nonlinear Block

A study was conducted in [11] to explore the cryptographic properties of four-neighbourhood CA. In the paper, five good candidate rules were selected based on their cryptographic properties. The rules 43350 and 51510 are cryptographically stronger among the five rules. In the NIST test suite [2], rule 43350 performed better. So this rule is used in the nonlinear block which computes the state of the CA cell q_i at time $t + 1$ as

Rule 43350: $q_i(t + 1) = q_{i-2}(t) \oplus q_{i+1}(t) \oplus (q_{i-1}(t) + q_i(t))$,

where $q_{i-2}(t)$, $q_{i-1}(t)$, $q_i(t)$, and $q_{i+1}(t)$ represent the state of the two left neighbours, self, and right-neighbour respectively at time t of the left-skewed four-neighbourhood CA, $\oplus$ and $+$ represent XOR and OR operations respectively. Rule 43350 provides high nonlinearity to the nonlinear block and the non-linearity increases rapidly with each iteration. The rule is balanced and exhibits good correlation immunity also.

3.2 Linear Block

Linear block uses a three-neighbourhood linear maximum-length CA. Two linear rules, rule 90 and 150 are used to realise the CA. These rules are defined as
Rule 90: $q_i(t + 1) = q_{i-1}(t) \oplus q_{i+1}(t)$
Rule 150: $q_i(t + 1) = q_{i-1}(t) \oplus q_i(t) \oplus q_{i+1}(t)$

The bit positions 1 and 29 uses rule 150 and all other 126 positions use rule 90 to realise the maximum length CA.

3.3 Nonlinear Mixing

The nonlinear mixing is achieved by using NMIX function [5] which is defined for two n-bit inputs X, Y, and output Z as follows:
$$z_i \leftarrow x_i \oplus y_i \oplus c_{i-1}$$
$$c_i \leftarrow x_0 y_0 \oplus \cdots \oplus x_i y_i \oplus x_{i-1} x_i \oplus y_{i-1} y_i$$
and $x_{-1} = y_{-1} = c_{-1} = 0, 0 \le i \le n - 1$.

We take 8-bits each from the nonlinear and linear block as input to NMIX and the most significant bit (MSB) is taken as the output from NMIX. We can see that all input bits are present in the computation of MSB. The output function is a 16-variable bent function of degree two and this mixing provides high nonlinearity.

3.4   Working of FResCA Cipher

FResCA is **F**ault-**Res**istant **C**ellular **A**utomata based Grain-like cipher. The cipher has an initialisation phase and a keystream generation phase. The output is suppressed in the initialisation phase which consists of 32 iterations. The number of iterations in initialisation phase is very less in comparison to 256 iterations in Grain. The 128-bit key and 128-bit IV are loaded to the nonlinear and linear blocks respectively. During this phase, the output is fed back to both the nonlinear and linear blocks as shown in Fig. 4. The output bit acts as the right neighbour for the rightmost linear cell and the XOR of the output bit and the leftmost bit of linear block acts as the right neighbour to the rightmost nonlinear cell in the initialisation phase. In each iteration, each bit in the nonlinear block changes its state according to the 4-neighbourhood CA rule 43350. In the linear block, the bits change according to 3-neighbourhood linear rule 90 except for bit locations 1 and 29 where rule 150 is used. Eight taps are taken from each of the nonlinear and linear blocks so that the number of input lines to the nonlinear mixing block is 16. The eight taps corresponds to the bit positions 1, 22, 43, 64, 65, 86, 107, and 128 in both the blocks. The tap positions are spaced equally other than the two central taps so that the output is influenced by all the bits in less iterations.

Thirty-two cycles are more than sufficient for all the 256 state bits to influence the input to the NMIX function and thereby influencing the output of NMIX, i.e., the keystream bit. So each keystream bit is influenced by all the 256 state bits. The first keystream bit z_1 (first 32 keystream bits are suppressed and are not available as output) involves 16 variables, 8 from the nonlinear block and 8 from the linear block.

If nonlinear bits are represented as $(b_1, \cdots, b_{128})$ and linear bits are represented as $(s_1, \cdots, s_{128})$, then z_1 is represented as

$z_1 = b_{128} \oplus s_{128} \oplus b_1 s_1 \oplus b_{22} s_{22} \oplus b_{43} s_{43} \oplus b_{64} s_{64} \oplus b_{65} s_{65} \oplus b_{86} s_{86} \oplus b_{107} s_{107} \oplus b_{86} b_{107} \oplus s_{86} s_{107}.$

The cryptographic properties of z_1 are measured. Nonlinearity, correlation-immunity, resiliency, and algebraic degree are 32256, 1, 1, and 2 respectively. Since we have resiliency value as 1, the Boolean function is balanced also.

The second keystream bit z_2, which is also suppressed, involves 41 variables (26 from the nonlinear block and 15 from linear block). The Boolean function corresponding to z_2 is

$$z_2 = b_{126} \oplus b_{127} \oplus b_{128} \oplus s_{127} \oplus (b_1 s_1) \oplus (b_1 s_2) \oplus (b_{105} b_{84}) \oplus (b_{105} b_{85}) \oplus (b_{105} b_{86})$$
$$\oplus (b_{105} b_{87}) \oplus (b_{105} s_{106}) \oplus (b_{105} s_{108}) \oplus (b_{106} b_{84}) \oplus (b_{106} b_{85}) \oplus (b_{106} b_{86}) \oplus (b_{106} b_{87})$$
$$\oplus (b_{106} s_{106}) \oplus (b_{106} s_{108}) \oplus (b_{107} b_{84}) \oplus (b_{107} b_{85}) \oplus (b_{107} b_{86}) \oplus (b_{107} b_{87}) \oplus (b_{107} s_{106})$$
$$\oplus (b_{107} s_{108}) \oplus (b_{108} b_{84}) \oplus (b_{108} b_{85}) \oplus (b_{108} b_{86}) \oplus (b_{108} b_{87}) \oplus (b_{108} s_{106}) \oplus (b_{108} s_{108})$$
$$\oplus (b_{127} b_{128}) \oplus (b_2 s_1) \oplus (b_2 s_2) \oplus (b_{20} s_{21}) \oplus (b_{20} s_{23}) \oplus (b_{21} s_{21}) \oplus (b_{21} s_{23}) \oplus (b_{22} s_{21})$$
$$\oplus (b_{22} s_{23}) \oplus (b_{23} s_{21}) \oplus (b_{23} s_{23}) \oplus (b_{41} s_{42}) \oplus (b_{41} s_{44}) \oplus (b_{42} s_{42}) \oplus (b_{42} s_{44}) \oplus (b_{43} s_{42})$$
$$\oplus (b_{43} s_{44}) \oplus (b_{44} s_{42}) \oplus (b_{44} s_{44}) \oplus (b_{62} s_{63}) \oplus (b_{62} s_{65}) \oplus (b_{63} s_{63}) \oplus (b_{63} s_{64}) \oplus (b_{63} s_{65})$$
$$\oplus (b_{63} s_{66}) \oplus (b_{64} s_{63}) \oplus (b_{64} s_{64}) \oplus (b_{64} s_{65}) \oplus (b_{64} s_{66}) \oplus (b_{65} s_{63}) \oplus (b_{65} s_{64}) \oplus (b_{65} s_{65})$$
$$\oplus (b_{65} s_{66}) \oplus (b_{66} s_{64}) \oplus (b_{66} s_{66}) \oplus (b_{84} s_{85}) \oplus (b_{84} s_{87}) \oplus (b_{85} s_{85}) \oplus (b_{85} s_{87}) \oplus (b_{86} s_{85})$$
$$\oplus (b_{86} s_{87}) \oplus (b_{87} s_{85}) \oplus (b_{87} s_{87}) \oplus (s_{106} s_{85}) \oplus (s_{106} s_{87}) \oplus (s_{108} s_{85}) \oplus (s_{108} s_{87})$$
$$\oplus (b_{105} b_{85} b_{86}) \oplus (b_{106} b_{107} b_{84}) \oplus (b_{106} b_{107} b_{85}) \oplus (b_{106} b_{107} b_{86}) \oplus (b_{106} b_{107} b_{87})$$
$$\oplus (b_{106} b_{107}\ s_{106}) \oplus (b_{106} b_{107} s_{108}) \oplus (b_{106} b_{85} b_{86}) \oplus (b_{107} b_{85} b_{86}) \oplus (b_{108} b_{85} b_{86})$$
$$\oplus (b_{21} b_{22} s_{21}) \oplus (b_{21} b_{22} s_{23}) \oplus (b_{42} b_{43} s_{42}) \oplus (b_{42} b_{43} s_{44}) \oplus (b_{63} b_{64} s_{63}) \oplus (b_{63} b_{64} s_{65})$$
$$\oplus (b_{64} b_{65} s_{64}) \oplus (b_{64} b_{65} s_{66}) \oplus (b_{85} b_{86} s_{85}) \oplus (b_{85} b_{86} s_{87}) \oplus (b_{106} b_{107} b_{85} b_{86}).$$

Algebraic degree increases from 2 to 4 in the second iteration itself and increases with each iteration. A Boolean function should have high algebraic degree for cryptographic security [6]. Presence of forty-one variables makes it impossible to compute the other crypto properties as the truth-table has 2^{41} entries.

4   Security of FResCA

We analyse the security of the cipher with respect to different attacks.

Meier-Staffelbach Attack Our cipher uses 4-neighbourhood CA in the non-linear block. It has been shown in [11] that a certain class of 4-neighbourhood CA resist Meier-Staffelbach attack. The nonlinear rule in FResCA is from that class. So the cipher is strong against the attack.

Linear Attacks First keystream bit of our cipher has a nonlinearity of 32256. The nonlinearity increases with each iteration. Keystream bits are available only from 33rd iteration onwards and the nonlinearity will be much higher at that stage.

Correlation Attacks The nonlinear CA rule 43350 exhibits good correlation property [11]. Output from this block is combined with the output from the maximum length CA block using NMIX function [5] which guarantees correlation immunity and balancedness in the output. Thus correlation attacks can be ruled out.

Algebraic Attacks Ciphers having high algebraic degree in their Boolean function are difficult to attack algebraically. The rate of increase in algebraic degree is high with each iteration in our cipher. This prevents algebraic attacks.

Scan-Based Side Channel Attacks This attack will succeed if the cipher is reversible. The combination of nonlinear and linear CA rules makes our cipher robust against this attack.

Experimental Results Our cipher was run on NIST test suite [2]. Input to the NIST test suite was a file containing 0.1 billion keystream bits. NIST test suite was allowed to partition the input to 100 keystreams where each keystream contains 1 million bits.

Our cipher with rule 43350 as the 4-neighbourhood rule passed all the tests for different key-IV pairs. Rule 51510, which is also thought to be promising [11], failed in some tests (failures relatively low in number). The same key-IV pairs were used to generate keystream bits for NOCAS cipher [13] which needs 64 cycles in the initialisation phase whereas FResCA needs only 32. NOCAS failed in non-overlapping tests but passed all other tests in the test suite.

Strength of the cipher against fault attack is discussed separately in the next section.

5   Strength of FResCA Against Fault Attacks

Grain is shown to be vulnerable against fault attacks. It is shown in [4] that the cipher can be broken by inserting fault into the LFSR state. Later, fault injection in NFSR state [12] is also shown to be successful.

5.1   Injecting Fault into Linear Block of Grain

Initially, the attack [4] tries to find out the fault location by analysing the keystream difference bits. If d_i, z_i, and z_i' are respectively the ith keystream difference bit, keystream bit, and keystream bit after fault injection, then $d_i = z_i \oplus z_i'$. Corresponding to each possible fault location i in the LFSR, a unique pattern in $\{d_i\}$ is found out.

The Boolean representation of Grain-128 output z_i contains $s_{i+13}s_{i+20}$ and $s_{i+60}s_{i+79}$ as terms. If any one of the four bits s_{13}, s_{20}, s_{60}, or s_{79} is faulted, then the output difference represents the value of an LFSR bit. As an example, if fault is injected at position 60, output difference is the value of s_{79}. In this way, each LFSR bit is revealed.

If we know the LFSR bits, we can generate linear equations involving NFSR bits from the regular keystream. The only exception is the involvement of the term $b_{i+12}b_{i+95}s_{i+95}$ and if $s_{i+95} = 0$, we get linear equation involving several bits of the current NFSR state. The keystream difference equations that are used to recover LFSR states can be reused here also.

Since Grain-128 algorithm is reversible, the cipher can be run backwards from the known current state to reach the initial state to reveal the key.

Prevention of the Attack in FResCA In our cipher, fault position cannot be found out as described in the attack. ΔGrain algorithm tries to find a unique pattern P_i corresponding to each each fault position i, $0 \leq i \leq 127$. The algorithm relies on the fact that the fault injected position will be represented by 1 while other bits are 0 and the availability of this 1 in the output through different taps at different instances of time provides the value of i. In our CA based linear block, a single 1 in the register generates more 1's in different cell positions with each iteration (unlike in Grain where the single 1 shifts its position with each iteration) and we cannot generate unique patterns corresponding to each fault position.

In phase 3 of the attack, the algorithm (algorithm 3) which finds the number of known LFSR bits also will fail as it uses ΔLFSR as used in ΔGrain algorithm because there will be more 1's in our cipher as opposed to a single 1 in ΔLFSR. In the case of Grain, the number of LFSR bits that are recovered depends on the fault location and the number of times the cipher is clocked after the fault is injected. In our case, during subsequent clocking after fault injection, the fault will not be preserved in a single cell and gets mixed with more and more neighbours with each iteration. We can find out exactly one linear bit if the fault location is 86 or 107 as $s_{86}s_{107}$ is the only term involving linear bits in the keystream function $z = b_{128} \oplus s_{128} \oplus b_1 s_1 \oplus b_{22}s_{22} \oplus b_{43}s_{43} \oplus b_{64}s_{64} \oplus b_{65}s_{65} \oplus b_{86}s_{86} \oplus b_{107}s_{107} \oplus b_{86}b_{107} \oplus s_{86}s_{107}$.

If we know all the linear bits (s_i's), we can try to find nonlinear bits (b_i's). Then the only nonlinear term in z_i (keystream bit) is $b_{86}b_{107}$. We cannot make it linear as was done in Grain where the only nonlinear term was $b_{12}b_{95}s_{95}$ and if s_{95} was zero, the whole equation becomes linear. In Grain, more iterations will produce more linear equations (shown in Fig. 4 - Algorithm "CountEquations" [4]) whereas in our cipher, more iterations will not be fruitful as the fault start mixing with more and more neighbours in each iteration.

We need to compute the initial state to find the key thereby breaking the cipher. Use of CA and combination of nonlinear and linear CA rules to produce keystream bits make the computation of initial state from the known present state of the cipher difficult. In our case, finding present state itself is not possible.

5.2 Injecting Fault into Nonlinear Block of Grain

After initialisation phase in Grain, if fault is injected into NFSR, it cannot propagate to LFSR. This attack [12], just like the previous attack, also starts by finding out the fault injection location. Over a large number of key-IV combinations, the nonlinear b-bits will provide unique keystream difference sequence for fault injection at a particular location thereby revealing the fault location. To enhance the attack, a table named Fault Traces Table which contains the list of corrupted bit locations after t iterations on fault injection at location f is also created.

To find out nonlinear bits, the feedback equation for b_{128} is used which contains seven degree-2 terms containing only nonlinear b-bits of the form $b_m b_n$. Moving the fault to either b_m or b_n will provide the value of the other as the difference. To get more linear equations involving b-bits, we use linear b-terms in z_i. Feedback fault is moved to one of the single b-bit output taps to get either the value of b-bit or linear equation involving several b-bits.

The three terms $b_{i+12}s_{i+8}$, $b_{i+95}s_{i+42}$, $b_{i+12}b_{i+95}s_{i+95}$ in z_i are exploited to determine the LFSR bits. They provide either the s-bit value or provide linear equation involving s-bits. These equations are solved to get the LFSR state.

Like in the previous attack, after NFSR and LFSR state is obtained, Grain is run backwards to get the key.

Prevention of the Attack in FResCA When fault is injected in the nonlinear block of our cipher, the fault propagation largely depends on the nonlinear CA rule used and the effect of the fault is propagated to the neighbouring cells on both sides of the cell where fault was injected. Because of the fast diffusion of the introduced fault, we will not be able to find unique pattern σ_f as in algorithm 1 of the attack so that fault location can be found out. Moreover, the computed fault traces in our cipher looks random as the nonlinear CA rule determines how the fault traces are spread.

It is not possible to determine the nonlinear bits in our cipher like the NFSR bits in Grain. The attack against Grain uses equations corresponding to z_i and b_{128}. In our cipher, we have only output z_i as there is no feedback path (which corresponds to b_{128} in Grain) for the nonlinear block. In the output equation for Grain, there are 7 single b-bit output taps, namely $b_2, b_{15}, b_{36}, b_{45}, b_{64}, b_{73}$, and b_{89} that are exploited in this phase whereas our cipher has only one, i.e., b_{128}. We cannot move a fault into single bit output tap as done in Grain as it is a simple left shift in Grain with each iteration. In our cipher, the number of 1's will be more and controlling them to occupy specific cell locations is practically impossible. This phase of the attack consults Fault Traces Table twice, but in our case, fault traces cannot be constructed in a similar manner.

We try to find out linear block bits just like how LFSR bits are found out in Grain assuming that we have already found out the nonlinear block bits. This phase uses the terms in z_i representation which has both b and s, like $b_m s_n$. In Grain, the induced fault propagates to some specified locations in NFSR without corrupting other b-bits of z_i. In our cipher, it is very difficult to guarantee this as more and more bits get corrupted because of the higher diffusion of the fault which is the inherent nature of the CA.

Computation of initial state from the known present state of the cipher thereby breaking the cipher is very difficult because of the use of CA and combination of nonlinear and linear CA rules to produce keystream bits as described in the previous attack.

6   Conclusion

We have proposed a 4-neighbourhood CA based Grain-like stream cipher. Its initialisation is 8 times faster than Grain. We have shown that it is strong against different attacks, in particular, fault attacks. Experimental results confirm our claim for its robustness.

References

1. The Estream Project. http://www.ecrypt.eu.org/stream/. Accessed 31 Mar 2016
2. The NIST Statistical Test Suite. http://csrc.nist.gov/groups/ST/toolkit/rng/. Accessed 31 Mar 2016
3. Banik, S., Maitra, S., Sarkar, S.: A differential fault attack on the grain family of stream ciphers. In: Proceedings of the CHES 2012-14th International Workshop, Leuven, Belgium, 9–12 September 2012
4. Berzati, A., Canovas, C., Castagnos, G., Debraize, B., Goubin, L., Gouget, A., Paillier, P., Salgado, S.: Fault analysis of grain-128. In: 2009 IEEE International Workshop on Hardware-Oriented Security and Trust, HOST 2009, pp. 7–14 (2009)
5. Bhaumik, J., RoyChowdhury, D.: Nmix: An ideal candidate for key mixing. In: SECRYPT 2009, Proceedings of the International Conference on Security and Cryptography, Milan, Italy, 7–10 July 2009, pp. 285–288 (2009)
6. Ding, C., Xiao, G., Shan, W.: The Stability Theory of Stream Ciphers. LNCS, 1st edn. Springer, Heidelberg (1991)
7. Ghosh, S., RoyChowdhury, D.: CASca: A CA based scalable stream cipher. In: Mohapatra, R.N., Chowdhury, D.R., Giri, D. (eds.) Mathematics and Computing. Springer Proceedings in Mathematics & Statistics, pp. 95–105. Springer, India (2015)
8. Hell, M., Johansson, T., Maximov, A., Meier, W.: A stream cipher proposal: Grain-128. In: 2006 IEEE International Symposium on Information Theory, pp. 1614–1618 (2006)
9. Hoch, J.J., Shamir, A.: Fault analysis of stream ciphers. In: Joye, M., Quisquater, J.-J. (eds.) CHES 2004. LNCS, vol. 3156, pp. 240–253. Springer, Heidelberg (2004)
10. Jose, J., Das, S., RoyChowdhury, D.: Inapplicability of fault attacks against triviumon a cellular automata based stream cipher. In: Proceedings of the Cellular Automata-ACRI 2014, Krakow, Poland, 22–25 September 2014, pp. 427–436 (2014)
11. Jose, J., RoyChowdhury, D.: Investigating four neighbourhood cellular automata as better cryptographic primitives. J. Discrete Math. Sci. Crypt. (to be published in 2016)
12. Karmakar, S., Roy Chowdhury, D.: Fault analysis of grain-128 by targeting NFSR. In: Nitaj, A., Pointcheval, D. (eds.) AFRICACRYPT 2011. LNCS, vol. 6737, pp. 298–315. Springer, Heidelberg (2011)
13. Karmakar, S., RoyChowdhury, D.: NOCAS: A nonlinear cellular automata based stream cipher. In: Automata 2011, Center for Mathematical Modeling, 21–23 November 2011, pp. 135–146. University of Chile, Santiago, Chile (2011)
14. Wu, C.K., Feng, D.: Boolean Functions and Their Applications in Cryptography. Advances in Computer Science and Technology, 1st edn. Springer, Heidelberg (2016)

Resilient Vectorial Functions and Cyclic Codes Arising from Cellular Automata

Luca Mariot[1,2(✉)] and Alberto Leporati[1]

[1] Dipartimento di Informatica, Sistemistica e Comunicazione,
Università degli Studi Milano-Bicocca, Viale Sarca 336, 20126 Milano, Italy
{luca.mariot,alberto.leporati}@unimib.it
[2] Laboratoire I3S, Université Nice-Sophia Antipolis,
2000 Route des Colles, 06903 Sophia Antipolis, France

Abstract. Most of the works concerning cryptographic applications of cellular automata (CA) focus on the analysis of the underlying local rules, interpreted as boolean functions. In this paper, we investigate the cryptographic criteria of CA global rules by considering them as vectorial boolean functions. In particular, we prove that the 1-resiliency property of CA with bipermutive local rules is preserved on the corresponding global rules. We then unfold an interesting connection between linear codes and cellular automata, observing that the generator and parity check matrices of cyclic codes correspond to the transition matrices of linear CA. Consequently, syndrome computation in cyclic codes can be performed in parallel by evolving a suitable linear CA, and the error-correction capability is determined by the resiliency of the global rule. As an example, we finally show how to implement the $(7,4,3)$ cyclic Hamming code using a CA of radius $r = 2$.

Keywords: Cellular automata · Boolean functions · S-boxes · Resiliency · Linear feedback shift registers · Cyclic codes · Hamming codes

1 Introduction

Cellular Automata (CA) provide an interesting framework for developing cryptographic primitives such as *stream* and *block ciphers*. The reason is twofold: first, depending on the local rule, CA can exhibit chaotic and unpredictable dynamic behaviors, making them possibly useful for *pseudorandom number generation* (PRNG), one of the most important building blocks in cryptography. Second, being a massively parallel model, CA can be efficiently realized in hardware, and thus they are interesting for implementing cryptographic applications on devices with limited computational resources.

Wolfram [10] was the first to pioneer the use of CA for keystream generation, using the elementary rule 30. However, the design was discovered to be insecure against the Meier-Staffelbach [7] and Koc-Apohan attacks [3], due to the fact that rule 30, when considered as a boolean function $f : \mathbb{F}_2^3 \rightarrow \mathbb{F}_2$, is not

© Springer International Publishing Switzerland 2016
S. El Yacoubi et al. (Eds.): ACRI 2016, LNCS 9863, pp. 34–44, 2016.
DOI: 10.1007/978-3-319-44365-2_4

1-resilient and has a low nonlinearity. Since then, some researchers [2,4] focused on the search of CA local rules having good cryptographic profiles.

To the best of our knowledge, there are no works in the literature addressing the cryptographic properties of CA *global rules*. The aim of this paper is to begin filling this gap by investigating CA as a particular kind of *vectorial boolean functions*. Specifically, we focus on the resiliency criterion, the reason being that resilient vectorial functions both have applications in stream ciphers and *error-correcting codes*.

We first show that the global rules of *bipermutive CA* are always at least 1-resilient, thus generalizing the result in [4] about bipermutive local rules. We then prove an equivalence between *linear CA* and linear *cyclic codes*. In particular, we show how the systematic encoding of cyclic codes actually corresponds to the preimage computation process of the all-zeros configuration in linear CA, while syndrome computation is equivalent to the application of the CA global rule, and can thus be performed in parallel. Leveraging on the theory of resilient vectorial functions, we remark that the resiliency order of a linear CA can be used to determine the minimum distance of its associated cyclic code. To sum up the results of the paper, we finally show how the $(7, 4, 3)$ cyclic Hamming code can be implemented using a CA of radius $r = 2$ and length $n = 7$.

The rest of the paper is organized as follows. Section 2 recalls some basic facts about cellular automata and vectorial boolean functions. Section 3 shows that the global rules of bipermutive CA are always at least 1-resilient. Section 4 recalls some key concepts about the theory of error-correcting codes, and presents the connection between linear cyclic codes and linear CA. Section 5 illustrates the results presented in the paper by showing how to simulate the $(7, 4, 3)$ cyclic Hamming codes using linear CA. Finally, Sect. 6 sums up the results presented in the paper and points out future directions of research on the subject.

2 Preliminaries on Cellular Automata and Boolean Functions

2.1 Cellular Automata

In what follows, we consider exclusively one-dimensional boolean cellular automata, formally defined below.

Definition 1. *A one-dimensional boolean cellular automaton (CA) is a triple* $\langle C, \delta, f \rangle$*, where* C *is a finite one-dimensional array of binary cells,* $\delta \in \mathbb{N}$ *is the diameter and* $f : \mathbb{F}_2^\delta \to \mathbb{F}_2$ *is the* local rule.

Given an array C of length $n \geq \delta$, the update of a CA is done as follows. If the diameter δ is odd with $\delta = 2r + 1$ for $r \in \mathbb{N}$, then each cell i in the range $\{r + 1, \cdots, n - r\}$ synchronously updates its state by applying rule f to the neighborhood $\{i - r, \cdots, i, \cdots, i + r\}$. Otherwise, if δ is even and $r = \delta/2$, then each cell i in the range $\{r, \cdots, n - r\}$ synchronously updates its state by applying f to the neighborhood $\{i - r + 1, \cdots, i + r\}$. In both cases, the parameter r is called the *radius* of the CA. The *global rule* of a CA $\langle C, \delta, f \rangle$ with array of length $n = m + \delta - 1$ is the function $F : \mathbb{F}_2^n \to \mathbb{F}_2^m$ defined as

$$F(C) = F(c_1, \cdots, c_n) = (f(c_1, \cdots, c_\delta), \cdots, f(c_{n-\delta+1}, \cdots, c_n)).$$

In what follows, we identify a CA $\langle C, \delta, f \rangle$ by its global rule $F : \mathbb{F}_2^n \to \mathbb{F}_2^m$.

The most common way to represent a CA is by means of the *truth table* of its local rule f. Since f depends on δ variables, it means that there exist a total of 2^{2^δ} possible local rules. Another convenient way of representing a CA rule f is through its *Wolfram code*, which is basically the decimal encoding of the truth table of f.

2.2   Vectorial Boolean Functions

A *boolean function* is a mapping $f : \mathbb{F}_2^n \to \mathbb{F}_2$. The boolean functions adopted in cryptography for the design of stream and block ciphers must satisfy several criteria, among which one of the most important is *resiliency*:

Definition 2. *A boolean function* $f : \mathbb{F}_2^n \to \mathbb{F}_2$ *is said to be t-resilient if, by fixing at most t input coordinates, the resulting restriction of f is* balanced, *i.e. its truth table is composed of an equal number of zeros and ones.*

A very well-known secondary construction to obtain a $(t+1)$-resilient function of $n + 1$ variables from a t-resilient function of n variables is to simply add (XOR) an additional variable, as shown in [9]. This method is formalized in the following result:

Proposition 1. *Let* $I = \{i_1, \cdots, i_{t+1}\} \subseteq \{1, \cdots, n\}$ *and* $J = \{j_1, \cdots, j_{n-t-1}\} = \{1, \cdots, n\} \setminus I$ *be complementary sets of indices. Additionally, let* $f : \mathbb{F}_2^n \to \mathbb{F}_2$ *be a boolean function of n variables defined as*

$$f(x_1, \cdots, x_n) = g(x_{j_1}, \cdots, x_{j_{n-t-1}}) \oplus x_{i_1} \oplus \cdots \oplus x_{i_{t+1}},$$

where $g : \mathbb{F}_2^{n-t-1} \to \mathbb{F}_2$ *is a boolean function of* $n - t - 1$ *variables. Then, f is t-resilient.*

Let $n \geq m$. A *vectorial boolean function* (also called a *S-box*) is a mapping $F : \mathbb{F}_2^n \to \mathbb{F}_2^m$ with n input variables and m outputs. By $f_1, \cdots, f_m : \mathbb{F}_2^n \to \mathbb{F}_2$ we denote the *coordinate functions* of F, that is, the m boolean functions which specify the value of each output bit of F:

$$F(x_1, \cdots, x_n) = (f_1(x_1, \cdots, x_n), f_2(x_1, \cdots, x_n), \cdots, f_m(x_1, \cdots, x_n)).$$

The *component functions* of F are defined as $v \cdot F$ for all $v \in \mathbb{F}_2^m \setminus \{\underline{0}\}$, where $\cdot$ denotes the scalar product modulo 2. Since

$$v \cdot F = v_1 f_1(x_1, \cdots, x_n) \oplus \cdots \oplus v_m f_m(x_1, \cdots, x_n),$$

it follows that the component functions are the linear combinations of the coordinate functions of F.

Remark 1. Let $F : \mathbb{F}_2^{m+\delta-1} \to \mathbb{F}_2^m$ be a one-dimensional boolean cellular automaton of length $n = m + \delta - 1$ defined by a local rule $f : \mathbb{F}_2^\delta \to \mathbb{F}_2$ of diameter δ. Since each output cell y_i depends only on the input cells $x_i, \cdots, x_{i+\delta-1}$ under application of the local rule, the coordinate functions of F are $f_i(x_1, \cdots, x_n) = f(x_i, \cdots, x_{i+\delta-1})$ for $i \in \{1, \cdots, m\}$.

We now define the resiliency property for vectorial functions.

Definition 3. *Let $F : \mathbb{F}_2^n \to \mathbb{F}_2^m$ be a vectorial function, and $1 \le t \le n$. Function F is said t-resilient if, by fixing any t input variables $x_{i_1}, \cdots, x_{i_t}$, the resulting restriction $\tilde{F} : \mathbb{F}_2^{n-t} \to \mathbb{F}_2^m$ is balanced, i.e. for all $y \in \mathbb{F}_2^m$ it follows that $|\tilde{F}^{-1}(y)| = 2^m$.*

Note that for $m = 1$ Definition 3 is actually equivalent to Definition 2 for boolean functions. The resiliency of a vectorial function can be characterized by the resiliency of its component functions, as the next result proved in [1] shows:

Proposition 2. *Let $F : \mathbb{F}_2^n \to \mathbb{F}_2^m$ be a vectorial boolean function in n variables and m outputs. Then, F is t-resilient if and only if for all $v \in \mathbb{F}_2^m \setminus \{\underline{0}\}$ the component function $v \cdot F$ is t-resilient.*

3   Resilient Vectorial Functions from Bipermutive CA

We now show that bipermutive cellular automata are always at least 1-resilient when considered as vectorial boolean functions. To this end, recall that a rule $f : \mathbb{F}_2^\delta \to \mathbb{F}_2$ of diameter $\delta \in \mathbb{N}$ is *bipermutive* if it is defined as

$$f(x_1, x_2, \cdots, x_{\delta-1}, x_\delta) = x_1 \oplus g(x_2, \cdots, x_{\delta-1}) \oplus x_\delta \quad (1)$$

for all $x = (x_1, x_2, \cdots, x_{\delta-1}, x_\delta) \in \mathbb{F}_2^\delta$, where $g : \mathbb{F}_2^{\delta-2} \to \mathbb{F}_2$. Clearly, by Proposition 1 any bipermutive local rule is also a 1-resilient boolean function. The following result characterizes the component functions of a cellular automaton based on a bipermutive rule:

Lemma 1. *Let $m, \delta \in \mathbb{N}$ and let $F : \mathbb{F}_2^{m+\delta-1} \to \mathbb{F}_2^m$ be a CA of length $n = m + \delta - 1$ defined by a bipermutive local rule $f : \mathbb{F}_2^\delta \to \mathbb{F}_2$. Then, for all $v \in \mathbb{F}_2^m \setminus \{\underline{0}\}$ the component function $v \cdot F$ is bipermutive as well.*

Proof. Let f be defined as in Eq. (1). Given $v \in \mathbb{F}_2^m \setminus \{\underline{0}\}$, denote the support of v as follows:

$$supp(v) = \{i_1, \cdots, i_k\} = \{i : v_i \ne 0\}. \quad (2)$$

Then, the component function $v \cdot F$ can be expressed as:

$$v \cdot F = x_{i_1} \oplus g(x_{i_1+1}, \cdots, x_{i_1+1+\delta-2}) \oplus x_{i_1+\delta-1} \oplus \cdots \oplus x_{i_k} \oplus g(x_{i_k+1}, \cdots, x_{i_k+\delta-2}) \oplus x_{i_k+\delta-1}. \quad (3)$$

Notice that the leftmost and rightmost variables x_{i_1} and $x_{i_k+\delta-1}$ appear exactly once in Eq. (3), thus they are never canceled. Let G be the boolean function defined as:

$$G(x_{i_1+1}, \cdots, x_{i_k+\delta-2}) = g(x_{i_1+1}, \cdots, x_{i_1+\delta-2}) \oplus x_{i_1+\delta-1} \oplus \cdots \oplus x_{i_k} \oplus g(x_{i_k+1}, \cdots, x_{i_k+\delta-2}). \quad (4)$$

Hence, the component function $v \cdot F$ has the form:

$$v \cdot F = x_{i_1} \oplus G(x_{i_1+1}, \cdots, x_{i_k+\delta-2}) \oplus x_{i_k+\delta-1}. \tag{5}$$

As a consequence, $v \cdot F$ is bipermutive. □

Combining Lemma 1 and Proposition 1, we get the following result:

Theorem 1. *Let $m, \delta \in \mathbb{N}$ and let $F : \mathbb{F}_2^{m+\delta-1} \to \mathbb{F}_2^m$ be a CA of length $n = m + \delta - 1$ defined by a bipermutive local rule $f : \mathbb{F}_2^\delta \to \mathbb{F}_2$. Then, F is at least 1-resilient.*

4   Linear CA and Linear Codes

4.1   Basics on Linear Codes

We now restrict our attention to the class of *linear resilient CA*, i.e. resilient CA whose local rule is a linear combination of the neighborhood cells. In this case, an interesting connection with *linear codes* can be observed. We first recall some basic facts about linear codes; for a thorough treatment of the subject, the reader can refer to [6].

Definition 4. *Let $n, m, d \in \mathbb{N}$ such that $n \geq m$, and let $q = \rho^\alpha$ be the power of a prime number ρ. A (n, m, d) linear code C is a m-dimensional subspace of the vector space $\mathbb{F}_q^n$, such that the Hamming distance between any two vectors $c_1, c_2 \in C$ (called codewords) is at least d. The parameters n, m and d are respectively called the length, the dimension and the minimum distance of C.*

In what follows, we focus on *binary linear codes*, where $q = 2$.

Since a (n, m, d) linear code C is a subspace of dimension m of $\mathbb{F}_2^n$, it is possible to specify it using a $m \times n$ matrix G whose rows form a set of m linearly independent codewords of C. Such a matrix G is called a *generator matrix* for code C. The encoding process simply amounts to multiplying a *message vector* $\mu \in \mathbb{F}_2^m$ by matrix G, thus obtaining the codeword $c = \mu G$. Another matrix associated to a linear code is its *parity check matrix*, which is useful for error correction. The parity check matrix for C is a matrix H of dimensions $(n-m) \times n$ such that $Hx^\top = \underline{0}$ if and only if $x \in C$. In general, the vector $s = Hx^\top$ is called the *syndrome* of $x \in \mathbb{F}_2^n$.

The *dual code* of a (n, m, d) linear code C is the set $C^\perp = \{x \in \mathbb{F}_2^n : x \cdot y = 0, \forall y \in C\}$, that is, the set of all vectors in $\mathbb{F}_2^n$ which are orthogonal to the codewords in C. The parity check matrix H of C is a generator matrix for $C^\perp$, and vice versa the generator matrix G of C is a parity check matrix for $C^\perp$. This means that $C^\perp$ is a code of length n and dimension $n - m$.

Notice that each codeword $c \in C$ defines a *ball* B_c of radius $t = \lfloor (d-1)/2 \rfloor$, since the minimum distance is d. Suppose now that a codeword $c \in C$ is transmitted over a noisy channel, and at most t errors occur, i.e. at most t bits of c are flipped. The received word z will always be inside ball B_c, thus making it possible to retrieve the original codeword by determining the center of the ball to which z belongs to. This procedure can be carried out in linear codes through *syndrome decoding* as follows. Let $c \in C$ be a codeword and $e \in \mathbb{F}_2^n$ be an *error pattern* introduced by the channel, having Hamming weight at most t. A received word can thus be expressed as $z = c \oplus e$. Given a parity check matrix H of C, the syndrome of z is $s = Hz^\top = H(c \oplus e)^\top = Hc^\top \oplus He^\top = He^\top$. In order to retrieve c, it thus suffices to determine the error pattern e corresponding to s, and output $c = z \oplus e$. This task can be performed by storing in a table the set of all possible error patterns of weight at most t together with their syndromes.

We now introduce the class of linear *cyclic codes*.

Definition 5. *A (n, m, d) linear code $C \subseteq \mathbb{F}_2^n$ is called* cyclic *if it is closed under cyclic shifts, i.e. for all $c = (c_1, c_2 \cdots, c_n) \in C$, it holds that $c' = (c_2, \cdots, c_n, c_1) \in C$.*

A cyclic code is described by its *generator polynomial* $g(x) = g_0 + g_1 x + \cdots + g_{n-m} x^{n-m}$, where $g_i \in \mathbb{F}_2$ for all $i \in \{0, \cdots, n-m\}$. If the m-bit message $\mu = (\mu_0, \cdots, \mu_{m-1})$ is represented by the polynomial $\mu(x) = \mu_0 + \mu_1 x + \cdots + \mu_{m-1} x^{m-1}$, then the polynomial corresponding to the codeword c is $c(x) = \mu(x)g(x)$. There exists a one-to-one correspondence between cyclic codes of length n and divisors of $x^n - 1$. In particular, a (n, m, d) code C is cyclic if and only if its generator polynomial $g(x)$ divides $x^n - 1$.

Given a (n, m, d) cyclic code C with generator polynomial $g(x)$ of degree $n-m$, the polynomial $h(x) = (x^n - 1)/g(x)$ of degree m is called the *parity check polynomial* of C. Analogously to the parity check matrix, $h(x)$ satisfies the property that the codeword associated to a polynomial $d(x)$ belongs to C if and only if $d(x)h(x) = 0$. The relationship between the generator/parity check polynomials of a cyclic code C and its generator/parity check matrices is given by the following result:

Theorem 2. *Let $C \subseteq \mathbb{F}_2^n$ be a (n, m, d) cyclic linear code with generator polynomial $g(x) = g_0 + g_1 x + \cdots + g_{n-m} x^{n-m}$ and parity check polynomial $h(x) = h_0 + h_1 x + \cdots + h_m x^m$. Then the following are respectively a generator and a parity check matrix for C:*

$$
G = \begin{pmatrix} g_0 & \cdots & g_{n-m} & 0 & \cdots\cdots\cdots\cdots & 0 \\ 0 & g_0 & \cdots & g_{n-m} & 0 & \cdots\cdots & 0 \\ \vdots & \vdots & \vdots & \ddots & \vdots & \vdots & \vdots \\ 0 & \cdots & & \cdots & 0 & g_0 & \cdots & g_{n-m} \end{pmatrix}, \quad H = \begin{pmatrix} h_m & \cdots & h_0 & 0 & \cdots\cdots\cdots\cdots & 0 \\ 0 & h_m & \cdots & h_0 & 0 & \cdots\cdots & 0 \\ \vdots & \vdots & \vdots & \ddots & \vdots & \vdots & \vdots \\ 0 & \cdots\cdots\cdots\cdots & 0 & h_m & \cdots & h_0 \end{pmatrix}.
$$

$$(6)$$

As a consequence of Theorem 2, the dual code $C^\top$ of a cyclic code is again a cyclic code of length n and dimension $n - m$.

One of the main advantages of cyclic codes is that they can be easily implemented using *Linear Feedback Shift Registers* (LFSR), as shown in [6, pp. 193–195]. In particular, if the parity check polynomial $h(x)$ of a (n, m, d) cyclic code is such that $h_0 \neq 0$, the codeword of a message $\mu \in \mathbb{F}_2^m$ can be generated by a LFSR of length m whose tap polynomial is the reciprocal $\tilde{h}(x) = h_m + h_{m-1} x + \cdots + x^m$

of $h(x)$. The registers are initialized to the values $\mu_0, \cdots, \mu_{m-1}$ of μ, and the LFSR is evolved for n steps. The output of length n produced by the LFSR is the codeword corresponding to μ. Notice that the first m output bits are exactly the original message μ, while the remaining $n - m$ are the parity check bits. This encoding procedure is called *systematic*, since the bits of the message appear unaltered in the corresponding codeword. If no errors are introduced by the channel, the decoding process is immediate since it just consists of truncating the codeword to its first m bits.

4.2   Linear CA and Cyclic Codes

A cellular automaton $F : \mathbb{F}_2^{m+\delta-1} \rightarrow \mathbb{F}_2^m$ is called *linear* if its local rule is defined as $f(x_1, \cdots x_\delta) = a_1 x_1 \oplus \cdots \oplus a_\delta x_\delta$, with $a_i \in \mathbb{F}_2$ for all $i \in \{1, \cdots, \delta\}$. The global rule of F is described by a $m \times (m + \delta - 1)$ *transition matrix* M_F of the following form:

$$
M_F = \begin{pmatrix} a_1 & \cdots & a_\delta & 0 & \cdots\cdots\cdots\cdots & 0 \\ 0 & a_1 & \cdots & a_\delta & 0 & \cdots\cdots\cdots & 0 \\ \vdots & \vdots & \vdots & \ddots & \vdots & \vdots & \vdots & \ddots & \vdots \\ 0 & \cdots\cdots\cdots\cdots & 0 & a_1 & \cdots & a_\delta \end{pmatrix}. \tag{7}
$$

In particular, when the CA is bipermutive and linear we have $a_1 = a_\delta = 1$. The application of the CA global rule F to a configuration $x \in \mathbb{F}_2^{m+\delta-1}$ corresponds to the multiplication $y = M_F x^\top$.

One can notice that the generator and parity check matrices of Eq. (6) in Theorem 2 have the same form of the linear CA matrix in Eq. (7). In particular, the systematic encoding for cyclic codes described above can be simulated through cellular automata. As observed in [5], computing a preimage of a spatially periodic configuration in a linear bipermutive CA is equivalent to a *concatenation* of LFSR, where the LFSR associated to the local rule is disturbed by the LFSR which generates the spatially periodic configuration. In our case, we are only interested in a preimage of a finite configuration. Thus the general scheme consists of the LFSR associated to the rule where the feedback is additively disturbed by the bits of the configuration. If one takes the all-zeros configuration $\underline{0}$, it can be observed that the resulting concatenated LFSR of Fig. 1 is equivalent to the LFSR used for the systematic encoding of a cyclic code. As a matter of fact, adding a sequence of zeros to the feedback of a LFSR does not change its dynamics. In the context of cellular automata, the system represented in Fig. 1 is equivalent to the computation of a preimage of $\underline{0} \in \mathbb{F}_2^{n-m}$, in particular the preimage determined by the m-bit block μ.

To summarise the discussion above, we have thus proved the following result:

Theorem 3. *Let $F : \mathbb{F}_2^{m+\varrho} \rightarrow \mathbb{F}_2^m$ be a linear cellular automaton defined by a local rule $f(x) = a_1 x_1 \oplus \cdots \oplus a_\delta x_\delta$ of diameter $\delta = \varrho + 1$ with $\varrho \in \mathbb{N}$, and let $g(x) = a_1 + a_2 x + \cdots + a_\delta x^\varrho$ be the polynomial associated to f. If $g(x)$ divides $x^n - 1$ where $n = m + \varrho$, then F is equivalent to a cyclic code C of length n and dimension m. The generator matrix of C is the CA matrix M_F associated to F, while $g(x)$*

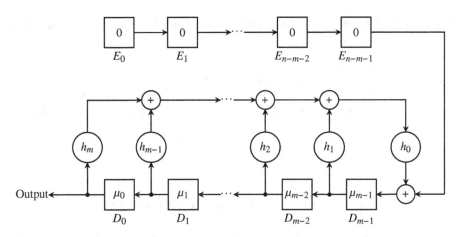

Fig. 1. Concatenation of a LFSR with a sequence of $n - m$ zeros, which computes a preimage $x \in F^{-1}(\underline{0})$.

is the generator polynomial of C. Additionally, let $\tilde{h}(x) = h_m + h_{m-1}x + \cdots + h_0 x^m$ be the reciprocal of the parity check polynomial $h(x) = (x^n - 1)/g(x)$, and let $\tilde{f}(x) = h_m x_1 \oplus \cdots \oplus h_0 x_{m+1}$ be the corresponding local rule. Then, the matrix $M_{\tilde{F}}$ associated to the linear CA $\tilde{F} : \mathbb{F}_2^{m+\varrho} \to \mathbb{F}_2^{\varrho}$ induced by rule $\tilde{f}$ is a parity check matrix for C, and $C = \tilde{F}^{-1}(\underline{0})$.

In other words, by Theorem 3 we can implement a linear cyclic code of length n and dimension m with a cellular automaton as follows:

1. Given m and $n = m + \varrho$ with $\varrho \in \mathbb{N}$, determine a local rule f of diameter $\delta = \varrho + 1$ such that the associated polynomial $g(x)$ divides $x^n - 1$.
2. Compute the reciprocal $\tilde{h}(x)$ of the parity check polynomial $h(x) = (x^n - 1)/g(x)$, and determine the corresponding local rule $\tilde{f}$ of diameter $m + 1$.
3. *Systematic encoding*: Let $\tilde{F} : \mathbb{F}_2^{m+\varrho} \to \mathbb{F}_2^{\varrho}$ be the linear CA of length n induced by $\tilde{f}$. A message $\mu \in \mathbb{F}_2^m$ is encoded by computing the preimage $x \in \tilde{F}^{-1}(\underline{0})$ whose leftmost m-bit block equals μ. This preimage can be computed by the LFSR in Fig. 1.
4. *Syndrome computation*: given $x \in \mathbb{F}_2^{m+\varrho}$, the syndrome of x is $s = \tilde{F}(x)$. If the syndrome s equals $\underline{0} \in \mathbb{F}_2^{\varrho}$ then x is a codeword of C. Otherwise, one can apply the syndrome decoding procedure to retrieve the original codeword.

The main advantage of the above procedure is that the computation of the syndrome can be performed in parallel, since it corresponds to the application of the CA global rule $\tilde{F}$ to the word $\tilde{x}$.

Notice that up to now we did not consider the minimum distance of the cyclic codes generated through linear CA, which is necessary in order to assess their error-correction capability. This is where the resiliency order of the CA comes into play. In particular, the connection between $(n, m, d - 1)$ general linear resilient functions and linear codes is given by the following theorem [8]:

Theorem 4. *A $(n, m, d-1)$ resilient linear function $F : \mathbb{F}_2^n \to \mathbb{F}_2^m$ is equivalent to a (n, m, d) linear code C.*

We already know from the previous section that all bipermutive CA are always at least 1-resilient, thus a linear and bipermutive CA which satisfies the hypotheses of Theorem 3 is equivalent to a linear cyclic code with minimum distance at least 2. More in general, we can refine Theorem 3 on account of Theorem 4 as follows:

Theorem 5. *Let $F : \mathbb{F}_2^{m+\varrho} \to \mathbb{F}_2^m$ be a linear CA satisfying the hypotheses of Theorem 3. If F is $(d-1)$–resilient, then the cyclic code associated to F has minimum distance d.*

5   Cyclic Hamming Codes Through Linear CA

To sum up the results presented in the previous section, we show an example of cyclic code generated by a linear CA. In particular we focus on *cyclic Hamming codes*, which are codes with minimum distance $d = 3$ and thus they can correct up to 1 error. The main reason for this choice is the simplicity of syndrome decoding in Hamming codes. As a matter of fact, the position of the column of the parity check matrix H containing the value of the syndrome is the position where the error occurred.

Example 1 (The $(7, 4, 3)$ Cyclic Hamming Code). Let $F : \mathbb{F}_2^7 \to \mathbb{F}_2^4$ be the linear CA induced by the local rule $f : \mathbb{F}_2^4 \to \mathbb{F}_2$ defined as $f(x) = x_1 \oplus x_2 \oplus x_4$. The associated polynomial is $g(x) = 1 + x + x^3$, while the CA matrix is:

$$M_F = \begin{pmatrix} 1\,1\,0\,1\,0\,0\,0 \\ 0\,1\,1\,0\,1\,0\,0 \\ 0\,0\,1\,1\,0\,1\,0 \\ 0\,0\,0\,1\,1\,0\,1 \end{pmatrix}. \tag{8}$$

The polynomial $g(x)$ divides $x^7 - 1$, and we have $h(x) = (x^7 - 1)/g(x) = 1 + x + x^2 + x^4$. Further, we can deduce from matrix M_F that F is 2-resilient. As a matter of fact, it is not difficult to see by exhaustive enumeration that each nonzero vector v results in a sum of rows which always have at least 3 ones. Hence, by Theorem 5 the code C associated to F is the $(7, 4, 3)$ cyclic Hamming code. Remark that $\tilde{h}(x) = 1 + x^2 + x^3 + x^4$ is the reciprocal of the parity check polynomial $h(x)$. The local rule $\tilde{f}$ associated to the polynomial $\tilde{h}(x)$ is $\tilde{f}(x) = x_1 \oplus x_3 \oplus x_4 \oplus x_5$, and thus it has radius $r = 2$. In particular, the Wolfram code representing the truth table of $\tilde{f}$ is 1768527510. The transition matrix of the linear CA $\tilde{F} : \mathbb{F}_2^7 \to \mathbb{F}_2^3$ induced by rule $\tilde{f}$ is the following:

$$M_{\tilde{F}} = \begin{pmatrix} 1\,0\,1\,1\,1\,0\,0 \\ 0\,1\,0\,1\,1\,1\,0 \\ 0\,0\,1\,0\,1\,1\,1 \end{pmatrix}. \tag{9}$$

Let $\mu = (0, 1, 1, 0) \in \mathbb{F}_2^4$ be a 4-bit message. The systematic encoding of μ under the Hamming code $(7, 4, 3)$ can be accomplished by computing the preimage x

of $(0,0,0)$ under the action of $\tilde{F}$, with the leftmost 4 bits of x initialized to μ. This process is depicted in Fig. 2. Hence, the codeword corresponding to μ is $x = (0,1,1,0,1,0,0)$.

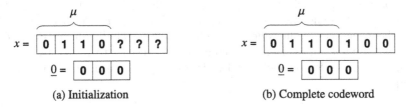

(a) Initialization   (b) Complete codeword

Fig. 2. Example of systematic encoding of $\mu = (0,1,1,0) \in \mathbb{F}_2^4$ using rule 1768527510, defined as $\tilde{f}(x) = x_1 \oplus x_3 \oplus x_4 \oplus x_5$.

Let us now assume that x is transmitted through a noisy channel and the fourth bit of x is flipped, thus yielding the word $\tilde{x} = (0,1,1,1,1,0,0)$. The receiver applies to $\tilde{x}$ the CA $\tilde{F}$ defined by rule 1768527510, thus obtaining the syndrome $s = F(x) = (1,1,0)$, as shown in Fig. 3(a). To correct the error, the receiver looks at the CA matrix $M_{\tilde{F}}$ and finds that the syndrome appears in the fourth column. Thus, the receiver knows that a transmission error has occurred in the fourth position of $\tilde{x}$, and the original codeword can be recovered as $\tilde{x} \oplus (0,0,0,1,0,0,0) = x$.

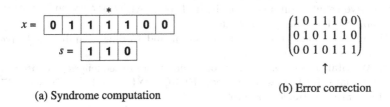

(a) Syndrome computation   (b) Error correction

Fig. 3. Example of error correction using rule 1768527510. The cell marked by $*$ indicates where the error occurred.

6   Conclusions and Future Directions

In this work, we began investigating the cryptographic properties of CA global rules, focusing on resiliency. In particular, we proved that the global rule of a bipermutive CA F is always at least 1-resilient, since each component of F is still a bipermutive boolean function. We then presented an equivalence between linear cyclic codes and linear CA, showing that syndrome computation in the former is equivalent to applying the global rule to the received word in the latter, and can thus be performed in parallel. Finally, the resiliency order of a linear and bipermutive CA can be used to determine the minimum distance of the corresponding cyclic code, and we applied these results by showing how the $(7, 4, 3)$ cyclic Hamming code can be implemented using a linear CA of radius $r = 2$.

There are several directions along which the present work can be extended, both on the cryptographic and on the coding-theoretic sides. For the cryptographic part, one could characterize the global rules of bipermutive CA in terms of other properties such as *nonlinearity* and *differential uniformity*. About the coding-theoretic part, cyclic codes form a broad class including for example *BCH* and *Reed-Solomon* codes. Hence, it could be interesting to investigate how to implement these codes through CA by elaborating on the method presented in this paper.

References

1. Carlet, C.: Boolean functions for cryptography and error-correcting codes. In: Crama, Y., Hammer, P.L. (eds.) Boolean Models and Methods in Mathematics, Computer Science, and Engineering. Cambridge University Press, New York (2010)
2. Formenti, E., Imai, K., Martin, B., Yunés, J.-B.: Advances on random sequence generation by uniform cellular automata. In: Calude, C.S., Freivalds, R., Kazuo, I. (eds.) Gruska Festschrift. LNCS, vol. 8808, pp. 56–70. Springer, Heidelberg (2014)
3. Koc, C.K., Apohan, A.M.: Inversion of cellular automata iterations. IEE Proc. Comput. Digit. Tech. **144**(5), 279–284 (1997). IET
4. Leporati, A., Mariot, L.: Cryptographic properties of bipermutive cellular automata rules. J. Cell. Aut. **9**(5–6), 437–475 (2014)
5. Mariot, L., Leporati, A.: On the periods of spatially periodic preimages in linear bipermutive cellular automata. In: Kari, J. (ed.) AUTOMATA 2015. LNCS, vol. 9099, pp. 181–195. Springer, Heidelberg (2015)
6. McEliece, R.J.: The Theory of Information and Coding. Cambridge University Press, New York (1985)
7. Meier, W., Staffelbach, O.: Analysis of pseudo random sequences generated by cellular automata. In: Davies, D.W. (ed.) EUROCRYPT 1991. LNCS, vol. 547, pp. 186–199. Springer, Heidelberg (1991)
8. Stinson, D.R.: Combinatorial Designs: Constructions and Analysis. Springer, Heidelberg (2004)
9. Siegenthaler, T.: Decrypting a class of stream ciphers using ciphertext only. IEEE Trans. Comput. **C–34**(1), 81–85 (1985)
10. Wolfram, S.: Cryptography with cellular automata. In: Williams, H.C. (ed.) CRYPTO 1985. LNCS, vol. 218, pp. 429–432. Springer, Heidelberg (1986)

Universality of 8-State Reversible and Conservative Triangular Partitioned Cellular Automata

Kenichi Morita[⊠]

Hiroshima University, Higashi-Hiroshima 739-8527, Japan
km@hiroshima-u.ac.jp

Abstract. A partitioned cellular automaton (PCA) is a subclass of a standard CA such that each cell is divided into several parts, and the next state of a cell is determined only by the adjacent parts of its neighbor cells. This framework is useful for designing reversible CAs. Here, we investigate isotropic three-neighbor 8-state triangular PCAs where a cell has three parts, and each part has two states. They are called elementary triangular PCAs (ETPCAs). There are 256 ETPCAs, and they are extremely simple since each of their local transition functions is described by only four local rules. In this paper, we study computational universality of nine kinds of *reversible* and *conservative* ETPCAs. It has already been shown that one of them is universal. Here, we newly show universality of another. It is proved by showing that a Fredkin gate, a universal reversible logic gate, can be simulated in it. From these results and by dualities, we can conclude six among the nine are universal. We also show the remaining three are non-universal. Thus, universality of all the reversible and conservative ETPCAs is clarified.

1 Introduction

A reversible cellular automaton (RCA) is a CA such that its global function is injective. Among various research topics on RCAs, computational universality of them is one of the important problems. Toffoli [12] first showed that a two-dimensional RCA is universal. Since then, studies on universality of one- and two-dimensional RCAs have been done extensively. As for two-dimensional RCAs, several very simple universal RCAs have been proposed. Margolus [4] presented a two-state universal block RCA with the Margolus neighborhood. Morita and Ueno [11] showed two kinds of 16-state universal RCAs using the framework of partitioned CAs (PCAs). Imai and Morita [3] gave a universal 8-state reversible triangular PCA (in the following sections it is denoted by T_{RU}) that has an extremely simple local function. In all these models, computational universality is shown by giving a configuration that simulates a Fredkin gate, a 3-input 3-output universal reversible logic gate.

A triangular CA is a one such that each cell is triangular-shaped, and communicates with its three neighbor cells. Here, we use the framework of a triangular

© Springer International Publishing Switzerland 2016
S. El Yacoubi et al. (Eds.): ACRI 2016, LNCS 9863, pp. 45–54, 2016.
DOI: 10.1007/978-3-319-44365-2_5

PCA (TPCA) to study reversible ones. It is a CA whose cell is divided into three parts. Each cell changes its state depending only on the three adjacent parts of its three neighbor cells, but not depending on the whole states of the three cells. This framework makes it easy to design reversible TPCAs. An elementary TPCA (ETPCA) is a TPCA where each part of a cell has only two states (hence a cell has eight states) and it is isotropic. ETPCAs are extremely simple, since each of their local transition functions is described by only four local rules.

In this paper, we investigate all the conservative (i.e., bit-conserving) and reversible ETPCAs (RETPCAs). There are nine conservative RETPCAs. It has been shown that one of them (denoted by T_{RU}) is computationally universal [3]. Here, we newly show another one, denoted by T_{RL}, is also universal. It is proved by showing that a Fredkin gate can be simulated in T_{RL}. From these results, and by the dualities among ETPCAs under reflection and conjugation, we can see six of them are universal. We also show that three are non-universal. Hence, universality of all the nine conservative RETPCAs is clarified.

2   Preliminaries

In this section, we give definitions on elementary triangular partitioned cellular automata (ETPCAs), their reversibility, and conservativeness. We also explain a method for showing computational universality of a reversible PCA.

2.1   Triangular Partitioned Cellular Automata (TPCAs)

A *partitioned cellular automaton* (PCA) is a subclass of a standard CA, where a cell is divided into several parts, and each part has a state set. The next state of a cell is determined by the states of the adjacent parts of the neighbor cells. A two-dimensional three-neighbor *triangular PCA* (TPCA) is a special kind of a PCA such that a cell is triangular-shaped, and divided into three parts.

We first consider an example of a TPCA whose behavior is determined by the set of local transition rules shown in Fig. 1. Note that each of the three parts of a cell has the state set $\{0, 1\}$, where 0 and 1 are represented by a blank and a particle (i.e., ●). Hence, each cell has eight states. We assume this TPCA is *isotropic* (or *rotation-symmetric*). Namely, for each local rule, the rules obtained by rotating the both sides of it by a multiple of 60° exist. Thus, the set of local rules in Fig. 1 specifies the *local function f* by which the next state of each cell is uniquely determined from the present states of the adjacent parts of the neighbor cells. Applying the local function f to all the cells in parallel, we obtain the *global function F*, which defines transition among configurations as in Fig. 2.

We say a PCA is *locally reversible* if its local function is injective, and *globally reversible* if its global function is injective. It is known that global reversibility and local reversibility are equivalent (Lemma 1). Thus, such a PCA is simply called a *reversible PCA* (RPCA). Note that, in [10], the lemma is given for one-dimensional PCAs, but it is easy to extend it for two-dimensional PCAs.

Lemma 1. [10] *A PCA A is globally reversible iff it is locally reversible.*

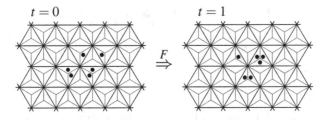

Fig. 1. Example of local rules of an isotropic TPCA, which define a local function

$t = 0$ $\qquad\qquad\qquad t = 1$

$$\overset{F}{\Rightarrow}$$

Fig. 2. Evolution of configurations by the global function F, which is induced by the local function shown in Fig. 1

By this lemma, to obtain a reversible CA, it is sufficient to give a locally reversible PCA. Thus, the framework of PCA makes it easy to design reversible CAs.

We can see that the local function defined by the set of local rules shown in Fig. 1 is injective, since there is no pair of local rules that have the same right-hand sides. Therefore, it is a reversible TPCA.

2.2   Elementary Triangular Partitioned Cellular Automata

An 8-state isotropic TPCA is called an *elementary TPCA* (ETPCA). Thus, each part of a cell has two states. ETPCAs are the simplest ones among two-dimensional PCAs. But, this class still contains many interesting PCAs as in the class of one-dimensional elementary CAs (ECAs) [13,14].

Since ETPCA is isotropic, and each part of a cell has the state set $\{0,1\}$, its local function is defined by only four local rules. Hence, an ETPCA can be specified by a four-digit number $wxyz$, as shown in Fig. 3, such that $w, z \in \{0,7\}$ and $x, y \in \{0, 1, \ldots, 7\}$. Thus, there are 256 ETPCAs. Note that w and z must be 0 or 7 because an ETPCA is deterministic and isotropic. The ETPCA with the number $wxyz$ is denoted by T_{wxyz}. The ETPCA in Fig. 1 is T_{0157}.

A *reversible ETPCA* is denoted by *RETPCA*. It is easy to see the following.

> An ETPCA T_{wxyz} is reversible iff
> $(w, z) \in \{(0, 7), (7, 0)\} \wedge$
> $(x, y) \in \{1, 2, 4\} \times \{3, 5, 6\} \cup \{3, 5, 6\} \times \{1, 2, 4\}$

Let T_{wxyz} be an ETPCA. We say T_{wxyz} is *conservative* (or *bit-conserving*), if the total number of particles (i.e., $\bullet$'s) is conserved in each local rule. Thus, the following holds.

> An ETPCA T_{wxyz} is conservative iff
> $w = 0 \wedge x \in \{1, 2, 4\} \wedge y \in \{3, 5, 6\} \wedge z = 7$

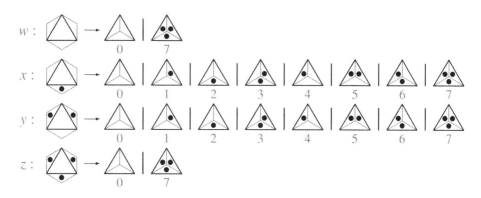

Fig. 3. Representing an ETPCA by a four-digit number $wxyz$, where $w, z \in \{0, 7\}$ and $x, y \in \{0, 1, \ldots, 7\}$. Vertical bars indicate alternatives of a right-hand side of a rule.

We can see that if an ETPCA is conservative, then it is reversible. This is because ETPCAs are isotropic. There are nine kinds of conservative RETPCAs.

Here, we give "aliases" to the nine conservative RETPCAs for the later convenience. Each of their local functions are shown in Fig. 4. Based on it, we denote a conservative RETPCA by T_{XY}, if its local function f is given by the set of local rules $\{(0), (1X), (2Y), (3)\}$, where $X, Y \in \{L, U, R\}$. For example, $T_{RU} = T_{0157}$. Note that L, U, and R stand for left-, U-, and right-turns of particles, respectively. Namely, the rule (1L) ((1U), and (1R), respectively) can be interpreted as the one where a coming particle makes left-turn (U-turn, and right-turn). The rules (2L), (2U), and (2R) are also interpreted similarly.

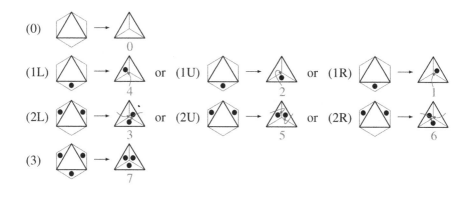

Fig. 4. Local function of a conservative RETPCA

2.3   Dualities in ETPCAs

We can define two kinds of dualities in ETPCAs. They are the duality under reflection, and the duality under conjugation, which are similarly defined as in the case of one-dimensional ECAs [13]. Dual ETPCAs are equivalent since they can simulate each other in a straightforward manner.

ETPCAs T and T' are called *dual under reflection*, if their local functions are mirror image of each other. It is denoted by $T \underset{\text{refl}}{\longleftrightarrow} T'$. Evolution of configurations in T is simulated by the mirror images of them in T' in an obvious way. We can see the following relations hold among nine conservative RETPCAs.

$$T_{\text{RL}} \underset{\text{refl}}{\longleftrightarrow} T_{\text{LR}}, \ T_{\text{RU}} \underset{\text{refl}}{\longleftrightarrow} T_{\text{LU}}, \ T_{\text{UR}} \underset{\text{refl}}{\longleftrightarrow} T_{\text{UL}}, \ T_{\text{RR}} \underset{\text{refl}}{\longleftrightarrow} T_{\text{LL}}, \ T_{\text{UU}} \underset{\text{refl}}{\longleftrightarrow} T_{\text{UU}}.$$

ETPCAs T and T' are called *conjugate* (or *dual under conjugation*), if their local functions are $0 - 1$ exchange of the other (i.e., renaming of the states). It is denoted by $T \underset{\text{conj}}{\longleftrightarrow} T'$. Obviously, evolution of configurations in T is simulated by the complemented configurations in T'. We can see the following relations hold.

$$T_{\text{RU}} \underset{\text{conj}}{\longleftrightarrow} T_{\text{UR}}, \ T_{\text{UL}} \underset{\text{conj}}{\longleftrightarrow} T_{\text{LU}}, \ T_{\text{RL}} \underset{\text{conj}}{\longleftrightarrow} T_{\text{LR}},$$
$$T_{\text{RR}} \underset{\text{conj}}{\longleftrightarrow} T_{\text{RR}}, \ T_{\text{LL}} \underset{\text{conj}}{\longleftrightarrow} T_{\text{LL}}, \ T_{\text{UU}} \underset{\text{conj}}{\longleftrightarrow} T_{\text{UU}}.$$

2.4   Turing Universality of RPCAs

An RPCA is called *Turing universal*, if any Turing machine is simulated in it. To prove Turing universality of an RPCA, it is sufficient to show any circuit composed of Fredkin gates [2] (Fig. 5) and delay elements is simulated in it. It is stated in Lemma 5.

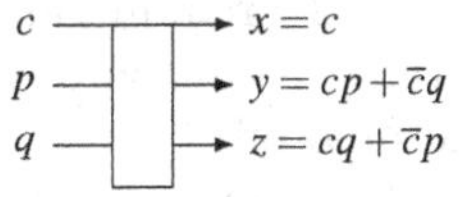

$$x = c$$
$$y = cp + \bar{c}q$$
$$z = cq + \bar{c}p$$

Fig. 5. Fredkin gate [2]. It is a 3-input 3-output reversible logic gate.

Lemma 5 can be derived, e.g., in the following way. First, any *reversible sequential machine* (RSM), in particular, a rotary element (RE), which is a 2-state 4-symbol RSM, is composed of Fredkin gates (Lemma 2). Next, any *reversible Turing machine* is constructed out of REs (Lemma 3). Finally, any (irreversible) Turing machine is simulated by a reversible one (Lemma 4). Thus, Lemma 5 follows. Note that the circuit that realizes a reversible Turing machine constructed by this method becomes an infinite (but ultimately periodic) circuit.

Lemma 2. [5,7] *Any RSM (in particular RE) can be simulated by a circuit composed of Fredkin gates and delay elements, which produces no garbage signals.*

Lemma 3. [6] *Any reversible Turing machine can be simulated by a garbage-less circuit composed only of REs.*

Lemma 4. [1] *Any (irreversible) Turing machine can be simulated by a garbage-less reversible Turing machine.*

Lemma 5. *An RPCA is Turing universal, if any circuit composed of Fredkin gates and delay elements is simulated in it.*

In [3], it is shown that any circuit composed of Fredkin gates and delay elements is simulated in T_{RU} (see Fig. 1). From this, and the dualities in ETPCAs, we have the following theorem.

Theorem 1. [3] *The conservative RETPCAs T_{RU}, T_{LU}, T_{UR}, and T_{UL} with infinite (but ultimately periodic) configurations are Turing universal.*

3   Universality of the RETPCA T_{RL}

We prove Turing universality of T_{RL}. Its local function is given in Fig. 6. In T_{RL}, if one particle comes, it makes right-turn, and if two come, they make left-turns.

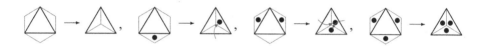

Fig. 6. Local function of the conservative RETPCA T_{RL}

It is easy to see that if the following elements and modules are implemented in T_{RL}, then any circuit composed of Fredkin gates and delay elements can be realized in it: (1) Signal and transmission wire. (2) Delay module. (3) Signal crossing module. (4) Fredkin gate module.

In T_{RL} a *signal* is represented by a single particle, and a *transmission wire* is composed of blocks (Fig. 7). A *block* is a stable pattern consisting of six particles as in Fig. 7 (note that a *pattern* is a finite segment of a configuration). A signal travels along a sequence of blocks as shown in Fig. 7.

To implement a delay module and a signal crossing module, we use a *signal control module*. It consists of a single particle that simply rotates (Fig. 8(a)), by which the trajectory of a signal can be altered as explained below. Since it is a pattern of period 6, a signal to be controlled must be given at a right timing.

A *delay module* is a pattern for fine adjustment of signal timing. Putting a signal control module near a transmission wire as in Fig. 8(b), an extra delay of 2 steps is realized. On the other hand, a large delay is implemented by appropriately bending a transmission wire. Note that a delay of odd steps is not necessary by the following reason. Assume a signal is in an up-triangle ($\triangle$) at $t = 0$. At $t = 1$ it must be in a down-triangle ($\triangledown$), then at $t = 2$ it is in an up-triangle,

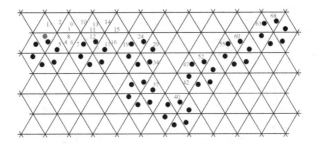

Fig. 7. A signal, and a transmission wire composed of blocks in T_{RL}. The signal travels along the wire. The number t $(1 \leq t \leq 68)$ shows the position of the signal at time t.

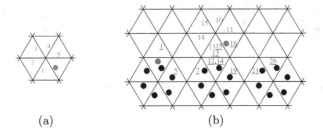

(a)   (b)

Fig. 8. (a) Signal control module, and (b) delay module of 2 steps in T_{RL}

and so on. Therefore, to interact two signals at a specified cell, they must be in the same type of triangles at $t = 0$. Thus, if both of the signals visit the same cell, then the difference of their arriving time is even.

A *signal crossing module* is for crossing two signals in the two-dimensional space. It consists of two signal control modules and transmission wires (Fig. 9).

To simulate a Fredkin gate, we implement a switch gate and an inverse switch gate (Fig. 10(a) and (b)). Since a Fredkin gate is composed of switch gates and inverse switch gates as in Fig. 10(c) [2], we can obtain a pattern that simulates a Fredkin gate, from those of a switch gate and an inverse switch gate.

In T_{RL}, a single cell works as a switch gate and an inverse switch gate as shown in Fig. 11. However, since it is not convenient to use one cell as a building unit for a larger circuit, we design a switch gate module and an inverse switch gate module from it. A *gate module* in the standard form is a pattern embedded in a rectangular-like region in the cellular space that satisfies the following (see Fig. 12): (1) It realizes a reversible logic gate. (2) Input ports are at the left end. (3) Output ports are at the right end. (4) Delay between input and output is constant.

Figure 13 shows a *switch gate module*, and an *inverse switch gate module*, each of which contains a (modified) signal crossing module, and three delay modules. The cells that work as switch gate and inverse switch gate are indicated by bold lines. The delay between input and output is 126 steps.

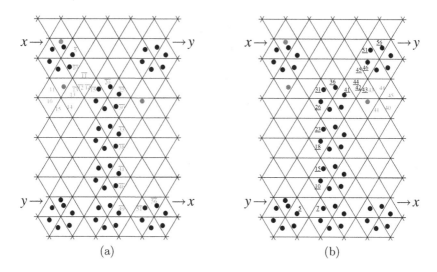

Fig. 9. Signal crossing module in T_{RL}. Trajectories of (a) signal x, and (b) signal y.

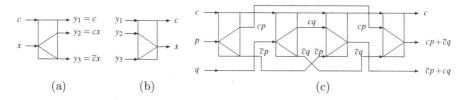

Fig. 10. (a) Switch gate. (b) Inverse switch gate, where $c = y_1$ and $x = y_2 + y_3$ under the assumption $(y_2 \to y_1) \wedge (y_3 \to \overline{y_1})$. (c) Fredkin gate composed of them [2].

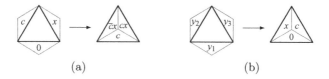

Fig. 11. A single cell of T_{RL} works as (a) a switch gate, and (b) an inverse switch gate

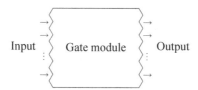

Fig. 12. Gate module in the standard form

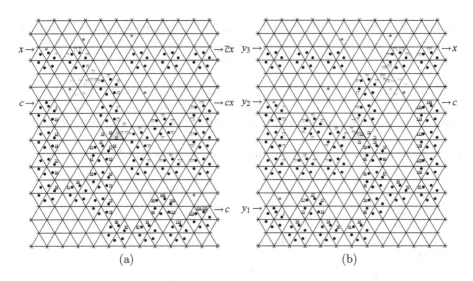

Fig. 13. (a) Switch gate module, and (b) inverse switch gate module in T_{RL}

A Fredkin gate module is obtained by connecting two switch gate modules, two inverse switch gate modules, five signal crossing modules, and many delay modules to form the circuit shown in Fig. 10(c). The complete configuration is found in [9]. Its size is of 30×131, and the input-output delay is 744 steps.

By above, and by the duality in ETPCAs, we have the following.

Theorem 2. *The conservative RETPCAs T_{RL} and T_{LR} with infinite (but ultimately periodic) configurations are Turing universal.*

4   Non-universality of the RETPCAs T_{RR}, T_{LL} and T_{UU}

T_{RR} has the set of local rules $\{(0), (1\mathrm{R}), (2\mathrm{R}), (3)\}$ (see Fig. 4). We can interpret $(1\mathrm{R})$, $(2\mathrm{R})$ and (3) to be the ones where all particles make right-turn. Therefore, *every* configuration has period 6, and thus T_{RR} is trivially non-universal. By a similar argument, T_{LL} is also non-universal.

In T_{UU}, we can interpret its local rules $(1\mathrm{U})$, $(2\mathrm{U})$ and (3) to be the ones where all particles make U-turn. Therefore, *every* configuration has period 2, and thus T_{UU} is again trivially non-universal.

Theorem 3. *The RETPCAs $T_{\mathrm{RR}}, T_{\mathrm{LL}},$ and T_{UU} are not Turing universal.*

5   Concluding Remarks

In this paper, nine conservative RETPCAs, which have extremely simple local functions, are studied. It was shown that T_{RL}, and T_{LR} are Turing universal

(Theorem 2), while T_{RR}, T_{LL}, and T_{UU} are not (Theorem 3). With Theorem 1 shown in [3], universality of all the nine conservative RETPCAs was clarified. Evolving processes of various configurations of T_{RL}, T_{RU}, and T_{UR} can be seen by movies in [9].

A non-conservative RETPCA T_{0347} also exhibits interesting behavior. Recently, existence of a glider and glider guns in T_{0347}, and its universality were shown in [8]. Investigation of other ETPCAs is left for the future study.

Acknowledgement. This work was supported by JSPS KAKENHI Grant Number 15K00019.

References

1. Bennett, C.H.: Logical reversibility of computation. IBM J. Res. Dev. **17**, 525–532 (1973)
2. Fredkin, E., Toffoli, T.: Conservative logic. Int. J. Theor. Phys. **21**, 219–253 (1982)
3. Imai, K., Morita, K.: A computation-universal two-dimensional 8-state triangular reversible cellular automaton. Theor. Comput. Sci. **231**, 181–191 (2000)
4. Margolus, N.: Physics-like model of computation. Physica D **10**, 81–95 (1984)
5. Morita, K.: A simple construction method of a reversible finite automaton out of Fredkin gates, and its related problem. Trans. IEICE Jpn. **E–73**(6), 978–984 (1990)
6. Morita, K.: A simple universal logic element and cellular automata for reversible computing. In: Margenstern, M., Rogozhin, Y. (eds.) MCU 2001. LNCS, vol. 2055, pp. 102–113. Springer, Heidelberg (2001)
7. Morita, K.: Reversible Computing (in Japanese). Kindai Kagaku-sha Co., Ltd., Tokyo (2012). ISBN 978-4-7649-0422-4
8. Morita, K.: An 8-State simple reversible triangular cellular automaton that exhibits complex behavior. In: Cook, M., Neary, T. (eds.) AUTOMATA 2016. LNCS, vol. 9664, pp. 170–184. Springer, Heidelberg (2016). doi:10.1007/978-3-319-39300-1_14
9. Morita, K.: Reversible and conservative elementary triangular partitioned cellular automata (slides with simulation movies). Hiroshima University Institutional Repository (2016). http://ir.lib.hiroshima-u.ac.jp/00039997
10. Morita, K., Harao, M.: Computation universality of one-dimensional reversible (injective) cellular automata. Trans. IEICE Jpn. **E72**, 758–762 (1989)
11. Morita, K., Ueno, S.: Computation-universal models of two-dimensional 16-state reversible cellular automata. IEICE Trans. Inf. Syst. **E75–D**(1), 141–147 (1992)
12. Toffoli, T.: Computation and construction universality of reversible cellular automata. J. Comput. Syst. Sci. **15**, 213–231 (1977)
13. Wolfram, S.: Theory and Applications of Cellular Automata. World Scientific Publishing, Singapore (1986)
14. Wolfram, S.: A New Kind of Science. Wolfram Media Inc., Champaign (2002)

Scalability of Non-uniform Cellular Automata Having only Point State Attractors

Nazma Naskar[1(✉)] and Sukanta Das[2]

[1] Department of Information Technology, Seacom Engineering College,
Howrah 711302, India
naskar.preeti@gmail.com
[2] Department of Information Technology,
Indian Institute of Engineering Science and Technology, Shibpur 711103, India
sukanta@it.iiests.ac.in

Abstract. In this paper, the concept of scalable non-uniform cellular automata (CAs) is discussed. The scalability of CA refers to its ability to accommodate more number of cells keeping the CA's dynamic behaviour unchanged. That is, a CA with n cell, converges to point state attractor from any seed also converges to point state attractor when another few cells are added. Using scalability of CA, a CA based scalable pattern classifier is introduced.

Keywords: Cellular Automata (CAs) · Scalability · Point state attractor · Reachability tree · Pattern classifier

1 Introduction

Over the years, researchers have been using cellular automata (CAs) as modeling tool. However, it has become apparent that many phenomena, such as chemical reactions occurring in a living cell, are found in nature which are not uniform. These new modeling requirement led to a new variant of CAs. As a result, non-uniformity in CAs has been introduced. In this paper, we consider $1D$ non-uniform binary CAs where cells follow wolfram rules [11]. Here, we concentrate on scalibility of CAs that are having only point state attractor. However, scalability of CA refers to its ability to accommodate more number of cells keeping the CA's dynamic behaviour unchanged. Moreover, we address the issue- whether it is possible to extend an n-cell CA to m-cell CA which always converges to point state attractor $(m > n)$.

Above problem has two issues- (1) designing of a CA having only point state attractors and (2) appending of one or more cells (m) to the n cell CA, such that $(n+m)$ cell CA contains only point state attractor in its state space. Solution to the first problem is reported in [3,7,9]. And the second problem is elaborated in Sects. 5.1 and 5.2. However, the procedures are based on *Reachability* tree and *Link* which are summarized in at Sect. 3. Section 4 enlist few essential term and property of CA having only point state attractor.

© Springer International Publishing Switzerland 2016
S. El Yacoubi et al. (Eds.): ACRI 2016, LNCS 9863, pp. 55–65, 2016.
DOI: 10.1007/978-3-319-44365-2_6

2   Preliminary of Cellular Automata

Cellular automaton (CA), a discrete dynamical system, consists of a lattice of cells. The states of cells are affected by their neighbors [10]. In the current work, we concentrate on the 1-dimensional 2-state 3-neighborhood (self, left and right neighbors) CAs. The next state of the ith cell of such CA is $S_i^{t+1} = f_i(S_{i-1}^t, S_i^t, S_{i+1}^t)$, where, f_i is the next state function; S_{i-1}^t, S_i^t and S_{i+1}^t are the present states of the left neighbor, self and right neighbor of the ith CA cell respectively.

Table 1. The rules 5, 73, 200 and 80

Present state:	111	110	101	100	011	010	001	000	Rule
(RMT)	(7)	(6)	(5)	(4)	(3)	(2)	(1)	(0)	
(i) Next state:	0	0	0	0	0	1	0	1	5
(ii) Next state:	0	1	0	0	1	0	0	1	73
(iii) Next state:	1	1	0	0	1	0	0	0	200
(iv) Next state:	0	1	0	1	0	0	0	0	80

The collection of states $\mathcal{S}^t(S_0^t, S_1^t, \cdots, S_{n-1}^t)$ of cells at time t is the configuration or (global) state of an n-cell CA at t. This work assumes that the boundary condition of such CA is open, and $S_{-1}^t = S_n^t = 0$ (null). The function $f_i : \{0, 1\}^3 \mapsto \{0, 1\}$ can be expressed in tabular form (Table 1). The decimal equivalent of the 8 outputs is traditionally called as 'rule' [11]. There are 2^8 (256) such rules. The first row of the Table 1 lists the possible 2^3 (8) combinations of the present states of $(i - 1)^{th}$, i^{th} and $(i + 1)^{th}$ cells at t. The last four rows indicate the next states of the ith cell at $(t + 1)$ for different combinations of the present states of its neighbors, forming the rules 5, 73, 200 and 84 respectively. Out of 256, only 14 rules are linear/additive [1]. The rest are nonlinear rules.

Traditionally, the cells of an automaton follow same rule. Such a CA is *uniform CA*. In a *non-uniform CA*, the cells may follow different rules. We need a rule vector $\mathcal{R} = \langle \mathcal{R}_0, \mathcal{R}_1, \cdots \mathcal{R}_i, \cdots \mathcal{R}_{n-1} \rangle$ for an n-cell non-uniform CA, where the cell i follows $\mathcal{R}_i$. In uniform CA $\mathcal{R}_0 = \mathcal{R}_1 = \cdots = \mathcal{R}_{n-1}$. The first row of Table 1 notes the combinations of the present states of three neighbors. Borrowing vocabulary from *Switching Theory*, we refer each combination as a *Rule Min Term (RMT)*. The column 011 of Table 1 is the RMT 3. The next states corresponding to this RMT are 0 for rule 5 and 1 for rule 73, and 1 for rule 200 and 0 for rule 84. The state of any RMT r of rule $\mathcal{R}_i$ express as $\mathcal{R}_i[r]$. Let us denote Z_8^i as the set valid RMTs of $\mathcal{R}_i$. Normally, $|Z_8^i| = 8$ but for null boundary CA $|Z_8^0| = |Z_8^{n-1}| = 4$.

The sequence of states generated (state transitions), during their evolution (with time), directs the CA behavior. The state transition diagram (Fig. 1a) of an automaton may contain *cyclic* and *acyclic* states. A state is called *cyclic* if it lies on some cycle. Cyclic states form attractors. The states 0000, 1100, 0100, 1000, 0111 and 1011 of Fig. 1a are the cyclic states that form attractors. In this work, we put our attention on those CA which contain only point state attractors. Hence, the CA of Fig. 1a is not our desired CA.

A CA state can also be viewed as a sequence of RMTs. For example, the state 1110 in null boundary condition can be viewed as $\langle 3764 \rangle$, where 3, 7, 6 and 4 are corresponding RMTs on which the transition of first, second, third and forth cells can be made. For an n-bit state, we get a sequence of n RMTs.

Definition 1. *Two RMTs r and s ($r \neq s$) are said to be equivalent to each other if $2r \bmod 8 = 2s \bmod 8$. Two RMTs r and s ($r \neq s$) are said to be sibling to each other if $\lfloor \frac{r}{2} \rfloor = \lfloor \frac{s}{2} \rfloor$.*

For example, RMTs 0 and 4 are equivalent to each other and RMTs 0 and 1 are sibling to each other.

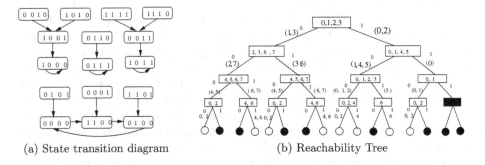

(a) State transition diagram   (b) Reachability Tree

Fig. 1. State transition diagram and reachability tree of CA $\langle 5, 73, 200, 80 \rangle$

3   Reachability Tree and Links

In this section, a characterization tool, named *Reachability tree* is introduced that uses both - CA states and RSs. Next we introduce *link* to establish relations among edges of the tree.

3.1   Reachability Tree

Reachability tree [2,4] is a discrete tool of characterizing 1-dimensional CA. It is a rooted and edge-labeled binary tree. The nodes are represented by $N_{i.j}$ where i ($0 \leq i \leq n$) is the level index, and j ($0 \leq j \leq 2^i - 1$) is the node number at ith level. The numbering of nodes in each level starts from left side.

Definition 2. *Reachability tree for an n-cell CA under null boundary condi-tion is a rooted and edge-labeled binary tree with $n+1$ levels, where $E_{i.2j} = (N_{i.j}, N_{i+1.2j}, l_{i.2j})$ and $E_{i.2j+1} = (N_{i.j}, N_{i+1.2j+1}, l_{i.2j+1})$ are the edges between nodes $N_{i.j} \subseteq Z_8^i$ and $N_{i+1.2j} \subseteq Z_8^{i+1}$ with label $l_{i.2j} \subseteq N_{i.j}$, and between nodes $N_{i.j}$ and $N_{i+1.2j+1} \subseteq Z_8^{i+1}$ with label $l_{i.2j+1} \subseteq N_{i.j}$ respectively ($0 \le i \le n-1$, $0 \le j \le 2^i - 1$). Following relations are maintained in the tree:*

1. $l_{i.2j} \cup l_{i.2j+1} = N_{i.j}$
2. $\forall r \in l_{i.2j}$ (resp. $\forall r \in l_{i.2j+1}$), RMT r of $\mathcal{R}_i$ is 0 (resp. 1) and RMTs $2r$ (mod 8) and $2r+1$ (mod 8) of $\mathcal{R}_{i+1}$ are in $N_{i+1.2j}$ (resp. $N_{i+1.2j+1}$)
3. $\bigcup_{0 \le j \le 2^i - 1} N_{i.j} = Z_8^i$, ($0 \le i \le n-1$)

If $l_{i.k} = \emptyset$ for any k, the edge $E_{i.k}$ (hence, $N_{i+1.k}$) does not exit. We call such an edge as a non-reachable edge. However, for each $r \in l_{i.2j}$ (resp. $r \in l_{i.2j+1}$), RMT r of $\mathcal{R}_i$ is 0 (resp. 1) and we get two RMTs $2r$ (mod 8) and $2r+1$ (mod 8) of $\mathcal{R}_{i+1}$ in $N_{i+1.2j}$ (resp. $N_{i+1.2j+1}$), and the edge is called 0-edge (resp. 1-edge).

Figure 1b shows the reachability tree of the CA of Fig. 1a (the RMTs of the CA rules are noted in Table 1). Under null boundary condition, only 4 RMTs are valid for left most and right most cells, and $Z_8^0 = \{0, 1, 2, 3\}$ and $Z_8^3 = \{0, 2, 4, 6\}$. Hence, the root $N_{0.0} = Z_8^0$. The label of edge $E_{0.0}$ is $\{1, 3\}$, as RMTs 1 and 3 of rule 5 are 0. We write RMTs of a label on the edge within a bracket. However, the label of edge $E_{2.7}$ is empty, that is $l_{2.7} = \emptyset$. This edge is non-reachable, and it can not connect any node of next level. Figure 1b marks such nodes as shaded. Since $Z_8^n = \emptyset$ for an n-cell CA, the leaf nodes are empty. Number of leaves (excluding shaded leaves as they don't exit) in Fig. 1b is 8, which is the number of reachable states. A sequence of edges from the root to a leaf node represents a reachable state, when 0-edge and 1-edge are replaced by 0 and 1 respectively. For example, 0011 is a reachable state in Fig. 1b. On the other hand, the states 1110 and 1111 are non-reachable states.

Reachability tree gives us information about reachable states. A sequence of edges $\langle E_{0.j_0} E_{1.j_1} \cdots E_{i.j_i} E_{i+1.j_{i+1}} \cdots E_{n-1.j_{n-1}} \rangle$ from root to a leaf associates a reachable state and at least one RS $\langle r_0 r_1 \cdots r_i r_{i+1} \cdots r_{n-1} \rangle$, where $r_i \in l_{i.j_i}$ and $r_{i+1} \in l_{i+1.j_{i+1}}$ ($0 \le i < n-1$, $0 \le j_i \le 2^i - 1$, and $j_{i+1} = 2j_i$ or $2j_i+1$). That is, the sequence of edges represents at least two CA states. Note that if RMT r_i is 0 (resp. 1) then $E_{i.j_i}$ is 0-edge (resp. 1-edge). Therefore, the reachable state is the next (resp. present) state of the state (resp. predecessor), represented as RMT sequence. Interestingly, there are 2^n RSs in the tree, but number of reachable states may be less than 2^n. However, a sequence of edges may associate m-number of RSs ($m \ge 1$), which implies, this state is reachable from m-number of different states.

3.2   CA State Space Through Reachability Tree

Unlike state transition diagram, reachability tree does not explicitly depict the transitions of states. In the tree, a sequence of edges from root to a leaf node associates a reachable state and at least one RMT sequence which corresponds to predecessor of the CA state. Through these predecessors, the relationship among the states can be traced.

Since the RSs and the states, both of an automaton can be traced in the tree, which RS corresponds to what state can be identified. To identify this correspondence, we form links among edges. The links are formed depending on whether the RMTs are self replicating (defined below) or not.

Definition 3. *An RMT x0y (resp. x1y) is said to be self replicating if RMT x0y (resp. x1y) is 0 (resp. 1).*

For example, RMT 2 (010) of rule 5 is self replicating, whereas all the RMTs except RMT 2 of rule 200 are self replicating (see Table 1). If an RMT $r \in l_{i.j}$ is not self replicating, then there is a link from the edge $E_{i.j}$ to $E_{i.k}$ ($j \neq k$). Depending on the values of j and k, we can classify the links in the following way: forward link (when $j < k$), backward link (when $j > k$) and self link (when $j = k$). The rules, followed to form links in a reachability tree, are noted below:

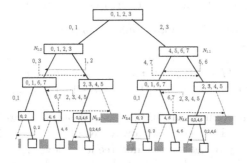

Fig. 2. Reachability tree of CA $\langle 12, 102, 192, 85 \rangle$ with links

(1) If RMT $r \in l_{0.j}$ is self replicating ($j = 0$ or 1),
    The edge $E_{0.j}$ is self linked for RMT r.
  Otherwise, if $j = 0$,
        there is a forward link from $E_{0.0}$ to $E_{0.1}$ for RMT r;
        else, there is a backward link from $E_{0.1}$ to $E_{0.0}$ for RMT r.

(2) If $E_{i-1.j}$ is self linked for RMT $r \in l_{i-1.j}$,
    and if s is self replicating
        where $s \in l_{i.2j}$ (resp. $s \in l_{i.2j+1}$) is $2r$ (mod 8) or $2r + 1$ (mod 8),
            then $E_{i.2j}$ (resp. $E_{i.2j+1}$) is self linked.
    But if s is not self replicating,
        then there is a forward link from $E_{i.2j}$ to $E_{i.2j+1}$ (resp. backward link from $E_{i.2j+1}$ to $E_{i.2j}$).

(3) If there is a link from $E_{i-1.j}$ to $E_{i-1.k}$ ($j \neq k$) for RMT $r \in l_{i-1.j}$,
    and $s \in l_{i.2j}$ (resp. $s \in l_{i.2j+1}$) is $2r$ (mod 8) or $2r + 1$ (mod 8),

then there is a link from $E_{i.2j}$ (resp. $E_{i.2j+1}$) to $E_{i.2k}$ while $s \in \{0, 1, 4, 5\}$ or to $E_{i.2k+1}$ while $s \in \{2, 3, 6, 7\}$.

[It is forward link if $j < k$, backward link if $j > k$]

Above definition of link guide to conclude following property.

Lemma 1. *There exist only two links from $E_{i.2k}$ and/or $E_{i.2k+1}$ to $E_{i.j}$ for RMTs s and r when $0 \leq i \leq n-1$, and s and r are sibling to each other, and only one link from $E_{n-1.m}$ to $E_{n-1.j}$ in a reachability tree $(0 \leq k \leq 2^i$ and $0 \leq j, m \leq 2^{i+1} - 1)$ [6].*

4   Cross Link

The consecutive forward and backward links may form loop, like $E_{i.j_1}(r_1) \to \cdots \to E_{i.j_q}(r_q) \to \cdots \to E_{i.j_m}(r_m) \to E_{i.j_1}$ $(0 \leq i \leq n-1)$. We call this link as *cross link*. We define the length of a cross link as the number of RMTs involved in the link. Here it is m. Cross Link is necessary condition to form multi state attractor. Here, we report some characteristics of cross link.

Theorem 1. *An n-cell CA contains multi-length cycle attractor, if a cross link among $E_{n-1.k}s$ exists [7].*

Theorem 2. *An RMT $r \in l_{i.j}$ can not be a part of a cycle, if the RMT is not involved in a self link or cross link $(0 \leq i \leq n-1, 0 \leq j \leq 2^i - 1)$.*

So, according to Theorem 2 only backward and only forward links are not our concern. According to Theorem 1, we always avoid cross link, that is, if cross link occur at level i, we try to get a cross link free level, level j $(0 \leq i \leq j \leq (n-1))$. Hence, at level j only self links exist. At level $j + 1$, few node behave like root node. We call these nodes as *root equivalent node*. And the corresponding sub-tree is called *connectionless sub-tree*. These two properties of linked tree help to restrict the growth of reachability tree. *Root equivalent node* and *connection-less sub-tree* can be defined as following:

Definition 4. *A node $N_{i.j}$ is said to be* root equivalent node *if each RMT $r \in l_{i-1.j}$ does not participate in cross link, where $1 \leq i < n-1, 0 \leq j \leq 2^{i+1} - 1$. The sub-tree, rooted at $N_{i.j}$, is said to be* connection-less sub-tree.

In Fig. 2, node $N_{1.0}$ and $N_{1.1}$ are root equivalent nodes. Whereas, corresponding sub-trees are connection-less sub-trees. RMTs $0, 1 \in l_{2.0}$, $0, 1 \in l_{2.4}$, $4, 5 \in l_{2.2}$ and $4, 5 \in l_{2.6}$ are self replicating RMTs. In third level four root equivalent nodes are present, which are $N_{3.0}$, $N_{3.2}$, $N_{3.4}$ and $N_{3.6}$. We call these nodes as root equivalent node, because, no link from sub-tree rooted at any one of these nodes goes to any other sub-tree. These connection-less sub-trees, produced by $N_{3.j}$ $(j \in \{0, 2, 4, 6\})$, holds sufficient information to synthesize CA having only point state attractors. It is further observed that two (or more) root equivalent nodes in an arbitrary tree can be similar, where the RMTs of the nodes are same. Therefore, the corresponding sub-trees are also same. In synthesis process, if we get such nodes, we can proceed only one and drop the another. Even if the RMTs of a root equivalent node $N_{i.j}$ is subset of another root equivalent node $N_{i.k}$, then also we can proceed with only node $N_{i.k}$. We call the node like $N_{i.j}$, as sub-node of $N_{i.k}$.

Definition 5. *The root equivalent node $N_{i.j}$ is said to be sub-node of another root equivalent node $N_{i.k}$ if $N_{i.j} \subseteq N_{i.k}$.*

In Fig. 2, $N_{3.0} = N_{3.4}$ and $N_{3.2} = N_{3.6}$. Further, $N_{3.0} \subset N_{3.2}$. Therefore, $N_{3.0}$ and $N_{3.4}$ are sub-node $N_{3.2}$ (or $N_{3.6}$). Hence, in next level, we can proceed with only $N_{3.2}$ (or $N_{3.6}$) drop the other nodes.

Lemma 2. *Maximum number of root equivalent nodes which are not sub-nodes of any other, at any level is 4.*

Proof. The nodes of any level are subset of 8 RMTs. Moreover, sibling RMTs are always paired in a node. Since we have 4 pairs of sibling RMTs, they can form at most 4 sets which are not sub-set of each other. Hence the proof.

5   Scalable CAs with only Point State Attractors

As stated earlier, *scalability* of CA refers to its ability to accommodate more number of cells keeping the CA's dynamic behaviour unchanged. Here we are concerned about those CAs (n cell) which have only point state attractor, and if the CA is extended upto ($n + m$) cell, then also it contains only point state attractors. However, Refs. [7,8] have reported the procedure of synthesis of CA having only point state attractors.

5.1   ($n + 1$)-cell CA from n-cell CA

Scalability of CAs are dependent on the behaviour of links. From the definition of links, it is clear that a link of level j depends on the link of level i ($i < j$, $0 \leq i \leq n - 2$). Let us consider an n-cell CA $\langle \mathcal{R}_0, \mathcal{R}_1, \cdots, \mathcal{R}_{n-1} \rangle$. The links at level i of the corresponding tree trigger the links of level j where $j > i$. However, the links of level i does not depend on that of level j ($i < j$). Hence, an n-cell CA is extended to ($n+1$)-cell CA with rule vector $\langle \mathcal{R}_0, \mathcal{R}_1, \cdots, \mathcal{R}_{n-1} \rangle$, the link of level i ($0 \leq i \leq n - 1$), will remain unaffected after extending the CA.

Now consider that the n-cell CA converges to point state attractor from any seed. Therefore, the corresponding reachability tree has no cross link at level $n - 1$. It is easy to show that if level i is cross link free, then there exists at least one rule as $\mathcal{R}_{i+1}$ which makes the level $i + 1$ cross link free. However this logic can not directly be applied to the levels $n - 1$ and n of the tree of ($n + 1$)-cell CA. Because, the odd RMTs of $\mathcal{R}_{n-1}$ are ignored in the n-cell CA (due to null boundary condition) but they are used in the ($n + 1$)-cell CA. Therefore, the odd RMTs of $\mathcal{R}_{i-1}$ may trigger a cross link at level $n - 1$, which may not get dissolved in level n of the tree of ($n + 1$)r- cell CA. However, following lemma guides us to get such ($n + 1$)-cell CA.

Lemma 3. *If an n-cell CA $\langle \mathcal{R}_0, \mathcal{R}_1, \cdots, \mathcal{R}_{n-1} \rangle$ converges to point state attractor from an seed then there exist an $(n+1)$-cell CA $\langle \mathcal{R}_0, \mathcal{R}_1, \cdots, \mathcal{R}'_{n-1}, \mathcal{R}_n \rangle$ that converges to point state attractor from an arbitrary seed. $\mathcal{R}'_{n-1}$ and $\mathcal{R}_{n-1}$ are equivalent where they act as the last rule.*

Proof. Let us consider, an n-cell $\langle \mathcal{R}_0, \mathcal{R}_1, \cdots, \mathcal{R}_{n-1} \rangle$ that converges to point state attractor from any seed. As null boundary CA is considered, the odd RMTs of last rule are ignored, so we can assume $\mathcal{R}_{n-1}$ as right independent rule[1]. Now, consider the last rule $\mathcal{R}'_{n-1}$, where each odd RMTs have equal next state value as its even sibling RMT. Hence, we can get a right independent rule (see footnote 1). As both of the sibling RMTs link to same edge (Lemma 1), so no cross link is formed. Thus, the CA $\langle \mathcal{R}_0, \mathcal{R}_1, \cdots, \mathcal{R}'_{n-1} \rangle$ also converges to point state attractor. For $(n + 1)$-cell CA $(\langle \mathcal{R}_0, \mathcal{R}_1, \cdots, \mathcal{R}'_{n-1}, \mathcal{R}_n \rangle)$, at n^{th} level few root equivalent nodes exist. There exist a $\mathcal{R}_n$ for which level n is cross link free.

5.2 $(n + m)$-cell CA from n-cell and m-cell CA

As it is possible to extend an n-cell CA $\langle \mathcal{R}_0, \mathcal{R}_1, \cdots, \mathcal{R}_{n-1} \rangle$ to the $(n + 1)$-cell CA $\langle \mathcal{R}_0, \mathcal{R}_1, \cdots, \mathcal{R}'_{n-1}, \mathcal{R}_n \rangle$, it can also be extended to $(n+2)$-cell CA with rule vector $\langle \mathcal{R}_0, \mathcal{R}_1, \cdots, \mathcal{R}'_{n-1}, \mathcal{R}'_n, \mathcal{R}'_{n+1} \rangle$, and so on. Scalability of CA also allows to append two CAs to get larger CA. That is, an n-cell CA $\langle \mathcal{R}_0, \mathcal{R}_1, \cdots, \mathcal{R}_{n-1} \rangle$ and an m-cell CA $\langle \mathcal{R}'_0, \mathcal{R}'_1, \cdots, \mathcal{R}'_{m-2}, \mathcal{R}'_{m-1} \rangle$ can produce the $(n + m)$ cell CA $\langle \mathcal{R}_0, \mathcal{R}_1, \cdots, \mathcal{R}''_{n-1}, \mathcal{R}''_0, \mathcal{R}'_1, \cdots, \mathcal{R}'_{m-2}, \mathcal{R}'_{m-1} \rangle$. However, due to null boundary condition, $\mathcal{R}_0$ and $\mathcal{R}_{n-1}$ are the special cases. To append an m-cell CA with an n-cell CA, $\mathcal{R}_{n-1}$ is converted to $\mathcal{R}''_{n-1}$, where $\mathcal{R}''_{n-1}$ is corresponding right independent rule of $\mathcal{R}_{n-1}$. The modification is similar as in extending n-cell CA to $(n + 1)$-cell CA. $\mathcal{R}'_0$ is also modified to $\mathcal{R}''_0$ where next states values of RMTs $4, 5, 6, 7$ of $\mathcal{R}'_0$ are modified based on root equivalent nodes $N_{n.j}$s of n-cell CA. Thus, our final CA has the rule vector $\langle \mathcal{R}_0, \mathcal{R}_1, \cdots, \mathcal{R}''_{n-1}, \mathcal{R}''_0, \mathcal{R}'_1, \cdots, \mathcal{R}'_{m-2}, \mathcal{R}'_{m-1} \rangle$.

However, $\mathcal{R}''_0$ and $\mathcal{R}'_0$ are not necessarily two different rules. If the node of an n-cell CA which are accounted as root equivalent node for the m-cell CA, are subset of $\{0, 1, 2, 3\}$, then $\mathcal{R}''_0$ and $\mathcal{R}'_0$ are the same rule. On the other hand, if at least one root equivalent node is subset of $\{4, 5, 6, 7\}$, the next state value of all equivalent RMTs will be same in $\mathcal{R}''_0$. For example, CA $\langle 10, 252, 140, 0 \rangle$ has only point state attractors in its state space. Also the CA $\langle 12, 240, 68 \rangle$ has only point state attractors in its state space. The CA $\langle 10, 252, 140, 0, 12, 240, 68 \rangle$ is also having only point state attractors in its state space. Here, $\mathcal{R}'_0 = \mathcal{R}''_0$ and $\mathcal{R}_{n-1} = \mathcal{R}''_{n-1}$. However, if two CAs having only point state attractors are blindly merged, then the final CA may contain multi-state attractors. For example, the CAs $\langle 10, 252, 136, 69 \rangle$ and $\langle 15, 195, 0, 64 \rangle$ are having only point state attractors, but the merged CA $\langle 10, 252, 136, 69, 15, 195, 0, 64 \rangle$ contains multi-state attractors in its state space. Hence, the third rule and the fourth rule of final CA are to

---

[1] A rule $\mathcal{R}$ is said to be *right independent rule*, if each sibling pairs of RMTs r, s have same next state value either 0 or 1 that is $\mathcal{R}[r] = \mathcal{R}[s]$.

be modified according to the above condition. If we follow the above rule of merging, we get the CA $\langle 10, 252, 136, 207, 255, 195, 0, 64 \rangle$ which always converge to point state attractor for an arbitrary seed.

Lemma 4. *The (n+m)-cell CA $\langle \mathcal{R}_0, \mathcal{R}_1, \cdots, \mathcal{R}''_{n-1}, \mathcal{R}''_0, \mathcal{R}'_1, \cdots, \mathcal{R}'_{m-2}, \mathcal{R}'_{m-1} \rangle$ converges to point state attractor if the n-cell CA $\langle \mathcal{R}_0, \mathcal{R}_1, \cdots, \mathcal{R}_{n-1} \rangle$ and m-cell CA $\langle \mathcal{R}'_0, \mathcal{R}'_1, \cdots, \mathcal{R}'_{m-2}, \mathcal{R}'_{m-1} \rangle$ converge to point state attractor for any seed, where $\mathcal{R}_0$ and $\mathcal{R}_{n-1}$ are converted to $\mathcal{R}''_0$ and $\mathcal{R}''_{n-1}$.*

Proof. Let us consider two CAs, CA of size n and CA of size m, contain only point state attractors in the CA state space. The m-cell CA is appended to n-cell CA. As n_1-cell CA is a CA having only point state attractors, following Theorem 1, at last level no cross link exists. Forward links and backward links are removed according to Theorem 2. Only self links are lefts. The leaf nodes are the root equivalent node. After appending the m-cell CA to n-cell CA, the linked tree of m cell CA does not get changed. The m cell CA is also a CA having only point state attractors. The last level is also cross link free. Hence, the last level of resultant CA is cross link free. Thus, resultant CA is having only point state attractors.

5.3 Design of a Classifier with Scalable CA

The proper hardware implementation of scaliblity property increases re-usability. The m-number of different CAs can be merged in $\frac{m(m+1)}{2}$ ways. Let us consider, Fig. 3, an N-cell CA is constructed using n_1-, n_2-, n_3-, n_4 cell CAs. These four different CAs can be used to construct 10 different CAs. However, this merging of CAs is not random event, rather we need to follow a sequence.

An n-cell CA with k point states can be viewed as k-class natural classifier [3]. Hence, the CAs that are having only point state attractors can be utilized to design a k-class pattern classifier. Here we consider the two class pattern classifier. Now these 4 CAs can independently act as pattern classifier. At the same time they can be classifier in combination.

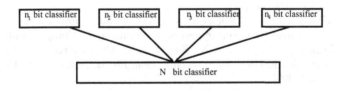

Fig. 3. Scalable classifier

To perform classification task on categorical/discrete attributes, each attribute is converted into binary form as per Thermometer Code [5]. The Fig. 3 also depicts the concept of scalable CA based pattern classifier.

As 24 CAs can be achieved from the Fig. 3 also 10 CA based pattern classifier may achieve. Table 2 shows few results on real-life data sets obtained from http://mlr.cs.umass.edu/ml/datasets. The CA $\langle 31, 206, 153, 222, 197, 192, 153, 222, 95 \rangle$ initially used for data set 'Haberman' which need 9-cell CA. This is used for 'Monk1' data set that needs 11 cell. The resultant CA is $\langle 31, 206, 153, 222, 197, 192, 153, 222, 255, 195, 0 \rangle$. Using Lemma 4, we get the CA $\langle 31, 206, 153, 222, 197, 192, 153, 222, 255, 255, 206, 153, 222, 197, 192, 153, 222, 95 \rangle$ and used for dataset 'tic-tac-toe'. Table 2 shows the result.

Table 2. CA based scalable pattern classifier

Data set	Number of attribute	CA size	CA
Haberman	3	9	31, 206, 153, 222, 197, 192, 153, 222, 95
monk1	6	11	31, 206, 153, 222, 197, 192, 153, 222, 255, 195, 0
tic-tac-teo	9	18	31, 206, 153, 222, 197, 192, 153, 222, 255, 255, 206, 153, 222, 197, 192, 153, 222, 95

6   Conclusion

This paper introduces the concept of scalability in non-uniform CA that always converges to point state attractor for any arbitrary seed. Using this scalability property of CA an efficient CA based scalable pattern classifier is also discussed.

References

1. Chaudhuri, P.P., Chowdhury, D.R., Nandi, S., Chatterjee, S.: Additive Cellular Automata – Theory and Applications. IEEE Computer Society Press, New York (1997). ISBN 0-8186-7717-1
2. Das, S.: Theory and applications of nonlinear cellular automata In VLSI design. Ph.D. thesis. Bengal Engineering and Science University, Shibpur, India (2007)
3. Das, S., Mukherjee, S., Naskar, N., Sikdar, B.K.: Characterization of single cycle CA and its application in pattern classification. Electr. Notes Theor. Comput. Sci. **252**, 181–203 (2009)
4. Das, S., Sikdar, B.K., Pal Chaudhuri, P.: Characterization of reachable/nonreachable cellular automata states. In: Sloot, P.M.A., Chopard, B., Hoekstra, A.G. (eds.) ACRI 2004. LNCS, vol. 3305, pp. 813–822. Springer, Heidelberg (2004)
5. Gallant, S.I.: Neural Networks Learning and Expert Systems. Mass, MIT Press, Cambridge (1993)
6. Nazma, M., Naskar, B.J.: Characterization and synthesis of non-uniform cellular automata with point state attractors. Ph.D. thesis. IIEST, Shibpur (2016)

7. Naskar, N., Adak, S., Maji, P., Das, S.: Synthesis of non-uniform cellular automata having only point attractors. In: Wąs, J., Sirakoulis, G.C., Bandini, S. (eds.) ACRI 2014. LNCS, vol. 8751, pp. 105–114. Springer, Heidelberg (2014)

8. Naskar, N., Chakraborty, A., Maji, P., Das, S.: Analysis of reachability tree for identification of cyclic and acyclic CA states. In: Sirakoulis, G.C., Bandini, S. (eds.) ACRI 2012. LNCS, vol. 7495, pp. 63–72. Springer, Heidelberg (2012)

9. Naskar, N., Das, S., Sikdar, B.K.: Characterization of nonlinear cellular automata having only single length cycle attractors. Journal of Cellular Automata 7(5–6), 431–453 (2012)

10. Von Neumann, J.: Theory of Self-Reproducing Automata. University of Illinois Press, Champaign (1966)

11. Wolfram, S.: Theory and application of cellular automata. World Scientific Publishing (1986)

The Garden of Eden Theorem for Cellular Automata on Group Sets

Simon Wacker[(✉)]

Karlsruhe Institute of Technology, Karlsruhe, Germany
simon.wacker@kit.edu
http://www.kit.edu

Abstract. We prove the Garden of Eden theorem for cellular automata with finite set of states and finite neighbourhood on right amenable left homogeneous spaces with finite stabilisers. It states that the global transition function of such an automaton is surjective if and only if it is pre-injective. Pre-Injectivity means that two global configurations that differ at most on a finite subset and have the same image under the global transition function must be identical.

Keywords: Cellular automata · Group actions · Garden of Eden theorem

The notion of amenability for groups was introduced by John von Neumann in 1929. It generalises the notion of finiteness. A group G is *left* or *right amenable* if there is a finitely additive probability measure on $\mathcal{P}(G)$ that is invariant under left and right multiplication respectively. Groups are left amenable if and only if they are right amenable. A group is *amenable* if it is left or right amenable.

The definitions of left and right amenability generalise to left and right group sets respectively. A left group set $(M, G, \rhd)$ is *left amenable* if there is a finitely additive probability measure on $\mathcal{P}(M)$ that is invariant under $\rhd$. There is in general no natural action on the right that is to a left group action what right multiplication is to left group multiplication. Therefore, for a left group set there is no natural notion of right amenability.

A transitive left group action $\rhd$ of G on M induces, for each element $m_0 \in M$ and each family $\{g_{m_0,m}\}_{m \in M}$ of elements in G such that, for each point $m \in M$, we have $g_{m_0,m} \rhd m_0 = m$, a right quotient set semi-action $\lhd$ of G/G_0 on M with defect G_0 given by $m \lhd gG_0 = g_{m_0,m} g g_{m_0,m}^{-1} \rhd m$, where G_0 is the stabiliser of m_0 under $\rhd$. Each of these right semi-actions is to the left group action what right multiplication is to left group multiplication. They occur in the definition of global transition functions of cellular automata over left homogeneous spaces as defined in [5]. A *cell space* is a left group set together with choices of m_0 and $\{g_{m_0,m}\}_{m \in M}$.

A cell space $\mathcal{R}$ is *right amenable* if there is a finitely additive probability measure on $\mathcal{P}(M)$ that is semi-invariant under $\lhd$. For example cell spaces with finite sets of cells, abelian groups, and finitely right generated cell spaces of

© Springer International Publishing Switzerland 2016
S. El Yacoubi et al. (Eds.): ACRI 2016, LNCS 9863, pp. 66–78, 2016.
DOI: 10.1007/978-3-319-44365-2_7

sub-exponential growth are right amenable, in particular, quotients of finitely generated groups of sub-exponential growth by finite subgroups acted on by left multiplication. A net of non-empty and finite subsets of M is a *right Følner net* if, broadly speaking, these subsets are asymptotically invariant under $\lhd$. A finite subset E of G/G_0 and two partitions $\{A_e\}_{e\in E}$ and $\{B_e\}_{e\in E}$ of M constitute a *right paradoxical decomposition* if the map $\_ \lhd e$ is injective on A_e and B_e, and the family $\{(A_e \lhd e) \cup (B_e \lhd e)\}_{e\in E}$ is a partition of M. The Tarski-Følner theorem states that right amenability, the existence of right Følner nets, and the non-existence of right paradoxical decompositions are equivalent. We prove it in [6] for cell spaces with finite stabilisers.

For a right amenable cell space with finite stabilisers we may choose a right Følner net $\mathcal{F} = \{F_i\}_{i\in I}$. The entropy of a subset X of Q^M with respect to $\mathcal{F}$, where Q is a finite set, is, broadly speaking, the asymptotic growth rate of the number of finite patterns with domain F_i that occur in X. For subsets E and E' of G/G_0, an (E, E')-tiling is a subset T of M such that $\{t \lhd E\}_{t\in T}$ is pairwise disjoint and $\{t \lhd E'\}_{t\in T}$ is a cover of M. If for each point $t \in T$ not all patterns with domain $t \lhd E$ occur in a subset of Q^M, then that subset does not have maximal entropy.

The global transition function of a cellular automaton with finite set of states and finite neighbourhood over a right amenable cell space with finite stabilisers, as introduced in [5], is surjective if and only if its image has maximal entropy and it is pre-injective if and only if its image has maximal entropy. This establishes the Garden of Eden theorem, which states that a global transition function as above is surjective if and only if it is pre-injective. This answers a question posed by Sébastien Moriceau at the end of his paper 'Cellular Automata on a G-Set' [4].

The Garden of Eden theorem for cellular automata over $\mathbb{Z}^2$ is a famous theorem by Edward Forrest Moore and John R. Myhill from 1962 and 1963, see the papers 'Machine models of self-reproduction' [2] and 'The converse of Moore's Garden-of-Eden theorem' [3]. This paper is greatly inspired by the monograph 'Cellular Automata and Groups' [1] by Tullio Ceccherini-Silberstein and Michel Coornaert.

In Sect. 1 we introduce E-interiors, E-closures, and E-boundaries of subsets of M. In Sect. 2 we introduce (E, E')-tilings of cell spaces. In Sect. 3 we introduce entropies of subsets of Q^M. And in Sect. 4 we prove the Garden of Eden theorem.

Preliminary Notions. A *left group set* is a triple $(M, G, \rhd)$, where M is a set, G is a group, and $\rhd$ is a map from $G \times M$ to M, called *left group action of G on M*, such that $G \to \mathrm{Sym}(M)$, $g \mapsto [g \rhd \_]$, is a group homomorphism. The action $\rhd$ is *transitive* if M is non-empty and for each $m \in M$ the map $\_ \rhd m$ is surjective; and *free* if for each $m \in M$ the map $\_ \rhd m$ is injective. For each $m \in M$, the set $G \rhd m$ is the *orbit of m*, the set $G_m = (\_ \rhd m)^{-1}(m)$ is the *stabiliser of m*, and, for each $m' \in M$, the set $G_{m,m'} = (\_ \rhd m)^{-1}(m')$ is the *transporter of m to m'*.

A *left homogeneous space* is a left group set $\mathcal{M} = (M, G, \rhd)$ such that $\rhd$ is transitive. A *coordinate system for $\mathcal{M}$* is a tuple $\mathcal{K} = (m_0, \{g_{m_0,m}\}_{m\in M})$, where $m_0 \in M$ and for each $m \in M$ we have $g_{m_0,m} \rhd m_0 = m$. The stabiliser G_{m_0} is denoted by G_0. The tuple $\mathcal{R} = (\mathcal{M}, \mathcal{K})$ is a *cell space*. The set $\{gG_0 \mid g \in G\}$ of left cosets of G_0 in G is denoted by G/G_0. The map $\lhd \colon M \times G/G_0 \to M$, $(m, gG_0) \mapsto g_{m_0,m} g g_{m_0,m}^{-1} \rhd m$ ($= g_{m_0,m} g \rhd m_0$) is a *right semi-action of* G/G_0 *on M with defect G_0*, which means that

$$\forall m \in M : m \lhd G_0 = m,$$
$$\forall m \in M \forall g \in G \exists g_0 \in G_0 : \forall \mathfrak{g}' \in G/G_0 : m \lhd g \cdot \mathfrak{g}' = (m \lhd gG_0) \lhd g_0 \cdot \mathfrak{g}'.$$

It is *transitive*, which means that the set M is non-empty and for each $m \in M$ the map $m \lhd \_$ is surjective; and *free*, which means that for each $m \in M$ the map $m \lhd \_$ is injective; and *semi-commutes with* $\rhd$, which means that

$$\forall m \in M \forall g \in G \exists g_0 \in G_0 : \forall \mathfrak{g}' \in G/G_0 : (g \rhd m) \lhd \mathfrak{g}' = g \rhd (m \lhd g_0 \cdot \mathfrak{g}').$$

The maps $\iota \colon M \to G/G_0$, $m \mapsto G_{m_0,m}$, and $m_0 \lhd \_$ are inverse to each other. Under the identification of M with G/G_0 by either of these maps, we have $\lhd \colon (m, \mathfrak{g}) \mapsto g_{m_0,m} \rhd \mathfrak{g}$.

A left homogeneous space $\mathcal{M}$ is *right amenable* if there is coordinate system $\mathcal{K}$ for $\mathcal{M}$ and there is a finitely additive probability measure μ on M such that

$$\forall \mathfrak{g} \in G/G_0 \forall A \subseteq M : ((\_ \lhd \mathfrak{g}) {\restriction}_A \text{ injective} \implies \mu(A \lhd \mathfrak{g}) = \mu(A)),$$

in which case the cell space $\mathcal{R} = (\mathcal{M}, \mathcal{K})$ is called *right amenable*. When the stabiliser G_0 is finite, that is the case if and only if there is a *right Følner net in $\mathcal{R}$ indexed by* $(I, \leq)$, which is a net $\{F_i\}_{i \in I}$ in $\{F \subseteq M \mid F \neq \emptyset, F \text{ finite}\}$ such that

$$\forall \mathfrak{g} \in G/G_0 : \lim_{i \in I} \frac{|F_i \smallsetminus (\_ \lhd \mathfrak{g})^{-1}(F_i)|}{|F_i|} = 0.$$

A *semi-cellular automaton* is a quadruple $\mathcal{C} = (\mathcal{R}, Q, N, \delta)$, where $\mathcal{R}$ is a cell space; Q, called *set of states*, is a set; N, called *neighbourhood*, is a subset of G/G_0 such that $G_0 \cdot N \subseteq N$; and δ, called *local transition function*, is a map from Q^N to Q. A *local configuration* is a map $\ell \in Q^N$, a *global configuration* is a map $c \in Q^M$, and a *pattern* is a map $p \in Q^A$, where A is a subset of M. The stabiliser G_0 acts on Q^N on the left by $\bullet \colon G_0 \times Q^N \to Q^N$, $(g_0, \ell) \mapsto [n \mapsto \ell(g_0^{-1} \cdot n)]$, and the group G acts on the set of patterns on the left by

$$\blacktriangleright \colon G \times \bigcup_{A \subseteq M} Q^A \to \bigcup_{A \subseteq M} Q^A,$$
$$(g, p) \mapsto \begin{bmatrix} g \rhd \operatorname{dom}(p) \to Q, \\ \qquad m \mapsto p(g^{-1} \rhd m). \end{bmatrix}$$

The *global transition function of* $\mathcal{C}$ is the map $\Delta \colon Q^M \to Q^M$, $c \mapsto [m \mapsto \delta(n \mapsto c(m \lhd n))]$.

A *cellular automaton* is a semi-cellular automaton $\mathcal{C} = (\mathcal{R}, Q, N, \delta)$ such that δ is $\bullet$-*invariant*, which means that, for each $g_0 \in G_0$, we have $\delta(g_0 \bullet \_) = \delta(\_)$. Its global transition function is $\blacktriangleright$-*equivariant*, which means that, for each $g \in G$, we have $\Delta(g \blacktriangleright \_) = g \blacktriangleright \Delta(\_)$.

For each $A \subseteq M$, let $\pi_A \colon Q^M \to Q^A$, $c \mapsto c {\restriction}_A$.

1   Interiors, Closures, and Boundaries

In this section, let $\mathcal{R} = ((M, G, \rhd), (m_0, \{g_{m_0,m}\}_{m \in M}))$ be a cell space.

In Definition 1 we introduce E-interiors, E-closures, and E-boundaries of subsets of M. In Lemma 3 we define surjective restrictions $\Delta^-_{X,A}$ of global transition functions to patterns. And in Theorem 1 we show that right Følner nets are those nets whose components are asymptotically invariant under taking finite boundaries.

Definition 1. *Let A be a subset of M and let E be a subset of G/G_0.*

1. The set

$$A^{-E} = \{m \in M \mid m \lessdot E \subseteq A\} \; \Big(= \bigcap_{e \in E} \bigcup_{a \in A} (\_ \lessdot e)^{-1}(a)\Big)$$

is called E-interior of A.

2. The set

$$A^{+E} = \{m \in M \mid (m \lessdot E) \cap A \neq \emptyset\} \; \Big(= \bigcup_{e \in E} \bigcup_{a \in A} (\_ \lessdot e)^{-1}(a)\Big)$$

is called E-closure of A.

3. The set $\partial_E A = A^{+E} \smallsetminus A^{-E}$ is called E-boundary of A.

Remark 1. Let $\mathcal{R}$ be the cell space $((G, G, \cdot), (e_G, \{g\}_{g \in G}))$, where G is a group and e_G is its neutral element. Then, $G_0 = \{e_G\}$ and $\lessdot = \cdot$. Hence, the notions of E-interior, E-closure, and E-boundary are the same as the ones defined in [1, Sect. 5.4, Paragraph 2].

Example 1. Let M be the Euclidean unit 2-sphere, that is, the surface of the ball of radius 1 in 3-dimensional Euclidean space, and let G be the rotation group. The group G acts transitively but not freely on M on the left by $\rhd$ by function application, that is, by rotation about the origin. For each point $m \in M$, its orbit is M and its stabiliser is the group of rotations about the line through the origin and itself.

Furthermore, let m_0 be the north pole $(0, 0, 1)^\intercal$ of M and, for each point $m \in M$, let $g_{m_0,m}$ be a rotation about an axis in the (x, y)-plane that rotates m_0 to m. The stabiliser G_0 of the north pole m_0 under $\rhd$ is the group of rotations about the z-axis. An element $gG_0 \in G/G_0$ semi-acts on a point m on the right by the induced semi-action $\lessdot$ by first changing the rotation axis of g such that the new axis stands to the line through the origin and m as the old one stood to the line through the origin and m_0, $g_{m_0,m}gg_{m_0,m}^{-1}$, and secondly rotating m as prescribed by this new rotation.

Moreover, let A be a curved circular disk of radius 3ρ with the north pole m_0 at its centre, let g be the rotation about an axis a in the (x, y)-plane by ρ radians, let E be the set $\{g_0 g G_0 \mid g_0 \in G_0\}$, and, for each point $m \in M$, let E_m be the set $m \lessdot E$. Because G_0 is the set of rotations about the z-axis and

$m_0 \trianglelefteq E = g_{m_0,m_0} G_0 g \triangleright m_0 = G_0 \triangleright (g \triangleright m_0)$, the set E_{m_0} is the boundary of a curved circular disk of radius ρ with the north pole m_0 at its centre. And, for each point $m \in M$, because $m \trianglelefteq E = g_{m_0,m} \triangleright E_{m_0}$, the set E_m is the boundary of a curved circular disk of radius ρ with m at its centre.

The E-interior of A is the curved circular disk of radius 2ρ with the north pole m_0 at its centre. The E-closure of A is the curved circular disk of radius 4ρ with the north pole m_0 at its centre. And the E-boundary of A is the annulus bounded by the boundaries of the E-interior and the E-closure of A.

Essential properties of and relations between interiors, closures, and boundaries are given in the next lemma. The upper bound given in its corollary follows from the last part of Item 7.

Lemma 1. *Let A be a subset of M, let $\{A_i\}_{i \in I}$ be a family of subsets of M, let e be an element of G/G_0, and let E and E' be two subsets of G/G_0.*

1. *$A^{-\{G_0\}} = A$, $A^{+\{G_0\}} = A$, and $\partial_{\{G_0\}} A = \emptyset$.*
2. *$A^{-\{G_0,e\}} = A \cap (\_ \trianglelefteq e)^{-1}(A)$, $A^{+\{G_0,e\}} = A \cup (\_ \trianglelefteq e)^{-1}(A)$, and $\partial_{\{G_0,e\}} A = A \smallsetminus (\_ \trianglelefteq e)^{-1}(A) \cup (\_ \trianglelefteq e)^{-1}(A) \smallsetminus A$.*
3. *$(M \smallsetminus A)^{-E} = M \smallsetminus A^{+E}$ and $(M \smallsetminus A)^{+E} = M \smallsetminus A^{-E}$.*
4. *Let $E \subseteq E'$. Then, $A^{-E} \supseteq A^{-E'}$, $A^{+E} \subseteq A^{+E'}$, and $\partial_E A \subseteq \partial_{E'} A$.*
5. *Let $G_0 \in E$. Then, $A^{-E} \subseteq A \subseteq A^{+E}$.*
6. *Let $G_0 \in E$ and let A be finite. Then, A^{-E} is finite.*
7. *Let G_0, A, and E be finite. Then, A^{+E} and $\partial_E A$ are finite. More precisely, $|A^{+E}| \leq |G_0| \cdot |A| \cdot |E|$.*
8. *Let $g \in G$ and let $G_0 \cdot E \subseteq E$. Then, $g \triangleright A^{-E} = (g \triangleright A)^{-E}$, $g \triangleright A^{+E} = (g \triangleright A)^{+E}$, and $g \triangleright \partial_E A = \partial_E (g \triangleright A)$.*
9. *Let $m \in M$, let $G_0 \cdot E \subseteq E$, and let $\iota \colon M \to G/G_0$, $m \mapsto G_{m_0,m}$. Then, $m \trianglelefteq \iota(A^{-E}) = (m \trianglelefteq \iota(A))^{-E}$, $m \trianglelefteq \iota(A^{+E}) = (m \trianglelefteq \iota(A))^{+E}$, and $m \trianglelefteq \iota(\partial_E A) = \partial_E(m \trianglelefteq \iota(A))$.*

Corollary 1. *Let G_0 be finite, let A be a finite subset of M, and let $\mathfrak{g}$ be an element of G/G_0. Then, $|(\_ \trianglelefteq \mathfrak{g})^{-1}(A)| \leq |G_0| \cdot |A|$.*

The restriction $\Delta^-_{X,A}$ of Δ given in Lemma 3 is well-defined according to the next lemma, which itself holds due to the locality of Δ.

Lemma 2. *Let $\mathcal{C} = (\mathcal{R}, Q, N, \delta)$ be a semi-cellular automaton, let Δ be the global transition function of $\mathcal{C}$, let c and c' be two global configurations of $\mathcal{C}$, and let A be a subset of M. If $c{\restriction}_A = c'{\restriction}_A$, then $\Delta(c){\restriction}_{A^{-N}} = \Delta(c'){\restriction}_{A^{-N}}$.*

Lemma 3. *Let $\mathcal{C} = (\mathcal{R}, Q, N, \delta)$ be a semi-cellular automaton, let Δ be the global transition function of $\mathcal{C}$, let X be a subset of Q^M, and let A be a subset of M. The map*

$$\Delta^-_{X,A} \colon \pi_A(X) \to \pi_{A^{-N}}(\Delta(X)),$$

$$p \mapsto \Delta(c){\restriction}_{A^{-N}}, \text{ where } c \in X \text{ such that } c{\restriction}_A = p,$$

is surjective. The map $\Delta^-_{Q^M,A}$ is denoted by Δ^-_A.

In the proof of Theorem 1, the upper bound given in Lemma 6 is essential, which itself follows from the upper bound given in Corollary 1 and the inclusion given in Lemma 5, which in turn follows from the equality given in Lemma 4.

Lemma 4. *Let m be an element of M, and let $\mathfrak{g}$ be an element of G/G_0. There is an element $g \in \mathfrak{g}$ such that*

$$\forall \mathfrak{g}' \in G/G_0 : (m \lhd \mathfrak{g}) \lhd \mathfrak{g}' = m \lhd g \cdot \mathfrak{g}',$$

in particular, for said $g \in \mathfrak{g}$, we have $(m \lhd \mathfrak{g}) \lhd g^{-1} G_0 = m$.

Lemma 5. *Let A and A' be two subsets of M, and let $\mathfrak{g}$ and $\mathfrak{g}'$ be two elements of G/G_0. Then, for each element $m \in (\_ \lhd \mathfrak{g})^{-1}(A) \smallsetminus (\_ \lhd \mathfrak{g}')^{-1}(A')$,*

$$m \lhd \mathfrak{g} \in \bigcup_{g \in \mathfrak{g}} A \smallsetminus (\_ \lhd g^{-1} \cdot \mathfrak{g}')^{-1}(A'),$$

$$m \lhd \mathfrak{g}' \in \bigcup_{g' \in \mathfrak{g}'} (\_ \lhd (g')^{-1} \cdot \mathfrak{g})^{-1}(A) \smallsetminus A'.$$

Lemma 6. *Let G_0 be finite, let F and F' be two finite subsets of M, and let $\mathfrak{g}$ and $\mathfrak{g}'$ be two elements of G/G_0. Then,*

$$|(\_ \lhd \mathfrak{g})^{-1}(F) \smallsetminus (\_ \lhd \mathfrak{g}')^{-1}(F')| \leq \begin{cases} |G_0|^2 \cdot \max_{g \in \mathfrak{g}} |F \smallsetminus (\_ \lhd g^{-1} \cdot \mathfrak{g}')^{-1}(F')|, \\ |G_0|^2 \cdot \max_{g' \in \mathfrak{g}'} |(\_ \lhd (g')^{-1} \cdot \mathfrak{g})^{-1}(F) \smallsetminus F'|. \end{cases}$$

Theorem 1. *Let G_0 be finite and let $\{F_i\}_{i \in I}$ be a net in $\{F \subseteq M \mid F \neq \emptyset, F \text{ finite}\}$ indexed by $(I, \leq)$. The net $\{F_i\}_{i \in I}$ is a right Følner net in $\mathcal{R}$ if and only if*

$$\forall E \subseteq G/G_0 \text{ finite} : \lim_{i \in I} \frac{|\partial_E F_i|}{|F_i|} = 0.$$

Proof. First, let $\{F_i\}_{i \in I}$ be a right Følner net in $\mathcal{R}$. Furthermore, let $E \subseteq G/G_0$ be finite. Moreover, let $i \in I$. For each $e \in E$ and each $e' \in E$, put $A_{i,e,e'} = (\_ \lhd e)^{-1}(F_i) \smallsetminus (\_ \lhd e')^{-1}(F_i)$. For each $\mathfrak{g} \in G/G_0$, put $B_{i,\mathfrak{g}} = F_i \smallsetminus (\_ \lhd \mathfrak{g})^{-1}(F_i)$. According to Definition 1,

$$\partial_E F_i = \left(\bigcup_{e \in E} (\_ \lhd e)^{-1}(F_i) \right) \smallsetminus \left(\bigcap_{e' \in E} (\_ \lhd e')^{-1}(F_i) \right)$$

$$= \bigcup_{e,e' \in E} (\_ \lhd e)^{-1}(F_i) \smallsetminus (\_ \lhd e')^{-1}(F_i) = \bigcup_{e,e' \in E} A_{i,e,e'}.$$

Hence, $|\partial_E F_i| \leq \sum_{e,e' \in E} |A_{i,e,e'}|$.

According to Lemma 6, we have $|A_{i,e,e'}| \leq |G_0|^2 \cdot \max_{g \in e} B_{i,g^{-1} \cdot e'}$. Put $E' = \{g^{-1} \cdot e' \mid e, e' \in E, g \in e\}$. Because E is finite, G_0 is finite, and, for each $e \in E$, we have $|e| = |G_0|$, the set E' is finite. Therefore,

$$\frac{|\partial_E F_i|}{|F_i|} \le \frac{1}{|F_i|} \sum_{e,e' \in E} |A_{i,e,e'}| \le \frac{|G_0|^2}{|F_i|} \sum_{e,e' \in E} \max_{g \in e} |B_{i,g^{-1} \cdot e'}|$$

$$\le \frac{|G_0|^2 \cdot |E|^2}{|F_i|} \max_{e' \in E'} |B_{i,e'}| \le |G_0|^2 \cdot |E|^2 \cdot \max_{e' \in E'} \frac{|F_i \smallsetminus (\_ \lhd e')^{-1}(F_i)|}{|F_i|} \underset{i \in I}{\to} 0.$$

In conclusion, $\lim_{i \in I} \frac{|\partial_E F_i|}{|F_i|} = 0$.

Secondly, for each finite $E \subseteq G/G_0$, let $\lim_{i \in I} \frac{|\partial_E F_i|}{|F_i|} = 0$. Furthermore, let $i \in I$, let $e \in G/G_0$, and put $E = \{G_0, e\}$. According to Item 2 of Lemma 1, we have $F_i \smallsetminus (\_ \lhd e)^{-1}(F_i) \subseteq \partial_E F_i$. Therefore,

$$\frac{|F_i \smallsetminus (\_ \lhd e)^{-1}(F_i)|}{|F_i|} \le \frac{|\partial_E F_i|}{|F_i|} \underset{i \in I}{\to} 0.$$

In conclusion, $\{F_i\}_{i \in I}$ is a right Følner net in $\mathcal{R}$.   □

2   Tilings

In this section, let $\mathcal{R} = ((M, G, \rhd), (m_0, \{g_{m_0,m}\}_{m \in M}))$ be a cell space.

In Definition 2 we introduce the notion of (E, E')-tilings. In Theorem 2 we show using Zorn's lemma that, for each subset E of G/G_0, there is an (E, E')-tiling. And in Lemma 7 we show that, for each (E, E')-tiling with finite sets E and E', the net $\{|T \cap F_i^{-E}|\}_{i \in I}$ is asymptotic not less than $\{|F_i|\}_{i \in I}$.

Definition 2. *Let T be a subset of M, and let E and E' be two subsets of G/ G_0. The set T is called (E, E')-tiling of $\mathcal{R}$ if and only if the family $\{t \lhd E\}_{t \in T}$ is pairwise disjoint and the family $\{t \lhd E'\}_{t \in T}$ is a cover of M.*

Remark 2. Let T be an (E, E')-tiling of $\mathcal{R}$. For each subset F of E and each superset F' of E' with $F' \subseteq G/G_0$, the set T is an (F, F')-tiling of $\mathcal{R}$. In particular, the set T is an $(E, E \cup E')$-tiling of $\mathcal{R}$.

Remark 3. In the situation of Remark 1, the notion of (E, E')-tiling is the same as the one defined in [1, Sect. 5.6, Paragraph 2].

Example 2. In the situation of Example 1, let E' be the set $\{g(g')^{-1}G_0 \mid e, e' \in E, g \in e, g' \in e'\}$ $(= \{g_0 g g_0' g^{-1} G_0 \mid g_0, g_0' \in G_0\})$ and, for each point $m \in M$, let $E'_m = m \lhd E'$. Because g^{-1} is the rotation about the axis a by $-\rho$ radians, the set $G_0 g^{-1} \rhd m_0$ is equal to E_{m_0} and the set $g G_0 g^{-1} \rhd m_0$ is equal to $E_{g \rhd m_0}$. Because $m_0 \lhd E' = g_{m_0,m_0} G_0 g G_0 g^{-1} \rhd m_0 = G_0 \rhd (g G_0 g^{-1} \rhd m_0) = G_0 \rhd E_{g \rhd m_0}$, the set E'_{m_0} is the curved circular disk of radius 2ρ with the north pole m_0 at its centre. And, for each point $m \in M$, because $m \lhd E' = g_{m_0,m} \rhd E'_{m_0}$, the set E'_m is the curved circular disk of radius 2ρ with m at its centre.

If the radius $\rho = \pi/2$, then the circle E_{m_0} is the equator and the curved circular disk E'_{m_0} has radius π and is thus the sphere M, and hence the set $T = \{m_0\}$ is an (E, E')-tiling of $\mathcal{R}$; if the radius $\rho = \pi/4$, then the curved circular disks E'_{m_0} and E'_S, where S is the south pole, have radii $\pi/2$, thus they are hemispheres, and hence the set $T = \{m_0, S\}$ is an (E, E')-tiling of $\mathcal{R}$; if the radius $\rho = \pi/8$, then the curved circular disks E'_{m_0} and E'_S have radii $\pi/4$, and it can be shown with spherical geometry that the set T consisting of the north pole m_0, the south pole S, four equidistant points m_1, m_2, m_3, and m_4 on the equator, and the circumcentres $c_1, c_2, \ldots, c_8$ of the 8 smallest spherical triangles with one vertex from $\{m_0, S\}$ and two vertices from $\{m_1, m_2, m_3, m_4\}$ (see Fig. 1).

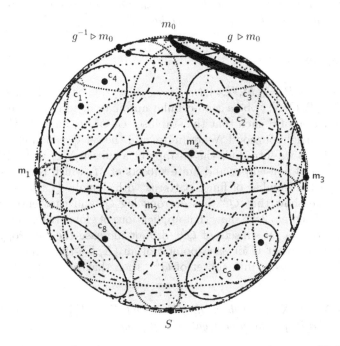

Fig. 1. The points m_0, S, m_1, m_2, m_3, m_4, $c_1, c_2, \ldots, c_8$ constitute an (E, E')-tiling of the sphere; the circles E_m about these points are drawn solid; the boundaries of the curved circular disks E'_m about these points are drawn dotted; the inclined circle about $g \triangleright m_0$ is the rotation $E_{g \triangleright m_0}$ of E_{m_0} by $\pi/8$ about the axis a; and the other inclined circles are rotations $g_0 \triangleright (E_{g \triangleright m_0})$ of $E_{g \triangleright m_0}$ about the z-axis, for a few $g_0 \in G_0$.

Theorem 2. *Let E be a non-empty subset of G/G_0. There is an (E, E')-tiling of $\mathcal{R}$, where $E' = \{g(g')^{-1}G_0 \mid e, e' \in E, g \in e, g' \in e'\}$.*

Proof. Let $\mathcal{S} = \{S \subseteq M \mid \{s \triangleleft E\}_{s \in S} \text{ is pairwise disjoint}\}$. Because $\{m_0\} \in \mathcal{S}$, the set $\mathcal{S}$ is non-empty. Moreover, it is preordered by inclusion.

Let $\mathcal{C}$ be a chain in $(\mathcal{S}, \subseteq)$. Then, $\bigcup_{S \in \mathcal{C}} S$ is an element of $\mathcal{S}$ and an upper bound of $\mathcal{C}$. According to Zorn's lemma, there is a maximal element T in $\mathcal{S}$. By definition of $\mathcal{S}$, the family $\{t \triangleleft E\}_{t \in T}$ is pairwise disjoint.

Let $m \in M$. Because T is maximal and $m \triangleleft E$ is non-empty, there is a $t \in T$ such that $(t \triangleleft E) \cap (m \triangleleft E) \neq \emptyset$. Hence, there are $e, e' \in E$ such that $t \triangleleft e = m \triangleleft e'$.

According to Lemma 4, there is a $g' \in e'$ such that $(m \lhd e') \lhd (g')^{-1}G_0 = m$, and there is a $g \in e$ such that $(t \lhd e) \lhd (g')^{-1}G_0 = t \lhd g(g')^{-1}G_0$. Therefore, $m = t \lhd g(g')^{-1}G_0$. Because $g(g')^{-1}G_0 \in E'$, we have $m \in t \lhd E'$. Thus, $\{t \lhd E'\}_{t \in T}$ is a cover of M.

In conclusion, T is an (E, E')-tiling of $\mathcal{R}$. $\square$

Lemma 7. *Let G_0 be finite, let $\{F_i\}_{i \in I}$ be a right Følner net in $\mathcal{R}$ indexed by $(I, \leq)$, let E and E' be two finite subsets of G/G_0, and let T be an (E, E')-tiling of $\mathcal{R}$. There is a positive real number $\varepsilon \in \mathbb{R}_{>0}$ and there is an index $i_0 \in I$ such that, for each index $i \in I$ with $i \geq i_0$, we have $|T \cap F_i^{-E}| \geq \varepsilon |F_i|$.*

3   Entropies

In this section, let $\mathcal{R} = ((M, G, \rhd), (m_0, \{g_{m_0,m}\}_{m \in M}))$ be a right amenable cell space, let $\mathcal{C} = (\mathcal{R}, Q, N, \delta)$ be a semi-cellular automaton, and let Δ be the global transition function of $\mathcal{C}$ such that the stabiliser G_0 of m_0 under $\rhd$, the set Q of states, and the neighbourhood N are finite, and the set Q is non-empty.

In Definition 3 we introduce the entropy of a subset X of Q^M with respect to a net $\{F_i\}_{i \in I}$ of non-empty and finite subsets of M, which is the asymptotic growth rate of the number of finite patterns with domain F_i that occur in X. In Lemma 8 we show that Q^M has entropy $\log |Q|$ and that entropy is non-decreasing. In Theorem 3 we show that applications of global transition functions of cellular automata on subsets of Q^M do not increase their entropy. And in Lemma 9 we show that if for each point t of an (E, E')-tiling not all patterns with domain $t \lhd E$ occur in a subset of Q^M, then that subset has less entropy than Q^M.

Definition 3. *Let X be a subset of Q^M and let $\mathcal{F} = \{F_i\}_{i \in I}$ be a net in $\{F \subseteq M \mid F \neq \emptyset, F \, finite\}$. The non-negative real number*

$$\mathrm{ent}_{\mathcal{F}}(X) = \limsup_{i \in I} \frac{\log |\pi_{F_i}(X)|}{|F_i|}$$

is called entropy of X with respect to $\mathcal{F}$.

Remark 4. In the situation of Remark 1, the notion of entropy is the same as the one defined in [1, Definition 5.7.1].

Lemma 8. *Let $\mathcal{F} = \{F_i\}_{i \in I}$ be a net in $\{F \subseteq M \mid F \neq \emptyset, F \, finite\}$. Then,*

1. $\mathrm{ent}_{\mathcal{F}}(Q^M) = \log |Q|$;
2. $\forall X \subseteq Q^M \forall X' \subseteq Q^M : (X \subseteq X' \implies \mathrm{ent}_{\mathcal{F}}(X) \leq \mathrm{ent}_{\mathcal{F}}(X'))$;
3. $\forall X \subseteq Q^M : \mathrm{ent}_{\mathcal{F}}(X) \leq \log |Q|$.

In the remainder of this section, let $\mathcal{F} = \{F_i\}_{i \in I}$ be a right Følner net in $\mathcal{R}$ indexed by $(I, \leq)$.

Theorem 3. *Let X be a subset of Q^M. Then, $\mathrm{ent}_{\mathcal{F}}(\Delta(X)) \leq \mathrm{ent}_{\mathcal{F}}(X)$.*

Proof. Suppose, without loss of generality, that $G_0 \in N$. Let $i \in I$. According to Lemma 3, the map $\Delta_{X,F_i}^- : \pi_{F_i}(X) \to \pi_{F_i^{-N}}(\Delta(X))$ is surjective. Therefore, $|\pi_{F_i^{-N}}(\Delta(X))| \leq |\pi_{F_i}(X)|$. Because $G_0 \in N$, according to Item 5 of Lemma 1, we have $F_i^{-N} \subseteq F_i$. Thus, $\pi_{F_i}(\Delta(X)) \subseteq \pi_{F_i^{-N}}(\Delta(X)) \times Q^{F_i \smallsetminus F_i^{-N}}$. Hence,

$$
\log|\pi_{F_i}(\Delta(X))| \leq \log|\pi_{F_i^{-N}}(\Delta(X))| + \log|Q^{F_i \smallsetminus F_i^{-N}}|
$$
$$
\leq \log|\pi_{F_i}(X)| + |F_i \smallsetminus F_i^{-N}| \cdot \log|Q|.
$$

Because $G_0 \in N$, according to Item 5 of Lemma 1, we have $F_i \subseteq F_i^{+N}$. Therefore, $F_i \smallsetminus F_i^{-N} \subseteq F_i^{+N} \smallsetminus F_i^{-N} = \partial_N F_i$. Because G_0, F_i, and N are finite, according to Item 7 of Lemma 1, the boundary $\partial_N F_i$ is finite. Hence,

$$
\frac{\log|\pi_{F_i}(\Delta(X))|}{|F_i|} \leq \frac{\log|\pi_{F_i}(X)|}{|F_i|} + \frac{|\partial_N F_i|}{|F_i|} \log|Q|.
$$

Therefore, because N is finite, according to Theorem 1,

$$
\mathrm{ent}_{\mathcal{F}}(\Delta(X)) \leq \limsup_{i \in I} \frac{\log|\pi_{F_i}(X)|}{|F_i|} + \left(\lim_{i \in I} \frac{|\partial_N F_i|}{|F_i|} \right) \cdot \log|Q| = \mathrm{ent}_{\mathcal{F}}(X). \qquad \square
$$

Lemma 9. *Let Q contain at least two elements, let X be a subset of Q^M, let E and E' be two non-empty and finite subsets of G/G_0, and let T be an (E, E')-tiling of $\mathcal{R}$, such that, for each cell $t \in T$, we have $\pi_{t \triangleleft E}(X) \subsetneqq Q^{t \triangleleft E}$. Then, $\mathrm{ent}_{\mathcal{F}}(X) < \log|Q|$.*

Corollary 2. *Let Q contain at least two elements, let X be a ▶-invariant subset of Q^M, and let E be a non-empty and finite subset of G/G_0, such that $\pi_{m_0 \triangleleft E}(X) \subsetneqq Q^{m_0 \triangleleft E}$. Then, $\mathrm{ent}_{\mathcal{F}}(X) < \log|Q|$.*

4   Gardens of Eden

In this section, let $\mathcal{R} = ((M, G, \triangleright), (m_0, \{g_{m_0,m}\}_{m \in M}))$ be a right amenable cell space and let $\mathcal{C} = (\mathcal{R}, Q, N, \delta)$ be a semi-cellular automaton such that the stabiliser G_0 of m_0 under $\triangleright$, the set Q of states, and the neighbourhood N are finite, and the set Q is non-empty. Furthermore, let Δ be the global transition function of $\mathcal{C}$, and let $\mathcal{F} = \{F_i\}_{i \in I}$ be a right Følner net in $\mathcal{R}$ indexed by $(I, \leq)$.

In Theorem 4 we show that if Δ is not surjective, then the entropy of its image is less than the entropy of Q^M. And the converse of that statement obviously holds. In Theorem 5 we show that if the entropy of the image of Δ is less than the entropy of Q^M, then Δ is not pre-injective. And in Theorem 6 we show the converse of that statement. These four statements establish the Garden of Eden theorem, see Main Theorem 1.

Definition 4. *Let c and c' be two maps from M to Q. The set $\mathrm{diff}(c, c') = \{m \in M \mid c(m) \neq c'(m)\}$ is called difference of c and c'.*

Definition 5. *The map Δ is called* pre-injective *if and only if, for each tuple $(c, c') \in Q^M \times Q^M$ such that $\operatorname{diff}(c, c')$ is finite and $\Delta(c) = \Delta(c')$, we have $c = c'$.*

In the proof of Theorem 4, the existence of a Garden of Eden pattern, as stated in Lemma 10, is essential, which itself follows from the existence of a Garden of Eden configuration, the compactness of Q^M, and the continuity of Δ.

Definition 6. *1. Let $c \colon M \to Q$ be a global configuration. It is called* Garden of Eden configuration *if and only if it is not contained in $\Delta(Q^M)$.*
2. Let $p \colon A \to Q$ be a pattern. It is called Garden of Eden pattern *if and only if, for each global configuration $c \in Q^M$, we have $\Delta(c){\restriction}_A \neq p$.*

Remark 5. 1. The global transition function Δ is surjective if and only if there is no Garden of Eden configuration.
2. If $p \colon A \to Q$ is a Garden of Eden pattern, then each global configuration $c \in Q^M$ with $c{\restriction}_A = p$ is a Garden of Eden configuration.
3. If there is a Garden of Eden pattern, then Δ is not surjective.

Lemma 10. *Let Δ not be surjective. There is a Garden of Eden pattern with non-empty and finite domain.*

Theorem 4. *Let δ be $\bullet$-invariant, let Q contain at least two elements, and let Δ not be surjective. Then, $\operatorname{ent}_{\mathcal{F}}(\Delta(Q^M)) < \log |Q|$.*

Proof. According to Lemma 10, there is a Garden of Eden pattern $p \colon F \to Q$ with non-empty and finite domain. Let $E = (m_0 \vartriangleleft \_)^{-1}(F)$. Then, $m_0 \vartriangleleft E = F$ and, because $\vartriangleleft$ is free, $|E| = |F| < \infty$. Because p is a Garden of Eden pattern, $p \notin \pi_{m_0 \vartriangleleft E}(\Delta(Q^M))$. Hence, $\pi_{m_0 \vartriangleleft E}(\Delta(Q^M)) \subsetneqq Q^{m_0 \vartriangleleft E}$. Moreover, according to [5, Item 1 of Theorem 2], the map Δ is $\blacktriangleright$-equivariant. Hence, for each $g \in G$, we have $g \blacktriangleright \Delta(Q^M) = \Delta(g \blacktriangleright Q^M) = \Delta(Q^M)$. In other words, $\Delta(Q^M)$ is $\blacktriangleright$-invariant. Thus, according to Corollary 2, we have $\operatorname{ent}_{\mathcal{F}}(\Delta(Q^M)) < \log |Q|$.   □

In the proof of Theorem 5, the fact that enlarging each element of $\mathcal{F}$ does not increase entropy, as stated in the next lemma, is essential.

Lemma 11. *Let X be a subset of Q^M and let E be a finite subset of G/G_0 such that $G_0 \in E$. Then, $\operatorname{ent}_{\{F_i^{+E}\}_{i \in I}}(X) \leq \operatorname{ent}_{\mathcal{F}}(X)$.*

Theorem 5. *Let $\operatorname{ent}_{\mathcal{F}}(\Delta(Q^M)) < \log |Q|$. Then, Δ is not pre-injective.*

Proof. Suppose, without loss of generality, that $G_0 \in N$. Let $X = \Delta(Q^M)$. According to Lemma 11, we have $\operatorname{ent}_{\{F_i^{+N}\}_{i \in I}}(X) \leq \operatorname{ent}_{\mathcal{F}}(X) < \log |Q|$. Hence, there is an $i \in I$ such that

$$\frac{\log |\pi_{F_i^{+N}}(X)|}{|F_i|} < \log |Q|.$$

Thus, $|\pi_{F_i^{+N}}(X)| < |Q|^{|F_i|}$. Furthermore, let $q \in Q$ and let $X' = \{c \in Q^M \mid c{\restriction}_{M \smallsetminus F_i} \equiv q\}$. Then, $|Q|^{|F_i|} = |X'|$. Hence, $|\pi_{F_i^{+N}}(X)| < |X'|$. Moreover, according to Item 3 of Lemma 1, we have $(M \smallsetminus F_i)^{-N} = M \smallsetminus F_i^{+N}$. Hence, for each

$(c, c') \in X' \times X'$, according to Lemma 2, we have $\Delta(c)\restriction_{M \smallsetminus F_i^{+N}} = \Delta(c')\restriction_{M \smallsetminus F_i^{+N}}$. Therefore,

$$|\Delta(X')| = |\pi_{F_i^{+N}}(\Delta(X'))| \le |\pi_{F_i^{+N}}(\Delta(Q^M))| = |\pi_{F_i^{+N}}(X)| < |X'|.$$

Hence, there are $c, c' \in X'$ such that $c \ne c'$ and $\Delta(c) = \Delta(c')$. Thus, because $\text{diff}(c, c') \subseteq F_i$ is finite, the map Δ is not pre-injective.   □

In the proof of Theorem 6, the statement of Lemma 12 is essential, which says that if two distinct patterns have the same image and we replace each occurrence of the first by the second in a configuration, we get a new configuration in which the first pattern does not occur and that has the same image as the original one.

Definition 7. *Identify M with G/G_0 by $\iota\colon m \mapsto G_{m_0, m}$. Let*

$$\blacktriangleleft\colon M \times \bigcup_{A \subseteq M} Q^A \to \bigcup_{A \subseteq M} Q^A, \quad (m, p) \mapsto \begin{bmatrix} m \lhd \text{dom}(p) \to Q, \\ m \lhd a \mapsto p(a). \end{bmatrix}$$

Remark 6. Let A be a subset of M, let p be map from A to Q, and let m be an element of M. Then, $m \blacktriangleleft p = g_{m_0, m} \blacktriangleright p$.

Definition 8. *Identify M with G/G_0 by $\iota\colon m \mapsto G_{m_0, m}$, let A be a subset of M, let p be map from A to Q, let c be map from M to Q, let m be an element of M. The pattern p is said to* occur at m in c *and we write $p \sqsubseteq_m c$ if and only if $m \blacktriangleleft p = c\restriction_{m \lhd A}$.*

Lemma 12. *Identify M with G/G_0 by $\iota\colon m \mapsto G_{m_0, m}$, let A be a subset of M, let N' be the subset $\{g^{-1} \cdot n' \mid n, n' \in N, g \in n\}$ of G/G_0, and let p and p' be two maps from $A^{+N'}$ to Q such that $p\restriction_{A+N' \smallsetminus A} = p'\restriction_{A+N' \smallsetminus A}$ and $\Delta_{A^{+N'}}^-(p) = \Delta_{A^{+N'}}^-(p')$. Furthermore, let c be a map from M to Q and let S be a subset of M, such that the family $\{s \lhd A^{+N'}\}_{s \in S}$ is pairwise disjoint and, for each cell $s \in S$, we have $p \sqsubseteq_s c$. Put*

$$c' = c\restriction_{M \smallsetminus (\bigcup_{s \in S} s \lhd A^{+N'})} \times \coprod_{s \in S} s \blacktriangleleft p'.$$

Then, for each cell $s \in S$, we have $p' \sqsubseteq_s c'$, and $\Delta(c) = \Delta(c')$. In particular, if $p \ne p'$, then, for each cell $s \in S$, we have $p \not\sqsubseteq_s c'$.

Theorem 6. *Let δ be $\bullet$-invariant, let Q contain at least two elements, and let Δ not be pre-injective. Then, $\text{ent}_{\mathcal{F}}(\Delta(Q^M)) < \log|Q|$.*

Proof. Suppose, without loss of generality, that $G_0 \in N$. Identify M with G/G_0 by $\iota\colon m \mapsto G_{m_0, m}$. Because Δ is not pre-injective, there are $c, c' \in Q^M$ such that $\text{diff}(c, c')$ is finite, $\Delta(c) = \Delta(c')$, and $c \ne c'$. Put $A = \text{diff}(c, c')$, put $N' = \{g^{-1} \cdot n' \mid n, n' \in N, g \in n\}$, put $E = A^{+N'}$, and put $p = c\restriction_E$ and $p' = c'\restriction_E$. Because $\Delta(c) = \Delta(c')$, we have $\Delta_{A^{+N'}}^-(p) = \Delta_{A^{+N'}}^-(p')$.

Because N is finite and, for each $n \in N$, we have $|n| = |G_0| < \infty$, the set N' is finite. Moreover, $G_0 \cdot N' \subseteq N'$. According to Item 5 of Lemma 1, because $G_0 \in N'$ and $A \neq \emptyset$, we have $E \supseteq A$ and hence E is non-empty. According to Item 7 of Lemma 1, because G_0, A, and N' are finite, so is E. Because E is non-empty, according to Theorem 2, there is a subset E' of G/G_0 and an (E, E')-tiling T of $\mathcal{R}$. Because G_0 and E are non-empty and finite, so is E'.

Let $Y = \{y \in Q^M \mid \forall t \in T : p \not\sqsubseteq_t y\}$. For each $t \in T$, we have $t \triangleleft p \notin \pi_{t \trianglelefteq E}(Y)$ and therefore $\pi_{t \trianglelefteq E}(Y) \subsetneqq Q^{t \trianglelefteq E}$. According to Lemma 9, we have $\mathrm{ent}_{\mathcal{F}}(Y) < \log |Q|$. Hence, according to Theorem 3, we have $\mathrm{ent}_{\mathcal{F}}(\Delta(Y)) < \log |Q|$.

Let $x \in Q^M$. Put $S = \{t \in T \mid p \sqsubseteq_t x\}$. According to Lemma 12, there is an $x' \in Q^M$ such that $x' \in Y$ and $\Delta(x) = \Delta(x')$. Therefore, $\Delta(Q^M) = \Delta(Y)$. In conclusion, $\mathrm{ent}_{\mathcal{F}}(Q^M) < \log |Q|$. □

Main Theorem 1 (Garden of Eden theorem; Edward Forrest Moore, 1962; John R. Myhill, 1963). *Let $\mathcal{M} = (M, G, \triangleright)$ be a right amenable left homogeneous space with finite stabilisers and let Δ be the global transition function of a cellular automaton over $\mathcal{M}$ with finite set of states and finite neighbourhood. The map Δ is surjective if and only if it is pre-injective.*

Proof. There is a coordinate system $\mathcal{K} = (m_0, \{g_{m_0,m}\}_{m \in M})$ such that the cell space $\mathcal{R} = (\mathcal{M}, \mathcal{K})$ is right amenable. Moreover, according to [5, Theorem 1], there is a cellular automaton $\mathcal{C} = (\mathcal{R}, Q, N, \delta)$ such that Q and N are finite and Δ is its global transition function.

In the case that $|Q| \leq 1$, the proof is trivial. Let it be the case that $|Q| > 1$. According to Theorem 4 and Item 1 of Lemma 8, the map Δ is not surjective if and only if $\mathrm{ent}_{\mathcal{F}}(\Delta(Q^M)) < \log |Q|$. And, according to Theorems 5 and 6, we have $\mathrm{ent}_{\mathcal{F}}(\Delta(Q^M)) < \log |Q|$ if and only if Δ is not pre-injective. Hence, Δ is not surjective if and only if it is not pre-injective. In conclusion, Δ is surjective if and only if it is pre-injective. □

Remark 7. In the situation of Remark 1, Main Theorem 1 is [1, Theorem 5.3.1].

References

1. Ceccherini-Silberstein, T., Coornaert, M.: Cellular Automata and Groups. Springer Monographs in Mathematics. Springer, Heidelberg (2010)
2. Moore, E.F.: Machine models of self-reproduction. In: Proceedings of Symposia in Applied Mathematics, vol. 14, pp. 17–33 (1962)
3. Myhill, J.R.: The converse of Moore's Garden-of-Eden theorem. Proc. Am. Math. Soc. **14**, 685–686 (1963)
4. Moriceau, S.: Cellular automata on a G-Set. Journal Cellular Automata **6**(6), 461–486 (2011)
5. Wacker, S.: Cellular automata on group sets and the uniform Curtis-Hedlund-Lyndon theorem. In: Cook, M., Neary, T. (eds.) AUTOMATA 2016. LNCS, vol. 9664, pp. 185–198. Springer, Heidelberg (2016). doi:10.1007/978-3-319-39300-1_15
6. Wacker, S.: Right Amenable Left Group Sets and the Tarski-Følner Theorem [math.GR]. arXiv:1603.06460

The Density Classification Problem in the Context of Continuous Cellular Automata

Barbara Wolnik[1], Marcin Dembowski[1(✉)], Witold Bołt[2,3],
Jan M. Baetens[3], and Bernard De Baets[3]

[1] Faculty of Mathematics, Physics and Informatics, Institute of Mathematics,
University of Gdańsk, 80-308 Gdańsk, Poland
marcin.dembowski@gmail.com
[2] Systems Research Institute, Polish Academy of Sciences,
Newelska 6, 01-447 Warsaw, Poland
[3] Department of Mathematical Modelling, Statistics and Bioinformatics, KERMIT,
Ghent University, Coupure Links 653, 9000 Gent, Belgium

Abstract. In this paper, we discuss the well-known density classification problem in the context of Continuous Cellular Automata, and recall that this problem cannot be solved in the classical sense. Yet, by slightly relaxing the assumptions on the output specification, we can identify a rich family of rules solving the problem.

1 Introduction

The density classification problem (DCP) was first introduced in [15], and then more formally presented in [19]. It concerns binary Cellular Automata (CAs) only and is very simple. The task is to find a CA that can indicate whether an initial configuration contains more 1s than 0s. The output should be given in such a way that all cells get the initial majority state. Unfortunately, it has been shown that the problem cannot be solved [6,16], *i.e.* there does not exist a CA that correctly solves the DCP for an arbitrary number of cells.

There exist, however, CAs that can give the proper outcome for many initial configurations. The most famous one is the GKL rule [15], which correctly classifies more than 80 % of the initial configurations. Similar CAs have been found using genetic algorithms [17,18]. Many researchers modified the original problem to obtain an infallible classifier. For instance, by allowing two CAs (instead of one) [14], endowing cells with memory [21], or using probabilistic CAs [10,12,20]. Another idea was to relax the output specification of the problem [8], by considering heterogeneous configurations with certain properties as valid answers. In such settings, reading the answer requires multiple time steps (and memory) or access to the states of multiple cells (global access).

Another direction in the quest for classifiers that correctly classify all initial configurations, is to use Continuous CAs (CCAs). For example, in [5] the authors present a large diffusion and small amplification CA, which can correctly solve

© Springer International Publishing Switzerland 2016
S. El Yacoubi et al. (Eds.): ACRI 2016, LNCS 9863, pp. 79–87, 2016.
DOI: 10.1007/978-3-319-44365-2_8

the DCP for any number of cells. However, the presented solution depends on a parameter, which needs to be chosen based on the number of cells, so this leads to a family of CCAs rather than a single CCA.

In this paper, we consider CCAs, and we look for an infallible classifier for any number of cells. We concentrate on one of the simplest families of CCAs, in which the local rule is affine in each variable. Recall that a function $f(x_1, \ldots, x_n)$ is affine in the variable x_i when for any fixed $x_1, \ldots, x_{i-1}, x_{i+1}, \ldots, x_n$ the function $f_i : [0, 1] \rightarrow [0, 1]$ given by $f_i(x_i) = f(x_1, \ldots, x_n)$ is affine, *i.e.* $f_i(x_i) = ax_i + b$ for some $a, b \in \mathbb{R}$. Such a family of CCAs was already investigated earlier [1,2,9], but was not used in the context of the DCP, except for our earlier attempts [4].

A preliminary examination of the family of Affine CCAs (ACCAs) has shown that, roughly speaking, finding a solution to the DCP is not possible (Theorem 2). Yet, by a slight alteration of the output specification, we found a broad family of density-conserving ACCAs of which most members solve this modified relaxed setting for any configuration irrespective of the system size.

The paper is organized as follows. In Sect. 2 we define the basic concepts and introduce the notation. Section 3 contains the definition of the DCP in the classical sense and the result on the non-existence of the solution. Section 4 presents the characterization of density-conserving ACCAs out of which many are solutions to the relaxed variant of the DCP which is presented in Sect. 5. Section 6 covers the results of experiments validating the theoretical findings.

2   Preliminaries

A one-dimensional two-state CA is a discrete dynamical system in which the space is subdivided into discrete elements, referred to as cells. Every cell is assigned one out of two states: 0 or 1. At every consecutive, discrete time step the state of the cells are updated according to some local rule. The new state of a cell depends only on its neighboring states at the previous time step. The neighborhood consists of the cell itself and its r left and r right neighbors (we assume that cells are arranged in a circular linear array). The number r will be referred to as the radius of the neighborhood, such that we can write $R = 2r + 1$ to denote the number of cells in the neighborhood. Binary CAs for which $r = 1$ will be referred to as Elementary CAs (ECAs) [22]. CCAs are a generalization of CAs where the states of the cells are real valued. Here, we assume that the value is in the range $[0, 1]$, and that the local rule can define any mapping from $[0, 1]^R$ to $[0, 1]$.

For further considerations, we introduce two sets:

$$[0, 1]^* = \bigcup_{n=1}^{\infty} [0, 1]^n, \quad \{0, 1\}^* = \bigcup_{n=1}^{\infty} \{0, 1\}^n,$$

referred to as the set of all configurations and the set of all binary configurations, respectively. Let the local rule $f : [0, 1]^R \rightarrow [0, 1]$ be given. On the set of all configurations, we define the global rule $F\colon [0,1]^* \to [0,1]^*$ by writing for $x \in [0,1]^n$:

$$F(x) = F(x_0, x_1, \ldots, x_{n-1}) = (x'_0, x'_1, \ldots, x'_{n-1}),$$

where:

$$x'_i = f(x_{i-r}, \ldots, x_i, \ldots, x_{i+r}), \tag{1}$$

and all operations on the indices are performed modulo n. Further, $F^t(x)$ will be used to denote the result of t-th application of F on the configuration x, corresponding to the t-th time step.

In this paper we will concentrate on local rules f that generalize the idea of "fuzzification" presented in [11], *i.e.* functions f that are affine in each variable. CCAs defined with such local rules will be referred to as ACCAs.

Formally speaking, we start by defining f on $\{0,1\}^R$. This can be done, for example, in tabular form by listing the 2^R binary tuples $\{N_0, N_1, \ldots, N_s\}$ (here and subsequently $s = 2^R - 1$) and mapping each tuple to a $l_i \in [0,1]$. We assume that the tuples $\{N_0, N_1, \ldots, N_s\}$ are arranged in such a way that N_i is the binary representation of the number i and $N_i(j)$ is the j-th digit, from left to right of N_i, *i.e.* $N_i = (N_i(R-1), N_i(R-2), \ldots, N_i(1), N_i(0)) \in \{0,1\}^R$ and $i = N_i(R-1) \cdot 2^{R-1} + N_i(R-2) \cdot 2^{R-2} + \cdots + N_i(1) \cdot 2^1 + N_i(0) \cdot 2^0$. The sequence $(l_0, l_1, \ldots, l_s)$ will be referred to as the lookup table (LUT) of the local rule f.

After defining f on $\{0,1\}^R$, we extend it to $[0,1]^R$. Obviously, the extension which is affine in each variable is unique, and can be expressed as a polynomial:

$$f(x_0, x_1, \ldots, x_{R-1}) = \sum_{i=0}^{s} l_i \left(\prod_{k=0}^{R-1} h(x_k, N_i(R-1-k)) \right), \tag{2}$$

where $h(x,1) = x$ and $h(x,0) = 1 - x$. It is clear that the function f we have just defined is affine in each of its variables and takes value l_i on N_i.

Table 1. LUT of a general ACCA for $r = 1$.

N_0	N_1	N_2	N_3	N_4	N_5	N_6	N_7
(0,0,0)	(0,0,1)	(0,1,0)	(0,1,1)	(1,0,0)	(1,0,1)	(1,1,0)	(1,1,1)
l_0	l_1	l_2	l_3	l_4	l_5	l_6	l_7

Example 1. If $r = 1$, then the set $\{0,1\}^R$ has only eight elements, and the corresponding LUT is given in Table 1.
Besides, Eq. (2) gives:

$$f(x,y,z) = l_0(1-x)(1-y)(1-z) + l_1(1-x)(1-y)z + l_2(1-x)y(1-z)$$
$$+ l_3(1-x)yz + l_4 x(1-y)(1-z) + l_5 x(1-y)z + l_6 xy(1-z) + l_7 xyz,$$

or in its canonical form:

$$f(x,y,z) = (l_7 - l_6 - l_5 - l_3 + l_4 + l_2 + l_1 - l_0)xyz + (l_6 - l_4 - l_2 + l_0)xy$$
$$+ (l_5 - l_4 - l_1 + l_0)xz + (l_3 - l_2 - l_1 + l_0)yz + (l_4 - l_0)x + (l_2 - l_0)y + (l_1 - l_0)z + l_0. \;\; \square$$

Note that if a function is affine in some variable, then it is monotone in this variable, hence the following theorem can be proven.

Theorem 1. *Assume that the function* $f : [0,1]^n \rightarrow [0,1]$ *is affine in each of its variables and let* $0 \le m \le M \le 1$. *If* $x \in [m, M]^n$, *then:*

$$\min \{f(y) \mid y \in \{m, M\}^n\} \le f(x) \le \max \{f(y) \mid y \in \{m, M\}^n\}.$$

In particular, we conclude that both the minimal and the maximal value of a local rule of an ACCA are included among the LUT values.

3   Nonexistence of a Solution of the DCP in the Classical Sense

Given a configuration $x \in [0,1]^n$, we define its density $\rho(x)$ as:

$$\rho(x) = \frac{1}{n} \sum_{i=0}^{n-1} x_i. \tag{3}$$

Clearly, for $x \in \{0,1\}^n$, $\rho(x)$ is equal to the fraction of 1's in the configuration x.

Let $\rho_0 \in]0,1[$. We say that a CCA defined by a local rule f *solves the DCP at threshold* ρ_0 *in the classical sense* if for all $x \in \{0,1\}^*$ it holds that:

$$\rho(x) < \rho_0 \Rightarrow \lim_{t \to \infty} F^t(x) = (0,0,\ldots,0),$$
$$\rho(x) > \rho_0 \Rightarrow \lim_{t \to \infty} F^t(x) = (1,1,\ldots,1). \tag{4}$$

Note that the problem is stated only for $x \in \{0,1\}^*$ instead of $[0,1]^*$. We say that a CCA defined by a local rule f *conserves the threshold* ρ_0 if for all $x \in \{0,1\}^*$ it holds that:

$$\rho(x) < \rho_0 \Rightarrow \rho(F(x)) \le \rho_0,$$
$$\rho(x) > \rho_0 \Rightarrow \rho(F(x)) \ge \rho_0. \tag{5}$$

Theorem 2. *Let* $\rho_0 \in]0,1[$. *There exists no ACCA that solves the DCP at threshold* ρ_0 *in the classical sense and that conserves the threshold* ρ_0.

This theorem is a consequence of the two lemmas given below. Each of them can be proved in the same way as the corresponding facts for CAs in [7,16].

Lemma 1. *Let us suppose that* f *is a local rule of some CCA, which solves the DCP at some threshold* $\rho_0 \in]0,1[$ *in the classical sense. If the function* f *is continuous, then* $f(0,0,\ldots,0) = 0$ *and* $f(1,1,\ldots,1) = 1$.

Lemma 2. *If the local rule* f *conserves the threshold* ρ_0, *and* $f(0,0,\ldots,0) = 0$, $f(1,1,\ldots,1) = 1$, *then for each* $x \in \{0,1\}^*$ *it holds that* $\rho(F(x)) = \rho(x)$.

Now, we can prove Theorem 2. We set the threshold $\rho_0 \in]0, 1[$ and assume that the f is a local rule of some ACCA which conserves the threshold ρ_0, and solves the DCP in the classical sense at the same threshold. From Lemma 1 we know that $l_0 = 0$ and $l_s = 1$. Thus, from Lemma 2 we get that $\rho(F(x)) = \rho(x)$ for each $x \in \{0,1\}^*$. Since f is the local rule of an ACCA, the last fact leads to $\rho(F(x)) = \rho(x)$ for each $x \in [0,1]^*$ according to [2]. Hence, the ACCA defined by local rule f conserves density, which is impossible.

4   Density-Conserving ACCAs

Motivated by Lemma 2, which shows a strong connection between density conservation and density classification, we analyze the behavior of density conserving ACCAs. For the sake of simplicity, we concentrate on the case of ACCAs defined by local rules with unit neighborhood radius ($r = 1$).

The proof of the following theorem is almost identical to the one presented in [3] for binary CAs, hence, it is omitted. A similar result is also reported for Stochastic CAs [13], and interestingly, the same system of equations is obtained there.

Theorem 3. *An ACCA defined by a local rule f and unit neighborhood radius ($r = 1$), conserves density if and only if the entries $l_0, \ldots, l_7 \in [0,1]$ in its LUT satisfy:*

$$\begin{cases} l_0 = 0, \\ l_1 + l_2 + l_4 = 1, \\ l_2 + l_5 = 1, \\ l_3 + l_5 + l_6 = 2, \\ l_7 = 1. \end{cases} \tag{6}$$

As a consequence of Theorem 3, we obtain that the local rule f of a density-conserving ACCA can be written as (cfr. Example 1):

$$f(x, y, z) = (l_6 + l_1 - 1)(x - z)y + l_4 x + l_2 y + l_1 z. \tag{7}$$

The solutions to System (6) obey the following condition:

$$(l_0, l_1, l_2, l_3, l_4, l_5, l_6, l_7) = (0, a, c, 1 - b, 1 - a - c, 1 - c, b + c, 1), \tag{8}$$

where $a, b, c \in [0,1]$ and $a, b \leq 1 - c$. The solution set depends on three parameters and can thus be presented graphically in the Cartesian coordinate system, as a pyramid P (Fig. 1(a)).

To analyze all density-conserving ACCAs effectively, one can take advantage of several symmetries that are present in the space. More precisely, upon defining the inversion of arguments I and conjugation C operators as:

$$f^I(x, y, z) = f(z, y, x) \text{ and } f^C(x, y, z) = 1 - f(1 - x, 1 - y, 1 - z),$$

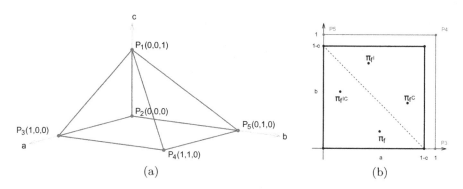

Fig. 1. (a) Parametrization of the set of density-conserving ACCAs with $r = 1$. (b) The location of the points π_f, π_{f^I}, π_{f^C}, $\pi_{f^{IC}}$ corresponding to local rules f, f^I, f^C and f^{IC}, respectively.

respectively, and noting that I commutes with C, i.e. for any local rule it holds that $f^{IC} = f^{CI}$. It is clear that if f defines an ACCA that conserves density, also f^I, f^C and f^{IC} define density-conserving ACCAs.

Let f be represented by some point π_f in the pyramid P. Then the points π_{f^I}, π_{f^C} and $\pi_{f^{IC}}$ corresponding to f^I, f^C and f^{IC}, respectively, lie in the same square cross-section (the pyramid P is cut with a plane parallel to the base). The points π_{f^I} and π_f are symmetric w.r.t. the centre of the square, while the points π_{f^C} and π_f are symmetric w.r.t. the main diagonal (Fig. 1(b)). The apex $P_1(0, 0, 1)$ of the pyramid corresponds to the identity rule (ECA 204), while the vertices $P_2(0,0,0)$, $P_3(1,0,0)$, $P_4(1,1,0)$, $P_5(0,1,0)$ of its base correspond to the following ECAs: the traffic-right rule (ECA 184), the shift-left rule (ECA 170), the traffic-left rule (ECA 226) and the shift-right rule (ECA 240). Since the dynamics of ACCAs defined by f, f^I, f^C and f^{IC} is identical, a behavioral analysis of ACCAs can be restricted to one of the quarters of the pyramid P.

5   Relaxed Formulation of the DCP for ACCAs

Since the classical DCP is not solvable using ACCAs (Theorem 2), we propose a slightly modified, relaxed formulation by altering the output specification. We will say that an ACCA defined by a global rule F solves the DCP at the threshold ρ_0 in the relaxed sense, if it holds that:

$$(\forall n \in \mathbb{N})\,(\exists T)\,(\forall x \in \{0,1\}^n)\,(\forall t \geq T) \left(\begin{cases} \rho(x) < \rho_0 \Rightarrow F^t(x) \in [0, \rho_0[^n \\ \rho(x) > \rho_0 \Rightarrow F^t(x) \in]\rho_0, 1]^n \end{cases} \right). \quad (9)$$

So, if the density of the initial vector x is smaller (respectively greater) than ρ_0, then all coordinates of $F^t(x)$ are smaller (respectively greater) than ρ_0, for t large enough. It turns out that we can simplify this condition, by means of the following theorem.

Theorem 4. *Assume that the local rule f of an ACCA with $r = 1$ conserves density. For any $v \in {]}0, \frac{1}{2}{[}$ it holds that:*

$$x \in [0, v]^n \Rightarrow F(x) \in [0, v]^n.$$

Analogously, for $v \in {]}\frac{1}{2}, 1{[}$ it holds that:

$$x \in [v, 1]^n \Rightarrow F(x) \in [v, 1]^n.$$

Following Theorem 4, we may rewrite Eq. (9) as:

$$(\forall n \in \mathbb{N})\, (\exists T)\, (\forall x \in \{0, 1\}^n) \left(\begin{cases} \rho(x) < \rho_0 \Rightarrow F^T(x) \in [0, \rho_0[^n \\ \rho(x) > \rho_0 \Rightarrow F^T(x) \in]\rho_0, 1]^n \end{cases} \right). \tag{10}$$

The two definitions are equivalent, since we know from Theorem 4 that if for some T it holds that $F^T(x) \in [0, \rho_0[^n$, then $F^t(x) \in [0, \rho_0[^n$ for every $t > T$, and similarly if $F^T(x) \in]\rho_0, 1]^n$, then $F^t(x) \in]\rho_0, 1]^n$ for every $t > T$.

6   Experimental Results

In this section we analyze the class of density-conserving ACCAs with regard to the solution of the relaxed DCP with threshold $\rho_0 = 0.5$. We measured the time T after which a correct classification answer was obtained, as given by (10). The class of density-conserving ACCAs was parametrized by $(a, b, c) \in P$, where P is the pyramid shown in Fig. 1(a). Recall that those parameters build the LUT used in Eq. (8). We sampled P with points (a_i, b_j, c_k), $i, j \leq k$, $i, j, k \in \{0, \ldots, 100\}$. The coordinates, a_p, b_p, c_p, are given by $0.01\,p$ and $a_i, b_j \leq 1 - c_k$. Then, for every such point, we measured T as the maximum of the number of iterations needed for reaching a classification answer, calculated over a set of initial configurations $\mathcal{I}$. If an answer was not reached within Λ iterations, the simulation was halted.

The experiment was conducted in two runs. In the first one, the test set $\mathcal{I}_{25}$ contained all binary initial configurations of $N = 25$ cells. Furthermore, we chose $\Lambda = 1000$. Apparently all points in the interior of the pyramid P were valid solutions, *i.e.* a classification answer was obtained in less than Λ iterations. The best ACCA found an answer in 73 iterations, and is given by the point $(0, 0, 0.05)$, or also $(0.01, 0.01, 0.05)$, $(0.94, 0.94, 0.05)$ and $(0.95, 0.95, 0.05)$, corresponding to f^I, f^C and f^{IC}, respectively. The results for the slice of the pyramid P in which the best solution was found, are presented in Fig. 2(a).

The second run invoked a set of $2 \cdot 10^6$ initial configurations which were randomly selected from the set $\mathcal{I}_{149}$ of all binary initial configurations with $N = 149$ cells. The time limit was set to $\Lambda = 20000$. Similarly to the case of $N = 25$, we found that every ACCA defined by a point in the interior of the pyramid P is a solution of the DCP. The best solution in this case was able to find an answer in 2918 iterations and is given by the points: $(0.0, 0.0, 0.02)$ and $(0.98, 0.98, 0.02)$ corresponding to f, f^I and f^C, f^{IC}, respectively. The results for the slice of pyramid P in which the best solution was found, are presented in Fig. 2(b).

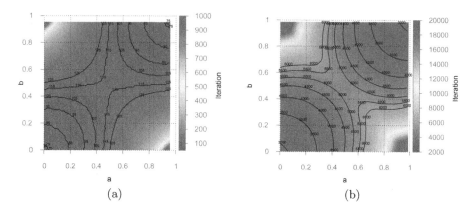

Fig. 2. Number of iterations needed to reach a classification answer, for:(a) $N = 25$, and (b) $N = 149$ cells.

In both settings the experiments show that density-conserving ACCAs, with a parametrization lying in the interior of the pyramid P solve the DCP at threshold $\rho_0 = 0.5$ in the relaxed sense. We conjecture that this property is not dependent on the number of cells, but this still has to be verified. The behavior of the ACCAs lying on the edges and faces of the pyramid seems to be more complex. It is already known that some of these ACCAs are solutions to the DCP. The properties of such ACCAs will be investigated in the future.

Acknowledgement. Calculations were carried out at the Academic Computer Centre in Gdańsk (TASK KDM).

References

1. Betel, H., Flocchini, P.: On the asymptotic behavior of fuzzy cellular automata. Electron. Notes Theoret. Comput. Sci. **252**, 23–40 (2009)
2. Betel, H., Flocchini, P.: On the relationship between Boolean and fuzzy cellular automata. Electron. Notes Theoret. Comput. Sci. **252**, 5–21 (2009)
3. Boccara, N., Fukś, H.: Number-conserving cellular automaton rules. Fundam. Inf. **52**(1–3), 1–13 (2002)
4. Bołt, W., Dembowski, M., Baetens, J.M., De Baets, B.: Solving the density classification problem by means of continuous cellular automata. In: Proceedings of the 21st International Workshop on Cellular Automata and Discrete Complex Systems (AUTOMATA 2015) - Exploratory Papers (2015)
5. Briceño, R., de Espanés, P.M., Osses, A., Rapaport, I.: Solving the density classification problem with a large diffusion and small amplification cellular automaton. Physica D **261**, 70–80 (2013)
6. Bušić, A., Fatès, N., Mairesse, J., Marcovici, I.: Density classification on infinite lattices and trees. Electron. J. Probab. **18**(51), 1–22 (2013)
7. Capcarrère, M.S., Sipper, M.: Necessary conditions for density classification by cellular automata. Phys. Rev. E **64**, 036113 (2001)

8. Capcarrère, M.S., Sipper, M., Tomassini, M.: Two-state, $r = 1$ cellular automaton that classifies density. Phys. Rev. Lett. **77**, 4969–4971 (1996)
9. Cattaneo, G., Flocchini, P., Mauri, G., Vogliotti, C., Santoro, N.: Cellular automata in fuzzy backgrounds. Physica D **105**(1–3), 105–120 (1997)
10. Fatès, N.: Stochastic cellular automata solutions to the density classification problem - when randomness helps computing. Theor. Comput. Syst. **53**(2), 223–242 (2013)
11. Flocchini, P., Geurts, F., Mingarelli, A., Santoro, N.: Convergence and aperiodicity in fuzzy cellular automata: revisiting rule 90. Physica D **142**(1–2), 20–28 (2000)
12. Fukś, H.: Nondeterministic density classification with diffusive probabilistic cellular automata. Phys. Rev. E **66**, 066106 (2002)
13. Fukś, H.: Probabilistic cellular automata with conserved quantities. Nonlinearity **17**(1), 159 (2003)
14. Fukś, H.: Solution of the density classification problem with two cellular automata rules. Phys. Rev. E **55**, R2081–R2084 (1997)
15. Gács, P., Kurdyumov, G.L., Levin, L.A.: One-dimensional uniform arrays that wash out finite islands. Problemy Peredachi Informatsii **14**(3), 92–96 (1978)
16. Land, M., Belew, R.K.: No perfect two-state cellular automata for density classification exists. Phys. Rev. Lett. **74**, 5148–5150 (1995)
17. Mitchell, M., Crutchfield, J.P., Das, R.: Evolving cellular automata with genetic algorithms: a review of recent work. In: Proceedings of the First International Conference on Evolutionary Computation and Its Applications (EvCA 1996) (1996)
18. de Oliveira, P.P., Bortot, J.C., Oliveira, G.M.: The best currently known class of dynamically equivalent cellular automata rules for density classification. Neurocomputing **70**(1–3), 35–43 (2006)
19. Packard, N.H.: Adaptation toward the edge of chaos. In: Kelso, J.A.S., Mandell, A.J., Shlesinger, M.F. (eds.) Dynamic Patterns in Complex Systems, pp. 293–301. World Scientific (1988)
20. Schüle, M., Ott, T., Stoop, R.: Computing with probabilistic cellular automata. In: Alippi, C., Polycarpou, M., Panayiotou, C., Ellinas, G. (eds.) ICANN 2009, Part II. LNCS, vol. 5769, pp. 525–533. Springer, Heidelberg (2009)
21. Stone, C., Bull, L.: Solving the density classification task using cellular automaton 184 with memory. Complex Syst. **18**(3), 329 (2009)
22. Wolfram, S.: Universality and complexity in cellular automata. Physica D **10**(1–2), 1–35 (1984)

Cellular Automata Dynamics
and Synchronization

A Spatial Sensitivity Analysis of a Spatially Explicit Model for Myxomatosis in Belgium

Jan M. Baetens[(✉)] and Bernard De Baets

KERMIT, Department of Mathematical Modelling, Statistics and Bioinformatics,
Ghent University, Coupure links 653, Ghent, Belgium
{jan.baetens,bernard.debaets}@ugent.be

Abstract. Motivated by their ability to mimic complex biological and natural processes, many spatially explicit models (SEMs) have been proposed during the last two decades for simulating such processes. Yet, a sensitivity analysis (SA) of such models is typically not performed, or model sensitivity is only studied over time on the basis of aggregated quantities, due to the lack of an appropriate framework. Taking a SEM for myxomatosis among European rabbits in Belgium as a model SEM, we conduct a spatial SA and investigate to what extent the sensitivity of this model varies spatially and whether or not this should become common practice when developing a SEM.

1 Introduction

Even though a sensitivity analysis (SA) is considered as a crucial step in the mathematical model development cycle [23,24], this step is often overlooked when it comes to the construction of spatially explicit models (SEMs) [12], like cellular automata (CAs) [29] and agent-based models (ABMs) [8]. The main reason for this lies in the fact that the spatial structure of such models cannot be neglected when analysing their sensitivity with respect to their inputs and parameters, whereas only very recently the first steps have been taken towards a theoretical underpinning of so-called spatial SAs [11,12,22]. Indeed, when referring to a SA in the field of SEMs, one typically means a study of how one or more aggregated quantities are affected by the SEM's inputs and/or parameters [15,17,20,27]. Still, it is to be expected that the sensitivity of such models is not necessarily spatially homogeneous, especially in the case of spatially heterogeneous inputs and/or parameters. Hence, for instance, the plausible range of model outputs might vary spatially, and likewise, different inputs and/or parameters might be the most important in different regions of the spatial domain. From a practical point of view, this implies that a small perturbation of a SEM's parameters might lead to considerable changes in the model outputs at some location, whereas these might be negligible elsewhere.

There are two main approaches two SAs of mathematical models, referred to as local and global SAs, respectively [23]. The former aims at quantifying the change in model outputs due to small perturbations of model inputs and/or

© Springer International Publishing Switzerland 2016
S. El Yacoubi et al. (Eds.): ACRI 2016, LNCS 9863, pp. 91–100, 2016.
DOI: 10.1007/978-3-319-44365-2_9

parameters, which is done by evaluating finite differences at specific points in the space of model inputs and/or parameters. Hence, the outcome of the SA might depend on the selected points in the parameter space. The most common method is the so-called one-at-a-time approach (OAT) in which one model input or parameter is perturbed at a time and the effect of this perturbation is determined [30]. Typically, the model input or parameter is changed with a given amount [15,20], but there are also studies where, for instance, a varying proportion of cells is swapped [6]. The main advantages of a local SA are that it is very intuitive and simple, while it is also computationally very efficient [11]. Besides, it works well when the plausible range of model inputs and/or parameters is known [7]. A global SA, on the other hand, is more comprehensive because it considers the full meaningful range of model inputs and/or parameters. As opposed to its local counterpart, these are varied simultaneously in order to quantify the interactions among them. Among the global SA methods, many trace back to Sobol's [26], or are extensions and variations thereof [25,28]. They are variance-based in that they decompose the variance of the model prediction into partial variances that represent the share in the total variance that is explained by the different model inputs and/or parameters. Only recently, Sobol's method has been extended to a spatial context [11,12]. For a more comprehensive overview of global SA methods, we refer the reader to [24].

The field of infectious disease modelling is one of the fields that has even not yet embraced non-spatial SA methods like Sobol's [26], let alone spatial SAs [31]. This is surprising because it can give insight into the plausible range of model outputs, while it can also help to allocate resources to follow-up experimentation and field study, to identify redundant parameters, and to determine the robustness of a modelling study's qualitative conclusions [2,18,24]. Furthermore, in the context of infectious disease modelling, it can help to identify those regions in the study areas where the simulation results are relatively robust, and hence where the required (human) resources and disease impacts can be estimated relatively reliably, irrespective of the uncertainty that might be involved in the model inputs and/or parameters.

Starting from an extension of the leading model simulating the spread of myxomatosis among European rabbits (*Oryctolagus cuniculus*) [3] to a spatially explicit context, we conduct a local spatial SA in order to quantify its robustness with respect to perturbations of the model parameters. We take myxomatosis as an exemplary infectious disease, because it has been well documented and the introduction of similar non-endemic epizootics is something that occurs increasingly often due to the ongoing globalization [14]. In Sect. 2 we present some basic facts on myxomatosis in general, and the epidemic wave that will be mimicked more in particular, after which we introduce the SEM for myxomatosis among European rabbits. The experimental setup is outlined in Sect. 3, while the results and conclusions of our study are presented in Sect. 4.

2 In Situ and in Silico Myxomatosis

2.1 Facts and Figures

Myxomatosis is caused by the myxoma virus that was released illegally in France in 1952 [4], after which it spread through Europe and decimated the endemic rabbit populations. In Belgium, the first cases were confirmed by the first half of September in several towns in the Northwest of the country, close to the French border where myxomatosis was confirmed by August 1953 [19]. This infectious disease then spread in an easterly direction and by the end of 1954 it had spread across the entire country, though the density of confirmed cases in the relatively clayey south of the country was significantly lower than in the more sandier north. This can be explained by the fact that rabbits prefer sandy soils to make their burrows [13], so that larger populations can be expected in the northern part of Belgium.

This infectious disease can be transferred by fleas or mosquitoes that have fed on infected rabbits and by direct contact with infected individuals [5]. Myxomatosis is often lethal for European rabbits [16], and leads to easily observable symptoms, such as skin tumors, fatigue and fever [10].

2.2 The Spatially Explicit Myxomatosis Model

The authors of [3] take the model of Anderson and May [1] as starting point for deriving a non-spatial model of myxomatosis for the European rabbit. The latter model is given by [1]:

$$
\begin{cases}
\dfrac{dS}{dt} = r\,(S + I + R) - \beta\,S\,I - m\,S\,, \\[2mm]
\dfrac{dI}{dt} = \beta\,S\,I - (\alpha + m + \nu)\,I\,, \\[2mm]
\dfrac{dR}{dt} = \nu\,I - m\,R\,, \\[2mm]
\dfrac{dD}{dt} = m\,(S + I + R) + \alpha\,I\,,
\end{cases}
\tag{1}
$$

where S [–], I [–], R [–] and D [–] represent the number of susceptible, infected, recovered and died individuals, respectively, r [T^{-1}] is the natural per capita birth rate, m [T^{-1}] is the natural per capita death rate, α [T^{-1}] is the additional per capita death rate of infected individuals caused by the disease, β [T^{-1}] is a measure of the contact rate between infected and susceptible individuals, and finally ν [T^{-1}] represents the per capita recovery rate.

As the focus of this paper is on a spatial SA, we do not distinguish between juvenile and adult individuals as in [3], but we take System (1) as starting point to devise a SEM for myxomatosis among European rabbits. More specifically, we conceive the spatial domain as an assembly of irregular polygons c_i as they typically arise in the framework of geographical information science. Besides, we discretize time in the sense that the number of individuals in every health class is updated in discrete time steps t, each of them corresponding with the same amount of time Δt [T]. The number of susceptible, infected, recovered and died individuals in a polygon c_i at time step t is referred to accordingly as $S(c_i,t)$, $I(c_i,t)$, $R(c_i,t)$ and $D(c_i,t)$, and the spatially explicit counterpart of System (1) can be written as:

$$
\begin{cases}
S(c_i,t+1) = S(c_i,t) + r\,\Delta t\big(S(c_i,t) + R(c_i,t)\big) - \underline{\beta}\,\Delta t\, S(c_i,t)\, I(c_i,t) - \\
\qquad \Delta t\, S(c_i,t) \displaystyle\sum_{c_j \in \mathcal{N}_i} \overline{\beta}\, O_{ij}\, I(c_j,t) - m\,\Delta t S(c_i,t) \\
I(c_i,t+1) = I(c_i,t) + \underline{\beta}\,\Delta t\, I(c_i,t)\, S(c_i,t) + \\
\qquad \Delta t\, S(c_i,t) \displaystyle\sum_{c_j \in \mathcal{N}_i} \overline{\beta}\, O_{ij}\, I(c_j,t) - (\epsilon\gamma + m + \epsilon(1-\gamma))\,\Delta t\, I(c_i,t) \\
R(c_i,t+1) = R(c_i,t) + \epsilon(1-\gamma)\,\Delta t\, I(c_i,t) - m\,\Delta t R(c_i,t) \\
D(c_i,t+1) = D(c_i,t) + m\,\Delta t\big(S(c_i,t) + I(c_i,t) + R(c_i,t)\big) + \epsilon\gamma\,\Delta t\, I(c_i,t)
\end{cases}
\tag{2}
$$

where $\mathcal{N}_i$ is the neighbourhood of polygon c_i that encloses all the polygons surrounding c_i with whose individuals the ones in c_i can interact O_{ij} [−] represents the proportion of c_i's circumference shared with c_j. Here, we will assume that c_i's neighbourhood encloses c_i itself and the polygons with which it shares at least a vertex. Further, $\underline{\beta}$ [T^{-1}] and $\overline{\beta}$ [T^{-1}] denote the short-range and long-range contact rates, respectively, ϵ [T^{-1}] is the reciprocal of the rabbit survival time, and finally, γ [−] is the disease mortality. Essentially, the model given by System (2) is a so-called continuous CA, also known as a coupled-map lattice.

3   Experimental Setup

Based on the average and maximum rabbit densities reported in [21], we assume a density of five individuals per hectare in Belgium. Further, given the fact that myxomatosis was introduced in 1953 through the nidi of infection in the border region between the north of France and Belgium [19], the initial condition was defined in such a way that infected populations were present just across the French side of the border at the end of August 1953. Based on the values reported in [3,21], we further took $r = 9.13 \times 10^{-3}$ d^{-1}, $m = 8 \times 10^{-3}$ d^{-1}, $\epsilon = 0.05$ d^{-1} and $\gamma = 0.8$ d^{-1}. For what concerns the short-range and long-range contact rates, we took the value reported in [3], namely $\underline{\beta} = \overline{\beta} = 2 \times 10^{-3}$ d^{-1}, thereby assuming that the contact rate between individuals living in the same cell is as high as the rate of contact between individuals living in neighbouring cells.

The local SA was performed by perturbing the model parameters one at a time at different points in their biologically meaningful range [3] (Table 1), and tracking the impact on the simulated number of infected individuals as

$$
\frac{I(c_i,t) - \widetilde{I}(c_i,t)}{\Delta p},
\tag{3}
$$

where p denotes an arbitrary parameter, and $\widetilde{I}(c_i, t)$ represents the simulated infected number of individuals if the model is evolved with a perturbed parameter. Further, $\Delta p = \delta p$ with δ a perturbation factor, which was chosen in such a way that the sum of squared errors at consecutive time steps between the finite difference approximation given by Eq. (3) and its backward counterpart was minimal, namely $\delta = 10^{-6}$. So, here we stick to the approach outlined in [23], though the magnitude of the parameter perturbations could be defined in a more natural way if relevant field data are available. Besides, we also kept track of the relative sensitivity, given by

$$p \frac{I(c_i, t) - \widetilde{I}(c_i, t)}{\Delta p}, \tag{4}$$

because this quantity allows for comparing the model sensitivity with respect to different parameters. Acknowledging the fact that $I(c_i, t)$ depends on both time and space, the computed sensitivities can be aggregated either over time (spatial sensitivity) or over space (temporal sensitivity). Throughout the remainder of this paper, we use the maximum and average operators respectively for this purpose.

Table 1. Parameter ranges and corresponding increments considered for the local SA of System (2)

Parameter	Range	Increment
ϵ	$[0.02, 0.1]$	$10 \, 10^{-3}$
γ	$[0.50, 0.99]$	$10 \, 10^{-3}$
r	$2/3 \, [0.5/365, 5/365]$	$2/3 \, 0.25/365$
m	$[6 \, 10^{-3}, 0.02]$	$0.5 \, 10^{-3}$
β	$[0.25 \, 10^{-3}, 0.01]$	$0.25 \, 10^{-3}$
$\overline{\beta}$	$[0.25 \, 10^{-3}, 0.01]$	$0.25 \, 10^{-3}$

All simulations were run in Mathematica (version 10.0.0, Wolfram Research Inc., Champaign, United States) on the high-performance computing infrastructure of Ghent University for 3000 time steps, corresponding with 1500 days as we chose $\Delta t = 0.5$ d.

4   Results

Figure 1 depicts a snapshot of the simulated fraction of infected individuals in the study area after 25 days (September 26, 1953), together with the location of the peak of the epidemic wave at every other 50 days until September 16, 1954. For the sake of comparison, the aforementioned fraction is expressed as the number of infected individuals in a given cell c_i over the maximum number of living individuals (susceptible, infected and recovered) in any of the cells, i.e. as $I(c_i, t)/\max_j(S(c_j, t) + I(c_j, t) + R(c_j, t))$. This figure unmistakably demonstrates that System (2) gives rise to travelling waves that propagate eastwards from the French-Belgian border where myxomatosis had been confirmed by the end of August 1953. Such waves have been observed for myxomatosis [9], so the present model is definitely capable of a evolving a qualitatively similar dynamics. Moreover, although we leave a sound validation of the presented model for a more comprehensive work, it should be mentioned that the occurrence of the in silico peaks roughly agrees in several seriously affected towns and villages (e.g. Antwerp, Ostend, Bruges, De Panne, ...) with those that were registered in situ [19].

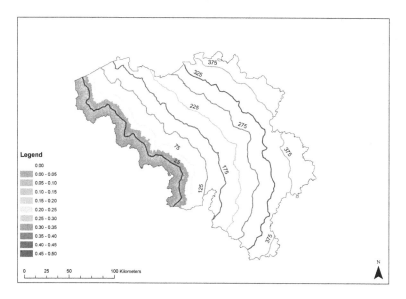

Fig. 1. Simulated proportion of infected individuals in the study area after 25 days (September 26, 1953), and location of the peak of the epidemic wave at every other 50 days until September 16, 1954

The temporal sensitivity of System (2) with respect to ϵ, γ, r and m is given in Fig. 2 for several points in the considered parameter ranges (cfr. Table 1). From the sensitivity plots in this figure it can be inferred that in some cases the magnitude and/or sign of the temporal sensitivity strongly depend(s) on the point in the parameter space that was perturbed, which is a known drawback of local SAs [11]. Still, these plots show that for most of the considered parameter values the temporal sensitivity approaches zero by the end of the simulation period, which can be understood by the fact that the same single steady state is reached, irrespective of the perturbation. It is clear that all parameters have a substantial impact on the simulated dynamics, from which we may conclude that none of them and none of the terms in the model equations are redundant. Still,

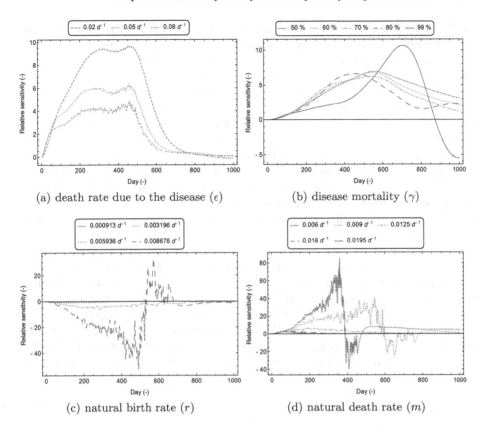

Fig. 2. Temporal sensitivity of System (2) with respect to the death rate due to the disease ϵ (a), the disease mortality γ (b), the natural birth rate r (c) and the natural death rate m (d).

it can be observed that the impact of the death rate due to the disease (ϵ) and the disease mortality (γ) are roughly the same. The effect of the natural death rate (m) and the natural birth rate (r) is for most of the considered parameter values less pronounced, even though the latter parameters can lead to the highest relative sensitivity values among the ones observed for the studied parameters. From Fig. 2(a) we further infer that a slight increase of the death rate due to the disease ϵ negatively affects the number of infected individuals, and that this effect is more pronounced as ϵ is lower. Although this seems contradictory at first, this can be understood by acknowledging that also the amount of available time for transmitting the disease decreases as ϵ increases, and so the rabbit survival time ϵ^{-1} decreases. A similar reasoning can be followed to understand the temporal sensitivity of System (2) with respect to the mortality rate γ, though this one can be come negative in the long run if evaluated for very high γ (e.g. $\gamma = 99\,\%$). On the other hand, a slight increase of the natural birth rate r leads to an increase in the number of infected individuals, and this effect becomes more pronounced as the perturbed parameter value is higher. Yet, when r is already very high (i.e. $r = 8.676$ d^{-1}), the opposite is true from a certain moment in time on. This tipping point occurs when the epidemic wave has covered the entire country, and rabbit populations countrywide can (partly) recover.

The spatial sensitivity of System (2) with respect to $\overline{\beta} = 5\,10^{-3}\,\mathrm{d}^{-1}$ is depicted in Fig. 3. Despite all model parameters are spatially homogeneous, the spatial sensitivity strongly depends on the location. Not only does the sensitivity increase with increasing distance from the source of infection (the border between France and Northwest of Belgium), as could have been anticipated, but regions at a similar distance from this source can have a completely different spatial sensitivity. This information cannot be derived from a classical SA, and it is to be expected that the spatial heterogeneity of the model sensitivity would increase even further when some of the model inputs and/or parameters would vary spatially.

This demonstrates that a SA of any SEM should be performed comprehensively so that it allows to investigate the sensitivity both from a temporal and a spatial point of view. In this way, one can identify the regions where the simulation results are still relatively reliable in the case of uncertain/imprecise model parameters and it allows to understand how sensitivity varies spatially both in terms of its magnitude and sign. A more comprehensive SA should, however, consist of both a global and local SA, where the former will allow to identify the most influential model parameter, whose effect can subsequently be analysed by conducting a local SA.

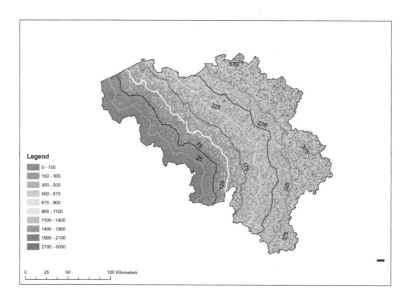

Fig. 3. Spatial sensitivity of System (2) with respect to the long-range contact rate $\overline{\beta} = 5\,10^{-3}\,\mathrm{d}^{-1}$.

Acknowledgements. This work was carried out using the STEVIN Supercomputer Infrastructure at Ghent University, funded by Ghent University, the Flemish Supercomputer Center (VSC), the Hercules Foundation and the Flemish Government.

References

1. Anderson, R.M., May, R.M.: Population biology of infectious diseases: Part 1. Nature **280**, 361–367 (1979)
2. Chitnis, N., Hyman, J.M., Cushing, J.M.: Determining important parameters in the spread of malaria through the sensitivity analysis of a mathematical model. Bull. Math. Biol. **70**, 1272–1296 (2008)
3. Dwyer, G., Levin, S.A., Buttel, L.: A simulation model of the population dynamics and evolution of myxomatosis. Ecol. Monogr. **60**, 423–447 (1990)
4. Fenner, F., Fantini, B.: The discovery of myxoma virus. In: Fenner, F., Fantini, B. (eds.) Biological Control of Vertebrate Pests: The History of Myxomatosis, an Experiment in Evolution, pp. 65–92. CABI Publishing, Wallingford, United Kingdom (1999)
5. Fenner, F., Ross, J.: The European Rabbit: The History and Biology of a Successful Colonizer. Oxford University Press, Oxford (1994)
6. Fisher, P., Abrahart, R.J., Herbinger, W.: The sensitivity of two distributed non-point source pollution models to the spatial arrangement of the landscape. Hydrol. Process. **11**, 241–252 (1997)
7. Frey, H.C., Patil, S.R.: Identification and review of sensitivity analysis methods. Risk Anal. **22**, 553–578 (2002)
8. Grimm, V., Railsback, S.F.: Individual-Based Modeling and Ecology. Princeton University Press, Princeton (2005)
9. Joubert, L., Leftheriotis, E., Mouchet, J.: La Myxomatose. L'Expansion Scientifique Française, Paris (1972)
10. Kritas, S., Dovas, C., Fortomaris, P., Petridou, E., Farsang, A., Koptopoulos, G.: A pathogenic myxoma virus in vaccinated and non-vaccinated commercial rabbits. Res. Vet. Sci. **85**, 622–624 (2008)
11. Ligmann-Zielinska, A., Jankowski, P.: Spatially-explicit integrated uncertainty and sensitivity analysis of criteria weights in multicriteria land suitability evaluation. Environ. Model. Softw. **57**, 235–247 (2014)
12. Lilburne, L., Tarantola, S.: Sensitivity analysis of spatial models. Int. J. Geogr. Inf. Sci. **23**, 151–168 (2009)
13. Lombardi, L., Fernández, N., Moreno, S., Villafuerte, R.: Habitat-related differences in rabbit (oryctolagus cuniculus) abundance, distribution, and activity. J. Mammal. **84**, 26–36 (2003). American Society of Mammalogists
14. Marano, N., Arguin, P.M., Pappaioanou, M.: Impact of globalization and animal trade on infectious disease ecology. Emerg. Infect. Dis. **13**, 1807–1809 (2007)
15. Marcot, B.G., Singleton, P.H., Schumaker, N.H.: Analysis of sensitivity and uncertainty in an individual-based model of a threatened wildlife species. Nat. Resour. Model. **28**, 37–58 (2015)
16. Marlier, D., Mainil, J., Sulon, J., Beckers, J.F., Linden, A., Vindevogel, H.: Study of the virulence of five strains of amyxomatous myxoma virus in crossbred New Zealand white/Californian conventional rabbits, with evidence of long-term testicular infection in recovered animals. J. Comp. Pathol. **122**, 101–113 (2008)

17. Massada, A.B., Carmel, Y., Koniak, G., Noy-Meir, I.: The effects of disturbance based management on the dynamics of mediterranean vegetation: A hierarchical and spatially explicit modeling approach. Ecol. Model. **220**, 2525–2535 (2009)

18. McLeod, R.G., Brewster, J.F., Gumel, A.B., Slonowsky, D.A.: Sensitivity and uncertainty analyses for a SARS model with time-varying inputs and outputs. Math. Biosci. Eng. **3**, 527–544 (2006)

19. Ministère de l'Agriculture: Service Vétérinaire: Bulletin sanitaire. Ministère de l'Agriculture, Service Vétérinaire, Brussels, Belgium (1953)

20. Rinaldi, P.R., Dalponte, D.D., Vénere, M.J., Clausse, A.: Cellular automata algorithm for simulation of surface flows in large plains. Simul. Model. Pract. Theory **15**, 315–327 (2007)

21. Lumpkin, S., Seidensticker, J.: Rabbits: The Animal Answer Guide. Johns Hopkins University Press, Baltimore (2011)

22. Saint-Geours, N., Lavergne, C., Bailly, J., Grelot, F.: Change of support in spatial variance-based sensitivity analysis. Math. Geosci. **44**, 945–958 (2012)

23. Saltelli, A., Chan, K., Scott, E.M.: Sensitivity Analysis. Wiley, West Sussex (2000)

24. Saltelli, A., Ratto, M., Andres, T., Campolongo, F., Cariboni, J., Gatelli, D., Saisana, M., Tarantola, S. (eds.): Global Sensitivty Analysis: The Primer. Wiley, Chichester (2008)

25. Saltelli, A.: Making best use of model evaluations to compute sensitivity indices. Comput. Phys. Commun. **145**, 280–297 (2002)

26. Sobol, I.M.: On sensitivity estimates for nonlinear mathematical models. Matematicheskoe Modelirovanie **2**, 112–118 (1990)

27. Tang, W., Jia, M.: Global sensitivity analysis of a large agent-based model of spatial opinion exchange: A heterogeneous multi-GPU acceleration approach. Ann. Assoc. Am. Geogr. **104**, 485–509 (2014)

28. Tarantola, S., Nardo, M., Saisana, M., Gatelli, D.: A new estimator for sensitivity analysis of model output: An application to the e-business readiness composite indicator. Reliab. Eng. Syst. Saf. **91**, 1135–1141 (2006)

29. von Neumann, J.: The general and logical theory of automata. In: Jeffres, L.A. (ed.) The Hixon Symposium on Cerebral Mechanisms in Behaviour, pp. 1–41. Wiley, Pasadena (1951)

30. Walsh, S., Brown, D.G., Bian, L., Allen, T.R.: Effects of spatial scale on data certainty: An assessment through data dependency and sensitivity analyses. In: Proceedings of the First International Symposium on the Spatial Accuracy of Natural Resource Data Bases, pp. 151–160. American Society for Photogrammetry and Remote Sensing (1994)

31. Wu, J., Dhingra, R., Gambhir, M., Remais, J.V.: Sensitivity analysis of infectious disease models: methods, advances and their application. J. R. Soc. Interface **10**, 20121018 (2013)

Regional Control of Boolean Cellular Automata

Franco Bagnoli[1,2]($\boxtimes$), Samira El Yacoubi[3,4], and Raul Rechtman[5]

[1] Department of Physics and Astronomy and CSDC, University of Florence,
Via G. Sansone 1, 50019 Sesto Fiorentino, Italy
`franco.bagnoli@unifi.it`
[2] INFN, Sez. Firenze, Firenze, Italy
[3] IMAGES Espace-Dev, University of Perpignan Via Domitia, Perpignan, France
`yacoubi@univ-perp.fr`
[4] Espace-Dev, UMR 228 IRD, UM, UAG, UR, Maison de la télédétection,
Montpellier, France
[5] Instituto de Energías Renovables, Universidad Nacional Autónoma de México,
Apartado Postal 34, 62580 Temixco, Morelos, Mexico
`rrs@ier.unam.mx`

Abstract. An interesting problem in extended physical systems is that of the regional control, *i.e.*, how to add a suitable control at the boundary or inside a region of interest so that the state of such region is near to a desired one. Many physical problems are modelled by means of cellular automata. It is therefore important to port control concepts to this discrete world. In this paper we address the problem of regional controllability of cellular automata via boundary actions, *i.e.*, we investigate the characteristics of a cellular automaton rule so that it can be controlled inside a given region only acting on the value of sites at its boundaries.

1 Introduction

Cellular Automata (CA) are widely used for modelling physical problems, ranging from physics to biology, medicine, ecology and economics [1]. In general, in these cases one is interested in finding the rule that best models the problem, then set the initial conditions and let the system evolve studying the emerging patterns. The advantage of using a model with respect to real experiments is that of being able to explore a wide range of parameters and that of performing measurements that are impossible in real systems. However, one is always concerned with the discrepancy between the model and the real system, differences that can amplify and lead to a complete disagreement between the experimental reality and the model.

An alternative approach with such a modelling problem was addressed by Bagnoli et al. [2]. If one has at his/her disposal experimental data and assumes that the numerical model is a good but not perfect approximation, one is confronted with the problem of synchronizing the model with the data. From a theoretical point of view, this control problem is equivalent to a "master-slave" control problem [3]: where is more convenient to perform measurements and apply them to the second system in order to get the adequate synchronization

© Springer International Publishing Switzerland 2016
S. El Yacoubi et al. (Eds.): ACRI 2016, LNCS 9863, pp. 101–112, 2016.
DOI: 10.1007/978-3-319-44365-2_10

with the minimum effort (*i.e.*, the optimal control)? The results depend on the CA rule. Clearly, rules that go into a unique final state are trivially easy to control, but they are also extremely unlikely to be a good model for any problem. Rules showing multiple attractors or chaotic behaviour are more interesting. Among them, the unexpected result of our previous study [2] is that chaotic ones are easier to control, since it is sufficient to block the spreading of the "difference" among master and slave and wait for an "automatic" synchronization. This is due to two factors: the "exploration" of the configuration space by the chaoticity of the rule and the discreteness of the state variables that makes the synchronized state stationary even if it is unstable with respect to finite perturbations [4].

The problem that we want to address here is that of forcing the appearance of a given pattern inside a region by imposing a suitable set of values to the sites that surround that region. In general, control problems have to be addressed splitting the problem into the *measurability* issue and the actual *controllability* one. The first topic relates with the problem of actually being able to measure some quantity in the target system. We skip this problem assuming being able to measure the instantaneous state of the system at will, and we focus on the second problem: that of driving a system into a given state acting only on the periphery of the given region.

This problem is related to the so-called regional controllability introduced by El Jai and Zerrik [5], as a special case of output controllability [6,7]. The regional control problem consists in achieving an objective only on a subregion of the domain when some specific actions are exerted on the system, in its domain interior or on its boundary. This concept has been studied by means of partial differential equations. Some results on the actions properties (number, location, space distribution) based on the rank condition have been obtained depending on the target region and its geometry, see for example Ref. [5] and the references therein. Regional controllability has been also studied using CA models. In Ref. [8], a numerical approach based on genetic algorithms has been developed for a class of additive CA in both 1D and 2D cases. In Ref. [9], an interesting theoretical study has been carried out for 1-D additive real valued CA where the effect of control is given through an evolving neighbourhood and a very sophisticated state transition function. However the study did not give a real insight in the regional controllability problem and the obtained theoretical results could not be exploited for other works. In the present article, we aim at providing (or introducing) a general framework for regional control problem by means of CA using the concept of Boolean derivatives. It focusses on boundary regional control and consists only on a 1D-CA.

The sketch of the paper is the following. In Sect. 2 we present some definitions and the concept of Boolean derivatives, which are the analogous of standard derivatives for discrete systems. In Sect. 3 we address the actual problem of regional control [10] and present some theorems and conjecture about the classification of controllable CA rules. In order to address the control problem numerically, in Sect. 4 we present a method for generating all pre-images of a target configuration for a given rule. Finally, conclusions are drawn in the last section.

2   Definitions and Boolean Derivatives

A CA is defined as a graph (the connections among a site and its neighbours), a set of states and one or more transition rules for the updating of the states according with the values of those of neighbours. The graph is defined by an adjacency matrix a such that $a_{ij} = 1$ if j is a neighbour of i and zero otherwise. The adjacency matrix needs not to be symmetric.

A lattice is a graph invariant by translation, i.e. a commutes with the shift matrices, which in one dimension are $S_{ij} = [[j = i \pm 1]]$, where $[[\cdot]]$ is the truth function, a generalization of the Kronecker delta which takes values 1 if $\cdot$ is true and zero otherwise. The connectivity degree of a node i is defined by $k_i = \sum_j a_{ij}$. In the following we shall consider one-dimensional lattices with homogeneous degree $K = 2k + 1$.

An automaton stays on a node i of the graphs and owns a state s_i^t at time t. In the simplest version, which is the one considered here, the state can only take the two values one and zero (Boolean automata). The state $\boldsymbol{n}_i^t$ of the neighbourhood of a site i at time t is given by the set of the states of the K connected sites $\boldsymbol{n}_i^t = \{s_{ij}^t | a_{ij} = 1\}$. For the one-dimensional lattice, $\boldsymbol{n}_i^t = \{s_{i-k}^t, \ldots, s_i^t, \ldots, s_{i+k}^t\}$.

The evolution of the automaton is given by the parallel application of a local rule f

$$s_i^{t+1} = f(\boldsymbol{n}_i^t). \tag{1}$$

The function f is a Boolean function of K Boolean arguments. Since all variables take Boolean values, it is possible to read the set of states of the neighbours $\{s_{i-k}^t, \ldots, s_i^t, \ldots, s_{i+k}^t\} \equiv \{x_0, x_1, \ldots x_{K-1}\}$ as a base-two number $X = \sum_{j=0}^{K-1} x_j 2^j; 0 \le X < 2^K$.

In order to indicate a rule in a compact way, one can use the Wolfram coding [11]. Just consider the set of values that the function takes for all possible configurations of the neighbourhood, ordered as a number in base two

$$\{f(0), f(1), \ldots, f(2^K - 1)\} \tag{2}$$

and read it as a base-two number $\mathcal{F} = \sum_{j=0}^{2^K - 1} f(j) 2^j; 0 \le \mathcal{F} < 2^{2^K}$. This notation is actually useful only for *elementary* (Boolean, $K = 3$) automata.

It is possible to define an equivalent of the usual derivatives for such discrete systems [12, 13]. Given a Boolean function

$$x' = f(x_1, x_2, \ldots, x_i, \ldots), \tag{3}$$

the Boolean derivative of x' with respect to x_i measures if x' changes when changing x_i, given the values of the rest of variables, and is defined as

$$\frac{\partial x'}{\partial x_i} = f(x_1, x_2, \ldots, x_i, \ldots) \oplus f(x_1, x_2, \ldots, x_i \oplus 1, \ldots), \tag{4}$$

where $\oplus$ is the sum modulus two (XOR operation). Essentially, the Boolean derivative is one if, given the arguments $\{x_1, x_2, \ldots, x_{i-1}, x_{i+1}, \ldots\}$, x' changes its value whenever x_i does.

This definition fulfils many of the standard properties of the derivative, and this is particularly evident is one expresses the rule f using only AND (multiplication) and XOR operations. For instance, the Boolean derivative of $f(x_1, x_2) = x_1 \oplus x_2$ with respect to x_1 is

$$\frac{\partial x_1 \oplus x_2}{\partial x_1} = x_1 \oplus x_2 \oplus (x_1 \oplus 1) \oplus x_2 = 1 \tag{5}$$

since $x \oplus x = 0 \; \forall x$. Analogously, the Boolean derivative of $f(x_1, x_2) = x_1 x_2$ with respect to x_1 is

$$\frac{\partial x_1 x_2}{\partial x_1} = x_1 x_2 \oplus (x_1 \oplus 1) x_2 = x_1 x_2 \oplus x_1 x_2 \oplus x_2 = x_2. \tag{6}$$

The derivative can be used to define an analogous of the Taylor series, which, for Boolean functions, is always finite. So for instance, expanding with respect to $x = 0$,

$$f(x) = f(0) \oplus f'(0)x = f(0) \oplus (f(0) \oplus f(1))x, \tag{7}$$

where f' is the derivative of f. It is immediate to verify the above identity by substituting the two possible values of x. In general

$$f(x \oplus y) = f(x) \oplus f'(x)y. \tag{8}$$

The derivative also obeys to the chain rule

$$\begin{aligned}
\frac{\partial f(g(x))}{\partial x} &= f(g(x)) \oplus f(g(x \oplus 1)) \\
&= f(g(x)) \oplus f(g(x) \oplus g'(x)) \\
&= f(g(x)) \oplus f(g(x)) \oplus f'(g(x))g'(x) = f'(g(x))g'(x).
\end{aligned} \tag{9}$$

Since in general a Boolean function depends on many variables $x_0, x_1, \ldots$, it is more compact to indicate a derivative as $f^{(i)}$ where i, in base two, indicates which variables are varied for taking the derivative. For instance,

$$f^{(1)}(x_0, x_1, \ldots) = \frac{\partial f(x_0, x_1, \ldots)}{\partial x_0}; \qquad f^{(2)}(x_0, x_1, \ldots) = \frac{\partial f(x_0, x_1, \ldots)}{\partial x_1};$$

$$f^{(3)}(x_0, x_1, \ldots) = \frac{\partial^2 f(x_0, x_1, \ldots)}{\partial x_0 \partial x_1}; \qquad \ldots \tag{10}$$

Using the Taylor (or McLaurin) expansion, it is evident that every rule can be written as a sum (XOR) of polynomials (AND) of the variables, for instance

$$f(x, y, z) = f_0 \oplus f_1 x \oplus f_2 y \oplus f_3 xy \oplus f_4 z \oplus f_5 xz \oplus f_6 yz \oplus f_7 xyz, \tag{11}$$

where $f_i = f^{(i)}(0)$ is the i-th derivative of f in zero (the McLaurin coefficient). The subscripts i of f_i, in base two, indicate the variables composing the polynomial.

The rule is uniquely identified by the set of values of the derivatives in zero, $\{f_0, f_1, \dots\}$, which therefore constitute an alternative to the set of values that the rule takes for all configurations, $\{f(0), f(1), \dots\}$, used in the Wolfram notation. For instance, the elementary rule W150 $= \{0, 1, 1, 0, 1, 0, 0, 1\}$, $i.e.$, $x_0 \oplus x_1 \oplus x_2$, can be identified by the McLaurin coefficients $\{0, 1, 1, 1, 0, 0, 0, 0\}$.

3 Regional Control of Cellular Automata

The problem that we address is the following: given a one-dimensional lattice and a Boolean rule f with a neighbourhood of size $K = 2k + 1$, which are the conditions on the rule so that a region of arbitrary size W can be driven to a given state q in a time T regardless of its initial state c, only acting on its boundary?

Let us denote by $c = \{c_1, \dots, c_{W-1}\}$ the state of the region to be controlled, see Fig. 1. The idea is to impose the state of all or some of the boundary sites, denoted as ℓ^t_{-1} (left sites) and r^t_W (right sites), for a given time T so that the value of the sites in the region $c^T = \{c^T_0, \dots, c^T_{W-1}\}$ be equal to the desired ones $q = \{q_0, \dots, q_{W-1}\}$, for every initial condition $c^0 = \{c^0_0, \dots, c^0_{W-1}\}$. If the control can be done in the minimum time $T = W/(2k)$ (the minimum time for letting a signal coming from the R or L regions to reach all c^T sites), the control is said to be optimal.

An interesting observation allows to switch from the boundary control to an initial-value control. Let us consider an initial-value problem as shown in Fig. 2, where we only fix an appropriate number of sites $\ell^0 = \{\ell^0_i\}$ at the left and $r^0 = \{r^0_j\}$ at the right of the region to be controlled, and then let the system evolve. If, in this way, we are able to obtain the desired values of q, it is sufficient to apply the sequence of ℓ^t_{-1} and r^t_W to obtain the desired boundary control. So we can limit our study to this initial value problem.

$$\dots \ell^0_{-1} \left| c^0_0 \ c^0_1 \ \dots \ c^0_{W-1} \right| r^0_W \ \dots$$

$$\dots \ell^1_{-1} \left| c^1_0 \ c^1_1 \ \dots \ c^1_{W-1} \right| r^1_W \ \dots$$

$$\vdots \quad \vdots \ \vdots \qquad \vdots \quad \vdots$$

$$\dots \ell^T_{-1} \left| q_0 \ q_1 \ \dots \ q_{W-1} \right| r^T_W \ \dots$$

Fig. 1. Regional control

From a theoretical point of view, we can restate the control problem in the following way. Each site in the target configuration c^T_i depends from a set of states at time 0

$$c^T_i = F(\ell^0, c^0, r^0), \tag{12}$$

$$\ldots\; \ell^0_{-3}\; \ell^0_{-2}\; \ell^0_{-1} \left| c^0_0\; c^0_1\; \ldots\; c^0_{W-1} \right| r^0_W\; r^0_{W+1}\; r^0_{W+2}\; \ldots$$

$$\ldots\; \ell^1_{-3}\; \ell^1_{-2}\; \ell^1_{-1} \left| c^1_0\; c^1_1\; \ldots\; c^1_{W-1} \right| r^1_W\; r^1_{W+1}\; r^1_{W+2}\; \ldots$$

$$\vdots\quad\vdots\quad\vdots \; \left| \; \vdots\quad\vdots \quad\quad\; \vdots \; \right| \; \vdots\quad\vdots\quad\vdots$$

$$\ldots\; \ell^T_{-3}\; \ell^T_{-2}\; \ell^T_{-1} \left| q_0\; q_1\; \ldots\; q_{W-1} \right| r^T_W\; r^T_{W+1}\; r^T_{W+2}\; \ldots$$

Fig. 2. Initial-value control

where we have indicated schematically the values of the set of sites of the region to be controlled (c) and those at its left (ℓ) and right (r). The function F is given by the repeated application of the local rule f. By using the chain rule Eq. (9) one can obtain the dependence of c_i^T from the sites at time 0

$$\frac{\partial c_i^T}{\partial \ell_j^0}, \qquad \frac{\partial c_i^T}{\partial c_n^0}, \qquad \frac{\partial c_i^T}{\partial r_m^0}. \tag{13}$$

We want to be able to impose an arbitrary configuration to c_i^T for any given c_j^0 by changing the values of ℓ^0 and/or e^0. This means that, for every initial configuration c^0, there should exist a set of ℓ^0 and r^0 such that there exists at least one ℓ_n^0 or r_m^0 such that

$$\frac{\partial c_i^T}{\partial \ell_n^0} = 1 \qquad \text{or} \qquad \frac{\partial c_i^T}{\partial r_m^0} = 1. \tag{14}$$

As expected, any linear rule (sum of degree-one polynomials, plus eventually a constant) is controllable [8], unless it only depends on the previous value of the same site.

One of the main results of this paper is that the rule is controllable if it is linear with respect to at least one of the peripheral sites (peripherally linear), i.e., for a generic function

$$x_i' = f(x_{i-k}, x_{i-k+1}, \ldots, x_i, \ldots, x_{i+k-1}, x_{i+k}), \tag{15}$$

if one has

$$\frac{\partial x'}{\partial x_{i+k}} = 1 \qquad \text{or} \qquad \frac{\partial x'}{\partial x_{i-k}} = 1, \tag{16}$$

which means that the rule can be written as

$$x_i' = g_\ell(x_{i-k}, x_{i-k+1}, \ldots, x_i, \ldots, x_{i+k-1}) \oplus x_{i+k}$$
$$\text{or} \qquad x_i' = x_{i-k} \oplus g_r(x_{i-k+1}, \ldots, x_i, \ldots, x_{i+k-1}, x_{i+k}), \tag{17}$$

for suitable functions g_ℓ or g_r, then the rule is peripheral. Let us consider the first option. In this case, the value of x_{i+k} can force the value of x' for every set of $\{x_{i-k}, x_{i-k+1}, \ldots, x_i, \ldots, x_{i+k-1}\}$. This means that $c_0^{W/k+1}$ depends linearly from r_W^0. Setting this value so that $c_0^{W/k+1} = q_0$, we can proceed to fix the value of $c_1^{R/k+1} = q_1$ by using its linear dependence on r_{W+1}^0 and so on. So, peripherally linear rules are controllable. For these rules, one only needs to apply the control to one side, therefore in this case it is possible to control a region from just one boundary. However, they are not optimal.

The double peripherally linear rules are optimally controllable. In this case, one divides the set of target sites in two (left and right half), and uses leftmost or rightmost sites to fix the value of the target region at the minimum time. Clearly, fully linear rules like W150 or W90 are optimally controllable.

A rule is not controllable if it depends in a multiplicative way on the previous value of the same site so that it can "fix" the value of that polynomial to zero. For instance, if

$$x_i' = f(x_{i-k}, x_{i-k+1}, \ldots, x_i, \ldots, x_{i+k-1}, x_{i+k})$$
$$= x_i g(x_{i-k}, \ldots, x_{i-1}, x_{i+1} \ldots, x_{i+k}), \tag{18}$$

it is impossible to force x' to one, if $x_i = 0$. By composing the rule, it is evident that the configuration $\{c_i^0 = 0\}$ "forces" $\{c_i^T = 0\}$ and thus is not controllable.

What about all other rules? Since we assume that they are not peripherally linear, the left-most and right-most sites appear in some polynomial together with other sites. By composing the rule backward in time, it implies that the sites in the L and R regions may appear, in the expression for the sites in the target region, in polynomials in which also sites of the control region appear, for instance

$$c_i^T = \ell_k^0 c_n^0 \oplus \ell_m^0 c_p^0 r_u^0. \tag{19}$$

This means that the configuration in which $c_n^0 = 0$ and $c_p^0 = 0$ cannot be controlled. Notice that the number and size of polynomial terms increases when composing the rule.

The rule may depend linearly on some other (non-peripherally) site and in some cases this is sufficient to make the rule controllable. However, in general this site is also involved in some polynomial of some other site to be controlled, and it may become not available for control. For instance, if

$$c_i^T = \ell_k^0 \oplus \ldots; \qquad \text{but} \quad c_j^T = \ldots \ell_k^0 c_n^0 \ldots \tag{20}$$

the state of ℓ_k^0 may be required to take value one for setting the value of c_j^T to one when $c_n^0 = 1$, and thus cannot be used to control c_i^T.

So in general, non-peripherally linear rules are not controllable, with exceptions. As shown in the following section, some of them are controllable, and some are not. For the moment we do not have a general criterion for discriminating among them.

4   Generating Preimages of a Configuration

In order to numerically test for controllability, one should in principle, for each initial configuration C^0 and all desired target configurations Q, search for the existence of a configuration of L^0 and R^0 that generates the target configuration, this for various sizes of the control region and time T. One can save some computational time by reversing the problem, starting from the target configuration. It is relatively easy to recursively generate all pre-images of a configuration, and thus test that they include all possible antecedents of the control region. If this is not the case, the rule is not controllable in such a time interval.

We pre-compute the look-up table of the rule $\tau[w] = f(w)$, for all values of the neighbourhood w (as numbers on base two). Let us consider a given target configuration $q = x = \{x_0, x_1, \ldots, x_{W-1}\}$. In order to keep indexing simple, the preimage will be denoted as

$$y = \{\underbrace{y_0, y_1, \ldots, y_{k-1}}_{L\text{region}}, \underbrace{y_k, \ldots, y_{k+L-1}}_{C\text{control region}}, \underbrace{y_{k+L}, \ldots, y_{2k+L-1}}_{R\text{region}}\}, \qquad (21)$$

where

$$x_0 = f(y_0, y_1, \ldots, y_{K-1}); \qquad x_1 = f(y_1, y_2, \ldots, y_K); \qquad \text{etc.}, \qquad (22)$$

and this iteration is to be repeated the desired number of times. All configurations $z_t = \{y_{tk}, \ldots, y_{tk+L-1}\}$ of the control region C (for all considered times t) are denoted *antecedents* of x.

The procedure starts generating the neighbourhood $y_0, y_1, \ldots, y_{K-1}$ given the value of the target site x_0, looking in the function table. For each of the found neighbourhoods, one continues searching for all possible values of y_K so that $x_1 = f(y_1, y_2, \ldots, y_K)$, given the already found values, and so on until all the y configuration is generated. One then continues generating all the pre-images at previous times. When the task is finished, the last recursive function ends, so the next value of the site under evaluation is tested, and so on.

Algorithm 1. This is the main loop. It constructs a matrix $C[x][t]$ that states if configuration x is controllable at time t.

$n = 0$ ▷ $n[t, z]$ will contain the number of occurrences...
                                    ▷ ...of antecedent z at time t
for all $0 \le x < 2^W$ **do**   ▷ x is the target configuration, as a base-2 number
    $p[0] \leftarrow x$ ▷ $p[t]$ will contain a "history" of preimages of x
    StartBacktracking$(0, T, W, k, p, n)$ ▷ Generation of preimages, from time $t = 0$

    for all $1 \le t \le T$ **do**
        $C[x, t] \leftarrow 1$ ▷ Assume that configuration x is controllable at time t
        for all $0 \le z < 2^W$ **do**   ▷ y is a possible antecedent
            if $n[t, z] = 0$ **then**   ▷ y is not an antecedent of x at time t
                $C[x, t] \leftarrow 0$ ▷ x is not controllable at time t
            end if
        end for
    end for
end for

Algorithm 2. StartBacktracking(t, T, W, k, p, n) begins building the preimage $p[t+1]$ generating the neighbourhood of the first site.

```
 1: procedure STARTBACKTRACKING(t, T, W, K, p, n)
 2:     s ← GetBit(c[t], 0)                          ▷ s is the first site
 3:     for all 0 ≤ w < 2^(2k+1) do                  ▷ w is a possible neighbourhood
 4:         if τ[w] = s then                         ▷ w is an accepted neighbourhood
 5:             p[t + 1] ← w                    ▷ Store w as the beginning of preimage
 6:             ContinueBacktracking(t, 1, T, W, k, p, n)      ▷ Add other sites, ...
 7:                                                   ▷ ...starting with i = 1
 8:         end if
 9:     end for
10: end procedure
```

Algorithm 3. ContinueBacktracking(t, i, T, W, k, p, n) extends the partial preimage $p[t+1]$ to site i.

```
procedure CONTINUEBACKTRACKING(t, i, T, W, k, p, n)
    s ← GetBit(p[t], i)                        ▷ s is the site under investigation
    w_p ← GetBits(p[t + 1], i, 2k)             ▷ w_p is the partial neighbourhood of s
    for s' = 0, 1 do                           ▷ s' is the missing site in the neighbourhood
        w ← SetBit(w_p, s', 2k)                ▷ w is the possible neighbourhood
        if τ[w] = s then                       ▷ w is an accepted neighbourhood
            p[t + 1] ← SetBit(p[t + 1], s', i + 2k)     ▷ Store s' in position i + 2k...
                                                         ▷ ...of preimage p[t + 1]
            if i + 1 = W + 2kt then                 ▷ Preimage completed
                z ← GetBits(p[t + 1], (t + 1)k, W)   ▷ The W central bits of p[t + 1]...
                                                     ▷ ...constitutes an antecedent z
                n[t, z] ← n[t, z] + 1                ▷ Count number of antecedents
                if t = T then                        ▷ Time limit reached
                    return
                else
                    StartBacktracking(t + 1, T, W, k, p, n)    ▷ Start another preimage
                end if
            else
                ContinueBacktracking(t, i + 1, T, W, k, p, n)       ▷ Add other sites
            end if
        end if
    end for
end procedure
```

After completing the enumeration of preimages, one checks if all antecedents at times $t = 1, 2, \ldots$ have been generated at least once. If so, the rule is controllable at time $T = -t$, otherwise it is not.

The pseudocode of the skeleton of the program is reported in Algorithms 1, 2 and 3 (the complete source in C language can be found in Ref. [14]).

With the use of this program is is easy to compute the controllability of rules for small regions and limited time span. We consider sizes up to $W = 6$ and times up to $T = 6$.

Let us consider the case $K = 5$ ($k = 2$). We denote the neighbourhood of a given site as $\{x_{ll}, x_l, x_c, x_r, x_{rr}\}$. As expected, any peripherally linear rule is controllable, like for instance $x_{ll} \oplus x_l x_c x_r x_{rr}$, and all double-peripherally linear rule s are optimally controllable, like for instance $x_{ll} \oplus x_l x_c x_r \oplus x_{rr}$. If the leftmost (or rightmost) site is not involved in any polynomial, the rule is still peripherally linear and thus controllable (although not optimally), like $x_l \oplus x_c x_r x_{rr}$.

Let us now consider non-peripherally linear rules, i.e., rules like $x_{ll} x_l \oplus x_c \oplus x_r x_{rr}$ or $x_{ll} x_{rr} \oplus x_c \oplus x_r x_l$. As reported in Table 1, it is not evident which structure is responsible for controllability. An indication may come from some estimation of the chaoticy of the rule (which implies a strong dependence on variation of inputs). It is possible to define the equivalent of Lyapunov exponents for cellular automata [4], which in principle depends on the trajectory and thus on the configuration. A rough idea of the chaoticity of the rule can be given by the average number of ones in the Jacobian for a random configuration, which is readily computable by evaluating the average value μ of all first-order derivatives over all possible configurations. We also tried to assign higher weight to peripheral derivatives with respect to central ones (μ').

The comparison between the values of μ and μ' and controllability is reported in Table 1 for some rules. The method can only say if a small region can be controlled in a limited amount of time. So, one can only state if a control can be found within this time limit. As shown in the Table, the chaotic indicator show some correlation with the minimum control time T_c, but this indicator is not exhaustive, since peripherally linear rules can be easily controlled even when

Table 1. The average number of ones in the derivative (μ) and the weighted version (μ') for some rules, compared with the minimal control time T_c for some values of N. For some rule the control time (if any) for $N = 6$ was longer than the available computational time, so N was reduced.

Rule	Lin. perif.?	μ	μ'	T_c	W
$x_{ll} \oplus x_l \oplus x_c \oplus x_r \oplus x_{rr}$	Yes	5	6	2	6
$x_{ll} \oplus x_l x_c x_r \oplus x_{rr}$	Yes	2.75	4.5	2	6
$x_l \oplus x_c \oplus x_r \oplus x_{rr}$	Yes	4	4	2	6
$x_l \oplus x_c \oplus x_r$	Yes	3	2	3	6
$x_{ll} \oplus x_l x_c x_r x_{rr}$	Yes	1.5	2.5	3	6
$x_{ll} x_{rr} \oplus x_l \oplus x_c \oplus x_r$	No	4	4	6	6
$x_{ll} x_{rr} \oplus x_c \oplus x_r$	No	3	3	6	4
$x_{ll} x_l \oplus x_c \oplus x_r x_{rr}$	No	3	3	6	5
$x_{ll} x_{rr} x_l \oplus x_c \oplus x_r$	No	2.75	2.25	5	4
$x_{ll} x_{rr} x_l \oplus x_c \oplus x_r$	No	2.75	2.25	> 6	5

they show relatively low chaoticity indicators, while non-peripherally linear rules may be hard or impossible to control even in the presence of moderately high chaoticity.

5 Conclusions

We introduced the interesting problem of regional controlling Cellular Automata (CA) only acting on the boundary of a given region. This problem has shown to be quite hard. We showed that it can be remapped into an initial-value problem and furnished an explicit solution for CA rules that are peripherally linear.

We developed a method for numerically analysing the pre-images of a given CA rule and check, for small sizes of the controllability region and small time intervals, the existence of a control. Better algorithms are needed for numerically investigating the problem in higher dimensions or on graphs and lattices with larger connectivity.

We investigated also the possible role of chaoticity indicators, but the conclusions are not definitive.

References

1. Kauffman, S.A.: Metabolic stability and epigenesis in randomly constructed genetic nets. J. Theor. Biol. **22**, 437 (1969); for a recent application, see Damiani, C., Serra, R., Villani, M., Kauffman, S.A., Colacci, A.: Cell-cell interaction and diversity of emergent behaviours. IET Syst. Biol. **5**, 137 (2011); Chorowski, J., Zurada, J.M.: Extracting rules from neural networks as decision diagrams. IEEE Trans. Neural Netw. **22**, 2435 (2012). For multiple applications, see the series of Proceedings of the Conference in ACRI: Cellular Automata for Research and Industry, LNCS, vol. 8751. Springer, Berlin (2014); ibid., vol. 7495. Springer, Berlin (2012); ibid., vol. 6350. Springer, Berlin (2010); ibid., vol. 5191. Springer, Berlin (2008); ibid., vol. 4173. Springer, Berlin (2006); ibid., vol. 3305. Springer, Berlin (2004); ibid., vol. 2493. Springer, Berlin (2002)
2. Bagnoli, F., Rechtman, R., El Yacoubi, S.: Control of cellular automata. Phys. Rev. E **86**(6), 066201 (2012)
3. Pecora, L.M., Carroll, T.L.: Synchronization in chaotic systems. Phys. Rev. Lett. **64**, 821 (1990)
4. Bagnoli, F., Rechtman, R.: Synchronization and maximum Lyapunov exponents of cellular automata. Phys. Rev. E **59**, R1307 (1999)
5. Zerrik, E., Boutoulout, A., El Jai, A.: Actuators and regional boundary controllability for parabolic systems. Int. J. Syst. Sci. **31**, 73–82 (2000)
6. Lions, J.L.: Controlabilité exacte des systèmes distribueés. C.R.A.S, Série I **302**, 471–475 (1986)
7. Russell, D.L.: Controllability and stabilizability theory for linear partial differential equations: recent progress and open questions. SIAM Rev. **20**, 639–739 (1978)
8. El Yacoubi, S., El Jai, A., Ammor, N.: Regional controllability with cellular automata models. In: Bandini, S., Chopard, B., Tomassini, M. (eds.) ACRI 2002. LNCS, vol. 2493, pp. 357–367. Springer, Heidelberg (2002)

9. Fekih, A.B., El Jai, A.: Regional analysis of a class of cellular automata models. In: El Yacoubi, S., Chopard, B., Bandini, S. (eds.) ACRI 2006. LNCS, vol. 4173, pp. 48–57. Springer, Heidelberg (2006)
10. El Jai, A., Simon, M.C., Zerrik, E., Prirchard, A.J.: Regional controllability of distributed parameter systems. Int. J. Control **62**, 1351–1365 (1995)
11. Wolfram, S.: Statistical mechanics of cellular automata. Rev. Mod. Phys. **55**, 601–644 (1983)
12. Vichniac, G.: Boolean derivatives on cellular automata. Physica D **45**, 63–74 (1990)
13. Bagnoli, F.: Boolean derivatives and computation of cellular automata. Int. J. Mod. Phys. C. **3**, 307 (1992)
14. http://francobagnoli.complexworld.net/capreimages

The Role of Randomness in Self-aggregative AntTree Approach

Urszula Boryczka[✉] and Mariusz Boryczka

Institute of Computer Science, University of Silesia, Sosnowiec, Poland
{urszula.boryczka,mariusz.boryczka}@us.edu.pl

Abstract. In some research works concerning biomimicry and data mining, new bio-inspired clustering algorithm has been proposed to deal with the difficult problem of a partitioning the data. In this work, a role of randomness in AntTree-based approach is discussed in clustering application. This proposition integrates the random mechanism of inserting ants in the tree representation of partitioning and the concept of attraction of the specific connections in the analyzed structure. In the same time, the role of shoving (dynamically changed) by the dissimilarity between objects has been analyzed. The comparative study concerning ant-based algorithm and the standard DBSCAN approach shows that this proposal achieves results comparable to the best classical approach's results. This approach shows that randomness improves the results in clustering offered by the AntTree algorithm.

Keywords: AntTree algorithm · Clustering · Deterministic · Randomness

1 Introduction

Many computer science's researchers focused on data mining tasks bear in their minds a question of how to organize observed data into fundamental structures, that is, to develop taxonomies. This task is answered by clustering analysis, which is an exploratory data examining instrument which aims at partitioning different objects into groups. The goal of this process is to maximize the degree of association between two objects whereas they belong to the same group with minimal differences. Then, clustering analysis can be used to discover structures in data without any prior knowledge. The result of this process ought to satisfy following criteria: homogeneity within the clusters and heterogeneity between clusters [5,8].

Thus, it is expected to obtain the greatest similarity between objects into a cluster as well as the greatest dissimilarity between objects from different clusters. One of the solution used to overcome these problems is an employment of centers or medoids that are hypothetical points in the search space. Every object is assigned using pre-defined distance metric to the nearest points.

Metaheuristics, such as Genetic Algorithms (GA), Ant Colony Optimization (ACO), Artificial Bee Colony (ABC) algorithm, and Artificial Immune System

© Springer International Publishing Switzerland 2016
S. El Yacoubi et al. (Eds.): ACRI 2016, LNCS 9863, pp. 113–122, 2016.
DOI: 10.1007/978-3-319-44365-2_11

have been efficiently applied to achieve optimal or approximately optimal partitioning without requiring prior knowledge about the data set to be clustered [7,9,10,13–15].

Some interesting properties can be observed in self-organizing method, called cellular ants. This approach combines insights from a classical swarm intelligence counterpart – ACO and from the artificial life representative – cellular automata. In Cellular Ants Clustering algorithm, data objects are treated as simple ants placed in a grid file, and through an interactive process via negotiations with neighbouring ants, in final phase, complex data sets are visualized by clusters. Ants in this decentralized system can autonomously check data similarity patterns in multi-dimensional space [1,3,11,12].

Divers phenomena in ants' behavior guided to self-organization. Mechanisms which found their way to partitioning objects are as follows: cemetery and larvae sorting [6], colonial odour and foraging behavior [4]. The ability of ants to build some ant-bridges or another structures using self-assembly could be employed in new ant clustering approach. Building chains of ants' bodies in order to connect leaves together are firstly used by Monmarche, Azzag et al. [2] to create a specific agglomerative, clustering algorithm. These types of self-assembly behavior have been observed with *Linepithema humiles* – Argentine ants and African ants of gender *Oecophylla longinoda*. In both cases, still not fully understandable, these structures disaggregate after a given period of time. From these phenomena, we can derive some features that will constitute a schema of a new approach to clustering, where ants create trees.

This tree-forming metaphor in ants is used to partition objects by allowing ants to form a specific tree dependency of objects. This structure is an equivalent of a hierarchical clustering technique. The discussed approach, called AntTree [2], contains of ants representing objects, which should be partitioned, according to the similarity between the analyzed data. Clustering algorithm discussed here, reorganize the analyzed data into subdivisions of higher similarity. It is a core issue to interpret the dependency structure. In this one, clusters are represented by sub-trees which are connected by the primary node, called here a suspension. Objects gathered in separate sub-trees represent clusters.

This paper is organized as follows. Section 2 presents some general considerations about different strategies to create an ant-based tree for clustering. Section 3 describes the performance of the method proposed in this work. Section 4 is devoted to the modifications of the AntTree approach. The experimental setup and the analysis of the results obtained from our empirical study is provided in Sect. 5. Finally, some general conclusions are drawn and possible future work is discussed.

2   The AntTree Algorithm and Its Performance

The AntTree approach is recognized as a hierarchical clustering algorithm. The structure of the resulting tree is not equal to a classical dendrogram. The main difference is that in the tree constructed by ants each node is represented by single object, while in the dendrogram data is located in leaves.

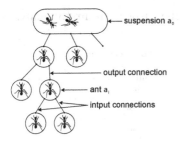

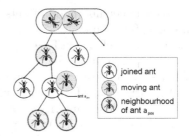

Fig. 1. Ants in tree construction

Fig. 2. Different states of ants in AntTree approach

In the AntTree algorithm each object from the input data set is represented by virtual ant. Each ant is located in the tree node. During the algorithm's performance, each ant is connected to the suspension. At first the tree consists only of the root which constitutes the artificial node, denoted as a_0 and called a suspension. At the beginning, ants are located in this suspension and then moves towards the correct point in the structure. This operation is repeated until every ant is located in the correct sub-tree. The relocation is determined by similarity measure between the moving ant and the local vicinity in which it actually is.

For each ant a_i, for $i \in (1, N)$, the following terms are defined [2]:

- the output connection for ant a_i defines the "parent" in the tree. There can be only one connection of this kind for each ant.
- the input connection for ant a_i can be considered as ant's legs. They represent the children for each node in the tree. Other ants can connect to the tree using these types of link.
- each object x_i is represented by an ant a_i.
- the thresholds of similarity and dissimilarity (τ_+ and τ_- meaning attractant and repellent of movement), determines the ant's behavior. This parameter describe whether the ant will be connected to the sub-tree or will it be moving towards other ants. During the algorithm performance, the thresholds will be locally updated by ant a_i, thanks to the self adaptive mechanism can be obtained.

The graphical illustration of these terms is presented in the Fig. 1. During the tree construction each ant a_i can be in one of the predefined states (Fig. 2):

Checking; each ant a_i can be moved in the suspension of the a_0 or relatively to the another ant (denoted as a_{pos}). It is impossible to join the ant in the level of leaves, directly. If the ant a_i is located in a_{pos}, then a_i is moved to the one of the neighbor of the node a_{pos}. The neighborhood of a_{pos} is determined by the gray nodes (see Fig. 1) – the parent and children of the analyzed a_{pos}, directly connected with the ant a_{pos}.

Joining; each ant, which is joined to the tree obtains one output connection to another ant and maximal L_{max} connections to remaining ants. The parameter L_{max} allows to control the number of descendant nodes in our tree.

We can see the neighborhood of ants as well as the suspension, firstly analyzed in the stage of checking.

The main part of an AntTree algorithm is the initialization phase. It can be treated as the set up each ant in the position a_0 – on the suspension and an arrangement of the default parameters for to thresholds: similarity $\tau_+(a_i)$ as well as dissimilarity threshold $\tau_+(a_i)$. We proposed the parameters' values as presented in Table 1.

Algorithm: Main AntTree

Initialization
while *exists unconnected ant a_i* **do**
   if $i = 1$ **then**
    | Suspension case
   else
    | Searching case
   end
end

Fig. 3. Pseudo-code of the main AntTree algorithm

If an object is located in the suspension, the suspension case is applied. In opposite instance the actions from searching case are carried out (Fig. 3). Firstly investigated or analyzed ant is settled directly in the suspension. For the rest of ants two cases should be examined. The first case corresponds to the suspension case. At the beginning of the algorithm, the created tree consists of the suspension only, so the first ant is instantly settled on the suspension. From this point for every following ant we need to decide whether to move towards the ant settled or to be placed on this suspension.

This decision is conditioned by values of similarity and dissimilarity thresholds for ant a_i. At first the ant a^+, which is the most similar to the ant a_i among all objects (ants) connected with the suspension is found. If the ant a_i is sufficiently similar to the ant a^+, accordingly to its probability thresholds, ant a_i moves towards the ant a^+. On the other hand, if the ant a_i is not similar to the ant a^+ and sufficiently dissimilar to it, then the ant a_i is settled on the suspension (Fig. 4). Then a new cluster is created. Thanks to this, a new sub-tree is obtained, which consists of objects strongly dissimilar to objects on other sub-tree joined to the suspension. In this way clusters significantly different are created. In case when a_i is not similar to the ant a^+, and is not sufficiently dissimilar to the ant a^+, the ant a_i stays on the suspension.

What is more, if the ant a_i is not similar to the ant a^+, and is not sufficiently dissimilar to the ant a^+, the similarity and dissimilarity thresholds for ant a_i change according the following rules [13]:

$$\tau_+(a_i) = \rho \cdot T_{Sim}(a_i) \quad \text{and} \quad \tau_-(a_i) = T_{Dissim}(a_i) + 0.1 \cdot (1 - \rho),$$

where ρ is an evaporation coefficient (in literature this value is established to 0.9), and T_{Sim} and T_{Dissim} are minimal and maximum values of the distance measure respectively. These thresholds are changing during the performance of our algorithm in accordance to the scheme presented in Table 1. We treat them

Table 1. Thresholds values proposed in our approach

For each ant a_i	Default	Min/max	Mean	Modified
Similarity threshold τ_+	1	$d_{max}(a_i)$	$d_{mean}(a_i)$	$\frac{d_{max}(a_i)+d_{mean}(a_i)}{2}$
Dissimilarity threshold τ_-	0	$d_{min}(a_i)$	$d_{mean}(a_i)$	$\frac{d_{min}(a_i)+d_{mean}(a_i)}{2}$

as an attractant τ_+ and a repellent of discussed action for the ant a_i. These values are used for making the algorithm more self aggregative. Due to the dynamic values, the tolerance of the ant a_i is changed (towards smaller values) for generation clusters of greater number of objects.

The thresholds actualization is accomplished for one of two reasons: if a_i was not connected and is still on the suspension, the thresholds are changed to increase the probability that is calculated in the following step; when a_i will be examined, the conditions allowing placing on the suspension or moving towards other ants will be fulfilled. If the ant a_i was connected to the suspension, the thresholds are updated, so the ant a_i would be more tolerant to subsequent ants' comparison.

Pseudo-code describing the work of algorithm in case when ant a_i is located on the suspension is presented in Fig. 5.

Algorithm: Suspension case

if *no ant a_0 is settled on the suspension*
then
  | Join a_i to a_0
else
  Find the ant a^+ most similar to ant a_i
  if $d(a_i, a^+) \geq I_{Sim}(a_i)$ **then**
    | Move a_i towards a^+
  else
    if *no free input connections for a_0*
    then
      | Decrease $T_{Sim}(a_i)$
      | Move a_i towards a^+
      | return
    end
    if $d(a_i, a^+) < T_{Dissim}(a_i)$ **then**
    | Join a_i to a_0
    else
    | Update T_{Ssim} and T_{Dissim}
    end
  end
end

Fig. 4. Pseudo-code of the suspension case of the AntTree approach

Algorithm: Searching case

Mark a_{pos} as an object where a_i is settled on
Determine a_k
if $d(a_i, a_{pos}) \geq I_{Sim}(a_i)$ **then**
  Choose a^+ as the most similar object to a_i in neighborhood of a_{pos}
  if $d(a_i, a^+) < T_{Dissim}(a_i)$ **then**
    if *a_{pos} does not posses input connections* **then**
      | Move a_i towards a_k
      | return
    end
    Join a_i to a_{pos}
  else
    | Update T_{Ssim} and T_{Dissim}
    | Move a_i towards a_k
  end
else
  | Move a_i towards a_k
end

Fig. 5. Pseudo-code of the searching case of the AntTree approach

3   A Deterministic AntTree Approach

The basic AntTree algorithm contains stochastic elements executed by ant moving towards randomly chosen nodes. Incorporation of determinism allows obtaining the same results for two different algorithm launches.

Another advantage of deterministic AntTree is the lack of similarity and dissimilarity thresholds and furthermore, a lack of any input parameters. The deterministic AntTree algorithm uses the phenomenon concerning the disconnection of a part of the created tree structure. The idea of the performance of the discussed approach is similar to the mechanism presented in the classical version: the ant a_i will be connected to the ant a_{pos} if the ant a_i is sufficiently dissimilar to the ant a^+, where the ant a^+ is the most similar to the ant a_i

among all ants connected to the a_{pos}. The difference is that the dissimilarity threshold depends solely on ants already connected to the a_{pos}. In the classical approach each ant possesses its local thresholds values. Thanks to this change, the similarity threshold is determined by the sub-tree structure itself.

In deterministic AntTree algorithm three cases can be distinguished. For each case the a_{pos} is defined as a position on which the currently analyzed ant a_i is located. If a_{pos} has at least one ant connected, then the ant a_i is connected to the a_{pos}. This means that the two first ants are automatically (without calculations) joined to the a_{pos}. The second case applies when a_{pos} has exactly two connected ants and the a_{pos} is visited for the first time. In this instance the ant a_{dis} is chosen, which is the most dissimilar to the ant a_i. The sub-tree created by the ant a_{dis} (meaning the ant a_{dis} and each ant connected recursively to the ant a_{dis}) will be disconnected from the a_{pos} and all ants created this sub-tree will be transferred to the suspension. Finally the ant a_i is linked to the a_{pos} in the spot of the ant a_{dis} (see Fig. 6).

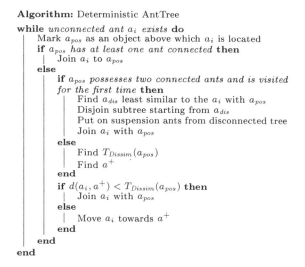

Algorithm: Deterministic AntTree

while *unconnected ant a_i exists* **do**
    Mark a_{pos} as an object above which a_i is located
    if a_{pos} *has at least one ant connected* **then**
        | Join a_i to a_{pos}
    else
        if a_{pos} *possesses two connected ants and is visited for the first time* **then**
            | Find a_{dis} least similar to the a_i with a_{pos}
            | Disjoin subtree starting from a_{dis}
            | Put on suspension ants from disconnected tree
            | Join a_i with a_{pos}
        else
            | Find $T_{Dissim}(a_{pos})$
            | Find a^+
        end
        if $d(a_i, a^+) < T_{Dissim}(a_{pos})$ **then**
            | Join a_i with a_{pos}
        else
            | Move a_i towards a^+
        end
    end
end

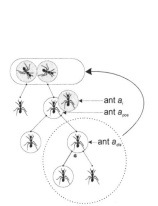

Fig. 6. Disjoining of sub-tree starting from a_{dis}

Fig. 7. Pseudo-code of the deterministic AntTree algorithm

The last case – minimum of two ants are connected to the a_{pos} and the a_{pos} is visited at least for the second time. Then the smallest probability value of $T_{Dissim}(a_{pos})$ between a_{pos} and the ants that are linked is calculated. The $T_{Dissim}(a_{pos})$ is defined as follows:

$$T_{Dissim}(a_{pos}) = \min d(a_x, a_y)|a_x, a_y \in \{\text{ants connected to } a_{pos}\}.$$

The conclusion is that in order to calculate T_{Dissim} the ant a_{pos} must have at least two ants connected to it. This assures that the first case of algorithm, where two first ants are linked without any calculations or similarity check. After establishing T_{Dissim}, the ant a^+ which is the most similar to the ant a_i among all ants connected to the a_{pos} is found. If the ant a_i is sufficiently dissimilar to the ant a^+, that is the $d(a_i, a^+) < T_{Dissim}(a_{pos})$ then the ant a_i is connected to the a_{pos}. In opposite case the ant a_i is moved towards a^+. During the algorithm performance for each node in the tree, the T_{Dissim} value always decreases, which assures the ending of the algorithm.

Pseudo-code for the deterministic AntTree algorithm is presented in Fig. 7.

4   Experiments and Results

For evaluating the performance of the clustering algorithm we suggest to use cluster validity indices. In literature several different scalar validity measures have been proposed which result to be more or less appropriate depending on our data and the specific application. There are several: Inter-Cluster Density, Dunn's Index, Generalized Dunn's Index (GDI), Classification Error (E_c), Cluster purity (P_c) and many others.

Examination of the AntTree algorithm has been performed for the following data sets: Iris, Survival, Knowledge, Glass and Wine. The testable values for parameter ρ are changed from 0.7 to 0.99 with the step 0.05. At the same time, four different initializations of the thresholds for similarity as well as dissimilarity values are examined (Table 2). The order of analyzed objects in data sets is the important factor in our analysis. The following data sets' order has been analyzed in our approach according to the following rules: default, descending, ascending and random. Each experiment has been averaged after 30 repetitions. The best

Table 2. The best results for each data set (with parameter values tested)

Data set	Method of sorting	Init. val. τ_+, τ_-	ρ	K	Dunn index	GDI index	E_c	P_c
Iris	Default	1, 0	0.90	3	0.174	0.427	0.089	0.925
	Descending	modified	0.99	3	0.174	0.402	0.096	0.930
	Descending	1, 0	0.90	3	0.174	0.386	0.125	0.903
Survival	Descending	modified	0.75	2	0.154	0.367	0.387	0.869
	Descending	modified	0.80	2	0.154	0.375	0.387	0.869
	Descending	modified	0.85	2	0.154	0.436	0.386	0.853
Glass	Ascending	min, max	0.95	6	0.272	0.392	0.352	0.687
	Default	modified	0.95	7	0.272	0.466	0.324	0.694
	Ascending	min, max	0.99	6	0.272	0.392	0.371	0.715
Knowledge	Default	modified	0.90	6	0.167	0.433	0.304	0.615
	Ascending	1, 0	0.75	7	0.167	0.488	0.307	0.612
	Ascending	1, 0	0.70	4	0.167	0.653	0.307	0.602
Wine	Default	min, max	0.98	3	0.478	0.685	0.133	0.893
	Ascending	modified	0.70	4	0.469	0.682	0.125	0.841
	Default	min, max	0.85	5	0.469	0.682	0.112	0.911

arrangements for the initial values are presented in Table 1. The preliminary study showed, that the coefficients used in τ_+ and τ_- are difficult to establish and it is hard to estimate the dependency between changes in τ_+ and τ_-. In Table 2 different methods of data ordering has been collated. Apart from the default order of data and comparing random order of objects with ascending and descending order, the best results has been obtained by sorting objects in descending manner for the data sets: Iris and Survival. On the other hand in other data sets better results outweighed for the ascending order. The random order is not sufficient enough – it did not bring good results even for mean values of similarity and dissimilarity thresholds. The best initialization of the thresholds is obtained for modified version (established and presented in Table 1).

To designate the effectiveness of the presented ant-based approaches against the background of classical clustering methods, we chose density-based DBSCAN algorithm (see Table 3). For the data sets: Glass and Wine the best turn to be the AntTree algorithm. For the remaining data sets the best approach could not be pointed out unanimously. The DBSCAN obtained slightly better results compared to the AntTree algorithm. However, it is imported to bear in mind, that in DBSCAN approach, the establishing of parameter ϵ and MinPts values is computationally expensive. This problem of matching values to parameters occurred in the AntTree approach as well. From the conducted research appeared that the DBSCAN cannot handle the Knowledge data set. It is also important to underline, that this approach has no random procedures and the results are not dependent on the initial order of objects.

Table 3. Comparative study for AntTree, deterministic AntTree and DBSCAN

Data set	Algorithm	Dunn index	GDI	E_c	P_c
Iris	AntTree	0.174	0.402	**0.096**	0.930
	Det. AntTree	0.174	0.367	0.172	0.886
	DBSCAN	0.202	0.694	**0.029**	0.972
Survival	AntTree	0.154	0.387	**0.375**	0.869
	Det. AntTree	0.154	0.464	0.387	0.637
	DBSCAN	0.123	0.566	0.389	0.871
Glass	AntTree	0.272	0.392	**0.352**	0.687
	Det. AntTree	0.280	0.484	0.401	0.638
	DBSCAN	0.231	0.538	0.503	0.881
Knowledge	AntTree	0.167	0.553	**0.307**	0.602
	Det. AntTree	0.167	0.594	0.373	0.548
	DBSCAN	0.188	0.287	0.675	0.777
Wine	AntTree	0.478	0.685	**0.133**	0.893
	Det. AntTree	0.469	0.672	0.169	0.909
	DBSCAN	0.083	0.561	0.375	0.835

Comparison of different types of algorithms shown that the AntTree approach predominates remaining counterparts considering variety of quality measures of clustering. This is because the number of objects that could not be assigned to any clusters is smaller. In case of data set Survival slightly better results of classification error have been obtained for the AntTree algorithm. Similar outcome occurred in three analyzed approaches for the rest of data.

Results obtained by the deterministic AntTree algorithm are slightly worse than for the classical AntTree algorithm. Much bigger differences in case of the classification error have been observed between the deterministic AntTree and the DBSCAN. For the deterministic AntTree approach the vice is creating bigger number of clusters than was expected. Comparing the complexity of algorithms and the manner of implementation, the Ant Tree approach is much complicated and demands the tuning of parameter values. Only the deterministic AntTree algorithm does not require such operations. It is important to point out the dependency between the performance of ant-based approaches and the order of objects in data sets. Therefore it is possible to improve the usability of these approaches by adding the preliminary objects' ordering. The advantage of the classical and deterministic AntTree algorithms is creating the tree of objects, by which the clustering can be conducted on different levels, comprising sub-level clusters. This hierarchical structure is a feature much desirable in real data sets. We also analyzed the results firstly presented in scientific work [16] and added the results of the Ant Tree approach.

Three approaches concerning ants are discussed: Lumer and Fieta algorithm, two versions of ant clustering algorithm based on Cellular Automata: SA^4C, and A^4C and our proposition. This study shows constantly progress in accuracy of clustering approaches based on the ant colony metaphor (Table 4).

Table 4. Comparative study – error rates

Data set	LF	SA^4C	A^4C	AntTree
Iris	4.45	2.94	1.31	0.09
Wine	4.52	2.71	1.13	0.15
Glass	4.79	3.55	1.84	0.40
Thyroid	6.75	5.00	4.10	0.26
Soybean	2.98	1.83	1.21	0.10

5 Conclusions

In this paper a bio-inspired AntTree algorithm has been presented. The interesting clustering process, based on the self-assembly behavior of natural ants, concerning forming engineering structures were discussed. Experimental results for clustering data sets reveals a promise carried by the proposed algorithm. While being computationally efficient and accurate, the probabilistic or stochastic nature of the ant activity in tree construction allows to avoid local optima which other algorithms may get stuck in. In our future work we will attempt to improve the government of the coefficient ρ occurred in the attractant and the repellent of the ant activity. We also want to further exploit the role of randomness, which now helped to create good results, with bigger accuracy of classification and the purity of clusters. In case of the AntTree approach, the construction of the sub-tree is more demanding but it is worth further analysis and improvement.

References

1. Albuquerque, P., Dupuis, A.: A parallel cellular ant colony algorithm for clustering and sorting. In: Bandini, S., Chopard, B., Tomassini, M. (eds.) ACRI 2002. LNCS, vol. 2493, pp. 220–230. Springer, Heidelberg (2002)
2. Azzag, H., Monmarche, N., Slimane, M., Venturini, G., Guinot, C.: AntTree: a new model for clustering with artificial ants. In: IEEE Congress on Evolutionary Computation. IEEE Press (2003)
3. Bitsakidis, N.P., Chatzichristofis, S.A., Sirakoulis, G.C.: Hybrid cellular ants for clustering problems. Int. J. Unconventional Comput. $11(2)$, 103–130 (2015)
4. Bonabeau, E., Dorigo, M., Theraulaz, G.: Swarm Intelligence. From Natural to Artificial Systems. Oxford University Press, New York (1999)
5. Bramer, M.: Principles of Data Mining. Springer, London (2007)
6. Deneubourg, J.-L., Goss, S., Franks, N., Sendova-Franks, A., Detrain, C., Chretien, L.: The dynamics of collective sorting: robot-like ant and ant-like robot. In: Meyer, J.A., Wilson, S.W. (eds.) First Conference on Simulation of Adaptive Behavior. From Animals to Animats, pp. 356–365 (1991)
7. Garai, G., Chaudhuri, B.B.: A novel genetic algorithm for automatic clustering. Pattern Recogn. Lett. $25(2)$, 173–187 (2004)
8. Han, J., Kamber, M.: Data Mining: Concepts and Techniques. Morgan Kaufmann, San Francisco (2001)
9. Kao, Y., Cheng, K.: An ACO-based clustering algorithm. In: Dorigo, M., Gambardella, L.M., Birattari, M., Martinoli, A., Poli, R., Stützle, T. (eds.) ANTS 2006. LNCS, vol. 4150, pp. 340–347. Springer, Heidelberg (2006)
10. Karaboga, D., Ozturk, C.: A novel clustering approach: artificial bee colony (ABC) algorithm. Appl. Soft Comput. $11(1)$, 652–657 (2011)
11. Moere, A.V., Clayden, J.J.: Cellular ants: combining ant-based clustering with cellular automata. In: 17th IEEE International Conference on Tools with Artificial Intelligence (ICTAI 2005), p. 184, November 2005. 8 pages
12. Moere, A.V., Clayden, J.J., Dong, A.: Data clustering and visualization using cellular automata ants. In: Sattar, A., Kang, B.-H. (eds.) AI 2006. LNCS (LNAI), vol. 4304, pp. 826–836. Springer, Heidelberg (2006)
13. Sheikh, R.H., Raghuwanshi, M.M., Jaiswal, A.N.: Genetic algorithm based clustering: a survey. In: Proceedings of the 2008 First International Conference on Emerging Trends in Engineering and Technology (ICETET), pp. 314–319 (2008)
14. Shelokar, P.S., Jayaraman, V.K., Kulkarni, B.D.: An ant colony approach for clustering. Anal. Chim. Acta 509, 187–195 (2004)
15. Tang, N., Vemuri, R.: An artificial immune system approach to document clustering. In: Proceedings of the 2005 ACM Symposium on Applied Computing, pp. 918–922 (2005)
16. Xu, X., Chen, L., He, P.: A novel ant clustering algorithm based on cellular automata. Web Intell. Agent Syst. Int. J. $5(1)$, 1–14 (2007)

Cutting the Firing Squad Synchronization

Antonios Dimitriadis[1], Martin Kutrib[2]($\boxtimes$), and Georgios Ch. Sirakoulis[1]($\boxtimes$)

[1] Department of Electrical and Computer Engineering,
Democritus University of Thrace, 67100 Xanthi, Greece
gsirak@ee.duth.gr
[2] Institut für Informatik, Universität Giessen, Arndtstr. 2, 35392 Giessen, Germany
kutrib@informatik.uni-giessen.de

Abstract. The firing squad synchronization problem on Cellular Automata (CA) has been studied extensively for many years, and a rich variety of synchronization algorithms have been proposed. From Mazoyer's paper it is known that a minimal-time solution with 6 states exists. The firing squad synchronization problem has also been studied for defective CA where a defective cell can still transmit information without processing it. In the present paper, we consider defective CA where the dynamic defects are such that a defective cell totally fails. The failures are permanent and may occur at any time in the computation. In this way the array is cut into two parts. The question addressed is how many cells in each part can still be synchronized and at which time steps. It is analyzed how many cells are synchronized, where and when this happens and how these three characteristics are connected with the position of the defective cell and the time at which the cell fails. Based on Mazoyer's 6-state algorithm, a solution for one-dimensional CA is proposed that synchronizes the maximal possible number of cells in each part.

1 Introduction

Nowadays it becomes possible to build massively parallel computing systems that consist of hundred thousands of processing elements. Each single component is subject to failure such that the probability of misoperations and loss of function of the whole system increases with the number of its elements. It was von Neumann [12] who first stated the problem of building reliable systems out of unreliable components. Here we consider one-dimensional CA as a model for homogeneously structured parallel systems as are linear processor arrays. Such devices of interconnected parallel acting finite-state machines have been studied from the viewpoint of fault tolerance in several ways. In [2] reliable arrays are constructed under the assumption that a cell (and not its links) at each time step fails with a constant probability. Moreover, such a failure does not incapacitate the cell permanently, but only violates its rule of operation in the step when it occurs. Under the same constraint that cells themselves (and not their links) fail (that is, they cannot process information but are still able to transmit it unchanged with unit speed) fault-tolerant computations have been investigated,

© Springer International Publishing Switzerland 2016
S. El Yacoubi et al. (Eds.): ACRI 2016, LNCS 9863, pp. 123–133, 2016.
DOI: 10.1007/978-3-319-44365-2_12

for example, in [4,13] where encodings are established that allow the correction of so-called K-separated misoperations, in [5] where the studies are in terms of syntactical pattern recognition, in [6,7,15,17,20] where the firing squad synchronization problem is considered in defective cellular arrays, and in [1] where the early bird problem [14] is investigated.

However, in the previous studies defective cells are considered such that cells still can transmit information without processing it. Here we consider defective CA where the dynamic defects are such that a defective cell totally fails. The failures are permanent and may occur at any time in the computation. In this way the array is cut into two parts. Our study is in terms of the famous Firing Squad Synchronization Problem (FSSP). It was raised by Myhill in 1957 and emerged in connection with the problem to start several parts of a parallel machine at the same time. The first published reference appeared with a solution found by McCarthy and Minsky in [11]. Roughly speaking, the problem is to set up a CA such that all cells change to a special state for the first time after the same number of steps. Many modifications and generalizations of the FSSP have been investigated. An overview can be found in [18].

From the perspective that a cell totally fails, the question addressed here is how many cells in each of the parts caused by the failure can still be synchronized and at which time steps. It is analyzed how many cells are synchronized, where and when this happens and how these three characteristics are connected with the position of the defective cell and the time at which the cell fails. Based on Mazoyer's 6-state algorithm, a solution for one-dimensional CA is proposed that synchronizes the maximal possible number of cells in each part. Implementations of the proposed algorithm show that the algorithm has an average of 78 % synchronization success, which means that in some cases a small number of cells could finally be remain unsynchronized.

2   Preliminaries

Let A denote a finite set of letters. Then we write A^* for the set of all finite words (strings) built with letters from A and A^+ for the set of all non-empty words. We use $\subseteq$ for set inclusion and $\subset$ for strict set inclusion. For a set S and a symbol a we abbreviatory write S_a for $S \cup \{a\}$.

A one-dimensional CA is a linear array of identical deterministic finite-state machines, called cells. Except for the leftmost cell and rightmost cell each one is connected to its both nearest neighbors. We identify the cells by positive integers. The state transition depends on the current state of a cell itself and the current states of its two neighbors, where the outermost cells receive a permanent boundary symbol on their free input lines.

Definition 1. *A cellular automaton (CA) is a system $M = \langle S, A, \#, \delta \rangle$, where S is the finite, nonempty set of cell states, $A \subseteq S$ is the nonempty set of input symbols, $\# \notin S$ is the permanent boundary symbol, $\delta : S_\# \times S \times S_\# \to S$ is the local transition function.*

A configuration c_t of M at time $t \geq 0$ *is a string of the form* #S^*#, *that reflects the cell states from left to right. The computation starts at time 0 in a so-called* initial configuration, *which is defined by the input* $w = a_1 a_2 \cdots a_n \in A^+$. *We set* $c_0 = $#$a_1 a_2 \cdots a_n$#. *During the course of its computation a CA steps through a sequence of configurations, whereby successor configurations are computed according to the global transition function* Δ: *Let* c_t *be a configuration reached at time* $t \geq 0$ *in some computation. Then its successor configuration* $c_{t+1} = \Delta(c_t)$ *is as follows. For* $2 \leq i \leq n-1$, $c_{t+1}(i) = \delta(c_t(i-1)), c_t(i), c_t(i+1))$, *and for the leftmost and rightmost cell we set* $c_{t+1}(1) = \delta($#$, c_t(1), c_t(2))$ *and* $c_{t+1}(n) = \delta(c_t(n-1), c_t(n), $#$)$, *for* $t \geq 0$. *Thus, the global transition function* Δ *is induced by* δ.

Next, we consider CA with dynamic defects. In [5] dynamic defects have been studied so that a defective cell can still transmit information without processing it. In this way the array is not cut into pieces. Here we investigate dynamic defects so that a defective cell totally fails, such failures are permanent and may occur at any time in the computation. In order to define CA with this type of defects more formally, a possible failure is seen as a weak kind of nondeterminism for the local transition function.

Definition 2. *A cellular automaton* $M = \langle S, A, $#$, \delta \rangle$ *is a* cellular automaton with (totally) dynamic defects *(TDCA), if* δ *is extended so that it may map any triple from* $S_{\#} \times S \times S_{\#}$ *to* $S_{\#}$, *that is, either to a state from* S *or alternatively to the boundary symbol* #.

If a cell works fine the local transition function maps to a state from S. Otherwise it maps to #. In the latter case, for the remaining computation the cell behaves as the boundary to its both neighbors. Since the transition function is not defined for #, the failure is permanent and the cell can be seen as totally defective. The time step at which a cell enters the boundary symbol from a non-boundary symbol is said to be the time step at which the cell *fails* or its *failure time*. We assume that initially all cells are intact and, thus, no cell fails at time 0.

3   The Firing Squad Synchronization Problem

Roughly speaking, the problem is to set up a CA such that all cells change to a special state for the first time after the same number of steps. Originally, the problem has been stated as follows: Consider a finite but arbitrary long chain of finite automata that are all identical except for the automata at the ends. The automata are called soldiers, and the automaton at the left end is the general. The automata work synchronously, and the state of each automaton at time step $t+1$ depends on its own state and on the states of its both immediate neighbors at time step t. The problem is to find states and state transitions such that the general may initiate a synchronization in such a way that all soldiers enter a distinguished state, the *firing state*, for the first time at the same time step. At the beginning all non-general soldiers are in the quiescent state.

Definition 3. *Let C be the set of all configurations of the form $\#GQQ \cdots Q\#$. The* Firing Squad Synchronization Problem *is to specify a CA $\langle S, A, \#, \delta \rangle$ so that for all $c \in C$,*

1. *there is a* synchronization time $t_f \geq 1$ *such that $\Delta^{t_f}(c) = \#FF \cdots F\#$,*
2. *for all $0 \leq t < t_f$, $\Delta^t(c) = \#X_1 X_2 \cdots X_n\#$ with $X_i \neq F$, $1 \leq i \leq n$, and*
3. *$\delta(Q, Q, Q) = \delta(\#, Q, Q) = \delta(Q, Q, \#) = Q$.*

While the first solution of the problem takes $3n$ time steps to synchronize n cells [11], Goto [3] was the first who presented a minimal-time solution that uses several thousand states (see [16, 21] for a reconstruction of this algorithm). The minimal solution time for the FSSP is $2n - 2$ [19].

Apart from time optimality there is a natural interest in efficient solutions with respect to the number of states or the number of bits to be communicated to neighbors. While there exists a time optimal solution where just one bit of information is communicated [10], the minimal number of states is still an open problem. Currently, a 6-state solution is known [9]. In the same paper it is proved that there does not exist a time-optimal 4-state algorithm. It is a challenging open problem to prove or disprove that there exists a 5-state solution.

Since the algorithm to be presented here relies on Mazoyer's solution, we next sketch the basic idea from [9].

Algorithm 4. The FSSP is solved by iteratively dividing the array of length n into parts on which the same algorithm is applied recursively (see Fig. 1). First the array is divided into two parts. Then the process is applied to both parts in parallel, etc. The cut-points are chosen so that one of the parts is twice as long as the other (up to the remainder of n modulo 3). Exactly when all cells are cut-points they enter the firing state synchronously.

In order to divide the array into two parts, the general sends two signals to the right. One Signal moves with speed 1, that is, one cell per time step, and the other signal speed $1/2$, that is, one cell every other time step. The fast signal is bounced at the right end and sent back to the left with speed. Both signals meet at position $2/3 \cdot n$ (up to the remainder of n modulo 3), where the cell becomes a general. Now the right part is treated as an array of length $(n + i)/3$, where $i \in \{0, 1, 2\}$ so that the synchronization starts with 0, 1, or 2 steps delay.

The next cut-point in the left part, which is at total position $(2/3)^2$, can be determined by another signal sent at initial time by the general at the left end. This signal moves with speed $2/7$. It meets the bounced signal from above at the required position. In order to determine the cut-point at total position $(2/3)^3$ in this way, the general has to send a further signal with speed $4/23$, and so on. Altogether, for a solution the general has to send a number of signals that depends on the length of the array.

In order to send this number of signals with a finite state set, an approach shown in [19] can be adopted. The idea is rather simple, the additional signals are generated and moved by trigger signals. The left-moving trigger signals themselves are emitted by the initial right-moving signal. Whenever a trigger

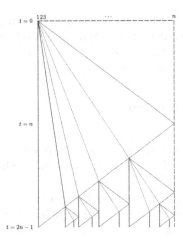

Fig. 1. Scheme of the time-optimal 6-state FSSP solution. The vertical solid lines are cells in the general state. For the sake of clarity not all signals are depicted.

signal reaches the leftmost cell, a new signal to be triggered is generated. Whenever a trigger signal reaches a triggered signal, the latter is moved. That way, the desired behavior is achieved, and a minimal-time solution for the FSSP is obtained.   □

4   Synchronization with a Totally Defective Cell

In this section we turn to consider the effect of a cell becoming totally defective on Mazoyer's algorithm that is extended. For non-defective CA, the algorithm runs in optimal time, that is, in time $2n - 2$ where n is the number of cells to be synchronized. For the case that a cell k with $1 < k < n$ fails the array is cut into two independent parts, that is, into the cells $1, 2, \ldots, k - 1$ on the left and the cells $k + 1, k + 2, \ldots, n$ on the right. The problem is now to synchronize these two parts independently of each other, if possible at all. However, this may yield extended synchronization times. The main goal in the sequel is to determine for a given situation how many cells can still be synchronized, and how many time steps are needed. The algorithm depends naturally on the time step at which a cell fails (recall that this is the time step at which it enters the boundary symbol from a non-boundary state) and its position in the array. For our notation, in the following we assume that at most one cell k with $1 < k < n$ fails at time step t_d with $0 < t_d \leq 2n - 2$.

In general, cell $k - 1$ has to detect that the failure occurred. This means, it has to distinguish between a boundary symbol to its right that is due to a failure and a boundary symbol that is initial. On the other hand, this distinction is irrelevant if the failure occurs when cell $k - 1$ has not received the initial signal. So, it is sufficient that each cell remembers the information whether or not its right neighbor is the boundary symbol when the cell receives the initial signal. To this end, no further copies of the states are used, but the remembering is successfully encapsulated in the transition function. In general, since the leftmost cell is cell 1, the running time of the initial signal to cell k is $k - 1$ time steps.

4.1 Analysis for the Left Part

When cell k fails at time t_d, its left neighbor enters a state that may depend on the fact that a failure occurs at the earliest at time $t_d + 1$. The actual behavior of cell $k - 1$ at time $t_d + 1$ depends on the position of the defective cell, that is, on k and on t_d.

Case 1: If $t_d \leq k - 3$, then the initial signal sent by the leftmost cell of the FSSP still did not arrive at cell $k - 1$ when its neighbor failed. The running time of this signal to cell $k - 1$ is $k - 2$ time steps. So, cell k acts a boundary cell for the FSSP that synchronizes all the $k - 1$ cells of the left part in $2(k - 1) - 2 = 2k - 4$ steps. This behavior does not apply to the case $k - 2 \leq t_d$. The reason is that the state of cell $k - 1$ at time $k - 2$ is given by the transition function that sees the quiescent state in cell k at time $k - 3$. So, if cell k fails at time $k - 2$, then the state of cell $k - 1$ does not reflect the bounced signal.

Case 2: Let $k - 2 \leq t_d \leq 2n - k - 1$. Then cell $k - 1$ was already reached by the initial signal and the synchronization is in progress. Therefore, the algorithm we consider is set up so that cell $k - 1$ informs the cells of the left part about the failure and to stop the running FSSP. To this end, it sends a signal to the left. This signal is started at time $t_d + 1$ and arrives at time $t_d + 1 + k - 2 = t_d + k - 1$. If the synchronization time $2n - 2$ of the running FSSP is after the arrival time of the signal in cell 1, none of the cells in the left part will fire according to the running FSSP. This happens if $2n - 2 \geq t_d + k - 1$ and, thus, $t_d \leq 2n - k - 1$.

Now the algorithm is further extended such that the signal that stops the running synchronization is additionally the initial signal of a new (mirrored) FSSP instance where the synchronization is initiated by the rightmost cell of the array. In particular, this implies that the left part is synchronized in $2(k - 1) - 2$ steps after the signal has been emitted. That is, the synchronization takes place at time step $t_d + 1 + 2(k - 1) - 2 = t_d + 2k - 3$.

It is worth mentioning that the mirrored FSSP costs extra states. Here we can trade states for a slowdown as follows. Cell $k - 1$ still sends the signal to the left in order to stop the running FSSP. If the signal arrives in cell 1 a new (non-mirrored) FSSP is initiated that synchronizes the left part in further $2(k - 1) - 2$ steps, that is, at time $t_d + 1 + k - 2 + 2(k - 1) - 2 = t_d + 3k - 5$. Since the new signal requires just one additional state, we trade one state for $k - 2$ additional time steps.

Case 3: Let $2n - k \leq t_d \leq 2n - 2$. In this case, the signal emitted by cell $k - 1$ to stop the running FSSP does not reach all cells of the left part before time step $2n - 2$ at which the running synchronization takes place. However, at time $t_d + x$ the signal has affected x cells, where $x \geq 1$. Setting $2n - 2 = t_d + x$ implies $x = 2n - 2 - t_d$. So, $2n - 2 - t_d$ cells are affected and, thus, not synchronized by the

Table 1. Summary of synchronization times and cells in the left part, where t_d denotes the time of failure, the columns with head *cells* show the number of cells synchronized, and t_f denotes the time step at which the cells are synchronized.

Left part		
t_d	cells	t_f
$[1, \ldots, k - 3]$	All	$2k - 4$
$[k - 2, \ldots, 2n - k - 1]$	All	$t_d + 2k - 3$
$[2n - k, \ldots, 2n - 2]$	$t_d - 2n + k + 1$	$2n - 2$

running FSSP. Conversely, this means that $k - 1 - (2n - 2 - t_d) = t_d - 2n + k + 1$ cells are synchronized at time step $2n - 2$.

For example, if $t_d = 2n - k$ then just one cell is synchronized. This is the leftmost cell that cannot be reached by the signal in due time. Setting $t_d = 2n - 2$ gives $k - 1$ synchronized cells. These are all cells in the left part since the synchronization takes place at the time cell k fails.

Table 1 summarizes the results for the left part.

4.2   Analysis for the Right Part

As for the left part, when cell k fails at time t_d, its right neighbor enters a state that may depend on the fact that a failure occurs at the earliest at time $t_d + 1$. The actual behavior of cell $k + 1$ at time $t_d + 1$ depends on the position of the defective cell, that is, on k and on t_d.

Case 1: If $t_d \leq k - 1$, then the initial signal sent by the leftmost cell of the FSSP still did not arrive at cell $k + 1$ when its left neighbor failed. The running time of this signal to cell $k + 1$ is k time steps. So, when cell $k + 1$ is still in the quiescent state with a boundary to its left, it can start a new instance of a FSSP that synchronizes the right part. Here we note that a quiescent cell next to the left boundary does not occur without a failure, since initially the leftmost cell is in the general state. The new instance is set up when cell $k + 1$ enters the general state at time $t_d + 1$. Then it takes another $2(n - k - 1) - 2$ steps to synchronize all the $n - k$ cells of the right part. That is, the right part is synchronized at time $t_d + 1 + 2(n - k - 1) - 2 = t_d + 2n - 2k - 3$.

Case 2: Let $k \leq t_d \leq n + k - 2$. Then cell $k + 1$ was already reached by the initial signal and the synchronization is in progress. Therefore, the algorithm we consider is set up so that cell $k + 1$ informs all cells of the right part about the failure and to stop the running FSSP. To this end, it sends a signal to the right. This signal is started at time $t_d + 1$ and arrives at time $t_d + 1 + n - k - 1 = t_d + n - k$. If the synchronization time $2n - 2$ of the running FSSP is after the arrival time of the signal in cell n, none of the cells in the right part will fire according to the running FSSP. This happens if $2n - 2 \geq t_d + n - k$ and, thus, $t_d \leq n + k - 2$.

Now, as for the left part, the algorithm is extended such that the signal that stops the running synchronization is additionally the initial signal of a new FSSP instance. This implies that the right part is synchronized in $2(n - k - 1) - 2$ steps after the signal has been emitted. That is, the synchronization takes place at time step $t_d + 1 + 2(n - k - 1) - 2 = t_d + 2n - 2k - 3$.

Case 3: Let $n + k - 1 \le t_d \le 2n - 2$. In this case, the signal emitted by cell $k + 1$ to stop the running FSSP does not reach all the cells of the right part before time step $2n - 2$ at which the running synchronization takes place. However, at time $t_d + x$ the signal has affected x cells, where $x \ge 1$. Setting $2n - 2 = t_d + x$ implies $x = 2n - 2 - t_d$. So, $2n - 2 - t_d$ cells are affected and, thus, not synchronized by the running FSSP. Conversely, this means that $n - k - (2n - 2 - t_d) = t_d - n - k + 2$ cells are synchronized at time step $2n - 2$.

For example, if $t_d = n + k - 1$ then just one cell is synchronized. This is the rightmost cell that cannot be reached by the signal in due time. Setting $t_d = 2n - 2$ gives $n - k$ synchronized cells. These are all cells in the right part since the synchronization takes place at the the time cell k fails.

Table 2 summarizes the results for the right part.

Table 2. Summary of synchronization times and cells in the right part, where t_d denotes the time of failure, the columns with head *cells* show the number of cells synchronized, and t_f denotes the time step at which the cells are synchronized.

Right part		
t_d	cells	t_f
$[1, \ldots, k - 1]$	All	$t_d + 2n - 2k - 3$
$[k, \ldots, n + k - 2]$	All	$t_d + 2n - 2k - 3$
$[n + k - 1, \ldots, 2n - 2]$	$t_d - n - k + 2$	$2n - 2$

5   Graphical Representation of Two Examples

In the first example a CA with 17 cells is considered. Let cell 9 fail at time step 15. A simulation of the original algorithm from [9] is depicted in the left part of Fig. 2. The boundary cells are represented in yellow. The cells to the right of the failure are left unsynchronized and are depicted in red, while the cells to the left of the failure which are still synchronized are drawn in orange.

At the right hand side of Fig. 2 the extended algorithm is simulated. In particular, all non-defective cells are synchronized (though the left and the right part fire independently at different time steps).

In the second example a CA with 26 cells is presented (see Fig. 3) and is supposed that cell 12 fails at time step 14. Again, at the left hand side of the figure a simulation of the original algorithm is shown. The colors are as before. Note, that none of the cells fires. At the right hand side of Fig. 3, a simulation based on the extended algorithm is presented. As in the first example, now all non-defective cells are synchronized, where the firing times for the left and right part necessarily differ.

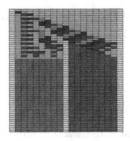 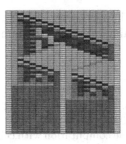

Fig. 2. Simulations of the first example. The original algorithm (left) and the extended algorithm (right). Boundary cells are depicted in yellow, finally synchronized cells in orange, and non-synchronized cells in red. (Color figure online)

Fig. 3. Simulations of the second example. The original algorithm (left) and the extended algorithm (right). Boundary cells are depicted in yellow, finally synchronized cells in orange, and non-synchronized cells in red. (Color figure online)

6   Conclusions

The time-optimal solution of the FSSP by Mazoyer has been considered for one-dimensional CA where at most one cell may totally fail, that is, it can neither process nor transmit information any longer. In order to synchronize as many cells as possible, the algorithm has been extended by several features. The proposed algorithm divides the initial array into two separated parts, which are treated independently. The number of cells that still can be synchronized and the synchronization times naturally depend on the position of the defective cell and the time at which it fails.

The new algorithm has been implemented with 14 states. It has been tested in experiments with all array lengths between 4 and 500 and for all possible failure times and positions. The tests were run on a commercially available Windows PC and took several days running time. It turned out that the algorithm has an average of 78 % synchronization success. Finally, by a case-by-case analysis the number of synchronized cells as well as their synchronization times were derived. A definition of the minimal time to solve the problem is not that obvious as it depends on the number of cells that are synchronized. Moreover, a formal proof would require that the precise configuration of an array at failure time is involved in the argumentation. However, it is not hard to see that the algorithm proposed here works in minimal time for the number of cells that it synchronizes.

References

1. Fay, B., Kutrib, M.: The fault-tolerant early bird problem. IEICE Trans. Inf. Syst. **E87–D**, 687–693 (2004)
2. Gács, P.: Reliable computation with cellular automata. J. Comput. Syst. Sci. **32**(1), 15–78 (1986)
3. Goto, E.: A minimal time solution of the firing squad problem. Course Notes for Applied Mathematics 298, Harvard University (1962)
4. Harao, M., Noguchi, S.: Fault tolerant cellular automata. J. Comput. Syst. Sci. **11**, 171–185 (1975)
5. Kutrib, M., Löwe, J.T.: Massively parallel fault tolerant computations on syntactical patterns. Future Gener. Comput. Syst. **18**, 905–919 (2002)
6. Kutrib, M., Vollmar, R.: Minimal time synchronization in restricted defective cellular automata. J. Inform. Process. Cybern. **EIK 27**, 179–196 (1991)
7. Kutrib, M., Vollmar, R.: The firing squad synchronization problem in defective cellular automata. IEICE Trans. Inf. Syst. **E78–D**, 895–900 (1995)
8. Maignan, L., Yunès, J.-B.: Experimental finitization of infinite field-based generalized FSSP solution. In: Wąs, J., Sirakoulis, G.C., Bandini, S. (eds.) ACRI 2014. LNCS, vol. 8751, pp. 136–145. Springer, Heidelberg (2014)
9. Mazoyer, J.: A six-state minimal time solution to the firing squad synchronization problem. Theoret. Comput. Sci. **50**, 183–238 (1987)
10. Mazoyer, J.: A minimal time solution to the firing squad synchronization problem with only one bit of information exchanged. Technical report TR 89–03, Ecole Normale Supérieure de Lyon (1989)
11. Moore, E.F.: The firing squad synchronization problem. In: Sequential Machines - Selected Papers, pp. 213–214. Addison-Wesley (1964)
12. von Neumann, J.: Probabilistic logics and the synthesis of reliable organisms from unreliable components. In: Automata Studies, pp. 43–98. Princeton University Press (1956)
13. Nishio, H., Kobuchi, Y.: Fault tolerant cellular spaces. J. Comput. Syst. Sci. **11**, 150–170 (1975)
14. Rosenstiehl, P., Fiksel, J.R., Holliger, A.: Intelligent graphs: networks of finite automata capable of solving graph problems. In: Graph Theory and Computing, pp. 219–265. Academic Press (1972)
15. Umeo, H.: A fault-tolerant scheme for optimum-time firing squad synchronization. In: Parallel Computing: Trends and Applications, North-Holland, pp. 223–230 (1994)
16. Umeo, H.: A note on firing squad synchronization algorithms. In: IFIP Cellular Automata Workshop 1996, p. 95. Universität Giessen (1996)
17. Umeo, H.: A simple design of time-efficient firing squad synchronization algorithms with fault-tolerance. IEICE Trans. Inf. Syst. **E87–D**, 733–739 (2004)
18. Umeo, H.: Firing squad synchronization problem in cellular automata. In: Meyers, R.A. (ed.) Encyclopedia of Complexity and System Science, pp. 3537–3574. Springer, New York (2009)
19. Waksman, A.: An optimum solution to the firing squad synchronization problem. Inform. Control **9**, 66–78 (1966)

20. Yunès, J.B.: Fault tolerant solutions to the firing squad synchronization problem. Techical report LITP 96/06, Institut Blaise Pascal (1996)
21. Yunès, J.B.: Goto's construction and Pascal's triangle: new insights into cellular automata synchronization. In: Symposium on Cellular Automata - Journées Automates Cellulaires, JAC 2008, pp. 195–203. MCCME Publishing House (2009)

A Field Based Solution of Mazoyer's FSSP Schema

Luidnel Maignan[1]([⊠]) and Jean-Baptiste Yunès[2]

[1] LACL, Université Paris-Est Créteil, Créteil, France
Luidnel.Maignan@u-pec.fr
[2] IRIF, Université Paris-Diderot, Paris, France
Jean-Baptiste.Yunes@univ-paris-diderot.fr

Abstract. Continuing our line of work on field based cellular automata programming we, here, focus our attention on an implementation of Mazoyer's schema for cellular synchronization problem. Due to its very special nature among the numerous solutions to the problem, we emphasize the power of cellular fields to construct cellular programs: clear semantic construction, modularity, automatic synthesis of finite state machines.

Keywords: Cellular automata · Cellular fields · Synchronization

1 Introduction

In this paper[1], we continue the line of work considering the well-know Firing Squad Synchronization Problem (FSSP) from the novel algorithmic point of view of field based cellular automata initiated in [3].

The problem is to provide a cellular automaton that can be started in different ways and on different numbers and topological arrangements of cells while always leading to a perfect synchronous never happened before event called "fire". The choices of the possible startings on one hand, and of the possible arrangements of cells on the other, lead to apparently different solutions to the problem [7–9].

The aforementioned paper presents a Balzer-like FSSP solution expressed in a direct, semantical, and modular way (see [2,3]). Classical presentations often use a description of an informal intuition of "signals" moving in a continuous space and then, magically "jump" to a finite description of a transition table that includes all the discrete subtleties (see [5,6,10] for examples). Our modularity is obtained by replacing the notion of signals by the concept of (cellular) fields. Fields are opened cellular automata modules that can be composed together to obtain either larger modules or a final classical closed cellular automaton. In these modules, we allow the use of unbounded integers and recursion, as usual in programming, in order to increase expressivity and clarity. The composition

---

[1] This work is partially supported by the French program ANR 12 BS02 007 01.

© Springer International Publishing Switzerland 2016
S. El Yacoubi et al. (Eds.): ACRI 2016, LNCS 9863, pp. 134–143, 2016.
DOI: 10.1007/978-3-319-44365-2_13

is therefore followed by a finitization step that reduces everything to a classical finite state cellular automata.

Acquaintance with this approach is assumed in this paper. To help, preliminary readings might be: the initial paper which deals with the unidimensional case as it is the case in this paper (see [3]) and the writing about the projection process details (see [4]).

Many advantages of this approach are advocated since the beginning: a clearer and more formal/semantical presentation of the solution, an easier and more understandable proof of correctness, a higher level of description allowing the use of recursion and unboundedness, a possible extension to other existing or new solutions, and a clean notion of projection to come back to a finite cellular automata in relation to automata synthesis and minimization.

The contribution of this paper is twofold. First we show what are the necessary variants of the modules built in previous works to build Mazoyer's solution. This sheds some lights on the underlying mechanism of this solution, especially to the critical step of the algorithm, namely the two-third/one-third division. Second, this is also a step forward in demonstrating the generality and advantages of the field-based approach as it allows arbitrary positions of one or many generals. We then give the synchronization times thus obtained. To the knowledge of the authors, this is the first such generalization of this solution.

The paper is organized as follows. In Sect. 2 we start by describing Mazoyer's solution and its peculiarities compared to previous works. We also describe our point of view on this solution in order to provide some guidance to the formal part. In Sect. 3 we describe formally our solution using an infinite recursive tree of fields representing the set of splittings. In Sect. 4 we say a few words about the benefits obtained with this approach.

2   Mazoyer's Solution and its Peculiarities

In this section, we list several points that make Mazoyer's solution remarkable and for which our solution provides alternatives or clarification.

[Symmetry] All the solutions already considered in our work are symmetric, either implementations of existing or new solutions. In particular, they split the whole space in two parts of equal sizes, then split theses parts into two and so on recursively like one can observe in Fig. 1a. Moreover, after each splitting, what happens in the right part is in some way a mirrored and properly scaled image of what happens in the whole (recursion). Mazoyer's solution is asymmetric, while being based on recursive division too, there is no mirroring; its computation is directed (from left to right). This can be easily observed by comparison in Fig. 1b.

[Remainders] Mazoyer's divides at two-third of the space and needs to deal with the three possible remainders of the division by 3, while Balzer's only need to take in account the parity of the length. We will see later how we solved this, but in the original solution this was treated with the help of some trick: a modular counter detects the remainder modulo 3 of the length, and some auxiliaries signals are launched, parallel to the anti-diagonal, that properly delay the launch of scaled copy of the whole process. This can be observed as the non uniform thickness signal going from the first right bouncing to the left cell in Fig. 1b.

[Stripes] Mazoyer's solution use modular counters as the figure clearly exhibits, and this is easily observed on the figure where a lot of stacked stripes are going from right to left. All these counters are dependent one from the other, providing sub-sampled counters as their thickness illustrated it.

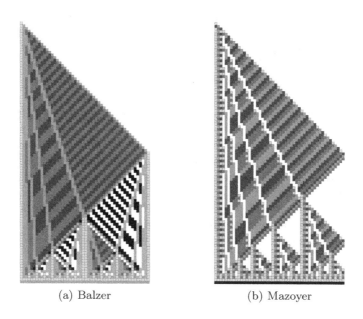

(a) Balzer   (b) Mazoyer

Fig. 1. Space-time diagrams of Balzer's and Mazoyer's solutions for 50 cells.

As our construction is based on a more abstract approach, we will obtain roughly the same schema (after all the "algorithm" is the same) but the final implementation will have some different properties that we will be able to observe on the space-time diagram, in particular our management of the remainders is slightly different and will not produce the stripes. Mazoyer's implementation uses clocking signals while we will use distance field (*i.e.* the right borders will never be aware of the remainder modulo 3 as it is unnecessary). Moreover, we will never mention any signals or speed but only semantical objects such as regions, distances, and cut points. At the end, the "fire" event will be triggered by a purely local decision (is the region of 0-edge size?) and this event will happen for every cell at the same time. This is a local decision with a global emergent effect.

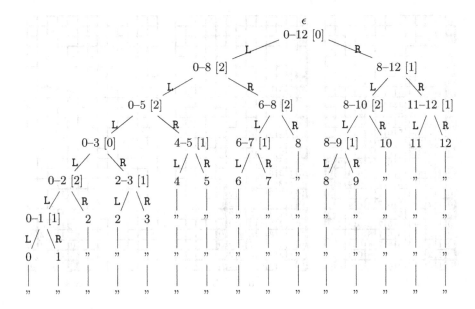

Fig. 2. Seven first levels of the infinite decomposition tree of a line of 13 cells. Each node of the tree is a region. The name of the regions are given by the labels on the path from the root. Unlabeled edges stand both for L and R.

3   Regions Fields and Splitting Fields

As all FSSP solutions, Mazoyer's solution is based on a recursive splitting of the space. This is the first thing that we need to model. Each splitting starts by dynamically determining the extent of the region and builds the corresponding left and right sub-regions of appropriate sizes. Since each region has two sub-regions, we label the regions with words on the alphabet $\{L, R\}$. The regions form an unbounded tree with the initial region (the whole space) ϵ at its root and with each region $u \in \{L, R\}^*$ having two sub-regions uL and uR. This region tree represents the recursive structure of the synchronization algorithm (see Fig. 2).

To represent a region u on the cellular space, we use three boolean fields lbrd^u, ins^u and rbrd^u. The field lbrd^u (resp. rbrd^u) is true at a given cell and timestep if this cell has identified that it is the left (resp. right) border of the region u. The field ins^u is true at a given cell and timestep if this cell has identified that it is strictly inside the region u. Figure 2 indicates the left and right borders of each region, those positions can be the same. The remaining tasks are to specify $\langle \mathrm{lbrd}^\epsilon, \mathrm{ins}^\epsilon, \mathrm{rbrd}^\epsilon \rangle$ and the process going from $\langle \mathrm{lbrd}^u, \mathrm{ins}^u, \mathrm{rbrd}^u \rangle$ to $\langle \mathrm{lbrd}^v, \mathrm{ins}^v, \mathrm{rbrd}^v \rangle$ for $v \in \{uL, uR\}$.

3.1   The Region ϵ

The fields $\langle \mathrm{lbrd}^\epsilon, \mathrm{ins}^\epsilon, \mathrm{rbrd}^\epsilon \rangle$ represent the whole line of cells as they are awaken by the general from neighbors to neighbors. We therefore introduce the field awk

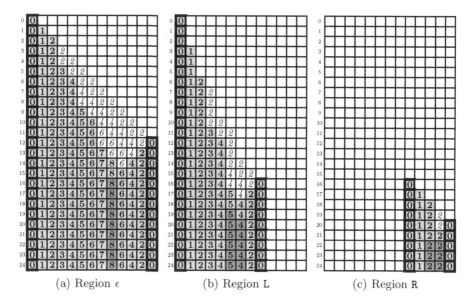

(a) Region ϵ (b) Region L   (c) Region R

Fig. 3. Fields lbrd^u, ins^u, rbrd^u, dst^u, and sta^u for $u \in \{\epsilon, \mathtt{L}, \mathtt{R}\}$

whose dynamics, where $\mathrm{N}(x)$ denotes the neighborhood of x, is:

$$\mathrm{awk}_t(x) = \exists y \in \mathrm{N}(x) \cup \{x\}; \mathrm{awk}_{t-1}(y). \tag{1}$$

Then a cell determines its "region state" when it is awake and do so by examining
its existing neighbors, as:

$$\begin{cases} \mathrm{lbrd}_t^\epsilon(x) = \mathrm{N}(x) = \{ \qquad\quad x+1\} \wedge \mathrm{awk}_t(x). \\ \mathrm{ins}_t^\epsilon(x) = \mathrm{N}(x) = \{x-1, x+1\} \wedge \mathrm{awk}_t(x). \\ \mathrm{rbrd}_t^\epsilon(x) = \mathrm{N}(x) = \{x-1 \qquad\quad\} \wedge \mathrm{awk}_t(x). \end{cases} \tag{2}$$

The dynamics of these fields is shown in spatio-temporal diagram of Fig. 3a:
blank cells represent the field awk^ϵ where it is false, cells for which either lbrd^ϵ
or rbrd^ϵ is true are drawn with a bold border, cells containing a strictly positive
value are those for which ins^ϵ is true.

3.2 Distance Information for Arbitrary Region u

The specificity of Mazoyer's schema is that, given a region u, its cut point is at the
two-third of the space. In order to determine it, we use the central building block
of all our solutions: a distance field. For the FSSP, this (integer) field usually
computes, for each cell, the distance to the nearest border using the hop-count
distance. For Balzer-like solutions, this allows to easily detect the middle of the
space as being the point the most far away from both borders. In other words,
the middle is the local maxima of the distance field. The simple modification

needed to use the same in order to obtain the two-third of the space is to add a weight in each direction and consider a "directed weighted-hop-count distance". Starting from any cell, a step to the right counts for one while a step to the left counts for two. With these weights, the two-third cut point is the most far away point from both borders. The weighted distance field equation to obtain the minimal distance to the borders is:

$$\mathrm{dst}_t^u(x) = \begin{cases} 0 & \text{if } \neg\mathrm{ins}_t^u(x) \\ \min(\mathrm{dst}_{t-1}^u(x-1)+1\,,\ \mathrm{dst}_{t-1}^u(x+1)+2) & \text{otherwise} \end{cases} \quad (3)$$

Figures 3a, b and c show the distance fields dynamics for different set of region fields $\langle \mathrm{lbrd}, \mathrm{ins}, \mathrm{rbrd}\rangle$. The blank cells are those where none of the region fields is true, the non-blank one have the obvious region field (either lbrd, ins, or rbrd) set to true. The distance value in bold cells (borders) and in the blank cells is obviously 0.

Regarding the distance field, one should consider that the region fields are determined by an arbitrary process. The most important property for the remainder of the construction is that for any cell, if a region field becomes true, it remains so forever. Of course, we also need some trivialities, e.g. that the left border is at the left of the right border. If these properties are respected, the distance field eventually converges to the correct distance values in a monotonous way as can be observed in Fig. 3.

3.3 Stability of the Distance Information

As usual, we also compute whether the distance value is stable, which means that it will not evolve anymore. The first stability case is when a cell is a border, i.e. when lbrd or rbrd are true. In this case the distance value equals to 0 and is stable. The other cases are when the distance value just obtained has been computed from a stable read from the left or the right. The monotonicity of the distance field evolution implies the stability of the distance value computed in this way. The stability field dynamics is given by the following equations (superscript u is omitted for the sake of readability):

$$\mathrm{sta}_t(x) = \bigvee \begin{cases} \mathrm{lbrd}_t(x) \vee \mathrm{rbrd}_t(x) \\ \mathrm{ins}_t(x) \wedge \mathrm{dst}_t(x) = \mathrm{dst}_{t-1}(x-1)+1 \wedge \mathrm{sta}_{t-1}(x-1) \\ \mathrm{ins}_t(x) \wedge \mathrm{dst}_t(x) = \mathrm{dst}_{t-1}(x+1)+2 \wedge \mathrm{sta}_{t-1}(x+1) \end{cases} \quad (4)$$

On Fig. 3, the stable cells are indicated with a gray background. One can note that their speed of evolution is exactly the speed of the signals set up in the Mazoyer's original solution. In the following, we often need to consider distance values only when they are stable (see Eqs. (5), (6), (7), and (8)). We introduce two notations corresponding to stable distances and an "equality" that can only be true for stable distances. We use ∞ with an absorbing property: $\infty + n = \infty$.

$$\mathrm{Dst}_t(x) = \begin{cases} \mathrm{dst}_t(x) & \text{if } \mathrm{sta}_t(x) \\ \infty & \text{otherwise;} \end{cases}$$

$$D_0 \simeq D_1 \iff D_0 = D_1 \wedge D_0 \neq \infty \wedge D_1 \neq \infty.$$

3.4   Cut Points of Region u and Sub-Regions uL and uR

The first thing to note is that we build the splitting with the distance field. This distance represents the weighted-hop-count to borders, and is therefore more concerned with edges between cells than by cells themselves. For that reason, it is better to adopt a edge-centric point of view. In the following, we number the cells from left to right from 0 to e, e being the number of edges, the number of cells is then $n = e + 1$.

When the number of edges is a multiple of 3, the local maximum of the distance field is exactly located at the cell $\frac{e}{3}$. There are $\frac{2e}{3}$ edges at its left and $\frac{e}{3}$ edges at its right and the cell $\frac{e}{3}$ is used both as right border for the left sub-region and as left border for the right sub-region. This corresponds to the dark gray cells in Fig. 3a, and to the right and left borders in Fig. 3b and c respectively.

When the number of edges is not a multiple of 3, the real cut point is supposed to be at position $\frac{e}{3}$, but this may fall between two cells (*i.e.* on an edge). The left approximation is therefore $\lfloor\frac{e}{3}\rfloor$ and the right is $\lceil\frac{e}{3}\rceil$. The left approximation is used as right border for the left sub-region and conversely for the right approximation. The region depicted in Fig. 3b has a number of edges $e_L = 2$ (mod 3) and the one of Fig. 3c has $e_R = 1$ (mod 3) and the positions of their dark gray cells are precisely at these approximations.

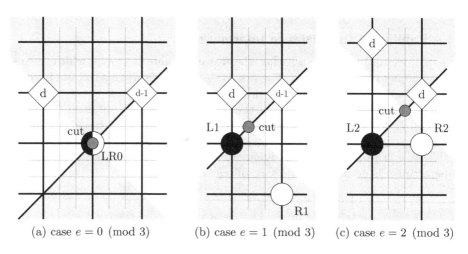

(a) case $e = 0$ (mod 3)   (b) case $e = 1$ (mod 3)   (c) case $e = 2$ (mod 3)

Fig. 4. Spatio-temporal approximation of the cut points: Time increases downward, cell positions increase rightward.

In order to construct these left and right approximations, we need everything to happen as if the real cut point (may it be on an edge) is really detected. This is crucial for the timing of the synchronization. It is possible to write a single formula for this detection process but since there are only three cases, it is clearer to spell out everything explicitly. Figure 4 shows the three cases on a refined grid. For instance, Fig. 4b shows the real cut point for a region of size

$e = 1 \pmod 3$ together with its past and future information cone (also called light-cone). In its past cone, the diamonds correspond to the nearest neighbor cells that are therefore examined to detect the cut point. Since the cut point is the point the most far away from both borders, if its distance value is c, then the left diamond should have distance value $d_1 = c - \frac{1}{3} \times 1$ and the right diamond $d_2 = c - \frac{2}{3} \times 2$. The fractions are the non-weighted distance to the cut point and the factor is the direction weights. Clearly $d_2 = d_1 - 1$ as shown in the diamonds. In the future cone of the cut point, its existence can be detected by the left (black circle) and right (white circle) approximation cells. The cases (a), (b), and (c) correspond exactly to the way the gray cells appear in Fig. 3a, b and c respectively. Equations (5) and (6) are obtained by taking the spatio-temporal position of the diamonds relatively to the black and white circles respectively. The fourth case of both formulas corresponds to the degenerated case of a 0-edge region, *i.e.* $e = 0$.

$$
\mathrm{lcut}_t(x) = \bigvee \begin{cases} \mathrm{Dst}_{t-1}(x-1) - 1 \simeq \mathrm{Dst}_{t-1}(x+1) & (\mathrm{LR0}) \\ \mathrm{Dst}_{t-1}(x) \quad -1 \simeq \mathrm{Dst}_{t-1}(x+1) & (\mathrm{L1}) \\ \mathrm{Dst}_{t-2}(x) \quad \simeq \mathrm{Dst}_{t-1}(x+1) & (\mathrm{L2}) \\ \mathrm{lbrd}_t(x) \wedge \mathrm{rbrd}_t(x) \end{cases} \tag{5}
$$

$$
\mathrm{rcut}_t(x) = \bigvee \begin{cases} \mathrm{Dst}_{t-1}(x-1) - 1 \simeq \mathrm{Dst}_{t-1}(x+1) & (\mathrm{LR0}) \\ \mathrm{Dst}_{t-2}(x-1) - 1 \simeq \mathrm{Dst}_{t-2}(x) & (\mathrm{R1}) \\ \mathrm{Dst}_{t-2}(x-1) \quad \simeq \mathrm{Dst}_{t-1}(x) & (\mathrm{R2}) \\ \mathrm{lbrd}_t(x) \wedge \mathrm{rbrd}_t(x) \end{cases} \tag{6}
$$

These two last equations detect the local maxima of the distance field. Its two slopes are also needed. Since all the neighbors of any cell located on the left side have the same nearest border, we can easily deduce that the difference between their values should be $+2$ by using the same reasoning on distance differences used above (Fig. 3b). Similarly, the difference should be -4 for the right slope cells.

$$
\mathrm{lins}_t(x) = \mathrm{Dst}_{t-1}(x-1) + 2 \simeq \mathrm{Dst}_{t-1}(x+1) \tag{7}
$$

$$
\mathrm{rins}_t(x) = \mathrm{Dst}_{t-1}(x-1) - 4 \simeq \mathrm{Dst}_{t-1}(x+1) \tag{8}
$$

The following equations only make explicit the corresponding region fields, while making sure that the right sub-region behaves as the whole space (compare Eqs. (10) and (11) with Eqs. (1) and (2)).

$$
\begin{cases} \mathrm{lbrd}_t^{u\mathsf{L}}(x) = \mathrm{lbrd}_t^{u}(x) \\ \mathrm{ins}_t^{u\mathsf{L}}(x) = \mathrm{lins}_t^{u}(x) \\ \mathrm{rbrd}_t^{u\mathsf{L}}(x) = \mathrm{lcut}_t^{u}(x) \end{cases} \tag{9}
$$

$$
\mathrm{rawk}_t^{u}(x) = \mathrm{rcut}_t^{u}(x) \vee \mathrm{rawk}_{t-1}^{u}(x-1) \tag{10}
$$

$$\begin{cases} \mathrm{lbrd}_t^{uR}(x) = \mathrm{rcut}_t^u(x) \ \wedge \ \mathrm{rawk}_t^u(x) \\ \mathrm{ins}_t^{uR}(x) = \mathrm{rins}_t^u(x) \ \wedge \ \mathrm{rawk}_t^u(x) \\ \mathrm{rbrd}_t^{uR}(x) = \mathrm{rbrd}_t^u(x) \ \wedge \ \mathrm{rawk}_t^u(x) \end{cases} \tag{11}$$

With this last touch, we fully reproduce the Mazoyer's schema. One can see that this matches the relations between the diagrams of Fig. 3.

Figure 5a illustrates the global behavior of our implementation. The "fire" event is triggered when a region of size 0-edge is built. A cell detects such event by observing if it is both its leftmost and rightmost cells of its region.

$$\mathrm{fir}_t(x) = \exists u \in \{\mathrm{L}, \mathrm{R}\}^*, \mathrm{lbrd}_t^u(x) \wedge \mathrm{rbrd}_t^u(x) \tag{12}$$

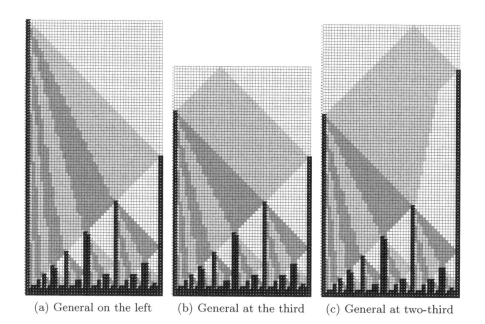

(a) General on the left   (b) General at the third   (c) General at two-third

Fig. 5. Stacking up of the regions reveals the global structure of the Mazoyer's schema.

4   Multi-generals, Synchronization Time, and Conclusion

As we state in the beginning, using fields has several benefits. Among them this solution is able to synchronize the space for many different initializations. The solution works for a general at any position.

The minimal synchronization time is achieved when the general in the left third of the space. More precisely, a line of size n with the general at position $g \in \{0, \ldots, e = n - 1\}$ synchronizes at time $\lceil \max(g + \frac{2e}{3}, e - g + \frac{e}{3}) + \frac{2e}{3} \rceil$.

Figure 5 shows the global structure of the spatio-temporal diagram generated by our solution for different position of the general. These figures are obtained by showing for each cell and timestep a color corresponding to the parity of the depth of the region having a "meaningful state".

The solution also works for many generals without any modifications since very little properties are needed from the region fields as explained earlier.

In this solution there exists a temporal dependency of order 2 (Eqs. (5) and (6)), but a close look will reveal that we don't need the full neighborhood of order two but only a temporal shift, it is a CA with memory (see [1]).

We did not implement the reduction to a finite CA, but as we did not modify any of the properties that are necessary to obtain such, the process we previously used will work (see [4]).

References

1. Alonso-Sanz, R., Martin, M.: Elementary cellular automata with memory. Complex Syst. **14**, 99–126 (2003)
2. Balzer, R.: An 8-state minimal time solution to the firing squad synchronization problem. Inf. Control **10**(1), 22–42 (1967). http://www.sciencedirect.com/science/article/pii/S0019995867900320
3. Maignan, L., Yunès, J.-B.: A spatio-temporal algorithmic point of view on firing squad synchronisation problem. In: Sirakoulis, G.C., Bandini, S. (eds.) ACRI 2012. LNCS, vol. 7495, pp. 101–110. Springer, Heidelberg (2012). http://dx.doi.org/10.1007/978-3-642-33350-7_11
4. Maignan, L., Yunès, J.-B.: Experimental finitization of infinite field-based generalized FSSP solution. In: Wąs, J., Sirakoulis, G.C., Bandini, S. (eds.) ACRI 2014. LNCS, vol. 8751, pp. 136–145. Springer, Heidelberg (2014). http://dx.doi.org/10.1007/978-3-319-11520-7_15
5. Mazoyer, J.: A six-state minimal time solution to the firing squad synchronization problem. Theoret. Comput. Sci. **50**(2), 183–238 (1987). http://www.sciencedirect.com/science/article/pii/0304397587901241
6. Noguchi, K.: Simple 8-state minimal time solution to the firing squad synchronization problem. Theoret. Comput. Sci. **314**(3), 303–334 (2004). http://www.sciencedirect.com/science/article/pii/S0304397503004250
7. Schmid, H., Worsch, T.: The firing squad synchronization problem with many generals for one-dimensional CA. In: Levy, J.J., Mayr, E.W., Mitchell, J.C. (eds.) Exploring New Frontiers of Theoretical Informatics. IFIP, vol. 155, pp. 111–124. Springer, Heidelberg (2004)
8. Swerinski, H.: Time-optimum solution of the firing-squad-synchronization-problem for n-dimensional rectangles with the general at an arbitrary position. Theoret. Comput. Sci. **19**, 305–320 (1982)
9. Umeo, H., Kubo, K., Takahashi, Y.: An isotropic optimum-time FSSP algorithm for two-dimensional cellular automata. In: Malyshkin, V. (ed.) PaCT 2013. LNCS, vol. 7979, pp. 381–393. Springer, Heidelberg (2013)
10. Waksman, A.: An optimum solution to the firing squad synchronization problem. Inf. Control **9**(1), 66–78 (1966). http://www.sciencedirect.com/science/article/pii/S0019995866901100

A Class of Minimum-Time Minimum-State-Change Generalized FSSP Algorithms

Hiroshi Umeo[✉] and Keisuke Imai

University of Osaka Electro-Communication,
Hastu-cho, 18-8, Neyagawa-shi, Osaka 572-8530, Japan
umeo@cyt.osakac.ac.jp

Abstract. The firing squad synchronization problem (FSSP, for short) on cellular automata has been studied extensively for more than fifty years, and a rich variety of FSSP algorithms has been proposed. Here we consider the FSSP from a view point of state-change-complexity that models the energy consumption of SRAM-type storage with which cellular automata might be built. In the present paper, we propose a class of minimum-time, minimum-state-change generalized FSSP (GFSSP, for short) algorithms for synchronizing any one-dimensional (1D) cellular automaton, where the synchronization operations are started from any cell in the array. We construct two minimum-time minimum-state-change GFSSP algorithms: one is based on Goto's algorithm, known as the first minimum-time FSSP algorithm that is reconstructed again recently in Umeo et al. [13], and the other is based on Gerken's one. These algorithms are optimum not only in time but also in state-change complexity.

1 Introduction

We study a synchronization problem that gives a finite-state protocol for synchronizing large-scale cellular automata. The synchronization in cellular automata has been known as a firing squad synchronization problem (FSSP) since its development, in which it was originally proposed by J. Myhill in Moore [6] to synchronize some/all parts of self-reproducing cellular automata. The problem has been studied extensively for more than fifty years, and a rich variety of synchronization algorithms has been proposed.

Here we consider the FSSP from a view point of state-change-complexity that models the energy consumption of SRAM-type storage with which cellular automata might be built. In the present paper, we propose a class of $n - 2 + \max(k, n - k + 1)$ minimum-time, $\Theta(n \log n)$ minimum-state-change generalized FSSP (GFSSP, for short) algorithms for synchronizing any one-dimensional (1D) cellular automaton of length n, where the synchronization operations are started from any cell k $(1 \leq k \leq n)$ in the array. We construct two minimum-time minimum-state-change GFSSP algorithms, one is based on Goto's algorithm, known as the first minimum-time FSSP algorithm that is reconstructed again

© Springer International Publishing Switzerland 2016
S. El Yacoubi et al. (Eds.): ACRI 2016, LNCS 9863, pp. 144–154, 2016.
DOI: 10.1007/978-3-319-44365-2_14

recently in Umeo et al. [13], and the other is based on Gerken's one. The Goto-based GFSSP algorithm is realized on a cellular automaton with 434 internal states and 13328 state-transition rules. The Gerken-based one is implemented on a cellular automaton with 215 internal states and 4077 state-transition rules. These algorithms are optimum not only in time but also in the state-change complexity. The implemented minimum-time GFSSP algorithms are the first ones having the minimum-state-change complexity.

In Sect. 2 we give a description of the 1D FSSP and review some basic results on FSSP and GFSSP algorithms. Section 3 gives new implementations and generalizations to the GFSSP algorithm having minimum-state-change complexity.

2   Firing Squad Synchronization Problem

2.1   Definition of Firing Squad Synchronization Problem

The firing squad synchronization problem (FSSP, for short) is formalized in terms of a model of cellular automata. Consider a 1D array of finite state automata. All cells (except the end cells) are identical finite state automata. The array operates in lock-step mode such that the next state of each cell (except the end cells) is determined by both its own present state and the present states of its right and left neighbors. All cells (*soldiers*), except one *general* cell, are initially in the *quiescent* state at time $t = 0$ and have the property whereby the next state of a quiescent cell having quiescent neighbors is the quiescent state. At time $t = 0$ the *general* cell is in the *fire-when-ready* state, which is an initiation signal to the array. The FSSP is stated as follows: given an array of n identical cellular automata, including a *general* on the left end which is activated at time $t = 0$, we want to give the description (state set and next-state transition function) of the automata so that, *at some future time*, all of the cells will *simultaneously* and, *for the first time*, enter a special *firing* state. The initial general is on the left end of the array in the original FSSP.

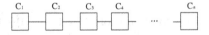

Fig. 1. A one-dimensional (1D) cellular automaton.

Figure 1 shows a finite 1D cellular array consisting of n cells, denoted by C_i, where $1 \leq i \leq n$. The set of states and the next-state transition function must be independent of n. Without loss of generality, we assume $n \geq 2$. The tricky part of the problem is that the same kind of soldiers having a fixed number of states must be synchronized, regardless of the length n of the array.

A formal definition of the FSSP is as follows: a cellular automaton $\mathcal{M}$ is a pair $\mathcal{M} = (\mathcal{Q}, \delta)$, where

1. $\mathcal{Q}$ is a finite set of states with three distinguished states G, Q, and F. G is an initial general state, Q is a quiescent state, and F is a firing state, respectively.
2. δ is a next state function such that $\delta : \mathcal{Q} \cup \{*\} \times \mathcal{Q} \times \mathcal{Q} \cup \{*\} \to \mathcal{Q}$. The state $* \notin \mathcal{Q}$ is a pseudo state of the border of the array.
3. The quiescent state Q must satisfy the following conditions: $\delta(Q, Q, Q) = \delta(*, Q, Q) = \delta(Q, Q, *) = Q$.

A cellular automaton $\mathcal{M}_n$ of length n, consisting of n copies of $\mathcal{M}$, is a 1D array whose positions are numbered from 1 to n. Each $\mathcal{M}$ is referred to as a cell and denoted by C_i, where $1 \leq i \leq n$. We denote a state of C_i at time (step) t by S_i^t, where $t \geq 0, 1 \leq i \leq n$. A *configuration* of $\mathcal{M}_n$ at time t is a function $\mathcal{C}^t : [1, n] \to \mathcal{Q}$ and denoted as $S_1^t S_2^t \dots S_n^t$. A *computation* of $\mathcal{M}_n$ is a sequence of configurations of $\mathcal{M}_n$, $\mathcal{C}^0, \mathcal{C}^1, \mathcal{C}^2, \dots, \mathcal{C}^t, \dots$, where $\mathcal{C}^0$ is a given initial configuration. The configuration at time $t + 1$, $\mathcal{C}^{t+1}$, is computed by synchronous applications of the next transition function δ to each cell of $\mathcal{M}_n$ in $\mathcal{C}^t$ such that:

$$S_1^{t+1} = \delta(*, S_1^t, S_2^t), \; S_i^{t+1} = \delta(S_{i-1}^t, S_i^t, S_{i+1}^t), \text{ and } S_n^{t+1} = \delta(S_{n-1}^t, S_n^t, *).$$

A *synchronized configuration* of $\mathcal{M}_n$ at time t is a configuration $\mathcal{C}^t$, $S_i^t = F$, for any $1 \leq i \leq n$.

The FSSP is to obtain an $\mathcal{M}$ such that, for any $n \geq 2$,

1. A synchronized configuration at time $t = T(n)$, $\mathcal{C}^{T(n)} = \overbrace{F, \cdots, F}^{n}$ can be computed from an initial configuration $\mathcal{C}^0 = G \overbrace{Q, \cdots, Q}^{n-1}$.
2. For any t, i such that $1 \leq t \leq T(n) - 1$, $1 \leq i \leq n, S_i^t \neq F$.

The generalized FSSP (GFSSP) is to obtain an $\mathcal{M}$ such that, for any $n \geq 2$ and for any k such that $1 \leq k \leq n$,

1. A synchronized configuration at time $t = T(k, n)$, $\mathcal{C}^{T(k,n)} = \overbrace{F, \cdots, F}^{n}$ can be computed from an initial configuration $\mathcal{C}^0 = \overbrace{Q, \cdots, Q}^{k-1} G \overbrace{Q, \cdots, Q}^{n-k}$.
2. For any t, i, such that $1 \leq t \leq T(k, n) - 1$, $1 \leq i \leq n, S_i^t \neq F$.

No cells fire before time $t = T(k, n)$. We say that $\mathcal{M}_n$ is synchronized at time $t = T(k, n)$ and the function $T(k, n)$ is a time complexity for the synchronization.

2.2 Some Related Results on FSSP and GFSSP

Here we summarize some basic results on FSSP algorithms.

- **Minimum-time FSSP algorithms with a general at one end**
  The FSSP problem was first solved by J. McCarthy and M. Minsky who presented a $3n$-step algorithm for n cells. In 1962, the first minimum-time,

i.e. $(2n - 2)$-step, synchronization algorithm was presented by Goto [3], with each cell having several thousands of states. Waksman [16] presented a 16-state minimum-time synchronization algorithm. Afterward, Balzer [1] and Gerken [2] developed an eight-state algorithm and a seven-state synchronization algorithm, respectively, thus decreasing the number of states required for the synchronization. In 1987, Mazoyer [4] developed a six-state synchronization algorithm which, at present, is the algorithm having the fewest states.

Theorem 1 (Goto [3], Waksman [16]). There exists a cellular automaton that can synchronize any 1D array of length n in minimum $2n - 2$ steps, where the general is located at a left (or right) end.

- **Generalized minimum-time FSSP algorithms**
  The generalized FSSP (GFSSP, for short) has also been studied, where an initial general can be located at any position in the array. The same kind of soldiers having a fixed number of states must be synchronized, regardless of the position k of the general and the length n of the array. Moore and Langdon [7] first studied the problem and presented a 17-state minimum-time GFSSP algorithm, i.e. operating in $n - 2 + \max(k, n - k + 1)$ steps for n cells with the general on the kth cell from left end of the array. See Umeo et al. [12] for a survey on GFSSP algorithms and their implementations. Concerning the GFSSP, it has been shown impossible to synchronize any array of length n in less than $n - 2 + \max(k, n - k + 1)$ steps, where the general is located on C_k, $1 \leq k \leq n$.

Theorem 2 (Moore and Langdon [7] (Lower Bounds)). The minimum-time in which the generalized firing squad synchronization could occur is no earlier than $n - 2 + \max(k, n - k + 1)$ steps, where the general is located on the kth cell from left end.

Theorem 3 (Umeo et al. [12]). There exists an 8-state cellular automaton that can synchronize any 1D array of length n in minimum $n - 2 + \max(k, n - k + 1)$ steps, where the general is located on the kth cell from left end.

3   A Class of Minimum-Time, Minimum-State-Change GFSSP Algorithms

3.1   Designing Minimum-Time GFSSP Algorithms

In this section we develop a general methodology for designing a minimum-time GFSSP algorithm based on freezing-thawing technique. We can construct a minimum-time GFSSP algorithm from any minimum-time FSSP algorithm with a general at one end. The *freezing-thawing technique* developed in Umeo [10] enables us to have an FSSP algorithm with an arbitrary synchronization delay for 1D arrays. The freezing-thawing technique can be employed efficiently for the design of a minimum-time, minimum-state-change GFSSP algorithms in Sects. 3.3 and 3.4. The technique is described as follows:

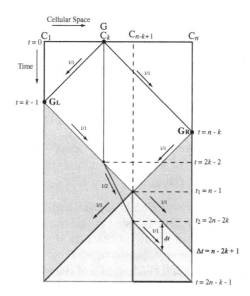

Fig. 2. Space-time diagram for the construction of minimum-time GFSSP algorithm.

Theorem 4 (Umeo [10]). *Let t_0, t_1, t_2 and Δt be any integer such that $t_0 \geq 0$, $t_1 = t_0 + n - 1$, $t_1 \leq t_2$ and $\Delta t = t_2 - t_1$. We assume that a usual synchronization operation is started at time $t = t_0$ by generating a special signal which acts as a general at the left end of 1D array of length n. We also assume that the right end cell of the array receives another special signals from outside at time $t_1 = t_0 + n - 1$ and $t_2 = t_1 + \Delta t$, respectively. Then, there exists a 1D cellular automaton that can synchronize the array of length n at time $t = t_0 + 2n - 2 + \Delta t$.*

Consider a cellular array C_1, C_2, ..., C_n of length n with an initial general on C_k, where $1 \leq k \leq n$. At time $t = 0$ the general sends a unit speed (1 cell/1 step) signal to both ends. The cell C_k keeps its state to indicate its initial position on the array. The signal reaches at the left and right ends at time $t = k - 1$ and $t = n - k$, respectively, and generates a new general, denoted as G_L and G_R at each end. In Fig. 2, we illustrate a space-time diagram for the GFSSP construction. Each general, G_L and G_R, starts minimum-time synchronization operations for the cellular space where the general is at its end by sending out a wake-up signal. At time $t = n - 1$ the two signals collide with each other on the cell C_{n-k+1} and the cellular space is divided into two parts by the collision. First, we consider the case where the initial general is in the left half of the given cellular space, i.e. $k \leq n - k + 1$. The wake-up signal generated by G_L reaches C_k at time $t = 2k - 2$, then collides with the wake-up signal generated by G_R. The larger part (left one in this case) is synchronized by a usual way, however, the small one is synchronized with time delay $\Delta t = n - 2k + 1$. The wake-up signal for the larger part splits into two signals on C_k, one is an original wake-up

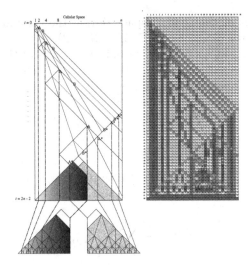

Fig. 3. An overview of the reconstructed Goto's FSSP algorithm (left) and its snapshots on 32 cells of the 166-state, 4378-transition-rule implementation in Umeo et al. [13].

signal and the other is a new slow signal which follows the wake-up signal at $1/2$-speed. Note that the wake-up signal for the smaller part (right one in this case) never reaches C_k. As for the synchronization for the smaller part, a freezing-signal is generated at time $t_1 = n - 1$ on C_{n-k+1} and the state configuration in the smaller part is frozen by the propagation of the $1/1$-speed right-going freezing signal. At time $t_2 = 2n - 2k$, the split slow signal reaches C_{n-k+1} and there a thawing signal is generated. The thawing signal thaws the frozen configuration progressively. Theorem 4 shows that the smaller part of length k is synchronized at time $t = 2n - k - 1$. The larger part is also synchronized at time $t = 2n - k - 1$. Thus, the whole space can be synchronized at time $t = 2n - k - 1 = n - 2 + \max(k, n - k + 1)$. Similar discussions can be made in the case where the initial general is in the right half of the cellular space. It is seen that any minimum-time FSSP algorithm with a general at one end can be embedded as a sub-algorithm for the synchronization of divided parts. A similar technique was used for solving FSSP with many generals in Schmid and Worsch [8]. Thus, we have:

Theorem 5. The schema given above can realize a minimum-time GFSSP algorithm by implementing two minimum-time FSSP algorithms with a general at one end.

3.2 State-Change Complexity

Vollmar [15] introduced a *state-change complexity* in order to measure the efficiency of cellular automata, motivated by energy consumption in certain SRAM-type memory systems. The state-change complexity is defined as the sum of *proper* state changes of the cellular space during the computations. A formal definition is as follows: Consider an FSSP (GFSSP) algorithm operating on n cells. Let $T(n)$ (resp., $T(k,n)$) be synchronization steps of the FSSP (GFSSP) algorithm. We define a matrix C of size $T(n) \times n$ ($T(n)$ rows, n columns) (resp., $T(k,n) \times n$ ($T(k,n)$ rows, n columns)) over $\{0,1\}$, where each element $c_{i,j}$ on ith row, jth column of the matrix C is defined:

$$c_{i,j} = \begin{cases} 1 & \mathbf{S}_i^j \neq \mathbf{S}_i^{j-1} \\ 0 & otherwise. \end{cases} \tag{1}$$

The state-change complexity $SC(n)$(resp., $SC_g(n)$) of the FSSP (GFSSP) algorithm is the sum of 1's elements in C defined as:

$$SC(n) = \sum_{j=1}^{T(n)} \sum_{i=1}^{n} c_{i,j}, \tag{2}$$

$$SC_g(n) = 1/n \sum_{k=1}^{n} \sum_{j=1}^{T(k,n)} \sum_{i=1}^{n} c_{i,j}. \tag{3}$$

Vollmar [15] showed that $\Omega(n \log n)$ state-changes are required for synchronizing n cells in $(2n-2)$ steps.

Theorem 6 (Vollmar [15]). $\Omega(n \log n)$ state-change is necessary for synchronizing n cells in minimum-steps.

Gerken [2] presented a minimum-time, $\Theta(n \log n)$ minimum-state-change FSSP algorithm with a general at one end.

Theorem 7 (Gerken [2]). $\Theta(n \log n)$ state-change is sufficient for synchronizing n cells in $2n-2$ steps.

Goto's algorithm (Goto [3]) has been known as the first minimum-time FSSP algorithm, however the paper itself has been a mysterious one for a long time due to its hard accessibility. Umeo [9] reconstructed the Goto's algorithm and it is noted in Umeo [11] that the algorithm has $\Theta(n \log n)$ minimum-state-change complexity. Mazoyer [5] also reconstructed the algorithm again. Yunès [17] gave a new construction of Goto-like algorithms using the Wolfram's rule 60. Recently, Umeo et al. [13] reconstructed the Goto's algorithm again and realized it on a cellular automaton having 166-state and 4378 transition rules.

Theorem 8 (Umeo [11], Umeo et al. [13]). The reconstructed Goto's algorithm has $\Theta(n \log n)$ state-change complexity for synchronizing n cells in $2n-2$ steps.

In order to get a minimum-time, minimum-state-change GFSSP algorithm, we embed the reconstructed Goto's algorithm and Gerken's one with a general at one end. The state-change complexity in the right and left parts in Fig. 2 is

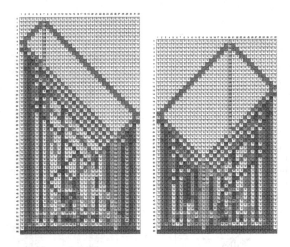

Fig. 4. Snapshots of configurations for Goto-based minimum-time, minimum-state-change GFSSP algorithm developed on $n = 32$ cells with a general on C_7 (left) and C_{20} (right), respectively.

$O((n - k + 1) \log(n - k + 1))$ and $O(k \log k)$, respectively, thus the total state-change-complexity of the constructed GFSSP algorithm is $O((n - k + 1) \log(n - k + 1)) + O(k \log k) \leq O(n \log n)$.

Thus, we have:

Theorem 9. There exists a minimum-time, minimum-state-change GFSSP algorithm.

3.3   An Implementation of Goto-Based Minimum-Time, Minimum-State-Change GFSSP Algorithm

The algorithm that Umeo [9] reconstructed is a non-recursive algorithm consisting of a marking phase and a $3n$-step synchronization phase. In the first phase, by printing a special marker in the cellular space, the entire cellular space is divided into many smaller subspaces, each length of which increases exponentially with a common ratio of two, that is 2^j, for any integer $j \geq 1$. The exponential marking is made by counting cells from both left and right ends of a given cellular space. In the second phase, each subspace is synchronized by starting a well-known conventional $3n$-step synchronization algorithm from center point of each divided subspace. Figure 3 illustrates an overview of the reconstructed Goto's algorithm. It can be seen that the overall algorithm does not call itself. Based on the reconstructed Goto's algorithm, we realize a minimum-time, minimum-state-change GFSSP algorithm on a cellular automaton with 434 internal states and 13328 state-transition rules. Figure 4 shows some snapshots for the constructed GFSSP algorithm on 32 cells with a general on C_7 (left) and C_{20} (right), respectively.

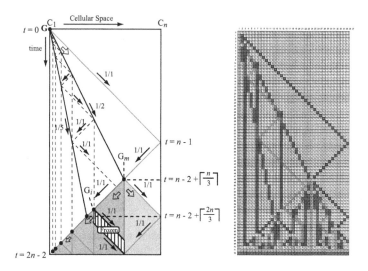

Fig. 5. Space-time diagram of Gerken's FSSP algorithm (left) and its snapshots on 37 cells.

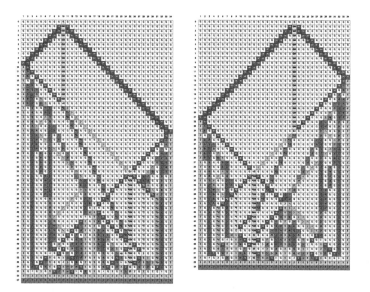

Fig. 6. Snapshots of configurations of Gerken-based minimum-time, minimum-state-change GFSSP algorithm developed on $n = 34$ cells with a general on C_{10} (left) and C_{22} (right), respectively.

3.4 An Implementation of Gerken-Based Minimum-Time, Minimum-State-Change GFSSP Algorithm

Gerken [2] constructed a minimum-time 157-state FSSP algorithm and showed that the algorithm has a minimum-state-change complexity. The algorithm is the first one having the $\Theta(n \log n)$ minimum-state-change complexity for synchronizing n cells with a general at one end. Figure 5 gives a space-time diagram for the algorithm (left) and some snapshots for the synchronization processes on 37 cells. Based on the algorithm, we realize a minimum-time, minimum-state-change GFSSP algorithm on a cellular automaton with 215 internal states and 4077 state-transition rules. Figure 6 shows some snapshots for the constructed GFSSP algorithm on 34 cells with a general on C_{10} (left) and C_{22} (right), respectively. Different snapshots can be found in Umeo et al. [14].

4 Summary

We studied the FSSP from a view point of state-change-complexity that models the energy consumption of SRAM-type storage with which cellular automata might be built. We have constructed two minimum-time minimum-state-change GFSSP algorithms: one is based on Goto's algorithm, known as the first minimum-time FSSP algorithm, and the other is based on Gerken's one. The Goto-based GFSSP algorithm is realized on a cellular automaton with 434 internal states and 13328 state-transition rules. The Gerken-based one is implemented on a cellular automaton with 215 internal states and 4077 state-transition rules. These algorithms are optimum not only in time but also in the state-change complexity. The implemented minimum-time GFSSP algorithms are the first ones having the minimum-state-change complexity.

References

1. Balzer, R.: An 8-state minimal time solution to the firing squad synchronization problem. Inf. Control **10**, 22–42 (1967)
2. Gerken, H.D.: Über Synchronisationsprobleme bei Zellularautomaten. Diplomarbeit, Institut für Theoretische Informatik, Technische Universität Braunschweig, p. 50 (1987)
3. Goto, E.: A minimal time solution of the firing squad problem. Dittoed course notes for Applied Mathematics 298, Harvard University, pp. 52–59 (1962)
4. Mazoyer, J.: A six-state minimal time solution to the firing squad synchronization problem. Theoret. Comput. Sci. **50**, 183–238 (1987)
5. Mazoyer, J.: A minimal-time solution to the FSSP without recursive call to itself and with bounded slope of signals. Unpublished draft version, pp. 1–25 (1997)
6. Moore, E.F.: The firing squad synchronization problem. In: Moore, E.F. (ed.) Sequential Machines, Selected Papers, pp. 213–214. Addison-Wesley, Reading MA (1964)
7. Moore, F.R., Langdon, G.G.: A generalized firing squad problem. Inf. Control **12**, 212–220 (1968)

8. Schmid, H., Worsch, T.: The firing squad synchronization problem with many generals for one-dimensional CA. In: Proceedings of IFIP World Congress, pp. 111–124 (2004)

9. Umeo, H.: A note on firing squad synchronization algorithms - a reconstruction of Goto's first-in-the-world optimum-time firing squad synchronization algorithm. In: Kutrib, M., Worsch, T. (eds.) Proceedings of IFIP Cellular Automata Workshop. 1996, Schloss Rauischholzhausen, Giessen, Germany, p. 65 (1996)

10. Umeo, H.: A simple design of time-efficient firing squad synchronization algorithms with fault-tolerance. IEICE Trans. Inf. Syst. E87-D(3), 733–739 (2011)

11. Umeo, H.: Firing squad synchronization problem in cellular automata. In: Meyers, R.A. (ed.) Encyclopedia of Complexity and System Science, vol. 4, pp. 3537–3574. Springer, New York (2009)

12. Umeo, H., Kamikawa, N., Nishioka, K., Akiguchi, S.: Generalized firing squad synchronization protocols for one-dimensional cellular automata - a survey. Acta Phys. Pol. B, Proc. Suppl. 3, 267–289 (2010)

13. Umeo, H., Hirota, M., Nozaki, Y., Imai, K., Sogabe, T.: A reconstruction of Goto's FSSP algorithm (2016, draft in submission)

14. Umeo, H., Imai, K., Sousa, A.: A Generalized Minimum-Time Minimum-State-Change FSSP Algorithm. In: Dediu, A.-H., Magdalena, L., Martín-Vide, C. (eds.) TPNC 2015. LNCS, vol. 9477, pp. 161–173. Springer, Switzerland (2015). doi:10. 1007/978-3-319-26841-5_13

15. Vollmar, R.: Some remarks about the efficiency of polyautomata. Inter. J. Theoret. Phys. 21(12), 1007–1015 (1982)

16. Waksman, A.: An optimum solution to the firing squad synchronization problem. Inf. Control 9, 66–78 (1966)

17. Yunès, J.B.: Goto's construction and Pascal's triangle: new insights into cellular automata synchronization. Proceedings of JAC 2008, 195–203 (2008)

Asynchronous Cellular Automata and Asynchronous Discrete Models-ACA

Collective Infotaxis with Reactive Amoebae: A Note on a Simple Bio-inspired Mechanism

Nazim Fatès[(✉)]

Inria Nancy – Grand Est, LORIA UMR 7503,
Vandœuvre-lès-Nancy, France
nazim.fates@loria.fr

Abstract. We study how to coordinate a team of agents to locate a hidden source on a two-dimensional discrete grid. The challenge is to find the position of the source with only sporadic detections. This problem arises in various situations, for instance when insects emit pheromones to attract their partners. A search mechanism named infotaxis was proposed to explain how agents may progressively approach the source by using only intermittent detections.

Here, we study the problem of doing a collective infotaxis search with agents that are almost memoryless. We present a bio-inspired model which mixes stochastic cellular automata and reactive multi-agent systems. The model, inspired by the behaviour of the social amoeba *Dictyostelium discoideum*, relies on the use of reaction-diffusion waves to guide the agents to the source. The random emissions of waves allows the formation of a group of amoebae, which successively act as emitters of waves or listeners, according to their local perceptions. We present a first study that shows that the model is worth considering and may provide a simple solution to coordinate a team to perform a distributed form of infotaxis.

Keywords: Bio-inspired models · Multi-agent systems · Infotaxis · Asynchronous cellular automata · Probabilistic cellular automata

1 Introduction

We study how to coordinate a team of agents to perform a collective search in a two-dimensional environment. The team of agents needs to locate a source which emits an information that can only be detected sporadically. This problem arises in various situations, for instance when insects emit pheromones to attract their partners. There are cases where the pheromones are dispersed by a turbulent environment, which makes it impossible to find the emitting source by simply following a gradient. As the pheromones are distributed in patches, the agents need to rely on random events and adapt their movement according to the detections they make. Vergassola et al. named *infotaxis* a search strategy which consists in maximizing the information gain on the location of the source [6].

© Springer International Publishing Switzerland 2016
S. El Yacoubi et al. (Eds.): ACRI 2016, LNCS 9863, pp. 157–165, 2016.
DOI: 10.1007/978-3-319-44365-2_15

Here, we study this problem in the context of cellular automata. Imagine a team of agents that are randomly dispersed on a two-dimensional grid. The teams needs to locate a particular cell, the *emitting source* but the agents have a very small internal memory and they have no map of their environment nor can they build one. Their perception is limited to the cells situated at a short distance from their location, and the information contained in these cells is minimal, typically, each cell can adopt only a few states. At each time step, the agents may detect the presence of the source (make a "hit"), but without knowing the direction of the source, *nor its distance*. The detection probability increases as one gets closer to the source and this is the only help that can guide the agents to the source. Given the fact that they made a hit or not, the agents can move or change the state of the cell they are located on. Under such circumstances, how can a team of agents achieve a form of coordination in order to efficiently locate the source?

One may call this problem the *distributed infotaxis problem* with memoryless agents. In contrast, (classical) infotaxis has been mainly studied with agents that remember where the hits occurred. This allows them to build a map of their environment according to the detections they have made. Since the detections are stochastic events, the map is progressively adjusted. Interestingly, it was shown that a good search strategy does not necessarily consist in always trying to approach the source. It also an advantage to move orthogonally to the estimated direction of the source in order to improve the process of locating the direction of source [6]. However, the use of a map in virtual agents or in real robots imposes a certain degree of complication. Different solutions have been proposed to simplify this scheme. In particular, Masson has proposed to use only a projection of the map of probabilities into a pre-determined form, where appears detection and non-detection terms [4]. Later on, this technique was extended by Zhang et al. to coordinate a team of robots [7].

We ask if we can further simplify the solution by using agents that *do not remember where previous detections have occurred*. In this context, the previous solutions cannot be used and the challenge is to find a method to guide the agents to the source in better way than a pure random walk.

In a previous work we considered the decentralised aggregation problem: the agents need to gather and form a compact group in a totally decentralised way with only local perceptions and no memory of their previous actions. We proposed to use a bio-inspired model, the social amoebae model, to perform this gathering task [2]. The aggregation scheme imitates the behaviour which occurs in the first phase of grouping in the social amoeba *Dictyostelim discoideum*. The mechanism relies on the asynchronous emission of reaction-diffusion waves in the environment: the amoebae alternatively speak and listen and these different roles are governed by simple random events (see more details in Ref. [2]). There is a trade-off to find between these two roles to ensure an efficient gathering process.

We modify this aggregation scheme to make the team of amoebae detect a hidden source. Informally, the system works as follows: in absence of information, an agent performs a random walk on the grid. When it makes a detection, which should be a rare event, it triggers a reaction-diffusion wave in the grid. This wave will propagate and attract the other agents towards the emitting agent. The repetition of these events will progressively help to form a group. However this group will not be static: the agents that are closer to the source will have a tendency to emit more often that the agents that are far from it. As a consequence, the group will progressively move towards the source and finally reach its target. The coordination of the group is ensured by the asynchronous nature of interactions: there are no leaders to take the decisions but instead each agent has the possibility to emit waves or to "listen" to the emissions of the others according to some particular stochastic behaviour that needs to be adjusted appropriately.

It can be noted that although seducing, the success of this scenario is not guaranteed. Indeed, this indirect communication process between agents, also called stigmergy, must take place in a group that is neither too compact nor too sparse. An excessive grouping of agents is detrimental because their movements occur in a more restricted zone than if they were absolutely free to wander on the grid. On the contrary, if they stay away from each other, the agents will have no tendency to move collectively to the source. In this note, we explore this trade-off with some first numerical simulations. We analyse if there are some particular conditions in which the amoebae-infotaxis model can be beneficial. We do not bring any definitive answer to the problem of distributed infotaxis but rather aim at showing that a simple search strategy with cellular automata is worthy of consideration.

2 Presentation of the Model

Our model is defined on a finite square grid denoted by $\mathcal{L} = \{1, \ldots, L\} \times \{1, \ldots, L\}$. This model, that we could name the `amobae-infotaxis model`, is composed of two interacting layers: the environment and the amoebae.

The *environment* is a cellular automaton composed of the cells of the grid. The states of the cells are taken in a finite set Q that will be specified below. The global state of the environment is called a *configuration* and the set of configurations is denoted by $Q^{\mathcal{L}}$. At each time step, each cell calculates its new state according to its own state and the states of its neighbours and a possible influence from the amoebae. In other words, the environment is a cellular automaton which is in interaction with a system of reactive agents.

The emitting source is modelled by a distinguished cell $\sigma \in \mathcal{L}$, whose location is fixed. As mentioned earlier, in this problem, the cells can only make binary detections and the probability of detection decreases with the distance to the emitting source. This property is modelled by the introduction of a probability detection field $\rho : \mathcal{L} \to [0, 1]$ which associates to each cell the probability to make a detection in this given cell. Here, we work with a field which follows an inverse square law; it is described with: $\rho(\sigma) = 1$ and

$$\forall c \neq \sigma, \rho(c) = \frac{K}{d(c, \sigma)^2},$$

where $d(c, c') = |c_x - c'_x| + |c_y - c'_y|$ is the Manhattan distance between two cells of the grid $c = (c_x, c_y)$ and $c' = (c'_x, c'_y)$, and where $K < 1$ is an arbitrary constant. Other authors have used an exponential decrease with the distance to the source. We prefer to use a $1/d^2$ function in order to allow the existence of a small, but non negligible, probability of detection in the cells that are far from the source. Note that this field does not make the problem non-local: the probabilities are simply some fixed parameters that cannot be "read" directly by the cells nor by the agents. Also note that this field may be computed by a local rule if one wishes to do so (by assigning a particular state to the source and computing the probabilities with a diffusion equation).

The *amoebae* are reactive agents: they are described by their positions on the grid and their internal state, which is binary and taken in the set $S = \{\text{rec}, \text{emi}\}$, which correspond to a receiver and emitter state, respectively. For a set of N amoebae, we will denote by $p = (p_i) \in \mathcal{L}^N$ the vector of all positions on the grid and by $s = (s_i) \in S^N$ the vector of all internal states. The quantity p_i and s_i thus denote the position and the internal state of the i-th amoeba, respectively.

With these notations, we can describe our model with a dynamical system F, which operates on the space $Q^{\mathcal{L}} \times \mathcal{L}^N \times S^N$. For an initial condition $(x^0, p^0, s^0) \in Q^{\mathcal{L}} \times \mathcal{L}^N \times S^N$, its evolution is described by the recursive equation: $(x^{t+1}, p^{t+1}, s^{t+1}) = F(x^t, p^t, s^t)$. Let us now describe how these quantities are calculated[1].

Evolution of the Cells. The set of states of the cells is given by $Q = \{\text{e}, \text{r}, \text{n}\}$, which respectively correspond to the *excited*, *refractory* and *neutral* states. This environment implements a simple reaction-diffusion law, called the Greenberg-Hastings model (see e.g. Ref. [1]). Informally, a cell becomes excited if it is neutral and (a) if it has at least one excited neighbour or (b) if it is excited externally by an amoeba. An excited cell always becomes refractory, and a refractory cell always become neutral.

To define this law, we introduce the function ξ_e that selects the excited cells around a given cell:

$$\xi_e(x, c) = \{d \in D, c + d \in \mathcal{L}, x_{c+d} = \text{e}\}$$

where $D = \{(0, 1), (0, -1), (1, 0), (-1, 0)\}$ represents the four cardinal directions. This means that our cellular automaton uses the von Neumann neighbourhood but note that it can also be easily applied to other types of neighbourhoods [2].

We then define the modified Greenberg-Hastings law of evolution of the cells with, for all $c \in \mathcal{L}$:

$$x_c^{t+1} = \begin{cases} \text{e if } x_c^t = \text{n and} & (\xi_e(x^t, c) \text{ is not empty} \\ & \text{or } \exists i, p_i^t = c \text{ and } s_i^t = \text{emi}) \\ \text{r if } x_c^t = \text{e} \\ \text{n otherwise.} \end{cases}$$

---

[1] We make a slight abuse in notations because we use the formalism of classical dynamical systems even though our function F is stochastic.

Evolution of the Amoebae. First, we need to describe the fact that some amoebae will *make a hit*, that is, detect the source with a given probability which depends on their location. To this end we introduce the sequence of random variables (H_t), where H_t tells whether a hit occurs on a given cell at a given time t:

$$\forall c \in \mathcal{L}, \; H_t(c) = \begin{cases} 1 & \text{with probability } \rho(c) \\ 0 & \text{with probability } 1 - \rho(c). \end{cases}$$

The behaviour of the amoebae is as follows: at each time step, independently of the other amoebae, each amoeba may follow a random movement according to the four cardinal directions with probability p_A, the *probability of agitation*. With probability $1 - p_A$, the "regular" behaviour is applied. Informally, this regular behaviour follows:

1. For an amoeba in the state rec, if it is standing on a neutral cell and sees one or several excited cells in its neighbourhood, it chooses one of these excited cells uniformly at random for its movement; otherwise, it stays static.
2. For an amoeba in the state emi, if it is standing on a neutral cell, it turns this cell to the excited state. It then remains in state emi with probability p_R, the *probability of reemission*.

The motivation for introducing the probability of agitation p_A is twofold: on the one hand, we add a randomness which ensures that the amoebae are not too static, on the other hand, this allows us to model the intrinsic noise that would exist in the movement of biological organisms or robots. The use of the probability of reemission p_R is not mandatory. It is simply here to allow several reaction-diffusion waves to be triggered when a hit occurs. As we will see below, these waves have an attractive force that groups the amoebae; this attractive force balances the dispersive force that is created by the random movements.

To write down this rule with our notations, we have:

- for $s_i^t = \text{rec}$, $s_i^{t+1} = \begin{cases} \text{emi} & \text{if } H_t(p_i^t) = 1 \\ \text{rec} & \text{otherwise,} \end{cases}$

- for $s_i^t = \text{emi}$, $s_i^{t+1} = \begin{cases} \text{emi} & \text{with proba. } p_R \\ \text{rec} & \text{with proba. } 1 - p_R. \end{cases}$

The positions evolve according to:

$$p_i^{t+1} = \begin{cases} B[p_i^t, \mathcal{U}(D)] & \text{with proba. } p_A \\ \mathcal{U}(\xi_e(x^t, p_i^t)) & \text{with proba. } 1 - p_A, \text{ if no hits occurs at time } t, \end{cases}$$

where

- $\mathcal{U}(X)$ is a random variable that selects an element uniformly in a set X,
- $B[c, d]$ is a function that equals $c + d$ if $c + d$ is in $\mathcal{L}$ and c otherwise,
- ξ_e is the set of excited cells neighbours to a given cell (see above).

The task is completed when an amoeba moves to the emitting source σ. The *detection time* is the smallest t which satisfies: $\exists i, p_i^t = \sigma$.

3   First Experiments

Recall that our purpose is simply to test the relevance of doing a collective form of infotaxis with (almost) memoryless agents. For the sake of simplicity, we arbitrarily fix the value of the constant in Eq. 2 to $K = 0.5$. Similarly, we fix the reemission probability to $p_R = 0.9$ in order to allow for multiple waves to be emitted when a 'hit' occurs. A first visual experiment will be presented for $L = 20$ and $N = 5$, and then statistics will be given for $L = 80$ and $N = 20$.

3.1   A Qualitative Observation

In our experiments, the amoebae are placed uniformly at random on the grid. The emitting source is placed at coordinates $(L/4, L/4)$ in order to make the problem more difficult. Indeed, if it were placed at the centre, the amoebae could more easily find it since they do not need to displace their centre of gravity.

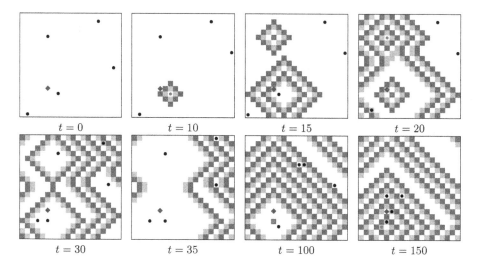

Fig. 1. Evolution of the system for $N = 5$ amoebae on a grid of size $L = 20$ with $K = 0.5$, $p_A = 0.2$, and $p_R = 0.9$; the emitting source is in blue (diamond shape); amoebae are shown as circles in black (**rec** state) or in purple (**emi** state). The colors of the grid cells are red, orange or white, which respectively correspond to the **e**, **r** and **n** states. [color online, see also the additional material given in the preprint HAL 01327983 https://hal.inria.fr/hal-01327983].

First, let us observe visually how a system with only 5 amoebae behaves for a small grid of size $L = 20$ and a small probability of agitation $p_A = 0.2$.

Figure 1 shows one particular random evolution of such a system. We see that various reaction-diffusion waves are emitted at different times when the hits occur. In this evolution two hits occur in a short time around $t = 20$, which allows us to observe how the reaction-diffusion annihilate when they meet frontally and how they merge when they meet orthogonally. This is the reason why it is important that the emission of waves do not occur simultaneously: as the reaction-diffusion waves annihilate when they meet, if all the amoebae were emitting at the same time, none of them could receive the information. In other words, some amoebae need to remain in the `rec` state in order to be able to "feel" the waves emitted by the other amoebae. In this evolution, after a hundred steps the amoebae are already regrouped around the emitting source and, at time $t = 150$, we are very close to the source detection event.

3.2   A Quantitative Experiment

We now make a second step by considering the statistical variations of the search time as a function of the agitation probability p_A. Indeed, p_A is the most important parameter in our study since it controls the average quantity of movement of the amoebae.

Taking the same settings as in the previous experiment, we observe the variation of the average detection time for a grid size of $L = 80$. We vary the agitation probability p_A from 0.1 to 1.0 with a step of 0.1 and the measure the detection time with 1000 random samples.

The results are shown on Fig. 2 and, interestingly, present a rather surprising behaviour of the system. It can be noted that a local minimum on the detection time is obtained for $p_A \sim 0.2$. (An additional sampling point is added at $p_A = 0.15$ to have a better observation of this zone.)

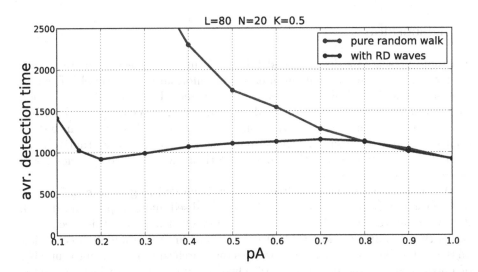

Fig. 2. Detection time for $N = 20$ amoebae as a function of the agitation probability p_A for $L = 80$ (in blue) with $K = 0.5$, $p_A = 0.1$, and $p_R = 0.9$. The curve in purple shows the detection time when the amoebae follow a pure random walk (reaction-diffusion waves are suppressed). (Color figure online)

We believe that the existence of this minimum corresponds to a balance between dispersive effect of the agitation and the grouping effect the reaction-diffusion waves. Indeed, if p_A is too small, the amoebae have a tendency to all aggregate on the same point – not the source ! – and to all remain almost static close to this point. As the random movements are rare, if an amoeba progressively gets far from the aggregation point, the waves emitted by the other amoebae will call it back to its starting point. On the contrary, when p_A is too high, the disorder introduced by the agitation is no longer beneficial because the information gained by "listening" to the other amoebae is "diluted" by the random movements.

For values of p_A which are even larger, that is, greater than 0.75, we observe that the detection time decreases again. This second effect is simply explained by considering the average number of movements per step: since the order of the system is already very weak (as p_A is high), it becomes more efficient to "mechanically" increase the average speed of the amoebae by moving more often.

In order to estimate what part of the behaviour is due to the reaction-diffusion waves and what part is due to the random movements, we estimated the average search time when there are no waves (we set $K = 0$). The corresponding curve on Fig. 2 shows no surprise: it is decreasing with p_A and, more precisely, the average detection time varies as $1/p_A$. This is expected since the amoebae follow a pure Brownian motion and do not interact. We can observe that for small values of p_A, the gain is important and for a similar average speed of movements, the search time with the amoebae-infotaxis search strategy may be divided a factor 5 with respect to the random walk strategy.

4   Discussion

This note presented a discrete model for performing a collective infotaxis task in an environment where only an intermittent information is available. The first experiments showed that the amoebae-infotaxis model can be a simple method to perform a collective search of a hidden source. The mechanism we described relies on the probabilistic and asynchronous nature of the detections: since these events are rare, the agents of the system (the amoebae) can alternatively act as emitters or receivers and thus coordinate their movements to get closer and closer to the emitting source.

A continuation of the experimental work is needed to get more insights on how to use virtual amoebae to solve the decentralised infotaxis problem. Indeed, it is not clear yet in which situations it is more efficient to use this mechanism rather than a simple random walk. It is also important to get a more precise view on the scaling laws of the system: how does the search time depend on the number of amoebae and on the size of the grid? There are also questions which regard the possible improvement of the model. Here, we presented a solution that uses only three states for the cellular automaton dynamics of the environment and two states for the agents, but the possibilities for further extending the behaviour of the agents are numerous, as for instance, making their emissions auto-adjust in order to have the correct balance between "listening" and "speaking".

In the context of applying the amoebae-infotaxis method in the context of distributed robotics [3,5], it would also be interesting to test the robustness of our scheme against several perturbations such as the introduction of obstacles in the grid or a non-regular distribution of the detection probabilities.

References

1. Berry, H., Fatès, N.: Robustness of the critical behaviour in the stochastic Greenberg-Hastings cellular automaton model. Int. J. Unconventional Comput. 7(1–2), 65–85 (2011)
2. Fatès, N.: Solving the decentralised gathering problem with a reaction-diffusion-chemotaxis scheme - social amoebae as a source of inspiration. Swarm Intell. 4(2), 91–115 (2010)
3. Fatès, N., Vlassopoulos, N.: A robust scheme for aggregating quasi-blind robots in an active environment. Int. J. Swarm Intell. Res. 3(3), 66–80 (2012)
4. Masson, J.-B.: Olfactory searches with limited space perception. Proc. Nat. Acad. Sci. 110(28), 11261–11266 (2013)
5. Silva, F., Correia, L., Christensen, A.L.: Modelling synchronisation in multirobot systems with cellular automata: analysis of update methods and topology perturbations. In: Sirakoulis, G.C., Adamatzky, A. (eds.) Robots and Lattice Automata. Emergence, Complexity and Computation, vol. 13, pp. 267–293. Springer International Publishing, Cham (2015)
6. Vergassola, M., Villermaux, E., Shraiman, B.I.: 'Infotaxis' as a strategy for searching without gradients. Nature 445(7126), 406–409 (2007)
7. Zhang, S., Martinez, D., Masson, J.-B.: Multi-robot searching with sparse binary cues and limited space perception. Front. Robot. AI 2(12) (2015). doi:10.3389/frobt.2015.00012

A Fast Parallel Algorithm for the Robust Prediction of the Two-Dimensional Strict Majority Automaton

Eric Goles[1,3]([✉]) and Pedro Montealegre[2]

[1] Facultad de Ingeniería Y Ciencias, Universidad Adolfo Ibáñez, Santiago, Chile
eric.chacc@uai.cl
[2] Université D'Orléans, INSA Centre Val de Loire, LIFO EA, 4022 Orléans, France
[3] Le Studium: Loire Valley Institute for Advanced Studies, Orléans, France

Abstract. Consider the *robust prediction* problem for some automaton as the one consisting in determine, given an initial configuration, if there exists a nonzero probability that some selected site change states, when the network is updated picking one site at a time uniformly at random. We show that the *robust prediction* is in **NC** for the two-dimensional, von Neumann neighborhood, *strict majority automaton*.

Keywords: Majority automata · Prediction problem · Asynchronous automata · Computational complexity · Fast parallel algorithm · Bootstap percolation

1 Introduction

The study of the dynamics of cellular automata and their relation with the computational complexity was introduced, to our knowledge, by Banks in the 70's [1,2]. The computational complexity of a cellular automaton is defined as its capability to simulate algorithms using certain configurations. In other words, to be Turing-Universal. These notions can be translated into decision problems, consisting in the prediction of state changes in some site, given an initial configuration. The complexity of the automaton is then related with the complexity of this type of decision problems, where the Turing Universality is translated as the **P-Completeness** of the prediction problem.

The class **NC**, which is a subclass of **P**, is known as the class of problems that can be solved with a *fast parallel algorithm*, which run in poly-logarithmic time in a PRAM machine using a polynomial number of processors. It is widely believed that **NC** $\neq$ **P**. The membership of the prediction problem of some **CA** in **NC**, suggest that this automaton is not capable of simulating algorithms in the sense above, since it can only simulate very simple circuits.

These perspectives have been studied by several authors, in the context of *sand piles* and the *chip firing game* [3–5,14], the *majority automaton* [13] and the *life without death* [11] in cellular automata, as well as when the dynamics

© Springer International Publishing Switzerland 2016
S. El Yacoubi et al. (Eds.): ACRI 2016, LNCS 9863, pp. 166–175, 2016.
DOI: 10.1007/978-3-319-44365-2_16

are not necessarily defined over a finite lattice but over some graph [7,9]. These results usually consider only synchronous dynamics, i.e., at each step the sites are updated at the same time. However, there exist some results around prediction problems with different updating schemes [6,8].

Another prediction problem considers the so-called *fully asynchronous* updating schemes, where in each time step a single site is updated, picked uniformly at random. The prediction problem in this context (that we call *robust-prediction*) consists in determining, given an initial configuration, if there exists a nonzero probability that some site change states. In other words, determine if there exists a sequence of site updates that produces the selected node to change states. In [13] it is suggested that this prediction problem belongs to the class **NC** restricted to two-dimensional majority cellular automata.

In this paper we show that the *robust prediction* problem is effectively in **NC** for the two-dimensional *strict majority automaton* with the von Neumann neighborhood. Our result is based on an algorithm on [9], which is used to solve a version of the prediction problem (the synchronous one) in the *freezing* version of the two-dimensional strict majority automaton. *Freezing* means that all sites that begin in or reach state 1, remain in that state forever.

In next section we begin by giving some formal definitions of the concept exposed above. In Sect. 3 we show the main result, and in Sect. 4 we give some conclusions.

2   Preliminaries

In the following $[n]$ denotes the set $\{1, \ldots, n\}$. For a node v in a graph $G = (V, E)$, we call $N(v)$ the neighborhood of v and $N[v] = N(v) \cup \{v\}$ the closed neighborhood of v. Let $U \subseteq V$ be a set of nodes, then $G[U]$ is the subgraph of G induced by the nodes in U.

An automata network (**AN**) of size n is a tuple $A = (G, F)$, where $G = (V, E)$ is a graph of size n. Each node $v \in V$ has a *state* in $\{0, 1\}$. Nodes in state 1 are called *active* while nodes in state 0 are called *inactive*. A *configuration* x of G is a state assignment to each node of G, represented by an element of $\{0, 1\}^n$. The configurations evolve according to a *global function* $F : \{0, 1\}^n \to \{0, 1\}^n$, composed of *node functions* $(f_v)_{v \in V(G)}$ such that $f_v : \{0, 1\}^{N[v]} \to \{0, 1\}$ depends only in the closed neighborhood of a node and $F(x) = (f_v(x))_{v \in V}$. Usually F is called the *rule* of the automata network. When G is a finite two-dimensional lattice with periodic boundary conditions, we say that the corresponding **AN** is a two-dimensional cellular automaton (**CA**). In this paper we will always consider the von Neumann neighborhood for **CA**'s (i.e., the four sites orthogonally surrounding a central site).

An *updating scheme* of an **AN** of size n is a function $\sigma : \mathbb{N} \to 2^{[n]}$, which defines which nodes are updated at each time step. An updating scheme σ is applied to an automata network $A = (G, F)$ as follows: define for $u \in V(G)$ and

$i \in \mathbb{N}$ the value of $(F^{\sigma(i)}(x))$ in the site u as:

$$(F^{\sigma(i)}(x))_u = \begin{cases} (F(x))_u & \text{if } u \in \sigma(i), \\ x_u & \text{otherwise.} \end{cases}$$

and $F^{\sigma,i}(x) = F^{\sigma(i)}(F^{\sigma,i-1}(x))$ with $F^{\sigma,0}(x) = x$. The synchronous updating scheme, represented by the function $sync \equiv [n]$, corresponds to the one where each site is updated at each time step. We denote $F^{sync,i} = F^i$, for any $i > 0$. In this paper all updating schemes which are not the synchronous one will be *sequential*, this is, for any $t > 0$ $|\sigma(t)| = 1$. In words, this means that at each time step we will update a single site. Notice that we do not ask the sequential updating schemes to be *fair*: some nodes may be updated several times, while others may not be updated at all. A sequential updating scheme is called *fully asynchronous* if at each time step the updated node is picked uniformly at random.

A node $v \in V$ is called *stable* for a pair (G, x) and some updating scheme σ of rule F, where G is a graph and x is a configuration of G, if $(F^{\sigma(t)}(x))_v = x_v$ for all $t > 0$. For any two n dimensional boolean vectors, $x, y \in \{0, 1\}^n$, we say that $x \leq y$ if $x_i \leq y_i$ for each $i \in [n]$. A rule F is called *monotone* if for each $x^1, x^2 \in \{0, 1\}^n$, $x^1 \leq x^2$ implies $F(x^1) \leq F(x^2)$. For any local rule F, we define the *freezing* version of F, denoted $\overline{F}$, as the rule defined as $(\overline{F}(x))_v = 1$ if $x_v = 1$ and $(F(x))_v$ otherwise.

The *Strict Majority* rule is the global function defined using the following local functions:

$$f_v(x) = \begin{cases} 1 & \text{if } \sum_{u \in N(v)} x_u > |N(v)|/2, \\ 0 & \text{otherwise.} \end{cases}$$

We call *Bootstrap Percolation* the freezing version of the strict majority rule.

2.1   Prediction Problems

As we said in the introduction, the computational complexity of an automata network can be characterized by different prediction problems. Let G be a graph and $v \in V(G)$ a special node, that we will call the *objective node*. In the following we will define three prediction problems, each of them consisting in deciding if a objective node will change states, given an initial configuration that evolves according to some fixed rule.

The first problem, called PREDICTION consists in determining if the objective node will change states in at most some given number of synchronous steps, given also an initial configuration. Formally the problem is stated as follows:

PREDICTION(F)
Input: A graph G, an initial configuration x, a vertex $v \in V(G)$ such that $x_v = 0$ and $T > 0$.
Question: Determine if $(F^T(x))_v = 1$.

The second problem, called EVENTUAL-PREDICTION is similar to PREDIC-TION. In this problem, the number of steps to decide a state change is not given, so the problem consists in determining if there exists a time step in which the objective node becomes active. In other words we ask if the objective node is stable for the synchronous updating. Formally the problem is stated as follows:

EVENTUAL-PREDICTION(F)
Input: A graph G, an initial configuration x and a vertex $v \in V(G)$ such that $x_v = 0$.
Question: Does there exists $T > 0$ such that $(F^T(x))_v = 1$?

The third problem is called ROBUST-PREDICTION, and the question is if there exists a nonzero probability that the objective node becomes active in at most some given number of steps, when the network is updated in a fully asynchronous updating scheme. In other words, if there exists a sequential updating scheme that makes the objective node to change. Formally the problem is stated as follows:

ROBUST-PREDICTION(F)
Input: A graph G, an initial configuration x, a vertex $v \in V(G)$ such that $x_v = 0$, and $T > 0$.
Question: Does there exists a sequential updating scheme σ such that $(F^{\sigma,T}(x))_v = 1$?

Let $\mathcal{G}$ be a family of graphs. We call PREDICTION (respectively EVENTUAL-PREDICTION, ROBUST-PREDICTION) restricted to $\mathcal{G}$ to the decision problem PREDICTION (respectively EVENTUAL-PREDICTION, ROBUST-PREDICTION) where the input graph is restricted to belong to $\mathcal{G}$.

Notice that PREDICTION(F) belongs to the class **P** for any rule F (whose node function is computable in polynomial time), because simulating the automaton for the given number of steps we can obtain the answer. Several examples exist for rules that are **P-Complete** both in general graphs and restricted to the two-dimensional case [9,11]. On the other hand, EVENTUAL-PREDICTION(F) is in general in **PSPACE**, and may be **PSPACE-Complete**. However, when the local function is a threshold function with symmetric weights (for example the strict majority rule), the problem becomes polynomial, since in that case the automaton reaches in at most a polynomial number of synchronous steps, a fixed point or a two-cycle [10]. Finally ROBUST-PREDICTION(F) is in general in **NP**, since a sequential updating scheme that makes the objective node active is a certificate that can verified in polynomial time.

In the following we will show that for the Strict Majority and Bootstrap Percolation rules, some of these problems restricted to the family of regular graphs of degree four are in **NC**.

2.2   Parallel Subroutines

In our algorithms we will use as subroutines some fast parallel algorithms to compute graph properties. These algorithms can be found in [12]. The connected components of a graph G are the equivalence classes of the connectivity relation over the vertices of G. The biconnected components of a graph are the equivalence classes of the relation over the edges of G, where two edges are related if they are both contained in the same cycle.

Proposition 1 ([12]). *There exist the following fast parallel algorithms:*

- **A Connected-Components algorithm**, *that receives as input the adjacency matrix of a graph of size n, and returns an array C of dimension n, such that $C(i) = C(j)$ if and only if nodes v_i and v_j are in the same connected component. The algorithm runs in time $\mathcal{O}(\log n)$ using $\mathcal{O}(n^2 \log n)$ processors in a CRCW PRAM[1].*
- **A Biconnected-Components algorithm**, *that receives as input the adjacency matrix of a connected graph of size n, and returns an array B of dimension $\binom{n}{2}$, such that $B(e_i) = B(e_j)$ if and only if edges e_i and e_j are in the same biconnected component. The algorithm runs in time $\mathcal{O}(\log^2 n)$ using $\mathcal{O}(n^2)$ processors CRCW PRAM.*
- **A Rooting-tree algorithm**, *that receives as input a tree T represented as the adjacency lists of its vertices and a special node r of T, and returns for each node v the value $p(v)$ which corresponds to the parent of v in the tree T rooted at r. The algorithm runs in time $\mathcal{O}(\log n)$ using $\mathcal{O}(n)$ processors in a CRCW PRAM.*
- **A Tree-level algorithm**, *that receives as input a tree T represented as the adjacency lists of its vertices, a special node r of T, and returns for each node v the value $l(v)$ which corresponds distance of node v to root r. The algorithm runs in time $\mathcal{O}(\log n)$ using $\mathcal{O}(n)$ processors in a CRCW PRAM.*

We will also use a fast parallel algorithm to solve EVENTUAL-PREDICTION for the Bootstrap Percolation rule.

Proposition 2 ([9]). *Let $\overline{F}$ be the Bootstrap Percolation rule. There exists an algorithm that solves EVENTUAL-PREDICTION($\overline{F}$) restricted to regular graphs of degree four, in time $\mathcal{O}(\log^2 n)$ using $\mathcal{O}(n^4)$ processors in a CRCW PRAM.*

This fast parallel algorithm, that we call **Algorithm 1** is based in the following characterization of nodes that are stable for the synchronous update of the Bootstrap Percolation rule.

Proposition 3 ([9]). *Let G be a regular graph of degree four, x be a configuration of G, and $v \in V(G)$ some node such that $x_v = 0$. Call $G[0, v]$ the connected component of $G[\{u \in V(G) : x_u = 0\}]$ that contains v. Then v is stable for (G, x) updated synchronously with the Bootstrap Percolation rule if and only if either v belongs to a cycle or to a path between two cycles in $G[0, v]$.*

---

[1] Concurrent-read Concurrent-write Parallel Random Access Machine: A RAM with several processors, which can read and write a shared memory.

Then, the fast parallel algorithm of [9] consists in finding the connected and biconnected components of the graph induced by the nodes initially inactive, and then detect if the objective node belongs to some cycle or a path between two cycles in that graph. If it is not, then from the above proposition necessarily the node eventually change states. In Sect. 3 we show that we can adapt this algorithm to find, in case that the objective node is not stable, the exact number of nodes that we must update in order to produce a change in the state of the objective node.

3   The Strict Majority Rule

Before enunciate the main theorem, we prove the following lemma.

Lemma 1. *Let G be a graph, x be a configuration of G, and $v \in V(G)$ a vertex such that $x_v = 0$. Then v is a stable node for the synchronous updating scheme of the Bootstrap Percolation rule if and only if v is stable for any sequential updating scheme of the Strict Majority rule.*

Proof. We will show that the property is true for any monotone rule F and its freezing version $\overline{F}$. We notice first that the monotonicity of F implies that $F^{\sigma,i}(x) \leq \overline{F}^i(x)$, for any $i > 0$, and sequential updating scheme σ. Indeed, from the definition of $\overline{F}$, for any configuration $y \in \{0,1\}^n$ and $k \in \mathbb{N}$, $F^{\sigma(k)}(y) \leq \overline{F}(y)$, in particular $F^{\sigma(1)}(x) \leq F(x)$. If we suppose then $F^{\sigma,i-1}(x) \leq \overline{F}^{i-1}(x)$, we obtain

$$F^{\sigma,i}(x) = F^{\sigma(i)}(F^{\sigma,i-1}(x)) \leq F^{\sigma(i)}(\overline{F}^{i-1}(x)) \leq \overline{F}^i(x).$$

where the first inequality follows from the monotonicity of F, and the second one from the base case. We obtain that if there exists an updating scheme σ and a time $t > 0$ such that $(F^{s,t}(x))_v = 1$, then $(\overline{F}^t(x))_v = 1$.

In the other direction, suppose that there exists a time $t > 0$ such that $(\overline{F}^t(x))_v = 1$. Call $U_i = \{u \in V(G) : (\overline{F}^{i-1}(x))_u = 0 \wedge (\overline{F}^i(x))_u = 1\}$ the set of the nodes that change states in step i (from 0 to 1, since $\overline{F}$ is *freezing*). Call now σ the updating scheme where sequentially update one by one the nodes in $U_1, \ldots, U_t$, starting from U_1, and choosing for each $i \in \{1, \ldots, t\}$ an arbitrary order in U_i. Call $t^* = \sum_{i=1}^{t} |U_i|$, then we have that for each $u \in U_i$ and $\sum_{j=1}^{i} |U_j| \leq k \leq t^*$, $(F^{\sigma,k}(x))_u = (\overline{F}^i(x))_u = 1$. Then, in particular $(F^{\sigma,t^*}(x))_v = 1$. □

Theorem 1. *Let F be the Strict Majority rule. Then* ROBUST-PREDICTION(F) *restricted to the family of regular graphs of degree four is in* **NC**.

Proof. Let (G, x, v, T) be an input of the ROBUST-PREDICTION(F) problem. We start checking, using **Algorithm 1**, that v is not stable in G and x for the Bootstrap Percolation rule updated with a synchronous updating scheme. If it does, our algorithm returns, indicating that the objective node is stable for any updating scheme of the strict majority rule.

In the following we suppose that v is not stable for the synchronous updating of Bootstrap Percolation rule. From Lemma 1 this means that there exists a sequential updating scheme σ for which v is not stable for the strict majority rule updated according to σ. This scheme will consist in the sequential updating of the nodes that change states at each step of the synchronous updating of the bootstrap percolation rule. We choose an arbitrary ordering if several nodes are updated at the same time step.

Let v_1, v_2, v_3 and v_4 the neighbors of v in G. Let $G[0] = G[\{u \in V(G) : x_u = 0\}]$ the induced graph of nodes initially inactive, and call $G[0; v]$ the connected component of $G[0]$ containing v. For $i \in \{1, 2, 3, 4\}$ call T_i the connected component of $G[0; v] - v$ that contain v_i.

Without loss of generality, suppose that v_1, v_2 and v_3 are the first three neighbors of v to become active before v in the synchronous update of the bootstrap percolation rule (in particular they can be initially active, in that case $T_i = \emptyset$). Notice that if $T_i \neq \emptyset$ then T_i is a tree. Indeed, if T_i contain a cycle C_i, then either v_i is contained in C or v_i is in a path P between C and v. In both cases each internal node of the path P will have two inactive neighbors, so v_i cannot change before v in a synchronous update of the Bootstrap Percolation rule, a contradiction.

Call T_i^0 the tree T_i, and for $t > 0$ call T_i^t the subtree of T_i that contains the inactive nodes after t synchronous updates of the bootstrap percolation rule. Notice that for any $t > 0$, the set $V(T_i^{t-1}) \backslash V(T_i^t)$ is the set of leafs of T_i^{t-1}, except possibly v_i. Indeed in time $t - 1$ each internal node of T_i^{t-1} has at least two inactive neighbors, every leaf has three active neighbors, and v_i is adjacent to v, which we suppose to become active after v_i. This implies that v_i will become active only once each node of T_i becomes active. Notice that if we sequentially update the leafs of the trees $T_i^0, T_i^1, \ldots$ we obtain a sequential updating scheme which produces a change of states in v_i in the minimum number of steps. Indeed, if there is a faster sequential updating scheme, that means that there is some $t > 0$ such that one leaf T_i^t was not updated, so it remains inactive. That implies that internal nodes of a path between such non updated leaf and v_i will have at least two inactive neighbors, preventing v_i to become active. We conclude that the minimum number of sequential steps to produce v_i to change states is $|T_i|$. We obtain that the objective node v changes in at most T steps if and only if $|T_1| + |T_2| + |T_3| + 1 \leq T$ (Fig. 1).

Let G be a regular graph of degree 4, v a node of G, and let v_1, v_2, v_3 and v_4 be the neighbors of v. We call G^{v,C_4} the graph obtained from G removing v, and replacing it with a cycle of length 4, called $C_4 = \{c_1, c_2, c_3, c_4\}$, such that for each $i \in \{1, 2, 3, 4\}$, the edge $\{v, v_i\}$ is replaced in G^{v,C_4} with $\{c_i, v_i\}$. Let x be a configuration of G such that $x_v = 0$, we call x^{v,C_4} the configuration of G^{v,C_4} such that $x_w^{v,C_4} = x_w$ if $w \neq v$ and $x_{c_i}^{v,C_4} = 0$ for $i \in \{1, 2, 3, 4\}$. Notice that from Proposition 3, T_i contains a cycle if and only if v_i is stable for (G^{v,C_4}, x^{v,C_4}) and the synchronous updating of the Bootstrap Percolation rule. We are now ready to present **Algorithm 2**.

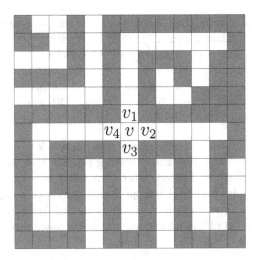

Fig. 1. Example of a configuration in the two-dimensional lattice. The objective node is v, which is not stable for the synchronous updating of the bootstrap percolation rule. Note that $|T_1| = 12$, $|T_2| = 11$ and $|T_3| = 5$, and that T_4 contains a cycle.

Algorithm 2

Input: A graph G of size n represented by its adjacency list, an array of dimension n representing a configuration x, a vertex $v \in V(G)$ and $T > 0$ such that $x_v = 0$.

Output: A boolean *out* that indicates if there exists an updating scheme σ such that $(F^{\sigma,T}(x))_v = 1$, where F is the Strict Majority rule.

1 Define for $i = \{1, 2, 3, 4\}$, $k_i \leftarrow \infty$.

2 Run **Algorithm 1** to check v is stable for (G, x) and the synchronous update of the bootstrap percolation rule. **If** it does not **then** continue, **else return** *out* $\leftarrow$ *false*.

3 Build the adjacency matrix of G^{v,C_4} and the configuration x_{v,C_4}.

4 **For** each v_i neighbor of v **do in parallel:**

   4.1 If $x_{v_i} = 1$ then $k_i \leftarrow 0$ and exit the for loop **else** contiue.

   4.2 Run **Algorithm 1** on input $(G^{v,C_4}, x^{v,C_4}, v_i)$ to check if v_i is stable for (G^{v,C_4}, x^{v,C_4}) and the synchronous update of the bootstrap percolation rule.

   4.3 if v_i is not stable **then**

      4.3.1 Use the **Connected Components Algorithm** of Proposition 1 to compute T_i, the connected component of $G[0, v] - v$ containing v_i.

      4.3.2 $k_i \leftarrow |T_i|$

5 Compute $t_1 \leftarrow \min\{k_1, k_2, k_3, k_4\}$, $t_2 \leftarrow \min\{k_1, k_2, k_3, k_4\}\backslash\{t_1\}$, $t_3 \leftarrow \min\{k_1, k_2, k_3, k_4\}\backslash\{t_1, t_2\}$ and $T^* \leftarrow t_1 + t_2 + t_3 + 1$.

7 If $T^* < T$ then *out* $\leftarrow$ *true* **else** *out* $\leftarrow$ *false*

The correctness of **Algorithm 2** is follow from the paragraphs above. About the complexity, **Algorithm 2** runs $\mathcal{O}(\log^2 n)$ time with $\mathcal{O}(n^4)$ processors, where the most expensive part is the runnings of **Algorithm 1** in steps **2** and **4.2**, running in $\mathcal{O}(\log^2 n)$ time with $\mathcal{O}(n^4)$ each. Steps **1**, **3**, **5** and **7** can be done in $\mathcal{O}(\log n)$ sequential time, steps **4.1**, **4.3.2** can be done in $\mathcal{O}(\log n)$ time using 4 processors. Finally step **4.3.1** can be done in time $\mathcal{O}(\log^2 n)$ and $\mathcal{O}(n^2)$ processors according to Proposition 1.   ◻

Remark 1. Notice that we can easily adapt **Algorithm 2** to output, in case that the objective node is not stable, the updating scheme that makes it change in the wished number of steps. Indeed, after step **4.3.2** we can compute for each subtree T_i the level of its nodes with respect to the root v_i, using the algorithms cited in Proposition 1. The updating scheme is then defined in decreasing order with respect to the level of the nodes, where tie cases are solved arbitrarily.

Corollary 1. *Let F be the strict majority rule. Then* ROBUST-PREDICTION(F) *restricted to the two-dimensional lattice is in NC.*

Remark 2. We can also adapt **Algorithm 2** to solve PREDICTION for the Bootstrap Percolation rule, restricted to the family of regular graphs of degree 4. Again, we can compute after step **4.2** the level of each node with respect to the corresponding subtree. The algorithm outputs *true* if there are three non stable neighbors of v whose trees have depth smaller than T.

Corollary 2. *Let F be the bootstrap percolation rule. Then* PREDICTION(F) *restricted to the two-dimensional lattice is in NC.*

4   Discussion

We had proven that the ROBUST-PREDICTION is in **NC** for the strict majority rule in the two dimensional lattice. This suggests, for example, that unless **NC** = **P** a two dimensional strict majority **CA** can not simulate monotone circuits that are not planar. However, the complexity of PREDICTION for the strict majority rule restricted to a two dimensional lattice is open. In [13] is conjectured that this problem is not **P-Complete**. The possibility that a monotone function, in two dimensions, and with a von Neumann neighborhood is capable of simulating non planar circuits is unlikely.

What about higher dimensions? In [9] it is shown that PREDICTION is **P-Complete** for the Bootstrap percolation rule for the family of graphs that admit nodes of degree greater than 4, and in [13] it is shown that in PREDICTION is **P-Complete** for the majority rule in the d-dimensional lattice, for $d \geq 3$. In the case of ROBUST-PREDICTION, the problem is in general in **NP**. In a future work we will show that when we are not restricted to a two dimensional lattice, both the Bootstrap Percolation and the Strict Majority rules are **NP-Complete**.

References

1. Banks, E.R.: Universality in cellular automata. In: SWAT (FOCS). IEEE Computer Society, pp. 194–215 (1970)
2. Banks, E.R.: Information processing and transmission in cellular automata, Technical Report AITR-233, MIT Artificial Intelligence Laboratory (1971)
3. Gajardo, A., Goles, E.: Crossing information in two-dimensional sandpiles. Theor. Comput. Sci. **369**, 463–469 (2006)
4. Goles, E., Margenstern, M.: Sand pile as a universal computer. Int. J. Mod. Phys. C **07**, 113–122 (1996)
5. Goles, E., Margenstern, M.: Universality of the chip-firing game. Theor. Comput. Sci. **172**, 121–134 (1997)
6. Goles, E., Montealegre, P.: Computational complexity of threshold automata networks under different updating schemes. Theor. Comput. Sci. **559**, 3–19 (2014). Non-uniform Cellular Automata
7. Goles, E., Montealegre, P.: The complexity of the majority rule on planar graphs. Adv. Appl. Math. **64**, 111–123 (2015)
8. Goles, E., Montealegre, P., Salo, V., Törmä, I.: Pspace-completeness of majority automata networks. Theor. Comput. Sci. **609**(Part 1), 118–128 (2016)
9. Goles, E., Montealegre-Barba, P., Todinca, I.: The complexity of the bootstraping percolation, other problems. Theor. Comput. Sci. **504**, 73–82 (2013). Discrete Mathematical Structures: From Dynamics to Complexity
10. Goles-Chacc, E., Fogelman-Soulie, F., Pellegrin, D.: Decreasing energy functions as a tool for studying threshold networks. Discrete Appl. Math. **12**, 261–277 (1985)
11. Moore, C.: Life without death is P-complete. Complex Syst. **10**, 437–447 (1996)
12. Jaja, J.: An introduction to parallel algorithms. Addison-Wesley Professional, New York (1992)
13. Moore, C.: Majority-vote cellular automata, Ising dynamics, and p-completeness. J. Stat. Phys. **88**, 795–805 (1997)
14. Moore, C., Nilsson, M.: The computational complexity of sandpiles. J. Stat. Phys. **96**, 205–224 (1999)

Asynchrony Immune Cellular Automata

Luca Mariot[1,2(✉)]

[1] Dipartimento di Informatica, Sistemistica e Comunicazione,
Università degli Studi Milano-Bicocca, Viale Sarca 336, 20126 Milano, Italy
luca.mariot@unimib.it
[2] Laboratoire I3S, Université Nice-Sophia Antipolis,
2000 Route des Lucioles, 06903 Sophia Antipolis, France

Abstract. We introduce the notion of asynchrony immunity for cellular automata (CA), which can be considered as a generalization of correlation immunity in the case of boolean functions. The property could have applications in cryptography, namely as a countermeasure for side-channel attacks in CA-based cryptographic primitives. We give some preliminary results about asynchrony immunity, and we perform an exhaustive search of $(3, 10)$–asynchrony immune CA rules of neighborhood size 3 and 4. We finally observe that all discovered asynchrony-immune rules are center-permutive, and we conjecture that this holds for any size of the neighborhood.

Keywords: Cellular automata · Cryptography · Asynchrony immunity · Correlation immunity · Nonlinearity · Side-channel attacks · Permutivity

1 Introduction

In the last years, research about cryptographic applications of cellular automata (CA) focused on the properties of the underlying local rules [6–8]. In fact, designing a CA-based cryptographic primitive using local rules that are not highly nonlinear and correlation immune could make certain attacks more efficient.

The aim of this short paper is to begin investigating a new property related to asynchronous CA called *asynchrony immunity* (AI), which could be of interest in the context of side-channel attacks. This property can be described by a three-move game between a user and an adversary. Let $r, m \in \mathbb{N}$, $n = m + 2r$ and $t \leq m$. The game works as follows:

1. The user chooses a local rule $f : \mathbb{F}_2^{2r+1} \to \mathbb{F}_2$ of radius r
2. The adversary chooses $j \leq t$ cells of the CA in the range $\{r, \cdots, m + r\}$.
3. The user evaluates the output distribution D of the CA $F : \mathbb{F}_2^{m+2r} \to \mathbb{F}_2^m$ and the distribution $\tilde{D}$ of the asynchronous CA $\tilde{F} : \mathbb{F}_2^{m+2r} \to \mathbb{F}_2^m$ where the t cells selected by the adversary are not updated
4. *Outcome*: if both D and $\tilde{D}$ equals the uniform distribution, the user wins. Otherwise, the adversary wins

© Springer International Publishing Switzerland 2016
S. El Yacoubi et al. (Eds.): ACRI 2016, LNCS 9863, pp. 176–181, 2016.
DOI: 10.1007/978-3-319-44365-2_17

A cellular automaton rule $f : \mathbb{F}_2^{2r+1} \to \mathbb{F}_2$ is called (t, n)–asynchrony immune if, for all lengths $2r < k \leq n$ and for all $j \leq t$, both the asynchronous CA $\tilde{F} : \mathbb{F}_2^k \to \mathbb{F}_2^{k-2r}$ resulting from not updating any subset of j cells and the corresponding synchronous CA $F : \mathbb{F}_2^k \to \mathbb{F}_2^{k-2r}$ are balanced, that is, the cardinality of the counterimage of each k-bit configuration equals 2^{2r}. Thus, asynchrony immune CA rules represent the winning strategies of the user in the game described above.

Notice the difference between the asynchrony immunity game and the t–resilient functions game [5]: in the latter, generic vectorial boolean functions $F : \mathbb{F}_2^n \to \mathbb{F}_2^m$ are considered instead of cellular automata, and the adversary selects both values and positions of the t input variables.

The side-channel attack model motivating our work is the following. Suppose that a CA of length n is used as an S-box in a block cipher, and that an attacker is able to inject clock faults by making t cells not updating. If the CA is not (t, n)–AI, then the attacker could gain some information on the internal state of the cipher by analyzing the differences of the output distributions in the original CA and the asynchronous CA.

In the remainder of this paper, we define the considered model of (asynchronous) CA in Sect. 2, and we formally introduce the definition of asynchrony immunity in Sect. 3, giving some basic theoretical results regarding this property. In particular, we show that AI is invariant under the operations of reflection and complement. We then perform in Sect. 4 an exhaustive search of $(3, 10)$–asynchrony immune cellular automata up to neighborhood size 4, computing also their nonlinearity values. We finally observe that all discovered rules are center-permutive, and we conjecture that this is a necessary condition for asynchrony immunity.

2   Preliminaries

In this work, we consider one-dimensional CA as a particular kind of *vectorial boolean functions*, i.e. mappings of the type $F : \mathbb{F}_2^n \to \mathbb{F}_2^m$ where $\mathbb{F}_2 = \{0, 1\}$ denotes the finite field with two elements. Here we cover only the essential concepts, referring the reader to [4] for further information on vectorial boolean functions.

A vectorial boolean function $F : \mathbb{F}_2^n \to \mathbb{F}_2^m$ (also called an (n, m)–function) is defined by m *coordinate functions* $f_i : \mathbb{F}_2^n \to \mathbb{F}_2$, where for all $x \in \mathbb{F}_2^n$ and $i \in \{0, \cdots, m-1\}$, the value of $f_i(x)$ specifies the output of the $i - th$ bit of F.

Let $r, m \in \mathbb{N}$ be positive integers and $f : \mathbb{F}_2^{2r+1} \to \mathbb{F}_2$ be a boolean function of $2r + 1$ variables. The *cellular automaton* of length $n = m + 2r$ and local rule f of radius r is the (n, m)–function $F : \mathbb{F}_2^n \to \mathbb{F}_2^m$ defined for all $x = (x_0, \cdots, x_{n-1}) \in \mathbb{F}_2^n$ as:

$$F(x_0, \cdots, x_{n-1}) = (f(x_0, \cdots, x_{2r}), f(x_1, \cdots, x_{2r+1}), \cdots, f(x_m, \cdots, x_{n-1})). \quad (1)$$

Thus, a CA F is defined by the synchronous application of the local rule f to all the central input variables $\{x_r, \cdots, x_{m+r}\}$. This means that, for all

$i \in \{0, \cdots, m-1\}$, the $i-th$ coordinate function of F is defined as $f_i(x) = f(x_i, \cdots, x_{i+2r})$.

Let $I = \{i_1, \cdots, i_t\} \subseteq [m] = \{0, \cdots, m-1\}$ be a subset of indices. The $t-$asynchronous CA $(t\text{–}ACA)$ $\tilde{F}_I$ induced by I on a CA $F : \mathbb{F}_2^{m+2r} \to \mathbb{F}_2^m$ is obtained by preventing the input variables $x_{i_1+r}, \cdots, x_{i_t+r}$ to update. In particular, for all indices $i_k \in I$ the coordinate function f_{i_k} equals the identity, while for the remaining indices $j \in J = [m] \setminus I$ function f_j still corresponds to the local rule f applied to the neighborhood $\{j, \cdots, j+2r\}$.

3   Basic Definition and Properties of Asynchrony Immunity

A CA $F : \mathbb{F}_2^{m+2r} \to \mathbb{F}_2^m$ is *balanced* if for all $y \in \mathbb{F}_2^m$ it holds that $|F^{-1}(y)| = 2^{2r}$. We formally define asynchrony immunity in CA as follows:

Definition 1. *Let $m, n, r, t \in \mathbb{N}$ be positive integers with $n = m + 2r$ and $t \le m$, and let $f : \mathbb{F}_2^{2r+1} \to \mathbb{F}_2$ be a local rule of radius r. Rule f is called (t, n)–asynchrony immune $((t, n)$–AI$)$ if, for all $0 < k \le m$ and for all sets $I \subseteq [k]$ with $|I| \le \min\{k, t\}$, both the CA $F : \mathbb{F}_2^{k+2r} \to \mathbb{F}_2^k$ and the t-ACA $\tilde{F}_I : \mathbb{F}_2^{k+2r} \to \mathbb{F}_2^m$ are balanced, i.e. $|F^{-1}(y)| = |\tilde{F}_I^{-1}(y)| = 2^{2r}$ holds for all $y \in \mathbb{F}_2^m$.*

Remark 1. The definition of (t, n)–asynchrony immunity implies in particular that the local rule f is itself balanced, i.e. $|f^{-1}(0)| = |f^{-1}(1)| = 2^{2r}$.

Among all possible $2^{2^{2r+1}}$ rules of radius r, we are interested in finding asynchrony immune rules that satisfy additional useful cryptographic properties, such as high nonlinearity. As a consequence, proving necessary conditions for a rule being (t, n)–AI helps one to prune the search space for possible candidates.

We begin by showing that asynchrony immunity is invariant under reflection and complement. To this end, recall that the *reverse* of a vector $x = (x_0, \cdots, x_{n-1})$ is the same vector in reverse order, i.e. $x^R = (x_{n-1}, \cdots, x_0)$, while the *complement* of x is the vector $x^C = (1 \oplus x_0, \cdots, 1 \oplus x_n)$. Given $f : \mathbb{F}_2^{2r+1} \to \mathbb{F}_2$, the *reflected* and *complemented* rules f^R and f^C are respectively defined as $f^R(x) = f(x^R)$ and $f^C(x) = 1 \oplus f(x)$, for all $x \in \mathbb{F}_2^{2r+1}$. For all $m \in \mathbb{N}$, the reflected and complemented CA $F^R : \mathbb{F}_2^{m+2r} \to \mathbb{F}_2^m$ and $F^C : \mathbb{F}_2^{m+2r} \to \mathbb{F}_2^m$ are defined for all $x \in \mathbb{F}_2^n$ as follows:

$$F^R(x) = F(x^R)^R = (f(x_{2r}, \cdots, x_0), \cdots, f(x_{n-1}, \cdots, x_m)), \qquad (2)$$

$$F^C(x) = \underline{1} \oplus F(x) = (1 \oplus f(x_0, \cdots, x_{2r}), \cdots, 1 \oplus f(x_m, \cdots, x_{n-1})). \qquad (3)$$

The following result shows that asynchrony immunity is preserved under reflection and complement.

Lemma 1. *Let $f : \mathbb{F}_2^{2r+1} \to \mathbb{F}_2$ be a (t, n)–AI local rule, with $n = m + 2r$ and $t \le m$. Then, the reflected and complemented rules f^R and f^C are (t, n)–AI as well.*

Proof. Let $0 < k \leq m$ and $I = \{i_1, \cdots, i_l\} \subseteq [k]$, with $l \leq \min\{k, t\}$.

For the reflected rule f^R, we know by Eq. (2) that $F^R(x) = F(x^R)^R$. It follows that the reflection of the l-ACA $\tilde{F}_I$ is defined as:

$$\tilde{F}_I^R(x) = \tilde{F}_J(x^R)^R = (f(x_{2r}, \cdots, x_0), \cdots, x_{j_1}, \cdots, x_{j_l}, \cdots, f(x_{k+2r-1}, \cdots, x_k)), \quad (4)$$

where $J = \{j_1, \cdots, j_l\}$ and $j_s = k - i_s$ for all $1 \leq s \leq l$. Rule f is (t, n)–AI and J is still a set of $l \leq t$ indices, thus $|F^{-1}(y)| = |\tilde{F}_J^{-1}(y)| = 2^{2r}$ for all $y \in \mathbb{F}_2^m$. Since the reverse operator is a bijection over both $\mathbb{F}_2^{k+2r}$ and $\mathbb{F}_2^k$, by Eq. (4) it results that $|(F^R)^{-1}(y)| = |F^{-1}(y)|$ and $|(\tilde{F}_I^R)^{-1}(y)| = |\tilde{F}_J^{-1}(y)|$. Thus, the reflected rule f^R is (t, n)–AI as well.

Analogously, for the complemented rule f^C the l-ACA $\tilde{F}_I$ is defined as:

$$\tilde{F}_I^C(x) = (1 \oplus f(x_0, \cdots, x_{2r}), \cdots, x_{i_1}, \cdots, x_{i_l}, \cdots, 1 \oplus f(x_k, \cdots, x_{k+2r-1})). \quad (5)$$

Hence we can compute $\tilde{F}_I^C$ by XORing $\tilde{F}_I$ with a bitmask composed of all 1s excepts in the positions $i_1, \cdots, i_l$. Since this operation is again a bijection over $\mathbb{F}_2^k$ and rule f is (t, n)–AI, it means that $|(F^C)^{-1}(y)| = |F^{-1}(y)| = 2^{2r}$ and $|(\tilde{F}_I^C)^{-1}(y)| = |\tilde{F}_I^{-1}(y)| = 2^{2r}$ for all $y \in \mathbb{F}_2^m$. Thus, f^C is also (t, n)–AI. □

4   Search of AI Rules up to 4 Variables

In order to search for asynchrony immune rules having additional cryptographic properties, by Remark 1 and Lemma 1 we only need to explore balanced rules under the equivalence classes induced by reflection and complement. We performed an exhaustive search among all elementary CA rules of radius $r = 1$ in order to find those satisfying (t, n)–asynchrony immunity with $t = 3$ and $n = 10$. The reason why we limited our analysis to these particular values is twofold. First, checking for asynchrony immunity is a computationally cumbersome task, since it requires to determine the output distribution of the t-ACA for all possible choices of at most t blocked cells. Second, the sizes of vectorial boolean functions employed as nonlinear components in several real-world cryptographic primitives, such as KECCAK [2], is not large.

In our quest for AI rules we also took into account the *nonlinearity* property, which is crucial in the design of several cryptographic primitives. Formally, a boolean function is *linear* if it is a linear combination of the input variables. The *nonlinearity* of a boolean function $f : \mathbb{F}_2^n \to \mathbb{F}_2$ is the minimum Hamming distance of f from all linear functions, and it equals $Nl(f) = 2^{-1}(2^n - W_{max}(f))$, where $W_{max}(f)$ is the maximum absolute value of the *Walsh transform* of f [3].

Up to reflection and complement, and neglecting the identity rule that is trivially AI for every length n and order t, we found that only rule 60 is $(3, 10)$–asynchrony immune. However, since rule 60 is linear it is not interesting from the cryptographic standpoint. We thus extended the search by considering all local rules of 4 variables defined on an asymmetric neighborhood. The corresponding CA F is defined as:

$$F(x_0, \cdots, x_{n-1}) = (f(x_0, x_1, x_2, x_3), \cdots, f(x_m, x_{m+1}, x_{m+2}, x_{m+3})). \quad (6)$$

The search returned a total of 18 rules satisfying $(3, 10)$–asynchrony immunity, among which several of them were nonlinear. Table 1 reports the Wolfram codes of the discovered rules, along with their nonlinearity values and algebraic normal form (ANF). One can notice from the ANF column in Table 1 that all discovered rules depend on the input variable x_1 in a linear way. This means that each rule can be written as $f(x_0, x_1, x_2, x_3) = x_1 \oplus g(x_0, x_2, x_3)$, where $g : \mathbb{F}_2^3 \to \mathbb{F}_2$. This means that the discovered rules are all *center-permutive*, i.e. by fixing the values of all variables except x_1 the resulting restrictions of the functions are permutations over $\mathbb{F}_2$. Remark that the elementary rule 60 is center permutive as well, being defined as $f(x_0, x_1, x_2) = x_1 \oplus x_2$. This seems to suggest that center-permutivity is a necessary condition for asynchrony immunity, a property that would greatly reduce the search space for possible AI candidates with interesting cryptographic properties. For future research, we thus plan to investigate the following conjecture:

Conjecture 1. Let $f : \mathbb{F}_2^d \to \mathbb{F}_2$ be a (t, n)–asynchrony immune rule of d variables. Then, rule f is center-permutive.

Table 1. List of $(3, 10)$–asynchrony immune CA rules of neighborhood size 4.

Rule	$Nl(f)$	$f(x_0, x_1, x_2, x_3)$	Rule	$Nl(f)$	$f(x_0, x_1, x_2, x_3)$
13107	0	$1 \oplus x_1$	14028	2	$x_1 \oplus x_0 x_3 \oplus x_2 x_3 \oplus x_0 x_2 x_3$
13116	4	$x_1 \oplus x_2 \oplus x_3 \oplus x_2 x_3$	14643	2	$1 \oplus x_1 \oplus x_0 x_3 \oplus x_0 x_2 x_3$
13155	2	$1 \oplus x_1 \oplus x_2 \oplus x_0 x_2 \oplus x_2 x_3 \oplus x_0 x_2 x_3$	14796	2	$x_1 \oplus x_3 \oplus x_0 x_3 \oplus x_0 x_2 x_3$
13164	2	$x_1 \oplus x_0 x_2 \oplus x_3 \oplus x_0 x_2 x_3$	15411	4	$1 \oplus x_1 \oplus x_3 \oplus x_2 x_3$
13203	2	$1 \oplus x_1 \oplus x_0 x_2 \oplus x_0 x_2 x_3$	15420	0	$x_1 \oplus x_2$
13212	2	$x_1 \oplus x_2 \oplus x_0 x_2 \oplus x_3 \oplus x_2 x_3 \oplus x_0 x_2 x_3$	15555	0	$1 \oplus x_1 \oplus x_2 \oplus x_3$
13251	4	$1 \oplus x_1 \oplus x_2 \oplus x_2 x_3$	15564	4	$x_1 \oplus x_2 x_3$
13260	0	$x_1 \oplus x_3$	26214	0	$x_0 \oplus x_1$
13875	2	$1 \oplus x_1 \oplus x_3 \oplus x_0 x_3 \oplus x_2 x_3 \oplus x_0 x_2 x_3$	26265	0	$1 \oplus x_0 \oplus x_1 \oplus x_3$

Another possible direction to explore is related to the maximum nonlinearity achievable by AI CA rules. For all even $d \in \mathbb{N}$, *bent* boolean functions $f : \mathbb{F}_2^d \to \mathbb{F}_2$ are those reaching the highest possible nonlinearity, which is $Nl(f) = 2^{d/2-1}$. Hence, an interesting question would be if it is possible to design an infinite family of bent AI CA.

A fact which could be useful for computer search of AI rules is that an infinite CA is *surjective* if and only if its finite counterpart is balanced for all lengths $n \in \mathbb{N}$, where balancedness corresponds to 0–AI. Thus, it would make sense to limit the search only to surjective CA, by adapting for instance Amoroso and Patt's algorithm [1].

Acknowledgements. The author wishes to thank the anonymous referees for their suggestions on how to improve the paper and extend the results for future research.

References

1. Amoroso, S., Patt, Y.N.: Decision procedures for surjectivity and injectivity of parallel maps for tessellation structures. J. Comput. Syst. Sci. **6**(5), 448–464 (1972)
2. Bertoni, G., Daemen, J., Peeters, M., Assche, G.V.: The Keccak reference (2011). http://keccak.noekeon.org/
3. Carlet, C.: Boolean functions for cryptography and error-correcting codes. In: Crama, Y., Hammer, P.L. (eds.) Boolean Models and Methods in Mathematics, Computer Science, and Engineering. Cambridge University Press, New York (2010)
4. Carlet, C.: Vectorial boolean functions for cryptography. In: Crama, Y., Hammer, P.L. (eds.) Boolean Models and Methods in Mathematics, Computer Science, and Engineering. Cambridge University Press, New York (2010)
5. Chor, B., Goldreich, O., Håstad, J., Friedman, J., Rudich, S., Smolensky, R.: The bit extraction problem of t-resilient functions. In: 26th Annual Symposium on Foundations of Computer Science, pp. 396–407. IEEE Press, New York (1985)
6. Formenti, E., Imai, K., Martin, B., Yunés, J.-B.: Advances on random sequence generation by uniform cellular automata. In: Calude, C.S., Freivalds, R., Kazuo, I. (eds.) Gruska Festschrift. LNCS, vol. 8808, pp. 56–70. Springer, Heidelberg (2014)
7. Leporati, A., Mariot, L.: Cryptographic properties of bipermutive cellular automata rules. J. Cell. Aut. **9**(5–6), 437–475 (2014)
8. Martin, B.: A walsh exploration of elementary CA rules. J. Cell. Aut. **3**(2), 145–156 (2008)

Asynchronous Simulation of Boolean Networks by Monotone Boolean Networks

Tarek Melliti[1], Damien Regnault[1], Adrien Richard[2(✉)], and Sylvain Sené[3]

[1] Université d'Évry Val-d'Essonne, CNRS, IBISC EA 4526, 91000 Évry, France
{tarek.melliti,damien.regnault}@ibisc.univ-evry.fr
[2] Université de Nice Sophia Antipolis, CNRS, I3S UMR 7271,
06900 Sophia-Antipolis, France
richard@unice.fr
[3] Aix-Marseille Université, CNRS, LIF UMR 7279, 13288 Marseille, France
sylvain.sene@lif.univ-mrs.fr

Abstract. We prove that the fully asynchronous dynamics of a Boolean network $f : \{0,1\}^n \to \{0,1\}^n$ without negative loop can be simulated, in a very specific way, by a monotone Boolean network with $2n$ components. We then use this result to prove that, for every even n, there exists a monotone Boolean network $f : \{0,1\}^n \to \{0,1\}^n$, an initial configuration x and a fixed point y of f such that: (i) y can be reached from x with a fully asynchronous updating strategy, and (ii) all such strategies contains at least $2^{\frac{n}{2}}$ updates. This contrasts with the following known property: if $f : \{0,1\}^n \to \{0,1\}^n$ is monotone, then, for every initial configuration x, there exists a fixed point y such that y can be reached from x with a fully asynchronous strategy that contains at most n updates.

Keywords: Boolean networks · Monotone networks · Asynchronous updates

1 Introduction

A *Boolean network* with n components is a discrete dynamical system usually defined by a global transition function

$$f : \{0,1\}^n \to \{0,1\}^n, \qquad x = (x_1, \ldots, x_n) \mapsto f(x) = (f_1(x), \ldots, f_n(x)).$$

Boolean networks have many applications. In particular, since the seminal papers of McCulloch and Pitts [13], Hopfield [7], Kauffman [9,10] and Thomas [19,20], they are omnipresent in the modeling of neural and gene networks (see [3,12] for reviews). They are also essential tools in Information Theory, for the network coding problem [1,5].

The structure of a Boolean network f is usually represented via its **interaction graph**, which is the signed digraph $G(f)$ defined as follows: the vertex set is $[n] := \{1, \ldots, n\}$ and, for all $i, j \in [n]$, there exists a positive (resp. negative) arc from j to i is there exists $x \in \{0,1\}^n$ such that

$$f_i(x_1, \ldots, x_{j-1}, 1, x_{j+1}, \ldots, x_n) - f_i(x_1, \ldots, x_{j-1}, 0, x_{j+1}, \ldots, x_n)$$

© Springer International Publishing Switzerland 2016
S. El Yacoubi et al. (Eds.): ACRI 2016, LNCS 9863, pp. 182–191, 2016.
DOI: 10.1007/978-3-319-44365-2_18

is positive (resp. negative). Note that $G(f)$ may have both a positive and a negative arc from one vertex to another. Note also that $G(f)$ may have *loops*, that is, arcs from a vertex to itself. The sign of a cycle of $G(f)$ is, as usual, the product of the signs of its arcs (cycles are always directed and without "repeated" vertices).

From a dynamical point of view, there are several ways to derive a dynamics from f, depending on the chosen *updating strategy*. With the so-called *synchronous* or *parallel strategy*, each component is updated at each step: if x^t is the configuration of the system at time t, then $f(x^t)$ is the configuration of the system at time $t+1$. Hence, the dynamics is just given by the successive iterations of f. On the opposite way, with the so-called *(fully) asynchronous strategy*, exactly one component is updated at each time. This strategy is very often used in practice, in particular in the context of gene networks [20]. More formally, given an infinite sequence $i_0 i_1 i_2 \ldots$ of indices taken in $[n]$, the dynamics of f resulting from an initial configuration x^0 and the asynchronous strategy $i_0 i_1 i_2 \ldots$ is given by the following recurrence: for all $t \in \mathbb{N}$ and $i \in [n]$, $x_i^{t+1} = f_i(x^t)$ if $i = i_t$ and $x_i^{t+1} = x_i^t$ otherwise.

All the possible asynchronous dynamics can be represented in a compact way by the so-called **asynchronous graph** $\Gamma(f)$, defined as follows: the vertex set is $\{0, 1\}^n$ and, for all $x, y \in \{0, 1\}^n$, there is an arc from x to y, called *transition*, if there exists $i \in [n]$ such that $f_i(x) = y_i \neq x_i$ and $y_j = x_j$ for all $j \neq i$. Note that f and $\Gamma(f)$ share the same information. The *distance* between two configurations x and y in $\Gamma(f)$, denoted $d_{\Gamma(f)}(x, y)$, is the minimal length of a path of $\Gamma(f)$ from x to y, with the convention that the distance is ∞ if no such paths exist. Note that $d_{\Gamma(f)}(x, y)$ is at least the Hamming distance $d_H(x, y)$ between x and y. A path from x to y in $\Gamma(f)$ is then called a **geodesic** if its length is exactly $d_H(x, y)$. In other words, a geodesic is a path along which each component is updated at most one. The **diameter** of $\Gamma(f)$ is

$$\mathrm{diam}(\Gamma(f)) := \max\{d_{\Gamma(f)}(x, y) : x, y \in \{0, 1\}^n, d_{\Gamma(f)}(x, y) < \infty\}.$$

In many contexts, as in molecular biology, the first reliable information are represented under the form of an interaction graph, while the actual dynamics are very difficult to observe [12,21]. A natural question is then the following: *What can be said about $\Gamma(f)$ according to $G(f)$ only?*

Robert proved the following partial answer [17, 18].

Theorem 1. *If $G(f)$ is acyclic then f has a unique fixed point y. Furthermore, $\Gamma(f)$ is acyclic and, for every configuration x, $\Gamma(f)$ has a geodesic from x to y.*

In other words, $d_{\Gamma(f)}(x, y) = d_H(x, y)$ for every $x \in \{0, 1\}^n$. However, the acyclicity of $G(f)$ is not sufficient for $\Gamma(f)$ to have a short diameter. Indeed, in a rather different setting, Domshlak [4] proved (a slightly stronger version of) the following result.

Theorem 2. *For every $n \geq 8$ there exists $f : \{0, 1\}^n \to \{0, 1\}^n$ such that $G(f)$ is acyclic and $\mathrm{diam}(\Gamma(f)) \geq 1.5^{\frac{n}{2}}$.*

Now, what can be said if $G(f)$ contains cycles? Thomas highlighted the fact that the distinction between positive and negative cycles is highly relevant (see [20,21] for instance). The subtlety and versatility of the influences of interactions between positive and negative cycles lead researchers to first focus on networks with only positive cycles or only negative cycles. In particular, the following basic properties was proved in [2,15,16]: *If $G(f)$ has no positive (resp. negative) cycles, then f has at most (resp. at least) one fixed point.* This gives a nice proof by dichotomy of the first assertion in Theorem 1.

In [14], the authors showed that the absence of negative cycles essentially corresponds to the study of **monotone networks**, that is, Boolean networks $f : \{0,1\}^n \to \{0,1\}^n$ such that

$$x \leq y \;\Rightarrow\; f(x) \leq f(y)$$

where $\leq$ is the usual partial order ($x \leq y$ if and only if $x_i \leq y_i$ for all $i \in [n]$). More precisely, they proved the following: *If $G(f)$ is strongly connected and without negative cycles, then there exists a monotone network $f' : \{0,1\}^n \to \{0,1\}^n$ such that: $G(f)$ and $G(f')$ have the same underlying unsigned digraph, and $\Gamma(f)$ and $\Gamma(f')$ are isomorphic.* Furthermore, they proved the following reachability result, that shares some similarities with Theorem 1.

Theorem 3. *If $f : \{0,1\}^n \to \{0,1\}^n$ is monotone, then, for every configuration x, $\Gamma(f)$ has a geodesic from x to a fixed point y of f.*

Here, we prove the following theorem, that shows that there may exist, under the same hypothesis, a configuration x and a fixed point y such that y is reachable from x with paths of exponential length only. This result contrasts with the previous one, and may be seen as an adaptation of Theorem 2 for monotone networks.

Theorem 4. *For every even n, there exists a monotone network $f : \{0,1\}^n \to \{0,1\}^n$, two configurations x and y such that y is a fixed point of f and*

$$\mathrm{diam}(\Gamma(f)) \geq d_{\Gamma(f)}(x,y) \geq 2^{\frac{n}{2}}.$$

The proof is by construction, and the idea for the construction is rather simple. Let A, B and C be the sets of configurations that contains $n/2 - 1$, $n/2$ and $n/2 + 1$ ones. Clearly, A, B and C are antichains of exponential size, and, in these antichains, obviously, the monotonicity of f doesn't apply. This leaves enough freedom to defined f on $A \cup B \cup C$ in such a way that subgraph $\Gamma(f)$ induced by $A \cup B \cup C$ contains a configuration x and fixed point y reachable from x with paths of exponential length only. To obtain a network as in the theorem, it is then sufficient to extend f on the whole space $\{0,1\}^n$ by keeping f monotone and without creating shortcuts from x to y in the asynchronous graph. This idea, that consists in using large antichains to construct special monotone functions, is also present in [6] and [8] for instance.

Let $f : \{0,1\}^n \to \{0,1\}^n$ be any Boolean network such that $G(f)$ has no negative loops. With the technic described above, we can go further and prove that $\Gamma(f)$ can be embedded in the asynchronous graph $\Gamma(f')$ of a monotone network $f' : \{0,1\}^{2n} \to \{0,1\}^{2n}$ in such a way that fixed points and distances between configurations are preserved. The formal statement follows. If $x, y \in \{0,1\}^n$, then the concatenation (x, y) is seen as a configuration of $\{0,1\}^{2n}$ and, conversely, each configuration in $\{0,1\}^{2n}$ is seen as the concatenation of two configurations in $\{0,1\}^n$. As usual, we denote by $\overline{x}$ the configuration obtained from x by switching every component.

Theorem 5 (Main Results). *Let $f : \{0,1\}^n \to \{0,1\}^n$. If $G(f)$ has no negative loops, then there exists a monotone network $f' : \{0,1\}^{2n} \to \{0,1\}^{2n}$ such that the following two properties holds. First, x is a fixed point of f if and only if $(x,\overline{x})$ is a fixed point of f'. Second, for all $x, y \in \{0,1\}^n$, $\Gamma(f)$ has a path from x to y of length ℓ if and only if $\Gamma(f')$ has a path from $(x,\overline{x})$ to $(y,\overline{y})$ of length 2ℓ.*

Theorem 4 is now an easy corollary of Theorem 5.

Proof (of Theorem 4 assuming Theorem 5). Let $r = 2^n$, and let $x^1, x^2, \ldots, x^r$ be any enumeration of the elements of $\{0,1\}^n$ such that $d_H(x^k, x^{k+1}) = 1$ for all $1 \le k < r$ (take the Gray code for instance). Let $f : \{0,1\}^n \to \{0,1\}^n$ be defined by $f(x^k) = x^{k+1}$ for all $1 \le k < r$ and $f(x^r) = x^r$. Let $x = x^0$ and $y = x^r$. Then y is the unique fixed point of f. Furthermore, since the set of transitions of $\Gamma(f)$ is $\{x^k \to x^{k+1} : 1 \le k < r\}$, we deduce that $d_{\Gamma(f)}(x, y) = 2^n - 1$. We also deduce that $G(f)$ has no negative loops (this is an easy exercise to prove that $G(f)$ has a negative loop if and only if $\Gamma(f)$ has a cycle of length two). Hence, by Theorem 5, there exists a monotone network $f' : \{0,1\}^{2n} \to \{0,1\}^{2n}$ such that $(y, \overline{y})$ is a fixed point and

$$d_{\Gamma(f')}((x,\overline{x}), (y,\overline{y})) = 2d_{\Gamma(f)}(x,y) = 2^{n+1} - 2 \ge 2^n.$$

$\square$

The paper is organized as follows. The proof of Theorem 5 is given in Sect. 2. A conclusion and some open questions are then given in Sect. 3.

2   Proof of Theorem 5

We first fix some notations:

$$
\begin{aligned}
\overline{x}^i &:= (x_1, \ldots, \overline{x_i}, \ldots, x_n) & (x \in \{0,1\}^n \text{ and } i \in [n]), \\
w(x) &:= |\{i \in [n] : x_i = 1\}| & (x \in \{0,1\}^n), \\
w(x,y) &:= w(x) + w(y) & (x, y \in \{0,1\}^n), \\
\Omega &:= \{(x,\overline{x}) : x \in \{0,1\}^n\}.
\end{aligned}
$$

The function f' in Theorem 5 is defined as follows from f.

Definition 1. *Given* $f : \{0,1\}^n \to \{0,1\}^n$*, we define* $f' : \{0,1\}^{2n} \to \{0,1\}^{2n}$
by: for all $i \in [n]$ *and* $x, y \in \{0,1\}^n$,

$$f_i'(x,y) = \begin{cases} f_i(x) & \text{if } y = \overline{x} \text{ or } \overline{y}^i = \overline{x} \\ \overline{x_i} & \text{if } w(x,y) = n \text{ and } y \neq \overline{x} \\ 1 & \text{if } w(x,y) = n+1 \text{ and } \overline{y}^i \neq \overline{x} \\ 0 & \text{if } w(x,y) = n-1 \text{ and } \overline{y}^i \neq \overline{x} \\ 1 & \text{if } w(x,y) \geq n+2 \\ 0 & \text{if } w(x,y) \leq n-2 \end{cases} \quad \text{and} \quad f_{n+i}'(x,y) = \overline{f_i'(\overline{y}, \overline{x})}.$$

Remark 1. $f_i'(x,y) = \overline{f_{n+i}'(\overline{y}, \overline{x})}$.

Remark 2. Let A, B and C be sets of configurations $(x,y) \in \{0,1\}^{2n}$ such that $w(x,y)$ is $n-1$, n and $n+1$, respectively (these are the three sets discussed in the introduction) (we have $\Omega \subseteq B$). One can see that f_i' behave as f_i when x and y are mirroring each other ($y = \overline{x}$) or almost mirroring each other ($\overline{y}^i = \overline{x}$); and in both cases, (x,y) lies in $A \cup B \cup C$. One can also see that f_i' equals 0 below the layer A and equals 1 above the layer C. The same remarks apply on f_{n+i}', excepted that f_{n+1}' behaves as the negation $\overline{f_i}$ in $A \cup B \cup C$. Hence, roughly speaking, f behaves as $(f, \overline{f})$ in the middle layer $A \cup B \cup C$, and it converges toward the all-zeroes or all-ones configuration outside this layer.

Lemma 1. *If* $G(f)$ *has no negative loops, then* f' *is monotone.*

Proof. Suppose, for a contradiction, that there exists $a, b, c, d \in \{0,1\}^n$ and $i \in [n]$ such that

$$(a,b) < (c,d) \text{ and } f_i'(a,b) > f_i'(c,d).$$

Then we have

$$n - 1 \leq w(a,b) < w(c,d) \leq n+1.$$

This leaves three possibilities.

Case 1: $w(a,b) = n-1$ *and* $w(c,d) = n+1$. Since $f_i'(a,b) = 1$, we fall in the first case of the definition of f_i', that is,

$$f_i'(a,b) = f_i(a) = 1 \text{ and } \overline{b}^i = \overline{a}.$$

Similarly

$$f_i'(c,d) = f_i(c) = 0 \text{ and } \overline{d}^i = \overline{c}.$$

Thus

$$(a,b) = (a, \overline{\overline{a}}^i) < (c,d) = (c, \overline{\overline{c}}^i).$$

So for all $j \neq i$, we have $a_j \leq c_j$ and $\overline{a_j} = (\overline{\overline{a}}^i)_j \leq (\overline{\overline{c}}^i)_j = \overline{c_j}$ thus $c_j \leq a_j$. So $a_j = c_j$ for all $j \neq i$, that is, $c \in \{a, \overline{a}^i\}$. Since $f_i(a) < f_i(c)$ we have $c = \overline{a}^i$, and since $a \leq c$ we deduce that $a_i = 0$. Thus $G(f)$ has a negative arc from i to i, a contradiction.

Case 2: $w(a, b) = n - 1$ *and* $w(c, d) = n$. As in Case 1, we have

$$f_i'(a, b) = f_i(a) = 1 \text{ and } \overline{b}^i = \overline{a}.$$

For $f_i'(c, d)$ we have two cases. Suppose first that

$$f_i'(c, d) = f_i(c) = 0 \text{ and } d = \overline{c}.$$

Then

$$(a, b) = (a, \overline{\overline{a}}^i) < (c, d) = (c, \overline{c}).$$

So for all $j \neq i$, we have $a_j \leq c_j$ and $\overline{a_j} = (\overline{a}^i)_j \leq \overline{c_j}$ thus $c_j \leq a_j$. So $a_j = c_j$ for all $j \neq i$, that is, $c \in \{a, \overline{a}^i\}$. Since $f_i(a) < f_i(c)$ we have $c = \overline{a}^i$, and since $a \leq c$ we deduce that $a_i = 0$. Thus $G(f)$ has a negative arc from i to i, a contradiction. The other case is

$$f_i'(c, d) = \overline{c_i} = 0 \text{ and } d \neq \overline{c}.$$

First, observe that for all $j \neq i$, if $c_j = 0$ then $a_j = 0$ thus $1 = (\overline{a}^i)_j \leq d_j$. Since $c_i = 1$ we deduce that $\overline{c} \leq d$. Now, suppose that $c_j = d_j = 1$ for some $j \in [n]$. Since $w(c, d) = n$, we deduce that there exists $k \neq j$ such that $c_k = d_k = 0$, and this contradicts $\overline{c} \leq d$. Thus, for all $j \in [n]$, either $d_j = 0$ or $d_j > c_j$, that is, $d \leq \overline{c}$. Thus $c = \overline{d}$, a contradiction.

Case 3: $w(a, b) = n$ *and* $w(c, d) = n + 1$. We obtain a contradiction as in Case 2.

So we have proven that f_i' is monotone for all $i \in [n]$. It remains to prove that f_{n+i}' is monotone. Using the monotony of f_i' for the implication we get:

$$
\begin{aligned}
(a, b) \leq (c, d) &\iff (\overline{c}, \overline{d}) \leq (\overline{a}, \overline{b}) \\
&\iff (\overline{d}, \overline{c}) \leq (\overline{b}, \overline{a}) \\
&\implies f_i'(\overline{d}, \overline{c}) \leq f_i'(\overline{b}, \overline{a}) \\
&\iff \overline{f_i'(\overline{b}, \overline{a})} \leq \overline{f_i'(\overline{d}, \overline{c})} \\
&\iff f_{i+n}'(a, b) \leq f_{i+n}'(c, d).
\end{aligned}
$$

$\square$

Lemma 2. *For all* $x \in \{0, 1\}^n$ *we have* $f(x) = x$ *if and only if* $f'(x, \overline{x}) = (x, \overline{x})$.

Proof. By definition we have

$$f(x) = x \iff f_i'(x, \overline{x}) = x_i \ \forall i \in [n].$$

So it is sufficient to prove that

$$f'(x, \overline{x}) = (x, \overline{x}) \iff f_i'(x, \overline{x}) = x_i \ \forall i \in [n].$$

The direction $\Rightarrow$ is obvious, and $\Leftarrow$ is a consequence of the following equivalences:

$$f_i'(x,\overline{x}) = x_i \iff \overline{f_{n+i}'(\overline{x},\overline{x})} = x_i$$
$$\iff f_{n+i}'(x,\overline{x}) = \overline{x_i}$$
$$\iff f_{n+i}'(x,\overline{x}) = (x,\overline{x})_{n+i}.$$

$\square$

Lemma 3. *For all* $x, y \in \{0,1\}^n$, *if* $\Gamma(f')$ *has a path from* (x,y) *to* Ω *then* $n - 1 \leq w(x,y) \leq n + 1$.

Proof. It is sufficient to prove that,

$$w(x,y) \leq n - 2 \Rightarrow f'(x,y) = 0 \quad \text{and} \quad w(x,y) \geq n + 2 \Rightarrow f'(x,y) = 1.$$

Let $i \in [n]$. If $w(x,y) \leq n - 2$ (resp. $w(x,y) \geq n + 2$) then $f_i'(x,y) = 0$ (resp. $f_i'(x,y) = 1$) by definition. Now, if $w(x,y) \leq n - 2$ then $w(\bar{y}, \bar{x}) \geq n + 2$ thus

$$f_{n+i}'(x,y) = \overline{f_i'(\bar{y}, \bar{x})} = \overline{1} = 0,$$

and if $w(x,y) \geq n + 2$ then $w(\bar{y}, \bar{x}) \leq n - 2$ thus

$$f_{n+i}'(x,y) = \overline{f_i'(\bar{y}, \bar{x})} = \overline{0} = 1.$$

$\square$

Lemma 4. *If* $G(f)$ *has no negative loops, then, for all* $x, y \in \{0,1\}^n$, *the following assertions are equivalent:*

(1) $x \to y$ *is a transition of* $\Gamma(f)$.
(2) $(x,\overline{x}) \to (y,\overline{x}) \to (y,\overline{y})$ *is a path of* $\Gamma(f')$.
(3) $(x,\overline{x}) \to (x,\overline{y}) \to (y,\overline{y})$ *is a path of* $\Gamma(f')$.
(4) $\Gamma(f')$ *has a path from* $(x,\overline{x})$ *to* $(y,\overline{y})$ *without internal vertex in* Ω.

Furthermore, the only possible paths of $\Gamma(f')$ *from* $(x,\overline{x})$ *to* $(y,\overline{y})$ *without internal vertex in* Ω *are precisely the ones in (2) and (3).*

Proof. Suppose that $\Gamma(f)$ has a transition $x \to y$, and let $i \in [n]$ be such that $y = \overline{x}^i$. We have $f_i'(x,\overline{x}) = f_i(x) \neq x_i$ thus $\Gamma(f')$ has a transition from $(x,\overline{x})$ to $(\overline{x}^i, \overline{x}) = (y, \overline{x})$. Since

$$f_{n+i}'(\overline{x}^i, \overline{x}) = \overline{f_i(\overline{x}, \overline{\overline{x}^i})} = \overline{f_i(x, \overline{\overline{x}^i})} = \overline{f_i(x)} = x_i \neq (\overline{x}^i, \overline{x})_{n+i},$$

$\Gamma(f')$ has a transition from $(\overline{x}^i, \overline{x})$ to

$$\overline{(\overline{x}^i, \overline{x})}^{n+i} = (\overline{x}^i, \overline{\overline{x}}^i) = (y, \overline{y}).$$

This proves the implication (1) $\Rightarrow$ (2). Now, if $\Gamma(f')$ contains the transition $(x,\overline{x}) \to (y,\overline{x})$ then there exists $i \in [n]$ such that $y = \overline{x}^i$ and $y_i = f_i'(x,\overline{x}) = f_i(x)$.

Thus $x \to y$ is a transition of $\Gamma(f)$. So we have (1) $\Longleftrightarrow$ (2) and we prove similarly that (1) $\Longleftrightarrow$ (3).

Since $[(2)$ or $(3)] \Rightarrow (4)$ is obvious, to complete the proof it is sufficient to prove that if $\Gamma(f')$ has a path P from $(x, \overline{x})$ to $(y, \overline{y})$ without internal vertex in Ω then either $P = (x, \overline{x}) \to (y, \overline{x}) \to (y, \overline{y})$ or $P = (x, \overline{x}) \to (x, \overline{y}) \to (y, \overline{y})$. Let a be the configuration following $(x, \overline{x})$ in P, and let b be the configuration following a in P. We will prove that $b = (y, \overline{y})$ and $a = (x, \overline{y})$ or $a = (y, \overline{x})$. We have $w(a) = n \pm 1$ and thus $w(b) \in \{n-2, n, n+2\}$, but if $w(b) = n \pm 2$ then we deduce from Lemma 3 that $\Gamma(f')$ has no paths from b to a configuration in Ω, a contradiction. Thus $w(b) = n$. Let $i \in [n]$ be such that $a = (\overline{x}^i, \overline{x})$ or $a = (x, \overline{x}^i)$. We have four cases.

Case 1: $a = (\overline{x}^i, \overline{x})$ *and* $w(a) = n - 1$. Since $w(a) = n - 1$ we have $x_i = 1$, and thus $f'_i(x, \overline{x}) = f_i(x) = 0$. Also $f'_i(a) = f'_i(\overline{x}^i, \overline{x}) = f_i(\overline{x}^i) = 0$ since otherwise $G(f)$ has a negative loop on vertex i. Let $1 \le j \le 2n$ be such that $b = \overline{a}^j$. Since $w(a) < w(b) = n$, we have $a_j = 0$ and $f'_j(a) = 1$. If $1 \le j \le n$ then $j \ne i$ (since $f'_i(a) = 0$) so $\overline{x}^j \ne \overline{x}^i$ and since $w(\overline{x}^i, \overline{x}) = n - 1$, we deduce from the definition of f' that $f'_j(a) = f'_j(\overline{x}^i, \overline{x}) = 0$, a contradiction. So $n < j \le 2n$. Let $k = j - n$. We have

$$f'_j(a) = f'_{n+k}(a) = f'_{n+k}(\overline{x}^i, \overline{x}) = \overline{f'_k(\overline{x}, \overline{x}^i)} = \overline{f'_k(x, \overline{x}^i)}.$$

Since $w(\overline{x}^i, \overline{x}) = n - 1$ we have $w(x, \overline{\overline{x}}^i) = n + 1$. So if $k \ne i$ we have $\overline{\overline{x}}^k \ne \overline{x}$. Thus by the definition of f' we have $f'_k(x, \overline{\overline{x}}^i) = 1$ thus $f'_j(a) = 0$, a contradiction. We deduce that $k = i$, that is, $j = n + i$. Thus $b = \overline{a}^{n+i} = (\overline{x}^i, \overline{\overline{x}}^i) \in \Omega$, and we deduce that

$$P = (x, \overline{x}) \to (y, \overline{x}) \to (y, \overline{y}).$$

Case 2: $a = (\overline{x}^i, \overline{x})$ *and* $w(a) = n + 1$. We prove with similar arguments that

$$P = (x, \overline{x}) \to (y, \overline{x}) \to (y, \overline{y}).$$

Case 3: $a = (x, \overline{\overline{x}}^i)$ *and* $w(a) = n - 1$. We prove with similar arguments that

$$P = (x, \overline{x}) \to (x, \overline{y}) \to (y, \overline{y}).$$

Case 4: $a = (x, \overline{\overline{x}}^i)$ *and* $w(a) = n + 1$. We prove with similar arguments that

$$P = (x, \overline{x}) \to (x, \overline{y}) \to (y, \overline{y}).$$

$\square$

Lemma 5. *If $G(f)$ has no negative loops, then for all $x, y \in \{0,1\}^n$, the following two assertions are equivalent:*

(1) *$\Gamma(f)$ has a path from x to y of length ℓ.*

(2) $\Gamma(f')$ *has a path from* $(x, \bar{x})$ *to* $(y, \bar{y})$ *of length* 2ℓ.

Proof. According to Lemma 4, $x^0 \to x^1 \to x^2 \to \cdots \to x^\ell$ is a path of $\Gamma(f)$ if and only if

$$(x^0, \overline{x^0}) \to (x^0, \overline{x^1}) \to (x^1, \overline{x^1}) \to (x^1, \overline{x^2}) \to (x^2, \overline{x^2}) \cdots \to (x^\ell, \overline{x^\ell})$$

is a path of $\Gamma(f')$. This proves (1) $\Rightarrow$ (2). To prove (2) $\Rightarrow$ (1) suppose that $\Gamma(f')$ has a path P from $(x, \bar{x})$ to $(y, \bar{y})$ of length 2ℓ. Let $(a^0, \overline{a^0}), (a^1 \overline{a^1}), \ldots, (a^p, \overline{a^p})$ be the configurations of P that belongs to Ω, given in the order (so $a^0 = x$ and $a^p = y$). According to Lemma 4, there exists $b^1, b^2, \ldots, b^p$ with $b^q \in \{(a^{q-1}, \overline{a^q}), (a^q, \overline{a^{q-1}})\}$ for all $1 \le q \le p$ such that

$$P = (a^0, \overline{a^0}) \to b^1 \to (a^1, \overline{a^1}) \to b^2 \to \cdots \to b^p \to (a^p, \overline{a^p}).$$

Thus $p = \ell$, and again by Lemma 4, $x^0 \to x^1 \to \cdots \to x^\ell$ is a path of $\Gamma(f)$. $\square$

Theorem 5 result from Lemmas 1, 2 and 5.

3   Conclusion and Open Questions

In this paper we have proved that the asynchronous graph of every n-component Boolean network without negative loop can be embedded in the asynchronous graph of a $2n$-component *monotone* Boolean network, in such a way that fixed points and distances between configurations are preserved. A consequence of this result, which was our initial goal, is that the asynchronous graph of a monotone network may have an exponential diameter. More precisely, it may exist a configuration x and a fixed point y reachable from x such that the distance between x and y is at least $2^{\frac{n}{2}}$. This contrasts with the fact that for every configuration x there exists a fixed point y such that the distance between x and y is at most n.

These results raise several questions. Could it be possible to embed, in a similar way, a n-component network *with* negative loops into a m-component monotone network? Maybe this would require m to be even larger than $2n$. Besides, the embedding we propose is based on the injection $x \mapsto (x, \bar{x})$ from $\{0, 1\}^n$ to the balanced words of length $2n$. The well-known Knuth's balanced coding scheme [11] provides a rather simple injection from $\{0, 1\}^n$ to the balanced words of length $n + 2 \log_2 n$ only. Could this technique be used to decrease the number of components in the host monotone network from $2n$ to $n + 2 \log_2 n$? Finally, it could be interesting to study the interaction graph of monotone networks with large diameter. Does it necessarily contain long cycles, or many disjoint cycles?

Acknowledgment. This work has been partially supported by the project PACA APEX FRI. We wish also to thank Pierre-Etienne Meunier, Maximilien Gadouleau and an anonymous reviewer for stimulating discussions and interesting remarks.

References

1. Ahlswede, R., Cai, N., Li, S.Y., Yeung, R.: Network information flow. IEEE Trans. Inf. Theory **46**(4), 1204–1216 (2000)
2. Aracena, J.: Maximum number of fixed points in regulatory Boolean networks. Bull. Math. Biol. **70**(5), 1398–1409 (2008)
3. Bornholdt, S.: Boolean network models of cellular regulation: prospects and limitations. J. R. Soc. Interface **5**(Suppl 1), S85–S94 (2008)
4. Domshlak, C.: On recursively directed hypercubes. Electron. J. Comb. **9**(1), R23 (2002)
5. Gadouleau, M., Richard, A., Fanchon, E.: Reduction and fixed points of Boolean networks and linear network coding solvability. ArXiv e-prints, December 2014
6. Gadouleau, M., Richard, A., Riis, S.: Fixed points of Boolean networks, guessing graphs, and coding theory. SIAM J. Discrete Math. **29**(4), 2312–2335 (2015)
7. Hopfield, J.: Neural networks and physical systems with emergent collective computational abilities. Proc. Nat. Acad. Sci. U.S.A. **79**, 2554–2558 (1982)
8. Julio, A., Demongeot, J., Goles, E.: On limit cycles of monotone functions with symmetric connection graph. Theoret. Comput. Sci. **322**(2), 237–244 (2004)
9. Kauffman, S.A.: Metabolic stability and epigenesis in randomly connected nets. J. Theor. Biol. **22**, 437–467 (1969)
10. Kauffman, S.A.: Origins of Order Self-Organization and Selection in Evolution. Oxford University Press, Oxford (1993)
11. Knuth, D.E.: Efficient balanced codes. IEEE Trans. Inf. Theory **32**(1), 51–53 (1986)
12. Le Novère, N.: Quantitative and logic modelling of molecular and gene networks. Nat. Rev. Genet. **16**, 146–158 (2015)
13. MacCulloch, W.S., Pitts, W.S.: A logical calculus of the ideas immanent in nervous activity. Bull. Math. Bio. Phys. **5**, 113–115 (1943)
14. Melliti, T., Regnault, D., Richard, A., Sené, S.: On the convergence of Boolean automata networks without negative cycles. In: Kari, J., Kutrib, M., Malcher, A. (eds.) AUTOMATA 2013. LNCS, vol. 8155, pp. 124–138. Springer, Heidelberg (2013)
15. Remy, E., Ruet, P., Thieffry, D.: Graphic requirements for multistability and attractive cycles in a Boolean dynamical framework. Adv. Appl. Math. **41**(3), 335–350 (2008)
16. Richard, A.: Negative circuits and sustained oscillations in asynchronous automata networks. Adv. Appl. Math. **44**(4), 378–392 (2010)
17. Robert, F.: Discrete Iterations: A Metric Study. Series in Computational Mathematics, vol. 6, p. 198. Springer, Heidelberg (1986)
18. Robert, F.: Les systèmes dynamiques discrets. Mathématiques et Applications, vol. 19, p. 296. Springer, Heidelberg (1995)
19. Thomas, R.: Boolean formalization of genetic control circuits. J. Theor. Biol. **42**(3), 563–585 (1973)
20. Thomas, R., d'Ari, R.: Biological Feedback. CRC Press, Boca Raton (1990)
21. Thomas, R., Kaufman, M.: Multistationarity, the basis of cell differentiation and memory. II. Logical analysis of regulatory networks in terms of feedback circuits. Chaos: an Interdisciplinary. J. Nonlinear Sci. **11**(1), 180–195 (2001)

Maxmin-ω: A Simple Deterministic Asynchronous Cellular Automaton Scheme

Ebrahim L. Patel[(⊠)]

Department of Mathematics, University of Portsmouth, Portsmouth PO1 3HF, UK
`ebrahim.patel@port.ac.uk`

Abstract. In this paper, we introduce the maxmin-ω system, a simple and intuitive model of asynchronous dynamics on a network. Each node in this system updates its state upon receiving a fixed proportion ω of inputs from neighbourhood nodes. We study the behaviour of nodal update times as a function of ω. Computational results suggest most complexity when ω is approximately 0.5. By implementing a cellular automaton (CA) under this maxmin-ω asynchronous scheme, we show some correspondence in complexity between timing and CA output. Moreover, our system can be interpreted by the useful modelling tool of max-min-plus algebra (MMP). We propose that the aforementioned results on complexity can be derived analytically via MMP.

1 Introduction

We introduce a simple asynchronous dynamical system, which we call maxmin-ω. The system acts on a network which, in this paper, will be a one-dimensional cellular automaton (CA) lattice (so the terms "nodes" and "cells" will be used interchangeably). There are a couple of crucial points that provide the attraction for studying this system: firstly, the update of cell states depends on local exchanges until the fraction ω is fulfilled; the maxmin-ω system is therefore deterministic, and is not only a departure from traditional asynchronous CA schemes (e.g., [1,2]) but differs from more recent work that looks at such local interactions that are stochastic [3]. Secondly, the parameter ω is shown to drive an interesting set of results – both in terms of the asymptotic timings and the implementation of a simple CA scheme – which leads us to suggest other, promising, applications other than CA.

2 The Maxmin-ω Model

In the maxmin-ω model a cell (node) state is updated at the end of a *cycle*. Consider a node i in a network of size N. The node carries a state that changes with time. Thus, we can plot points on the real line, representing time, corresponding to when these changes occur. We refer to the points as the *update times* of the nodal state. Let $x_i(k)$ denote the kth update time for the ith node.[1] Once each

---

[1] We choose x and not t as we will study update time as a 'state' itself; this is consistent with the literature [9].

© Springer International Publishing Switzerland 2016
S. El Yacoubi et al. (Eds.): ACRI 2016, LNCS 9863, pp. 192–198, 2016.
DOI: 10.1007/978-3-319-44365-2_19

node in the neighbourhood of i has completed its kth cycle (where k is also called a *cycle number*), it sends the updated state to i. The transmission of such a state from node j to i takes *transmission time* $\tau_{ij}(k)$. The update (or computation) of the state of node i takes a *processing time*, and it is represented in the kth cycle by $\xi_i(k)$.

Now, suppose each node updates its state upon receiving a fraction ω of inputs from its neighbourhood ($\omega \in [0, 1]$). We define the "ω^{th} input" as the last of the fraction ω of inputs arriving at i. Then the $(k+1)^{\text{th}}$ update time of node i is given by the following recurrence relation.

$$x_i(k+1) = x_{(\omega)}(k) + \xi_i(k+1) \tag{1}$$

where $x_{(\omega)}(k)$ represents the kth time of arrival of the ωth input from the neighbourhood of i; if k is clear from context, we denote this $x_{(\omega)}$ for short. If there are n nodes in the neighbourhood of i, then $x_{(\omega)}$ practically represents the time of arrival of the mth input where $m = \lceil \omega n \rceil$. Once node i receives the m inputs, it processes its new state; this takes time duration $\xi_i(k+1)$. Once processed, node i sends its state to downstream nodes at time $x_i(k+1)$, which is also the update time of i.

Figure 1 gives a flavour of the effect of maxmin-ω on CA using the same initial CA state and same CA rule. When $\omega = 1$ the CA space-time pattern resembles the synchronous CA pattern. This is because when $\omega = 1$, nodal states are updated upon arrival of *all* neighbourhood inputs, so there is no loss of information between the network states in the traditional synchronous model (where all nodes update at the same time) and this asynchronous system. On the other hand, the synchronous pattern is lost when $\omega < 1$.

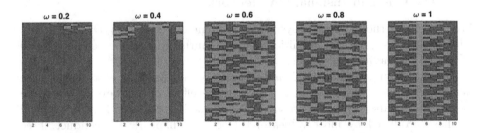

Fig. 1. CA space-time patterns as a function of ω for the maxmin-ω system. The underlying lattice comprises 10 cells. Each cell takes on one of two states, 1 and 0; state 1 is coloured light and state 0 is coloured dark.

2.1 Asymptotic Behaviour

Define the function $\mathcal{M}$ as the mapping $\mathcal{M} : \mathbb{R}^N \to \mathbb{R}^N$ whose components $\mathcal{M}_i$ are of the form of Eq. (1). We represent a system of N such equations by the following.

$$\boldsymbol{x}(k+1) = \mathcal{M}(\boldsymbol{x}(k)) \tag{2}$$

for $k \geq 0$, where $\boldsymbol{x}(k) = (x_1(k), x_2(k), \ldots, x_N(k))$.

Denote by $\mathcal{M}^p(\boldsymbol{x})$ the action of applying $\mathcal{M}$ to a vector $x \in \mathrm{IR}^N$ a total of p times, i.e., $\mathcal{M}^p(\boldsymbol{x}) = \underbrace{\mathcal{M}(\mathcal{M}(\cdots(\mathcal{M}(\boldsymbol{x}))\cdots))}_{p \text{ times}}$.

Definition 1. *If it exists, the* cycletime vector *of $\mathcal{M}$ is $\chi(\mathcal{M})$ and is defined as* $\lim_{k\to\infty}(\mathcal{M}^k(\boldsymbol{x})/k)$.

Definition 2. *For some $k \geq 0$, consider the set of vectors*

$$\boldsymbol{x}(k), \boldsymbol{x}(k+1), \boldsymbol{x}(k+2), \ldots \in \mathrm{IR}^N$$

where $\boldsymbol{x}(n) = \mathcal{M}^n(\boldsymbol{x}(0))$ for all $n \geq 0$. The set $x_i(k), x_i(k+1), x_i(k+2), \ldots$ is called a periodic regime *of $i \in \mathrm{IN}$ if there exists $\mu_i \in \mathrm{IR}$ and a finite number $\rho_i, \in \mathrm{IN}$ such that*

$$x_i(k + \rho_i) = \mu_i + x_i(k).$$

The period *of the regime is ρ_i and $\chi_i = \mu_i/\rho_i$ is the cycletime of i. The smallest k for which the periodic regime exists is called the* transient time.

Under our initial conditions, K_i will be finite (see Theorem 1) and so, maxmin-ω always yields a periodic regime with the following system-wide quantities.

$$K = \max_i\{K_i\}, \quad \rho = \mathrm{LCM}_i(\rho_i), \quad \chi = (1/N)\sum_{i=1}^{N}\chi_i.$$

2.2 The One-Dimensional CA Network

We implement the maxmin-ω system on the one-dimensional (1D) CA lattice. This lattice has a natural definition of neighbourhood, i.e., the neighbourhood $\mathcal{N}_i$ of cell i of radius r is $\{i - r, \ldots, i - 1, i, i + 1, \ldots, i + r\}$ [6].[2]

From now on, we take $\xi_i(k)$ and $\tau_i(k)$ to be independent of k, so they are denoted ξ_i and τ_i, respectively. A study of the effect of r is beyond the scope of this short paper, suffice it to say that the results presented here are typical of those produced by most values of r (see [5], Chap. 5). We conduct three experiments with $N = 50$ and $r = 10$; they may best be described by the following.

Algorithm 1. *1. Choose $\xi_i, \tau_i \in \mathbb{Z}$ both from the uniform distribution (with equal probability) where $1 \leq \xi_i \leq \xi_{max}$ and $1 \leq \tau_i \leq \tau_{max}$.*
2. Taking an initial vector, $\boldsymbol{x}(0)$, run the maxmin-ω system for each ω value from 0.05 to 1, in steps of 0.05 (so there are 20 maxmin-ω systems to run).
3. For each maxmin-ω system, record the period ρ and cycletime χ.
4. Repeat above three steps 100 times to obtain, for each maxmin-ω system above, 100 independent periods and cycletimes.

---

[2] We take a finite lattice, so cells may be regarded as being arranged in a ring.

5. *For each maxmin-ω system, record the mean and median of the 100 periods and cycletimes obtained.*

We know that transient time K is always finite, therefore we don't exhibit transient time results here. We are most interested in the period ρ, which we take as a measure of the complexity of the system.

In experiment (i), we initialise to $\boldsymbol{x}(0) = \boldsymbol{0} = (0, 0, \ldots, 0)$ for all 100 runs; in experiment (ii), for each of the 100 runs, the elements of $\boldsymbol{x}(0) \in \mathbb{Z}$ are selected uniformly with equal probability where $0 < x_i(0) \leq 10$. In both of these experiments, we take $(\xi_{\max}, \tau_{\max}) = (10, 10)$. Experiment (iii) is a repeat of the second experiment but now taking $(\xi_{\max}, \tau_{\max}) = (20, 20)$. Figures 2 and 3 plot the results, a few notable features of which are as follows.

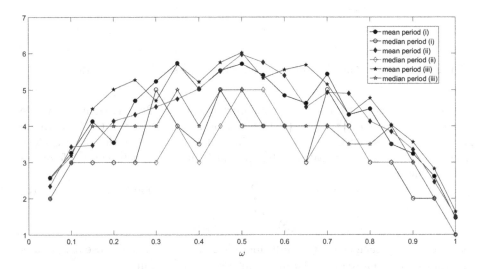

Fig. 2. Periods for the three experiments on the size 50 lattice with $r = 10$.

1. Under different initial conditions, the cycletime is almost identical. This is why we only alter the parameters ξ_i and τ_i in experiment (iii).
2. Increasing $(\xi_{\max}, \tau_{\max})$ values implies a larger cycletime; this fits with intuition since larger ξ_i and τ_i values would delay the processing of nodal states; subsequently the system takes longer to settle into some periodic behaviour.
3. The period curve is maximal when $\omega \approx \frac{1}{2}$. This forms part of a symmetrical curve, with smallest values at the two extremes of $\omega \approx 0$ and $\omega \approx 1$.

3   Cellular Automata in Maxmin-ω Time

Let $s_i(k)$ denote the (CA) state of a cell i at cycle $k \in \mathbb{N}$, so that the state of the system at cycle k is represented by the vector $\boldsymbol{s}(k) = (s_1(k), s_2(k), \ldots, s_N(k))$.

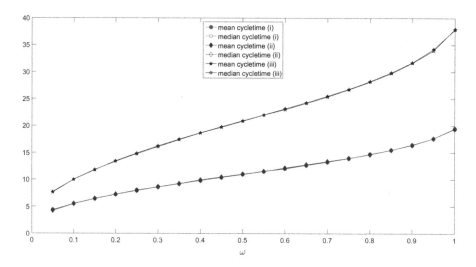

Fig. 3. Cycletimes for the three experiments on the size 50 lattice with $r = 10$.

Suppose a cell is contained in a neighbourhood of size $2r + 1$; then a CA rule is a function $f : \{0,1\}^{2r+1} \rightarrow \{0,1\}$ given by $s_i(k + 1) = f(\mathcal{N}(s_i(k)))$, where $\mathcal{N}(s_i(k))$ denotes the CA states of $\mathcal{N}_i$ in cycle k. Note that the same cycle k does not imply the same real time $t \in \mathbb{R}$; this is due to asynchrony. We focus on the CA rule

$$s_i(k + 1) = \sum_{\substack{j \,\in\, \mathcal{N}_i \\ x_j(k) + \tau_{ij} \leq x_{(\omega)}(k)}} s_j(k) \bmod 2 \tag{3}$$

i.e., the state of each cell is the sum (modulo 2) of the states of those neighbours of i that arrive before or at the same time as the ωth input.

3.1   Classification

To numerically classify the CA space-time output as a function of ω, we use two measures in tandem, as provided by Marr and Hütt in [7]. The first measure is the *Shannon entropy* $S \in [0, 1]$, which relies on the densities of CA states 0 and 1 in the time series of the evolving CA states of a cell. The second measure we employ is the *word entropy* $W \in \mathbb{R}_+$, which depends on the occurrence of blocks of constant states in the time series of a cell. CA space-time patterns can now be classified according to their S and W values; a large S or W value generally signifies large complexity of CA pattern.

3.2   CA Results

For each maxmin-ω system of Algorithm 1, we also implemented the CA rule of Eq. (3). That is, steps 3, 4, and 5 were extended to record Shannon and word entropies from the 100 runs. Here, we present these CA results.

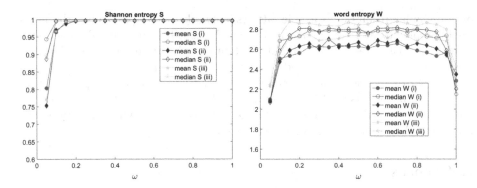

Fig. 4. CA entropies for the three experiments of Sect. 2.2

Again, we generated results for the three experiments of Sect. 2.2. The initial CA state (when $k = 0$) was randomised for each of the 100 runs, and each CA was iterated 250 times. The corresponding entropy results are in Fig. 4.

4 Max-min-plus Algebra

The maxmin-ω system of Eq. (2) can be reinterpreted in terms of a curious branch of mathematics called *max-min-plus algebra* (MMP) [5]. We leave the details of MMP to the highly accessible expositions in [8,9]. What we must state here is that once maxmin-ω is represented as a max-min-plus function then transient time, period, and cycletime are readily understood concepts. The following theorem (see [9], Theorem 12.7 for proof) provides some significance.

Theorem 1. *If the cycletime vector $\chi(\mathcal{M})$ of a max-min-plus function $\mathcal{M}$ exists for some finite vector x (i.e. where all elements of x are finite), then it exists for all finite vectors x and $\chi(\mathcal{M})$ is independent of the initial condition x.*

This theorem explains why our cycletime is invariant under different initial conditions (see Fig. 3). As for the periods being similar (except, perhaps, in experiment (iii)), this can be explained analytically by the "Duality Theorem" [10], a result that shows that the period is dependent on network structure and the parameters ξ_i and τ_i. MMP thus looks to be a promising way to study maxmin-ω analytically.

5 Discussion

We have shown that a simple, deterministic, asynchronous system produces intriguing results. In line with the periods, CA complexity for the simple rule we have employed appears maximal when ω is not near 0 or 1 (see Fig. 4). A natural extension is to study the effect on different CA rules. Moreover, while this work focused on the 1D lattice, preliminary work suggests that it is also possible to obtain similar results for variable lattices/networks [5]. In particular, the maximal complexity at $\omega \approx 1/2$ seems universal, regardless of network type. This leads us to ask whether this 'middle system complexity' exists in applications such as neural networks and epidemic processes on a network.

The reason for the name "maxmin-ω" is now evident. A MMP representation is a first step towards analytically understanding the complexities of maxmin-ω and any associated information exchange system (such as virus transmission), not only CA. We have conjectured ways to make progress in this in [5].

References

1. Schönfisch, B., de Roos, A.: Synchronous and asynchronous updating in cellular automata. BioSystems **51**(3), 123–143 (1999)
2. Fatès, N., Morvan, M.: An experimental study of robustness to asynchronism for elementary cellular automata. Complex Syst. **16**, 1–27 (2005)
3. Bouré, O., Fatès, N., Chevrier, V.: Probing robustness of cellular automata through variations of asynchronous updating. Nat. Comput. **11**(4), 553–564 (2012)
4. Patel, E.L., Broomhead, D.: A max-plus model of asynchronous cellular automata. Complex Syst. **23**(4), 313–341 (2014)
5. Patel, E.L.: Maxmin-plus models of asynchronous computation, Ph.D. thesis. University of Manchester (2012)
6. Wolfram, S.: Statistical mechanics of cellular automata. Rev. Mod. Phys. **55**(3), 601 (1983)
7. Marr, C., Hütt, M.T.: Topology regulates pattern formation capacity of binary cellular automata on graphs. Physica A **354**, 641–662 (2005)
8. Baccelli, F., Cohen, G., Olsder, G.J., Quadrat, J.-P.: Synchronization Linearity: An Algebra for Discrete Event Systems. Wiley, New York (1992)
9. Heidergott, B., Olsder, G.J., van der Woude, J.W.: Max Plus at Work: Modeling and Analysis of Synchronized Systems: A Course on Max-Plus Algebra and its Applications. Princeton Series in Applied Mathematics, vol. 13. Princeton University Press, Princeton (2006)
10. Gaubert, S., Gunawardena, J.: The duality theorem for min-max functions. Comptes Rendus de l'Académie des Sciences-Series I-Mathematics **326**(1), 43–48 (1998)

Cellular Automata Modelling
and Simulation

Chance-Constrained Water Supply Operation of Reservoirs Using Cellular Automata

Mohammad Hadi Afshar[✉] and Mohammad Azizipour

School of Civil Engineering, Iran University of Science and Technology,
Tehran, Iran
{mhafshar, m_azizipour}@iust.ac.ir

Abstract. This paper presents the application of a novel Cellular Automata approach for the efficient and effective solution of chance-constrained water supply reservoir operation problems. The method is based on the observation that a low value of the penalty parameter would lead to partial enforcement of the constraints. The constraints of the operation problem namely operation and reliability constraint, are dealt differently. A high enough value of the penalty parameter is used for the first set while a lower than enough value is used for the second set leading to complete enforcement of the first set of the constraint and partial fulfillment of the second set. Since the proper value of the penalty parameter to be used for the reliability constraints is not known *a priori*, an adaptive method is, therefore, proposed to find the proper value. For this, the problem is first solved for the optimal operation using a zero value of the penalty parameter. The value of the penalty parameter is then adjusted using the reliability of the optimal operation obtained. At each iteration, the penalty parameter is increased if the current reliability is less than the target reliability and deceased if otherwise. The proposed model is used for the optimal water supply operation of Dez reservoir in Iran over short, medium and long term for different target reliabilities and the results are presented and compared with those of a Genetic algorithm. The proposed model is shown to produce comparable results to the GA for water supply problem with much reduced computational effort.

Keywords: Reliability · Cellular automata · Reservoir operation

1 Introduction

Optimal use of water from an available reservoir system is an important issue in water resources management. Many attempts have been made by researchers to achieve best possible performance of the reservoir system. Various optimization techniques have been used for optimal reservoir operation represented by a set of releases or storages. While most of the methods developed were used for optimal operation of reservoirs disregarding the importance of reliability, some researchers proposed methods to solve chance constrained reservoir management problems. Askew (1974) used SDP to derive optimum reservoir operating policy considering reliability constraints. A DP procedure was developed by Sniedovich (1979) to solve reliability-constrained reservoir operation problems. Simonovic and Marino (1980) proposed a three-level solution algorithm for a multipurpose reservoir and solved reservoir management problem by reliability

© Springer International Publishing Switzerland 2016
S. El Yacoubi et al. (Eds.): ACRI 2016, LNCS 9863, pp. 201–209, 2016.
DOI: 10.1007/978-3-319-44365-2_20

programming. A reliability programming technique was introduced for multiple-multipurpose reservoir system (Simonovic and Marino 1982). Marino and Mohammadi (1983) applied a model based on a chance-constrained linear programming (CCLP) and DP to determine the optimum monthly releases from a multipurpose reservoir. Sreenivasan and Vedula (1996) used CCLP formulation for a multipurpose reservoir to determine the maximum annual hydropower produced while meeting irrigation demand at a specified reliability.

Recently a new method of optimization namely cellular automata (CA) has been introduced for the solution of water resources problems. The theory of CA as a self-reproducing model was first developed during the 1950s by Ulam (1952). Ulam's work was later extended by Von Neumann (1966) to model biological systems. Since then, CA has been extensively used for the simulation of many complex physical problems with great success. While CA was originally proposed as a simulation method to reproduce complex processes, it is now being widely used to solve optimization problems of different engineering disciplines due to its interesting features such as simplicity and computational speed.

The first application of the CA to water resources problem was proposed by Keedwell and Khu (2005) in which a CA was used to produce initial solutions for a GA model for optimal design of water distribution network. Guo et al. (2007a) hybridized a Non-dominated Sorting GA (NSGAII) with CA and used it for multi-objective design of both water distribution and storm sewer networks. The first use of CA as a stand-alone optimizer in water resources problems is due to Guo et al. (2007b) proposing a CA model for the optimal design of storm-sewer networks. While most of researches used an ad hoc transition rule based on engineering judgments and physical characteristics of the considered problem, Afshar and Shahidi (2009) were the first to propose a CA model with a mathematically derived transition rule and used it for optimal solution of reservoir operation problems. More recently, Afshar (2013) extended the model of Afshar and Shahidi (2009) for optimal hydropower operation of multi-reservoir systems. The method was used for solving the well-known four-reservoir and ten-reservoir problems and the results were compared with those obtained by GA and PSO methods indicating superiority of the method to heuristic search methods. Application of CA with mathematically derived transition rule for optimal design of sewer networks was first introduced by Afshar (2013). The nodes of the network were used as CA cells with the corresponding elevation as cell states. Afshar and Rohani (2012) extended the method of Afshar (2013) to a hybrid two-stage CA method for optimal design of sewer networks. Comparison of the results with those obtained by GA, PSO and ACO demonstrated the efficiency and effectiveness of the proposed hybrid method.

In this study, a Cellular Automata (CA) method is developed to determine optimal operating policy of a single reservoir for a specified reliability. In the proposed method, the constraints of the operation problem, namely operational and reliability constraints are enforced differently. A high enough value of the penalty parameter is used for the first set while a lower than enough value is used for the second set leading to complete enforcement of the first set and partial fulfillment of the second set. Since the proper value of the penalty parameter to be used for the reliability constraints is not known a priori, an adaptive method is, therefore, proposed to find the proper value. For this, the problem is first solved for the optimal operation using a zero value of the penalty parameter. The value of the penalty parameter is then adjusted using the reliability of the optimal operation obtained. The proposed model is used for optimal water supply operation of Dez reservoir in Iran and the results are presented and compared with those of the GA for short, medium and long term operation periods to demonstrate the efficiency and effectiveness of proposed method for reservoir operation problems of different scales. The model is shown to be superior to the GA in every regards such as computational effort, optimality and reliability of the final solution.

2 Proposed Cellular Automata Method for Chance Constrained Water Supply Operation of a Single Reservoir

The single-objective operation of reservoirs can be either benefit-based or reliability-based. In a benefit-based operation, the reservoir is operated such that the net benefit of the operation is maximized while the reliability-based operation is concerned with maximizing the reliability of meeting a set of pre-defined demand over the operation period. While simultaneous consideration of benefit and reliability requires the use of bi-objective optimization methods, a simpler and more practical problem is often encountered in which predefined target reliability is to be met in a benefit-based reservoir operation. In these problems, commonly referred to as chance constrained reservoir operation problem, the objective is to find a set of releases, or storages, such that a predefined pattern of demands, water or energy, are observed with a predefined reliability while optimizing the objective function over the operation period. Different operational policies represented by different objectives are defined and used for operation of single or multi-reservoir systems. Here the chance constrained water supply operation of a single reservoir is defined by an operation policy that minimizes the total squared deviation (TSD) of releases from a predefined pattern of demands defined as:

$$Min \quad F_w = \frac{\sum_{t=1}^{N}(D_t - R_t)^2}{D_{max}^2} \tag{1}$$

Subject to:

$$S_{t+1} = S_t + Q_t - R_t \quad t = 1, \ldots, N \tag{2}$$

$$S_{min} \le S_t \le S_{max} t = 1, \ldots, N+1 \tag{3}$$

$$R_{min} \le R_t \le R_{max} \quad t = 1, \ldots, N \tag{4}$$

$$Pr[R \ge D] \ge R_T \tag{5}$$

Where R_t, D_t, S_t and Q_t are water release from reservoir, demand, water storage and inflow to reservoir at period t, respectively; D_{max} is the maximum demand over the operation period; N is the total number of operation periods; S_{min} and S_{max} are minimum and maximum allowable reservoir storage, respectively; R_{min} and R_{max} are minimum and maximum water release from reservoir, respectively; and R_T is the target reliability. Here Eq. 2 represents the continuity equation in the reservoir, Eqs. 3 and 4 represents the maximum and minimum allowable water storage & monthly release volumes from reservoir, and Eq. 5 is the reliability constraint requiring that the probability of monthly releases from the reservoir being greater than water demand should be at least equal to the target reliability.

The optimization problem in hand, chance-constrained operation of a single reservoir, contains two set of constraints of different nature. The operational constraints represented by Eqs. (2, 3 and 4) are of explicit nature and can, therefore, be easily enforced while searching for the optimal solution. However, the reliability constraint, represented by Eq. (5) is of implicit type and its imposition requires an iterative method. The first step for the application of CA to reliable reservoir operation problem is to recast the reliability constraints into more explicit form for easier handling. Defining A' as a subset of $A = \{1, 2, 3, \ldots, N\}$ with N' members, the reliability constraint is written as:

$$R_t \geq D_t \quad t \in A' \tag{6}$$

subject to the condition that N' is equal to or greater than $N * R_T$, where N' represents the total number of periods for which the corresponding reliability constraints are realized ensuring an operation of desired target reliability R_T. The reliability constraints defined by Eq. (6) is now in more useful form for the application of CA as it is explicitly defined in terms of the reservoir release as the decision variable of the problem. The second step for the application of CA to the problem in hand is to recast the problem into an unconstrained optimization problem. For this, a penalty method is used in which the constraints of problem are embedded into the objective function. This leads to following unconstrained optimization problem defined as:

$$MinPF = F + \alpha * \sum_{t=1}^{N} (CV_O)_t^2 + \beta * \sum_{t=1}^{N} (CV_R)_t^2 \tag{7}$$

where F stands for the original objective function, PF is the penalized objective function of the problem, $(CV_O)_t$ represents the maximum violation from operational constraints, $(CV_R)_t$ is the maximum violation from reliability constraint, and α, β are penalty coefficients for operational and reliability constraints, respectively.

Application of CA to any optimization problem requires that four primary components of the CA model namely: cells, cell state, cell neighborhood, and the transition or updating rule are defined. For the operation problem in hand, the cells are taken as discrete points in time representing the beginning and the end of each period of the operation as suggested by Afshar and Shahidi (2009). The cell states representing the decision variables of the optimization problem is, therefore, taken as the reservoir storage at these discrete points. The surrounding cells are considered as the neighborhood cells. The transition rule for an arbitrary cell, j, is derived by requiring that the problem objective function (7) should be minimized with respect to the cell state, S_j, while all other cell states are kept constant. Assuming pre-defined arbitrary initial values for all cell states denoted by S_j^k, j = 1, 2, ... , N, the updated value of the jth cell states S_j^{k+1} is obtained by solving the following sub-optimization problem defined on the neighborhood of cell j as:

$$Min \quad (PF_w)_j = \left(D_{j-1} - R_{j-1}^{k+1}\right)^2 + \left(D_j - R_j^{k+1}\right)^2 + \alpha * \left[(CV_O)_j^2 + (CV_O)_{j-1}^2\right]^{k+1}$$
$$+ \beta * \left[(CV_R)_{j-1}^2 + (CV_R)_j^2\right]^{k+1} \tag{8}$$

Here, R_{j-1}^{k+1} and R_j^{k+1} are the updated release volumes at period $j-1$ and j, respectively. Rewriting (8) in terms of $\Delta S_j = S_j^{k+1} - S_j^k$ and its analytical solution leads to the following updating rule:

$$\Delta S_j = \frac{\left(D_j - R_j^k\right) - \left(D_{j-1} - R_{j-1}^k\right) + \alpha * \left[(CV_O)_j^2 + (CV_O)_{j-1}^2\right]^k + \beta * \left[(CV_R)_{j-1} + (CV_R)_j\right]^k}{2 + 2 * B_O * \alpha + 2 * B_R * \beta} \tag{9}$$

where B_O and B_R are binary variables with zero value if the solution at iteration k is feasible regarding operational and reliability constraints, respectively and with unit values otherwise.

It is a well-known fact that the value of the penalty coefficient in the penalty method determines the level of constraint satisfaction. With a zero value for the penalty coefficient, the constraints would not be taken into account as if an unconstrained problem is solved. With a large enough value of the penalty parameter for which any infeasible solution having a total cost greater than any feasible solution, the constraints are totally enforced. For any value between zero and large enough value of the penalty parameter, the constraints are partially enforced depending on how close the penalty parameter is to the proper value. This means that assuming a proper value for the operational penalty parameter α and a zero value for the reliability penalty parameter β would lead to an operationally feasible solution with the reliability constraint totally disregarded. This, in fact, leads to the model of Afshar and Shahidi (2009) proposed for optimal operation of single reservoirs without reliability considerations. Increasing the value of the reliability penalty parameter β would logically lead to operationally feasible solutions of higher reliability. This suggests that the penalty parameter β could be gradually increased until the desired target reliability is reached. This process, however, could be time consuming since no prior knowledge of the proper magnitude of the penalty coefficient is in hand.

An adaptive method is, therefore, proposed to find the proper value of the reliability penalty parameter β. Having fixed the operational penalty parameter value, the problem is first solved using a zero value of the penalty coefficient β leading to a solution with a reliability R lower than the target reliability R_T. At each iteration, the penalty coefficient is adjusted using the following relation:

$$\beta^{new} = \left[\beta^{old} + \left(R_T - R^{old}\right)\right] \tag{10}$$

Where R^{old} is the reliability of the solution obtained using the previous value of the reliability penalty parameter β^{old}. For a penalty coefficient less than proper value, the reliability of the solution R^{old} is less than the target reliability leading to an increase in the updated value of the penalty parameter β^{new} and vice versa. The iterative process of updating is continued until the current reliability is equal to the target reliability.

3 Model Application and Results

In this section, efficiency and effectiveness of the proposed model is illustrated for chance-constrained operation of "Dez" reservoir in southern district of Iran. To assess the effect of the problem scale on the performance of the model, three different operation periods of 5, 20 and 40 years are considered here. The average annual inflow to the reservoir and annual demand, are estimated at 5900 MCM and 5303 MCM, respectively. The active storage volume of reservoir is 2510 MCM. The minimum and maximum admissible storage volumes are 830 and 3340 MCM, respectively, while maximum and minimum water release volumes is considered as 1000 MCM and 0, respectively.

The proposed CA model is used to solve the chance-constrained operation of Dez reservoir over three different operation periods with different target reliabilities for water supply operation. Table 1 presents the solution cost, CPU time, reliability of the solution obtained by the proposed model, number of adaptive iterations required, and the final value of the operational penalty parameter β for different target reliabilities of water supply operation. It is seen that the proposed method has been generally converged in a few iteration And, therefore, been able to find the optimal solution within few seconds which illustrates the efficiency of the proposed method for water supply operation.

Table 1. Results of water supply operation for periods of 60, 240 and 480 months

Months	R_T	Solution cost	CPU time (sec)	Reliability	Iterations	Final β
60	0.6	2.36	0.18	0.6	6	0.73
	0.65	2.42	0.18	0.65	5	0.8
	0.7	2.49	0.19	0.7	6	0.93
240	0.6	8.92	1.41	0.6	10	0.48
	0.65	9.2	1.04	0.65	7	0.55
	0.7	9.5	1.3	0.7	9	0.64
480	0.6	20.09	3.33	0.6	11	0.5
	0.65	20.66	2.82	0.65	9	0.56
	0.7	21.3	1.97	0.7	6	0.64

The problem under consideration is also solved here using a GA model for comparison purpose. Considering the storage volume as the decision variables of the GA, a real-coded GA with tournament selection is used in which the tournament size is randomly selected. A *single-point* crossover with probability of 0.9 and random weighted averaging after the crossover site, and a *1-bit* mutation procedure with probability of 0.01 is used to produce the off-springs. Population size is set 50, 100 and 200 for operation periods of 60, 240 and 480 months, respectively, and an exhaustive maximum number of generations equal to 20000 is used for all runs to make sure of the GA convergence.

Performance of the proposed CA method is compared with that of GA in Table 2. In this table, the solution costs and the ratio of the computational times required by the GA and CA (t_{GA}/t_{CA}) at three generation numbers are shown for different target reliabilities and operation periods. It is seen that the GA has been able to produce superior solutions to the proposed CA method within all three generation numbers for the smaller operation periods of 60 and 240 months. For the longest operation period of 480 months, however, CA is seen to produce results comparable to that of GA. To be more specific, the CA is seen to produce solutions of the same cost with that of GA solutions with a computational cost 433, 564, and 1015 times less than those required by the GA indicating on the computational efficiency of the proposed method.

Table 2. Comparison of results obtained by GA and proposed CA

Period	R_T	Generation	Total cost		(t_{GA}/t_{CA})
60	0.6	5000	2.07	2.36	283
		10000	1.77		567
		20000	1.55		1133
	0.65	5000	1.89	2.42	233
		10000	1.75		472
		20000	1.73		944
	0.7	5000	2.5	2.49	232
		10000	2.34		468
		20000	2.14		937
240	0.6	5000	8.55	8.92	128
		10000	6.71		257
		20000	6.05		513
	0.65	5000	8.59	9.20	155
		10000	6.82		310
		20000	6.29		618
	0.7	5000	9.21	9.50	135
		10000	7.65		272
		20000	6.84		543
480	0.6	5000	31.14	20.09	200
		10000	21.04		400
		20000	16.24		799
	0.65	5000	32.85	20.66	207
		10000	23.99		414
		20000	18.38		829
	0.7	5000	33.06	21.30	341
		10000	23.88		681
		20000	19.39		1362

4 Conclusions

A novel Cellular Automata approach was developed for the efficient and effective solution of reliability-based reservoir operation problems. The method is based on different treatments of the operational and reliability constraints of the problem. A high enough value of the penalty parameter is used for the operational constraints while a lower than enough value is used for the reliability constraint leading to complete fulfillment of the first set of the constraint and partial enforcement of the second set. Since, the proper value of the penalty parameter for the reliability constraint is not known *a priori*, an adaptive method is introduced to find its proper value. For this, the optimal operation problem is first solved using a zero value of penalty parameter and is adjusted considering the reliability of optimal operation obtained. At each iteration, the penalty parameter is decreased if the current reliability is greater than the target reliability and increased if otherwise. The proposed method were applied to optimal water supply operation of Dez reservoir in Iran considering various target reliability for periods of 5, 20, and 40 years and the results are presented and compared with those obtained by a GA. The results indicated the superiority of the proposed method to the GA in both efficiency and effectiveness of the method.

References

Afshar, M.H., Shahidi, M.: Optimal solution of large-scale reservoir operation problems cellular automata versus heuristic search methods. Eng. Optim. **41**, 275–293 (2009)

Afshar, M.H., Rohani, M.: Optimal design of sewer networks using cellular automata-based hybrid methods: discrete and continuous approaches. Eng. Optim. **44**, 1–22 (2012)

Afshar, M.H.: A cellular automata approach for the hydro-power operation of multi-reservoir systems. Water Manage. (2013). doi:10.1680/wama.11.00105

Askew, A.J.: Optimum reservoir operating policies and the imposition of a reliability constraint. Water Resour. Res. **10**, 51–56 (1974)

Guo, Y., Keedwell, E.C., Walters, G.A., Khu, S.-T.: Hybridizing cellular automata principles and NSGAII for multi-objective design of urban water networks. In: Obayashi, S., Deb, K., Poloni, C., Hiroyasu, T., Murata, T. (eds.) EMO 2007. LNCS, vol. 4403, pp. 546–559. Springer, Heidelberg (2007a)

Guo, Y., Walters, G.A., Khu, S.T., Keedwell, E.C.: A novel cellular automata based approach to optimal storm sewer design. Eng. Optim. **39**(3), 345–364 (2007b)

Keedwell, E., Khu, S.T.: A hybrid genetic algorithm for the water distribution networks. J. Eng. Appl. Artif. Intell. **18**, 461–472 (2005)

Marino, M.A., Mohammadi, B.: Reservoir management: a reliability programming approach. Water Resour. Res. **19**, 613–620 (1983)

Neumann, V.J.: Theory of Self-Reproduction Automata. University of Illinois press, Urbana (1966). Edited by A. Burks

Simonovic, S.P., Marino, M.A.: Reliability programming in reservoir management: 1. single multipurpose reservoir. Water Resour. Res. **16**, 844–848 (1980)

Simonovic, S.P., Marino, M.A.: Reliability programming in reservoir management: 3. system of multipurpose reservoirs. Water Resour. Res. **18**, 735–743 (1982)

Sniedovich, M.: Reliability-constrained reservoir operation control problems: 1. methodological issues. Water Resour. Res. **15**, 1574–1582 (1979)

Sreenivasan, K.R., Vedula, S.: Reservoir operation for hydropower optimization: a chance-constrained approach. Sadhan-Acad. Proc. Eng. Sci. **21**, 503–510 (1996)

Ulam, S.M.: Random process and transformations. In: Proceedings of the International Congress of Mathematics, vol. 2, pp. 264–275 (1952, held in 1950) (1952)

Cognitive Map Routing

Mohcine Chraibi[(✉)] and David Haensel

Jülich Supercomputing Centre, Research Centre Jülich, Jülich, Germany
{m.chraibi,d.haensel}@fz-juelich.de
http://fz-juelich.de/ias/jsc/cst

Abstract. We introduce a framework to navigate agents in buildings, inspired by the notion of "the cognitive map". It allows to route agents depending on their spacial knowledge. With help of an event-driven mechanism, agents acquire new information about their surroundings, which expands their individual cognitive map.

1 Introduction

The simulation of pedestrian dynamics provides important results for different applications. For architects the analysis of people flow is interesting during the planning of new facilities and exit routes. For organizers of large scale events a simulation of pedestrians could help to appraise the location.

Hoogendoorn et al. [5] divided pedestrian dynamics decision making into three levels, the strategic, tactical and operational level. The pre trip route planning and the choice of the final destination is done in the strategical level. It should be mentioned that at the strategical level no information about actual circumstances is available. Short term decisions like obstacle avoidance or route changes depending on actual situation are done at the tactical level. At this level additional information is available, like people flow or smoked rooms. At the operational level the pedestrian motion is modeled including interaction with other pedestrians.

Current routing mechanisms in pedestrian dynamics simulations are mostly based on shortest path calculation or quickest path approximation. Some of them already feature perception of congestion and jams in front of doors [6]. This perception leads to another route choice for some individual agents. But most of the routing implementations do not take individual knowledge or behavior into consideration. It is for example unrealistic to assume that pedestrians in a shopping mall take the shortest path only because they are knowledgeable about the exits in building. In contrast one should assume that most pedestrians do not even know more than one emergency exit. To resign individual knowledge assumes that every agent has perfect knowledge of the actual building.

To reach more realistic simulations it seems necessary to take some individual factors into consideration. Individual knowledge is the basis for those individuality. It is needed for individual decision making and social behavior.

Another important feature, the human perception, is often missing in actual implementation. If we want to consider dynamic circumstances which influence

© Springer International Publishing Switzerland 2016
S. El Yacoubi et al. (Eds.): ACRI 2016, LNCS 9863, pp. 210–218, 2016.
DOI: 10.1007/978-3-319-44365-2_21

the route choice we need to have a perception layer. The information gathered from this perception layer should then be written in the aforementioned knowledge representation. This shows, that a versatile knowledge representation combined with perception possibilities and decision making is needed.

2   Related Work

Cognitive Map. The cognitive map is a concept introduced and analyzed by E.C. Tolman [12]. From his experiments with rats he deduced that rats are not simply navigating by stimuli and response but rather discover the space and store their acquired knowledge in a structured way. This so called *cognitive map* enables rats to make decisions while navigating.

B. Kuipers later analyzed the cognitive map from a more technical point of view [7,8]. In his work he described that the cognitive map aggregates information from observations to route description and fixed features which later are integrated in topological and the metric relations. An overview of the interaction between those five types of information can be seen in Fig. 1 from [8, p.11].

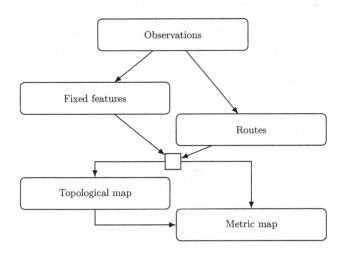

Fig. 1. Five different types of information of a cognitive map according to Kuipers [8, p. 11]

Individual Behavior. Individual behavior in pedestrian dynamics simulation is handled in different ways. Braun et al. implemented individual behavior in the operational level by introducing new parameters like dependence (need of help) and altruism (willingness to help) and by introducing groups (like families) [3]. Those new parameters change the force calculation in the underlying social force model by Helbing [4]. Pelechano et al. used the operational level too but also took individual knowledge of the building into consideration in the way finding [10]. Pan implemented a modular framework for human and social behavior which features typical behavior like queuing and leader following [9]. This new framework is also analyzed and compared with other evacuation simulations.

On the tactical level several works about way finding were performed. The book of Arthur and Passini [1, chap. 5.] gives a good overview of the way finding in general and especially the process of finding a specific way. In [2] the route choice during a fire is discussed. They pay attention on the decision process and the way people choose the emergency exit (for example closed or open doors). In addition they discuss the influence of evacuation signs and the delay time after fire alarm.

Modeling human behavior, perception and cognition is a complicated task. It is not the goal of this work to reach realistic human behavior or even to understand human cognition, but to emulate the behavior simplified enough to reach adequate simulations. With the created framework a powerful and extensible set of tools was build to model and emulate realistic behavior.

For achieving individual behavior and basic reasoning in pedestrian dynamics simulations it is necessary to have a versatile spatial knowledge representation. For this reason a simplified version of the cognitive map proposed by Tolman [12] was implemented and used for each agent separately (Sect. 3). To model the information gathering of pedestrians a sensor structure was build to enrich the information stored in the cognitive map (Sect. 3.4). Moreover the stored knowledge is used for individual decision making (Sect. 3.5). The aforementioned three modules are encapsulated in the new created cognitive map router. Figure 2 shows an overview of the build modules which are described in detail in the following sections.

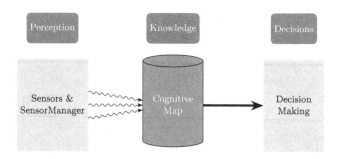

Fig. 2. Overview of the interaction between the modules.

3   Representing Knowledge with a Cognitive Map

The knowledge representation is the central module for the new routing mechanism. It has to fulfil several requirements. One of them is the possibility to represent different spatial knowledge. Another one is the possibility to store knowledge individually to achieve the goal of individual behaviour.

For the data structure we use the concept of the cognitive map proposed by Tolman [12] which is widely used in robotics navigation. Due to the fact that the navigation is used for agents in evacuation simulations inside a building we omit some parts of the cognitive map concept. A metric map (Sect. 3.1) and a memory of used routes (Sect. 3.2) constitute our new cognitive map (Sect. 3.3). The metric map represents the notion which the simulated pedestrian has about the building whereas the memory of used routes constitutes a simple remembrance.

3.1   The Metric Map (NavigationGraph)

The metric map constitutes the notion of the building an agent has. Therefore it has to represent the knowledge of first order as well as the knowledge of second order. As aforementioned elements of second order could be modeled as properties of elements of first order. Therefore we have to care about first order elements mostly.

For the first order knowledge we decided to use a graph based structure. That is why we had to identify sub rooms and doors with vertices and edges. In contrast to some former routing algorithm we identify the sub rooms as vertices and the doors as edges.

This is reasonable in order to have a versatile structure for adding information to a certain edge. In our representation an edge represents the intersection between sub rooms, which is needed to guide agents from room to room instead of guiding them from door to door. Another advantage is the possibility to store different information for different edges directions. For example leaving a room towards a corridor is rated better than the other direction. This structure gives us the possibility to have an idea about leaving the sub room in the first place, which would be difficult if doors are vertices. The chosen structure has some downsides as well. When it comes to accurate distance calculations some problems appear. It is possible to create a sparse graph to model pedestrians with incomplete knowledge of a building.

Edge-Weight Calculation. The calculation of optimal routes is based on the weight of each edge. These depend primarily on the distance and other factors which represent the second order knowledge.

Let $e_i \in E$ be an edge of the navigation graph $G = G(V, E)$.

$$F_i := \{f_k \in F_i \mid f_k \in \mathbb{R} \wedge f_k > 0\} \qquad (|F_i| < \infty)$$

is the **set of corresponding factors** for e_i. The elements of F_i are called **edge-factors**.

$$f^{(i)} := \prod_{f_k \in F_i} f_k$$

is called the **accumulated edge-factor**.

Let x_i be the length of the edge e_i and F_i the set of corresponding factors for e_i. Then is

$$w_i := x_i \cdot \prod_{f_k \in F_i} f_k = x_i \cdot f^{(i)} \tag{1}$$

the **edge-weight** of e_i.

Edge-factors and sensors are highly related to the decision making process. The decision making is based on the edge-weight, to decide for an optimal route. Thus the edge-factors have a high influence on the chosen route.

3.2   Used Routes Memory

The smaller part of the cognitive map is the memory of used routes, which is for the purpose of representing the pedestrians remembrance. We store every edge which was chosen by the decision making in the same order. With this we can reconstruct the chosen path. An application could be a sensors which avoids the agent from going backwards.

3.3   Putting it All Together: The Cognitive Map

Even if this cognitive map is a drastic simplification of Tolmans cognitive map it is less complex and still fits our needs.

In the simulation each agent has its individual cognitive map. These maps are accessed through the *CognitiveMapStorage* class which also takes care of the creation of the initial cognitive maps. The creation itself is done by *CognitiveMapCreator* classes which are passed to the *CognitiveMapStorage* and executed when needed. With these *CognitiveMapCreators* it is possible to create different cognitive maps, in matter of information content, to simulate pedestrians with different knowledge. It is also possible to use different creators for different agents. The current implementation features two creators the *CompleteCognitiveMapCreator* which creates a complete cognitive map and an *EmptyCognitiveMapCreator* which creates an empty cognitive map. Further creators can be easily implemented.

3.4   Gathering Information

With the proposed cognitive map we have a versatile structure for the later discussed decision making. The decision making is based on the edge weight and thereby on the edge factors. Therefore it is important that the cognitive map in general and the edge factors in particular are up to date to make current decisions.

The information gathering module is responsible for this update process. It provides a framework for reproducing simplified human perception. It is able to manipulate edge factors as well as an entire edge or vertex.

For gathering information a sensor structure was build. These sensors are managed and executed by an event driven sensor manager. Those events could be triggered in every time step during the execution of the router. Therefore the sensors are executed individually for each agent.

3.5 Making Decisions

The last module of the proposed routing framework is the decisions making module. With the already defined edge-factors and the deduced edge-weight it was nearby to calculate optimal routes in the given navigation graph. But due to the fact, that some agents may have a sparse navigation graph it is possible that an agent does not know any complete exit route. There for we distinguish between agents with enough knowledge to find a complete exit route and agents with less knowledge. The first group uses a global optimization algorithm and the second uses a local algorithm. Till now there is a strong separation of strategies of this two groups, but for more realistic behavior a combination of both strategies would be advisable.

4 Simulation Results

To showcase the flexibility of our new routing framework we analyze the impact of different configurations on the route choice and thus on the whole simulation. The implemented routing framework is adjustable in many different ways. This leads to a lot of possible configurations, which we can not analyze in all aspects. That is why we choose some configurations for the analysis. As first we study the impact of single sensors when used with complete cognitive maps. For the analysis we conduct 50 simulations for each configuration of interest with different initial conditions. The initial conditions influence mainly the position of pedestrians in a certain sub room.

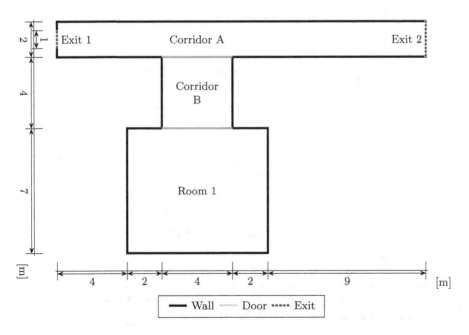

Fig. 3. The geometry (T-Junction) used for analyzing the *DensitySensor*.

The initial conditions are different among the 50 simulations of one configuration but equal for different configurations. With this setup we want to minimize the influence of random effects. For some configurations we compare the total evacuation time with the total evacuation time obtained using the global shortest path router [6]. The total evacuation time is the duration until the last agent has left the building. For comparing evacuation times we use Welch's t-test [13]. This test has the null hypothesis that the expected values of the distributions of the two samples are the same using the mean value. Rejecting this null hypothesis means that the expected values are significantly different. All tests are calculated with R's [11] intrinsic t-test method. All agents have a complete initial cognitive map and thus "know" every sub room and door in the building. The only additional information which could be added is knowledge of second order.

For the analysis of the `DensitySensor` we conducted simulations with the geometry shown in Fig. 3. Exit 1 is smaller than exit 2 and should cause some congestion. In addition the way from room 1 to exit 1 is shorter than the way

Table 1. Comparison of total evacuation time frequencies of simulations with *DensitySensor* and without sensors. We conducted 50 simulations each. The simulations are all done with complete cognitive maps.

t [s]	Freq.	With sensor	Without sensor		Freq.
59	4	8%	0%		0
60	9	18%	0%		0
61	8	16%	0%		0
62	9	18%	0%		0
63	11	22%	0%		0
64	7	14%	0%		0
65	2	4%	0%		0
...	...	...	...		...
81	0	0%	2%		1
82	0	0%	2%		1
83	0	0%	10%		5
84	0	0%	28%		14
85	0	0%	32%		16
86	0	0%	16%		8
87	0	0%	8%		4
88	0	0%	2%		1

p-value $< 2.2 \cdot 10^{-16}$ (Result of Welch's t-test)

mean (Total evac. time):   61.86s 84.76s

to exit 2. We distributed 140 agents in room 1. Without any sensors the agents take the direct path to the exit 1. This leads to a high density and a congestion in front of the emergency exit. With the `DensitySensor` the exit 2 is used too and the agents are distributed better. Depending on the actual density when arriving at corridor A the agents decides whether to go to exit 1 or to exit 2. The total evacuation time is significant lower with the `DensitySensor` than without. Table 1 shows the comparison of the total evacuation times.

5   Conclusion

In this work we implemented a versatile and knowledge based routing framework for pedestrian dynamics. With this framework we propose a adjustable method for emulating human knowledge, perception and decision making. This work does not claim investigating and understanding the nature of human behavior, rather its goal is to create tools to ease the implementation of new behavioral models.

The framework consists out of three modules: the perception module (`Sensors` and `SensorManager`), the knowledge module (`Cogntivemap`) and the decision making module. For the knowledge representation we proposed a simplified cognitive map which reduces the complexity of the model but represents all needed knowledge. For the perception module we implemented a sensor structure and for the decision making we provide a local and a global optimization algorithm. We showed that the sensors have a high impact on the simulation and are suitable for reproducing human behavior. Especially the sensor module is highly extendable and could thereby fulfill even additional requirements later. For all module the cognitive map is the central module to read information from or to write information into. Due to the object oriented design and the modularization it is possible to exchange or adjust modules independently from each other.

There are several extensions and improvements which could be part of future works. Some of them are related to problems which arose during the implementation or the analysis and some are suggestions for possible extensions. One of the most important tasks would be a verification of simulations with empirical data. This task is not just important for this routing framework but for the pedestrian dynamics simulations in general. The next tasks are directly related to our new routing framework and suggestions for further improvements.

The perception module offers further extension possibilities. We already implemented several sensors and showed their impact on the result of simulations. For simulating certain situations and circumstances sensors are a good option. That is why it is advisable to design and implement further sensors. They enrich information and help to emulate realistic behavior.

The decision making should always use all knowledge which is available for the certain agent. Additional the strategies could be mixed up to emulate more realistic behavior.

References

1. Arthur, P., Passini, R.: Wayfinding: People Signs and Architecture. McGraw-Hill Book Co., New York (1992)
2. Benthorn, L., Frantzich, H.: Fire alarm in a public building: How do people evaluate information and choose evacuation exit? Technical Report 3082, Departement of Fire Safety Engineering, Lund University (1996)
3. Braun, A., Musse, S., de Oliveira, L., Bodmann, B.: Modeling individual behaviors in crowd simulation. In: 2003 16th International Conference on Computer Animation and Social Agents, pp. 143–148, May 2003
4. Helbing, D., Farkas, I., Vicsek, T.: Simulating dynamical features of escape panic. Nature **407**, 487–490 (2000)
5. Hoogendoorn, S.P., Bovy, P.H.L., Daamen, W.: Microscopic pedestrian wayfinding and dynamics modelling. In: Schreckenberg, M., Sharma, S.D. (eds.) Pedestrian and Evacuation Dynamics, pp. 123–155 (2002)
6. Kemloh Wagoum, A.U.: Route choice modelling and runtime optimisation for simulation of building evacuation. Dr., Jülich (2013)
7. Kuipers, B.: Modeling spatial knowledge. Cogn. Sci. **2**(2), 129–153 (1978)
8. Kuipers, B.: The cognitive map: Could it have been any other way? In: Pick Jr., H.L., Acredolo, L.P. (eds.) Spatial Orientation, pp. 345–359. Springer, Heidelberg (1983)
9. Pan, X.: Computational modeling of human and social behaviors for emergency egress analysis. Ph.D. thesis, Stanford University (2006)
10. Pelechano, N., O'Brien, K., Silverman, B., Badler, N.: Crowd simulation incorporating agent psychological models, roles and communication. In: 1st International Workshop on Crowd Simulation (2005)
11. R Core Team R: A Language and Environment for Statistical Computing. R Foundation for Statistical Computing, Vienna, Austria (2014)
12. Tolman, E.C.: Cognitive maps in rats and men. Psychol. Rev. **55**(4), 189–208 (1948)
13. Welch, B.: The generalization of student's problem when several different population variances are involved. Biometrika **34**(1/2), 28–35 (1947)

Characteristics of Pedestrian and Vehicle Flows at a Roundabout System

Hicham Echab[✉], Hamid Ez-Zahraouy, Nourddine Lakouari, and Rachid Marzoug

Laboratoire de Magnétisme et de Physique des Hautes Energies (URAC 12),
Département de physique, Faculté des sciences, Université Mohammed V Rabat,
B.P. 1014 Rabat, Morocco
hichamechab@gmail.com

Abstract. For the purposes of optimizing vehicle flow and improving the crossings pedestrian safety, it is important to understand pedestrians-vehicles behaviors. This paper proposes a cellular automata model to study the interactions of crossings pedestrian and traffic flow on a single lane roundabout. The boundary is controlled by the injecting rates α_1, α_2 and the extracting rate β. Meanwhile, the crossing pedestrian decision is modeled with a gap acceptance rule. The results show that, pedestrian (resp. vehicular) flow can benefit from small (resp. large) gap acceptance to decrease the interferences vehicles-pedestrians. Likewise, we found that the crosswalk location play a chief role in improving the satisfaction of both pedestrians and vehicles. However, the use of slowdown sections provokes a decrease in pedestrians-vehicles interactions and increases the traffic capacity.

Keywords: Cellular automata · Roundabout · Pedestrians · Phase diagram · Satisfaction rate

1 Introduction

Interactions between different traffic participants (e.g. pedestrians, cars, buses, etc.) have attracted considerable attention of researchers from various domains. Numbers of models have been proposed for describing different traffic phenomenon [1–10]. Among different models, Cellular automaton (CA) has been adopted extremely and well received as a good tool to study and analyze the evolution of mixing traffic dynamics [11–19]. Feng et al. [17] proposed a cellular automata model to evaluate walkers' facilities before its implementation, Zhang et al. [18] proposed a cellular automata model to study the effect of the traffic light control on the pedestrians flow, Xie et al. [19] investigated the characteristics of the traffic flow on a road with a signalized crosswalk in the framework of CA model. Therefore, the present study aims to investigate the effect of crossings pedestrian on traffic flow at a roundabout system using the CA model. Also, the effects of some parameters design such as the crosswalk position and the speed limit zone on the traffic flow and the behavior of crossings pedestrian will be investigated. The paper is organized as follows. Section 2 we explain the model. Results and discussions are presented in Sect. 3. The conclusion is given in Sect. 4.

© Springer International Publishing Switzerland 2016
S. El Yacoubi et al. (Eds.): ACRI 2016, LNCS 9863, pp. 219–226, 2016.
DOI: 10.1007/978-3-319-44365-2_22

2   Model and Method

2.1   Roundabout Model

The sketch of the model is shown in Fig. 1-(a), where the system consists of eight chains of length L_2 connected to a closed chain (i.e. ring) of length L_1. All chains are single lane and one-way. Also, each lane is designed with a crosswalk. This later is defined as a discrete grid $L_{CW} * W_{CW}$ and it is located in one cell of the lane at position P_{CW}. Here, L_{CW} and W_{CW} denote the crosswalk length and width respectively. Vehicles enter from odd-numbered lanes and exit from even numbered ones. In the ring vehicles move orderly and counter clockwise.

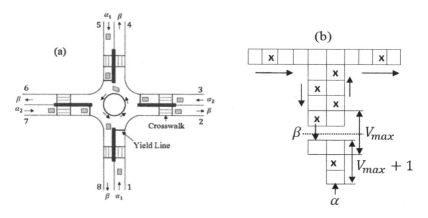

Fig. 1.   (a) Sketch of the roundabout, (b) the injection rule with $V_{max} = 2$.

2.2   Crossing Pedestrian

In this paper, pedestrians arrive at waiting zone (i.e. grey area) at each time step with probability P_{pa}. Pedestrian can make decision to cross according to the distance between the crosswalk and the first vehicle before the crossing line, i.e., if the available distance is greater than the threshold d_{AC}, the pedestrian will cross, otherwise he/she will not. We note that pedestrian can cross from right side to left one (i.e. right crossing) and vice versa (i.e. left crossing). On the other hand, to keep conformity between pedestrians, we divide the crosswalk into two sides by a partition line: one for the right pedestrian while the other is for the left ones. Also, we assume that the walkers cannot change their directions (i.e. pedestrians follow each other in one direction). To describe the motion of a pedestrian, we adopt the Nagel and Schreckenberg (NS) model [1]; where all pedestrians are handled in parallel during one time step according to the three rules:

i.   Acceleration: $V_i^p \rightarrow Min\left(V_i^p + 1, V_{max}^p\right)$

ii. Deceleration: $V_i^p \rightarrow Min(V_i^p, d_i^p)$

iii. Movement: $x_i^p \rightarrow x_i^p + V_i^p$

Where V_i^p and x_i^p denote the velocity and position of the pedestrian i respectively. The maximum velocity and the gap between pedestrians are denoted as V_{max}^p and d_i^p respectively. According to Ref. [20], the maximum velocity of walker under easy mind is no more than 1.4 m/s (i.e. $V_{max}^p = round\left(\dfrac{1.4}{0.6}\right) = 2$, where 0.6 presents the dynamic space of a pedestrian [21]). We note that pedestrian can cross the road in two stages by using the splitter island.

2.3 Vehicles' Movement Rules

To describe the motion of a vehicle, we use the NS model [1]; where all vehicles are handled in parallel during one time step according to the four rules:

i.   Acceleration: $V_j(t + 1) = min(V_{max}, V_j(t) + 1)$
ii. Deceleration: $V_j(t + 1) = min(V_j(t), d_j)$, $d_j = x_{j+1}(t) - x_j(t)$
iii. Randomization: with the braking probability P_b; $V_j(t + 1) = max(0, V_j(t) - 1)$
iv. Movement: $x_j(t + 1) = x_j(t) + V_j(t + 1)$

Where x_j and V_j designate the position and velocity of the vehicle j respectively. The maximum velocity and the gap are denoted as V_{max} and d_j respectively.

All vehicles obey these updating rules, except the nearest vehicle to crosswalk must move slowly and adjust its velocity according to the gap d_j as follow:

$$d_j = \begin{cases} x_{j+1}(t) - x_j(t) & \text{if the crosswalk is empty} \\ x_{CW} - x_j(t) & \text{else} \end{cases}$$

Where x_{CW} is the crosswalk location.

2.4 Roundabout Rules

In the entry lanes, if the first cell is empty, a new vehicle is added with rate α_1 or α_2. However, the rate β controls the exit lanes, if the position of the leading vehicle is superior to the lane length, it is removed from the road with rate β, else it has to slow down and brake in the last site with rate $1 - \beta$. The inclusion of the exit probability can be related to the traffic status in the exit direction. it is important to note that, each road inflow is controlled by an injecting rate α_i (i = 1, 3, 5, 7), but for less complexity and to get better insights into the traffic dynamics, we suppose that each opposite roads are controlled by the same injecting rate, also we take the same extracting rate β for all exit lanes.

The exit lane is selected for each vehicle with probability P_{exit} upon entrance to the entry lane and it remains unchanged. On the other hand, the rules of the roundabout give priority to the circulating flow, in other word, the incoming vehicle (i.e. vehicle on the entry lane) should yield to the vehicles in the ring, then it allowed to enter the ring if the left quadrant is empty or the oncoming vehicle (i.e. the leading vehicle on the left quadrant) displays its indicator for informing the others of his exit direction. Simultaneously, an oncoming vehicle can leave the ring if the gap between the vehicle and the last vehicle at its desired exit direction is inferior to its velocity.

3   Results and Discussion

In the simulation, the parameters $L_1 = 40, L_2 = 60, L_{CW} = 8, W_{CW} = 4,$ $V_{max} = 2, P_b = 0, \beta = 1$ and $P_{pa} = 0.2$ are used. The results are averaged over 40000 time steps after 10000 time steps for 50 independent runs.

At the beginning, we are interested in investigating the effect of the threshold of acceptable gap d_{AC} on the traffic behavior. In this respect, based on the vehicle flux in the circulating lane and the average pedestrian flux as order parameters, Fig. 2 presents the phase diagrams of the system in the (α_1, α_2) space. The results shown that when d_{AC} is large (Fig. 2-a), the phase diagram presents two regions: Free-Free (F-F), here pedestrians and vehicles can move freely, i.e., pedestrians have no influence on the inflow and the outflow due to the small values of injecting rates. Congested-Congested (C-C), the congested state is reached for both pedestrians and vehicles, in this situation the interactions between vehicles and pedestrians in the entry and/or exit lanes increase owing to the large values of injecting rates. In contrast, when d_{AC} is small (Fig. 2-b), in addition to the two previous regions, a new region appears: Congested-Free (C-F), here pedestrians are able to make a decision to cross with shorter gap which enlarges the pedestrian free region but increases delay to vehicles. It is important to note that the short acceptable gap rises the collisions between crossings pedestrian and vehicles.

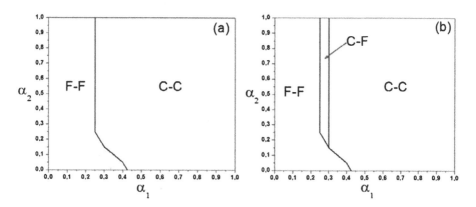

Fig. 2. Phase diagram in the (α_1, α_2) space, (a) $d_{AC} = 4$ and (b) $d_{AC} = 2$.

The position of the crosswalk has an important effect on traffic characteristics. Figure 3 presents the phase diagram for different crosswalk location. It is evident that as P_{CW} increases the vehicles free region enlarges. This result can be understood by looking at the density profile of the entry and exit lanes (see Fig. 4). In the entry lane, when P_{CW} is close to yield line, the oscillations can be observed but become weak and the density increases as one approaches to crosswalk. In contrast, when P_{CW} is far from yield line, a planar profile is observed before the crosswalk (i.e. the congested state takes place), here the interruptions to the inflow caused by walkers rise; therefore, the number of incoming vehicles becomes smaller. However, in the exit lane, we obtained the same profile on the both cases where the density is great only before the crosswalk; this means that the congested state of circulating lane is determined by the crosswalk location in the exit lane especially when it closer to exit point.

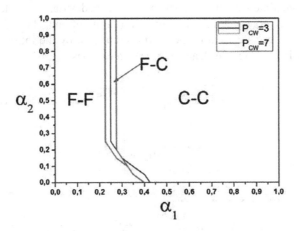

Fig. 3. Phase diagram in the (α_1, α_2) space for different values of P_{CW}.

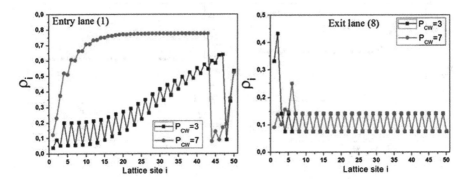

Fig. 4. Density profile ρ_i as function of site number i for different values of P_{CW} where $\alpha_1 = 0.27$ and $\alpha_2 = 0.3$.

To reduce this impact we propose that the crosswalk positions are not the same at the entry and exit lanes, i.e., P_{CW}^{EN} (resp. P_{CW}^{EX}) is the position of the crosswalk in the entry (resp. exit) lane. For this purpose, we calculate the average satisfaction rates $\eta_v = \dfrac{V_i}{V_{max}}$ and $\eta_p = \dfrac{V_i^p}{V_{max}^p}$ (i.e. the proportion of vehicles or pedestrians that move at their desired velocity) [22]. In this context, Fig. 5 presents the behavior of the satisfaction rates as a function of the injecting rate α_1. It can be obviously inferred from the figure that, when the crosswalk positions are different, the vehicle satisfaction rate increases on the circulating lane (83% $\leq \eta_v$), the exit lanes $\left(97\% \leq \eta_v\right)$ but on the entry lanes we obtained the same satisfaction rate (18% $\leq \eta_v \leq$ 90%). Also, we can see clearly that the pedestrian satisfaction rate increases slightly (24% $\leq \eta_p$). In this situation, pedestrians take more time to travel between the two crosswalk splits at the splitter island which decrease their number during one time step, thereby decreasing the pedestrians-vehicles interactions. From this result, we conclude that the inflow (i.e. flow of entry lanes) is affected not only by the interruptions caused by pedestrians, but also by the interactions between vehicles and the increasing of α_1 leads to more interactions.

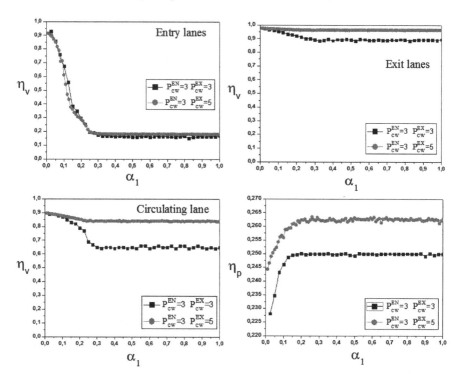

Fig. 5. Satisfaction rates as function of injecting rate α_1 for different values of P_{cw}^{EN} and P_{cw}^{EX}, where $\alpha_2 = 0.3$.

Usually, entry/exit roads have a slowdown section (i.e. speed limit zone) before the crosswalk, used to prepare vehicle to yield to pedestrians. In other words, there is a section of length L_S where vehicles will be forced to slow down within velocity V_{Smax}.

Figure 6 shows the behavior of the satisfaction rates as a function of the injecting rate α_1. It is found that the existences of speed limit zones increase the pedestrian satisfaction rate (24% $\leq \eta_p$), the vehicle satisfaction rate on the circulating lane (92% $\leq \eta$), exit lane (99% $\leq \eta$) and on the entry lane (25% $\leq \eta$), because vehicles apt to move slower before the crosswalk which reduces the interferences pedestrians-vehicles, and thus increases the number of vehicles that can go through the crosswalk. Indeed, the speed limit zones can effectively increase the performance of the system.

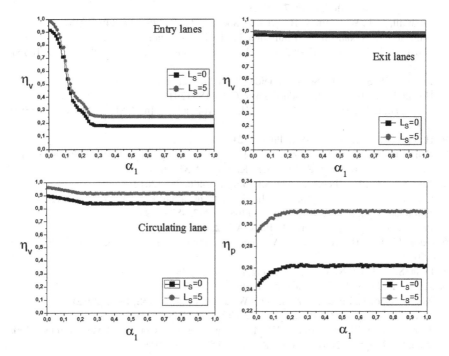

Fig. 6. Satisfaction rates as function of injecting rate α_1 for different values of L_S where $P_{CW}^{EN} = 3, P_{CW}^{EX} = 6$ and $\alpha_2 = 0.3$.

4 Conclusion

In summary, we have studied the effect of crossings pedestrian on the traffic flow at a single lane roundabout using a cellular automaton model. The boundary is controlled by the injecting rates α_1, α_2 and the extracting rate β. The pedestrians have the right of way over vehicles on crosswalk. The simulations are carried out to investigate the characteristics of traffic on different conditions. It has been observed that, the interferences between vehicles and pedestrians do not affect the traffic flow when the injecting rates are small. In contrast, when the injecting rates are large, the interferences act an important role in the system where both pedestrians and vehicles reach their congested state. Furthermore, we have examined how the crosswalk location influences the dynamic of pedestrians and vehicles. We have found that the traffic can avail from the crosswalk position in the entry and exit lanes to improve the satisfaction rate of vehicles. Moreover, the traffic can be improved by the use of slowdown sections before the crosswalk.

References

1. Nagel, K., Schreckenberg, M.: J. Phys. I **2**(12), 2221–2229 (1992)
2. Helbing, D.: Rev. Mod. Phys. **73**, 1068 (2001)
3. Lighthill, M.J., Whitham, G.B.: Proc. R. Soc. London A **299**, 317–345 (1955)
4. Nagatani, T., Nakanishi, K., Emmerich, H.: J. Phys. A: Math. Gen. **31**(24), 5431 (1998)
5. Echab, H., Lakouari, N., Ez-Zahraouy, H., Benyoussef, A.: Int. J. Mod. Phys. C **27**, 1650009 (2016)
6. Barlovic, R., Santen, L., Schadschneider, A., Schreckenberg, M.: Eur. Phys. J. B **5**, 793 (1998)
7. Huang, D.W.: Internat. J. Modern. Phys. C **21**, 189 (2010)
8. Echab, H., Lakouari, N., Ez-Zahraouy, H., Benyoussef, A.: Int. J. Mod. Phys. C **26**, 1550100 (2015)
9. Huang, D.W.: Internat. J. Mod. Phys. C **21**, 189 (2010)
10. Echab, H., Lakouari, N., Ez-Zahraouy, H., Benyoussef, A.: Phys. Lett. A **380**, 992 (2016)
11. Yamamoto, K., Kokubo, S., Nishinari, K.: Phys. A **379**, 654 (2007)
12. Xin, X.Y., Jia, N., Zheng, L., Ma, S.F.: Phys. A **406**, 287 (2014)
13. Cherry, C., Donlon, B., Yan, X.D.: Int. J. Inj. Control Saf. Promot. **19**, 320 (2012)
14. Muramatsu, M., Irie, T., Nagatani, T.: Phys. A **267**, 487 (1999)
15. Perez, G.J., Tapang, G., Lim, M.: Phys. A **312**, 609 (2002)
16. Gang, L., Jing, H., Zhiyong, L., Wunian, Y., Xiping, Z.: Int. J. Mod. Phys. B **29**, 1550100 (2015)
17. Feng, S.M., Ding, N., Chen, T., Zhang, H.: Phys. A **392**, 2847 (2013)
18. Zhang, Y., Duan, H.: Tsinghua Sci. Technol. **12**, 214 (2007)
19. Xie, D., Gao, Z., Zhao, X., Wang, D.Z.W.: J. Transp. Eng. **138**, 1442 (2012)
20. Zhang, J., Wang, H., Li, P., Zhejiang, J.: Univ. Sci. 835 (2004)
21. Transportation Research Board: HCM. National Research Council, Washington DC (2000)
22. Wan, B., Rouphail, N.M.: Transp. Res. Rec. **1878**, 58 (2004)

An Enhanced Cellular Automata Sub-mesh Model to Study High-Density Pedestrian Crowds

Claudio Feliciani[1(✉)] and Katsuhiro Nishinari[2,3]

[1] Department of Advanced Interdisciplinary Studies,
Graduate School of Engineering, The University of Tokyo, Tokyo 153-8904, Japan
feliciani@jamology.rcast.u-tokyo.ac.jp
[2] Research Center for Advanced Science and Technology, The University of Tokyo,
Tokyo 153-8904, Japan
[3] Department of Aeronautics and Astronautics, Graduate School of Engineering,
The University of Tokyo, Tokyo 113-8656, Japan

Abstract. This study presents an alternative mesh system for the floor-field Cellular Automata model which allows reproducing relevant phenomena observed in high density crowds. Sub-mesh positions are created at the edges and at the corners of adjacent cells to increase the mobility in dense crowds. Special rules are introduced to constrain the use of those additional positions and recreate some behavioral features observed in reality. The model was calibrated and validated using empirical data showing good agreement, while similar results could not be obtained using the standard mesh. Finally it was shown that the introduction of the corner sub-mesh position enhances the quality of the results in case of diagonal motion. The model presented here may allow a more accurate investigation of the crowd accidents occurred in the past and prevent a potential re-occurrence in the future.

1 Introduction

Cellular Automata (CA) has been extensively used in the frame of pedestrian dynamics. After the appearance of the first studies at the end of the 20th century [4] there has been an increasing interest in the possibilities given by the use of CA to predict some of the collective phenomena observed in pedestrian crowds. With the evolution of the IT capabilities and the improved computing power, CA models have been used in increasingly larger scenarios with airport terminal or large international events being within the possibilities offered by the system [15]. Additionally, the maximum number of agents has increased, with simulations dealing with hundreds of thousands of agents reported [10] and mid-size simulations running faster than real-time.

Besides performance and technical improvements, recently proposed pedestrian CA models allow to consider complex social structures such as groups [1], which can have a large influence on the overall results. Moreover, models including different walking speeds have been proposed to account, for example, for the situation in which a given fraction of the crowd is composed by elderly [2,13].

© Springer International Publishing Switzerland 2016
S. El Yacoubi et al. (Eds.): ACRI 2016, LNCS 9863, pp. 227–237, 2016.
DOI: 10.1007/978-3-319-44365-2_23

Finally, an anticipation model has been proposed to reproduce the anticipation behavior observed in bidirectional flows [14].

However, while additional features to consider specific aspects of crowds are continuously proposed, the standard mesh used in CA simulations has been almost unchanged since the introduction of the first models. Although some modifications have been proposed throughout the years, such as the real-coded lattice gas model [18] or an hexagonal mesh [19] (both mostly to improve the diagonal motion still being one of weak points of CA), the size of the grid has been almost unchanged, limiting therefore the maximum density allowed in simulations.

Empirical evidence shows that densities up to 8.4 persons m^{-2} [11] are possible in safe controlled experiments and density related to fatal accidents has been estimated as being close to 10 persons m^{-2} [8]. Nonetheless, CA models still typically employ a $0.4\,m \times 0.4\,m$ mesh, based on data collected by Weidmann [17]. Some researchers proposed different approaches to increase the maximum density allowed, for example by overlapping pedestrians [3], employing a finer mesh [12,16] or introducing a force field [9] (which indirectly consider higher densities).

In this study we present a different approach by introducing a sub-mesh model which allows increasing the maximum density achieved in simulations while including some of the behaviors observed in high-density crowds. A similar concept had been introduced in the past [7], but the mesh employed did not allow an accurate reproduction of the diagonal motion. With the model proposed here we aim at allowing a more accurate prediction of high-density crowds by reproducing some typical behavioral patterns and increasing the mobility within the grid to account, for example, for percolation-like phenomena observed in highly congested scenarios [5].

2   Cellular Automata Model

In this section, the sub-mesh system and the basic transition rules are described and discussed. The fundamental rules of the sub-mesh model (transition probabilities, update sequence, conflict resolution,...) are based on the classic floor-field model (for which a comprehensive description, including some of the particular features used here, is given in [14]). This section will focus on the peculiarities of the sub-mesh concept and shows the differences with similar approaches which appeared in the past.

2.1   Computational Mesh

Figure 1 shows the conventional grid and the sub-mesh grid proposed here. In the conventional approach a square cell is used to approximate the area occupied from a single pedestrian. Pedestrians' motion is therefore simulated by having agents moving from one cell to the next one at each iteration.

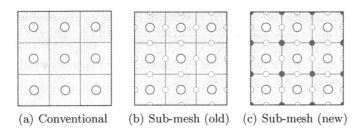

(a) Conventional   (b) Sub-mesh (old)   (c) Sub-mesh (new)

Fig. 1. Comparison between the conventional and the sub-mesh approach. Sub-mesh locations are indicated with small circles.

If TASEP (Totally Asymmetric Simple Exclusion Process) rules are strictly applied only one pedestrian is allowed per cell and therefore the maximum density reached using conventional grid is 6.25 persons m^{-2} (using a mesh of 0.4 m $\times$ 0.4 m size). In the sub-mesh approach we decided to add some locations at the boundaries between the cells to increase mobility and allow high-density simulations. In a former approach [7] sub-mesh locations were added between the edges of adjacent cells (Fig. 1(b)). However we found that in case of diagonal geometries such approach may result in largely inaccurate results. To overcome this problem we added some additional positions in the corners as shown in Fig. 1(c). As a consequence, this study will focus on the sub-mesh grid using both edge and corner positions and the following discussion on the model and its rule will focus on the newest approach (Fig. 1(c)).

It is important to notice that while center positions are all equivalent, there exist two types of sub-mesh positions depending on the number of cells which they share. Specifically, sub-mesh positions being located at the edges share their location with two adjacent cells, while sub-mesh positions being located at the corners share their location with four neighbor cells. We can therefore assume that pedestrians occupying an edge sub-mesh position are half in one cell and half in the adjacent one. A similar argument can be used for corner pedestrians, but the shared value will be one quarter in this case.

We can now introduce the concept of occupancy which we will use to count the number of pedestrians for each cell. Considering the above arguments the occupancy for each cell (n_{cell}) can be defined as:

$$n_{cell} = n_{center} + \frac{1}{2} \cdot n_{edge} + \frac{1}{4} \cdot n_{corner} \tag{1}$$

where $n_{center} \in \{0,1\}$, $n_{edge} \in \{0,1,2,3,4\}$ and $n_{corner} \in \{0,1,2,3,4\}$ represents the number of pedestrians in the center, the edges and the corners respectively. n_{cell} is 0 when the cell is completely empty and 4 when all the positions are occupied. By using the sub-mesh approach densities 4-times higher than the conventional model ($25\,m^{-2}$) are therefore technically possible. However we want to limit the maximum density achieved to values slightly over $10\,m^{-2}$. This can be done by fixing a maximum value of n_{cell}, defined as n_{max} (or maximum occupancy), above which motion to any position of the given cell is not allowed.

This approach, besides limiting the maximum density to reasonable values, it allows to recreate a percolation-like behavior because different cells may reach maximum occupancy showing different configurations. From this point of view the sub-mesh approach differs from a grid-scaling approach, in which at maximum density all cells are equally occupied.

2.2   Transition Rules

By only considering the rules described so far the sub-mesh approach would not be much different from an overlapping extension. One of the distinguishing characteristic of the sub-mesh approach lies in the timing rules which apply for the motion to and from the sub-mesh positions.

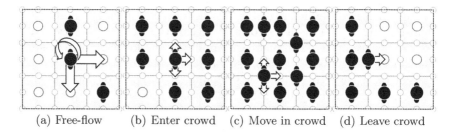

(a) Free-flow   (b) Enter crowd   (c) Move in crowd   (d) Leave crowd

Fig. 2. Different scenarios for a right-walking pedestrian.

Figure 2 illustrates some typical situations which may be encountered in simulation. Two cases need to be distinguished: motion to a cell center and motion to a sub-mesh position (either edge or corner). The former case will be used to reproduce phenomena observed during free-flow or low-density conditions, while the sub-mesh will be dedicated to high-density considerations. The different rules applying to free-flow and congested motion are summarized as follows:

1. If a neighboring cell center is empty a given pedestrian is allowed to move there the following iteration if maximum occupancy is not exceeded. In other words we can say that a pedestrian being in a situation like the one illustrated in Fig. 2(a) or (d) at the time step t_n can move to the next cell center at t_{n+1} if occupancy n_{cell} for the given cell will not go beyond the maximum occupancy n_{max}. Under low density conditions pedestrians move like in the conventional CA mesh from one cell center to the other.

2. Pedestrians are allowed to move into a sub-mesh position only after having waited a minimum number of t_{wait} iterations (and only if the maximum occupancy will not be exceeded). This rule applies to both pedestrians moving from a cell center and those already being in a sub-mesh position before transition. This rule represents one of the distinguishing points of the sub-mesh approach proposed here. The presence of this rule means that motion to a sub-mesh location or between them is slower compared to center-to-center

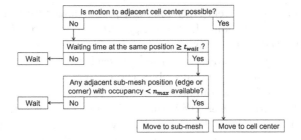

Fig. 3. Transition rules for cell center and sub-mesh positions summarized.

motion. The motivation hidden behind this rule is that pedestrians do actually move even in congested situations, but their speed is significantly lower and they may have to turn their body to fit between adjacent pedestrians (this last observation is one of the inspirations of the sub-mesh system).

The transition rules described above are schematically summarized in Fig. 3. In addition to the rules introduced earlier we decided to use the exchange probability which allows to avoid head-on collisions by exchanging (or tunneling) the position of two pedestrians being in front of each other and pointing toward opposite directions. To adapt the tunneling method to the sub-mesh approach introduced here we decided to add a penalty to avoid an over-use of this option. For instance a pair of pedestrians walking in different directions may exchange their position if the following two conditions are satisfied:

1. The pair has been waiting in the same position for a time longer than $2 \cdot t_{wait}$.
2. The randomly chosen exchange probability p is smaller or equal than a fixed parameter $p_E \in [0, 1]$. By setting $p_E = 1$ every time that the temporal condition above is satisfied tunneling will occur. Setting $p_E = 0$ will result in no position exchange at all.

The transition probabilities are computed using the standard equations of the floor field model and pedestrians choose their next step according to the transition which has the highest probability. Parallel update is used and in case of a conflict between two pedestrians for the same position, one of the two is chosen with equal probability.

3   Results

3.1   Calibration and Validation

The model presented above was calibrated and validated using empirical data resulting from the observation of a bidirectional flow formed by commuters passing a corridor in a subway station (details are given in [6]). Two different scenarios were considered: a normal and a heavily congested case. In the normal case the total flow observed is relatively low and pedestrians simply had to reduce their speed to avoid collisions. In the congested case a deadlock was observed with some of the pedestrians having to stop briefly.

In the simulation, the inflow recorded for each side of the corridor during the observation was used as input, while the output was computed using the simulation model and later compared with the experimental data as shown in Fig. 4(a) and (b) (total flow is given there). Overall density variation was also compared (see Fig. 4(c) and (d)) and a density map showing the location with highest density was generated at the end of the simulation (see Fig. 4(e) and (f)). 500 simulations were performed for each case.

In general, both the total flow and the density show a satisfactory agreement with the empirical results. Although a comparison is not possible, the density map obtained from simulation reflects the qualitative observation that the densest crowd formed at the right side of the corridor (in the congested case). In particular, using the sub-mesh positions and the waiting time, the double peak observed in the congested case was correctly reproduced.

It is however important to remark that a slightly different set of parameters had to be used. As Table 1 shows, the parameters which had to be adjusted for both cases (normal and congested) generally reflect the partially different attitude observed in the respective situations.

Table 1. Model parameters calibrated using different scenarios. k_S, k_D, k_A and k_W are the values of the static, dynamic, anticipation and wall floor field respectively; α_D and β_D are the diffusion and decay of the dynamic field and d_A is the anticipation distance. Walking velocity is set at $1.4\,\mathrm{m \cdot s^{-1}}$.

Parameter	Normal	Congested	Parameter	Normal	Congested
k_S	8.5	13.0	k_A	8.5	13.0
k_W		0.75	d_A		4
k_D		6.0	α_D		0.25
p_E		0.275	β_D		0.25
n_{max}		2	t_{wait}		1

3.2   Comparison with the Conventional Model

To grasp the fundamental differences with the conventional model we performed the congested-case simulation using the standard CA mesh by setting $n_{max} = 1$ and $t_{wait} = 0$. Two different values for p_E were used as given in Fig. 5 which presents the results.

In none of the two cases the double peak (or similar shapes) observed in reality is correctly reproduced. In addition, low values for p_E (generally < 0.10) resulted almost constantly in a complete gridlock as both groups of pedestrians had to stop in front of each other's (simulations were aborted when the given inflow couldn't be reached). This shows that, while the exchange probability

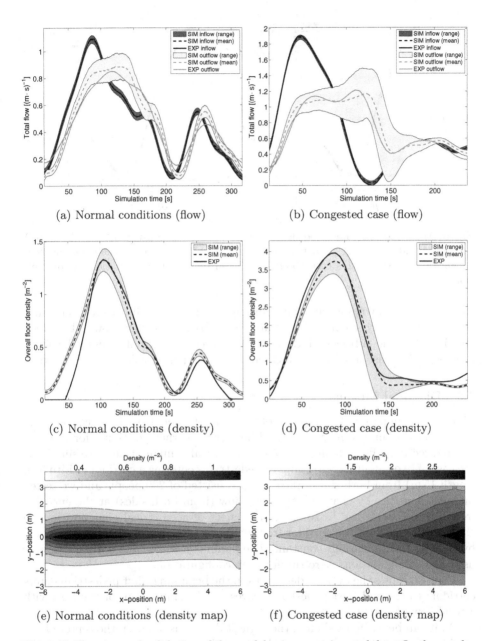

(a) Normal conditions (flow)

(b) Congested case (flow)

(c) Normal conditions (density)

(d) Congested case (density)

(e) Normal conditions (density map)

(f) Congested case (density map)

Fig. 4. Calibration and validation of the model using experimental data. In the graphs representing the flow, dark colors are used for the total inflow and light colors for the total outflow. Thick lines show the experimental result, while dotted line the average simulation result (with the surrounding surface being the variation among the several simulations). In the density maps the effect of the wall floor field is evident; in the congested case a higher density is correctly predicted on the right side. SIM refers to simulation, EXP to experiment.

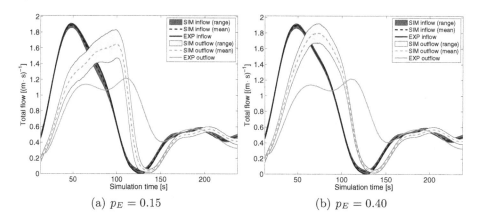

(a) $p_E = 0.15$ (b) $p_E = 0.40$

Fig. 5. Measured and simulated flow in the congested case using the standard mesh ($n_{max} = 1$ and $t_{wait} = 0$). p_E acts as a sort of filter blocking part of the incoming flow. When set too low (in this case about < 0.10) in most of the simulations a complete stop occurred.

has an effect in avoiding head-on collisions, its role is similar to a filter which regulates how much counter-flow is allowed to pass through a crowd. The waiting time and the sub-mesh introduced here create a sort of buffer allowing a temporary increase in density which enhances the permeability of the crowd.

3.3   Diagonal Motion

Finally we compared the original (old) sub-mesh model (without corner positions) and the improvement proposed here (with corner positions) for the case of a bidirectional flow having different geometrical configurations. We simulated the case of two equally large groups of pedestrians entering a corridor (width 5 m, length 15 m) from both sides. Each group consisted of 200 people and we tested different densities by changing the total flow (from both sides) at the entrance from 1.0 to 2.0 (m · s)$^{-1}$. To assess the effect of geometrical configuration we changed the angle of the corridor from 0° (horizontal) to 26.56° and finally 45° by keeping the dimensions constant. The parameter-set for the normal case was used and 50 simulations were run for each configuration.

Figure 6 shows the average density from the beginning (first pedestrian enters corridor) to the end (last pedestrian leaves) of the simulation for the case with a total flow of 2.0 (m · s)$^{-1}$.

As it can be easily predicted, the highest density is found in the center of the corridor, around 4.0 m^{-2}. In general the density maps are quite similar for the three angles considered, although it appears that in both models the geometry tends to change the distribution of crowd in the center. As it can be observed, in the horizontal case the highest-density region is elongated by reproducing the shape of the corridor. However in the 45° case a more concentric configuration is observed. Similar characteristics were found in the 1.0 (m · s)$^{-1}$ case which is not reported here.

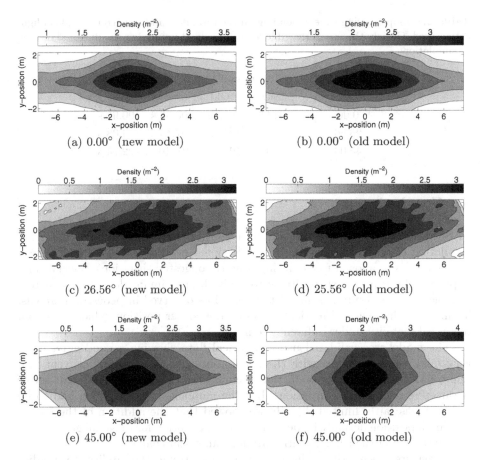

Fig. 6. Average density in the different regions of the corridor for the case with a total flow of $2.0\,(\mathrm{m}\cdot\mathrm{s})^{-1}$. All the cases have been rotated to facilitate visualization and comparison. In the $26.56°$ case the discrete configuration used in the model results in a light distortion.

Concerning the absolute values, it has to be remarked that an higher maximum density is found in the $45°$ case compared the other two cases. This behavior can be understood considering the group crossing time (the time required by the crowd to completely leave the corridor) given in Table 2.

As Table 2 shows, while in the low density scenario both models (old and new) perform well when the geometry is changed, for the in $2.0\,(\mathrm{m}\cdot\mathrm{s})^{-1}$ case in the $45°$ configuration a longer crossing time is required, which creates a denser crowd in the center of the corridor. In the model not using the edge sub-mesh position the effect of the geometry is quite strong and the average crossing time increases of more than $20\,\%$ because of the change in geometry. The use of the corner position allows reducing this deviation, although an error slightly larger than $5\,\%$ is still observed.

Table 2. Group crossing time depending on the total flow and the geometrical configuration used. Clearly the use of the edge location helped improving the diagonal motion in simulations.

Total flow Model	$1.0\ (m \cdot s)^{-1}$		$2.0\ (m \cdot s)^{-1}$	
	New	Old	New	Old
0.00°	104.33 s	103.19 s	96.95 s	100.97 s
26.56°	108.69 s	107.16 s	97.43 s	104.08 s
45.00°	109.17 s	108.11 s	102.91 s	122.74 s

4 Conclusions

In this study we introduced an alternative grid system to be employed for the simulation of dense crowd scenarios. Additional positions are created between adjacent cells to allow a usage during heavily congested situations. Special rules apply for the use of such positions to limit the maximum density within reasonable limits and mimic some of the behaviors observed in pedestrian crowds. To improve the diagonal motion we added the corner position, which allows an increased mobility under different geometries.

The model was validated using empirical data showing a good agreement, especially when compared with the results obtained by using the conventional approach. To increase the prediction accuracy we had to use a different set of parameters for different situations, but the number of values which had to be adapted was fairly limited. Finally we showed that the addition of the corner sub-mesh position actually helped improving the motion for diagonal geometries, greatly reducing the error resulting from geometrical changes.

Given its peculiarities, in particular concerning the ability to predict percolation-like phenomena, the model presented here may be used, in addition to pedestrian dynamics, in fields such as material engineering (for example to simulate conductive properties in fiber-reinforced materials) or fluid dynamic (for porous medium in particular).

Acknowledgments. This work was financially supported by JSPS KAKENHI Grant Number 25287026 and the Doctoral Student Special Incentives Program (SEUT RA) of the University of Tokyo. In addition the authors would like to thank Tokyo Metro Co., Ltd for helping us obtaining the experimental data used for model calibration.

References

1. Bandini, S., Crociani, L., Gorrini, A., Vizzari, G.: An agent-based model of pedestrian dynamics considering groups: a real world case study. In: 2014 IEEE 17th International Conference on Intelligent Transportation Systems (ITSC), pp. 572–577. IEEE (2014)

2. Bandini, S., Crociani, L., Vizzari, G.: Pedestrian simulation: considering elderlies in the models and in the simulation results. In: Andó, B., Siciliano, P., Marletta, V., Monteriù, A. (eds.) Ambient Assisted Living. Biosystems & Biorobotics, vol. 11, pp. 11–21. Springer, Switzerland (2015)

3. Bandini, S., Mondini, M., Vizzari, G.: Modelling negative interactions among pedestrians in high density situations. Transp. Res. Part C Emerg. Technol. **40**, 251–270 (2014)

4. Blue, V., Adler, J.: Emergent fundamental pedestrian flows from cellular automata microsimulation. Transp. Res. Rec. J. Transp. Res. Board **1644**, 29–36 (1998)

5. Federici, M.I., Gorrini, A., Manenti, L., Vizzari, G.: An innovative scenario for pedestrian data collection: the observation of an admission test at the university of milano-bicocca. In: Weidmann, U., Kirsch, U., Schreckenberg, M. (eds.) Pedestrian and Evacuation Dynamics 2012, pp. 143–150. Springer, Switzerland (2014)

6. Feliciani, C., Nishinari, K.: Phenomenological description of deadlock formation in pedestrian bidirectional flow based on empirical observation. J. Stat. Mech: Theory Exp. **2015**(10), P10003 (2015)

7. Feliciani, C., Nishinari, K.: An improved cellular automata model to simulate the behavior of high density crowd and validation by experimental data. Physica A Stat. Mech. Appl. **451**, 135–148 (2016)

8. Helbing, D., Johansson, A., Al-Abideen, H.Z.: Dynamics of crowd disasters: an empirical study. Phys. Rev. E **75**(4), 00046109 (2007)

9. Henein, C.M., White, T.: Macroscopic effects of microscopic forces between agents in crowd models. Phys. A Statis. Mech. Appl. **373**, 694–712 (2007)

10. Lümmel, G., Rieser, M., Nagel, K.: Large scale microscopic evacuation simulation. In: Klingsch, W.W.F., Rogsch, C., Schadschneider, A., Schreckenberg, M. (eds.) Pedestrian and Evacuation Dynamics 2008, pp. 547–553. Springer, Heidelberg (2010)

11. Oberhagemann, D.: Static and dynamic crowd densities at major public events. Technical Report March, Vereinigung zur Förderung des Deutschen Brandschutzes (2012)

12. Sarmady, S., Haron, F., Talib, A.Z.: Simulating crowd movements using fine grid cellular automata. In: 2010 12th International Conference on Computer Modelling and Simulation (UKSim), pp. 428–433. IEEE (2010)

13. Shimura, K., Ohtsuka, K., Vizzari, G., Nishinari, K., Bandini, S.: Mobility analysis of the aged pedestrians by experiment and simulation. Pattern Recogn. Lett. **44**, 58–63 (2014)

14. Suma, Y., Yanagisawa, D., Nishinari, K.: Anticipation effect in pedestrian dynamics: modeling and experiments. Phys. A **391**(1), 248–263 (2012)

15. Szymanezyk, O., Dickinson, P., Duckett, T.: Towards agent-based crowd simulation in airports using games technology. In: O'Shea, J., Nguyen, N.T., Crockett, K., Howlett, R.J., Jain, L.C. (eds.) KES-AMSTA 2011. LNCS, vol. 6682, pp. 524–533. Springer, Heidelberg (2011)

16. Was, J., Lubaś, R.: Towards realistic and effective agent-based models of crowd dynamics. Neurocomputing **146**, 199–209 (2014)

17. Weidmann, U.: Transporttechnik der Fussgänger: Transporttechnische Eigenschaften des Fussgängerverkehrs (Literaturauswertung). ETH, IVT (1993)

18. Yamamoto, K., Kokubo, S., Nishinari, K.: Simulation for pedestrian dynamics by real-coded cellular automata (RCA). Phys. A **379**(2), 654–660 (2007)

19. Yanagisawa, D., Nishi, R., Tomoeda, A., Ohtsuka, K., Kimura, A., Suma, Y., Nishinari, K.: Study on efficiency of evacuation with an obstacle on hexagonal cell space. SICE J. Control Meas. Syst. Integr. **3**(6), 395–401 (2010)

A Cellular Automata-Like Scheduler and Load Balancer

Jakub Gasior$^{(\boxtimes)}$ and Franciszek Seredynski

Cardinal Stefan Wyszynski University, Warsaw, Poland
j.gasior@uksw.edu.pl

Abstract. The paper presents a general framework to study issues of effective load balancing and scheduling in highly parallel and distributed computing environments. We propose a novel approach based on the concept of the *Sandpile* cellular automaton: a decentralized multi-agent system working in a critical state at the edge of chaos. Our goal is providing fairness between concurrent job submissions by minimizing slowdown of individual applications and dynamically rescheduling them to the best suited resources.

Keywords: Cellular automata · Self-organization · Load-balancing

1 Introduction

Two fundamental issues in dynamic load-balancing and rescheduling domains are *workload sharing* and *job migration*. In situations, whereby newly created jobs arrive into the system, some resources can become heavily loaded while others are idle or only lightly loaded. Therefore, the main objective of workload sharing is to develop some assignment algorithms to transfer or migrate the jobs from heavily to lightly loaded machines so that no nodes are idle, when there are other requests waiting to be processed. Some important aspects to consider are to decide when a physical resource should migrate part of its workload, which part of the workload must be moved, and where it should be moved.

To realize this goal, we propose a decentralized and self-organizing multi-agent system based on the *Sandpile* CA model. Given a set of agents, which have only partial knowledge of local resources and submitted workload, it is possible to design a set of simple local rules, so that a smart behavior emerges from them at a global system level. The working hypothesis of our approach relies on the *Self-Organized Criticality* theory (SOC) described by Bak in [2]. The goal of our algorithm is to reduce the average response time of arriving jobs by equalizing the *Slowdown* between neighboring computing nodes. The performance of our scheme is evaluated in terms of several performance metrics in relation to multiple variations of arrival and processing times as well as the number of submitted jobs.

The remainder of this paper is organized as follows. In Sect. 2, we present the works related to the distributed scheduling and load balancing in distributed

© Springer International Publishing Switzerland 2016
S. El Yacoubi et al. (Eds.): ACRI 2016, LNCS 9863, pp. 238–247, 2016.
DOI: 10.1007/978-3-319-44365-2_24

computing systems. In Sect. 3, we describe the proposed scheduling problem. Section 4 presents the dynamic load balancing and scheduling scheme based on the *Sandpile* model. The experimental evaluation of the proposed approach is given in Sect. 5. We end the paper in Sect. 6 with some conclusions and indications for future work.

2   State of the Art

Distributed scheduling has been widely studied in the context of real-time systems, when jobs have deadline constraints. Due to the distributed nature of such systems, several concurrent jobs originating from different users are likely to compete for the resources. Traditionally, schedulers aim at minimizing the overall completion time of a job [5]. However, in a multi-user setting, it is important to maintain some fairness between users: we do not want to favor a user with a large number of small jobs compared to another with fewer larger jobs. Similarly, if jobs can be submitted at different entry points of the distributed system, we do not want that the location of the user to impact his experienced running time [6].

There are several studies complementary to our work, which focus on how to share the available resources among several users. For example, in [1] authors employed a scheduling policy utilizing the solution to a linear programming problem in order to maximize the system capacity. Closer to our problem, Viswanathan in [12] proposed a distributed scheduling strategy specifically designed to handle large volumes of computationally intensive and arbitrarily divisible workloads submitted for processing involving multiple sources and processing nodes. In [7] authors proposed a distributed scheduling solution ensuring a fair and efficient use of the available resources by providing a similar share of the platform to every application through stretch optimization.

In [9] authors proposed a skeleton for dynamic load balancing through *gossiping*: rather than a fully-operative scheduling system, the authors aim at illustrating the application potentials of gossiping protocols. Similarly, in [8] authors described a distributed load balancing algorithm based on building a consensus between nodes. To reach the consensus nodes communicate within a homogeneous architecture via gossiping protocol.

Finally, in [10] authors employed a *Sandpile* model for non-clairvoyant load-balancing of jobs in large-scale decentralized systems. The model works with two different interconnection topologies, based on a ring and a small-world graph and aims to minimize the sizes and quantities of the avalanches by using a gossiping-based version of the multi-agent system. Instead of propagating a real avalanche, the gossiping protocol forwards the avalanche virtually until a new state of equilibrium is found. The proposed solution was found to reduce the overhead of intermediate migrations and increase the overall throughput of the system, however it employed a simple FIFO local allocation scheme and did not consider the impact of resulting rescheduling events on the overall performance of the considered platform.

3   Scheduling Problem

3.1   Problem Definition

Our system model is based on the architecture introduced in [11] and consists of a set of geographically distributed computing nodes $M_1, M_2, ..., M_m$, which are connected to each other via a wide area network. Each node M_i is described by a parameter m_i, which denotes the number of identical processors P_i and its computational power s_i, characterized by a number of operations per unit of time it is capable of performing.

Individual users $(U_1, U_2, ..., U_n)$ submit their jobs to the system, expecting their completion before a required deadline. Job (denoted as J_k^j) is jth job produced (and owned) by user U_k. J_k stands for the set of all jobs produced by user U_k, while $n_k = |J_k|$ is the number of such jobs. Each job has varied parameters defined as a tuple $< r_k^j, size_k^j, t_k^j, d_k^j >$, specifying its release date r_k^j; its size $1 \leq size_k^j \leq m_m$, that is referred to as its processor requirements or *degree of parallelism*; its execution requirements t_k^j defined by a number of operations and deadline d_k^j.

The goal of the scheduler is to find the allocation and the time of execution for each job. The distribution of the jobs must be done in such a way that the system's throughput is optimized. To do so, an optimal trade-off between the processing overhead and the degree of knowledge used in the balancing process must be sought. Formally, the objective is to allocate a batch of local jobs to the available nodes M_i and minimize the global system *Slowdown* ς_{max} thereby enforcing a fair trade-off between all submitted jobs.

4   Dynamic Load Balancing and Scheduling Based on a Sandpile Model

4.1   The Sandpile Model

Our proposed solution (pseudo-code is presented in Algorithm 1) is a local neighborhood diffusion approach which employs overlapping domains to achieve system-wide load balancing and fairness between individual nodes. Each computational node M_i is associated with a scheduling agent A_i who decides the processing order of allocated jobs. Agents gather up-to-date information in each transition time constructing complete availability summary (i.e., *workload index*) and communicating it to neighboring nodes, so that each node can schedule submitted jobs efficiently. The state of the platform is based on the availability of computational nodes to receive and execute newly submitted jobs.

Agents inform their nearest neighbors of their estimated workload indices and update this information throughout program execution (Algorithm 1: Lines 9–11). Due to heterogeneity of both system and workload, our work employs a complex workload index, comprised of two parameters: *Maximum Completion Time*, C_{max}^i of the local job queue on machine M_i and size (or duration) of the

Algorithm 1. Pseudo-code of the *CA-Stretch* Scheduling Algorithm

1: **Input:** Q: Node's M_i local job queue
2: **Input:** r_{new}: Release time of the job J_{new}
3: **Input:** p_{new}: Processing time of the job J_{new} on machine M_i
4: **Input:** S_i: Current state of the machine M_i
5: **Input:** V_i: Neighborhood of the machine M_i

6: *Initialize Iteration Counter, $T \leftarrow 0$*
7: **for all** $A_i \in A$ **do** {In parallel}
8:    *Trigger(J_{new})*
9:    *Calculate Completion Time of Local Job Queue, C_{max}^i.*
10:   *Calculate Free Time Slot Duration, $\tau_i = freeTimeSlot(Q, r_{new}, p_{new})$.*
11:   *Exchange information about Workload Index with machines in V_i.*
12:   *Update Cell State, $S_i(t_n) = f(S_i(t_{n-1}), V_i(t_{n-1}))$*

13:   **if** $S_i ==$ *Overloaded* **then**
14:      **while** $S_i ==$ *Overloaded* **do**
15:         **for all** $M_i \in V_i$ **do**
16:            *Sort machines in V_i by non-decreasing Time Slots, $\tau_1 \leq \tau_2 \leq ... \leq \tau_n$.*
17:            *Send job J_{new} to the machine with the longest Time Slot, τ_i.*
18:         **end for**
19:      **end while**
20:   **else**
21:      **if** $\tau \geq p_{new}$ **then**
22:         *Add job J_{new} to machine's M_i queue.*
23:         *Schedule job J_{new} in the free Time Slot, τ_i.*
24:      **else**
25:         **for all** $M_i \in V_i$ **do**
26:            *Sort machines in V_i by non-decreasing Time Slots, $\tau_1 \leq \tau_2 \leq ... \leq \tau_n$.*
27:            *Send job J_{new} to the machine with the longest τ_i.*
28:         **end for**
29:      **end if**
30:   **end if**
31:   *Update Iteration Counter, $T \leftarrow T + 1$*
32: **end for**

available *Time Slot*, τ_i denoting the amount of unallocated processor's time in machine's M_i schedule. The calculation of the first parameter is straightforward and doesn't require further discussion. In order to describe the evaluation of the second parameter comprising our workload index we will use an example depicted in Fig. 1 visualizing five jobs scheduled for execution on exemplary node with two processing elements.

Variables below the Gantt chart $(d_1^1, ..., d_1^5)$ represent deadline values of each job in the local queue. Let us further assume that a new job J_{new} will be released to the system at time r_{new} with execution time p_{new} and deadline d_{new}. The process necessary to compute the size of a free *Time Slot* τ_i on node M_i that can be allocated to the new job J_{new} (if any) is presented in Algorithm 1. In the

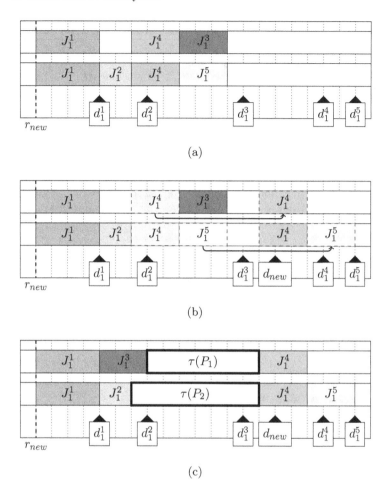

Fig. 1. Estimation of the available *Time Slot* on node M_i: Jobs J_1, J_2 and J_3 are processed as soon as possible, while jobs J_4 and J_5 are processed as late as possible. The size of the available free *Time Slot* τ may differ between processors.

example of Fig. 1(b), deadline d_{new} of the new job J_{new} lies between deadlines d_3 and d_4, respectively. Thus, the earliest starting time for the job J_{new} is after jobs J_1, J_2, and J_3 (that is all jobs with $d_j < d_{new}$) have been completed. Similarly, the latest completion time for the job J_{new} must ensure that jobs J_4 and J_5 (that is all jobs with $d_j > d_{new}$) will not miss their deadlines, and also that deadline d_{new} is not exceeded. In practice, it enforces rescheduling of jobs J_4 and J_5 to the end of the local job queue as visualized in Fig. 1(b).

Let us further assume that a variable c_k denotes the moment at which $k-1$ job in the queue is expected to finish its execution. It can be calculated by adding the remaining execution time of the $k-1$ jobs to the starting time r_{new}, as follows:

$$c_k = r_{new} + \sum_{j=1}^{k-1} p_j. \tag{1}$$

Then, assuming that the new job J_{new} would be at position k in the local queue, we can calculate the size of the available *Time Slot* τ_i that can potentially be devoted to job J_{new} between the moment at which the previous job is going to finish (c_k), and the deadline of the new job (d_{new}) or the last moment at which next job must start (x_{k+1}), whichever comes first:

$$\tau = min(d_{new}, x_{k+1}) - c_k. \tag{2}$$

As visible in Fig. 1(c), the above procedure is performed individually for each processor in the considered node. By combining the data from separate processors in each node we are able to provide a complete availability overview necessary for construction of the *workload index* employed in the latter phases of the dynamic rescheduling process performed by the proposed *Sandpile* CA-based scheduler.

Whenever a resource becomes overburdened in comparison with its neighbors, its local *Maximum Completion Time*, C^i_{max} exceeds the local average by a specified *threshold* value $\left(C^i_{max} - \overline{C^i_{max}} > C_{threshold}\right)$. For simplicity's sake we employ in our work a value of threshold equal to $C_{threshold} = 1$. Resources in such a state are considered as *Overloaded*. They will send all incoming traffic to their neighbors, as well as any surplus workload that cannot be completed in a required time frame (i.e., before deadline).

Resource that are not overburdened with workload can be considered as *Underloaded*. Their estimated *Maximum Completion Time*, C^i_{max} is lower than the local average $\left(\overline{C^i_{max}} - C^i_{max} > C_{threshold}\right)$, while the available free *Time Slot* duration is usually longer than the local average $\left(\tau_i > \overline{\tau}\right)$ and they are capable of accepting excessive workload from their *Overloaded* neighbors, as well as any incoming workload submitted by users. Resources in the *Balanced* state are characterized by the estimated *Maximum Completion Time*, C^i_{max} close to the local average $\left(|C^i_{max} - \overline{C^i_{max}}| \leq C_{threshold}\right)$. They will run jobs, which exist in their local queue and will accept new jobs as well. Such a state can be alternatively triggered by estimation of the free *Time Slots* slightly smaller than the local average $\left(0 \ll \tau_i < \overline{\tau}\right)$ ensuring that they are capable of meeting the deadline constraints of their local jobs.

If the arrival of the job triggers the *Overloaded* transition rule (i.e., causes workload imbalance), the excessive jobs will be sent to one of the available neighbors. Scheduling agent will find a set of neighboring nodes which are suitable to execute the job J_{new}. Nodes are first sorted in a descending order according to the available *Time Slots* and the job J_{new} is sent to a machine with the longest available free *Time Slot* (Algorithm 1: Lines 13–19). In a case of nodes in *Underloaded* and *Balanced* states, the job J_{new} will be added to their local queue.

As long as the schedule can be accommodated before the required deadline, a job will be allocated for execution in the available *Time Slots* (Algorithm 1: Lines 22–23). Alternatively, an excessive job will be sent to one of the neighboring nodes (Algorithm 1: Lines 25–28). Because this process may trigger new events in the adjacent nodes, the avalanches (migrations of jobs) will iteratively continue throughout the the entire system until a global state of equilibrium is achieved.

5   Experimental Analysis and Performance Evaluation

5.1   Simulation Testbed

To study the performance of the proposed dynamic load balancing and rescheduling algorithm, we have conducted several simulation experiments under three system scales: a small-scale system composed of $m = 16$ nodes, a medium-scale system composed of $m = 64$ nodes and a large-scale system composed of $m = 144$ nodes. The number of processing elements m_i in each node M_i was generated by a Gaussian probability distribution function with parameters $\mathcal{N}(6, 1)$. The computational capacity (or speed) s_i of the processing elements was similarly generated with parameters $\mathcal{N}(4, 1)$ [Instructions/Time Unit], while a nominal bandwidth of the network connecting every two nodes was assumed to be generated with parameters $\mathcal{N}(2, 1)$ [Instructions/Time Unit].

The number of users submitting their jobs to the system was fixed at 8, 32, and 72 for the small-scale, medium-scale, and large-scale systems, respectively. The execution requirements of submitted jobs t_k^j were normally distributed with parameters $\mathcal{N}(10, 3)$ [Instructions]. Each job J_k^j was composed of a number of threads $size_k^j$ uniformly selected from the following set $\mathcal{U}\{1, 2, 3, 4\}$.

In the following simulation experiments, the efficiency of the analyzed job scheduling methods was measured in terms of:

- **Makespan:** the total running time of all jobs, defined as $C_{max} = max\{C_{max}^i, i = 1, 2, ..., m\}$, that is completion time of the last finalized job;
- **Flowtime:** the time job J_k^j spends in the system, defined as the difference between its completion time and the release date, $F_k^j = C_k^j - r_k^j$;
- **System Utilization:** the percentage of processing power allocated to successfully executed jobs out of the total processing power available in the system;
- **Slowdown:** the ratio of the response time under the concurrent scheduling policy $(C_k^j - r_k^j)$ over its response time in dedicated mode, i.e., $\frac{C_k^j - r_k^j}{p_k^j}$;

5.2   Comparison with Classic Sandpile CA-Based Scheduler

Experiments aimed to compare the performance of the proposed dynamic load balancing scheme (referred to further as *CA-Stretch*) with a classic *Sandpile* CA-based scheduler operating according to rules designed by Bak in [3] and denoted as *BTW-CA*. In order to adjust the *BTW-CA* model to heterogeneous conditions considered in this work, we employed a simple *workload index* calculated as the *Maximum Completion Time*, C_{max}^i of the local job queue on each computational node M_i. Transition rules of the *BTW-CA* scheme were analogous to ones employed in the proposed job scheduling algorithm, however the size of the available *Time Slot* τ_i was not taken into consideration. That way, we were able to indirectly investigate the impact of incorporated rescheduling mechanics aiming to minimize the *Slowdown* metric by making use of any unallocated *Time Slots* in the local schedule.

The conducted experiments aimed to analyze the behavior of the *CA-Stretch* scheduler in multiple scenarios with increasing complexities, where static schedulers are often unable to approach optimal solutions. We conducted several simulations with a constant workload size equal to $n = 5000$ jobs, scheduled within each system scale by a variable number of clients. We present the comparative performance analysis of our proposed job scheduling algorithm in Fig. 2, detailing the achieved *Makespan, Flowtime, System Utilization* and *Slowdown* results.

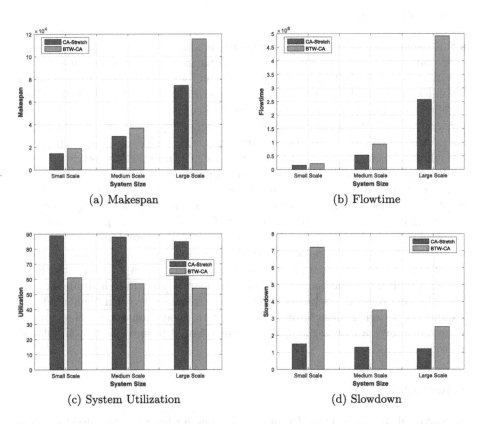

(a) Makespan

(b) Flowtime

(c) System Utilization

(d) Slowdown

Fig. 2. Performance results of conducted experiments for a total of $n = 5000$ jobs scheduled within $m = 16, 64$ and 144 nodes: (a) Makespan, (b) Flowtime, (c) System Utilization, (d) Slowdown.

As depicted, with an increase of the number of available resources, better scheduling decisions are being made which results in better performance. Once again, the *CA-Stretch* achieves better performance of both analyzed scheduling strategies. It can be attributed to the employed reshuffling and rescheduling mechanisms in the proposed *CA-Stretch* scheme and its capability to equalize the workload in the local balancing domain. As a results, the number of concurrent requests submitted by the users has less negative impact on the scheduler's effectiveness.

On the other hand, a classic *Sandpile* scheduler exhibits worse performance as it is forced, in many circumstances, to allocate computationally expensive jobs to already overloaded resources. Obviously, the best results were achieved for the *Slowdown* metric (Fig. 2(d)), which is a direct effect of implementing this metric as the main performance objective in our *Sandpile* CA-based scheduling scheme. In fact, a nearly equal *Slowdown* values in all considered size scenarios suggest that our goal of achieving fairness between multiple job submissions was accomplished.

6   Conclusion

In this paper we have proposed a novel parallel and distributed algorithm based on the *Sandpile* CA model for dynamic load balancing and rescheduling of jobs in a distributed computing environment. In our solution, computing resources are under the control of agents which can interact locally within an established neighborhood. In such a system, jobs arrive to resources and accumulate similarly to grains of sand. When a given agent detects any inequalities, it sends excessive jobs to his neighbors, often starting an avalanche, which may be propagated throughout the entire system until a new state of equilibrium is met.

We presented the rules of local interactions among agents providing a global behavior of the system. We also addressed common issues of resource heterogeneity by taking several parameters into account such as processing power of computing nodes and a number of threads of submitted job requests. Proposed decentralized scheduling approach is particularly convenient for large-scale distributed environments. The objective of our scheduler was to ensure fairness among applications, by minimizing the *Slowdown* metric of all submitted jobs. Our solution inherits the benefits of both static and dynamics scheduling strategies. The proposed algorithm is robust and scalable due to implemented on-demand rescheduling mechanisms, which have a great impact on enhancing its performance over a classic *Sandpile* scheduler tested in implemented simulated environment.

References

1. Al-Azzoni, I., Down, D.G.: Dynamic scheduling for heterogeneous desktop grids. J. Parallel Distrib. Comput. **70**(12), 1231–1240 (2010)
2. Bak, P., Tang, C., Wiesenfeld, K.: Self-organized criticality: an explanation of the 1/f noise. Phys. Rev. Lett. **59**, 381–384 (1987)

3. Bak, P., Tang, C., Wiesenfeld, K.: Self-organized criticality. Phys. Rev. A **38**, 364–374 (1988)
4. Beaumont, O., Carter, L.: Centralized versus distributed schedulers for multiple bag-of-task applications. In: 20th International Parallel and Distributed Processing Symposium, IPDPS 2006, p. 10, April 2006
5. Benoit, A., Marchal, L., Pineau, J.-F., Robert, Y., Vivien, F.: Scheduling concurrent bag-of-tasks applications on heterogeneous platforms. IEEE Trans. Comput. **59**(2), 202–217 (2010)
6. Brasileiro, F., Araujo, E., Voorsluys, W., Oliveira, M., Figueiredo, F.: Bridging the high performance computing gap : the ourgrid experience. In: Proceedings of the Seventh IEEE International Symposium on Cluster Computing and the Grid, CCGRID 2007, pp. 817–822, Washington, D.C., USA. IEEE Computer Society (2007)
7. Celaya, J., Marchal, L.: A fair decentralized scheduler for bag-of-tasks applications on desktop grids. In: 2010 10th IEEE/ACM International Conference on Cluster, Cloud and Grid Computing (CCGrid), pp. 538–541, May 2010
8. Franceschelli, M., Giua, A., Seatzu, C.: Load balancing over heterogeneous networks with gossip-based algorithms. In: Proceedings of the 2009 Conference on American Control Conference, ACC 2009, pp. 1987–1993, Piscataway, NJ, USA. IEEE Press (2009)
9. Jelasity, M., Montresor, A., Babaoglu, O.: A modular paradigm for building self-organizing peer-to-peer applications. In: Di Marzo Serugendo, G., Karageorgos, A., Rana, O.F., Zambonelli, F. (eds.) ESOA 2003. LNCS (LNAI), vol. 2977, pp. 265–282. Springer, Heidelberg (2004)
10. Laredo, J., Bouvry, P., Guinand, F., Dorronsoro, B., Fernandes, C.: The Sandpile scheduler. Cluster Comput. **17**(2), 1–14 (2014)
11. Tchernykh, A., Schwiegelshohn, U., Yahyapour, R., Kuzjurin, N.: On-line hierarchical job scheduling on grids with admissible allocation. J. Sched. **13**(5), 545–552 (2010)
12. Viswanathan, S., Veeravalli, B., Robertazzi, T.G.: Resource-aware distributed scheduling strategies for large-scale computational cluster/grid systems. IEEE Trans. Parallel Distrib. Syst. **18**(10), 1450–1461 (2007)

The Evacuation Process Study with the Cellular Automaton Floor Field on Fine Grid

Tomasz M. Gwizdałła[(⊠)]

Department of Solid State Physics, University of Łódź,
Pomorska 149/153, 90-236 Łódź, Poland
tomgwizd@uni.lodz.pl

Abstract. The modification of Cellular Automaton Floor Field based simulation of evacuation is presented. The typical approach, where the pedestrian occupies single cell, usually of size $0.4 \times 0.4\,\mathrm{m}^2$. is modified by assumption that the single person can occupy 2 cells. The rules of motion are presented and the basic characteristics as well as comparison with the one-cell model are shown.

1 Introduction

There is a large number of approaches which are devoted to study the process of motion or even evacuation of people under different conditions (see e.g. [1,2]). Also Cellular Automata were extensively studied as a tool for analyzing the evacuation process. It can be suggested that the initial attempts follow the experience of their authors coming from other areas of CA interest, like traffic analysis [3] or collective processes [4].

From our point of view those papers are of much interest where the unconventional approach to the problem of pedestrian's size is presented. We can enlist here e.g. [5], where the model of two cells occupying person is used to show the people flow in public transportation. From the same group it comes the paper [6] where the elliptic-like shape of person corresponds to the interpretation of social distance. Here however, the persons are localized in the centers of cells. The choice of the size of individual, exceeding the typical one cell and going beyond the circular or four-fold symmetry, comes from real observations and practice [7–9]. It was shown that the axes of the personal space (PS) connected with the single individual was as great as approximately 2.5m × 0.5m. In our paper we are not going to deal with the psychological notion of PS but we want to follow the observation about the asymmetric shape of person. We should point out that the definition of the size appropriate for single person (as expressed in cells) is the crucial problem of fine-grid approaches since we have to strictly distinguish the models where we can use the CA definition and rules and models which are close to macroscopic, dynamical analysis. It seems that the upper limit can be found in [10].

© Springer International Publishing Switzerland 2016
S. El Yacoubi et al. (Eds.): ACRI 2016, LNCS 9863, pp. 248–257, 2016.
DOI: 10.1007/978-3-319-44365-2_25

2   Model

The system under consideration follows a lot of earlier attempts. We especially want to refer here to papers [11,12]. The room is presented as a two-dimensional array of $n_x \times n_y$ cells. The size of edge of every cell is typically assumed as 0.4 m. The value assigned to every cell has to somehow describe the distance to the closest exit. Such an array of numbers is called the Floor-Field (FF). In the paper we use generally two schemes of creating FF, but several properties characterizes both methods. The room is bounded with the wall and the FF values are for the wall's cells significantly higher than for all other positions. The number of doors is arbitrary fixed and all cells corresponding to the doors are assigned the value $FF_{door} = 1$. Subsequently one of the enlisted methods can be used.

- The one following the Varas' scheme - According to this algorithm we start from the location of doors and try to assign values for the adjacent cells. They can be either incremented by 1 ($FF_{new,proposed} = FF_{neighbor,set} + 1$) when they adjoin vertically or horizontally, or by some predefined value λ ($FF_{new,proposed} = FF_{neighbor,set} + \lambda$) when they adjoin diagonally. The value of λ can be understood as a parameter of procedure and for the cases studied in this paper, which are limited to the empty spaces we should mention $\lambda = 2$ as the critical value. Above this value, the Varas' procedure produces the Manhattan metric what can be observed in Fig. 1. Certainly, approaching the cell from different directions we can obtain different values, so finally we choose the lowest one.
- The Euclidean scheme - According to this scheme the FF for a particular cell is calculated from the formula

$$FF_{i,j} = min\{k : 1 + \sqrt{(i - door_i^k)^2 + (j - door_j^k)^2}\} \qquad (1)$$

where k enumerates the positions of doors i and j are the coordinates of cell and simultaneously describe the corresponding coordinates of doors. Like in the previous case, having more doors we can obtain different values of FF and always the lowest one is chosen.

In further parts of paper we consider only the presented above static Floor Fields and all results are the effects of this static description and some procedures implemented for the individuals' motion. In our calculations we used three different models of Floor Field: the Varas model with $\lambda = 1.5$, the Varas model with $\lambda = 2.5$ and the Euclidean model. The comparison of models for reduced sizes of rooms are shown in Fig. 1.

The crucial point of this paper is the proposition of enlargement of individuals' silhouette. Typically one assumes that one cell of dimensions $0.4 \times 0.4 \, \text{m}^2$ can be occupied by one person. Such an assumption can lead to un unrealistic estimations for people density. It can be easily shown that we can assemble up to $2.5 \times 2.5 = 6.25$ person per square meter. Although the values close to the

	6.5	7.0	7.5	8.0	
	5.5	6.0	6.5	7.0	
	4.5	5.0	5.5	6.5	
	3.5	4.0	5.0	6.0	
	2.5	3.5	4.5	5.5	
1	2.0	3.0	4.0	5.0	
1	2.0	3.0	4.0	5.0	
	2.5	3.5	4.5	5.5	
	3.5	4.0	5.0	6.0	
	4.5	5.0	5.5	6.5	
	5.5	6.0	6.5	7.0	
	6.5	7.0	7.5	8.0	

	7.0	8.0	9.0	10	
	6.0	7.0	8.0	9.0	
	5.0	6.0	7.0	8.0	
	4.0	5.0	6.0	7.0	
	3.0	4.0	5.0	6.0	
1	2.0	3.0	4.0	5.0	
1	2.0	3.0	4.0	5.0	
	3.0	4.0	5.0	6.0	
	4.0	5.0	6.0	7.0	
	5.0	6.0	7.0	8.0	
	6.0	7.0	8.0	9.0	
	7.0	8.0	9.0	10	

	6.1	6.4	6.8	7.4	
	5.1	5.5	6.0	6.7	
	4.2	4.6	5.2	6.0	
	3.2	3.8	4.6	5.5	
	2.4	3.2	4.2	5.1	
1	2.0	3.0	4.0	5.0	
1	2.0	3.0	4.0	5.0	
	2.4	3.2	4.2	5.1	
	3.2	3.8	4.6	5.5	
	4.2	4.6	5.2	6.0	
	5.1	5.5	6.0	6.7	
	6.1	6.4	6.8	7.4	

Fig. 1. Three models of Floor Field: left - Varas $\lambda = 1.5$, center - Varas $\lambda = 2.5$, right - euclidean.

presented one were presented for example for so-called "One Million March" by El-Baz ([13]: $5\,persons/\mathrm{m}^2$, $2.15\,ft^2/person$) we think that such values may be appropriate for static situations. When we assume the possibility of motion the above value seems to be visibly exaggerated. On the other hand we should point out that the size of the contour of person's silhouette projection usually exceeds the value of 0.4 m as well as 0.56 m, the value of diagonal of single cell.

The motion of individual is performed in the same way as it was presented in our earlier paper [12]. The pedestrian chooses always the direction of the lowest possible Floor Field value what, generally, corresponds to the path to the closest exit. Among those empty cells in the neighbourhood of analyzed one which have the same FF value we choose one randomly. With the probability 0.05 the possible move is not performed what corresponds to the random panic effect. The main properties of our model can be presented as follows (the visualization of the discussed situations is shown in Fig. 2).

- Since we consider two-cell sized individual we have to redefine slightly the determination of the direction of motion. Usually we consider the value assigned to the potentially next cell. Now we take into account the sum of values in the cells which could be occupied by the individual after the move.
- The pedestrian has either 4 or 8 possibilities of motion. The choice of particular number depends on the parameters of simulation. In the case presented as (a) where only 4 directions parallel to the axes are allowed we, due to similarities, say about von Neumann update while the case (c) we present as Moore update.
- The usual motion of the person is performed front-facing. We distinguish two possible versions of motion. With the first one we accept the arbitrary direction

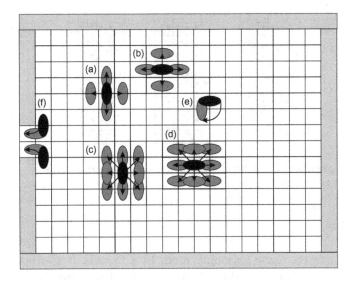

Fig. 2. The acceptable moves of pedestrian according to the two-cell approach. For details, see text.

of person. In the further part we call it "arbitrary motion" (but with different updates or neighbourhoods). This situation is shown in situations (b) and (d) where pedestrians moves sideways in the direction of door. The typical motion, called "front set" is shown in mentioned earlier cases (a) and (c).

- If we want to disable the sideways moves we have to force the individual to change his/her direction. The appropriate move is shown as situation as (e). In order to determine the correct direction we define, except of FF array, the array of gradients. The pedestrian, who has to move front-facing, changes his direction in compliance with the direction of gradient. The gradient is calculated as a direction parallel to the axis and leading into the cell with the lowest possible value of FF. In the ambiguous situations, like for Varas' model with $\lambda = 2.5$ we choose such direction of gradient which distinguishes it from the $\lambda = 1.5$ case. The comparison of gradient array is shown in Fig. 3.

- We include also some specific procedure of avoiding the deadlock near doors. When two pedestrians block themselves, like in situation (f) we allow both of them to slide through the door sideways.

- The follow generally the rules constructed for the one-cell model in our previous paper [12]. It corresponds especially to the situations of conflict between two or more individuals. In the situation when two persons try to move into the same final cell, the random selection between these two persons is performed. It concerns the typical steps as well as the rotation described as the case (e).

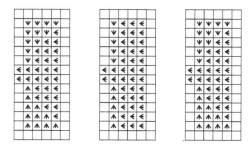

Fig. 3. Three models of Floor Field - gradient directions: left - Varas $\lambda = 1.5$, center - Varas $\lambda = 2.5$, right - euclidean.

3   Results

All calculations were made for empty room 14×18 cells. It corresponds to the room size $5.6\,\mathrm{m} \times 7.2\,\mathrm{m}$. According to this notation, Figs. 1 and 3, shown earlier, correspond to the size 12×4 and Fig. 2 presents correctly the considered room. For simplicity we will define the horizontal axis in the figures as the X-axis and the vertical one as the Y-axis. It means that in our simulations the length of the room along the X-axis is always greater than that along the Y one. In the majority of presented results the location of door is the same as in the Varas' paper, i.e., they are located in the middle of shorter wall. In some further calculations, the positions of doors are changed.

The short view at the Figs. 1 and 3 makes it possible to say that two FF configurations: Varas' with $\lambda = 1.5$ and the Euclidean one are similar one to another. Only the small sections of room are shown in Fig. 3 but those presented ones are the most important for creating deadlocks and, finally, for the overall evacuation time.

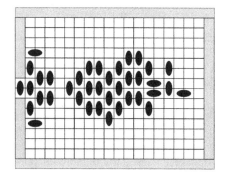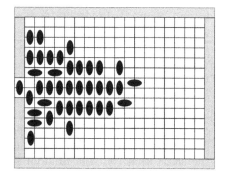

Fig. 4. The snapshot of simulation of about 40 individuals for two FF models. On the left $\lambda = 2.5$, on the right the Euclidean one.

In the Fig. 4 we show the snapshot of two simulations for two different Floor Field definitions. On both pictures there are visible about 40 pedestrians among 50, which were initially distributed randomly in the room. The pattern formed by the individuals is explicitly different. Some unexpected effect is that the accumulation of people at the wall containing the door is observed rather for Euclidean FF. For this model we could expect the earlier convergence into the middle of the room. Very interesting observation can be made when we compare Fig. 4 with the Fig. 4 of original paper by Varas et al. [11]. The authors show there an artificial configuration of pedestrians sampled along the diagonals heading to the exit. Both our configurations are much more realistic.

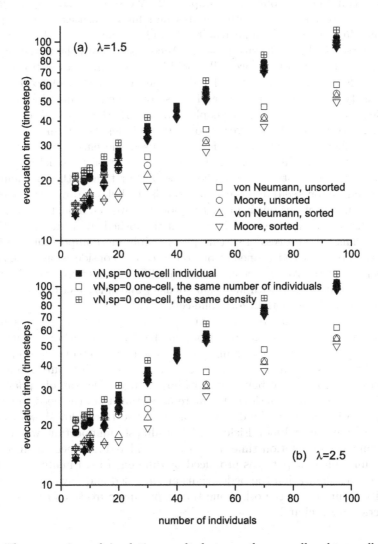

Fig. 5. The comparison of simulation results between the one-cell and two-cell models.

Figure 5 is prepared in such a way that it enables to compare the results obtained with the proposed two-cell model with the ones obtained within the one-cell model described in our former paper [12]. Taking into account the parameters of simulation we choose here 4 combinations of von Neumann and Moore update as well as sorted and unsorted pedestrian management. The sorting of persons is in more detail described in [12] (see especially Fig. 4) and is dedicated to prevent the rising of unreal gaps between the people. It is expected that sorting should lead to shortening of evacuation time. The plots are prepared for the initial number of pedestrians from 5 to 95. The highest number may seem unrealistic but we intentionally choose it since it corresponds to the higher value of density ($\rho = 0.75$) considered in our earlier paper [12]. We should also emphasize that the proximity of results for both updates and high densities is the expected effect since in this case the final result is mainly influenced by the jam at the exit. Similarly, the lower density ($\rho = 0.079$) corresponds to the initial presence of 10 persons. Every plot for two-cell model is compared with the two plots for one-cell model, the first one is calculated for the same number of people (so the initial density is two times smaller) and the second one is prepared for the same initial density (so the number of people is doubled). Here as well as for other simulations every point is the average over 10000 independent runs.

Figure 5 shows that for both FF models used the effects are similar, the differences are almost invisible. The results for the two-cell model are close to those for the same density except of two cases. The first one is the von Neumann, unsorted update (one-cell) and the second one is the behavior for lower densities. When the number of persons is lower the plots for two-cell model start to group into two distinctly visible sets. They are distinguished by a fact of sorting of the individuals. The process of sorting plays visibly more important role in our model as compared with the one-cell one but it can be considered as more typical for higher densities. We expect also that the difference between von Neumann and Morse update vanish with increasing density and this effect can be observed for two-cell model better than for a one-cell.

In the Fig. 6 we want to check, which of the steering parameters has an influence on the results obtained for our model. Since the former figure show some effect of dependency on sorting process, the first two plots are prepared in order to distinguish both cases. It can be seen that, except of some quantitative differences, the qualitative behavior does not change. The way of update, here the number of positions considered is more important than the need to preserve the correct orientation in the direction of exit. The third plot shows that the selection of particular Floor Field model is almost unimportant when taking into account the evacuation time. It can be considered unexpected since Fig. 4 shows visibly different patterns produced by different FFs. Finally, it turns out that for one configuration the pedestrians are huddled and have to wait for the possibility to move, for the other one they move quite freely and the effects of both tactics are similar.

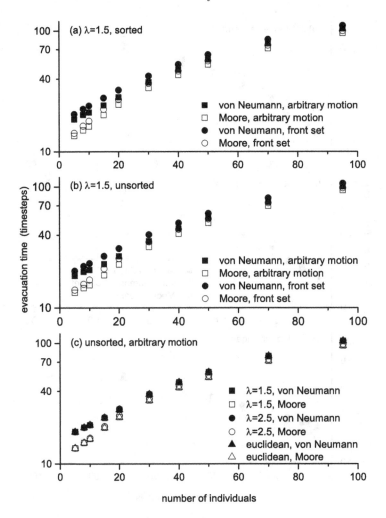

Fig. 6. Two-cell model. Dependence of results on different simulation parameters.

In the Fig. 7 we show whether the effects observed for the one location of door is reproduced for other orderings. We consider three other configurations, in more detail described in paper [12] (see e.g. Fig. 7). Generally: in the configuration (b) the door is in the middle of longer wall (X), (c) - two doors are located in the corners of shorter wall (Y), (d) - two doors are located in the corners of longer wall (X). Once more it turns out that the size of neighbourhood considered is the crucial factor. An interesting observation is that the configuration (d) produces result significantly different from all others. Firstly, the value of evacuation time is almost two times lower that for other cases. Usually we explain such differences with the increase of the width of exit and the decrease of distance between the exit and the farthest point in the room. Here, in order to observe the effect, we

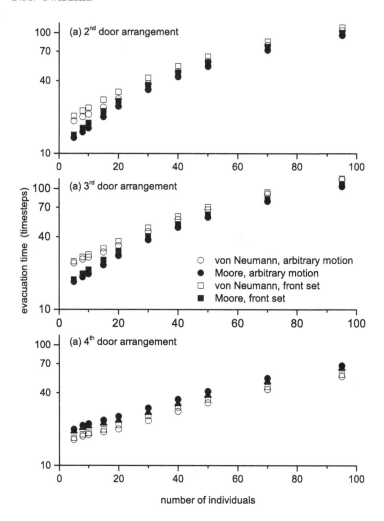

Fig. 7. Two cell model. Results for different doors configurations.

have to combine both these features while every single feature does not produce any result what can be observed in plots (a) and (b) when compared to earlier figures.

An interesting information about the evacuation process is that about the possible scaling of the result. In our model almost all lines can be scaled with the linear dependence with the slope similar to that one for one-cell model which corresponds to a higher density case. Only for the last configuration of exits (d) the better approximation is the Euclidean one. We can also remark on the patterns presented in the Fig. 4. We performed some undocumented observations concerning people leaving the building with similar door arrangement and proportionally greater size.

We observed that the choice of pattern in the figure mentioned above depends strongly on the dynamics of the process. Although we are unable to present now the snapshots from these observations we noticed that for the quiet motion, the left pattern can be observed, while for rapid evacuation it resembles the right one. This makes it possible to ask question whether the typical Manhattan metric with the two-cell pedestrian model does nicely conform to some customs of people.

References

1. Zheng, X., Zhong, T., Liu, M.: Modeling crowd evacuation of a building based on seven methodological approaches. Build. Environ. **44**, 437–445 (2009)
2. Henein, C.M., White, T.: Microscopic information processing and communication in crowd dynamics. Phys. A Stat. Mech. Appl. **389**, 4636–4653 (2010)
3. Burstedde, C., Klauck, K., Schadschneider, A., Zittartz, J.: Simulation of pedestrian dynamics using a two-dimensional cellular automaton. Phys. A Stat. Mech. Appl. **295**, 507–525 (2001)
4. Perez, G.J., Tapang, G., Lim, M., Saloma, C.: Streaming, disruptive interference and power-law behavior in the exit dynamics of confined pedestrians. Physica A Stat. Mech. Appl. **312**, 609–618 (2002)
5. Gudowski, B., Wąs, J.: Modeling of people flow in public transport vehicles. In: Wyrzykowski, R., Dongarra, J., Meyer, N., Waśniewski, J. (eds.) PPAM 2005. LNCS, vol. 3911, pp. 333–339. Springer, Heidelberg (2006)
6. Wąs, J.: Multi-agent frame of social distances model. In: Umeo, H., Morishita, S., Nishinari, K., Komatsuzaki, T., Bandini, S. (eds.) ACRI 2008. LNCS, vol. 5191, pp. 567–570. Springer, Heidelberg (2008)
7. Gérin-Lajoie, M., Richards, C.L., McFadyen, B.J.: The negotiation of stationary and moving obstructions during walking: anticipatory locomotor adaptations and preservation of personal space. Mot. Control **9**, 242–269 (2005)
8. Chraibi, M., Seyfried, A., Schadschneider, A.: Generalized centrifugal-force model for pedestrian dynamics. Phys. Rev. E **82**, 046111 (2010)
9. Darekar, A., Lamontagne, A., Fung, J.: Dynamic clearance measure to evaluate locomotor and perceptuo-motor strategies used for obstacle circumvention in a virtual environment. Hum. Mov. Sci. **40**, 359–371 (2015)
10. Sarmady, S., Haron, F., Talib, A.: Simulating crowd movements using fine grid cellular automata. In: 2010 12th International Conference on Computer Modelling and Simulation (UKSim), pp. 428–433 (2010)
11. Varas, A., Cornejo, M.D., Mainemer, D., Toledo, B., Rogan, J., Munoz, V., Valdivia, J.A.: Cellular automaton model for evacuation process with obstacles. Phys. A Stat. Mech. Appl. **382**, 631–642 (2007)
12. Gwizdałła, T.M.: Some properties of the floor field cellular automata evacuation model. Phys. A Stat. Mech. Appl. **419**, 718–728 (2015)
13. El-Baz, F.: Million man march. http://www.bu.edu/remotesensing/research/completed/million-man-march/

A Comparison of a Proposed Dynamical Direct Verification of Lattice's Configuration and a Forecast Behavior Parameter on a Cellular Automata Model to Task Scheduling

Tiago Ismailer Carvalho[✉], Murillo Guimarães Carneiro,
and Gina Maira Barbosa Oliveira

Faculdade de Computação, Universidade Federal de Uberlândia, Uberlândia, Brazil
ismailerpc@gmail.com, {mgcarneiro,gina}@ufu.br

Abstract. This paper compares two strategies to evolve cellular automata (CA) rules avoiding an undesirable dynamical behavior. Here long-cycle rules are considered inappropriate, specially the chaotic rules. The first approach employs a forecast parameter to guide a genetic algorithm (GA) toward rules out of the region where long-cycle rules are most probably to happen. The second one is proposed here and directly evaluates the lattice convergence in the spatio-temporal evolution to classify the cycle as long (or not). The problem taking in account here is the task scheduling for multiprocessor architectures. CA-based schedulers use two stages: (a) learning, where a GA is used to find rules to schedule an specific program graph and (b) operation, where the evolved rules are used to schedule new instances. The experimental results show that both approaches are able to find more CA rules with adequate dynamical behavior in both stages. Moreover, a reasonable improvement of makespan in the operation phase is obtained by controlling the CA dynamics.

1 Introduction

Although composed by very simple components with local interactions, cellular automata (CA) generate a complex and unpredictable behavior. Besides, they can exhibit a rich variability of dynamic behaviors and control this dynamics is an important point in several works using CA. For example, if the CA model is dealing with pattern recognition tasks it is important to construct CA rules with a short-cycle attractor, most probably, fixed-point rules. On the other hand, if one is using a CA model to cryptography the best probable behavior is the chaotic one.

Here we investigate two different strategies to evolve CA transitions by means of a genetic algorithm (GA) obtaining rules classified in a desirable behavior (or at least they are used to avoid the undesirable behavior). Both strategies for CA dynamics control were investigated in the context of task scheduling in multiprocessor architectures. Since the initial proposal of a scheduler based on CA [8], the scheduling approach has been evaluated in many CA-based models [3, 4, 7–10, 12]. As in the original approach, as in several studies which followed it, the scheduler model comprises two main stages: (i) a learning phase, in which a GA is used to evolve CA rules able to schedule a specific parallel program over a multiprocessor architecture;

© Springer International Publishing Switzerland 2016
S. El Yacoubi et al. (Eds.): ACRI 2016, LNCS 9863, pp. 258–268, 2016.
DOI: 10.1007/978-3-319-44365-2_26

and (ii) an operating phase, in which the CA rules previously evolved are applied to different parallel programs aiming to obtain a good scheduling performance. Recently, a nonstandard CA neighborhood called pseudo-linear was evaluated in a scheduler model based on synchronous updating [4]. In this strategy the neighborhood can be formed by nonlocal cells. This scheduler showed more suitable results for scheduling than other previous models, which employ the standard CA neighborhood [3] or other pseudo-linear neighborhoods proposed for this problem [7, 8]. The scheduler model that uses this new neighborhood was named SCAS-HP and it has returned good results of makespan (the task who finishes last). Further investigations about the dynamical behavior of the evolved rules was presented in [10] showing that the use of the pseudo-linear neighborhood leads to a higher probability of occurrence of chaotic behavior rules. On the other hand, when applying the CA-based scheduling, the desired behavior is the fixed-point, or, at least, a periodic rule with short cycle length. Thus, a strategy to avoid the chaotic rules was presented in [10], in which the forecast dynamical parameter known as sensitivity [1] was used to guide the GA when evolving rules with the desired dynamics. A similar approach had previously been used quite successfully in the well-known problem named Density Classification Task [13]. The resulting scheduler, called SCAS-HPµ, showed promising results.

In order to analyze the influence of the dynamical control of cellular automata rules, a second approach called SCAS-HPρ is proposed and investigated here. It takes into account the dynamical behavior of the CA rules by penalizing the makespan of non-ordered rules. The rule dynamics is calculated by checking the cycle length over its evolved lattice. The idea behind SCAS-HPρ is formally defined in this paper.

2   Models Based on CA for Task Scheduling

Task scheduling is a classical computing problem where a set of computational tasks that compose a parallel application are allocated in the nodes of a multiprocessor architecture. We consider Task Static Scheduling Problem (TSSP), one simple variation of the problem where all information about tasks is known a priori. The problem is NP Complete and diverse approaches had been applied to solve it. The biggest motivation for CA-based schedulers is their ability to extract knowledge of the scheduling process and reuse it in other instances. Some previous works exhibit good results in the use of CA-based approaches to TSSP [3, 4, 8–10]. Such models are combined with evolutionary algorithms due to the high cardinality of rules space [6]. Lately a CA based scheduler was applied in real time embedded systems [10] and in parallel machines schedule [12]. In the TSSP a parallel application is represented by a weighted directed acyclic graph $G = (V, E)$. V is the set of N tasks of the parallel program. There is a precedence constraint relation between tasks i and j if the result produced by task i has to be available to task j, before it starts. E is the set of precedence relations between tasks. Each nodes and edges has weights: w_{nodes} describes the processing time required to execute a given task on any processor and w_{edges} describes the communication time between pairs of tasks i and j, in case they are located in distinct processors. The aim is to found a task distribution in such that the precedence constraints are satisfied and the runtime - or makespan - is minimized. Figure 1 shows an example of a program graph named Gauss18 [10].

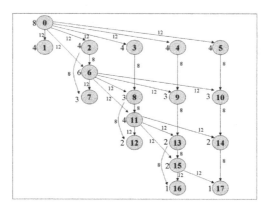

Fig. 1. Gauss18 program graph: represents the Gaussian elimination algorithm

Different CA models were already applied to TSSP. Seredynski [7] presented a CA-based scheduler with standard definitions and linear neighborhood. Both methods of updating - sequential and parallel – were investigated being that the results obtained with the sequential updating better. This model is unable to gain advantage of the CA's massive parallelization and later in [3] the parallel updating was applied obtaining a similar performance. In [4] a non-linear neighborhood was presented increasing the scheduler performance a lot. In a CA-based scheduler, each lattice cell is associated with a task of the program graph. For each k-processors in the architecture, the lattice has k states possible per cell so each cell state designates that the corresponding task is allocated in a processor. Makespan T associated to a given lattice is calculated using a scheduling policy that defines the order of the tasks within each processors. Here we present three different variations of CA based schedulers and they differ on the way of handling the undesirable rules which inherits a chaotic behavior. SCAS-HP [4] and SCAS-HPμ [10] parameters and definitions are out of scope of this work but results about his dynamics and performance is a contribution of this paper. Later a new scheduler SCAS-HPρ will be presented.

2.1 Previous Models: SCAS-HP and SCAS-HPμ

Here we summarize SCAS-HP characteristics [4]. In the learning phase the search for good rules for TSSP is performed by a GA. The population of rules R is evaluated by the following process. Firstly the deterministic construction heuristic DHLFET [1] is applied to obtain an allocation that defines the initial lattice configuration. Then, the rule R is applied over the lattice by τ time steps. The final lattice configuration determines where each task is allocated. After, the scheduling policy d-level [4] defines the running order of tasks in each processor. Finally, the R evaluation is equal to the makespan of the scheduling obtained using it. SCAS-HP employs a pseudo-linear neighborhood. It preserves the simple structure of regular neighborhoods, uses the radius parameter and it is able to capture relations among computational tasks in the program graph. To determine the neighbors of a cell C a subset of predecessors and successors of the correspondent task of C is created based on the program graph. The radius parameter determines the numbers of tasks selected to belong to the neighborhood. The task selection order is determined by a selected heuristic.

SCAS-HPμ [10] is a scheduler which started from the previous SCAS-HP. It was shown that many of the rules evolved in SCAS-HP have a chaotic behavior. To diminish the number of chaotic rules a low value of Binder sensitivity (μ) parameter [1] is desirable. The GA used in the learning phase incorporates the parameter in two aspects [13]. The fitness function was made by the weighted average of the original fitness PM and the parameter-based heuristic $P\mu$. PM is the makespan while $P\mu$ increases on how far the rule parameter value is from a selected band. Another novelty is the biased reproduction and mutation where 10 rules are generated from the crossover and mutation methods [4] and the rule with the lower value of μ is selected.

2.2 SCAS-HPρ

SCAS-HPρ is based on the SCAS-HP technique [4], but it employs the penalty parameter ρ to control the CA dynamics during the learning mode. The dynamics of a rule is determined by checking the cycle length over its evolved lattice and ρ considers the dynamical behavior by penalizing the makespan of non-ordered rules.

In SCAS-HPρ, an initial lattice, which denotes the allocation of the tasks by DHLFET heuristic, is evolved by a CA rule by τ time steps. The penalty parameter ρ then is applied by (i) finding the dynamic class of the rule and (ii) applying the penalization. Formally, let us consider $t = \tau$ and $t' \in \{1, 2, ..., C\}$ which represents the subsequent time steps to evolve, the dynamic class D of each rule is defined as:

$$D(t, t') = \begin{cases} t', \text{if } d(t, t') = 0 \\ \infty, \text{otherwise} \end{cases} \quad (1)$$

where t' and ∞ respectively means the dynamic classes until and above C cycle length. The function d verifies if the subsequent evolved lattices, what is denoted as:

$$d(t, t') = \sum_i \sigma_i^t - \sigma_i^{(t+t')} \quad (2)$$

with $d(t, t') = 0$ meaning the evaluated rule forms a cycle with length t'.

In following the fitness of CA rules are penalized according to the parameter ρ which applies a penalization rate for each dynamical class, such as follows:

$$\rho = [\rho_1, ..., \rho_k, ..., \rho_C; \rho_\infty] \quad (3)$$

where ρk and $\rho\infty$ represent penalization rates for rules with short and long cycle lengths, respectively. While none or very small penalization rates are recommended for fixed-point and short-cycle rules, big penalization rates are suggested for long-cycle rules. An overview about ρ is given by Algorithm 1 which shows the main steps related to the application of the parameter. One can see in lines 1–2 that ρ is applied over a final lattice which was evolved by τ time steps. Lines 3–6 denotes the search for cycles by evolving the final lattice for more C steps, and lines 7–11 shows the application of the penalization over the makespan obtained by the rule, which is represented by $S(\sigma, t)$, according to its dynamical behavior.

Algorithm 1: Penalty parameter ρ

1 $t = \tau$;
2 $t' = 1$;
3 do
4 | $k = D(t, t')$ //(Eq. 1);
5 | $t' = t' + 1$;
6 while $k = \infty$ and $t' \leq C$;
7 $F_0 = S(\sigma, t) + \rho_k * S(\sigma, t)$;
8 for $j = 1 \rightarrow (t' - 1)$ do
9 | $F_j = S(\sigma, t + j) + \rho_k * S(\sigma, t + j)$;
10 end
11 $F = \min_j F_j$;
12 return F

---

3   Experimental Results

This section presents results related to dynamical behavior analysis of the three CA-based scheduling models showed in the previous section. They are evaluated in terms of dynamical behavior and makespan performance considering the learning and operation modes. In the simulations, four program graphs have been considered: Gauss18, Rand30, Rand40 and Rand50, also investigated in [4, 10]. Aiming to study the rule behavior it is need to select a dynamic classification scheme. The scheduler proposed in [4] look at most at the five last CA's lattice configuration. For that reason rules with cycle above 5 and complex rules are also undesirable. As a consequence, we adopted an approximate scheme similar to the one proposed by Li [4] in which a rule can be classified into five classes: Null (N), Fixed-Point (F), Two-Cycle (T), Short-Cycle (S) and Long-Cycle (L). Long-Cycle collapses 3 behaviors: (i) periodic rules with cycle length >5; (ii) complex rules and (iii) chaotic rules.

In all computer simulations presented here, the parameters of the evolutionary algorithm are: population size gaP = 200, simple tournament gaTour = 2, crossover rate gaCross = 100 %, mutation rate per bit gaMut = 3 % and number of generations gaGen = 200. For each simulation, the GA was runned by 100 times. The CA parameters in both learning and operation mode are: time steps $\tau = 3\,N$, where N denotes the number of tasks in the program graph, radius = 3 for 2 processors and radius = 1, for 3 and 4 processors. For the dynamics control: (i) SCAS-HPρ parameters are: penalization vector

ρ is: [0 %, 10 %, 20 %, 30 %, 40 %; 100 %]; (ii) the desirable μ bands used in SCAS-HPμ for each architecture (number of processors P) are 0.25 to 0.35 (P = 2), 0.35 to 0.45 (P = 3) and 0.40 to 0.50 (P = 4).

3.1 Dynamic Behavior of Evolved Rules in Leaning Mode

Figures 2 and 3 show the best rule found in each GA running is applied over 100 randomly sampled lattices. The final lattice (after applying the CA transition rule for τ steps) is then classified according to its dynamical behavior [9]. One can see that both approaches SCAS-HPμ and SCAS-HPρ were able to deal with the undesirable behavior (long-cycle rules). In addition, each one of them performed better in different graphs: SCAS-HPμ in gauss18 and rand50, and SCAS-HPρ in rand30 and rand40. Considering 2 processors, 83.50 % of SCAS-HP rules are classified as long-cycle, while SCAS-HPμ and SCAS-HPρ has 40 % and 22.25 %, respectively. With 3 and 4 processors, the SCAS-HP long-cycle rules are 41 % and 69 %, respectively, while using SCAS-HPμ theses numbers decay to 7.50 % and 16 %, or when SCAS-HPρ is used to 6.50 % and 36.75 %. In general, an average reduction of 33 % of long-cycle rules is noticed when taking together both approaches that avoid those rules. Moreover, the SCAS-HPρ scheduler was able to find more rules in the most desirable behavior (fixed-point rules) at the same time that it avoids the long-cycle rules.

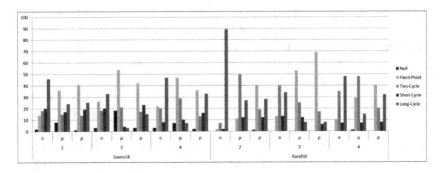

Fig. 2. Dynamic behavior of rules evolved for Gauss18 and Rand50 in learning phase

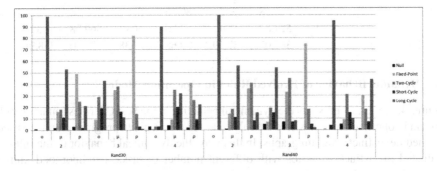

Fig. 3. Dynamic behavior of rules evolved for Rnd30 and Rand40 in learning phase

3.2 Quality of Schedule in Learning Phase

Table 1 shows the makespan performance of the three CA-based schedulers considered in this work. The results refer to the learning mode and they comprehend multiprocessor systems with 2, 3 and 4 processors. BEST denotes the makespan result of the best rule found considering all GA runs, while AVG is the average makespan which is calculated by taking the best rule found in each GA run. The geometric mean is presented at the last row of the table. SCAS-HP outperforms SCAS-HPμ and SCAS-HPρ, especially considering the average values. This result is explained by the fitness functions used in the schedulers with dynamics control which must consider makespan performance (as SCAS-HP fitness do) and also other desired skills, making the convergence to a lower makespan harder. The fitness function penalize rules with undesired μ values in SCAS-HPμ and penalize rules with undesired behavior in SCAS-HPρ, so the GA does not search only for the best allocation of the tasks, but also reckons the rule dynamical behavior. However, when considering just the best makespan found in all the runs, all scheduler's performance is similar. In fact, SCAS-HPρ returned better values than SCAS-HP in two scenarios, and vice versa. SCAS-HPμ was overcame by at least one of the other two schedulers in 5 scenarios (out of 12), but this advantage is not so expressive as the resultant geometric mean shows.

Table 1. Comparison of CA-based schedulers perfomance in learning phase

Grafo	P	SCAS-HP		SCAS-HPμ		SCAS-HPρ	
		AVG	BEST	AVG	BEST	AVG	BEST
Gauss18	2	44,55	44	45,15	44	44,15	44
	3	45,52	44	46,65	44	45,65	44
	4	44	44	44	44	44	44
Rand30	2	1224,22	1222	1225,19	1222	1228,78	1222
	3	898,75	853	929,75	865	890,63	**850**
	4	822,75	778	853,55	778	815,72	778
Rand40	2	984,87	983	985,49	983	986,31	983
	3	705.12	**682**	821,96	688	701,83	688
	4	585,67	563	605,91	564	597,03	**557**
Rand50	2	632	624	631,60	624	634	624
	3	566,28	**532**	580,76	548	569,64	**532**
	4	527,87	**500**	553,20	508	569,88	532
Geo. Mean	–	347,07	357,29	379,68	359,38	370,70	358,98

3.3 Dynamic Behavior of Evolved Rules in Operation Mode

Figures 4, 5, 6, and 7 presents the dynamical behavior of the best CA rules found in each GA run in operation mode, where the rules learned over a given program graph are used to schedule distinct program graphs. In this way, the dynamical behavior of the rules is evaluated in distinct scenarios with different number of tasks, neighborhood, initial lattice, and so on. Considering all experiments the percentage of rules identified as long-cycle rules was 66.19 % for SCAS-HP, 19.56 % in SCAS-HPμ and 30.47 % for SCAS-HPρ. The μ parameter approach kept the reduction of this rules approximately by one third while the penalty parameter strategy reduced the long-cycle rules amount in a half. The difference of results between μ and ρ approaches is more expressive considering rules trained using Gauss18 and Rand50, being that the long-cycle rules number are 2.5 times higher using ρ. On the other hand, the percentage of rules identified as fixed-point rules was 8.91 % for SCAS-HP, 26 % in SCAS-HPμ and 43.52 % for SCAS-HPρ. These results corroborate what was observed in learning phase about the dynamic behavior: the sensitivity parameter avoids more long-cycle rules (chaotic) and the penalty parameter obtains more desired rules (fixed-point). However, in operation mode these differences are more expressive.

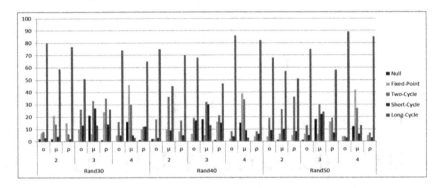

Fig. 4. Dynamic behavior of rules evolved in Gauss18 applied on the other program graphs

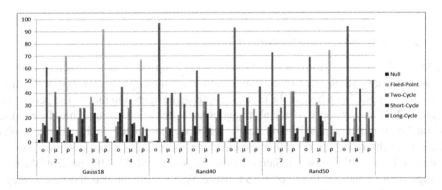

Fig. 5. Dynamic behavior of rules evolved in Rand30 applied on the other program graphs

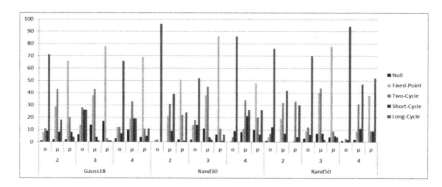

Fig. 6. Dynamic behavior of rules evolved in Rand40 applied on the other program graphs

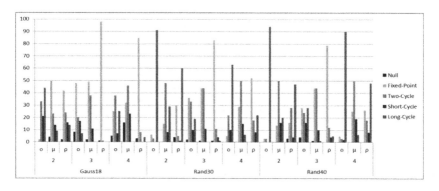

Fig. 7. Dynamic behavior of rules evolved in Rand50 applied on the other program graph

3.4   Quality of Schedule in Operation Mode

Table 2 evaluates the performance of the schedulers in operation mode. Each row corresponds to the geometric mean of the makespan obtained using rules evolved in learning phase when applied to schedule the other 3 graphs in the operation mode. The geometric mean in BEST shows both dynamical strategies are better when learning rules for rand30 and rand40 program graphs. In addition, the sensitivity parameter obtained better results considering the reuse for rand50 rules while the technique without dynamic control strategy is better in the reuse for Gauss18 rules. In general, SCAS-HPµ presents the best average performance in terms of BEST while SCAS-HPρ showed the best average performance in terms of AVG.

Table 2. Perfomance of rules evolved in learning phase applied to other program graphs

Grafo	SCAS-HP		SCAS-HPµ		SCAS-HPρ	
	AVG	BEST	AVG	BEST	AVG	BEST
Gauss18_rules	1097,25	809,37	1155,76	818,12	1123,02	831,54
Rand30_rules	374,71	296,24	372,80	281,80	328,76	291,65
Rand40_rules	412,66	332,21	412,88	323,79	410,35	322,06
Rand50_rules	454,69	343,01	443,01	331,38	455,84	343,66
Geo.Mean	527,02	406,56	529,840	**396,58**	**512,63**	404,76

4 Conclusions

Two approaches to control the dynamical behavior of CA rules found by an evolutionary algorithm were compared here. The sensitivity parameter μ analyzes the CA rules in order to classify their transition in the range $[0, 1]$, in which low and high values of μ denote, respectively, rules most likely being ordered and chaotic. Further, the penalty parameter ρ analyzes the lattices evolved by CA rules in a way the dynamic is directly captured and the penalization guides the evolutionary search.

Approaches μ and ρ were compared in the context of CA-based models for task scheduling problem (TSSP). The justification is simple: chaotic rules are expected to provide random allocation of the tasks while complex and long-cycle rules are supposed to present unstable behavior. Therefore the control approaches can drive the learning process toward short-cycle rules. Considering the learning mode, μ and ρ were able to reduce the number of long-cycle rules, but μ returns a slightly more expressive reduction, and ρ can get closer to the best behavior (fixed-point). That is, μ is more effective in the control of undesirable behavior but ρ gives a more refined result. Regarding the ability of the evolved rules to schedule new instances of TSSP, it was possible to note that the dynamical control made in the learning phase from a specific program graph is somehow preserved when this rule is applied to a new instance of the problem. Therefore, both strategies μ and ρ meet the objective for which they were designed. Additionally, the particularities of each approach was kept in the operation mode: μ is stronger to avoid long-cycle rules and ρ obtains more refined rules (fixed-point). A more formal method of comparing results is considered as a future work. Also, as a continuity of this work we plan to investigate a mixed approach in which the good characteristics of each approach are preserved.

Regarding the controlled schedulers performance, the average makespan found was a little bit worse than the results obtained with the free-dynamics model, while the best values found were very similar. This decay was expected since the search performed by controlled models must found not only lower makespan but also well behavioured rules, embarrassing GA convergence. On the other hand, the results obtained in operation mode, in general, shows that the controlled-behaviour rules return lower makespan when submitted to other program graphs, which is the major motivation to avoid chaotic rules. However, some situations must be clarified. For example, the controlled schedulers returned a poorly performance when scheduling rand30 using rules evolved for other graphs. We suspect that this graph structure is more suitable for random allocations and thus it is not a good example for TSSP.

Acknowledgments. Authors are grateful to Fapemig, CNPq and CAPES

References

1. Adam, T.L., Chandy, K.M., Dickson, J.R.: A comparison of list schedules for parallel processing systems. Commun. ACM **17**, 685–690 (1974)
2. Binder, P.M.: Parametric ordering of complex systems. Phys. Rev. E. **49**(3), 2023 (1994)
3. Carneiro, M.G., Oliveira, G.M.B.: Cellular automata-based model with synchronous updating for task static scheduling. In: Proceedings of Automata, pp. 263–272 (2011)
4. Carneiro, M.G., Oliveira, G.M.B.: Synchronous cellular automata-based scheduler initialized by heuristic and modeled by a pseudo-linear neighborhood. Nat. Comput. **12**(3), 339–351 (2013)
5. Li, Wentian, Packard, N.: The structure of elementary cellular automata rule space. Complex Syst. **4**, 281–297 (1990)
6. Mitchell, M.: Computation in cellular automata: a selected review. In: Non-standard Computation, pp. 385–390 (1996)
7. Oliveira, G.M.B., Vidica, P.M.: A coevolutionary approach to cellular automata-based task scheduling. In: Sirakoulis, G.C.H., Bandini, S. (eds.) ACRI 2012. LNCS, vol. 7495, pp. 111–120. Springer, Heidelberg (2012)
8. Seredynski, F., Zomaya, A.: Sequential and parallel cellular automata-based scheduling algorithms. IEEE Trans. Parallel Distrib. Syst. **13**(10), 1009–1023 (2002)
9. Swiecicka, A., Seredynski, F., Zomaya, A.: Multiprocessor scheduling and rescheduling with use of cellular automata and artificial immune system support. IEEE Trans. Parallel Distrib. Syst. **17**(3), 253–262 (2006)
10. Carvalho, T.I., Oliveira, G.M.B.: Searching for non-regular neighborhood cellular automata rules applied to scheduling task and guided by a forecast dynamical behavior parameter. In: Proceedings of ECAL, pp. 538–545 (2015)
11. Boutekkouk, F.: A cellular automaton based approach for real time embedded systems scheduling problem resolution. In: Silhavy, R., Senkerik, R., Oplatkova, Z.K., Prokopova, Z., Silhavy, P. (eds.) Artificial Intelligence Perspectives and Applications. AISC, vol. 347, pp. 13–22. Springer, Heidelberg (2015)
12. Kucharska, E., et al.: Cellular Automata approach for parallel machine scheduling problem. Simulation **92**(2), 165–178 (2016). doi:10.1177/0037549715625120
13. Oliveira, G.M.B., de Oliveira, P.P.B., Omar, N.: Evolving solutions of the density classification task in 1D cellular automata, guided by parameters that estimate their dynamic behavior. Artif. Life **7**, 428–436 (2000)

Modeling of Wind Flow and Its Impact on Forest Fire Spread: Cellular Automata Approach

Omar Jellouli[1]([✉]), Abdessamed Bernoussi[1], Mina Amharref[1], and Mustapha Ouardouz[2]

[1] GAT Team, Faculty of Sciences and Techniques, B.P. 416, Tangier, Morocco
jellouliomar@gmail.com, a.samed.bernoussi@gmail.com, amharrefm@yahoo.fr
[2] MMC Team, Faculty of Sciences and Techniques, B.P. 416, Tangier, Morocco
ouardouz@gmail.com

Abstract. In this paper, we propose a model of wind flow and its impact on the forest fire spread by using Cellular Automata (CA) approach. The wind model determines the wind flow and speed according to the topography of the studied area and climate data. While in a previous work we took into consideration only uniform wind direction and speed, in this one we have improved the forest fire model which takes into account both the physical attributes (Topography, land use, nature and density of vegetation) and the climatic parameters (humidity, wind) by considering wind flow. As an application we consider a region in the North of Morocco.

Keywords: Modeling · Cellular automata · Spreadability · Wind flow · Forest fire

1 Introduction

Forest fires are the causes of numerous and irreversible damages with deep ecological and socio-economic impacts. Thus, the scientific community meets the challenge addressed by forest fires as an interesting and a complex phenomenon requiring a multi-disciplinary approaches [5,11,14]. Modeling and simulation have been applied to fire fighting and management for many years, particularly in order to predict fire behavior and spread in forests under various scenarios of weather conditions.

Wind and topographic slopes are commonly considered to be the main factors determining wildfires spreadability [2]. Wind has the effect of tilting the flame forward, increasing convection and radiation transfer of energy to the unburnt fuel and inducing faster rate of spreads. Slope effect is often described as being similar, because it tends to make the ground and the fuel closer [9,10,13]. A comprehensive understanding of the wind-flame interaction is one of the major challenges in the prediction of forest fire propagation [15].

In a previous work [8] we presented and illustrated the simulation results of a Cellular Automata (CA) model describing the dynamics of a forest fire spread

© Springer International Publishing Switzerland 2016
S. El Yacoubi et al. (Eds.): ACRI 2016, LNCS 9863, pp. 269–279, 2016.
DOI: 10.1007/978-3-319-44365-2_27

on a mountainous landscape taking into account the main parameters that affect this phenomenon (the type and density of vegetation, the wind speed and direction and humidity). However we have considered an uniform wind direction and uniform speed (or power) in the studied zone.

In this work, we consider the problem of modelling the wind flow using the CA approach and its impact on fire spread. Wind and slope effects on fire behavior have been studied separately and then coupled. The combined effects of wind flow and slope will indeed produce a variety of unusual yet significant effects on spread rate. The result of the wind-slope analysis was coupled with the model proposed in [8] to take into account the dynamic behavior of wind flow.

The improved model was applied to the watershed Oued Laou area (north Morocco) and compared to previous simulation in [8]. A software based on JAVA object oriented was developed to be used as a decision aid tool for strategies in control and prevention against forest fire [1,7].

2   Modeling of Wind Flow Using CA Approach

2.1   Generalities on CA

We recall the definition of CA model.

Cellular Automata, first introduced by von Neumann (1966), have been extensively used as models for complex systems (Wolfram 1994). Cellular automata have also been applied to several problems in biology, fluid dynamics, nerves model excitable media, forest fire or training pattern..., where local interactions are involved [3,4,6,12]. In spite of their structural simplicity, CA exhibit complex dynamical behavior and can describe many physical systems and processes. Cellular automata (CA) are discrete dynamical systems formed by a set generally of identical objects called cells. These cells are endowed with a state which changes at every discrete step of time according to a predetermined rule.

Definition 1. *A cellular automaton is defined by the quadruple* $\mathcal{A} = (\mathcal{L}, \mathcal{S}, N, f)$ *where:*

- $\mathcal{L}$ *is a d-dimensional lattice of cells c which are arranged depending on space dimension and cell shape. In a two-dimensional domain, a cell will be denoted by* $c_{i,j}$,
- $\mathcal{S}$ *denotes a discrete state set. It is a finite commutative ring given by* $\mathcal{S} = \{0, 1, \cdots, k-1\}$ *in which the usual operations use modular arithmetics,*
- $\mathcal{N}$ *is a map which assigns to each cell* $c \in \mathcal{L}$ *a subset of* $\mathcal{L}$ *given by* $\mathcal{N} : c \longmapsto \mathcal{N}(c) \subseteq \mathcal{L}$. *n is the cardinality of the set* $\mathcal{N}(c)$ *which defines the neighborhood size,*
- *f is a local function which associates local configurations with states, i.e. it defines maps from* $\mathcal{N}(c)$ *to* $\mathcal{S}$. *It can be given by:*

$$f : \mathcal{S}^{N(c)} \longrightarrow \mathcal{S}$$
$$s_t(N(c)) \longrightarrow s_{t+1}(c)$$

2.2   CA Model of Wind Flow

Wind and slope are commonly accepted to be major environmental factors affecting the manner in which wildfires propagate. These two parameters have been observed as having a significant effect on fire behavior.

CA approach was used to model the wind spreadability. Our CA is determined as follow:

1. **The lattice:** a two-dimensional lattice of cells with boundary conditions type. Each cell denoted by c_{ij} has its own physical attributes (topographic slope, land use).
2. **The states set $\mathcal{S}$:** we consider various combinations of wind directions and speeds level. We adopt the following notation, for example N means direction from South to North, E means direction from West to East, etc. Double or triple direction is the combination of two or three directions in the same cell, generally observed when there is an obstacle due to topography. We note: $NE = N \oplus E$ (double direction), $NSE = N \oplus S \oplus E$ (triple direction), etc. (Fig. 1(b)). So to define the CA states set of wind flow model we consider all the possible combination of wind directions and power for each cell.
We denote I: No wind and R: Riptide wind.

   The states set is summarized in Table 1. The levels 0, 1, 2 and 3 represent respectively standard, weak, medium and strong wind speeds (The choice of the levels is made according to the studied area).

   The states set of wind flow model is given as $\mathcal{S} = \{I, R, N0, N1, N2, N3, S0, ..., SEW3\}$ with $Card\mathcal{S} = 50$.
3. **The neighborhood:** in this work we consider the von Neumann neighborhood type in order to compare the obtained result with the previous work result in which we used the von Neumann neighborhood type too.
4. **The transition rules:** we consider two influences
   • Land use: Surface roughness creates friction that slows the wind at low altitude Fig. 1(a). It is extracted by using earth observation techniques.
   • Topographic slopes: The presence of relief can cause a riptide in the wind on different directions and speed Fig. 1(b). Slopes are determined and classified in different classes of levels from DTM (Digital Terrain Model).

   Each cell is characterized by two parameters $c_{ij}\{T^{t_i}(.), P^{t_i}(.)\}$. We consider the following notations:

Table 1. States representation according to speed (Sp) and direction (D)

Sp \ D	N	S	E	W	NE	NW	SE	SW	NSE	NSW	NEW	SEW1
Level 0	N0	S0	E0	W0	NE0	NW0	SE0	SW0	NSE0	NSW0	NEW0	SEW0
Level 1	N1	S1	E1	W1	NE1	NW1	SE1	SW1	NSE1	NSW1	NEW1	SEW1
Level 2	N2	S2	E2	W2	NE2	NW2	SE2	SW2	NSE2	NSW2	NEW2	SEW2
Level 3	N3	S3	E3	W3	NE3	NW3	SE3	SW3	NSE3	NSW3	NEW3	SEW3

$ALt(c_{ij})$: Altitude level

cc_{ij}: Cell in the neighborhood of c_{ij} upwind

$c_{ij}^{\frac{\pi}{2}}$: Cell obtained by rotation of $\frac{\pi}{2}$ from the cell c_{ij}

$c_{ij}^{\frac{-\pi}{2}}$: Cell obtained by rotation of $\frac{-\pi}{2}$ from the cell c_{ij}

The following example illustrate the position of above denoted cells in case of a wind from West to East.

$\alpha^{[t_i]}(c_{ij})$: Index of wind flow between t_i and t_{i+1}

$T^{t_i}(c_{ij})$: Wind type at time t_i
$\begin{cases} \bullet \text{ Riptide} \\ \bullet \text{ Normal: unidirectional} \\ \bullet \text{ Double: Double direction} \\ \bullet \text{ Triple: Triple direction} \end{cases}$

$T_r^{[t_i]}(c_{ij})$: Wind type received from neighboring cells between t_i and t_{i+1}

$P^{t_i}(c_{ij})$: Wind speed at time t_i
$\begin{cases} \bullet \text{ Level 0 of wind speed } (P_s) \\ \bullet \text{ Level 1 of wind speed} \\ \bullet \text{ Level 2 of wind speed} \\ \bullet \text{ Level 3 of wind speed} \end{cases}$

$P_r^{[t_i]}(c_{ij})$: Wind speed received from neighboring cells between t_i and t_{i+1}

The transition rules of wind flow are separated in two phases:

• Phase of exchanging wind between cells: the wind flow from one cell to another. In each iteration a direction of wind is associated to a neighboring cell upwind. The direction is fixed according to the two characterization $T^{t_i}(.), P^{t_i}(.)$ of the cell.

$$\text{if } ALt(cc_{ij}) < ALt(c_{ij}) \text{ then } cc_{ij} \begin{cases} T_r^{[t_i]}(cc_{ij}) = Riptide \\ P_r^{[t_i]}(cc_{ij}) = P_s \end{cases}$$

$$\text{else } cc_{ij} \begin{cases} T_r^{[t_i]}(cc_{ij}) = Normal \\ P_r^{[t_i]}(cc_{ij}) = \frac{P^{t_i}(c_{ij})}{\alpha^{[t_i]}(c_{ij})} \end{cases}$$

$\alpha^{[t_i]}(c_{ij})$ represents the number of cells where the wind will be distributed after crashing with higher altitude. Using the von Neumann neighborhood type $\alpha^{[t_i]}(c_{ij}) = \{1, 2, 3\}$, the rare case of wind volteface is not considered.

To determine the value of $\alpha^{[t_i]}(c_{ij})$ we have to treat furthermore cells $c_{ij}^{\frac{\pi}{2}}$ and $c_{ij}^{\frac{-\pi}{2}}$.

$$\text{if } ALt\left(c_{ij}^{\frac{\pi}{2}}\right) \geq ALt(c_{ij}) \text{ then } c_{ij}^{\frac{\pi}{2}} \begin{cases} T_r^{[t_i]}\left(c_{ij}^{\frac{\pi}{2}}\right) = Normal \\ P_r^{[t_i]}\left(c_{ij}^{\frac{\pi}{2}}\right) = \frac{P^{t_i}(c_{ij})}{\alpha^{[t_i]}(c_{ij})} \end{cases}$$

$$\text{else } c_{ij}^{\frac{\pi}{2}} \begin{cases} T_r^{[t_i]}\left(c_{ij}^{\frac{\pi}{2}}\right) = Riptide \\ P_r^{[t_i]}\left(c_{ij}^{\frac{\pi}{2}}\right) = P_s \end{cases}$$

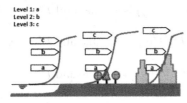
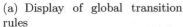

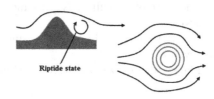

(a) Display of global transition rules

(b) Display of local transition rules, represent also the state NSE1

Fig. 1. Wind flow principle

$$
\text{if } ALt\left(c_{ij}^{\frac{-\pi}{2}}\right) \ge ALt\left(c_{ij}\right) \text{ then } c_{ij}^{\frac{-\pi}{2}}
\begin{cases}
T_r^{[t_i]}\left(c_{ij}^{\frac{-\pi}{2}}\right) = Normal \\[2mm]
P_r^{[t_i]}\left(c_{ij}^{\frac{-\pi}{2}}\right) = \dfrac{P^{t_i}(c_{ij})}{\alpha^{[t_i]}(c_{ij})}
\end{cases}
$$

$$
\text{else } \; c_{ij}^{\frac{-\pi}{2}}
\begin{cases}
T_r^{[t_i]}\left(c_{ij}^{\frac{-\pi}{2}}\right) = Riptide \\[2mm]
P_r^{[t_i]}\left(c_{ij}^{\frac{-\pi}{2}}\right) = P_s
\end{cases}
$$

Consequently,

$$
\begin{cases}
\text{if } ALt\left(c_{ij}^{\frac{\pi}{2}}\right) \ge ALt\left(c_{ij}\right) \text{ and } ALt\left(c_{ij}^{\frac{-\pi}{2}}\right) \ge ALt\left(c_{ij}\right) & \text{then } \alpha^{[t_i]}(c_{ij}) = 1 \\[2mm]
\text{if } ALt\left(c_{ij}^{\frac{\pi}{2}}\right) \ge ALt\left(c_{ij}\right) \text{ or } ALt\left(c_{ij}^{\frac{-\pi}{2}}\right) \ge ALt\left(c_{ij}\right) & \text{then } \alpha^{[t_i]}(c_{ij}) = 2 \\[2mm]
\text{if } ALt\left(c_{ij}^{\frac{\pi}{2}}\right) < ALt\left(c_{ij}\right) \text{ and } ALt\left(c_{ij}^{\frac{-\pi}{2}}\right) < ALt\left(c_{ij}\right) & \text{then } \alpha^{[t_i]}(c_{ij}) = 3
\end{cases}
$$

- Phase of wind characteristic for each own cell:

*Direction: depends on the altitude level of the upwind cells. Indeed, if the cell is in the trajectory of the wind source then it takes the same direction, otherwise it will split (double or triple direction) according to a parameter $\alpha^{[t_i]}(c_{ij})$.

$$
\begin{cases}
\text{if } \alpha^{[t_i]}(c_{ij}) = 1 \text{ then } T^{t_{i+1}}(c_{ij}) = Normal \\
\text{if } \alpha^{[t_i]}(c_{ij}) = 2 \text{ then } T^{t_{i+1}}(c_{ij}) = Double \\
\text{if } \alpha^{[t_i]}(c_{ij}) = 3 \text{ then } T^{t_{i+1}}(c_{ij}) = Triple
\end{cases}
$$

*Speed: the wind speed of each cell is a function of wind speeds received by the neighboring cells defined by:

$$
P^{t_{i+1}}(c_{ij}) = \frac{P_r^{[t_i]}(cc_{ij})}{\alpha^{[t_i]}(cc_{ij})} + \frac{P_r^{[t_i]}\left(c_{ij}^{\frac{\pi}{2}}\right)}{\alpha^{[t_i]}\left(c_{ij}^{\frac{\pi}{2}}\right)} + \frac{P_r^{[t_i]}\left(c_{ij}^{\frac{-\pi}{2}}\right)}{\alpha^{[t_i]}\left(c_{ij}^{\frac{-\pi}{2}}\right)}
$$

Example: The determination of state in the wind flow model is explained with these examples:

– The state of c_{ij} will be N1 at time t_{i+1} if $T^{t_{i+1}}(c_{ij})$ is normal and $P^{t_{i+1}}(c_{ij})$ is level 1.
– The state of c_{ij} will be NE3 at time t_{i+1} if $T^{t_{i+1}}(c_{ij})$ is double and $P^{t_{i+1}}(c_{ij})$ is level 3.
– The state of c_{ij} will be SEW1 at time t_{i+1} if $T^{t_{i+1}}(c_{ij})$ is triple and $P^{t_{i+1}}(c_{ij})$ is level 1.

Remark: The wind speed levels are determined by a classification of the maximum and minimum wind speed of the studied area.

5. **Initial condition:** It is chosen according to the studied area and the weather data.
6. **Boundary condition:** We choose a reflexive boundary conditions. This choice is made to ensure a wind flow from one outside to the other in through the inner domain.

2.3   Application to the Watershed Oued Laou (North Morocco)

The watershed of Oued Laou was the subject of the case study. It is located in the North of Morocco, Rif region, with a big biogeographical interest in amphibians and reptiles. It covers $18\,Km^2$ and is located between 35.45 north latitude and west longitude -5.083 Fig. 2. This choice was made because of periodic wildfires occurring in summer and the availability of data (DTM, satellite images and weather).

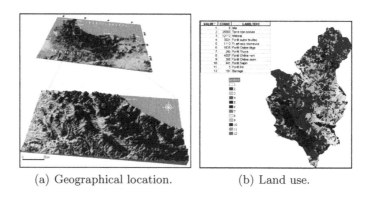

(a) Geographical location.   (b) Land use.

Fig. 2. Description of the studied area.

For the simulation we use the altitude data from the DTM Fig. 3(d) as in [8]. This region is generally characterized generally in Summer (period of forest fire) by West to East winds.

We first simulate the wind flow according to the topographic slopes and the land use of the watershed Oued Laou using the CA model developed in the Subsect. 2.2. Wind direction and speed for each cell are then stored to be used in forest fire model as input data.

The simulation result in Fig. 3 shows that:

– The speed level is always powerful in height altitude levels
– Places with high speed level (red color in Fig. 3(c)) are concurred with places of high topographic slopes in Fig. 3(d).

🌳 **State 0: Not burned vegetation.** 🔥 **State 3: Ash.**
🕯 **State 1: ignited vegetation.**   **State 4: Bare soil.**
🔥 **State 2: Burning vegetation.**

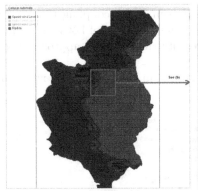

(a) i=100 of wind flow simulation   (b) Zoom in i=100 of wind flow simulation

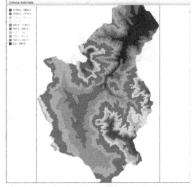

(c) i=250 of wind flow simulation   (d) Classification of the different altitude levels in the watershed of Oued Laou.

Fig. 3. Wind flow for the study area. (Color figure online)

3 Coupling Wind and Fire Models

3.1 The Improved Forest Fire Model

We recall the forest fire model developed in [8]. In that previous work, CA model for the dynamical prediction of the forest fires spread has been proposed. The model takes into account the fundamental parameters that influence the speed and direction of fire (humidity, wind direction and speed, vegetation types and density and the altitude levels). These parameters have combined effects.

The model is based on **the states set** $\mathcal{S} = \{0, 1, 2, 3, 4\}$ of the fire spread model where:

We improve the transition rules given in [8] by coupling the wind flow and fire spread models to illustrate the dynamic behavior of both the wind flow and fire spread. The flow chart Fig. 4 presents the coupling approach between the two models.

The parameters affecting the fire spread in the **transition rules** are:

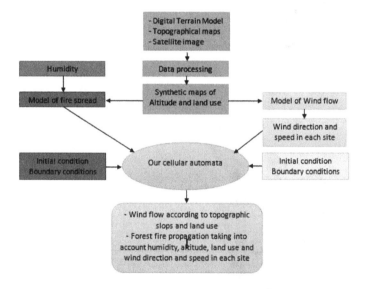

Fig. 4. Flow chart for coupling wind flow and fire spread models

1. **Vegetation type and density:** Burning velocity in each cell changes according to the type and density of vegetation (represented by a burning duration T_{fire}).
2. **Humidity:** We consider three rate of humidity α_0, α_1 and α_2 which are representing respectively dry, wet and very wet rate. We denote the humidity by H. The humidity affect the burning duration T_{fire}, i.e.

if $H=\alpha_0$ then T_{fire} will be a short duration,
if $H=\alpha_1$ then T_{fire} will be a long duration and
if $H=\alpha_2$ then T_{fire} will be a very long duration, fire will not propagate.

3. **Wind direction:** In order to set a specific fire spread direction, we modify the transition rules to verify neighborhood set $N(c_{ij})$ by neglecting inactive cells, i.e. cells where the wind flow will not spread. Those cells are determined previously by the model of wind flow developed in Subsect. 2.2.

4. **Wind speed:** According to wind speed level determined by the wind flow model in Subsect. 2.2, we define radius of the neighborhood set $N(c_{ij})$. The transition rules are represented as follows:

$$
\text{if } s_{t_i}(c_{ij}) = 0 \text{ then } s_{t_{i+1}}(c_{ij}) = \begin{cases} 1 & \text{if } \begin{array}{l} s_{t_0}(c_{ij}) \text{ contains plant and} \\ \exists kl \mid c_{kl} \in N(c_{ij}) \text{ with } s_{t_i}(c_{kl}) = 1 \\ \text{and } H < \alpha_2 \end{array} \\ 0 & \text{otherwise} \end{cases}
$$

$$
\text{if } s_{t_i}(c_{ij}) = 1 \text{ then } s_{t_{i+1}}(c_{ij}) = 2
$$

$$
\text{if } s_{t_i}(c_{ij}) = 2 \text{ then } s_{t_{i+1}}(c_{ij}) = \begin{cases} 3 & \text{if } t_i = T_{fire} \\ 2 & \text{otherwise} \end{cases}
$$

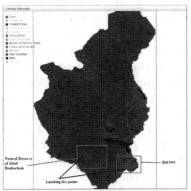

(a) i=0: Synthetic map of land use in the watershed of Oued Laou and launching fire points.

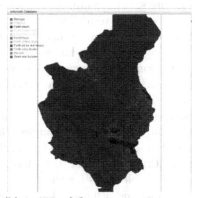

(b) i=200 of fire propagation coupled with wind flow model

(c) i=470 of fire propagation coupled with **wind flow model**

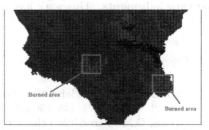

(d) i=470 of fire propagation with a **uniform wind parameters**

Fig. 5. Different stages of the fire spread.

if $s_{t_i}(c_{ij}) = 3$ then $s_{t_{i+1}}(c_{ij}) = 4$
if $s_{t_i}(c_{ij}) = 4$ then $s_{t_{i+1}}(c_{ij}) = 4$

3.2 Simulation Results

For the simulation, we consider two launching fire points in the Natural Reserve of Jebel Bouhachem and in Bab Taza Fig. 5(a) which are the most vulnerable areas and which present a big risk of forest fire [8]. The simulation results, presented in Fig. 5, show that the burned area in the Natural Reserve of Jebel Bouhachem and Bab Taza using the model with dynamic wind parameters is larger than the result of model with uniform wind parameters. This is due to the multi-direction and different speed of wind instead of taking those two parameters as uniform.

4   Conclusion

In this paper we present a CA model for the wind flow and its impact on the fire spread. The wind flow model takes into account the topographic slope and the land uses. It determines the wind direction and speed in each site and how it spreads according to altitude levels. In the framework of this research, a proper methodology to simulate this phenomenon has been developed by using a computer aiding tool which has allowed us to view the simulation results based on CA transition rules. It was used to improve the previous fire forest spread model proposed in [8]. It will be very useful by determining exactly the behavior of the wind flow which is the main parameter affecting fire spread. The proposed methodology has been applied to simulate the wind flow in an area: Watershed Oued Laou, Morocco, and coupled the two models to obtain the final result of improved model. The parameters in this model have random behavior, so it will be interesting to consider a stochastic CA. The model of wind flow can be used to asses suitable areas for wind turbine. It will be better to have a visualization of this model and other similar ones using 3D software. Such problems are under investigation.

Acknowledgments. This work has been supported by the project PPR2 OGI-Env and the International network TDS, Academie Hassan II of sciences and Techniques.

References

1. Bernoussi, A.: Spreadability, vulnerability and protector control. Math. Model. Nat. Phenom. **5**(07), 145–150 (2010)
2. Byram, G.M.: Forest fire behavior. In: Davis, K.P. (ed.) Forest Fire: Control and Use, p. 90123 (1959)
3. Chopard, B., Droz, M.: Cellular Automata Modeling of Physical Systems. Cambridge University Press, Cambridge (2005)

4. Deutsch, A., Dormann, S.: Cellular Automaton Modeling of Biological Pattern Formation: Characterization, Applications, and Analysis. Springer Science and Business Media, New York (2007)

5. Encinas, A.H., Encinas, L.H., White, S.H., del Rey, A.M., Sanchez, G.R.: Simulation of forest fire fronts using cellular automata. Adv. Eng. Softw. **38**, 372–378 (2007)

6. Good, R.B., McRae, R.H.D.: The challenges of modeling natural area ecosystems. In: Proceedings of 8th Biennial Conference and Bushfire Dynamics Workshop, Canberra, Australia, pp. 475–484 (1989)

7. Jellouli, O., Bernoussi, A., Amharref, M., El Yacoubi, S.: Vulnerability and protector control: cellular automata approach. In: Was, J., Sirakoulis, G.C., Bandini, S. (eds.) ACRI 2014. LNCS, vol. 8751, pp. 218–227. Springer, Heidelberg (2014)

8. Jellouli, O., Bernoussi, A., Maâtouk, M., Amharref, M.: Forest fire modelling using cellular automata: application to the watershed Oued Laou (Morocco). Math. Comput. Model. Dyn. Syst. **22**(5), 493–507 (2016). doi:10.1080/13873954.2016.1204321

9. Morandini, F., Simeoni, A., Santoni, P.A., Balbi, J.H.: A model for the spread of fire across a fuel bed incorporating the effects of wind and slope. Combust. Sci. Technol. **177**(7), 1381–1418 (2005)

10. Ntinas, V.G., Moutafis, B.E., Trunfio, G.A., Sirakoulis, G.C.: GPU and FPGA parallelization of fuzzy cellular automata for the simulation of wildfire spreading. In: Wyrzykowski, R., Deelman, E., Dongarra, J., Karczewski, K., Kitowski, J., Wiatr, K. (eds.) PPAM 2015. LNCS, vol. 9574, pp. 560–569. Springer, Heidelberg (2016). doi:10.1007/978-3-319-32152-3_52

11. Progias, P., Sirakoulis, G.C.: An FPGA processor for modelling wildfire spread. Math. Comput. Model. **57**(5–6), 1436–1452 (2013)

12. Slimi, R., El Yacoubi, S.: Spreadable cellular automata: modelling and simulation. Int. J. Syst. Sci. **40**(5), 507–520 (2009)

13. Sharples, J.J.: Review of formal methodologies for wind slope correction of wildfire rate of spread. Int. J. Wildland Fire **17**(2), 179–193 (2008)

14. Trunfio, G.A., D'Ambrosio, D., Rongo, R., Spataro, W., Di Gregorio, S.: A new algorithm for simulating wildfire spread through cellular automata. ACM Trans. Model. Comput. Simul. **22**, 1–26 (2011). ISSN 1049-3301

15. Viegas, D.X.: Slope and wind effects on fire propagation. Int. J. Wildland Fire **13**(2), 143–156 (2004)

Modelling of Climate Change Impact on Water Resources: Cellular Automata Approach

Hamidou Kassogué[1]([✉]), Abdessamed Bernoussi[1], Mina Amharref[1],
and Mustapha Ouardouz[2]

[1] GAT Team, Faculty of Sciences and Techniques, 416, Tangier, Morocco
hamidoukass@gmail.com, a.samed.bernoussi@gmail.com, amharrefm@yahoo.fr
[2] MMC Team, Faculty of Sciences and Techniques, 416, Tangier, Morocco
ouardouz@gmail.com

Abstract. In this work, we consider the cellular automata approach for modelling the climate change impact on water resources. This consists on coupling physical terrain attributes like altitude, soil type and land use, for a given region with the corresponding climate projections (temperature and precipitation). The system evolves under a water cycle dynamics governed by mass conservation principle. We apply the model to a basin in northern Morocco using a simulation tool we designed.

Keywords: Modelling · Cellular automata · Climate change · Water resource

1 Introduction

Climate change is a worrying problem for the entire humanity. Indeed the equilibrium existing in the environment is dangerously threatened. This change has a negative and harmful impact on the survival of humans, plants and animals. According to scientists [1] the negative effects due to global warming are the most frequent. The most noticeable ones are: ice melting, sea level rising and intense heat waves. In addition, extreme events such as droughts, storms, floods, heat waves and frosts are not unusual but common. Various climate models like General Circulation Models (GCM) [2] or Radiative Convective Models (RCM) [3] and Earth-system Models of Intermediate Complexity (EMICs) [4] are developed to predict climate change and anticipate its effects.

In this paper, we consider the impact of climate change on water resources: groundwater and surface water. They both undergo a great loss in their volume because of the evaporation due to above mentioned heat waves. Because of this water cycle monitoring model is required to assess the actual state of these water resources. Various models exist in literature. In this work, we adopt a discrete model approach based on cellular automata (CA) [5,6]. Continuous approach like partial differential equations can lead to a complicated equation which will be difficult to implement in real situations. Cellular automata offer wide kinds of

S. El Yacoubi et al. (Eds.): ACRI 2016, LNCS 9863, pp. 280–290, 2016.
DOI: 10.1007/978-3-319-44365-2_28

implementations in various areas. They are more efficient computationally and are more suitable to model the dynamics of complex systems.

The CA model presented in this paper consists in discretizing the study area into meshes called cells with pre-defined size. Each cell has its own physical terrain attributes (altitude, soil type and land use) and climatic attributes (temperature and precipitation). The transition rules that govern the evolution of the system enable the determination of the groundwater and surface water using the mass conservation principle. The climate projections over a long period help us to assess the climate change impact on water resources.

We designed the simulation tool using Java object oriented programming. The simulation results are of a basin in north Morocco where the physical terrain attributes were carried out using a previous work through digital terrain model, geological maps and satellite images processing [7,8]. For the climatic data, we used Maroc-Meteo stored values [9] and climate projections presented in [10].

2   Problem Statement

The groundwater and the surface water are two principal freshwater resources available in a terrain. Their recharging results from the processes of the water cycle (precipitation, evaporation/evapotranspiration, infiltration and runoff):

- The groundwater recharging is due to the infiltration which depends closely on the soil type and the land use.
- The surface water recharging is due to the runoff which depends essentially on the altitude.

Although the precipitation is very helpful to the recharging process, the freshwater resources still undergo a great loss of their volume because of evaporation. This is so especially with the global warming predicted in climate change models. So, the question is how to assess the impact of climate change on water resources?

3   Problem Approach

The principle of our approach is based on:

- modelling and monitoring water cycle using cellular automata taking into account the physical terrain attributes (altitude, soil type and land use).
- coupling our cellular automaton model with the scenarios of a selected climate model as input data (temperature and precipitation).
- determining as output the water resources: the groundwater, the surface water and the evaporated water.

This approach is illustrated in the Fig. 1. Let us start by recalling some generalities on climate change.

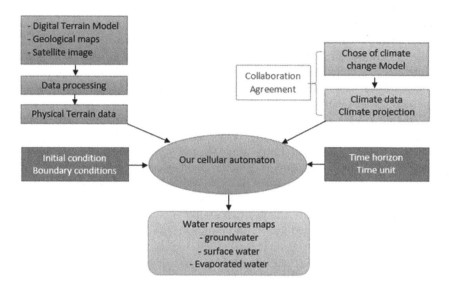

Fig. 1. Modelling of climate change impact on water resources principle using CA

3.1   Generalities on Climate Change

Climate changes refer to all changes in climate during an extended period of time. The climate parameters considered in our study are temperature and precipitation. In order to assess the climate projections, it is necessary to choose a climate model. In literature there are a multitude of climate models (GCM [2], RCM [3], EMICs [4]). Most of them are coupled with an ocean circulation model, a sea ice model and an atmospheric chemistry model. These climate models use a mesh with a spatial resolution between 100 and 300 Km^2. To estimate climate change in smaller scale, we need to use disintegration methods like anomalies method, quantile-quantile or time regimes [11]. To calibrate the climate projections an adjustment is made with real climate data of passed known periods.

3.2   Presentation of the Cellular Automaton Model

According to the problem statement, the water cycle constitutes a spatio-temporal dynamical system. We present briefly the cellular automaton model [7,8] for the water cycle.

The CA model is

$$\mathcal{A} = (\mathcal{L}, \mathcal{N}, \mathcal{S}, f) \tag{1}$$

where:

– The lattice is

$$\mathcal{L} = \{c_{ij}; \ i, j \in \mathbb{Z}\} \tag{2}$$

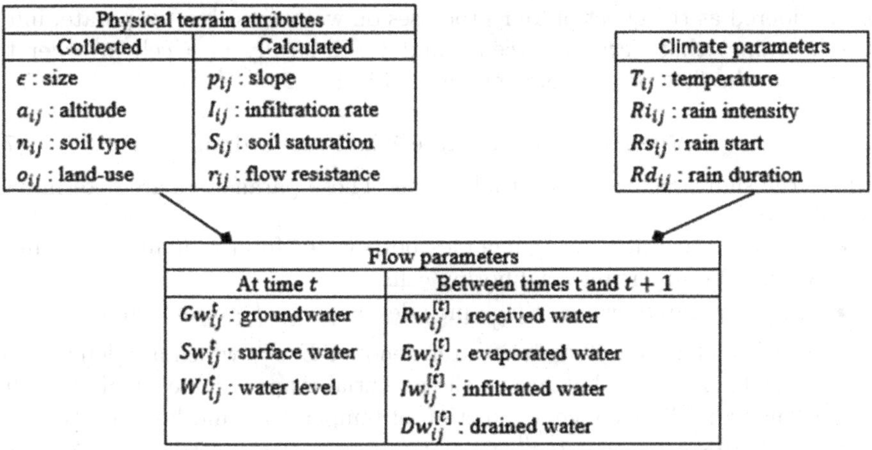

Physical terrain attributes		Climate parameters
Collected	Calculated	
ϵ : size	p_{ij} : slope	T_{ij} : temperature
a_{ij} : altitude	I_{ij} : infiltration rate	Ri_{ij} : rain intensity
n_{ij} : soil type	S_{ij} : soil saturation	Rs_{ij} : rain start
o_{ij} : land-use	r_{ij} : flow resistance	Rd_{ij} : rain duration

Flow parameters	
At time t	Between times t and $t+1$
Gw_{ij}^{t} : groundwater	$Rw_{ij}^{[t]}$: received water
Sw_{ij}^{t} : surface water	$Ew_{ij}^{[t]}$: evaporated water
Wl_{ij}^{t} : water level	$Iw_{ij}^{[t]}$: infiltrated water
	$Dw_{ij}^{[t]}$: drained water

Fig. 2. Physical terrain attributes, climatic and flow parameters for a cell c_{ij}

where each cell c_{ij} is a terrain mesh which has a set of physical terrain attributes, climatic parameters and flow parameters (Fig. 2).

– The neighborhood for a cell is the set of m adjacent cells expressed by

$$\mathcal{N}(c_{ij}) = \{c_{kl} \in \mathcal{L}; \ d(c_{ij}, c_{kl}) \leq 1\} \tag{3}$$

where d is a distance on $\mathcal{L} \times \mathcal{L}$ equivalent to the norm L_∞ defined in [6].

– The set of states is

$$\mathcal{S} = \{0, 1, 2, 3\} \tag{4}$$

whose values correspond to the amount of groundwater and surface water contained in a cell as:

0 : no saturation and no water in surface,
1 : saturation and no water in surface,
2 : no saturation and water in surface,
3 : saturation and water in surface.

Then, the CA configuration $s_t : c_{ij} \in \mathcal{L} \to s_t(c_{ij})$ at a time t is given by

$$s_t(c_{ij}) = \begin{cases} 0, & \text{if } Gw_{ij}^t(i,j) < S_{ij} \text{ and } Sw_{ij}^t(i,j) = 0 \\ 1, & \text{if } Gw_{ij}^t(i,j) = S_{ij} \text{ and } Sw_{ij}^t(i,j) = 0 \\ 2, & \text{if } Gw_{ij}^t(i,j) < S_{ij} \text{ and } Sw_{ij}^t(i,j) > 0 \\ 3, & \text{if } Gw_{ij}^t(i,j) = S_{ij} \text{ and } Sw_{ij}^t(i,j) > 0 \end{cases} . \tag{5}$$

– The transition function

$$f : \mathcal{S}^m \to \mathcal{S}$$
$$s_t(\mathcal{N}(c_{ij})) \mapsto s_{t+1}(c_{ij}) \tag{6}$$

is considered as the effect of four processes on water (receive, evaporate, infiltrate, draine) that occur between t and $t + 1$ locally in a cell in order to determine the flow parameters enumerated in Fig. 2:

$$f \equiv \text{receive} \oplus \text{evaporate} \oplus \text{infiltrate} \oplus \text{draine} \qquad (7)$$

where the sign $\oplus$ refer to a mutual action. Those parameters are determined as follows:

- The received water $Rw_{ij}^{[t]}$ includes both water from rainfall and drained water from upstream neighboring cells.
- The evaporated water $Ew_{ij}^{[t]}$ includes a part of groundwater denoted $Egw_{ij}^{[t]}$ and a part of surface water denoted $Esw_{ij}^{[t]}$ which are determined using Thornthwate balance on the potential evaporation evaluated by the Blaney-Criddle balance as function of temperature and land-use [12].
- The infiltrated water $Iw_{ij}^{[t]}$ depends on the soil saturation and the infiltration rate. We use the Horton formula [12].
- The drained water $Dw_{ij}^{[t]}$ toward the downstream neighboring cells depends on the slope, the water level and the flow resistance. We use the Chezy-Manning formula [12].
- The water level Wl_{ij}^{t} depends on the cell size and the surface water.
- The groundwater Gw_{ij}^{t+1} and the surface water Sw_{ij}^{t+1} at $t+1$ are determined by the mass conservation principle:

$$Gw_{ij}^{t} + Sw_{ij}^{t} + Rw_{ij}^{[t]} = Gw_{ij}^{t+1} + Sw_{ij}^{t+1} + Ew_{ij}^{[t]} + Dw_{ij}^{[t]}, \qquad (8)$$

$$Gw_{ij}^{t} + Iw_{ij}^{[t]} = Gw_{ij}^{t+1} + Egw_{ij}^{[t]}. \qquad (9)$$

The model takes into account fixed (no exchange water) and reflexive (exchange water) boundary conditions. We have implemented in previous works the model to flood problem in two Moroccan regions [7,8].

3.3   Coupling CA with Climate Change Scenarios

The coupling of climate change scenarios with the cellular automaton consists on:

- Considering a discretized period of time;
- Saving as input the climatic parameters of cells in Fig. 2 for each time interval;
- Simulating the water cycle in the considered terrain and storing as output the groundwater, surface and evaporated water for each time interval.

For this, we have designed a simulation tool of the CA model using Java object oriented programming as a part of a decision aided software for real time monitoring of water cycle. It offers various features. We have also assessed the water resources and the vulnerability to flood. For the physical terrain data, we used digital terrain models for altitude, geological maps for soil type and satellite images for land-use. All the earth observation data was processed and homogenized before integration in the model.

4   Application

As an application we consider a region in the northern Moroccan. We will start by presenting the studied region with its physical terrain attributes and climate attributes, and then we will present the simulation results.

4.1   Study Region

The studied region, Oued Boukhalef basin, leading to the Atlantic Ocean, is located in Tangier (northern Morocco) between 35.702 and 35.775 northern latitudes and west longitudes 5.855 and 5.948. It covers an area of 34.3 Km^2.

The CA Component

- The lattice is constituted by hexagonal cells covering 468.75 m^2. The lattice geometry as shown in Fig. 3 is obtained superposing maps of altitude, soil type and land use [8].
- The neighborhood for a cell is given by the formula (3).
- The set of states and the transition function are given respectively by the formulas (4) and (6).

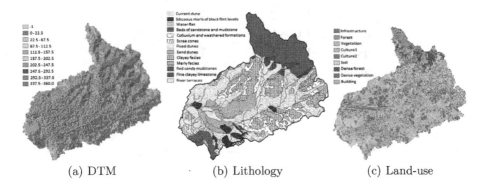

(a) DTM   (b) Lithology   (c) Land-use

Fig. 3. Oued Boukhalef basin (northern Morocco) with physical terrain attributes

The Physical Terrain Data. The region presents a great variation in altitude (3 to 275 m). Figure 3(a) shows the digital terrain model (DTM) in 2D view. The variation on soil type (Fig. 3(b)) presents twelve classes and nine classes for the land use (Fig. 3(c)).

Climate Data. For climate data, we use the values in Table 1 which refer to the average climate in Tangier estimated by Maroc-Meteo for the period 1984–2014 [9]. We use it as reference climate data.

Table 1. Climate data of Tangier considered for the period 1984–2014 [9]

	Sept	Oct	Nov	Dec	Jan	Feb	Mar	Apr	May	Jun	Jul	Aug
Temperature (°C)	22.5	19	16	13.5	12	13	13.75	15	17.75	21	23.5	23.5
Precipitation (mm)	20	74	115	137	105	80	60	70	40	10	2	2

We use the climate projection of the same region as given in the thesis [10] for the Moroccan territory. The projected values intervals for the period 2021–2050 are given in Table 2 with respect to the seasons. The values indicate a climate warming. The temperature will increase between +1 and +2 °C and the precipitation will vary between −25 % and +30 %. We simulate the water resources evolution under the low and upper projected values per season as respectively pessimistic and optimistic climate scenarios. Figure 4 illustrates the chosen climate evolution scenarios in comparison with the reference climate data. The rainfall is shifted in the projected cases and the temperature has a similar variation for the three climate scenarios.

Table 2. 2021–2050 climate projections per season for Morocco, from [10].

Season	Temperature (°C)	Precipitation (%)
Autumn	+1.4 to +1.8	+5 to +30
Winter	+1 to +1.4	−25 to −5
Spring	+1.4 to +1.7	+5 to +20
Summer	+1.4 to +2	−10 to −5

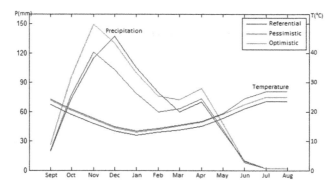

Fig. 4. Comparison of climate projections with the reference climate data

4.2   Simulation Results

For each scenario, we simulate under the following considerations:

- The precipitation P_m starts the first day of the month m over the whole region. The average annual rain days is 74 for the corresponding period. We consider the rain days per month (RD) in relation to the corresponding precipitation:

$$\mathrm{RD}_m = \frac{74 \times P_m}{\sum_{m=1}^{12} P_m}.$$

- The time unit is one hour and the water unit is the millimeter.
- Reflexive boundary condition for cells of the Atlantic coast and fixed type for the rest.
- For the initial condition, we have followed water resources with the above average climate values for a single year from September to August. 95 % of the lattice has almost no groundwater and no surface water at the simulation end.
- Each color connotes a class of water in millimeter:

■ > 50   ■]37.5, 50]   ■]25, 37.5]   ■]12.5, 25]   ■]0, 12.5]   ■ =0

Groundwater. The average groundwater of each cell (obtained from simulation per hour) is shown in Fig. 5 for the both pessimistic and optimistic scenarios.

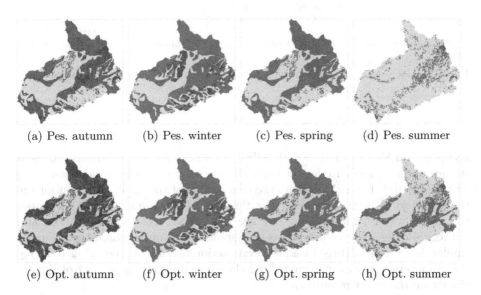

(a) Pes. autumn   (b) Pes. winter   (c) Pes. spring   (d) Pes. summer

(e) Opt. autumn   (f) Opt. winter   (g) Opt. spring   (h) Opt. summer

Fig. 5. Groundwater per season for pessimistic (Pes.) and optimistic (Opt.) climate scenarios in the region.

In the pessimistic case we notice an important increase of groundwater for several zones in autumn while the values remain similar for the two scenarios in winter and even increase during spring and summer in optimistic case.

Surface Water. The average surface water of each cell (obtained from simulation per hour) is shown in Fig. 6 for the both pessimistic and optimistic scenarios.

For each season, the surface water is more important in the case of optimistic climate scenario than in the pessimistic one. The difference is more notable in winter and spring than the autumn and summer.

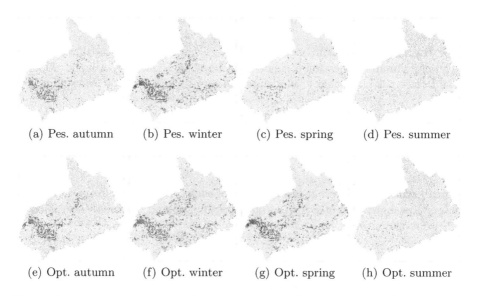

(a) Pes. autumn   (b) Pes. winter   (c) Pes. spring   (d) Pes. summer

(e) Opt. autumn   (f) Opt. winter   (g) Opt. spring   (h) Opt. summer

Fig. 6. Surface water per season for pessimistic (Pes.) and optimistic (Opt.) climate scenarios in the region.

Evaporated Water. To assess the effect of evaporation on the groundwater and surface water we simulate for the three climate scenarios (referential, pessimistic and optimistic). Figure 7 presents the comparison of the water variation for the three scenarios during one year. For the case of pessimistic climate scenario, the groundwater and surface water are much lower than the referential and optimistic cases. The values between referential and optimistic cases are more similar. But for all of three cases, the evaporation remains similar. Thus reducing the evaporation process can contribute closely to improve the impact of climate change on the water resources.

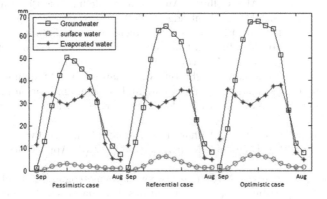

Fig. 7. Comparison of annual water resources for three climate scenarios in the region.

5   Conclusion and Perspectives

In this paper, we have proposed a cellular automaton model to assess the climate change impact on water resources. The model consists on coupling physical terrain attributes with climate projections to follow the water cycle. As an application we have considered the case of a region in north Morocco. The simulation results show that the groundwater is more important than the surface water over the region but the evaporation has a considerable effect on the two later waters.

For rainfall and temperature, we have considered the climate projections as deterministic events in the model. In an outlook, it will be interesting to consider stochastic cellular automata approach since the climatic parameters are random events. In addition, to improve our approach it is worth to consider a 3D cellular automaton to describe the water cycle. Such problems are under investigations.

Acknowledgments. This work has been supported by the project PPR2-OGI-Env and the international network TDS, Academy Hassan II of Sciences and Techniques.

References

1. IPCC: Climate Change 2014: Synthesis Report. Contribution of Working Groups I, II and III to the Fifth Assessment Report of the Intergovernmental Panel on Climate Change [Core Writing Team, R.K. Pachauri and L.A. Meyer (eds.)], 151 p. IPCC, Geneva (2014)
2. Phillips, N.A.: The general circulation of the atmosphere: a numerical experiment. Q. J. R. Meteorol. Soc. **82**(352), 123–154 (1956)
3. Ramanathan, V., Coakley, J.A.: Climate modelling through radiative-convective models. Rev. Geophys. Space Phys. **16**(4), 465–489 (1978)
4. Claussen, M., Ganopolski, A., Schellnhuber, J., Cramer, W.: Earth system models of intermediate complexity. Glob. Change Newsl. **41**, 4–6 (2002)

5. Chopard, B., Droz, M.: Cellular Automata Modelling of Physical Systems. Cambridge University Press, Cambridge (1998)
6. Ammor, N., El Jai, A., El Yacoubi, S.: Regional controllability with cellular automata models. In: Bandini, S., Chopard, B., Tomassini, M. (eds.) ACRI 2002. LNCS, vol. 2493, pp. 357–367. Springer, Heidelberg (2002)
7. Kassogué, H., Bernoussi, A., Amharref, M., Maatouk, M.: Modelling of flow by cellular automata, vulnerability to flooding and erosion: application to the region of Oued Laou (Morocco). In: 7th Workshop of TamTam, Tangier, Morocco, 04–08 May (2015)
8. Kassogué, H., Bernoussi, A., Amharref, M., Maatouk, M.: A Two Scale Cellular Automaton for Flow DYnamics Modeling (2CAFDYM). Appl. Math. Model. (in press)
9. Maroc-Meteo, Decemeber 2015. http://www.marocmeteo.ma/?q=fr/climat_villes
10. Driouech, F.: Distribution des précipitations hivernales sur le Maroc dans le cadre d'un changement climatique: descente d'échelle et incertitudes. Ph.D. thesis, Toulouse University (2010)
11. Habets, F., et al.: Impact du changement climatique sur les ressources en eau du bassin versant de la Seine. Programme PIREN-SEINE (2011)
12. Maidment, D.R.: Handbook of Hydrology. McGraw-Hill Inc., London (1993)

Simulations of Debris/Mud Flows Invading Urban Areas: A Cellular Automata Approach with SCIDDICA

Valeria Lupiano[1], Guillermo E. Machado[2], Gino M. Crisci[1], and Salvatore Di Gregorio[3(✉)]

[1] Department of Biology, Ecology and Earth Sciences,
University of Calabria, 87036 Rende, Italy
{valeria.lupiano, crisci}@unical.it
[2] Faculty of Engineering, National University of Chimborazo,
Riobamba, Ecuador
gmachado@unach.edu.ec
[3] Department of Mathematics and Computer Science,
University of Calabria, 87036 Rende, Italy
salvatore.digregorio@unical.it

Abstract. Different methodologies are used for modelling flow-like landslides. A critical point concerns the flooding of town areas, which cannot be assimilated straight to a morphology, especially, when the urban tissue is very irregular with narrow streets and setting of buildings, which reflect historical contingencies. SCIDDICA is a competitive (related to PDE approach) Cellular Automata model for 3-dimensions simulation of flow-like landslides. This paper presents innovations to the transition function of SCIDDICA-SS2, which manage opportunely building data in the cells corresponding to the urban tissue. That permits to simulate the complete evolution of landslides, from the detachment area to its exhaustion almost on the same precision level. This is an advantage for hazard and risk analyses in threatened zones. Improved SCIDDICA-SS2 was applied successfully to the well-known 2009 debris flows of Giampilieri Superiore also in comparison with simulation results of the previous versions.

Keywords: Cellular Automata · Modelling and Simulation · Debris flow · Natural hazard · SCIDDICA · Giampilieri Superiore

1 Introduction

Flow-like landslides of different types: debris flows, mudflows, lahars, rock avalanches are extremely dangerous surface flows, which can generate destructions with casualties in inhabited areas, especially in urban zones. Modelling and simulations of such natural disasters could be an important tool for hazard and risk mitigation and management in threatened regions.

Such complex fluid-dynamical phenomena are modelled through different standard approaches: empirical models, based on smart correlations of phenomenon observables, simple rheological and hydrological models, which assume acceptable

© Springer International Publishing Switzerland 2016
S. El Yacoubi et al. (Eds.): ACRI 2016, LNCS 9863, pp. 291–302, 2016.
DOI: 10.1007/978-3-319-44365-2_29

simplifications, numerical methods approximating PDE [1, 2]. These various approaches can produce discordant results [3], because different objectives of the simulations could involve different levels of precision for different types of data. Simulation results have to be accurately interpreted according to the model features. Simulations produce usually a large amount of data, whose usage in validation stage is devoted to a comparison with real event data that are almost approximate in the evolution phase, but usually detailed for the final effects that represent secure comparison terms.

Cellular Automata (CA) represent an alternative numerical method for modelling dynamical complex systems, which evolve on the basis of local interactions of their constituent elements. A Cellular Automaton evolves in a discrete space-time. Space is partitioned in cells of uniform size, each cell embeds a finite states automaton (a computing unit), all the cells change simultaneously state according a transition function of the states of the neighbor cells, where the neighborhood conditions are determined by a pattern invariant in time and space [4]. An extension of classical CA, MCA, Multicomponent (alias Macroscopic) CA, was developed in order to model large scale (extended for kilometers) phenomena [4, 5]. MCA need a large amount of states, in order to describe "macroscopic" properties of the space portion corresponding to the cell; such states may be formally represented by means of sub-states (e.g., sub-state altitude, i.e., the average value of altitude in the cell), which specify the characteristics to be attributed to the state of the cell. This involves several advantages in the case of surface flows; quantities concerning the third dimension, i.e. the height, may be easily included among the MCA sub-states, e.g., the thickness of debris in the cell, permitting models in two dimensions, working effectively in three dimensions; limits of discreteness may be partially overcome, permitting valid refinements; e.g. debris in a cell can be expressed as a thickness, but a further specification could be introduced by specifying the sub-states "center mass co-ordinates".

Two MCA models were developed for flow-like landslide, SCIDDICA (several versions since 1987, e.g. [6–12]) for subaerial/subaqueous debris/mud/gra-nular flows and LLUNPIY for primary and secondary lahars [13–15].

A critical point of these models concerns the flooding of town areas; previous solutions assimilated the urban tissue to a morphology and provided for a cell dimension enough small to permit that the cell corresponds nearly entirely to a piece of the road-bed (altitude of the road-bed) or to a piece of building (altitude of the building).

When part of the urban tissue consists of narrow streets and very irregular setting of buildings, due to historical contingencies, such a solution could involve an extremely large amount of cells, if the complete evolution of landslides from the detachment area to its exhaustion has to be simulated. That could implicate unsustainable computing time with the number of cells multiplied at least some hundreds times, if we consider that the model validation and following hazard analyses can imply thousands of simulations [16].

An extension of SCIDDICA-SS2 [7, 8, 11] was developed and applied in order to overcome these problems. A new sub-state that encodes building data, is introduced and AMD (the algorithm of minimization of differences [5], first step for determining cell outflows) was expanded in order to account for different heights (part of the road-bed, parts of buildings) inside the same cell. Simulation results of the well-known catastrophic landslide that overran Giampilieri Superiore in 2009 are excellent.

A short presentation of SCIDDICA-SS2 with a detailed specification of extended AMD is in the next section, the third section reports and compares different simulations of Giampilieri debris flows, conclusions and comments appear at the end.

2 SCIDDICA-SS2 Extension to Urban Areas

SCIDDICA-SS2 [7, 8, 11], SCIDDICA-SS3 [9, 10, 12] and LLUNPIY [13–15] are our front-rank models for simulations of flow-like landslides. The extension of SCIDDICA-SS2 to urban areas and applied to Giampilieri events, could be introduced easily in SCIDDICA-SS3 that represents a more precise version, but involving long running times, or in LLUNPIY, an adaptation of SCIDDICA-SS3 to lahar features. The following description of SCIDDICA-SS2 considers only the part of subaerial flows, without lacking of generality; a successive section presents the extended AMD.

2.1 Main Specifications of SCIDDICA-SS2

The hexagonal CA model SCIDDICA-SS2 is the quintuple: $< R, X, S, P, \tau >$ where:

- $R = \{(x, y)|\ x, y \in \mathbb{N}, 0 \leq x \leq l_x, 0 \leq y \leq l_y\}$ is the set of points with integer co-ordinates, which individuate the regular hexagonal cells, covering the finite region, where the phenomenon evolves. $\mathbb{N}$ is the set of natural numbers.
- $X = \{(0, 0), (1, 0), (0, 1), (-1, 1), (-1, 0), (0, -1), (-1, -1)\}$, the neighborhood index, identifies the geometrical pattern of cells, which influence state change of the central cell: the central cell (index 0) itself and the six adjacent cells (indexes 1,..,6).
- S is the finite set of states of the finite automaton, embedded in the cell; it is equal to the Cartesian product of the sets of the considered sub-states (Table 1). The new sub-state C specifies the type of cell: normal cell; detachment cell, where the landslide originates (the detachment depth is encoded in the C value); urban cell, whose C value encodes the parts of cell at different altitudes together with the differences in altitude from the road-bed.

Table 1. Sub-states

Sub-states	Description
C, A, D	Type of Cell, cell Altitude, erodible soil Depth
T, X, Y, K	Debris Thickness, co-ordinates X and Y of the debris barycenter inside the cell, Kinetic Head
E_T, E_X, E_Y, E_K (6 components)	External debris flow normalized to a Thickness, External flow co-ordinates X and Y, Kinetic Head of External flow
I_T, I_X, I_Y, I_K (6 components)	Internal debris flow normalized to a Thickness, Internal flow co-ordinates X and Y, Kinetic Head of Internal flow

- P is the set of the global physical and empirical parameters (Table 2), which account for the general frame of the model and the physical characteristics of the phenomenon, the choice of some parameters is imposed by the desired precision of simulation where possible, e.g., cell dimension; the value of some parameters is deduced by physical features of the phenomenon, e.g., turbulence dissipation, even if an acceptable value is fixed by the simulation quality by attempts, triggered by comparison of discrepancies between real event knowledge and simulation results.

Table 2. Physical and empirical parameters (with their physical dimensions)

Parameters	Description
a, t	cell **apothem** (m), **temporal** correspondence to a CA step (s)
p_f	friction coefficient **parameter** (°)
$d_t, d_e, p_e,$	energy **dissipation** by **turbulence** (-) and **erosion** (-); parameter of **progressive**
t_m	erosion (-); **mobilization** threshold (m)

- τ: $S^7 \rightarrow S$ is the cell deterministic state transition, it accounts for the components of the phenomenon, the "elementary processes" that are sketched in the next section.

2.2 Outline of SCIDDICA-SS2 Transition Function

A MCA step involves the ordered application of the following elementary processes, which constitute the transition function; every elementary process implies the state updating. In the formulae, neighborhood index for sub-states and related variables is specified by subscript, if it is not referred to central cell; ΔQ means Q value variation, multiplication is explicitly ".".

Debris Outflows. Outflows computation is performed in two steps: determination of the outflows f_i towards the neighbor i, $1 \leq i \leq 6$, by the new AMD (described in Sect. 2.3) according to "heights" of the cell neighborhood and determination of the shift of the outflows [5, 7, 8].

The outflow could be represented as an ideal cylinder, tangent the next edge of the central hexagonal cell, whose barycenter corresponds to the debris barycenter inside the central cell, in direction to the center of the neighbor cell. The part of the outflow, which overcomes the central cell, constitutes the external flow, specified by external flow sub-states, while the remaining part, the internal flow, is specified by internal flow sub-states. Shift "Δs" is computed according to the following simple formula, which averages the movement of all the mass as the barycenter movement of a body on a constant slope θ with a constant friction coefficient: $\Delta s = v \cdot t + g \cdot (\sin\theta - p_f \cos\theta) \cdot t^2 / 2$ with "g" gravity acceleration and initial velocity $v = \sqrt{(2 \cdot g \cdot K)}$ [7, 8].

Turbulence Effect. A turbulence effect is modelled by a proportional kinetic head loss at each SCIDDICA step: $-\Delta K = d_t \cdot K$. This formula involves that a velocity limit is asymptotically imposed de facto, for a maximum slope value.

Soil Erosion. When the kinetic head value overcomes an opportune threshold ($K > t_m$), depending on the soil features, then a mobilization of the detrital cover occurs proportionally to the quantity overcoming the threshold: $p_e \cdot (K - t_m) = \Delta T = -\Delta D$ (the erodible soil depth diminishes as the debris thickness increases), the kinetic head loss is: $-\Delta K = d_e \cdot (K - t_m)$.

Flows Composition. When outflows and their shifts are computed, the new situation involves that external flows leave the cell, internal flows remain in the cell with different co-ordinates and inflows (trivially derived by the values of external flows of the neighbor cells) have to be added. The new value of T is given, considering the balance of inflows and outflows with the remaining debris mass in the cell. A kinetic energy reduction is considered by loss of flows, while an increase is given by inflows: the new value of the kinetic head is deduced from the computed kinetic energy. X and Y are calculated as the average weight of the co-ordinates considering the remaining thickness in the central cell, the thickness of internal flows and the inflows.

2.3 AMD Adaptation for not Homogeneous Cells in SCIDDICA-SS2

The lack of homogeneity regards different altitudes for parts of the same cell. It involves a distinction of different rates of the cell area (normalized to unit), to which different altitudes and debris thicknesses correspond.

The following specification of AMD holds for SCIDDICA-SS2 with cells divided in two parts "R" (road-bed) and "B" (Building) with two areas of different altitude Preliminary definitions are given in the Table 3.

Table 3. Definitions for AMD adapted to urban areas

a_i	area rate related to the "R" part of the neighbor cell i, $0 \leq i \leq 6$
A_i	area rate related to the "B" part of the neighbor cell i, $0 \leq i \leq 6$
d	distributable quantity (as height) in the central cell
h_i	height of the "R" part of the neighbor cell i, $0 \leq i \leq 6$
H_i	height of the "B" part of cell i, $0 \leq i \leq 6$
f_i	flow toward the "R" part of the neighbor cell i, $0 \leq i \leq 6$
F_i	flow toward the "B" part of the neighbor cell i, $0 \leq i \leq 6$
h_i', H_i'	$h_i' = h_i + f_i$, $H_i' = H_i + F_i$, $0 \leq i \leq 6$

The values of the heights for the central cell is obtained by the sum of altitude and kinetic head for both the parts; the values of the heights for the adjacent cells is obtained by the sum of altitude and debris thickness for both the parts.

The adapted AMD (Table 4) finds f_i and F_i, $0 \leq i \leq 6$ that minimize:

$$\sum_{\{(i,j) \mid 0 \leq i \leq j \leq 6\}} \left(\left| h_i' - h_j' \right| + \left| H_i' - H_j' \right| + \left| h_i' - H_j' \right| \right)$$

Table 4. AMD adapted to urban areas

Initialization:	a	both the "R" and "B" parts of all the neighbors are "admissible" to receive flows; R and B are the sets of admissible cell parts
Cycle:	b	$q = (d + \Sigma_{i \in R} (h_i \cdot a_i) + \Sigma_{i \in B} (H_i \cdot A_i))/(\Sigma_{i \in R} (a_i) + \Sigma_{i \in B} (A_i))$ is the "average height" for the set R *and* B of admissible cell parts.
	c	$h_x \geq q$, $(H_X \geq q)$ implies x (X) eliminated from R (B).
End of cycle:	d	go to step < b > until no cell is eliminated
Results:	e	$f_i = (q - h_i)\, a_i$ for $i \in R$; $f_i = 0$ *for* $i \notin R$. $F_i = (q - H_i)\, A_i$ for $i \in B$; $F_i = 0$ *for* $i \notin B$

3   Giampilieri Superiore Debris Flow Simulations

3.1   1st October 2009 Landslides Event

On the October 1st 2009 a severe meteorological event stroke the Peloritani Mountains (NE Sicily). The intense rainfall caused floods and triggered many debris and mud flows that brought 37 fatalities, numerous injured, several damages to public and private buildings, railways, roads, infrastructures, electric and telephonic networks, thousands of evacuated persons. The Department of Civil Protection of Sicilian Region has mapped more than 600 landslides, in an area, which stretched approximately for 50 km^2. Analysis of the rainfall event indicates a cumulative rainfall depth of 225 mm obtained in 9 h from the data recorded at the S. Stefano di Briga rain-gauge, with a peak of rainfall intensity of about 22 mm/min. The area is susceptible to the formation of debris flows due to lithological characteristics, complex tectonic history, high gradient of slopes (30–60°) and landscapes characterized by narrow gullies with hydraulic torrential regime.

Giampilieri Superiore was one of the most wounded villages by these catastrophic events. The village is located on the eastern slopes of the Peloritani Mountains on left side of Giampilieri River. In particular, it rises on an alluvial fan and is crossed by various creeks, tributaries of the Giampilieri River. All of them are characterized by small catchments with extension ranging from 0.03 km^2 to 0.1 km^2 [17]. The path of Sopra Urno creek, inside the urbanized area, was turned into a road (Chiesa Street, Fig. 1b). During the paroxysmal pluvial event of 1st October, several debris flows (Fig. 1a) were mobilized from the slope behind the village. Many of these channeled before in the drainage network and after in the Chiesa Street, reached Giampilieri Superiore, producing dramatic effects in terms of loss of human lives and damages of buildings.

The severity of the rainfall event was not the only cause of the disaster. In fact, other factors contributed to slope failures in the Giampilieri case, as Ardizzone et al. [18] stressed: abandoned terraced slopes lacking proper drainage and unmaintained dry walls; furthermore some village streets cover part of creek beds.

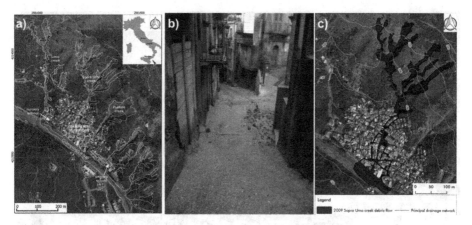

Fig. 1. (a) October 2009 debris flows occurred in Giampilieri Superiore, obtained by interpretation of aerial photo; (b) Example of Chiesa Street that during a normal rainfall event becomes the bed of the Sopra Urno creek; (c) Sopra Urno creek debris flow

3.2 Application of SCIDDICA SS2 to Sopra Urno Debris Flow

For testing the innovation introduced in SCIDDICA-SS2, we considered the Sopra Urno debris flow (mapped in Fig. 1c). SCIDDICA-SS2 and SCIDDICA–SS3 were calibrated and validated [10, 12, 15] on all debris flows occurred in Giampilieri Superiore area. The same parameters were used for simulations of this extended model. Genetic Algorithms were used for some key parameters related to energy dissipation in the previous versions of SCIDDICA; an analogous applications of Genetic Algorithm could improve the simulation quality.

Sopra Urno debris flow caused the largest number of casualties and damages, due to the fact that the flow crossed the village. Three experiments have been performed: the first one on a DTM (Digital Terrain Model), the second and third one on a DEM (Digital Elevation Model). The terms DTM and DEM are often confused. The principal difference between the two digital models lies in the fact that the DEM takes into account all objects on the ground (vegetation, buildings and other artifacts), while the DTM shows the geodesic surface. The difference between the two models is more evident in urban areas where buildings prevail.

First experiment, shown in Fig. 2a and a', simulates the event, by considering the elevation at ground level in the urbanized area. The flows at the change of slope, reduce the speed, and give rise to the typical fan shape of debris.

A second test (Fig. 2b and b') was performed using a DEM, which was obtained from manipulation of DTM by inserting urban data related to buildings and roads and by approximating altitude to road-bed. The flows, when reached the urbanized area, insinuates among the buildings. The results show a good capability of the model to simulate the debris run-out, particularly, in the upslope parts of the basins, while in the downslope urbanized area, the reproduction of the real events is less accurate. In fact, significant differences do exist in the lateral spreading characteristics of the run-out, as the streets inundated by the debris in the real event are different from those resulting

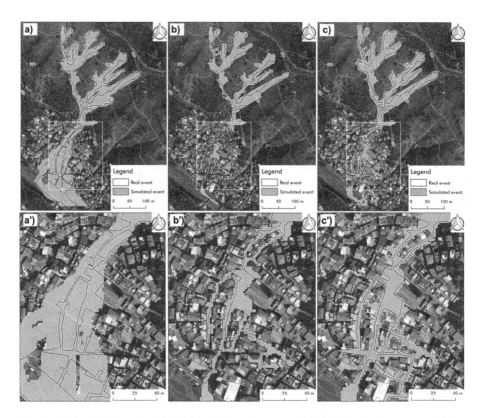

Fig. 2. (a) simulated event on DTM; b) simulated event on DEM; c) simulated event considering the improvement introducing in SCIDDICA; (a′), (b′) and (c′) enlargement of urban area

from simulation. This is related to both the inevitable approximation errors in the process of data elaboration from square cells to hexagonal cells, and to DEM accuracy. The presence of buildings in urban areas involves a greater difference of elevation between the ground and the same buildings, for the same corresponding cell. It induces an approximation in the assessment of the average elevation of cells that are partially covered by a building and by a terrain or a street. Results show that the program could be refined in the reproduction of debris flow propagation into highly urbanized areas, where streets are narrow.

The third experiment, regards this improvement just as described in the preceding paragraphs (cfr. Sect. 2). The improvement was been obtained by a better cell discretization. It allows a better positioning. It is possible to note (Fig. 2 c and c′) as the path of flows is better represented in urbanized areas, compared to the previous cases and to real event. The flows, which inundate the urban area, follow the path of the roads; the simulated travel times improve, resulting much closer to the realty; the real event lasted 5-6 min, case 2 length is 10 min, case 3 length is 7 min.

In Table 5 are reported the values of the evaluation (or fitness) function e, where R is the set of cells involved in the real event and S the corresponding one for simulated event. This function returns values from 0 (completely wrong simulation) to 1 (perfect match); values greater than 0.7 (precision lack in input data) are considered good results. Note how the match is increased in the urban path after the optimization of the model. If we consider only the urban sector, the evaluation function rises from 0.82 to 0.91 (Table 5). The evaluation formula accounts for necessity to compare results of different dimensions, so square (cubic) root normalizes surface (volume) measures.

Table 5. Evaluation function in study area

Case	$e = \sqrt{\frac{R \cap S}{R \cup S}}$ complete event	$e = \sqrt{\frac{R \cap S}{R \cup S}}$ just urbanized area
1	0,73	0.49
2	0,77	0.71
3	0,82	0.91

SCIDDICA is a semi-empirical model, whose parameters are fixed almost definitively in validation phase with the "equivalent fluid" hypothesis [5, 7–9, 19]. Its simulations may be compared with other simulations of the same event, which are performed by the continuous models FLO-2D and TRENT-2D [20].

FLO-2D is a commercial code, adopted worldwide for debris flow phenomena modelling and delineating flood hazards. It is a pseudo 2-D model in space which adopts depth-integrated flow equations. Hyperconcentrated sediment flows are simulated considering the flow as a monophasic non-linear Bingham fluid. The basic equations implemented in the model consist mainly of the continuity equation; in FLO-2D the bed is fixed and all the debris mass is initially available (the erosion is not considered) [20]. Larger Giampilieri areas are covered in FLO-2D simulations in comparison with the real event and SCIDDICA results.

TRENT-2D is a code developed for the simulation of hyperconcentrated sediment transport and debris flows. It is based on a two-phase approach, in which the interstitial fluid is water and the granular phase is modelled according to the dispersive pressure theory of Bagnold, applied to the debris flows. The reference model has a more specific physical base, it is biphasic and able to reproduce the erosion and deposition processes [20]. Small areas, which were invaded in the real event and in SCIDDICA simulation, result untouched in TRENT-2D simulation and vice versa.

SCIDDICA simulations start from detachment area and continue considering erosion before town invasion; results about this first phase lack for both the results of FLO-2D and TRENT-2D.

4 Conclusions

This paper presents SCIDDICA-SS2 improvements for simulating the part of debris flows that invade the urban areas. The less precision, related to momentum, of this version in comparison with SCIDDICA-SS3 and LLUNPIY does not worse simulations in urban areas, because there is a larger turbulence.

Validation has been carried out by simulating Sopra Urno debris flow occurred on October 1st, 2009 in the Giampilieri Superiore territory.

An accurate study was performed in order to obtain the most accurate reproduction of the observed event. In AMD is introduced a new sub-state, which encodes building data, so as to take into account the cells that contain buildings and soil simultaneously. This means that elements at different heights coexist in the same cell. Such model extension adapts very well to this problem. In fact, simulation results of Giampilieri Superiore debris flows are first-rate and may be evaluated still better, because fitness function was applied to the full area of the partially flooded cells.

A comparison with "continuous" models was performed: Flo-2D simulations involve invasion of a very larger area than real event [20]; TRENT-2D approximate well the real event in urban area, which is comparable with SCIDDICA simulations [20].

AMD needs to be improved for flow determination when the building parts of two adjacent cells occupy a common edge. Future work will solve such a minor problem. Another important goal is modelling situations, where part of debris flows runs into tunnels (or channels modified in tunnels) cross the urban area.

The new features of SCIDDICA-SS2 could be very important for hazard and risk analyses in threatened towns by flow-like landslides after a calibration of its parameters on real events, occurred in their territory. Giampilieri area was cultivated until recently, according to agricultural techniques (fine terracing and control of water runoff), introduced during the "Saracen" dominion. The abandonment of the land cultivation and of this cultural heritage is enhancing the natural hazard because of soil deterioration, which cannot emerge easily from the physical data, but can be better captured by empirical parameters, tuned in simulation phase of real events.

The efficiency of possible hazard mitigation works could also be tested by simulations, but solutions have to be evaluated on long times, because the risk (e.g. dams) could be transferred onto future events.

References

1. Iovine, G., Di Gregorio, S., Sheridan, M.F., Hideaki, M.: Modelling, computer-assisted simulations, and mapping of dangerous phenomena for hazard assessment. Environ. Model. Softw. **22**(10), 1389–1391 (2007)
2. Manville, V., Major Jon J., Sagents, S.A.: Modeling lahar behavior and hazards. In: Modeling Volcanic Processes, The Physics and Mathematics of Volcanism, pp. 300–330. Cambridge University Press, Cambridge (2013)
3. Canuti, P., Casagli, N., Catani, F., Falorni, G.: Modeling of the guagua pichincha volcano (Ecuador) lahars. Phys. Chem. Earth **27**, 1587–1599 (2002)
4. Di Gregorio, S., Serra, R.: An empirical method for modelling and simulating some complex macroscopic phenomena by cellular automata. Future Gener. Comput. Syst. **16**(2/3), 259–271 (1999)
5. Avolio, M.V., Di Gregorio, S., Spataro, W., Trunfio, G.A.: A theorem about the algorithm of minimization of differences for multicomponent cellular automata. In: Sirakoulis, G.C., Bandini, S. (eds.) ACRI 2012. LNCS, vol. 7495, pp. 289–298. Springer, Heidelberg (2012)

6. Barca, D., Di Gregorio, S., Nicoletta, F.P., Sorriso Valvo, M.: Flow-type landslide modelling by cellular automata. In: Mesnard, G. (ed.) Proceeddings of the Internat AMSE Conference on "Modelling and Simulation", Cairo, Egypt, March 2–4, vol. 4A, pp. 3−7. AMSE Tassin-la-Demi-Lune (1987)
7. Avolio, M.V., Lupiano, V., Mazzanti, P., Di Gregorio, S.: Modelling combined subaerial-subaqueous flow-like landslides by cellular automata. In: Umeo, H., Morishita, S., Nishinari, K., Komatsuzaki, T., Bandini, S. (eds.) ACRI 2008. LNCS, vol. 5191, pp. 329–336. Springer, Heidelberg (2008)
8. Mazzanti, P., Bozzano, F., Avolio, M.V., Lupiano, V., Di Gregorio, S.: 3D numerical modelling of submerged and coastal landslides propagation. In: Mosher, D.C., Shipp, R.C. (eds.) Submarine Mass Movements and Their Consequences. Advances in Natural and Technological Hazards Research, vol. 28, pp. 127–139. Springer, The Netherlands (2010)
9. Avolio, M.V., Di Gregorio, S., Lupiano, V., Mazzanti, P.: SCIDDICA-SS3: a new version of cellular automata model for simulating fast moving landslides. J. Supercomputing **65**(2), 682–696 (2013)
10. Lupiano, V., Avolio, M.V., Di Gregorio, S., Peres, D.J., Stancanelli, L.M.: Simulation of 2009 debris flows in the Peloritani Mountains area by SCIDDICA-SS3. In: Proceedings of the 7th International Conference on Engineering Mechanics, Structures, Engineering Geology (EMESEG 2014), Salerno, Italy, 3–5 June, pp. 53–61 (2014)
11. Lupiano, V., Avolio, M.V., Anzidei, M., Crisci, G.M., Di Gregorio, S.: Susceptibility assessment of subaerial (and/or) subaqueous debris-flows in archaeological sites, using a cellular model. In: Lollino, G., et al. (eds.) Engineering Geology for Society and Territory, vol. 8, pp. 405–408. Springer, Switzerland (2015)
12. Lupiano, V., Peres, D.J., Avolio, M.V., Cancelliere, A., Foti, E., Spataro, W., Stancanelli, L.M., Di Gregorio, S.: Use of the SCIDDICA-SS3 model for predictive mapping of debris flow hazard: An example of application in the Peloritani Mountains area. In: Proceedings of PDPTA 2015, Las Vegas, Nevada, USA, 27–30 July, pp. 625−663 (2015)
13. Machado, G., Lupiano, V., Crisci, G.M., Di Gregorio, S.: LLUNPIY preliminary extension for simulating primary lahars: Application to the 1877 Cataclysmic Event of Cotopaxi Volcano. In: SIMULTECH Proceedings of 5th International Conference on Simulation and Modeling Methodologies, Technologies and Applications, 21–23 July 2015, Colmar, Alsace, France, pp. 367−376 (2015)
14. Machado, G., Lupiano, V., Avolio, M.V., Gullace, F., Di Gregorio, S.: A cellular model for secondary lahars and simulation of cases in the Vascún Valley, Ecuador. J. Comput. Sci. **11**, 289–299 (2015). doi:10.1016/j.jocs.2015.08.001
15. Lupiano, V., Machado, G., Crisci, G.M., Di Gregorio, S.: A modelling approach with macroscopic cellular automata for hazard zonation of debris flows and lahars by computer simulations. Int. J. Geol. **9**, 35–46 (2015)
16. D'Ambrosio, D., Spataro, W., Rongo, R., Iovine, G.G.R.. Genetic algorithms, optimization, and evolutionary modeling. In: Shroder, J.F., Baas, A.C.W. (eds.) Treatise on Geomorphology, vol. 2, pp. 74–97. Academic Press, San Diego (2013)
17. Stancanelli, L.M., Bovolin, V., Foti E.: Application of a dilatant - viscous plastic debris flow model in a real complex situation, River, Coastal and Estuarine Morphodynamics. In: RCEM 2011, pp. 45–64. Tsinghua University Press, Beijing (2011)
18. Ardizzone, F., Basile, G., Cardinali, M., Casagli, M., Del Conte, S., Del Ventisette, C., Fiorucci, F., Garfagnoli, F., Gigli, G., Guzzetti, F., Iovine, G., Mondini, A.C., Moretti, S., Panebianco, M., Raspini, F., Reichenbach, P., Rossi, M., Tanteri, L., Terranova, O.: Landslide inventory map for the Briga and the Giampilieri catchments, NE Sicily, Italy. J. Maps **8**(2), 176–180 (2012)

19. Hungr, O.: Numerical modelling of the motion of rapid, flow-like landslides for hazard assessment. KSCE J. Civ. Eng. **13**(4), 281–287 (2009)
20. Stancanelli, L.M., Foti, E.: Comparative assessment of two different debris flow propagation approaches – blind simulations on a real debris flow event. Nat. Hazards Earth Syst. Sci. **15**(4), 735–746 (2015)

Car Accidents at the Intersection with Speed Limit Zone and Open Boundary Conditions

Rachid Marzoug[✉], Hicham Echab, Noureddine Lakouari, and Hamid Ez-Zahraouy

Laboratoire de Magnétisme et de Physique Des Hautes Energies (URAC 12),
Département de Physique, Faculté Des Sciences, Université Mohammed V Rabat, B.P. 1014,
Rabat, Morocco
rachid.marzoug@gmail.com

Abstract. Using cellular automata model, we numerically study the traffic characteristics and the probability P_{ac} of car accidents to occur at the intersection of
two roads under open boundary conditions. Beside the free flow (phase I),
jamming phase (phase III) and maximum current (phase IV) the phase diagram
exhibits a new phase (phase II) which take place for $\beta < 0.4$ (β is the extracting
rate). Moreover, the investigation of probability of the occurrence of car accidents
has shown that the probability P_{ac} increases with increasing the extraction rate β
and exhibits a maximum at the transition point from the free flow to the congestion
phase. However, when β exceeds the value 0.4, the probability P_{ac} doesn't depends
on β. Furthermore, simulation results show that the speed limit zone (SLZ) can
improve the road safety, where the probability P_{ac} decreases with increasing
length of SLZ. Likewise, we found that there is a critical injection rate α_c, below
which both roads must be equiprobable. However, above which, one road must
always have priority in order to reduce the risk of collisions.

Keywords: Cellular automata · Intersection · Car accidents · Speed limit zone ·
Open boundary

1 Introduction

Traffic problems have attracted a lot of researchers' attentions in many fields, and several
models have been proposed [1–3]. In particular, cellular automata model (CA) is widely
used to simulate traffic due to its simplicity. The first model for studying traffic flow
using CA has been proposed by Cremer and Ludwig [4]. In this model, particles jump
only with one site. Actually, among the most known models that investigate vehicular
traffic, we find Nagel-Schreckenberg (NaSch) model [3]. It is a probabilistic model based
on one-dimensional cellular automata. It contains a path discretized into cells. Also, the
time and speeds are discretized. The updating of cell states is done in a parallel manner
respecting clear rules. In this model, the particles can move with more than one site.
However, this model studies the vehicular traffic only with one kind of vehicles (homogeneous case). After, the impact of heterogeneous of traffic on the flow is studied in the
open and periodic boundaries [19, 23].

© Springer International Publishing Switzerland 2016
S. El Yacoubi et al. (Eds.): ACRI 2016, LNCS 9863, pp. 303–311, 2016.
DOI: 10.1007/978-3-319-44365-2_30

Recently, numerous studies have been carried [5–7]. In real traffic-flow systems the traffic conflict and accidents are frequently induced at intersections. Therefore, the control and the optimization of traffic flux at the intersection are essentially important to solve city traffic problems. The first simple CA model for urban traffic systems was proposed by Biham, Middleton and Levine (BML) [8]. Recently, the control of flow at intersection is widely studied with diverse features; at signalized [9, 10] and non signalized intersection [11, 12], intersection with specific boundary [13], and T-shaped intersection [14]. However, the car accidents at the intersection are seldom studied. The investigation of car accidents is very important because it is associated directly with humane life. Boccara et al. proposed the first conditions for occurrence of car accidents in the NaSch model [15]. Recently, Marzoug et al. [16] studied car accident at the intersection of two roads under periodic boundary conditions.

In fact, we often find speed limit zones in the roads because of the public works, tunnels, etc. In these zones the velocity of cars is reduced to a given value. The impact of speed limit zone on the rear-end collision in the homogeneous traffic is studied in [17, 18].

Our aim in this paper, on the one hand, is to analyze the traffic characteristics and the effects of open boundaries (injecting and extracting rates) on the probability (P_{ac}) of car accidents to occur when vehicles don't respect the priority rules at the intersection (sideswipe crashes). On the other hand, determine the impact of speed limit zone on this type of accidents.

This paper is arranged as follow: we define the model and car accidents conditions in the Sect. 2. Section 3 deals with simulation results and discussion. Section 4 is devoted to a conclusion.

2 Model and Method

2.1 Movement of Vehicles and Heterogeneity of Traffic

We consider two perpendicular roads of length L, which cross in the middle (Fig. 1). In the first road (R1), vehicles move from the top to the bottom. However, in the second road (R2), vehicles move from the left to the right, under open boundary conditions. At the left boundary of each road a particle is injected in the first cell with probability α (injection rate) if it is empty. At the right boundary, the particle is removed with probability β (extracting rate) if $V_i + x_i > L$ (V_i and x_i are the velocity and position of the vehicle, respectively) (Fig. 1).

Each chain is divided on L cell with the same size, where each cell can either occupied by a car or being empty. The intersection cell can be occupied by only one vehicle. Moreover, the time is also discretized. Furthermore, each vehicle can take discrete-valued velocities: 0, 1, 2…V_{max}. Here we consider two types of vehicles; fast vehicles ($V_{max} = V_{f\,max} = 5$) and slow ones ($V_{max} = V_{s\,max} = 1$). F_f and F_s denote the fraction of the fast and slow vehicles, respectively ($F_s = 1 - F_f$).

At each step of time, the vehicle is characterized by its position and its velocity. The new position x_i of a vehicle at the time $t + 1$ can be determined by applying the NS model [3], where all of the vehicle locations are updated in a parallel manner. We note

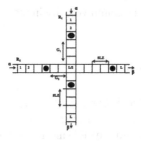

Fig. 1. Scheme of the intersection.

also that the fast vehicles can overtake the slow ones according to the rules proposed in [19], in this paper, the overtaking is certain if the conditions are satisfied.

2.2 Priority Rules and Car Accident Condition

The traffic flow at the intersection of two roads can be controlled via the following rules:

1- Priority is given to the faster car.

2- If both the approaching cars have the same velocity, the priority is given to the nearest car (G_{min}). $G_{1,2}$ is the distance of the vehicle to the intersection cell in the road R1,2.

3- If both the approaching cars have the same distance and they are the same kind (slow-slow or fast-fast), then the priority is given to one road with probability $P = 0.5$.

The car does not have the priority will be decelerates and its velocity is: $V_i = G_{1,2}$.

In fact, some drivers don't respect the priority rules at the intersection. This behavior can cause many traffic conflicts and even car accidents. In this paper we study the probability (P_{ac}) of car accidents to occur when vehicles don't respect the priority rules at the intersection. That means, car accident occur when two cars reach the intersection at the same time: t1 = t2, with $t_{1,2} = G_{1,2}/V_{1,2}$. $t_{1,2}$ is the time necessary for a car on R1,2 to reach the intersection.

If this condition is satisfied, then the accident occurs with a probability p'.

The probability of car accident P_{ac} is defined as follows:

$$P_{ac} = \frac{1}{T} \sum_{t=t_0+1}^{t_0+T} \frac{1}{N} n_i$$

Where;

N: is the total number of vehicles in the system.

t_0: is temporary time.

T: is the statistical time-steps.

If the car accident condition is satisfied, then $n_i = 1$. Otherwise $n_i = 0$. Hence, P_{ac} is the probability for the car accident to occur per time per car.

We consider a region in each road that presents the speed limit zone (SLZ). It is situated at 40 cells after the intersection (Fig. 1), where the velocities of vehicles can't exceed VL. VL represents the maximum velocity in the speed limit zone. The length of this zone is denoted by Lz.

3   Results and Discussion

We consider that both roads R1 and R2 have the same length L = 500 cells. SLZ length is Lz = 40. The system runs for 20000 iterations. The calculation is done for the last 5000 time-steps. We denote the flow of R1 and R2 by J1 and J2 respectively and the total flow of the system by $J_T = (J_1 + J_2)/2$.

Figure 2 illustrates the total flow as a function of injecting rate for several values of β. JT increases for small values of α until it reaches its maximum, and then undergoes a decrease for β < 0.4, after JT remains almost constant.

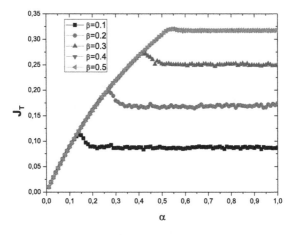

Fig. 2. Total flow as a function of injecting rate for several values of extracting rate. With $F_s = 0.2$ and $L_z = 40$.

For more details we present in Fig. 3 the phase diagram of the system in the space parameter (α, β). The phase diagram is a very important tool that allows us to determine how the system varies depending on the control parameters and study all the states of a system [20, 22].

In comparison with one road where the phase diagram exhibits at maximum three phases [24, 25], in our case, beside the free flow (phase I), jamming phase (phase III) and maximum current (phase IV) the phase diagram exhibits a new phase (phase II) which take place for β < 0.4. Once β exceeds this value, the new phase disappears. Such a phase is characterized by a decreasing of flow from its maximum to the platoon. Moreover, for β ≥ 0.4 the system is in the maximum current phase, here, the flow is not dependent on β, even if we increase the extracting rate, the flow remains the same. Furthermore, the line α = β does not separate the free phase and the jamming phase.

In the following sections, we will focus our study on the probability P_{ac} and the different parameters that can influence it.

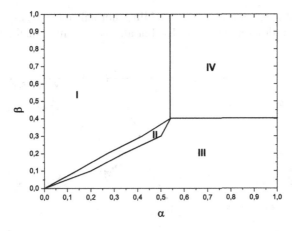

Fig. 3. Phase diagram in the space parameters (α, β). $F_s = 0.2$, and $L_z = 40$.

Figure 4 illustrates that the probability P_{ac} exhibits two maximum for small values of β. The first one is situated at $\alpha \approx \beta$. At this critical point, the flow starts to disrupt because $\alpha \geq \beta$. Indeed, P_{ac} presents three regions as a function of α. In the first region, P_{ac} rises to its first maximum, and then decreases. In the second region, P_{ac} increases with further injection rate α until it reaches the second maximum. In the third region, the car accidents probability remains constant and no longer depends on α.

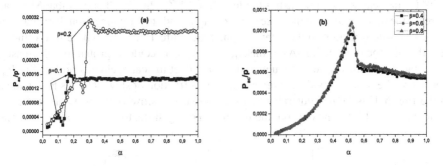

Fig. 4. Car accidents probability as a function of α. (a) for low values of β. (b) for $\beta \geq 0.4$.

Moreover, this figure shows that as the extraction rate β increases, the car accidents probability P_{ac} increased correspondingly and it exhibits only one maximum. When β is high, the flow grows and the number of vehicles that pass through the intersection increase correspondingly, which enhance the risk of collision. However, when β exceeds the value 0.4, the probability P_{ac} presents the same behavior even if we increase β (due to the maximum current).

Another noticeable result of our study shows that the probability P_{ac} depends strongly on the SLZ.

Figure 5 shows the car accidents probability (normalized by p') as a function of the injection rate α for different values of Lz. For all cases we have qualitatively the same behavior.

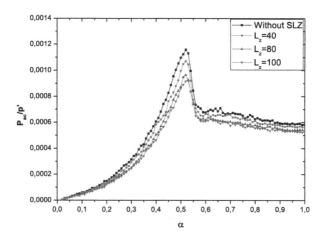

Fig. 5. P_{ac} as a function of α for different values of SLZ length. With β = 0.8 and F_s = 0.2.

In contrast with the rear-end collision [17], the car accident probability in our case (sideswipe crashes) depends strongly on the length of the speed limit zone. The probability P_{ac} decreases with increasing the length of SLZ. This result shows that SLZ can increase the road safety. The increase of SLZ length leads to the congestion. It propagates in the opposite direction to the intersection, which infect this last, where few vehicles pass through the intersection. As a consequence, the car accidents probability decreases.

In fact there are various parameters that can affect the car accidents probability P_{ac}. Therefore, the probability P_{ac} for several values of fraction of slow vehicles F_S is shown in the Fig. 6 This figure illustrates that the increase of slow vehicles enhance the car accidents probability. In addition, the maximum of P_{ac} shifts to the low values of α and

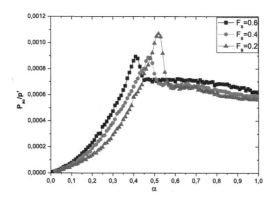

Fig. 6. P_{ac} as a function of α for different values of fraction of slow vehicles. With β = 0.8 and L_z = 40.

it is situated at the transition point from the free flow to the jamming phase. The presence of slow vehicles in the roads obligates fast ones to pile up behind them, which leads to the formation of the waiting queues at the intersection in both roads. Consequently, the conflict between vehicles of R1 and R2 increases.

Until now, we considered that both roads are equiprobable. So, it is very important to know how the priority can affect the car accidents probability at the intersection.

Figure 7 displays a comparison between two cases: in the first one, both roads are equiprobable, however, in the second case, R1 is favored (it always has priority).

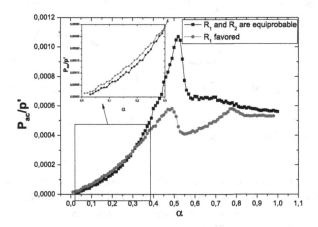

Fig. 7. Effect of priority on the probability P_{ac}. With $\beta = 0.8$, $F_s = 0.2$ and $L_z = 40$.

For the lows values of α, we have the same qualitative behavior in both cases, where P_{ac} increases with increasing α. However, P_{ac} in the second case presents a fluctuation in the region $0.45 < \alpha < 0.8$ and presents two maximums at $\alpha \approx 0.5$ and $\alpha \approx 0.8$, respectively. We note the existence of a critical injection rate $\alpha_c \approx 0.3$ below which, P_{ac} increases when a road is favored. However, above which P_{ac} increases when roads have the same probability of priority. For low values of α there is the formation of waiting queues at the intersection on the road R2 with enough space in from of them, which enhance the conflict between vehicles. However, for high values of α, vehicles are blocked for more time because of the intersection and high density, which decrease the car accidents probability.

This result can give us an idea about how we must control the vehicular traffic at the intersection in order to increase the road safety. When the injection rate is low, both roads must be equiprobable. However, when the number of entering vehicles increases one road must be favored over the other.

For more details, we plotted density profile of each road in both cases (Fig. 8). For low values of α, the priority has no effect on the occupation rate because there are few vehicles on the roads. However, for high value α, the number of vehicles increases and the priority has an important effect. In the second case, the occupation rate of R1 before the intersection decreases, because this road is always favored. However, vehicle on R2 are blocked which increases the occupation rate of this road.

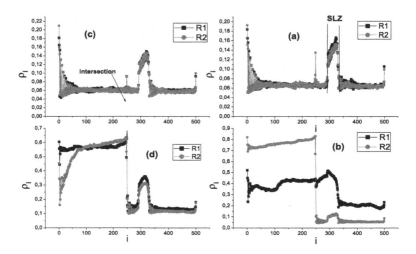

Fig. 8. Density profile as a function of lattice site, (a) R1 is favored and $\alpha = 0.2$. (b) R1 is favored and $\alpha = 0.9$. (c) R1 and R2 are equiprobable and $\alpha = 0.2$. (d) R1 and R2 are equiprobable and $\alpha = 0.9$.

In road R1 a lot of vehicles pass through the intersection and they arrive quickly to the SLZ. That's why the occupation rate increases in this region. However, the occupation rate in R2 is low, because the majority of vehicles are blocked due to the intersection and few vehicles reach SLZ.

4   Conclusion

In summary, we have studied the flow and car accidents probability to occur at the intersection of two roads under open boundary conditions. In our study, we have three defects: two localized defects (intersection and SLZ) and moving defect (slow vehicles). We tried to determine the impact of each defect on the car accidents probability.

Beside the free flow (phase I), jamming phase (phase III) and maximum current (phase IV) the phase diagram exhibits a new phase (phase II) which take place for $\beta < 0.4$. Once β exceeds this value the new phase disappears. Moreover, the probability P_{ac} increases with increasing β and exhibits a maximum at the transition point from the free flow two the congestion phase. However, when β exceeds the value 0.4, the probability P_{ac} not depends on β. Furthermore, simulation results show that the SLZ can improve the road safety, where the probability P_{ac} decreases with increasing length of SLZ. In addition, we found that the heterogeneity of traffic affects also the car accidents probability. Car accidents occur more likely when the number of slow vehicles on the road increases. Likewise, we found that there is a critical injection rate αc, below which both roads must be equiprobable. However, above which, one road must always have priority in order to reduce the risk of collisions.

References

1. Lighthill, M.J., Whitham, G.B.: Proc. Roy. Soc. A **229**, 281 (1955)
2. Daganzo, C.: Transp. Res. B **28**(4) (1994)
3. Nagel, K., Schreckenberg, M.: J. Phys. I (France) **2**, 2221 (1992)
4. Cremer, M.: J. Ludwig. Comput. Simul. **28**, 297 (1986)
5. Bentaleb, K., Lakouari, N., Marzoug, R., Ez-Zahraouy, H., Benyoussef, A.: Phys. A **413**, 473 (2014)
6. Echab, H., Lakouari, N., Ez-Zahraouy, H., Benyoussef, A.: Int. J. Mod. Phys. C **27**, 1650009 (2016)
7. Lakouari, N., Ez-Zahraouy, H., Benyoussef, A.: Phys. Lett. A **378**, 3169 (2014)
8. Biham, O., Middelton, A.A., Levine, D.A.: Phys. Rev. A **46**, R6124 (1992)
9. Belbasi, S., Ebrahim Foulaadvand, M.: J. Stat. Mech. P 07021 (2008)
10. Foulaadvand, M., Belbasi, S.: J. Phys. A: Math. Theor. **44**, 105001 (2011)
11. Foulaadvand, M., Amal, N.: Europhys. Lett. **80**, 60002 (2007)
12. Embley, B., Parmeggiani, A., Kern, N.: Phys. Rev. E **80**, 041128 (2009)
13. Marzoug, R., Ez-Zahraouy, H., Benyoussef, A.: Phys. Scr. **89**, 065002 (2014)
14. Li, X.-G., Gao, Z.-Y., Jia, B., Zhao, X.-M.: Int. J. Mod. Phys. C **20**, 501 (2009)
15. Boccara, N., Fuks, H., Zeng, Q.: J. Phys. A **30**, 3329 (1997)
16. Marzoug, R., Ez-Zahraouy, H., Benyoussef, A.: Int. J. Mod. Phys. C **26**, 1550007 (2015)
17. Zhang, W., Yang, X., Sun, D., Qiu, K., Xia, H.: J. Phys. A: Math. Gen. **39**, 9127 (2006)
18. Li, X., Kuang, H., Fan, Y., Zhang, G.: Int. J. Mod. Phys. C **25**, 1450036 (2014)
19. Ez-Zahraouy, H., Jetto, K., Benyoussef, A.: Chin. J. Phys. **44**, 486 (2006)
20. Helbing, D., Hennecke, A., Treiber, M.: Phys. Rev. Lett. **82**, 4360 (1999)
21. Lee, H.Y., Lee, H.W., Kim, D.: Phys. Rev. E **62**, 4737 (2000)
22. Kerner, B.S., Klenov, S.L., Wolf, D.E.: J. Phys. A: Math. Gen. **35**, 9971 (2002)
23. Ez-Zahraouy, H., Jetto, K., Benyoussef, A.: Eur. Phys. J. B **40**, 111 (2004)
24. Cheybani, S., Kertész, J., Schreckenberg, M.: Phys. Rev. E **63**, 016107 (2000)
25. Cheybani, S., Kertész, J., Schreckenberg, M.: Phys. Rev. E **63**, 016108 (2000)

A Cellular Automata Model with Repulsive Pheromone for Swarm Robotics in Surveillance

Danielli A. Lima[(✉)], Claudiney R. Tinoco, and Gina M.B. Oliveira

Universidade Federal de Uberlândia - Faculdade de Computação,
Av. João Naves de Ávila, 2121 - Santa Mônica, Uberlândia, MG 38408-100, Brazil
{danielli,claudineyrt,gina}@ufu.br

Abstract. This study proposes an inverted ant cellular automata (IACA) model for swarm robots performing the surveillance task. A new distributed coordination strategy is described here, which was designed with a cellular automata-based modeling and using a repulsive pheromone-based search. The environmental structure is well-known to all robots and their current positions are shared by the team. Besides, they communicate indirectly through the repulsive pheromone, which is available to each robot as an information about its neighborhood. The pheromone is deposited at each time step by each robot, over its current position and neighborhood cells. The pheromone is also evaporated as the time goes by. All next movement decisions are stochastic giving a non-deterministic characteristic to the model. Simulation results are presented, by applying the proposed model to different environmental conditions.

Keywords: Cellular automata · Ants · Swarm robots · Surveillance

1 Introduction

Each member of a multi-agent system must be capable to achieve its objectives autonomously adapting it-self to environmental changes. An intelligent global behavior is desirable, which can be generated by modeling each individual agent of the system and the interactions among them [1]. It is well-known that a distributed and coordinated behavior can emerge from individual interactions in complex systems. In this context, there are several works that have investigated the application of cellular automata-based models to swarm robotics [2,3]. Swarm systems are characterized by a global dynamics reflecting some synergy among the swarm members [4]. Swarm robotics models that mimic the natural collective behavior have being recently investigated, such as the pheromone interaction employed by ants colonies (ACO) [1] and the communication between glows-worms lights [5]. In this context, some works use a combination of cellular automata (CA) and ACO [6] and others use IAS (Inverted Ant System) [7]. The IAS [7] is a technique based on the biological ants behavior that uses the indirect global communication denominated stigmergy. Unlike ACO [8], that provides a

© Springer International Publishing Switzerland 2016
S. El Yacoubi et al. (Eds.): ACRI 2016, LNCS 9863, pp. 312–322, 2016.
DOI: 10.1007/978-3-319-44365-2_31

chemical attraction between agents through the pheromone interaction, an opposite behavior emerges in IAS since it employs a repulsive pheromone type. This kind of pheromone is also observed in natural ants and it is used to indicate risk or danger. Stigmergy is considered one of the factors that decisively contributes to enlarge the capabilities of a single ant. Colonies use the stigmergy to coordinate their activities in a distributed way [9]. There are many coordinating tasks being investigated in swarm robotics, such as, foraging [10], search and rescue [11]. Another relevant task in robotics is surveillance [12], which consists in monitoring the behavior, the activities, or other environmental changing information, protecting people or objects [7,13,14]. Surveillance involves environmental exploration and the area must be covered by the robots. Therefore, the swarm uses cooperation and communication strategies to cover the environment, in a reasonable period of time.

In the present work, a navigation model called IACA based on cellular automata modeling and inverted ant pheromone communication was proposed for robots performing the surveillance task. The environment is modeled by a lattice of square cells composed by two layers. Simulations were carried out to evaluate the model in different situations and environments. They were made to (i) measure the time taken by the robots team to perform the surveillance task; (ii) analyze the evaporation process; (iii) analyze the coverage and exploration. By simulation results it was possible to observe that the resultant behavior returns an efficient task execution and the inverted pheromone employment causes scattered paths with low or none collisions.

2   Model Description

Initially, a two-dimensional map representing the environment is constructed. It is divided in square cells and the resultant lattice has two layers. The first layer is the pheromone lattice where the cell's pheromone amount is stored. A continues state is assigned to each cell of the pheromone lattice. The state value is between 0 and τ_{max} for the non-wall cells cells. Additionally, a value representing ∞ is assigned for all wall cells. The second layer is the physical lattice, in which the current robots' positions and the walls cells are represented. A discrete state is assigned to each cell of the physical grid. There are three possible values: free, wall and robot. Figures 1(a) and (b) show two examples of physical grids, where the walls cells are represented in gray, the free cells are represented in white and the cells with red circles represent the current robots' positions. One robot in the grid cannot overlaps another or a wall cell. The pheromone layer relative to the environment E_2 is shown in Fig. 1(c).

The IACA model is divided in two levels: one is related to the individual robot's behavior and the other is related to the team's global behavior. The team's behavior is related to robot-robot and environment-robot interactions.

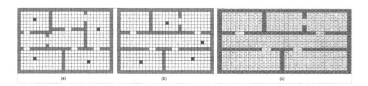

Fig. 1. Rooms 20×30 size. (a) Environment E_1 with 7 rooms. (b) Environment E_2 with 6 rooms. Four robots are represented in red in each environment and they are performing the surveillance task. (c) Pheromone grid. (Color figure online)

2.1 Individual Behavior

The behavior model of each robot can be described by a four finite state machine (FSM), as shown in Fig. 2. In IACA model, the robots start their movements at time step 0 and the task is finished (when the robots stop their movements) after a predefined number of time steps (T).

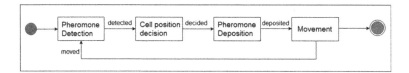

Fig. 2. Individual behavior represented by a finite state machine adapted from [7].

The **pheromone detection** state in the FSM represents the robot's pheromone reading process. The current amount of pheromone in each cell x_{ij} is a resultant from the previous pheromone deposition due to robots' steps followed by an evaporation process. This reading comprises the Moore neighborhood cells considering the robot's vision radius r_v. The robot access all the neighborhood pheromone values x_{ij}, which size is defined as $m = (2r_v + 1)^2$. The robot access the x_{ij} values from its neighborhood cells to make the next movement decision.

The **decision process** is represented by the next cell choice, which will drive the next robot's movement. This choice is based on the amount of the repulsive pheromone deposited in the neighborhood cells. The amount of pheromone in a determined cell x_{ij} will define the probability $P(x_{ij})$ of this cell to be chosen in the next time step. If the pheromone amount is big, then the probability is low. On the other hand, if the cell has a small amount of pheromone, it has a high probability to be chosen. The total pheromone deposited in the neighborhood cells as a whole is given by $\rho_{max}^t = \sum_{k=1}^{m} x_{ij}^t$. Equation 1 shows the function used to determine the probability of each cell x_{ij} of the current neighborhood to be the next robot position in the time step $t + 1$. Using this equation, a stochastic choice is made to decide the next position.

$$P(x_{ij})^{t+1} = \frac{\rho_{max}^t - x_{ij}^t}{\sum_{k=1}^{m} \rho_{max}^t - x_{ij}^t} \tag{1}$$

Each robot deposits pheromone over its current and neighborhood cells, to signalize its presence to the other members of the swarm. The **pheromone deposition** state in the FSM represents the process in which the robot increases the amount of pheromone over its current position x_{ij} and in the corresponding neighborhood cells $x_{(i+a)(j+b)}$, where $-r_v \leq a < 2 \times r_v$ and $-r_v \leq b < 2 \times r_v$. If a neighborhood cell is a wall, then the pheromone is not deposited. There is a maximum amount of pheromone $\tau_{\max}$ that each cell can receive, avoiding an uncontrolled growth of pheromone. Equation 2 represents the amount of pheromone deposited in one time step. The constants δ and σ represents, respectively, the pheromone rate and the dispersion rate.

$$\rho_{ij}^{t+1} = \delta \times e^{-\frac{x_{ij} - x_{(i+a)(j+b)}}{\sigma r_v{}^2}} \tag{2}$$

The pheromone updating is computed by Eq. 3:

$$x_{ij}^{t+1} = x_{ij}^t + (\tau_{\max} - x_{ij}^t) \times \rho_{ij}^{t+1} \tag{3}$$

By analyzing Eqs. 2 and 3, one can observe that in a first visit to a cell with no pheromone the robot deposits the maximum amount of pheromone $\tau_{\max}$ multiplied by the δ constant before its departure. However, in the next time steps, this value will be continuously evaporated until a robot crosses the cell's neighborhood again. On the other hand, the robot deposits an attenuated amount of pheromone ($<< \tau_{\max}$ and given by σ parameter) over its neighborhood, which will be also submitted to an evaporation process in the next time.

The **movement** state is the FSM is the final step that represents the robot's transition from one cell x_{ij} to another $x_{(i+a)(j+b)}$ in the robot neighborhood. This action will be accomplished by the robots' individual control, which is responsible to decide how to control robot's components to make the desired step.

The CA model investigated here is not standard since the transition rule changes the state of two cells of the neighborhood. This transition starts with a stochastic local rule which taking in account the pheromone amount in each cell of the robot neighborhood. Each robot movement corresponds to change its current position to an adjacent cell. Besides that, the CA modifies the neighborhood cells updating the pheromone amount. Finally, the cell occupied by the robot becomes free, and the free neighborhood's cell chosen by the stochastic rule as its next position, becomes the new robot's position.

2.2   Global Behavior

The global behavior comprehends two processes: the first is the evaporation process and the second represents the interaction between the robots and the environment. The pheromone **evaporation** is a global process performed in all the cells of the environment (except the wall cells) at the end of each time step t according to a constant β. The evaporation process is represented by Eq. 4. In the first time step ($t = 0$), each cell x_{ij} receives a pheromone amount equal to 0.

In the subsequent time steps, each cell visited by a robot or in its neighborhood has its pheromone increased according to Eqs. 2 and 3. Besides, all the non-wall cells in the environment having a pheromone different from zero have their values decreased by a β constant as in Eq. 4.

$$x_{ij}^{t+1} = x_{ij}^t - (\beta \times x_{ij}^t) \tag{4}$$

Each robot tries to move to a cell of its neighborhood defined by its vision radius r_v. The employment of the inverted pheromone - and its inherit repulsive force [15] - to guide robot's movements returns trajectories almost-free of conflicts due to the robots spreading effect. However, specific conflict cases are solved by a random decision process: if two robots try to move into the same cell, a random choice decides which robot that will perform the movement, while the loser has to wait until the next time step. The conflicts avoidance between a robot and a wall is solved using a high value of pheromone, in this case, $\rho = \infty$.

From these interactions between the robots and the environment (pheromone dynamics), and between the robots themselves (collision avoidance), emerges a complex behavior that makes the swarm of robots able to efficiently solve the surveillance task. These interactions produce a robot-robot repulsion and prevent collisions, improving the exploration and increasing the covered area.

3   Experiments

The experiments presented in this section were carried out using virtual environments implemented in C language aiming to: (i) evaluate different evaporation rates, (ii) evaluate different team size N to perform the task, (iii) evaluate the team performance related to the environment coverage, (iv) evaluate the team performance in the surveillance task. All the simulation experiments were conducted in 20×30 cells lattice environments, each cell was defined as a 14×14 cm square. This size is sufficiently large to accommodate a robot inside the cell, since the robot size was adopted according to a real e-puck dimension: a circular robot with 7 cm of diameter. This configuration results in a 2.8×4.2 m environment, which is adequate to analyze the performance of a e-pucks' team performing surveillance. Figure 1 presents the two lattice environments used to conduct the experiments. All the simulations were carried out using the following parameters: $T = 1000$ steps, $\sigma = 0.43$, $r_v = 1$, $\delta = 0.7$ and $\tau_{max} = 50$, values were defined by preliminar experiments with the model and they were adjusted based on the adaptation of the values proposed for a continuous model in [13].

The first experiment was conducted to refine the evaporation rate corresponding to the β constant in Eq. 4, which was varied using six different values: {0.001, 0.005, 0.01, 0.05, 0.1, 0.2}. It was accomplished using the E_1 environment. The number of iterations was $T = 1000$ and $N = 3$ robots were used. The amount of pheromone from each cell x_{ij} was captured in the step $T = 1000$ for each β variation. Figure 3 shows the temperature graphics for the six β variations. The red cells have high pheromone levels, while the dark blue cells have low or null pheromone levels. It is important to note that each graphic has a different color scale, because the highest temperature (dark red color) depends on the maximum pheromone level (θ_{max}) found at the end of the simulation. It is possible to observe in Fig. 3(a) that final lattice does not have a significant variation on x_{ij} value, because all the cells have high pheromone levels (red and orange cells), except for the blue cells corresponding to the environment walls. This situation is not adequate for a good coverage strategy because it turns the movement choice a random process, since the cells have almost the same probability to be chosen, not taking account the cells previously visited by the swarm. The best evaporation rates were those used in the simulations related to Fig. 3(b) and (c) ($\beta = 0.005$ and $\beta = 0.01$), because the cells have a good variability in the color scales. It represents that the robot can choose a cell in its neighborhood using the pheromone information. The higher evaporation rates were used in Fig. 3(d), (e) and (f). It is possible to conclude that they are not appropriate, because of the large number of dark blue regions. This absence of pheromone information affects the task conclusion and the robot decision movement is a random choice.

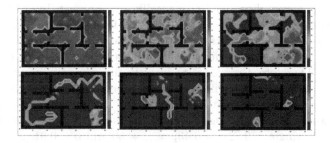

Fig. 3. Maps of amount of pheromone according to different evaporation rates (a) $\beta = 0.001$ and $\theta_{max} = 50$. (b) $\beta = 0.005$ and $\theta_{max} = 46$. (c) $\beta = 0.01$ and $\theta_{max} = 45$. (d) $\beta = 0.05$ and $\theta_{max} = 40$. (e) $\beta = 0.1$ and $\theta_{max} = 35$. (f) $\beta = 0.2$ and $\theta_{max} = 35$. (Color figure online)

A second analysis was conducted using $N = 3$ robots to verify the environment coverage employing the same β variation used in the first experiment. The number of times each cell x_{ij} have been visited during 1000 time steps was computed in each simulation. These values were used to construct temperature graphics, in which a high number of dark blues cells represents a simulation with low coverage, indicating a poor surveillance performance. Figure 4 shows that robots made good environmental coverage for almost all β values. The simulation $\beta = 0.2$ returned the worst performance, due to one room was overloaded with robots visits, while other rooms were missing visits. It is also possible to observe in $\beta = 0.05$ and $\beta = 0.1$ simulations that there are several blue points inside some individual rooms, indicating that some positions were never or few times visited by the robots. Therefore, considering both pheromone (Fig. 3) and coverage (Fig. 4) analyses we conclude that $\beta = 0.005$ and $\beta = 0.01$ evaporation rates leads the team to the best behaviors.

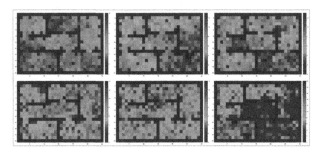

Fig. 4. Maps of cell steps according to different evaporation rates (a) $\beta = 0.001$ and $s_{max} = 12$. (b) $\beta = 0.005$ and $s_{max} = 16$. (c) $\beta = 0.01$ and $s_{max} = 16$. (d) $\beta = 0.05$ and $s_{max} = 14$. (e) $\beta = 0.1$ and $s_{max} = 14$. (f) $\beta = 0.2$ and $s_{max} = 20$, using $N = 3$, $T = 1000$ and $\sigma = 0.43r_v$. (Color figure online)

The appropriate team size N to perform the task is an important feature to be considered in a swarm of robots for an specific environment. In order to analyze this characteristic, the team size was varied using four different values $N = \{1, 2, 3, 4\}$ and they were used to perform the surveillance for E_2 environment. Since there are 7 rooms in this environment, the task could be solved putting one robot in each room. Therefore, the goal is to identify the minimum number of robots in the team to solve this task with a reasonable performance, that is, each room needs to be checked by at least one robot after a short interval of time. The experiment was conducted using $T = 1000$ steps and $\beta = 0.01$. By inspecting Eqs. 2, 3 and 4 using $\delta = 0.7$, $\sigma = 0.43$, $\tau_{max} = 50$ and $\beta = 0.01$, it was possible to conclude that after a cell is visited and a pheromone is deposited on it, and it takes at least 100 time steps to be almost evaporated (considering the case that no robot returns to this position to reinforce the pheromone trace). Therefore, if a dark blue cell is found at time $T = 1000$, it means that this position has not been visited by any robot for at least 100 time units. Figure 5 shows the pheromone in each cell x_{ij} after $T = 1000$ steps. Figure 5(a) shows the result of the first experiment performed with just one robot ($N = 1$). It was possible to note that 4 rooms were not recently visited, since they just have dark blue cells. It represents that a unique robot is not able to perform this task alone. Figure 5(b) shows the resultant pheromone temperature graphic using 2 robots in the team. Although it was possible to observe at least one cell in each room with a different color, it is still possible to observe a lot of dark blue cells in each room, meaning that a large portion of these rooms were not recently visited, embarrassing the surveillance task. Therefore, 2 robots is still not enough to complete the task. Starting from 3 robots (Fig. 5(c) and (d)), it is possible to notice that the team performance is good. Although we have 1 room in Fig. 5(c) with a great number of dark blue cells, this same room has a hot region indicating that a robot was inside it at time $T = 1000$ and this region was started to be coverage again. Figure 5(d) indicates that all rooms received a good recent exploration but as the previous analysis suggested we can considered a waste of resources to use

Fig. 5. Maps of pheromone amount according to the number of robots (a) $N = 1$ and $\theta_{max} = 46$. (b) $N = 2$ and $\theta_{max} = 45$. (c) $N = 3$ and $\theta_{max} = 45$. (d) $N = 4$ and $\theta_{max} = 46$. (Color figure online)

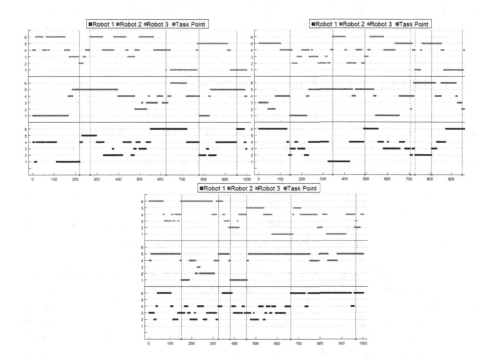

Fig. 6. The IACA performance according to different evaporation rates (a) $\beta = 0.001$. (b) $\beta = 0.01$. (c) $\beta = 0.1$. (Color figure online)

4 robots. Finally, we conclude that the appropriate team size for this environment configuration uses 3 robots.

A final experiment was carried out to deeper analyze the team performance by registering the number of visits in each room during the 1000 time steps. Figure 6 exhibits three graphics summarizing the simulation conducted using room E_2, each one corresponding to a different evaporation rate $\beta = \{0.001, 0.01, 0.1\}$. The graphics were elaborated registering the current localization of each robot at each time step. The y-axis represents the rooms and the x-axis represents iterations. Each red vertical line indicates that one cycle of the surveillance was completed, that is, the iteration when the robots cooperatively visited all the 6 rooms. Each robot is initialized in a different room. The graphics show that IACA system with $\beta = 0.001$ is able to conclude the first cycle of surveillance at the iteration 219. In the simulations using $\beta = 0.01$ and $\beta = 0.1$ the IACA system executes more efficiently the task concluding the first cycle at the iterations 145 and 152, respectively. Moreover, İACA system with $\beta = 0.001$ concludes 5 cycles of the surveillance task, considering all the 1000 steps of simulation. On the other hand, using $\beta = 0.01$ and $\beta = 0.1$, the number of cycles concluded is increased to 7 and 6, respectively. This result corroborates that the pheromone evaporation rate is an important parameter of the model to induce a better swarm performance. Considering the β values evaluated and using 3 robots to explore the environment E_2, the best performance was achieved using $\beta = 0.01$.

4   Conclusions and Further Comments

This work proposes and investigates a new control model for swarms of robots based on two-dimensional cellular automata and inverted pheromone dynamics called IACA. Our model is dedicated to the surveillance task, which is very relevant to collective robotics due to [14] (i) it is included in a broad class of robotics problems; (ii) surveillance is largely used for the study of robot-robot cooperation, (iii) many real-world applications for robotics are samples of surveillance robots.

The major characteristics of IACA model are: (i) the environment is modeled as a cellular automata lattice formed by identical square cells; (ii) each robot is controlled by an individual finite state machine that switches over a 4-state cycle; (iii) each time a robot passes a cell while exploring, it leaves a trace in the environment, being that the repulsive pheromone is deposited in the current cell but also in the adjacent ones (in a attenuated value); (iv) the pheromone is submitted to an evaporation process aiming to enable visited cells to be checked again after some time delay, (v) the vision ability is considered in a such way that the robot is able to identify a pheromone trace inside its vision radius; (vi) the next step choice is stochastic and based on a probability which is inversely proportional to the pheromone amount of the neighborhood cells; (vii) the pheromone dynamics allows almost-free collisions trajectories; (viii) the robot-robot conflict avoidance are treated in a non-deterministic way.

Using simulations on virtual environments it was possible to evaluate the IACA model in terms of coverage performance, exploration analysis and the best evaporation rate. It was possible to conclude that the proposed model is adequate to control a team of robots for surveillance returning an efficient performance in this task. For a better utilization of this model, it is possible to refine its parameters according to robots and environment's specifications.

A forthcoming work is about the implementation of this model using simulation platforms with real-world robotic architectures, allowing a more realistic analysis of the model. We have already started this investigation and some new relevant issues have appeared related to the need of synchronization and the model dependency on the accuracy of the localization and orientation of robots. In a future investigation we intend to identify the common behavior returned by the proposed model, independently from the parameters values adopted.

Aknowledgments. GMBO thanks to CAPES, CNPq and Fapemig.

References

1. Kıran, M.S., Gündüz, M., Baykan, Ö.K.: A novel hybrid algorithm based on particle swarm and ant colony optimization for finding the global minimum. Appl. Math. Comput. **219**(4), 1515–1521 (2012)
2. Ferreira, G.B.S., Vargas, P.A., Oliveira, G.M.B.: An improved cellular automata-based model for robot path-planning. In: Mistry, M., Leonardis, A., Witkowski, M., Melhuish, C. (eds.) TAROS 2014. LNCS, vol. 8717, pp. 25–36. Springer, Heidelberg (2014)
3. Behring, C., Bracho, M., Castro, M., Moreno, J.: An algorithm for robot path planning with cellular automata. In: Bandini, S., Worsch, T. (eds.) Theory and Practical Issues on Cellular Automata, pp. 11–19. Springer, Heidelberg (2001)
4. Biswas, S., Das, S., Debchoudhury, S., Kundu, S.: Co-evolving bee colonies by forager migration: a multi-swarm based Artificial Bee Colony algorithm for global search space. Appl. Math. Comput. **232**, 216–234 (2014)
5. Quang, N.N., Sanseverino, E.R., Di Silvestre, M.L., Madonia, A., Li, C., Guerrero, J.M.: Optimal power flow based on glow worm-swarm optimization for three-phase islanded microgrids. In: AEIT Annual Conference-From Research to Industry, pp. 1–6. IEEE (2014)
6. Ioannidis, K., Sirakoulis, G.C., Andreadis, I.: Cellular ants: a method to create collision free trajectories for a cooperative robot team. Rob. Auton. Syst. **59**(2), 113–127 (2011)
7. Calvo, R., de Oliveira, J.R., Figueiredo, M., Romero, R.A.F.: Bio-inspired coordination of multiple robots systems, stigmergy mechanims to cooperative exploration, surveillance tasks. In: 2011 IEEE 5th International Conference on Cybernetics and Intelligent Systems (CIS), pp. 223–228. IEEE (2011)
8. Dorigo, M., Birattari, M., Blum, C., Clerc, M., Stützle, T., Winfield, A. (eds.): Ant Colony Optimization and Swarm Intelligence, vol. 5217. Springer, Heidelberg (2008)
9. Yingying, D., Yan, H., Jingping, J.: Multi-robot cooperation method based on the ant algorithm. In: Proceedings of the 2003 IEEE on Swarm Intelligence Symposium, SIS 2003, pp. 14–18. IEEE (2003)
10. Castello, E., Yamamoto, T., Libera, F.D., Liu, W., Winfield, A.F., Nakamura, Y., Ishiguro, H.: Adaptive foraging for simulated, real robotic swarms: the dynamical response threshold approach. Swarm Intell. **10**(1), 1–31 (2016)
11. Kantor, G., Singh, S., Peterson, R., Rus, D., Das, A., Kumar, V., Pereira, G., Spletzer, J.: Distributed search, rescue with robot, sensor teams. In: Yuta, S., Asama, H., Prassler, E., Tsubouchi, T., Thrun, S. (eds.) Field and Service Robotics, pp. 529–538. Springer, Heidelberg (2006)
12. Saska, M., Vakula, J., Preucil, L.: Swarms of micro aerial vehicles stabilized under a visual relative localization. In: 2014 IEEE International Conference on Robotics and Automation (ICRA), pp. 3570–3575. IEEE (2014)

13. Calvo, R., de Oliveira, J.R., Romero, R.A., Figueiredo, M.: A bioinspired coordination strategy for controlling of multiple robots in surveillance tasks. Int. J. Adv. Softw. **5**(3 & 4), 146–165 (2012)
14. Falleiros, E.L.S., Calvo, R., Ishii, R.P.: PheroSLAM: a collaborative and bioinspired multi-agent system based on monocular vision. In: Gervasi, O., Murgante, B., Misra, S., Gavrilova, M.L., Rocha, A.M.A.C., Torre, C., Taniar, D., Apduhan, B.O. (eds.) ICCSA 2015. LNCS, vol. 9156, pp. 71–85. Springer, Heidelberg (2015)
15. Wei-Guo, S., Yan-Fei, Y., Bing-Hong, W., Wei-Cheng, F.: Evacuation behaviors at exit in CA model with force essentials: a comparison with social force model. Physica A: Stat. Mech. Appl. **371**(2), 658–666 (2006)

Neuro-Radiosurgery Treatments: MRI Brain Tumor Seeded Image Segmentation Based on a Cellular Automata Model

Leonardo Rundo[1,2(✉)], Carmelo Militello[2], Giorgio Russo[2,3,4],
Pietro Pisciotta[2,4,5], Lucia Maria Valastro[3,4],
Maria Gabriella Sabini[3,4], Salvatore Vitabile[6], Maria Carla Gilardi[2],
and Giancarlo Mauri[1]

[1] Dipartimento di Informatica, Sistemistica e Comunicazione (DISCo),
Università degli Studi di Milano-Bicocca, Milan, Italy
leonardo.rundo@disco.unimib.it
[2] Istituto di Bioimmagini e Fisiologia Molecolare - Consiglio Nazionale
delle Ricerche (IBFM-CNR), Cefalù, PA, Italy
[3] UOS di Fisica Sanitaria, Azienda Ospedaliera per l'Emergenza Cannizzaro,
Catania, Italy
[4] Laboratori Nazionali del Sud (LNS),
Istituto Nazionale di Fisica Nucleare (INFN), Catania, Italy
[5] Università degli Studi di Catania, Catania, Italy
[6] Dipartimento di Biopatologia d Biotecnologie Mediche (DIBIMED),
Università degli Studi di Palermo, Palermo, Italy

Abstract. Gross Tumor Volume (GTV) segmentation on medical images is an open issue in neuro-radiosurgery. Magnetic Resonance Imaging (MRI) is the most prominent modality in radiation therapy for soft-tissue anatomical districts. Gamma Knife stereotactic neuro-radiosurgery is a mini-invasive technique used to deal with inaccessible or insufficiently treated tumors. During the planning phase, the GTV is usually contoured by radiation oncologists using a manual segmentation procedure on MR images. This methodology is certainly time-consuming and operator-dependent. Delineation result repeatability, in terms of both intra- and inter-operator reliability, is only obtained by using computer-assisted approaches. In this paper a novel semi-automatic segmentation method, based on Cellular Automata, is proposed. The developed approach allows for the GTV segmentation and computes the lesion volume to be treated. The method was evaluated on 10 brain cancers, using both area-based and distance-based metrics.

Keywords: Gamma Knife treatments · MR imaging · Brain tumors · Cellular Automata · Semi-automatic segmentation

1 Introduction

Target volume segmentation is still a challenging and open issue in neuro-radiosurgery. Gross Tumor Volume (*GTV*) is usually delineated on morphologic medical images (i.e. Computed Tomography or Magnetic Resonance Imaging) by means of a fully

© Springer International Publishing Switzerland 2016
S. El Yacoubi et al. (Eds.): ACRI 2016, LNCS 9863, pp. 323–333, 2016.
DOI: 10.1007/978-3-319-44365-2_32

manual procedure in the clinical practice, since current Treatment Planning Systems (TPS) do not implement automatic or semi-automatic segmentation tools. Of course, this procedure is time consuming, because dozens of slices have to be manually contoured by radiation oncologists. However the primary issue that affects manual segmentation tasks is operator-dependency. The repeatability of the lesion boundaries delineation may be ensured only by using automatic/semi-automatic methods, supporting the clinicians in the segmentation task. This improves the assessment of the treatment response during patient follow-up and cancer staging. As demonstrated in [1], semi-automated approaches provide more reproducible measurements compared to conventional manual tracing, in terms of both intra- and inter-operator reliability.

MRI is emerging as the most important imaging modality in radiation therapy for soft-tissue anatomical districts, complementing the use of CT in target delineation. MRI provides several advantages over CT, including high quality detailed images and excellent soft-tissue contrast, especially concerning the extent of brain cancer [2]. In particular, brain MRI provides high quality images revealing detailed information concerning the extent of abnormalities, showing thus a great potential in radiotherapy planning of brain tumors [3].

Leksell Gamma Knife® (Elekta, Stockholm, Sweden) is a device for stereotactic mini-invasive neuro-radiosurgery to deal with untreatable brain diseases for traditional surgery or radiotherapy, such as inaccessible benign or malignant tumors, arteriovenous malformations, and trigeminal neuralgia [4]. This technology employs radioactive beams which are focused on the planned *GTV* through a metal helmet. Time constraints are crucial in neuro-radiosurgery treatment planning. Especially, in Gamma Knife treatments a neurosurgeon installs a stereotactic head frame on the patient, under local sedation, just before MRI acquisition for the forthcoming treatment planning phase. In this way, head movement during imaging and treatment execution is kept under control and the target areas can be accurately localized. After a personalized radiation plan using the Leksell Gamma Plan® TPS, the head frame is locked onto the Gamma Knife metal helmet and the actual treatment will be immediately executed.

In this paper a novel semi-automatic segmentation method, based on a pure *Cellular Automata (CA)* model, is proposed. This approach allows for the target segmentation and automatically calculates the lesion volume to be treated with stereotactic neuro-radiosurgery. To evaluate the effectiveness of the proposed approach, initial MR image segmentation tests, using both area-based and distance-based metrics, were performed on 10 brain cancers undergone Leksell Gamma Knife. Despite CyberKnife® (Accuray Inc., Sunnyvale, CA) is an alternative neuro-radiosurgery system that uses different technologies and allows to treat several anatomical districts, the presented work is equally valid for CyberKnife treatment delivery for brain tumors.

This manuscript is organized as follows: Sect. 2 introduces an overview of brain lesion segmentation on MR images; Sect. 3 describes the proposed segmentation method; Sect. 4 depicts the experimental results obtained in the segmentation tests; finally, conclusive remarks and future developments are provided in Sect. 5.

2 Background

An overview of the literature works regarding MRI brain lesion segmentation in radiation therapy scenarios is presented. In [5] a localized region-based active semi-automatic contouring method, using *Level Set functions* [6], was applied on brain MRI to obtain clinical target volumes. Analogously, a semi-automatic approach using *Hybrid Level Sets (HLS)* was presented in [7], in which the segmentation is simultaneously driven by region and boundary information.

Machine Learning techniques were often exploited. The authors of [8] evaluated two fully automated brain MRI tumor segmentation approaches: supervised *k-Nearest Neighbors (kNN)* and automatic *Knowledge-Guided (KG)* methods. *kNN* achieved slightly better results than *KG*. A similar approach based on *Support Vector Machine (SVM)* discriminative classification was proposed in [9]. In supervised learning, however, a training phase is mandatory. Hall et al. [10] extensively compared literal and approximate *Fuzzy C-Means* unsupervised clustering algorithms, and a supervised *computational Neural Network*, in brain MRI segmentation. This study suggested comparable experimental results between supervised and unsupervised learning.

Considering this experimental finding, our group has already proposed a MR brain *GTV* segmentation approach, based on unsupervised *Fuzzy C-Means Clustering (FCM)* for Gamma Knife treatment support [11, 12]. Nevertheless the method is inevitably semi-automatic, operator-dependence is reduced because user intervention is limited to the selection of a bounding region containing the tumor zone and no parameter setup is required. Since sometimes either edema or necrosis could be present in some lesions, which must be included into the planned target volume in radiotherapy clinical practice, some morphological refinements are required.

An interesting work by Hamamci et al. [13] presented a semi-automatic segmentation tool, called "Tumor-Cut" for brain tumors segmentation for radiosurgery applications, especially in Cyberknife® radiosurgery treatments. A method based on *Cellular Automata (CA)* is used on input contrast enhanced T1-weighted MR images. First, the iterative *CA* framework solves the shortest path problem. Then, an implicit *Level Set* surface is evolved on a tumor probability map, which combines tumor and background strengths obtained separately by two independent *CA* algorithm executions. User interaction consists in drawing the maximum diameter of the tumor on the corresponding axial slice.

3 Materials and Methods

In this section, first MRI data concerning the subjects enrolled in this study are reported, and then a novel semi-automatic tumor segmentation approach on brain MRI axial slices concerning Gamma Knife patients is presented.

The proposed method results in a simple but effective application based merely on *Cellular Automata* model, by initializing adaptively foreground and background seeds in a smart fashion.

3.1   Brain Cancer Dataset Description

The study was performed on a real dataset composed of 10 brain metastatic lesions concerning patients undergone neuro-radiosurgery. All available MRI series were acquired on the Gyroscan Intera 1.5T MR Scanner (Philips Medical System, Eindhoven, the Netherlands), a few hours before the Gamma Knife treatment and then utilized for the planning phase. MR images were "T1w FFE" (T1-weighted Fast Field Echo) contrast-enhanced sequences. Two different instances of input MR images are shown in Fig. 1.

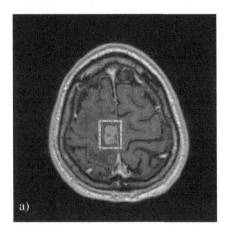 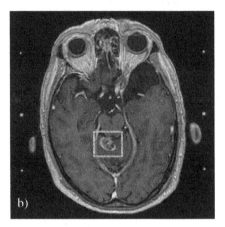

Fig. 1. Examples of input MR axial slices with the rectangular bounding area, selected by the user, containing the lesion: (a) heterogeneous tumor; (b) tumor with necrosis (dark core)

3.2   The Proposed Segmentation Approach

Since the region connectedness is ensured by *CA*, segmentation results are represented by connected-regions with unbroken edges even if necroses or cysts are present. This fact is very important in radiation therapy treatment planning, since tumor delineation is a critical step that must be performed accurately and effectively. Moreover, since in cancer imaging we are dealing with non-uniform intensity distributions, local image statistics should be used instead of global image statistics [5]. *CA* model is very suitable due to its own local update rules.

The user has just to select a bounding area containing the tumor zone and no parameter setup is required (see Fig. 1). Operator-dependence is thus minimized by reducing the degree of user interaction. We chose a draggable rectangular tool, because it is very simple Region of Interest (ROI) selection tool [14].

A detailed flow diagram of the overall segmentation method is shown in Fig. 2. In the following, the various processing steps are described.

Pre-processing. Masked input images, after the bounding region selection accomplished by the user, are pre-processed in order to improve the segmentation process. The range of intensity values of the selected part is expanded to enhance the *GTV* extraction.

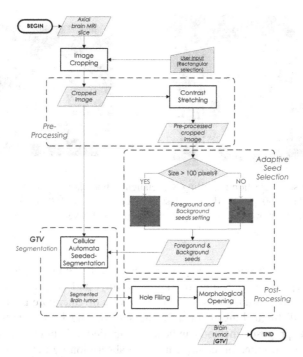

Fig. 2. Flow diagram of the proposed brain tumor *GTV* segmentation method. The pipeline can be divided in four main stages: (i) pre-processing to improve the segmentation process; (ii) adaptive seed selection to choose suitable foreground and background seed pixels; (iii) *GTV* segmentation using a *CA* model; (iv) post-processing to refine the achieved segmentation results

The input intensity values are linearly stretched into the double-precision full dynamic range $[0, 1]$.

Adaptive Seed Selection. A strategy for the choice of both the foreground (tumor) and background seeds was designed ad hoc. Especially, according to the flow diagram in Fig. 2, seed selection depends only on the size of the image cropped by the operator and then it is fully automatic. Since also very small regions could be present (approximately 5 mm diameter), such as in initial and final tumor slices, a discrimination based on the dragged area is necessary:

- If its size is greater than 100 pixels, nine foreground pixels in the central zone and eight background pixels at the border of the cropped image are selected (Fig. 3a), to provide significant samples for the *CA* algorithm inizialization;
- Otherwise, to avoid the access to pixels outside the cropped image, only five foreground pixels in the central zone and four background pixels at the corners are selected (Fig. 3b).

Foreground tumor seed-points are set according to the center coordinates of the cropped image, hence the only trivial requirement for the operator is that the rectangular bounding region must be centered on the tumor. This strategy implements a highly robust seed selection procedure.

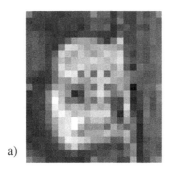
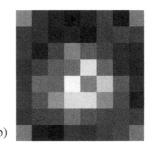

a)   b)

Fig. 3. Adaptive seed selection according to rectangular boundary region dragged by the user: (a) size greater than 100 pixels; (b) size less than or equals to 100 pixels. Foreground and background seeds are shown using transparent blue and red pixels, respectively (Color figure online)

GTV Segmentation. A two labeled *CA* segmentation is the most efficient schema for classifying a hyper-intense lesion from the healthy part of the brain. In fact, in contrast-enhanced MR brain scans, metastases have a brighter core than periphery and distinct borders distinguishing them from the surrounding healthy brain tissue [15]. Nevertheless, the proposed method can be safely applied to both benign and malignant brain tumors, since it relies on contrast medium absorption by tumor tissues.

In some instances, either central or adjacent areas of the lesions could comprise necrotic material [16]. For radiotherapeutic purposes, also these necrotic areas must be considered in the clinical target volume during the treatment planning phase. Our method is able to segment correctly heterogeneous tumors, even when foreground seeds are located in necrotic core proximity.

Cellular Automata (CA) are one of the oldest models of bio-inspired computing and were studied by John von Neumann in the late 1940s [17]. The goal was to design self-replicating artificial systems that make up a discrete universe consisting of a bi-dimensional mesh of finite state machines (cells), interconnected locally with each other, which will produce a complex global emergent behavior. Each cell changes its own state synchronously depending on its own state and on the states of the neighbor cells, at the previous discrete time step, as determined by a local update rule [18]. All cells use the same update rule so that the system is homogeneous like many physical and biological systems. The most common cellular automata are discrete in both space and time and process a lattice of d-dimensional sites $\mathbf{p} \in Z^d$. The *CA* formalism has been used to model and simulate several phenomena in dynamic complex systems. In image processing, $\mathbf{p}$ represents a pixel ($d = 2$) or a voxel ($d = 3$).

In [19] image segmentation problem is treated as a labeling process, where K colonies of bacteria compete each other for the domination according to a *CA* model. The authors named this method "GrowCut". Formally, a bi-directional deterministic cellular automaton is defined by a triplet $A := (S, N, f)$, where: S is the non-empty state set; N is the set of the n neighbors of a particular cell; $f : S^n \rightarrow S$ is the local transition rule, which, given the states of the neighborhood cells at the current time step t, maps the cell state at the next $t + 1$ time step. Let $\mathbf{p} \in Z^d$ be a cell location, the most used neighborhood definitions are von Neumann neighborhood and Moore neighborhood that use ℓ_1 and ℓ_∞ norms, respectively.

In "GrowCut" *CA* formulation, the cell state is a triple $S_\mathbf{p} := (l_\mathbf{p}, \theta_\mathbf{p}, \mathbf{c}_\mathbf{p})$, where: $l_\mathbf{p}$ is the label of the current cell; $\theta_\mathbf{p} \in [0, 1]$ is the strength value of the current cell; $\mathbf{c}_\mathbf{p}$ is the feature vector associated to the cell $\mathbf{p}$ according to image content.

The automaton is initialized with the previously calculated seeds, by labeling foreground and background seeds. The maximum strength value is assigned to labeled cells, while unlabeled cells are set to $\theta_\mathbf{p} = 0$. Cell states are then updated synchronously at each iteration, until convergence condition is reached (i.e. any cell does not change its own state). State transitions occur if the attacker force of a neighbor cell $\mathbf{q}$ (we used the Moore 8-neighborood), defined by its strength $\theta_\mathbf{q}^t$ and a distance between $\mathbf{c}_\mathbf{p}$ and $\mathbf{c}_\mathbf{q}$ feature vectors, is greater than the current cell strength $\theta_\mathbf{p}^t$:

$$g(\mathbf{c}_\mathbf{p}, \mathbf{c}_\mathbf{q}) \cdot \theta_\mathbf{q}^t > \theta_\mathbf{p}^t \tag{1}$$

where $g(\mathbf{c}_\mathbf{p}, \mathbf{c}_\mathbf{q})$ is a pixel similarity function, which is monotonically decreasing and bounded. This property ensures the algorithm convergence. Especially, as explained in [13], *CA* model with the gradient magnitude $g(\mathbf{c}_\mathbf{p}, \mathbf{c}_\mathbf{q}) = e^{-\|\mathbf{c}_\mathbf{p} - \mathbf{c}_\mathbf{q}\|_2}$ is equivalent to the shortest path algorithm. This deduction has been derived from [20], in which Sinop & Grady presented a unifying graph theoretic framework for seeded image segmentation depending on the used norm in the objective function optimization. In particular, the shortest path algorithm uses an ℓ_∞ norm.

The main advantage of using *CA* algorithms against graph-theoretic formulations is the ability to obtain a multi-label solution in a simultaneous iteration. In addition, the local transition rules are simple to interpret, and it is possible to impose prior knowledge, specific to the problem, into the segmentation approach [13].

Post-processing. Finally, a pair of morphological refinements is also required to enhance the *CA* segmentation results. A hole filling operation is first applied to remove possible holes at tumor boundaries. Successively, a morphological opening with a disk structuring element (1 pixel radius) is employed to smooth the *GTV* contour shape by unlinking poorly connected pixels.

4 Experimental Results

To evaluate the accuracy of the proposed segmentation method, several measures have been calculated by comparing the automatically segmented *GTV*s against those manually contoured by a neurosurgeon (considered as our "gold standard"). Supervised evaluation was used to quantify the goodness of the segmentation outputs.

Area-based metrics and distance-based metrics were calculated for all tumor slices of each MR image series, according to the definitions reported in [12, 21]. Figure 4a and b show two segmentation results achieved using the *CA* algorithm. It is appreciable how the proposed segmentation approach obtains correct results even with inhomogeneous input data.

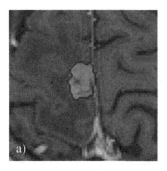 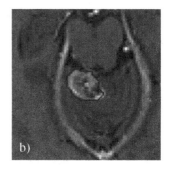

Fig. 4. Brain lesion segmentation using the proposed approach based on *CA* model: (a) and (b) are the outputs of the MR images shown in Fig. 1a and b, respectively. (2 × zoom factor)

4.1 Segmentation Evaluation Metrics

Area-based metrics quantify the similarity between the segmented regions through the proposed method (R_A) and the "gold standard" (R_T). Thus, the regions containing "true positives" ($R_{TP} = R_A \cap R_T$), "false positives" ($R_{FP} = R_A - R_{TP}$), and "false negatives" ($R_{FN} = R_T - R_{TP}$) are defined. In our experimental trials, according to the formulations in [12], we used the most representative evaluation measures: Dice similarity index $DSI = 2|R_{TP}|/(|R_A| + |R_T|) \times 100$, Jaccard index $JI = |R_A \cap R_T|/|R_A \cup R_T| \times 100$, Sensitivity $SE = |R_{TP}|/|R_T| \times 100$, and Specificity $SP = (1 - |R_{FP}|/|R_A|) \times 100$.

In order to evaluate the contour discrepancy, the distance between the automatically generated boundaries (defined by the vertices $A = \{\mathbf{a}_i : i = 1, 2, \ldots, K\}$) and the manually traced boundaries ($T = \{\mathbf{t}_j : j = 1, 2, \ldots, N\}$) was also estimated. Accordingly, the distance between each element of the automatic *GTV* contour and the set T must be defined: $d(\mathbf{a}_i, T) = \min_{j \in \{1,2,\ldots,N\}} \|\mathbf{a}_i - \mathbf{t}_j\|$. The following distances (expressed in pixels) were calculated: Mean Absolute Difference $MAD = (1/K) \sum_{i=1}^{K} d(\mathbf{a}_i, T)$, Maximum Difference $MAXD = \max_{i \in \{1,2,\ldots,K\}} \{d(\mathbf{a}_i, T)\}$, and the Hausdorff distance $HD = \max\{h(T, A), h(A, T)\}$ (where $h(T, A) = \max_{\mathbf{t} \in T} \{\min_{\mathbf{a} \in A} \{d(\mathbf{t}, \mathbf{a})\}\}$ and $d(\mathbf{t}, \mathbf{a}) = \sqrt{(t_x - a_x)^2 + (t_y - a_y)^2}$).

4.2 Segmentation Results

The values of both area-based and distance-based metrics obtained in the experimental *GTV* segmentation tests are shown in Table 1. High *DSI* and *JI* values prove segmentation accuracy and reliability. In addition, sensitivity and specificity average values involve the correct detection of the "true" pathological areas as well as the ability of not detecting wrong parts within the segmented tumors. The achieved distance-based indices are in line with area-based metrics. Hence, good performances were obtained also with heterogeneous tumors, since the *CA* algorithm delineates accurately irregular and complex shapes. The achieved segmentation results are comparable with the state of the art.

Table 1. Area-based and distance-based metrics calculated on the MRI dataset composed of 10 brain cancers. The achieved average values and standard deviations are reported

	DSI%	JI%	SE%	SP%	MAD	MAXD	HD
AVG ± SD	93.82 ± 2.77	88.47 ± 4.93	92.90 ± 1.75	96.33 ± 2.26	0.465 ± 0.140	1.301 ± 0.409	1.576 ± 0.234

5 Conclusions and Future Works

In this paper an original application of *Cellular Automata* is presented. This computational technique is used to segment brain tumors in neuro-radiosurgery scenarios. The developed methodology can be integrated in the current clinical practice, by supporting physicians in the target delineation task during treatment planning. The proposed semi-automatic segmentation approach was tested on MR images concerning 10 real brain cancers, by calculating both area-based and distance-based metrics. The achieved experimental results are very encouraging and they show the effectiveness of our approach.

However, it is not always possible to identify the actual tumor extent using only the MRI modality. The combination of multimodal imaging might address this important issue. Surgery, chemotherapy and radiation therapy may alter the acquired MRI data concerning the tumor bed. Therefore, further studies are planned to use a multimodal target segmentation, which combines MRI and ^{11}C-Methionine - Positron Emission Tomography (MET-PET) [22]. Thereby, MR images will show the morphology of the *GTV*, while PET images will convey information on metabolically active regions (Biological Target Volume, *BTV*) [23]. The proposed approach for *GTV* segmentation on brain MRI, properly integrated with *BTV* segmentation, would provide a support for an accurate identification of the Clinical Target Volume (*CTV*) to be treated during Gamma Knife treatments.

In the near future, we are going to address the issues related to necrotic areas and enhancement region distinction in brain tumors on MR images. In fact, radionecrosis of brain cancers is a critical aspect, since it has become more frequent with the advent of aggressive radiation treatment options such as stereotactic radiosurgery [16].

References

1. Joe, B.N., Fukui, M.B., Meltzer, C.C., Huang, Q.S., Day, R.S., Greer, P.J., Bozik, M.E.: Brain tumor volume measurement: comparison of manual and semiautomated methods. Radiology 212(3), 811–816 (1999). doi:10.1148/radiology.212.3.r99se22811
2. Khoo, V.S., Joon, D.L.: New developments in MRI for target volume delineation in radiotherapy. Br. J. Radiol. **79**, S2–S15 (2006). (Special Issue 1), doi:10.1259/bjr/41321492
3. Beavis, A.W., Gibbs, P., Dealey, R.A., Whitton, V.J.: Radiotherapy treatment planning of brain tumours using MRI alone. Br. J. Radiol. **71**(845), 544–548 (1998). doi:10.1259/bjr.71. 845.9691900
4. Luxton, G., Petrovich, Z., Jozsef, G., Nedzi, L.A., Apuzzo, M.L.: Stereotactic radiosurgery: principles and comparison of treatment methods. Neurosurgery **32**(2), 241–259 (1993). doi:10.1227/00006123-199302000-00014

5. Aslian, H., Sadeghi, M., Mahdavi, S.R., Mofrad, F.B., Astarakee, M., Khaledi, N., Fadavi, P.: Magnetic resonance imaging-based target volume delineation in radiation therapy treatment planning for brain tumors using localized region-based active contour. Int. J. Radiat. Oncol. Biol. Phys. **87**(1), 195–201 (2013). doi:10.1016/j.ijrobp.2013.04.049

6. Lankton, S., Tannenbaum, A.: Localizing region-based active contours. IEEE T. Image Process. **17**(11), 2029–2039 (2008). doi:10.1109/TIP.2008.2004611

7. Xie, K., Yang, J., Zhang, Z.G., Zhu, Y.M.: Semi-automated brain tumor and edema segmentation using MRI. Eur. J. Radiol. **56**(1), 12–19 (2005). doi:10.1016/j.ejrad.2005.03.028

8. Mazzara, G.P., Velthuizen, R.P., Pearlman, J.L., Greenberg, H.M., Wagner, H.: Brain tumor target volume determination for radiation treatment planning through automated MRI segmentation. Int. J. Radiat. Oncol. Biol. Phys. **59**(1), 300–312 (2004). doi:10.1016/j.ijrobp.2004.01.026

9. Bauer, S., Nolte, L.P., Reyes, M.: Fully automatic segmentation of brain tumor images using support vector machine classification in combination with hierarchical conditional random field regularization. In: Fichtinger, G., Martel, A., Peters, T. (eds.) MICCAI 2011, Part III. LNCS, vol. 6893, pp. 354–361. Springer, Heidelberg (2011). doi:10.1007/978-3-642-23626-6_44

10. Hall, L.O., Bensaid, A.M., Clarke, L.P., Velthuizen, R.P., Silbiger, M.S., Bezdek, J.C.: A comparison of neural network and fuzzy clustering techniques in segmenting magnetic resonance images of the brain. IEEE T. Neural Networ. **3**(5), 672–682 (1992). doi:10.1109/72.159057

11. Rundo, L., Militello, C., Vitabile, S., Russo, G., Pisciotta, P., Marletta, F., Ippolito, M., D'Arrigo, C., Midiri, M., Gilardi, M.C.: Semi-automatic brain lesion segmentation in Gamma Knife treatments using an unsupervised fuzzy C-Means clustering technique. In: Bassis, S., Esposito, A., Morabito, F.C., Pasero, E. (eds.) Advances in Neural Networks: Computational Intelligence for ICT, Smart Innovation, Systems and Technologies, vol. 54, pp. 15–26, Springer International Publishing (2016). doi:10.1007/978-3-319-33747-0_2

12. Militello, C., Rundo, L., Vitabile, S., Russo, G., Pisciotta, P., Marletta, F., Ippolito, M., D'Arrigo, C., Midiri, M., Gilardi, M.C.: Gamma Knife treatment planning: MR brain tumor segmentation and volume measurement based on unsupervised fuzzy C-Means clustering. Int. J. Imaging Syst. Technol. **25**(3), 213–225 (2015). doi:10.1002/ima.22139

13. Hamamci, A., Kucuk, N., Karaman, K., Engin, K., Unal, G.: Tumor-cut: segmentation of brain tumors on contrast enhanced MR images for radiosurgery applications. IEEE T. Med. Imaging **31**(3), 790–804 (2012). doi:10.1109/TMI.2011.2181857

14. Rother, C., Kolmogorov, V., Blake, A.: Grabcut: interactive foreground extraction using iterated graph cuts. ACM T. Graphic. **23**(3), 309–314 (2004). doi:10.1145/1186562.1015720

15. Ambrosini, R.D., Wang, P., O'Dell, W.G.: Computer-aided detection of metastatic brain tumors using automated three-dimensional template matching. J. Magn. Reson. Imaging **31**(1), 85–93 (2010). doi:10.1002/jmri.22009

16. Chin, L.S., Ma, L., DiBiase, S.: Radiation necrosis following Gamma Knife surgery: a case-controlled comparison of treatment parameters and long-term clinical follow up. J. Neurosurg. **94**(6), 899–904 (2001). doi:10.3171/jns.2001.94.6.0899

17. Von Neumann, J.: Theory of Self-Reproducing Automata. Univ. of Illinois Press, Urbana (1966). Edited and completed by Arthur Burks

18. Kari, J.: Theory of cellular automata: a survey. Theor. Comput. Sci. **334**(1–3), 3–33 (2005). doi:10.1016/j.tcs.2004.11.021

19. Vezhnevets, V., Konouchine, V.: GrowCut: Interactive multi-label ND image segmentation by cellular automata. In: Proceedings of Graphicon, pp. 150–156 (2005)

20. Sinop, A.K., Grady, L.: A seeded image segmentation framework unifying graph cuts and random walker which yields a new algorithm. In: 11th IEEE International Conference on Computer Vision, ICCV 2007, pp. 1–8 (2007). doi:10.1109/ICCV.2007.4408927

21. Fenster, A., Chiu, B.: Evaluation of segmentation algorithms for medical imaging. In: 27th Annual International Conference of the Engineering in Medicine and Biology Society, IEEE-EMBS 2005, pp. 7186–7189 (2005). doi:10.1109/IEMBS.2005.1616166

22. Miwa, K., Matsuo, M., Shinoda, J., Aki, T., Yonezawa, S., Ito, T., Asano, Y., Yamada, M., Yokoyama, K., Yamada, J., Yano, H., Iwama, T.: Clinical value of [^{11}C]Methionine PET for stereotactic radiation therapy with intensity modulated radiation therapy to metastatic brain tumors. Int. J. Radiat. Oncol. Biol. Phys. **84**(5), 1139–1144 (2012). doi:10.1016/j.ijrobp.2012.02.032

23. Stefano, A., et al.: An automatic method for metabolic evaluation of Gamma Knife treatments. In: Murino, V., Puppo, E. (eds.) ICIAP 2015. LNCS, vol. 9279, pp. 579–589. Springer, Heidelberg (2015). doi:10.1007/978-3-319-23231-7_52

Decentralized Estimation of Forest Fire Spread Using Mobile Sensors

Guillaume Schlotterbeck, Clement Raïevsky, and Laurent Lefèvre[✉]

LCIS, University Grenoble Alpes, 26000 Valence, France
`laurent.lefevre@lcis.grenoble-inp.fr`

Abstract. This paper presents a study of the ability to build an observer for a complex system using a decentralized multi-agent system for the coordination of mobile sensors. The environment is modeled using a CA model representing forest fire spread. The initial distribution for the different species in the vegetation is generated using a Perlin algorithm. Implementation is realized on GPGPU. A coherence measure for the observation error is defined. The observation itself is realized with mobile sensors and a decentralized coordination of the trajectories. We analyze the balance between individual and collective behaviours of agents which is required to achieve the best performance with respect to the chosen coherence measure. The collective behaviour of the mobile sensors is based on pheromones usage, inspired from ants behaviour.

Keywords: Mobile sensors · Multi agent systems · State estimation · Distributed parameters system · Forest fire spread · Cellular automata · Parallel computing

1 Introduction

In this paper, we present our work on the ability of a multi-agent system (MAS) to observe a dynamic 2D complex system. By observing a complex system, we mean building a representation of its internal state based on partial and local measures of it. A multi-agent system (MAS) is a set of artificial entities (agents) which interact with each other. These entities' action selection is autonomous and based on a partial representation of their environment, on internal states, and on the interactions that occur in the group. In our case, the agents can be seen as mobile sensors.

Observation of complex system is an interesting problem because understanding and control of this kind of systems require a dynamic representation of their states as precise as possible.

The complex system we chose to observe is the propagation of a forest fire. Cellular Automata (CA) are particularly suitable for modelling dynamic systems at a mesoscopic[1] level, especially to represent the spreading phenomenon [2], and that is why we chose them to simulate fire front propagation.

---

[1] In terms of behavioural rules mimicking the physical interactions and translating them into a fully discrete universe [1].

© Springer International Publishing Switzerland 2016
S. El Yacoubi et al. (Eds.): ACRI 2016, LNCS 9863, pp. 334–343, 2016.
DOI: 10.1007/978-3-319-44365-2_33

Sensors' placement is a crucial point of the 2D complex systems observation problem. Existing work tackling this point focus on methods to maximize an observability measure. For example, [3] use an observability matrix singular value based measure, an observability grammian singular value based measure or the Popov-Belevitch Hautus rank test. Empirical approaches based on genetic algorithms are also presented in [4]. The main differences with our approach is that they are off-line and only consider static sensors.

Our main objective is both to determine and maximize the ability of a group of agents (mobile sensors) to build an estimation of the state of a complex dynamical system as close as possible to its actual state. To do so, we study the relationship between the collective behaviour of a group of autonomous mobile sensors and the difference between the estimate they build of a system and its actual state. In our simulations, the agents move in the simulated forest while it is burning and collectively build a virtual map of its state according to their local observations. This map is the estimate they build and changes only when the agents update it with their observations. As we are using the MAS approach, the behaviour of the agents is decentralized: each agent has its own local perceptions of the forest and acts accordingly. The challenge is thus to find a local behaviour that allows the group to reach its global goal to build an estimation as precise as possible. The strategy we explored to coordinate the agents is inspired by ant colonies. The only communication between agents is through the environment: when moving, agents leave a trail of virtual pheromone along their path. These pheromones are detectable by the other agents. This kind of communication is inspired by stigmergy [5]. Unlike ants however, agents are not able to communicate directly with each-other. Furthermore, to keep our algorithm decentralized, we prevent the agents to fetch informations from the estimated state that they construct collectively. They also do not have (and do not try to get) any knowledge about the fire propagation rules.

We studied two collective behaviours that seemed intuitively interesting: (1) homogeneously distribute the agents over the environment, (2) make the agents go where the environment is changing. The main contribution of this paper is thus to compare decentralized mobile sensors coordination strategies in terms of estimation quality.

In Sect. 2, we present a formal definition of the CA used to simulate the environment. Then we present in Sect. 3 the observability measure we used to evaluate the collective behaviour of the MAS which is described in Sect. 4. In Sect. 5, we describe the implementation of the whole system and the results obtained through simulations. Finally we analyse those results and draw some conclusion about our approach in Sect. 6.

2   Forest Fire Front Propagation Simulation Using CA

The environment we defined is a 2D domain with periodic boundary condition. Geometrically, it is a toroidal surface (to exclude any boundary effect). The width of the environment is noted W and its heigh H.

2.1 Cellular Automaton Definition

Cellular Automata (CA) may be defined by a quadruple $A(L, S, N, f)$ according to the definition presented in [6] where:

- L is a 2-dimensional lattice of cells c. $L = \{0, 1, ..., W - 1\} \times \{0, 1, ..., H - 1\}$. so a point c on this space have two components noted c_w and c_h.
- S denotes a discrete state set: $S = \mathbb{N} \times \mathbb{N} \times \mathbb{N} \times \mathbb{R}^+ \times \{0, 1\} \times \mathbb{N}$. Elements in S are denote s. We note $s(c, t)$ the state of the cell c at the time $t \in \mathbb{R}^+$. The different sub-states are:
  - $s_T \in \mathbb{N}$: The quantity of remaining combustible.
  - $s_I \in \mathbb{N}$: The fire intensity (heat).
  - $s_F \in \mathbb{N}$: The necessary of neighbour's heat (intensity) to ignite the cell.
  - $s_R \in \mathbb{R}^+$: The neighbourhood's radius.
  - $s_B \in \{0, 1\}$: A boolean which is true when the cell is burning.
  - $s_Q \in \mathbb{N}$: The amount of pheromone (Ph) at the cell.
  Sub-states s_F and s_R are constant. An indexed notation is used to denote sub-states of a cell. *e.g.* we note $s_T(c, t)$ the remaining combustible in cell c at time t. The global state at time t is defined by $s(t) \in S^{card(L)}$.
- N is a mapping which defines the cell's neighbourhood set. It is given by $N(c) = \{c' \in L \mid \|c' - c\|_{WH} =< s_R(c, .)\}$ where $\|c' - c\|_{WH}{}^2$ is the modular[3] distance we defined on the toroidal surface of the environment.
- f is a transition function which allows us to calculate the cell's state at time $t + 1$. This function depends on the cell's neighbourhood state. It can be defined by $s(c, t + 1) = f(c, t)$ and is described below.

The algorithm of this function is as follow: when a plant ignites, its heat intensity (s_I) is incremented at each time step and its remaining combustible (s_T) is decremented. To ignite, a plant has to be in a hot enough neighbourhood, *i.e.* when the sum of cells intensities (s_I) in its neighbourhood (N) in range (s_R) is greater or equal to its flammability (s_F). When all combustible in a cell has burned, the fire is finished and the heat intensity falls to 0.

The next section presents our approach to generate initial condition of the environment.

2.2 Initial Conditions

To evaluate the ability of a MAS to build a precise estimate, we need to simulate a sufficiently complex system. To generate rich dynamics in a CA, the environment is required to exhibit local differences [7]. We therefore chose to use three virtual plants with specific dynamics and a probabilistic initial distribution of these plants in the environment based on Perlin Noise [8].

---

[2] $\|c' - c\|_{WH} = \sqrt{((c'_w - c_w) \mod W)^2 + ((c'_h - c_h) \mod H)^2}$.
[3] $x \mod y = x - y.\lfloor \frac{x}{y} \rfloor$.

Fig. 1. Example of initial conditions of the cellular automata

The three kinds of plant we defined are:

- **Tree:** Has the biggest starting amount of combustible ($s_T = 200$, *i.e.* a tree burns during 200 iterations). Has a flammability of 70 ($s_F = 70$) and a range of 2 ($s_R = 2$). *i.e.* A tree ignites if the sum of fire intensities within a range of 2 cells is at least 70.
- **Shrub:** $s_T = 70$. It has a range of 1 and a flammability of 2.
- **Grass:** $s_T = 1$. $s_R = 1$ and $s_F = 1$.

Figure 1 shows an example of initial conditions. White, black and gray pixels represent grass, trees, and shrub respectively.

2.3   Implementation

In our CA implementation, all cells are synchronously updated using the same algorithm. The computation of this kind of SIMD (*Single instruction Multiple Data*) algorithm benefits greatly of GPGPU (General-purpose processing on graphics processing units) [9]. Figure 2 shows six successive states of the fire front

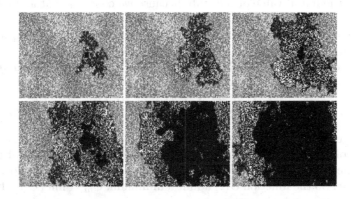

Fig. 2. Forest fire front propagation. Black pixels represent burned cells (ashes), white ones burning cells and gray ones plants. Among those, darkest pixels represent trees, and lightest ones grass.

propagation. We can see in these snapshots that the shape of the fire front is chaotic and sufficiently complex to be interesting.

The next section presents the observability problem we try to tackle and mathematical tools we use to evaluate the quality of our solution.

3   Observation Quality Evaluation

The purpose of observability is to construct a representation of the state of the system called the state's estimate. The main problem is that the state of the system is only partially accessible directly with sensors. There are two main approaches to tackle this problem, building a mathematical model of the system in order to compute what cannot be measured on one hand, and try to determine the best positions for the sensors in order to get sufficient information about the system on the other hand. We chose the second approach since mathematical models are not always possible to obtain and our aim is to use a MAS as a set of mobile sensors to get the best estimation of the current state of the system. In order to evaluate the quality of our MAS-built estimation, we need some evaluation of its quality. To do so, we defined a distance between the estimate built by the MAS and the "actual" state, simulated by the CA. Before presenting this distance and the way we construct the estimated state, we will present the definition of the estimate.

We denote the estimate of cell $c \in L$ at time t as follows:

$$\hat{s}(c,t) = \begin{cases} s(c,t) & \text{if } c \in V(t) \\ \hat{s}(c,t-1) & \text{otherwise} \\ \hat{s}(c,0) = s(c,0) \ \forall c \in L \end{cases} \tag{1}$$

where $V(t)$ is the set of directly measured cells (by the MAS in our case). V is formally defined in Sect. 4.1. The value of the estimate is not changed when a cell is not directly measured by a sensor at time t. We set the initial value of the estimate to the initial value of the state because we consider that an unexplored cell is correct.

We define the predicate eq that test the equality of 2 states. So $eq(s,s') = 1$ if all substates, except s_Q, of s and s' are equal; 0 otherwise.

We define the coherence C between the global state and his estimate as:

$$C(t) = \frac{1}{|L|} \sum_{c \in L} eq(s(c,t), \hat{s}(c,t)) \tag{2}$$

Since agents trajectories and fire propagation are (macroscopically) continuous, the coherence $C(t)$ is mathematically continuous. At the end of the simulation (when the fire is over), the state $s(c,t)$ is constant over L. So $C(t)$ can only increase. So the function $C(t)$ admit a minimum: $C_m = \min_t C(t)$. It occurs when the estimation is the worst.

We use C_m as the measure of the quality of our MAS-built estimate. This measure, computed off-line and a posteriori, allowed us to compare various sets of parameters of the MAS's behaviour.

The next section presents our decentralized MAS approach to build an estimate $\hat{s}$ of the system's state that maximize C_m.

4   Multi-agents System

In our implementation, the agents constituting the MAS choose their next action (move) at each CA time step. Our definition of an agent is as follows.

4.1   Definition

An agent is a mobile entity moving in the environment defined by the CA. We denote $p_i(t)$ the position of agent i at time t in $[0; W[\times[0; H[$. Agents speed, v, is constant and they can only chose their direction, $\theta_i(t)$. We note n the number of agents. Agents cannot communicate directly with each others, are not affected by fire, and have a circular field of view with a constant radius r_a. We define the set V_i as the coordinates of the cells directly observed by agent i: $V_i(t) = \{c \in L \ / \ \|p_i(t) - c\|_{WH} \leq r_a\}$. Finally, we define a set V as the union of all $V_i(t)$ and which contains the coordinates in L of all the cells measured by the MAS collectively.

As previously stated, agents leave a trail of virtual pheromone (Ph) along their path. Agents are able to detect this pheromone in range r_{Ph}. The amount of pheromone is modelled by the sub-state Q of the CA. As shown in the algorithm of the CA state update function f (2), the amount of pheromone in a cell is decreasing linearly over time. At each time step, agents leave a quantity Q_0 of pheromone in their current cell.

In the next section, we describe how agents decide which direction they will follow a each time step.

4.2   Agents Reactive Behaviour

Agents are homogeneous, they all use the same decision making process to choose their direction. Each agent chose its direction $\theta_i(t)$ according to a combination of three directions $(\theta_1, \theta_2, \theta_3)$ associated with three rules:

1 *Inertia*: This rule keeps the direction from the previous time step and ensures smooth trajectories. For agent i, we have:

$$\theta_{1i}(t) = \theta_i(t-1) \tag{3}$$

2. *Pheromone repulsion*: The direction associated with this rule is the one pointing to the lowest concentration of pheromone in range r_{Ph}. We introduced this rule to ensure a homogeneous distribution of the agents over the environment. Indeed, if there is a lot of agents in the same place, there will be a

great amount of pheromone, repelling the agents from this area. The following equation describe how the direction associated with this rule is computed.

$$\theta_{2i}(t) = \arg \left(-\sum_{c \in V_i^{\text{Ph}}(t)} \frac{s_Q(c,t)}{Q_0} \frac{c - \lfloor p_i(t) \rfloor}{\|c - \lfloor p_i(t) \rfloor\|_{WH}^2} \right) \tag{4}$$

where $V_i^{\text{Ph}}(t) = \{c \in L \mid 0 < \|c - \lfloor p_i(t) \rfloor\|_{WH} < r_{\text{Ph}}\}$ is the set of cell coordinates that are within the pheromone perception range of the agent. The parameter of the function arg() is $\mathbb{R}^2$. If we place a point in an orthonormal basis, arg() return the angle from horizontal axe.

3. *Focus on fire*: This rule gives the direction where there is the greater number of burning cells in a specific range r_f. This rule tends to make agents go where the fire front is active. Our intuitive motivation to add this rule was to focus observations where the environment is changing and where the estimate has to be updated.

$$\theta_{3i}(t) = \arg \left(\sum_{c \in V_i^f(t)} s_B(c,t) \frac{c - \lfloor p_i(t) \rfloor}{\|c - \lfloor p_i(t) \rfloor\|_{WH}} \right) \tag{5}$$

where $V_i^f(t) = \{c \in L \mid 0 < \|c - \lfloor p_i(t) \rfloor\|_{WH} < r_f\}$ is the set of cell coordinates that are within the fire perception range of the agent.

The final direction chosen by agents is computed according to the following equation:

$$\theta_i(t) = \frac{k_1 \theta_{1i}(t) + k_2 \theta_{2i}(t) + k_3 \theta_{3i}(t)}{k_1 + k_2 + k_3} \tag{6}$$

where k_1, k_2, and k_3 are weights that can be adjusted to modify the agent's behaviour. In Sect. 5, we present our approach to select those weights according to the minimal estimation coherence C_m they give to the MAS.

The next section gives some information about the MAS implementation and numerical values we used in simulation.

4.3   Implementation

The main bottleneck of the simulation is the concurrent access by the agents to the CA's data (*e.g.* the amount of pheromone $Q(c,t)$). To reduce the negative influence of this bottleneck on the simulation performance, we chose to implement agents using GPGPU as well. This allowed us to complete a simulation of 2200 iterations on a 1280×720 cell environment with 200 agents in an acceptable time ($\approx 45\,$s).

The simulation parameters were:

Width of the environment	W	1280
Height of the environment	H	700
Number of agents	n	200
Agents' field of view radius	r_a	12
Radius of pheromone detection	r_{Ph}	24
Radius of fire detection	r_f	30
Amount of pheromone dropped by the agents	Q_0	64
Linear speed of the agents (cells/iteration)	v	3
Weight of the inertia rule in the agents' direction choice	k_1	1

As initial conditions, we disposed the agents at random positions and with random orientations. There are two initial fire spots at $(\frac{W}{4}, \frac{H}{3})$ and $(\frac{3W}{4}, \frac{2H}{3})$. These initial spots are 4×4 cells large squares. We stop the simulation when there is no burning cell left and when the estimate is perfect (*i.e.* $\forall c \in L$, $s_B(c, t_f) = 0$ and $\hat{s}(c, t_f) = s(c, t_f)$. In this configuration, 220 iterations are required to explore 99 % of the environment. Once those parameters set, we studied the influence of the two remaining parameters, k_2 (the weight of the rule making agents going away from pheromones) and k_3 (the weight of the rule making agents going towards burning cells) on the overall quality of the observation process C_m. The results of this study are presented in the next section.

5   Results and Discussions

In order to evaluate the relation between the weights of the three decision rules and the overall observation quality and to find the best values of these parameters we carried out a systematic exploration of the parameter space. We then compared the obtained solution with some objective references.

5.1   Simulations, Parameters Optimization

Our aim was to find the weights of the decision rules that maximize C_m. To do that, we fixed the parameter k_1 to 1 and we did different simulations varying geometrically k_2 and k_3 from 0.01 to 100. We changed the parameters values geometrically between each simulation to get a more systematic exploration of the parameter space because the θ_i are combined using a mean.

This parameter space exploration indicated that high values for k_2, which drive the agents away from pheromones, give better results (higher minimal coherence C_m). Conversely, focusing agents' exploration on the fire front does not improve this criterion. Overall, the best values for the two considered parameters are: $k_2 = 35$ and $k_3 = 0.6$.

To get a more objective evaluation of the quality of this set of parameters, we used the following references.

5.2   Comparison with References Implementation

We can define two kinds of reference behaviour for the agents: static agents and Brownian agents, moving randomly.

For static agents, only the estimate of initially seen cells will be correct. So we can directly compute the coherence $C(t) = C_m = 11.5\%$ if the agents do not overlap. This value is the lower bound of the observation quality and far below the observed ones which are above 90 %.

To build the dynamic reference, we used the average of three random behaviours with three different steering speeds (linear speed remaining constant). The overall coherence $C(t)$ of these three behaviours and their average are depicted in Fig. 3 along with the best behaviour we found during the parameter space exploration. It appears that the MAS-built estimate is always better than the one built by random agents and that the MAS's exploration of the environment is faster.

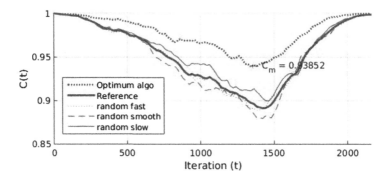

Fig. 3. Comparison between empiric optimum solution and dynamic references

We did the same analysis with 50 agents and we obtained the same result: it is better to ensure a homogeneous distribution of the agents than to focus exploration where the dynamic of the environment is high. This was a surprising result for us. Indeed, we thought that the smaller the number of agents, the higher the need to focus on the changing parts of the environment. The simulation results proved this hypothesis wrong.

6   Conclusion and Perspectives

This paper describes a multi-agent system which coordinates the trajectories of mobile sensors in order to achieve the state estimation of a cellular automata representing a 2D fire front propagation dynamic model. We used a completely decentralized approach to the problem of dynamic complex system observation and that's what distinguish our work from existing approaches which use either centralized methods or examine static systems.

The collective coordination of the agents combines two behaviours: the first one is inspired by ant's pheromones-related behaviours and aims at distributing mobile sensors homogeneously in space. The second one makes the agents move toward areas where the CA cells are changing to keep the estimate faithful. Using this kind of decentralized coordination mechanisms brings both resilience (no single point of failure) and scalability to the approach.

To evaluate the performance of this coordination mechanism, we defined a distance measure between the CA-simulated state of the forest fire front and the estimate collectively built by the agents. Simulations were carried out using GPGPU and showed that the best performance is obtained by privileging the pheromone-based behaviour over the change-seeking one.

The main research avenue we plan to explore is the introduction of more complex coordination mechanisms taking into account the built estimate and using local, direct, inter-agent communication. Other future work includes the refinement of the observation quality measure, observing more complex, periodic, systems such as chemical reactions, or populations.

References

1. Chopard, B.: Cellular automata modeling of physical systems. Computational Complexity: Theory, Techniques, and Applications, pp. 407–433 (2012)
2. El Yacoubi, S., El Jai, A.: Cellular automata modelling and spreadability. Math. Comput. Model. **36**(9–10), 1059–1074 (2002)
3. Waldraff, W., Dochain, D., Bourrel, S., Magnus, A.: On the use of observability measures for sensor location in tubular reactor. J. Process Control **5**(6), 497–505 (1998)
4. Liu, W., Gao, W.C., Sun, Y., Xu, M.J.: Optimal sensor placement for spatial lattice structure based on genetic algorithms. J. Sound Vibr. **317**, 175–189 (2008)
5. Dorigo, M., Bonabeau, E., Theraulaz, G.: Ant algorithms and stigmergy. Future Gener. Comput. Syst. **16**(8), 851–871 (2000)
6. Yacoubi, S.E.: A mathematical method for control problems on cellular automata models. Int. J. Syst. Sci. **39**(5), 529–538 (2008)
7. Green, D.G.: Simulated effects of fire, dispersal and spatial pattern on competition within forest mosaics. Vegetatio **82**(2), 139–153 (1989)
8. Parberry, I.: Designer worlds: procedural generation of infinite terrain from real-world elevation data. J. Comput. Graph. Tech. (JCGT) **3**(1), 74–85 (2014)
9. Laville, G.: Thèse de Doctorat - Exécution efficace de systèmes multi-agents sur GPU (2013)

Evacuation Dynamics in Room with Multiple Exits by Real-Coded Cellular Automata (RCA)

Kazuhiro Yamamoto[✉] and Riku Nonomura

Department of Mechanical Science and Engineering, Nagoya University, Nagoya, Japan
kazuhiro@mech.nagoya-u.ac.jp

Abstract. In this study, we have simulated evacuation dynamics in a room with multiple exits by Real-Coded Cellular Automata (RCA). Here, we have focused on the number of exits which is related with the evacuation dynamics. For comparison, the room without corridors was also considered. Evacuation time and the size of bottleneck formed at the exit were examined by changing the number of exits. Especially, we discussed the evacuation dynamics toward the exit, which could be affected by the corridors in the room. As the number of evacuees was increased, it took more time for evacuation, but it was observed that the evacuation time unexpectedly depended on the number of exits, which was caused by each exit location. Apparently, less effects of corridors on the evacuation time was found. This is because the evacuation time without corridors was decreased when all evacuees could move freely but were forced to concentrate at the exit.

Keywords: Evacuation dynamics · Bottleneck · Exit · Cellular automata

1 Introduction

Recently, various types of disasters have been occurring all over the world, and many people could become victims. In particular, a fire breaks out almost every day in Japan, and the number of building fires has exceeded 30,000 a year. To mitigate the loss and the damages when the fire breaks out, the source of the fire must be identified as early as possible, and an appropriate evacuation route must be secured. However, since available information on the fire could be limited, evacuees may panic [1]. Therefore, the smooth and appropriate evacuation is actually difficult in the real situation.

At present, Wada et al. have been developing the emergency rescue evacuation support system (ERESS) to support the rescue and evacuation process when a disaster occurs [2]. For safety management, this system provides real-time information for evacuees and supports emergency action. To realize this system, the behaviors of evacuees must be analyzed and whether a disaster has occurred must be judged. Since an actual disaster involves many factors, such as the shape of a building, the number of evacuees, and the state of the disaster, a demonstration experiment assuming the actual disaster is difficult to perform from the perspective of the cost and safety. Therefore, for collecting various types of data, a numerical simulation by assuming the actual disaster would be useful.

© Springer International Publishing Switzerland 2016
S. El Yacoubi et al. (Eds.): ACRI 2016, LNCS 9863, pp. 344–352, 2016.
DOI: 10.1007/978-3-319-44365-2_34

By referring to a model experiment [2], the present study simulated the evacuation dynamics using the real-coded cellular automata (RCA). The model experiment reproduced the evacuation with multiple exits in one room. By performing the numerical simulation, the present study examined the evacuation situation in which some exits for evacuation were limited under the emergency accidents. Focusing on the number of exits of the room, we discussed the evacuation dynamics by investigating the change in evacuation time at different number of evacuees initially allocated in the room. Moreover, the present study examined evacuation situations with and without corridors by setting partition walls in the room.

In general, evacuees are confirmed to concentrate at the exit. Then, for the safety management, multiple exits are set to disperse the evacuees moving in several directions [3–5]. In the ERESS, by leading evacuees to a safe exit, quick evacuation planning must be attained. Therefore, in the present study, we tried to reduce the bottleneck during the evacuation when evacuees moved toward the exit. In the numerical simulation, the floor field which determined the evacuation route was updated to lead the evacuees to another exit.

2 Numerical Method

Here, we explain our approach which is applied for evacuation at arbitrary velocity and directions [6, 7]. The idea is quite similar to stochastic approach in lattice gas model [8, 9]. In the conventional CA model, the direction of each pedestrian or evacuee is limited to four (or eight). Their velocity must be constant. In RCA, the direction and the velocity can be set freely, by considering the stochastic process to reposition them right on the grid [6, 7, 9]. We apply this method to the simulation of the evacuation in the room with multiple exits. The numerical procedure is explained briefly.

The update rule of RCA for evacuation motion is determined by the floor field, which is applied to each evacuee's motion randomly. The speed of all evacuees can be changed. The update rules are the same as the original RCA rule. The room in this study has four exits, which is shown in Fig. 1. The room size and the location of exits are roughly shown in this figure, which were referred to experiments [2]. One example of the floor field of the room using all exits is shown in Fig. 2, where the exit width is 1.2 m. The floor field was determined by the distance from the nearest exit. It was the static floor field, corresponding to the shortest distance to the exit. Then, when some exits were not used, the different floor field was initially applied in the simulation.

Next, the calculation conditions are explained. The lattice spacing was set to be 0.4 m [9] and the time step was 1/3 s. The velocity of all evacuees was 1.6 m/s [7]. The evacuation time was examined by changing the number of evacuees initially allocated in the room N (hereinafter referred to as the initial allocation number, N). Additionally, a similar simulation was performed when corridors were not considered in the room to examine the effect of corridors on the evacuation dynamics. To avoid the dependence of the initial positions of evacuees, the average evacuation time was obtained. Then, the evacuation simulation was conducted for 10 times by changing initial allocation of

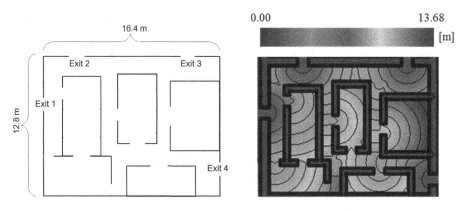

Fig. 1. Room size and exit location   **Fig. 2.** Floor field using four exits

evacuees, and the average evacuation time was calculated. Once the number of exits was set, the floor field was not changed.

3   Results and Discussion

3.1   Evacuation in Room with Corridors

First, we simulated evacuation dynamics in room with corridors. Figure 3 shows the results for $N = 40$. Only exit 2 was used. As shown in this figure, evacuees were congested in a part of the corridors at $t = 2$ s. At $t = 14$ s when most of evacuees reached the exit, a bottleneck was formed. Even when the number of exits was increased, evacuees were confirmed to be still congested at the exit. However, as the number of exits was increased, the size of the bottleneck at the exit became smaller. This is because the flow of evacuees was dispersed due to the increase in the number of exits.

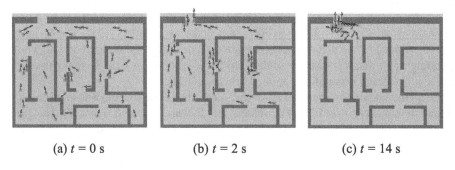

(a) $t = 0$ s   (b) $t = 2$ s   (c) $t = 14$ s

Fig. 3. The position of evacuees in the room using exit 2; $N = 40$

Figure 4 shows the relationship between the initial allocation number N and the evacuation time T_E. When N was below 20, the evacuation time was almost constant regardless of the exit location. The reason for this was that the bottleneck was not formed under this condition. The evacuation time was simply determined by the evacuee who was at a farthermost place from the exit. When the initial allocation number exceeded 20, the evacuation time tended to be similar when one, two, three, and four exits were used. However, in the case of two exits, the evacuation time was longer when exits 1 and 2 were used than when the other two exits were used.

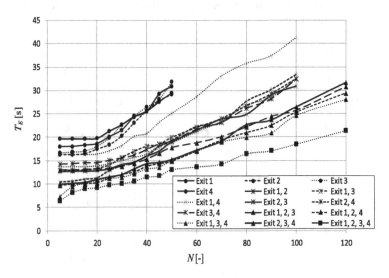

Fig. 4. Comparison of evacuation time at different number of exits

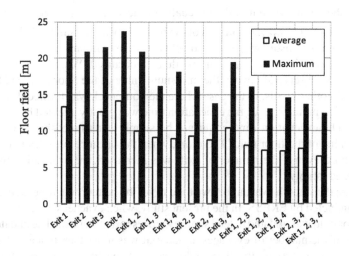

Fig. 5. Comparison of floor field at different number of exits

It was observed that the evacuation time unexpectedly depended on the number of exits. To identify the reason, the floor field was compared at different number of exits. In Fig. 5, the maximum value of the floor field was shown in black. The value expressed in white indicates the average value of the floor fields at $N = 50$. As shown in this figure, the distance for each evacuee to the exit reasonably decreased as the number of exits increased. However, no large difference was observed between values of the floor field when exits 1 and 2 were used and when only exit 2 was used. Therefore, the distance for each evacuee to the exit was not shortened when the exits 1 and 2 were used, although one more exit was available.

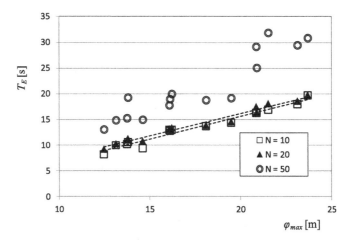

Fig. 6. Correlation of maximum floor field and evacuation time

Figure 6 shows the correlation between the maximum value of the floor field φ_{max} and the evacuation time T_E. Here, the initial allocation number N was changed to 10, 20, and 50. As shown in this figure, the evacuation time T_E increased with the maximum value of the floor field φ_{max}, regardless of the initial allocation number N. When $N = 10$ and 20, a linear relationship was observed between the maximum value of the floor field and the evacuation time, as long as no bottleneck occurred. When $N = 50$, no linear relationship was observed between the maximum value of the floor field and the evacuation time. In other words, in the case where the bottleneck was formed due to a large initial allocation number, since the evacuation time was greatly affected by the situation at the exit. The evacuation time could not be simply determined based only on the maximum value of the floor field. Therefore, when the distance between two exits was relatively short, even if the number of exits was increased, the evacuation time could not be reduced largely.

To realize the smooth evacuation, we tried to set the better route for evacuees, which could be conducted by ERESS. In the present study, when evacuees concentrated at one exit, the floor field was updated to lead some evacuees to another exit. The update process was simple: if the number of evacuees at one exit was more than twice as larger than those at the adjacent exits, the floor field was updated to set the floor field of the uncrowded exit. The evacuation using exits 1 and 2 were tested. Specifically, when evacuees concentrated at exit 2, the floor field only for evacuees congested at exit 2 was replaced by that of exit 1 to lead them toward exit 1 (or vice versa). Figure 7 shows results by comparing the evacuation time when evacuees were led or not led. As shown in this figure, no large difference was observed in the evacuation time when N was below 20. On the other hand, for $N > 40$, the evacuation time was shortened when evacuees were led. By comparing Fig. 7 with Fig. 4, it was found that the situation where the evacuation time was prolonged even when exits 1 and 2 were used was improved. In other words, evacuees congested at the particular exit were led to another exit; consequently, the bottleneck which inhibited the smooth evacuation could be avoided.

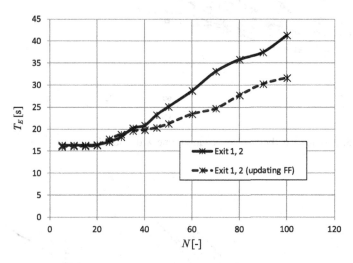

Fig. 7. Comparison between evacuation time with and without guiding evacuees by updating floor field (FF)

3.2   Evacuation in Room Without Corridors

Finally, a simulation was performed in which there were no corridors in the room. In experiments, all partitions in the room were removed. The widths of all exits were still the same (1.2 m), and the relationship between the initial allocation number N and the evacuation time T_E was compared with and without corridors. Even for cases without corridors, 10 simulations were conducted. Figure 8 shows the comparison results. As shown in this figure, the difference between the evacuation time with and without corridors is relatively small, except for the cases with two exits 1, 2. That is, less effect of corridors on the evacuation time was found. This may be because the evacuation time without corridors must be decreased when all evacuees could move freely but were forced to concentrate at the exit. It was also found that, even without corridors, the evacuation time increased as the initial allocation number was increased.

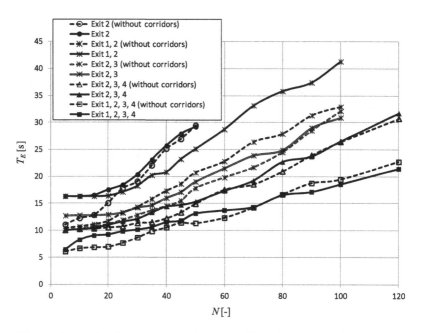

Fig. 8. Comparison between evacuation time with and without corridors in room

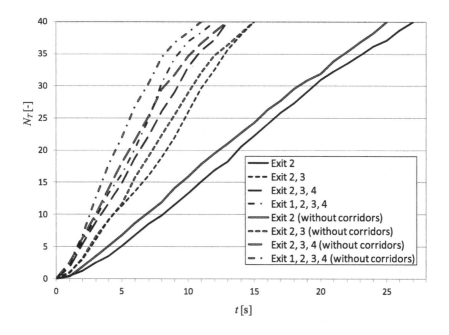

Fig. 9. Time-variations of total number of evacuees from all exits for $N = 40$

Then, we focused on the number of evacuees who had passed through all exits, which must be related with the bottleneck formed at the exit. This is because the evacuation time was considered to be determined by the situation around the exit, regardless of the existence of corridors. Figure 9 shows the number of evacuees who had passed through all exits until a certain time, N_T. Two cases with and without corridors were considered for $N = 40$. Without corridors, N_T always became larger. When there were no corridors, evacuees could reach the exit in a short time. However, the bottleneck was formed in the early stage, so the number of evacuees who could pass through the exit was confined. When there were corridors, evacuees moved along the corridors toward the exit. Consequently, the time required for each evacuee to reach the exit was dispersed, and the size of the bottleneck formed at the exit became smaller, resulting in the same evacuation time as that without corridors.

4   Conclusions

The present study simulated the evacuation with multiple exits by considering the room in experiments. The results are summarized as follows:

(1) When the initial allocation number N exceeded 20, the evacuation time slightly increased with N due to interference among evacuees. After the bottleneck appeared along the corridors or at the exit, the evacuation time increased linearly.
(2) The evacuation time could be shortened by increasing the number of exits. When the distance between exits was short, the length of the route toward the exit was not shortened. In this case, the evacuation time could not be reduced. This situation was improved by leading evacuees congested at one exit toward another exit.
(3) When there were no corridors in the room, evacuees moved freely toward the exit. More evacuees concentrated at the exit, and the bottleneck was formed; consequently, the evacuation time was prolonged. However, no large difference between the evacuation time with and without corridors. When there were corridors, the time required for each evacuee to reach the exit was prolonged because they had to move along the corridors. However, the size of bottleneck was smaller with corridors than that without corridors. As a result, the difference between the evacuation time with and without corridors was small.

These are useful information for developing the safety management by ERESS system.

References

1. Helbing, D., Farkas, I., Vicsek, T.: Simulating dynamical features of escape panic. Nature **407**, 487–490 (2000)
2. Mori, K., et al.: Development of emergency rescue evacuation support system (ERESS) in panic-type disasters: disaster recognition algorithm by support vector machine. IEICE Trans. Fundam. **E96-A**, 649–657 (2013)
3. Burstedde, C., et al.: Simulation of pedestrian dynamics using a two-dimensional cellular automaton. Phys. A **295**, 507–525 (2001)

4. Kirchner, A., Schadschneider, A.: Simulation of evacuation processes using a bionics-inspired cellular automata model for pedestrian dynamics. Phys. A **312**, 260–276 (2002)
5. Nishinari, K., et al.: Extended floor CA model for evacuation dynamics. IEICE Trans. Inf. Syst. **E87-D**, 726–732 (2004)
6. Yamamoto, K., Kokubo, S., Nishinari, K.: New approach for pedestrian dynamics by real-coded cellular automata (RCA). In: Yacoubi, S., Chopard, B., Bandini, S. (eds.) ACRI 2006. LNCS, vol. 4173, pp. 728–731. Springer, Heidelberg (2006)
7. Yamamoto, K., Kokubo, S., Nishinari, K.: Simulation for pedestrian dynamics by real-coded cellular automata (RCA). Phys. A **379**, 654–660 (2007)
8. Malevanets, A., Kapral, R.: Continuous-velocity lattice-gas model for fluid flow. Europhys. Lett. **44**, 552–558 (1998)
9. Hashimoto, Y., Chen, Y., Ohashi, H.: Immiscible real-coded lattice gas. Comput. Phys. Commun. **129**, 56–62 (2000)

Crowds, Traffic and Cellular Automata - CT&CA

A CA-Based Model of Dyads in Pedestrian Crowds: The Case of Counter Flow

Luca Crociani[1]([✉]), Andrea Gorrini[1], Katsuhiro Nishinari[2], and Stefania Bandini[1,2]

[1] Department of Informatics, Systems and Communication,
Complex Systems and Artificial Intelligence Research Center,
University of Milano - Bicocca, Viale Sarca 336 - Edificio U14, 20126 Milano, Italy
{luca.crociani,andrea.gorrini,stefania.bandini}@disco.unimib.it
[2] Research Center for Advance Science and Technology, The University of Tokyo,
4-6-1 Komaba, Meguro-ku, Tokyo 153-8904, Japan
tknishi@mail.ecc.u-tokyo.ac.jp

Abstract. The calibration and validation of pedestrian dynamics simulation require the acquisition of empirical evidences of human behaviour. In this framework, this paper firstly presents the results of an experimental study focused on the negative impact of counter flow and grouping on pedestrian speed. In particular, we focused on two member groups (dyads) as the most frequently observed and basic interacting element of crowds. On the basis of the behavioural effects observed with the experiment, a novel cellular automaton is proposed to represent the different behaviour of individuals and dyads, with particular reference to the group spatial alignment and the dynamic leader-follower structure. This has been demonstrated to modulate the speed of dyads by maintaining the spatial cohesion among the two members. In addition, the model is also able to reproduce the significant impact of flow ratio observed in the experiment results.

Keywords: Cellular automata · Pedestrian dynamics · Groups · Experiment

1 Introduction

The role of advanced computer-based systems for the simulation of the dynamical behaviour of pedestrians is becoming a consolidated and successful field of research and application, thanks to the possibility to test the efficiency, comfort and safety of urban crowded facilities evaluating key performance indicators (e.g., travel time, perceived density, waiting time).

The development of simulation systems requires a cross-disciplinary methodology to calibrate and validate the model according to benchmark information about pedestrian behaviours and wayfinding decisions. In particular, the validation of simulations requires to test the model itself and the related simulation results by means of empirical studies about pedestrian dynamics. In this framework, this paper firstly introduces the results of an experiment focused on the impact of flow ratio and grouping (*dyad*) on pedestrian dynamics in a controlled laboratory setting. The final aim is the design and validation of a CA-based model focused on the reproduction of the observed effects of

© Springer International Publishing Switzerland 2016
S. El Yacoubi et al. (Eds.): ACRI 2016, LNCS 9863, pp. 355–364, 2016.
DOI: 10.1007/978-3-319-44365-2_35

flow ratio and grouping, with particular reference to heterogeneous speed profiles and group cohesion mechanism.

Considering groups in the simulation models has been generally neglected until the last decade, in which microscopic modelling of individual behaviour represented the main focus of this research field. Recent empirical studies on pedestrian groups [8,22], on the other hand, brought much interests on this element and many approaches considering its presence in the simulations have been proposed [13,20]. In particular, the granulometric distribution of pedestrian flows is strongly affected by two-members groups, which represent the most frequently observed and basic interacting elements of crowds [9]. Analyses of pedestrian dynamics not considering this aspect have a reduced accuracy, since grouping was found to impact the overall dynamics of the crowd movements [19] and evacuation dynamics [13]. This is due to the need to maintain spatial cohesion among members to communicate while walking. In particular, group proxemic behaviour generates different spatial configuration while walking at variable density conditions [12,22]: *line abreast* pattern at low density, *diagonal* pattern at medium density and *river-like* pattern at high density.

The proposed methodological approach represents a complete *analysis-synthesis* cycle [2], employing the results of an empirical study on the impact of groups in pedestrian counter flow for the design and calibration of a CA-based model. Furthermore, a first novel contribution of this work sees the employment of a simulation system for pedestrian and crowd dynamics (ELIAS38) to help the design of the experiment itself, using thus results from the synthesis side to support the analysis. The observed quantitative data from the experiment allowed the configuration of a set of ad-hoc rules that are able to reproduce a valid behaviour of the simulated pedestrians and groups.

In the literature the issue of defining formal computational models about pedestrian dynamics has been tackled from different perspectives:

- *Physical* approach [5,10] represents pedestrians as particles subject to forces (e.g., attraction and repulsive forces), in analogy with fluid dynamics;
- *Cellular Automata* approach [3,6,14] represents pedestrians as occupied states of the cells. Pedestrian interactions are based on the *floor field* method: a virtual traces that influence pedestrian transitions and movements;
- *Agent-based* approach [7,17] represents pedestrians as heterogeneous, situated and autonomous entities moving according to behavioural rules and specifications. Higher level aspects of behaviour, such as wayfinding, are also considered.

The hereby presented CA model is specifically tailored for the simulation of the experiment procedures, towards the extension of the simulation platform ELIAS38 for a validated simulation of pedestrian groups. In the experiment singles and dyads of participants walked in a corridor at different counter flow ratio. Both types of pedestrian are represented in the CA model by basic behavioural specifications which allow them to reach their destination. In addition, groups members interact through refined proxemic rules, by defining in the model a dynamic (*leader-follower*) structure.

The paper is structured as the following: the case study and the experiment results are proposed in Sect. 2. The CA model is presented in Sect. 3, with results in Sect. 4. The paper concludes with final remarks about the validation process of the CA model.

Fig. 1. A video frame of the analysed measurement area of the experiment (procedure No. 2).

2 Experimental Study

The experiment was performed on June 13, 2015 at the Research Center for Advance Science and Technology of The University of Tokyo (Tokyo, JAPAN). The objective of the study was to test the following hypotheses:

– Hp 1: The increase of flow ratio negatively impacts the speed;
– Hp 2: Dyads walk slower than singles, to maintain spatial alignment.

The experiment has been designed with the support of the ELIAS38 simulation tool, analysing different counter flow scenarios in order to avoid excessive level of density in the measurement area. The simulation results allowed to correct critical aspects of the procedures, like the dimension of the measurement area and flow ratio configuration.

In this paper we denote the *flow ratio* as the rate between the minor flow and the total flow in bidirectional scenarios. Flow ratio was managed as independent variable among four different experimental procedures: a unidirectional flow (flow ratio = 0) and three different configurations of bidirectional flow (flow ratio = .167, .333, .5). The setting was designed as a corridor-like scenario, composed of: (*i*) the measurement area in the centre (10 m × 3 m); (*ii*) two side buffer zones to allow pedestrians reaching a stable speed (2 m × 3 m); (*iii*) two starting areas (12 m × 3 m).

The starting positions were drawn on the floor with coloured cross signs (lateral distance 0.5 m, longitudinal distance 1.5 m). The number of dyads per line and the positions of members (e.g., line-abreast, river-like patter) were homogeneously distributed among the starting positions. At the start signal, all participants were asked to walk toward the opposite side of the corridor. Each procedure was repeated four times, asking participants to change their starting positions.

The sample was composed of 54 male students of The University of Tokyo (from 18 to 25 years old). 24 participants were randomly paired (44 % of the total, as observed in [9]) and asked to walk close to each other during the experiment reproducing the locomotion behaviour of dyad members (no instructions were given to them about the spatial pattern). The rest of participants walked as individual pedestrians. The recorded video images have been analysed by using the PeTrack software [4], which allowed to automatically track pedestrians' trajectories. A screenshot from the video footages of the experiment is shown in Fig. 1.

Table 1. The experiment and simulation results about pedestrian speeds and alignment of dyads.

Flow ratio	Grouping	EXP speed [m/s]	EXP X-align	EXP Y-align	SIM speed [m/s]	SIM X-align	SIM Y-align
0	Total	$1.31 \pm .10$	-	-	$1.26 \pm .07$	-	-
	Singles	$1.32 \pm .11$	-	-	$1.29 \pm .06$	-	-
	Dyads	$1.30 \pm .09$	$.53 \pm .21$	$.23 \pm .25$	$1.23 \pm .07$	$.51 \pm .05$	$.18 \pm .07$
0.167	Total	$1.20 \pm .13$	-	-	$1.22 \pm .09$	-	-
	Singles	$1.22 \pm .15$	-	-	$1.26 \pm .07$	-	-
	Dyads	$1.16 \pm .10$	$.42 \pm .13$	$.23 \pm .24$	$1.17 \pm .08$	$.50 \pm .04$	$.25 \pm .07$
0.333	Total	$1.07 \pm .09$	-	-	$1.17 \pm .12$	-	-
	Singles	$1.08 \pm .10$	-	-	$1.23 \pm .09$	-	-
	Dyads	$1.05 \pm .09$	$.35 \pm .17$	$.31 \pm .22$	$1.10 \pm .11$	$.51 \pm .03$	$.29 \pm .10$
0.5	Total	$1.08 \pm .10$	-	-	$1.18 \pm .12$	-	-
	Singles	$1.10 \pm .10$	-	-	$1.22 \pm .09$	-	-
	Dyads	$1.07 \pm .11$	$.41 \pm .13$	$.26 \pm .20$	$1.09 \pm .12$	$.50 \pm .02$	$.30 \pm .05$

2.1   Experimental Results

A two-factors analyses of variance[1] (two-way ANOVA) was conducted to test the impact of *flow ratio* and *grouping* on speed (see Table 1 and Fig. 5). Results showed a significant effect for the flow ratio factor [$F(3,856) = 242.777$, p value $< .000$] and a significant effect for the grouping factor [$F(1,856) = 26.946$, p value $< .000$]. No significant interaction among the two factors was found [$F(3,856) = 1.008$, p $= .388$]. A linear regression showed that the overall speed of participants was affected by the increase of flow ratio [$F(1,862) = 546.039$, p value $< .000$, R-square of .388; speed $= 1.287 - .489$ * flow ratio]. A post hoc Tukey test showed that the speed of participants at flow ratio $= .333$ and flow ratio $= .5$ did not differ significantly at p $= .406$. In conclusion, results partially confirmed the Hp 1, showing that the increase of flow ratio from 0 to .333 significantly affected the overall speed of participants.

A post hoc Tukey test showed that the speed of singles and dyads among the procedures No. 1 (flow ratio $= 0$) did not differ significantly at p $= .05056$. The average speed of singles (1.13 m/s $\pm .08$) and dyads (1.09 m/s $\pm .06$) among procedures No. 2, No. 3 and No. 4 differed significantly at p value $< .000$. In conclusion, results partially confirmed the Hp 2, showing that in case of counter flow dyads walked in average the 4 % slower than singles, due to the need of group members to preserve spatial alignment in case of local situations of density.

The alignment of dyads on the X-axis ($.43$ m $\pm .17$ SD) and the Y-axis ($.26$ m $\pm .23$ SD) was measured as the gap between the positions of members and the geometrical centre of the group (*centroid*) (see Table 1). A series of one factor analyses of variance (one-way ANOVA) showed a significant impact of the flow ratio on the X-alignment of dyads [$F(3,188) = 9.531$, p value $< .000$]. A non significant impact of the flow ratio on the Y-alignment was found [$F(3,188) = 1.197$, p value $= .312$]. A linear regression analysis showed a significant impact of the X-alignment on the speed of dyads [$F(1,190) = 32.180$, p value $< .000$, with an R-square of .145; speed of dyads $= 1.017 + .381$ * X-alignment]. A non significant impact was found for the Y-alignment on speed

---

[1] All the analyses presented in this work have been conducted at the p $< .01$ level.

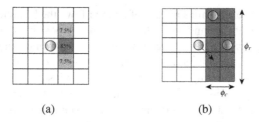

(a)   (b)

Fig. 2. (a) Configuration of the probabilities of movement for the free flow case. (b) The grey area is considered for the evaluation of movement: the central pedestrian, moving towards the right, will much probably perform a movement towards south-east, due to the other pedestrians belonging to the counter flow.

$[F(1,190) = 4.344$, p value $= .038$, with an R-square of 0.022; speed of dyads $= 1.165 - .150 *$ Y-alignment]. In conclusion, the increase of flow ratio negatively affected the alignment of dyads on the X-axis and consequently their speed.

In case of counter flow, dyads walked in average the 4 % slower than singles, due to the need to maintain spatial cohesion. As generally observed (see e.g., [9]), in condition of relatively low local density dyads walk side by side with a line abreast pattern. Results of the experiment showed that dyads split due the local condition of density in counter flow situations; consequently they slow down to regroup and maintain cohesion, arranging their spatial pattern with detriment of speed (*leader-follower* structure).

3   A Simulation Model Considering Dyads

A Cellular Automaton (CA) based on ad-hoc rules has been designed to simulate the experiment procedures. As generally applied in the field of pedestrian simulation [3, 14], this CA is based on a grid of square cells of $40 \times 40 \, \mathrm{cm}^2$ size that reproduce the environment and the space occupation of a person. Each cell can be occupied by one pedestrian at most and this generates a maximum density of 6.25 ped/m², covering the range of densities usually observed [21]. The assumed duration of the discrete time step is 0.3 s. In this way, a unique desired speed of 1.333 m/s is simulated, in accordance with the average speed observed with the experiment procedures. Given the objective of this work to analyse the impact of flow ratio and proxemic behaviour on the speed of dyads, possible approaches from the literature for the management of heterogeneous speeds [1] have not been considered.

The movement of the simulated pedestrians is modelled with simple rules leading them towards the other extreme of the corridor. In particular, at each time-step all pedestrians can choose between the three forward cells next to its position or alternatively to maintain the current position. The set of forward cells is configured ad-hoc for the two direction of flows. To allow the pedestrians to produce more smooth trajectories and avoid sudden changes of direction, the probability distribution for choosing the next cell in absence of other nearby persons is configured as shown in Fig. 2(a). The probability to move in the forward cell is configured as 85 % for these tests, while the remaining 15 % is equally distributed among the two other closer cell to the target.

To model a plausible dynamics in case of counter flow, the behaviour of pedestrians is modelled to let them understand where to move next, by possibly minimising conflicts with the surrounding persons. The choice is performed according to a *perception* phase: the pedestrian evaluates the situation in rectangular areas of $\phi_r \times \phi_c$ cells in front of the possible movements by counting the number of persons inside. Cell closer to counter flow pedestrians are considered less convenient, thus during the simulation pedestrians tend to choose cells behind other persons moving in the same direction. This allows the generation of the well-known *lane formation* effect of pedestrian dynamics [16] and also to achieve realistic average speed of pedestrians comparing to the observed experiment scenarios (see results in the next section). For the time being, quantitative analysis on the capability of the model to generate and maintain lanes in counter flow situations [15] has not been performed, but it will be subject of future works.

This mechanism is exemplified in Fig. 2(b), where the couple of calibration parameters (ϕ_r, ϕ_c) of this component is set to $(10, 2)$ as for the executed tests. After the evaluation, a probabilistic choice is performed, making choices to converge towards less dense zones. This perception component is inspired by the model proposed in [18].

For simplicity, in this model we adopted a *shuffled sequential* update rule, avoiding a-priori the generation of conflicts. It is known in the literature that this update strategy can lead to a higher and unrealistic simulation of flows at high pedestrian density in the scene [11]. To improve the simulated dynamics, we introduced a probability p_c for which a pedestrian can choose as well an already occupied position, generating a conflict. If this happens, the pedestrian will hold its position for the current step. For our tests, this probability has been set to about 0.6.

The objective of the experiment procedures performed and described in this paper was to verify the impact of counter flow ratio and grouping on speed. The behaviour of dyads was therefore a primary element of this model, representing its novel part. To maintain the observed *cohesion* of the dyad members, their behaviour is modelled with a dynamic *leader-follower* structure, by means of a set of ad-hoc rules defined for each member type. The structure of one group varies over time and the leader is temporary defined as the person which is forward to the other, with respect to their direction. In

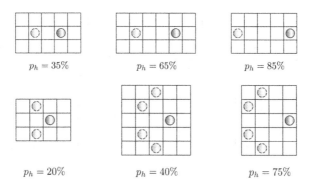

Fig. 3. Configuration of the probability p_h of the leader according to the possible positions of the follower (dashed circle).

case of line abreast pattern (much frequent in this model due to the space discretisation) the mechanism is inhibited and the two members move according to the general rule of movement, to allow a better usage of the space.

The *follower* has a simpler behaviour and it is much probably driven by the position of the other member. At each step, the distance between the two members is calculated with the *manhattan* metrics. If this value is ≤ 2 cells, then the follower has a 80 % probability of moving in the closer cell to the leader and 20 % of choosing a movement with the base rule. The probability to follow rises to 100 % if the leader is over the 2 cells threshold of distance.

Differently, the behaviour of the leader is more aimed at reaching the target, but it is also described by a tendency to hold its position and wait for the follower to allow a re-composition. This tendency is managed with a probability p_h to not move at a given step, varied according to the positions of the two members. The configuration of this probability is graphically explained by Fig. 3. The possible cases are divided as: (*i*) the dyad walk with a river-like pattern and (*ii*) the two members are not aligned. This allowed to reproduce the experiment results and to maintain the distances among dyads members within the achieved range.

4   Simulation Results

A simulation campaign was performed to test and validate the model mechanism described in the previous section. The simulated environment has been designed with a grid of 85×8 cells ($34\,m \times 3.2\,m$), describing the complete experimental setting (comprising the measurement area, the buffer zones and starting areas). As for the experiment, data about speed and trajectories of singles and dyads have been recorded only from the measurement area. The same number and proportion of singles and dyads was reproduced with the simulations. 10 iterations were run per each procedure.

The same statistics have been calculated on simulation results (see Table 1 and Fig. 5). Results showed a significant effect for the flow ratio factor [$F(3,3014) = 3.788$, p value $< .000$] and a significant effect for the grouping factor [$F(1,3014) = 6.643$, p value $< .000$]. Moreover, results showed a significant interaction among the two factors [$F(3,3014) = 3.788$, p value $< .000$]. A linear regression showed a significant and negative impact of the flow ratio on speed [$F(1,3020) = 277.131$, p value $< .000$, R-square of 0.084; speed $= 1.252 - 0.165 *$ flow ratio]. A post hoc Tukey test showed that the speed among the simulated procedures No. 3 (flow ratio $= .333$) and No. 4 (flow ratio $= .5$) did not differ significantly at $p = .993$. In conclusion, the simulations confirmed the experiment results, showing that the increase of flow ratio from 0 to .333 negatively affected the overall speed of the simulated pedestrians.

The average simulated speed of singles ($1.24\,m/s \pm .09$) and dyads ($1.14\,m/s \pm .11$) differed significantly at p value $< .000$ among all procedures. In conclusion, the simulation results confirmed the ones achieved by means of the experiment, showing the effectiveness of the implemented group cohesion mechanism among dyad members, which moved in average the 8 % slower than singles.

A series of one factor analysis of variance (one-way ANOVA) were conducted to test the impact of flow ratio on dyads X-alignment ($.51\,m \pm .04$ SD) and Y-alignment

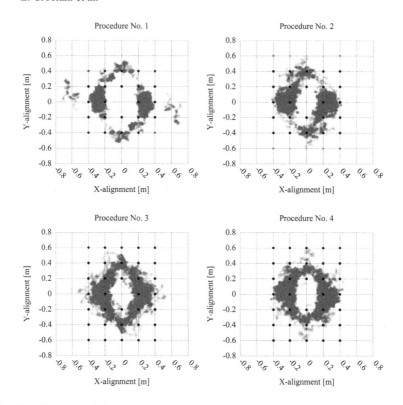

Fig. 4. The alignment of dyad among the experiment (red dots) and simulation (black dots) results. The charts report the aggregated positions of dyads, with a transparent effect to emphasise their distribution. (Color figure online)

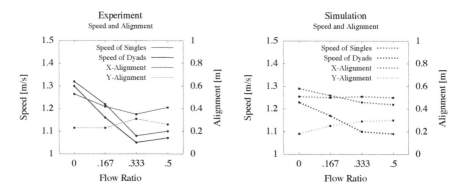

Fig. 5. A comparison among the experiment and simulation results.

(.25 m $\pm$ .09 SD) (see Table 1 and Fig. 4). Results showed a non significant impact of flow ratio on the X-alignment [F(3,147) = .574, p value = .633]. A significant impact of flow ratio on the Y-alignment was found [F(3,147) = 21.630, p value < .000]. In conclusion, the introduced cohesion mechanism was quite effective in simulating the group proxemic behaviour: the average distance between members on the X and Y-alignment and their relative positions have been plausibly reproduced. However, the dynamic arrangement of spatial patterns of dyads according to the counter flow ratio did not completely fit with the experiment results, due to space discretisation by itself.

5 Conclusions and Future Works

According to the proposed methodological framework, an experimental study on the impact of counter flow and grouping on pedestrian dynamics was performed for sake of the design and validation of a CA-based model. The results of the experiment showed that the two hypotheses Hp 1 and Hp 2 were partially confirmed: the increase of flow ratio from 0 to .333 negatively impacts the overall speed of pedestrians; the difference between the speeds of singles and dyads is confirmed in case of counter flow and it is explained by the need of maintaining the spatial cohesion by the group members.

On the basis of the achieved results and observed behaviour, a CA model focused on the reproduction of the group proxemic behaviour has been designed. The model reproduces the dynamics by means of simple ad hoc rules, which can be calibrated by means of several parameters. In particular, individuals choose their movement direction according to the position of their target and the perception of nearby pedestrians. In this way, they try to avoid conflicts with counter flow. Dyad members, instead, are modelled with a dynamic leader-follower structure that aims at preserving the observed cohesion and spatial patterns during the simulations.

A set of simulations, reproducing the experiment procedures, was performed to validate the proposed mechanisms of the model. Results showed that the model is able to reproduce the observed effects of flow ratio and grouping on the speed of pedestrians (as shown in Fig. 5). Furthermore, the spatial patterns reproduced by the model are also similar to the observed results, demonstrating the effectiveness of the leader-follower behavioural rules.

Acknowledgement. The experiment was performed within the authorization of The University of Tokyo. The authors thank Claudio Feliciani, Zhao Pengfei, Barbara Lodigiani, Antonio Menolascina and Prof. Giuseppe Vizzari for their valuable contributions.

References

1. Bandini, S., Crociani,L., Vizzari, G.: Heterogeneous pedestrian walking speed in discrete simulation models. In: Proceedings of Traffic and Granular Flow 2013. pp. 273–279. Springer International Publishing (2015)
2. Bandini, S., Gorrini, A., Vizzari, G.: Towards an integrated approach to crowd analysis and crowd synthesis: a case study and first results. Pattern Recogn. Lett. **44**, 16–29 (2014)
3. Blue, V.J., Adler, J.L.: Cellular automata microsimulation for modeling bi-directional pedestrian walkways. Transp. Res. Part B **35**(3), 293–312 (2001)

4. Boltes, M., Seyfried, A.: Collecting pedestrian trajectories. Neurocomputing **100**, 127–133 (2013)
5. Chraibi, M., Seyfried, A., Schadschneider, A.: Generalized centrifugal-force model for pedestrian dynamics. Phys. Rev. E **82**(4), 46111 (2010)
6. Crociani, L., Lämmel, G.: Multidestination pedestrian flows in equilibrium: a cellular automaton-based approach. Comput. Aided Civil Infrastruct. Eng. **31**(2016), 432–448 (2016)
7. Crociani, L., Piazzoni, A., Vizzari, G., Bandini, S.: When reactive agents are not enough: tactical level decisions in pedestrian simulation. Intelligenza Artificiale **9**(2), 163–177 (2015)
8. Duives, D., Daamen, W., Hoogendoorn, S.: Influence of group size and group composition on the adhered distance headway. Transp. Res. Procedia **2**, 183–188 (2014)
9. Gorrini, A., Bandini, S., Vizzari, G.: Empirical investigation on pedestrian crowd dynamics and grouping. In: Proceedings of Traffic and Granular Flow 2013. pp. 83–91. Springer International Publishing (2015)
10. Helbing, D., Molnar, P.: Social force model for pedestrian dynamics. Phys. Rev. E **51**(5), 4282 (1995)
11. Kirchner, A., Nishinari, K., Schadschneider, A.: Friction effects and clogging in a cellular automaton model for pedestrian dynamics. Phys. Rev. E **67**(5), 56122 (2003)
12. Moussaïd, M., Perozo, N., Garnier, S., Helbing, D., Theraulaz, G.: The walking behaviour of pedestrian social groups and its impact on crowd dynamics. PloS One **5**(4), e10047 (2010)
13. Müller, F., Wohak, O., Schadschneider, A.: Study of influence of groups on evacuation dynamics using a cellular automaton model. Transp. Res. Procedia **2**, 168–176 (2014)
14. Nishinari, K., Kirchner, A., Namazi, A., Schadschneider, A.: Extended floor field CA model for evacuation dynamics. IEICE Trans. Inf. Syst. **87**(3), 726–732 (2004)
15. Nowak, S., Schadschneider, A.: Quantitative analysis of pedestrian counterflow in a cellular automaton model. Phys. Rev. E **85**(6), 066128-10 (2012)
16. Schadschneider, A., Klingsch, W., Klüpfel, H., Kretz, T., Rogsch, C., Seyfried, A.: Evacuation dynamics: empirical results, modeling and applications. In: Meyers, R.A. (ed.) Encyclopedia of Complexity and Systems Science, pp. 3142–3176. Springer, New York (2009)
17. Shao, W., Terzopoulos, D.: Autonomous pedestrians. Graph. Models **69**(5–6), 246–274 (2007)
18. Suma, Y., Yanagisawa, D., Nishinari, K.: Anticipation effect in pedestrian dynamics: modeling and experiments. Physica A **391**(1–2), 248–263 (2012)
19. Templeton, A., Drury, J., Philippides, A.: From mindless masses to small groups: conceptualizing collective behavior in crowd modeling. Rev. Gen. Psychol. **19**, 215–229 (2015)
20. Was, J., Lubas, R., Mysliwiec, W.: Proxemics in discrete simulation of evacuation. In: Proceedings of the 10th International Conference on Cellular Automata for Research and Industry, ACRI 2012, pp. 768–775 (2012)
21. Weidmann, U.: Transporttechnik der fussgänger - transporttechnische eigenschaftendes fussgängerverkehrs (literaturstudie). Literature Research 90, Institut füer Verkehrsplanung, Transporttechnik, Strassen- und Eisenbahnbau IVT an der ETH Zürich (1993)
22. Zanlungo, F., Ikeda, T., Kanda, T.: Potential for the dynamics of pedestrians in a socially interacting group. Phys. Rev. E **89**(1), 012811 (2014)

Cellular Automata Model of Dyads Dynamics in a Pedestrian Flow by Rigid Body Approximation

Kenichiro Shimura[1(✉)], Stefania Bandini[2,1], and Katsuhiro Nishinari[1]

[1] Research Center for Advanced Science and Technology, The University of Tokyo,
4-6-1, Komaba, Meguro-Ku, Tokyo, 153-8904, Japan
shimura@tokai.t.u-tokyo.ac.jp

[2] Department of Informatics Systems and Communication, The University of Milano Bicocca,
Viale Sarca 336 - U14, 20126 Milan, Italy

Abstract. In this study, pedestrian flow considering group especially for dyads is modelled in cellular automata (CA). Rigid body approximation is made based on the assumption of that the dyads are bonded with strong psychophysical relationship and have strong intention to stay together. Multi cell CA is applied for dyads and transition rules associating to their stress reducing behaviour are designed. Simulations are carried out to reproduce pedestrian flow in a pavement. Investigations are carried out to clarify how proportion of dyad and pedestrian density affect the pedestrian flow and spatial pattern of dyads. Although it has been known that dyads keeps line-abreast pattern at low density flow and river-like pattern at high density flow by observation study, but this is the first study which considers the detailed mechanisms to reproducing such phenomena by modelling and simulation.

Keywords: Cellular automata · Pedestrian · Crowd dynamics · Group · Dyad

1 Introduction

Pedestrian congestion has become an everyday affair in urban life. Understanding and modelling the pedestrian dynamics would help us to make a solution to solve the urban congestion. Numerous studies regarding to modelling the pedestrian motion have been performed by variety of researchers but most of those studies only focus on a pedestrian flow with singles. It is clear by observing the real world that the pedestrians are forming groups in many occasions. This fact suggests the importance of modelling and under-standing the pedestrian flow when singles and groups are mixed. In this study, modelling and simulation analysis are carried out focusing on dyads (group consist of two members). The importance of study on group dynamics is also emphasised by some observation studies. Federici et al. [1] shows that 34 % of the observed pedestrians are singles while 66 % are in groups, as composed of 19 % of dyads, 4 % larger groups. Gorrini et al. [2] shows that 16 % of the observed pedestrians are singles while 84 % are in groups, as composed of 44 % of dyads, 17 % triples and 23 % four members groups. These works shows that the percentage of individual singles in pedestrian flow is small while dyads take most of the proportions. Major characteristic of groups is to form

© Springer International Publishing Switzerland 2016
S. El Yacoubi et al. (Eds.): ACRI 2016, LNCS 9863, pp. 365–375, 2016.
DOI: 10.1007/978-3-319-44365-2_36

particular spatial arrangement due to their stress reducing behaviour as apparent of their psychophysical relationship [3]. Particularly for dyads, typical spatial arrangements are line-abreast and river-like pattern which are group members walk forming a side by side line perpendicular to the walking direction and forming a backward and forward line parallel to the walking direction, respectively as shown in Fig. 1. Costa [3] also suggests that strong psychophysical relationship makes the group members tend to keep line-abreast pattern when the pedestrian flow is in low density and they tend to keep river-like pattern in high density situation due to stress reducing behaviour. Further observation study carried out by Federici et al. [1] shows that 97 % of dyads is characterized by line-abreast pattern, 3 % by river-like pattern and Gorrini et al. [2] shows that 94 % of dyads is characterized by line-abreast pattern, 6 % by river-like pattern. Both observations are carried out for low density situation where the pedestrian flow is under free flow condition. But unfortunately there is not enough observation studies exist regarding to how dyads behaves in high density situation except brief report by Helbing et al. [4]. By this means, dynamics of mixed pedestrian flow of singles and dyads is yet unclear. The aim of this paper is to clarify how the interaction of dyads and singles affect the pedestrian dynamics. First, we propose a cellular automata (CA) model to describe mixed pedestrian flow. The model is designed based on Rule 184 of Elementary CA [5] with stochastic process where the exact solution is derived by Derrida et al. [6] and theoretical expression of associated flow is shown by Schadschneider et al. [7]. Then density effect to the flow and spatial patterns of dyads are examined by various simulations. In recent studies, group dynamics is simulated by detailed modelling of the group members [8–10]. Although it exhibits adequate results but large calculation cost is required since interpersonal distances of each member are calculated for every update. This paper introduces a new approach especially for dyads to neglect the detailed modelling of group members. For modelling the dyads, it is assumed that the dynamics of dyads is driven by strong psychophysical relationship which yields strong tendency to minimise the interpersonal distance between the members and as result, it increases the rigidity of the group. When such relationship is strong enough, at the ultimate limit, it is considered that the dyad only takes particular spatial pattern. Thus, the dyad is approximately modelled as a rigid body where only line-abreast and river-like pattern are considered neglecting intermediate spatial patterns.

Fig. 1. The typical spatial arrangement of walking dyads (a) line-abreast pattern, and (b) river-like pattern.

2 Modelling

We consider a narrow pavement where the width is just as narrow as only two people can walk side by side. Implementing this environment in CA lattice leads us to set N by 2 lattice with periodic boundary condition. Each cell has three states that are vacant, occupied by a single pedestrian and occupied by a member of a dyad. Figure 2 illustrates the environmental setting and graphical representations.

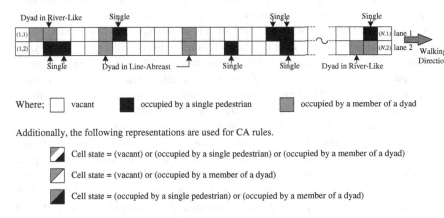

Fig. 2. The graphical representation used for this model.

2.1 CA Rules for Singles

Single pedestrians move one cell ahead with transition probability P_s if the cell is empty (*c.f.* Figure 3 (a) and (b)). This motion corresponds to one dimensional asymmetric simple exclusion process (ASEP) [6, 7]. Additionally single pedestrian overtakes other singles or dyads where the rules are illustrated in Fig. 3(c) and (d). The overtaking only occurs with probability O_s if the front cell is occupied by a single pedestrian or occupied by a member of a dyad, and if the cell at directly on his side and cell at diagonally in front is vacant. Otherwise when the above conditions are unsatisfied, the single pedestrian stops at the current cell.

(a)   (b)   (c)   (d)

Fig. 3. Rules associating to a single pedestrian moving forward in (a) lane 1, (b) lane 2. And a single pedestrian overtaking others in ahead (c) lane 1, (d) lane 2.

2.2 CA Rules for Dyads

When a group is consisted of two members, it is defined as dyad or often called the couples. There is no distinction between genders. The group here defined as multiple numbers of pedestrians bonded with psychophysical relationship and behaves together in the same manner sharing the same aim and motivation. The distinction of characteristics for singles and groups in pedestrian simulation can be interpreted as difference in grain size and associated behavioural parameters while both of them partly shares the same characteristics as they walk forward towards their destination point. Groups also have peculiar dynamics within the group induced by the members. One of the most affective dynamics of such to the macro properties of pedestrian flow is the leader and follower interactions which characterises the spatial pattern, occupancy area and interpersonal distances between group members. This paper assumes the group which members are bonded with strong psychophysical relationship. This assumption allows us to simplify modelling the peculiar dynamics within the group. Strong psychophysical relationship produces the cohesion between members not to separate each other, so members tend to keep the minimum interpersonal distance at all times. Such bonding between members makes them more difficult to change the spatial pattern and makes the group rigid. Although groups are forming particular stable patterns and are continuously changing from one stable pattern to another, but the details of transient states can be neglected from our consideration. This is because, if the members of rigid group have strong motivation to move fast to minimise their interpersonal distances, then spatial patterns should change fast enough compared to the changing rate of spatial position of surrounding pedestrians. For this reason the rigid dyad does not take arbitrary pattern lather it takes the preliminary defined stable patterns. For example, when the dyad in line-abreast pattern change its formation to river-like, there should be some intermediate spatial patterns but if this change occurs fast enough then the effect of those intermediate states to the surrounding pedestrian flow would be small enough. Thus in our dyad model, it is considered that two of the members are always staying together with keeping the closest interpersonal distance and so multi-cell CA such that a dyad is defined to be occupying two adjacent cells at all time is applied. The behaviour of dyad is then represented in CA as two adjacent particles moves together as a set under the same rule associated to three characteristic behaviours such as simple forwarding movement without changing the formation, the formation change from line-abreast to river-like pattern and vice versa.

2.2.1 Dyads, Simple Forwarding Movement

Dyads move forward similar to that for singles as previously shown. If there is space ahead of them, the dyad moves forward by one cell with probability P_g by keeping their formation pattern. Figure 4(a) shows the CA rules that a dyad in line-abreast pattern moves forward. The dyads in line-abreast pattern moves forward without changing its spatial pattern only when there is no singles behind and adequate space ahead. If there are singles behind the dyad, the dyads would feel psychological stress to give way for them and induces formation change to river-like pattern as discussed in later section. Figure 4(b) and (c) shows the condition that a dyad in river-like pattern moves forward. Dyads prefer to keep their formation in line-abreast pattern whenever possible. This possibility is controlled by surrounding available space as seen in the observation studies. And so the dyads in river-like pattern moves forward keeping its spatial pattern only when there is not enough space to change the formation to line-abreast pattern and adequate space ahead.

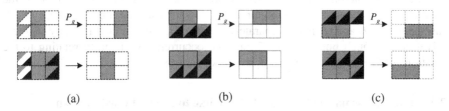

Fig. 4. Rules associating to a dyad moving forward without changing the formation pattern, (a) line-abreast pattern. (b) and (c) river-like pattern.

2.2.2 Dyads, Formation Change of Line-Abreast to River-like Pattern

It is known that when the pedestrian density increases, the dyads more likely keeps river-like lather than a line-abreast pattern. We comprehend this phenomenon as a spontaneous action by dyads due to stress reducing behaviour. Dyads in line-abreast pattern sense some stresses to keep their formation pattern when there are other pedestrians around. To reduce such stresses induced by surrounding factors, dyad changes its formation to river-like from line-abreast pattern by some probability. We consider the dyads are motivated to change formation by following two factors. 1, Formation change by collision avoidance that is dyads tend to reduce their stress which induced by obstruction of their own walking path. 2, Dyads gives way to other singles of those who come from the behind since singles often walk faster than dyads and gives stress to slow walking dyads to move away from its walking path. These two factors are modelled in CA rule as illustrated in Fig. 5(a), (b) and Fig. 5(c), (d), (e) respectively. Figure 5(a) and (b) show the CA rules for dyads change formation from line-abreast to river-like pattern by probability O_{lr} when there is someone ahead of them. This movement appears as results of dyads try to avoid their walking path being obstructed by others and is referred to the former factor. Figure 5(c), (d) and (e) show the situation when there is singles

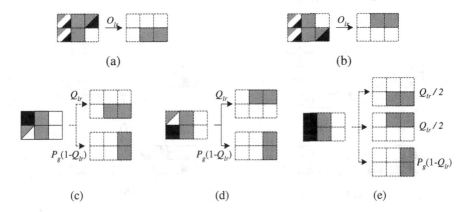

Fig. 5. Rules associating to a dyad changing the formation form line-abreast to river-like pattern.

behind of the dyad and there is no one ahead which refers to the latter factor. The dyad has choice of either changing its formation or moves forward. The probability of changing the formation to river-like is Q_{lr} and if the dyad is chosen not change the formation, then it moves forward remaining its line-abreast pattern by probability P_g. It is also note that O_{lr} and Q_{lr} needs separately evaluated since they are driven by different motivations although both O_{lr} and Q_{lr} are the occurrence probability relating to the formation change from line-abreast to river-like pattern.

2.2.3 Dyads, Formation Change of River-like to Line-Abreast Pattern

Member of dyads in rigid group minimise their interpersonal distance and prefer to keep line-abreast pattern whenever possible. And so the dyads in river-like change their formation to line-abreast pattern by some probability when there is adequate available space. Changing the formation to line-abreast pattern often obstructs the walking path of others so required space are those two spaces directly beside the dyad members. When these spaces are available at vicinity and there is not a single nor a dyad at diagonally behind, the dyad in river-like pattern may changes its formation to line-abreast pattern without obstructing the walk path of others. So the dyad can comfortably change its formation without sensing a stress induced by pedestrians behind. The associated CA rules of this condition are illustrated in Fig. 6(a), (b), (c) and (d) where the possibility of changing formation form river-like to line-abreast pattern is noted as q_{rl}. Additionally

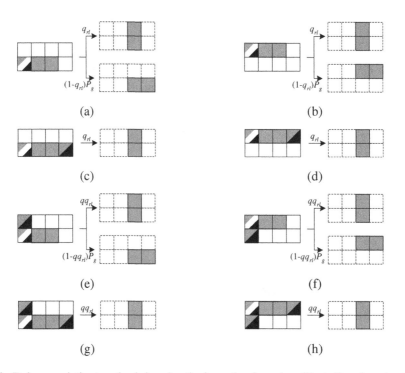

Fig. 6. Rules associating to a dyad changing the formation form river-like to line-abreast pattern.

to this, when the dyad does not change its formation pattern (where the probability is 1-q_{rl}) and there is a vacancy ahead of the line-abreast dyad, it has a possibility of moving forward with keeping its formation pattern similar to that shown in Fig. 4. The probability of such motion is given as $P_g(1- q_{rl})$ and the associated CA rules are shown in Fig. 6 (a), (b). Moreover, Fig. 6(e), (f), (g) and (h) show the rules relating to the situation that single or a dyad exist at diagonally behind. When the dyad in river-like changes the formation to line-abreast pattern, the dyad obstructs the walking path of a single or a dyad who are approaching from diagonally behind and so the dyad may senses some psychological stress. The dyad has choice of either changing its formation or moves forward depends on the level of stresses. The action which induces less stress is chosen by comparing not being in line-abreast pattern against that obstructing the walking path of pedestrians behind the dyad. For some river-like dyads who have strong intention to stay side by side, they may change to line-abreast pattern without caring the pedestrians behind because they percept larger stress induced by not being in line-abreast pattern. The value qq_{rl} is the probability expressing the occurrence of such ignorance behaviour. And so small value qq_{rl} is assigned for sensible or cooperative dyads. Additionally to this, when the dyad does not change its formation pattern and there is a vacancy ahead of the line-abreast dyad, it has a possibility of moving forward with keeping its formation pattern as for the former rule.

3   Results and Discussions

Simulation is carried out to investigate the effect of densities on dyad's formation pattern and pedestrian flow. The pedestrian consists of singles and dyads, so total number of pedestrian n is the sum of singles n_s and sum of member of dyads n_m so number of dyads n_c is given as $n_m/2$. Then the pedestrian density ρ is defined as ratio between numbers of pedestrian n to the lattice size $2 \times N$ with periodic boundary condition. The proportion of pedestrians classified as dyads θ with respect to overall pedestrian is n_m/n and so the proportion of singles is $1-\theta = n_s/n$. For the initial condition, singles and members of dyads associated to the density $\rho(1-\theta)$ and $\rho\theta$, respectively are randomly placed along the lattice assuming that all dyads are initially in line-abreast pattern. The image output of the simulation is shown in Fig. 7 where (a) is for the initial condition and (b), (c) are for the snap shot after sufficient iteration. The values of parameters are set as $P_s = 1$,

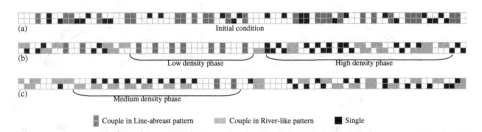

Fig. 7. The image output of the simulation. ($P_s = 1$, $O_s = 1$, $P_g = 0.7$, $O_{lr} = 1$, $Q_{lr} = 1$, $q_{rl} = 1$, $qq_{rl} = 0$, $\rho = 0.5$ and $\theta = 0.65$).

$O_s = 1$, $P_g = 0.7$, $O_{lr} = 1$, $Q_{lr} = 1$, $q_{rl} = 1$, $qq_{rl} = 0$, $\rho = 0.5$ and $\theta = 0.65$. This parameter setting is to simulate the interaction of singles and slow walking dyads who are cooperative to surrounding pedestrians.

Thee spatial phases for low, medium and high density are repeatedly appears throughout the simulation. Example of typical spatial pattern appears at low, medium and high density phase are illustrated in Fig. 7(b) and (c). It appears that at low density, most of the dyads keep line-abreast pattern. Toward medium density phase, singles move faster than dyads so the singles penetrate into the interstitial site between dyads to cause interactive behaviour such as overtaking and formation change of line-abreast dyads to river-like pattern. Such behaviours cause the separation of walking lane for singles and dyads in medium density phase. Figure 7(c) shows the phenomenon of that singles and river-like dyads are making a line formation and separately walking in different lane. Together with these spatial structure, some dyads are keeping line-abreast pattern when reasonable space is available. And at high density, singles are trapped in between dyads whom keeping river-like formation trying to let singles to path through. The dependency of dyad's formation pattern on local density seen in these result are consistency to reported observed phenomena [1–3].

At first, we look at the effects of dyads' formation pattern to the pedestrian flow. A plot of mean flow with respect to total density is so called a fundamental diagram. Figure 8(a) illustrates the fundamental diagram of when there exist only line-abreast dyads at entire simulation period with no formation change. This dynamics only contains the CA rule shown in Fig. 4(a). The obtained diagram is identical to that for ASEP based single lane single particle traffic model [7] since, in this case, two particles are lined up in side by side formation on each lane and moves together. Contrary to this, Fig. 8(b) illustrates the fundamental diagram of when there exist only river-like dyads. The dynamics contains the CA rule shown in Fig. 4(b), (c) and 6 with $q_{rl} = qq_{rl} = 0$. It is seen that the dyads being in river-like formation has the effect of increasing the maximum flow and associated total density. The reason for this is that, for river-like model, two adjacent particles line up in moving direction moves together by one cell in a single update step. And so the maximum flow at $P_g = 1$ for river-like case is 2/3 at total density of 2/3 giving that the maximum flow for line-abreast is 0.5.

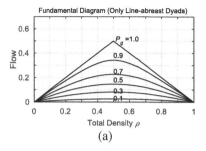
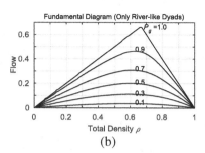

Fig. 8. Fundamental diagrams of when (a) only Line-abreast dyads and, (b) only River-like dyads in the lattice.

And to reveal more in detail about how the total pedestrian density ρ affects the dyads formation and associated flow, further calculation are carried out for the case of various proportions of dyads θ. The values of parameters P_s, O_s, P_g, O_{lr}, Q_{lr}, q_{rl}, qq_{rl} are set as same as those for Fig. 7. Figure 9(a) and (c) illustrates how the presence ratio of line-abreast and river-like pattern of dyads varies with respect to total pedestrian density for given θ. And associated fundamental diagrams are illustrated in Fig. 9(b) and (d), respectively. Every simulation initially start with all dyads are in line-abreast pattern so the initial presence ratio of line-abreast dyad is unity. When pedestrian consists of only dyads where $\theta = 1$, there is no interaction with singles so no formation change occurs, thus initially assigned line-abreast pattern is kept during entire simulation time. Therefore, the fundamental diagram for this case is identical for that illustrated in Fig. 8(a) when $P_g = 0.7$. On the other hand, when $\theta = 0$, it is a situation that only singles are present in the lattice. As previously mentioned that the fundamental diagrams for line-abreast dyads are identical to those for singles. So Fig. 9(b) and (d) when $\theta = 0$ are identical to Fig. 8(a) when $P_g = 1$ since $P_s = 1$ in this simulation. When dyads and singles are mixed, initially all dyads are in line-abreast pattern, then the presence of river-like dyads start increases as increasing ρ. These phenomena appear as result of two interacting motion of dyads against singles, that against singles in front and that against singles at behind. The former CA rules are shown in Fig. 5(a), (b), Fig. 6(a), (b), (c) and (d). And the latter CA rules are shown in Fig. 5(c), (d), (e), Fig. 6 (e), (f), (g) and (h). The case of Fig. 9 (a) includes the interactions induced by dyads having backward perception. So dyads are always making cooperative action which doesn't obstruct the walking path of singles at behind. This is the meaning of parameter setting of $O_{lr} = 1$ and $qq_{rl} = 0$. Contrary to this, when dyads have no backward perception, the action made by dyads would have defective effect to singles at behind. The parameter settings correspond to such situation are $O_{lr} = 0$ and $qq_{rl} = 1$ and the result is illustrated in Fig. 9(c). Comparing Fig. 9(c) to Fig. 9(a), the increase rate of river-like pattern with respect to the total density is slower. This is due to the lack of backward perception which reduces the opportunity of line-abreast dyads to change their formation to river-like pattern. Additionally, if those dyads gain the backward perception as shown in Fig. 5(c), (d) and (e) then the opportunity of changing to river-like pattern would increase. It is also seen that the intersection of line-abreast and river-like presence ratio occurs when both presence ratio is 0.5. This situation represents the mean number of line-abreast and river-like dyads are balanced. Figure 9(a) shows that the values of ρ for the intersection point increases as increasing θ, but the profile is reversed for Fig. 9(c). This is relating to the presence of backward perception of dyads and the mechanisms of associating pattern change. The mechanism of the former (Fig. 9(a)) is dominated by interaction of dyads between singles at behind and the latter (Fig. 9(c)) is dominated by interaction of dyads between singles in front. The line-abreast dyad without backward perception change its formation to river-like only when there is congestion ahead of it. Since the dyads generally walk slower than singles (where in this simulation $P_s = 1.0$ and $P_g = 0.7$), when fast walking singles caught up with preceding line-abreast dyad, those singles are trapped behind the dyad and the jam is locally produced unless the dyad change formation to river-like. When succeeding line-abreast dyad encounters to the jam, it gains the opportunity for changing the formation to river-like pattern. And so the dyads without backward perception have higher possibility of changing the formation to river-like pattern when the occurrence possibility of local jam is larger. The occurrence possibility of local jam is larger when total density ρ is lower, proportion of dyads θ is higher and presence ratio of line-abreast dyads is higher. Thus the intersection point shifts to larger ρ with respect to decrease of θ as seen in Fig. 9 (b). If the preceding line-abreast dyad has backward perception, then the dyad may change formation to river-like and those single can path through. So the associated flow appears higher than that for dyads without backward perception as seen in Fig. 9 (b) and (d). And so the dyads with backward perception have higher possibility of changing the formation to river-like pattern when the mobility of single is larger. The mobility of singles is larger when total density ρ is lower, proportion of dyads θ is lower and presence ratio of line-abreast dyads is higher. Thus the intersection point shifts to larger ρ with respect to increase of θ as seen in Fig. 9(a).

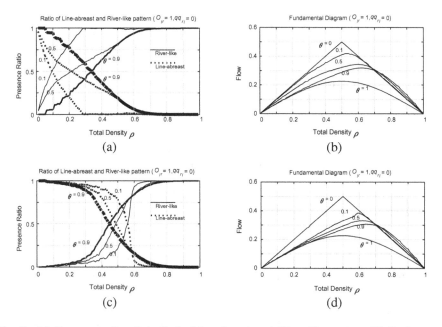

Fig. 9. (a) Presence ratio of dyads in Line-abreast and River-like pattern (b) fundamental diagrams when dyads has backward perception ($O_{lr} = 1$ and $qq_{rl} = 0$). (c) and (d) those for dyads has no backward perception ($O_{lr} = 0$ and $qq_{rl} = 1$). Which calculated for various dyad's proportion θ as numbered on each graph.

4   Conclusion

A cellular automata model of mixed flow of singles and dyads is introduced by approximating dyads as rigid bodies. Investigations are carried out to clarify how flow and dyad's spatial arrangement are affected by pedestrian density and proportion of dyads. The phenomenon that more dyads take river-like pattern as increasing the total pedestrian density is validly reproduced. The advantage of introducing the rigid body approximation is to make the algorithm simple and reduces the number of iteration loop but adequate for simulation. Yet disadvantage remains as not capable to represent the arbitrary group shape. Although the simulation is carried out for two lanes problem in this study but the model is easily extensible to arbitrary environment.

References

1. Federici, M.L., Gorrini, A., Manenti, L., Vizzari, G.: Data collection for modeling and simulation: case study at the university of milan-bicocca. In: Sirakoulis, G.Ch., Bandini, S. (eds.) ACRI 2012. LNCS, vol. 7495, pp. 699–708. Springer, Heidelberg (2012)
2. Gorrini, A., Bandini, S., Vizzari, G.: Empirical investigation on pedestrian crowd dynamics and grouping. Traffic Granular Flow **13**, 83–91 (2014)
3. Costa, M.: Interpersonal distances in group walking. J. Nonverbal Behav. **34**(1), 15–26 (2010)
4. Moussaïd, M., Niriaska, P.N., Simon, G.S., Dirk Helbing, D., Guy Theraulaz, G.: The walking behaviour of pedestrian social groups and its impact on crowd dynamics. PLoS ONE **5**(4), e10047 (2010)
5. Wolfram, S.: Cellular Automata and Complexity: Collected Papers. Addison-Wesley Publishing Company, Reading (1994)
6. Derrida, B., Evans, M.R., Hakim, V., Pasquier, V.: Exact solution of a 1D asymmetric exclusion model using a matrix formulation. J. Phys. A: Math. Gen. **26**, 1493 (1993)
7. Schadschneider, A., Schreckenberg, M.: Cellular automaton models and traffic flow. J. Phys. A: Math. Gen. **26**, L679–L683 (1993)
8. Bandini, S., Rubagotti, F., Vizzari, G., Shimura, K.: A cellular automata based model for pedestrian and group dynamics: motivations and first experiments. In: Malyshkin, V. (ed.) PaCT 2011. LNCS, vol. 6873, pp. 125–139. Springer, Heidelberg (2011)
9. Bandini, S., Rubagotti, F., Vizzari, G., Shimura, K.: An agent model of pedestrian and group dynamics: experiments on group cohesion. In: Pirrone, R., Sorbello, F. (eds.) AI*IA 2011. LNCS, vol. 6934, pp. 104–116. Springer, Heidelberg (2011)
10. Bandini, S., Manzoni, S., Mauri, G., Redaelli, S., Vanneschi, L., Bandini, S., Manenti, L., Manzoni, S.: Generation of pedestrian groups distributions with probabilistic cellular automata. In: Sirakoulis, G.Ch., Bandini, S. (eds.) ACRI 2012. LNCS, vol. 7495, pp. 299–308. Springer, Heidelberg (2012)

Enhanced Multi-parameterized Cellular Automaton Model for Crowd Evacuation: The Case of a University Building

Dimitrios Tsorvas[1], Ioakeim G. Georgoudas[1], Franciszek Seredynski[2], and Georgios Ch. Sirakoulis[1(✉)]

[1] Laboratory of Electronics, Department of Electrical and Computer Engineering, Democritus University of Thrace, 67100 Xanthi, Greece
{dtsorvas,igeorg,gsirak}@ee.duth.gr
[2] Department of Mathematics and Natural Sciences, Cardinal Stefan Wyszynski University in Warsaw, 01-938 Warsaw, Poland
f.seredynski@uksw.edu.pl

Abstract. This work investigates the impact of interactions among individuals and their environment during evacuations in a University Building. The proposed CA-based model aims at simplifying the simulation process and at accomplishing successful modeling of evacuation processes of moderate density. Thus, the model is effectively parameterised by incorporating variable speeds, acceleration, massive physical pressure onto individuals, adoption and efficient location of leading persons. Remarkable features that characterise crowd evacuation are prominent; transition from uncoordinated to coordinated movement due to common purpose, arching in front of exits, herding behavior. Finally, the validation of the model includes further qualitative and quantitative analysis, which is based on the comparison of the flow-density and speed-density response of the model with corresponding literature derived distributions.

Keywords: Crowd modelling · Cellular automata · Evacuation · Flow-density diagram · Speed-density diagram · Acceleration · Leaders

1 Introduction

Safety of people during evacuation strongly depends on their environment (fellow people and surroundings), as well as on the design and the spatial arrangement of the area that they are present. Thus, deep understanding of how people make up their minds in evacuation processes is rather helpful in order to minimize the corresponding risk. A common approach for predicting the moving behaviour of a large number of people is to emulate the crowd as a homogeneous mass, which behaves like a flowing liquid [1]. But this approach considers that the crowd consists of individuals identical and unable to think. Therefore, the need is evident for approaching the crowd as consisting of people who have critical capacity and think in order to react to the stimulus that they receive from their environment. In such critical situations, there is always a tendency for individuals to follow the crowd [2]. Moreover, there is a strong possibility, due to apparent

© Springer International Publishing Switzerland 2016
S. El Yacoubi et al. (Eds.): ACRI 2016, LNCS 9863, pp. 376–386, 2016.
DOI: 10.1007/978-3-319-44365-2_37

danger, people to react hastily and to block an output that could be passed safely, provided that they had retained their composure. Another interesting attribute that characterises crowd movement is that the widening of a corridor does not always accelerate the corresponding movement of a crowd [3]. Nevertheless, it should be noted that the simulation of a crowd consisting of discrete individuals with different properties, obviously entails additional complexity. Modern computational resources provide scientific community with the ability to overcome such problems and to develop models that are based on the motion of each individual.

In this study, the adoption of Cellular Automata (CA) as the main computational tool facilitates the simulation process. CA are featured by massive parallelism and they are very effective in simulating physical systems. They can capture the essential features of systems, where global behaviour arises from the collective effect of simple components that interact locally [4]. Furthermore, CA can act as an alternative to Partial Differential Equations (PDEs) [5]. Thus, they could effectively approach multi-parameterised systems that are mathematically described by differential equations, such as evacuation. Literature review proves that CA constitute a robust crowd modeling method. They have been extensively adopted to examine crowd behaviour from various aspects. More particularly, herding behaviour [6, 7] along with obstacle avoidance [8, 9] has been thoroughly investigated. Bi-directional pedestrian behaviour [10] and friction effects [11] have been elaborated. Furthermore, the impact of environmental conditions [12] and proxemics [13] have been studied. Inertial effects [14] and leader effect [15] as well as the assumption that pedestrians behave as particles subject to long-range forces [16] have also been modeled with the use of CA.

This study examines interactions among people and between people and environment during evacuations. The proposed model is CA-based and its scope is to simplify the process of simulation in terms of computational speed and complexity yet to achieve adequately accurate modeling of the evacuation process with microscopic and macroscopic characteristics, in cases of moderate density. Simulation process emerges features that characterise crowd evacuation being themselves indicative of the correctness of the method; transition from uncoordinated to coordinated movement due to common purpose, arching in front of exits, herding behavior. Moreover, the model incorporates the concept of leading individuals, namely persons who have the ability to lead the crowd towards an exit. These individuals equipped with electronic devices such as modern mobile phones and combined with sensors could provide information to the administrator for appointing more efficient evacuating responses. Finally, the evaluation process includes further qualitative and quantitative analysis. The later is based on the comparison of the flow-density and speed-density response of the model with corresponding representations from literature.

In the following, the major theoretical principles of the proposed evacuation model are presented (Sect. 2). In Sect. 3, simulation scenarios and corresponding results are presented and discussed, in order to indicate the prominent features of the model and to evaluate its response. Conclusions and future perspectives are provided in Sect. 4.

2   The Theoretical Background of the Model

The model is CA-based, thus the modeling of the phenomenon of evacuation is based on lattices that discretises the space into a grid of two dimensions $L \times M$. This grid is homogeneous and isotropic, and the cells of the CA can exist in two possible states, either free or occupied by only one pedestrian. Each cell is equal to the minimum size that a person can occupy, i.e. 0.3 m × 0.3 m [17]. This space enables modeling of moderate and high density crowd evacuation situations. This model adopts the Moore neighborhood of radius three cells, indicating that the state of each cell is influenced by its neighboring cells. The renewal of the state of each cell takes place synchronously for all cells. Moreover, for each individual, the choice of direction is an important factor of the model, since it realises the driving mechanism of the model. It is adopted the idea of the floor potential, which generates an attraction field among pedestrians and exits [2]. This field is incorporated in the table of weights, which contains for each cell its distance from the exit. This attraction A is mathematically described by the following formula:

$$
A = \begin{cases} A_0, & \text{if } (x_i, y_i) \text{ an exit} \\ exp\left\{ -min\left[\sqrt{(x_i - x_o)^2 + (y_i - y_o)^2} \right] \right\}, & \text{if } (x_i, y_i) \text{ not an obstacle} \\ 0, & \text{if } (x_i, y_i) \text{ an obstacle} \end{cases} \quad (1)
$$

where A_o indicates the maximum attraction, whereas (x_i, y_j) and (x_o, y_o) represent the coordinates of the cell (i, j) and the exit respectively.

During a simulation step, each individual chooses to move to one of the eight possible orientations of the neighborhood. The movement is designed to approximate the direction which is closer to the exit. The mechanism of movement results from a possible approach of the space, which is mainly based on the Euclidean distance metric d_e for two dimensions and is calculated by the equation:

$$
d_e = \sqrt{(x_i - x_o)^2 + (y_i - y_o)^2} \quad (2)
$$

Moreover, aiming at a more realistic movement representation of a person in case of parallel movement, Manhattan distance is used along with the metric of Euclidean distance. The former is much faster when considering the required calculations and it is expressed by the relationship:

$$
d_m = |x_i - x_o| + |y_i - y_o| \quad (3)
$$

The gradual reduction of values that correspond to the table of distances and they are generated by the formula above, defines the direction of travel, thus providing a kind of sense of space to the pedestrians. This model, as being CA-generated is able to create complex phenomena from simple interactions between cells. Algorithmically, the simulation is a two-fold process that is based on two tables; the first is the one that contains the topology of the building, the individuals and other objects, and the second one, which is of the same size and contains for each cell a number that corresponds to the distance from the nearest exit (Fig. 1).

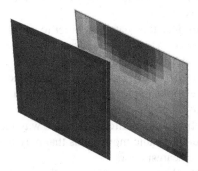

Fig. 1. Parallel optical representation of data/simulation table (left) with the weights table (right) as drafted by the model developed in Matlab. The gradation of colors in the table weights represents the variation in the distance.

Furthermore, while aiming at a more realistic representation of the evacuation process, factors that affect movement characteristics are taken into consideration. Such a parameter is the velocity of the pedestrians, which varies from person to person. In this model, three different speed levels are incorporated, thus extending the dimension of the active neighbourhood of cells from 3×3 up to 7×7. Thus, an individual that occupies a cell is enabled to get along with greater speeds. Consequently, people with different speeds (U) cover different distances (x) in the same time (t). This fact is mathematically represented by the formula below:

$$
\begin{cases}
U1 = x \times t \\
U2 = 2x \times t \\
U3 = 3x \times t
\end{cases}
\tag{4}
$$

However, the modeling of speed is not a static process but it is adapted on the current conditions during each simulation step. More specifically, a person who can move with maximum speed is able to be transferred to the corresponding cell only in the case that all intermediate cells are free. Provided that there is at least one intermediate cell that is occupied then the person will adjust her/his motion dynamically and will move at a lower speed proportional to the distance that the obstruction lies.

In cases of normal visibility, anyone can quite easily find the exit and reach the optimal route. However, when the exit is not so apparent, evacuation is less effective and more often has a longer duration. The majority of people try to move straight to the position, where they believe that the exit lies, but usually they end up moving near the walls. Then they move in one of these two directions to locate the exit. In case that they meet other people along the way, the tendency is to form groups that collectively move towards one direction. Nevertheless, simulations show that neither the herding nor the individualistic behavior perform effectively [2]. Most chances of survival summons a mix of these two behaviors; individualism allows some people to find the exit and grouping behavior ensures that even more teams will follow such a course. This approach combined with the incorporation of leaders within simulation process may provide very satisfactory results in terms of evacuation.

This model tries to introduce this feature in order to simulate evacuation more realistically. Thus, the model assigns to each person randomly a value to a parameter called "panic flag", whereby the ability to manage panic situations will depend. The range is chosen to vary from one to ten to integer values [1, ..., 10]. The more this value increases the more possible is the person to approach the panic behaviour. It is worth noting that in such a condition, the route of the individual towards the exit is not the optimal. A secondary algorithm is activated that differentiates the way that the person reaches the exit by introducing rush due to panic movements that may form wrong choices in the process of exiting from the nearest door.

Furthermore, aiming at enhancing the realism of the simulation the model takes into consideration the fact that the speed is not constant, but continuously variable depending on the density and topology of the space available. Therefore the acceleration is a parameter that is incorporated. The term of acceleration Acc is defined as follows:

$$Acc = \frac{1}{\tau_\alpha}\left(u_a^o e_a - v_a\right) \tag{5}$$

where e_α is the direction that the pedestrian wants to move, y_a^o is the desired speed and ν_α the actual speed. The deviation from the speed y_a^o leads to a bias for achieving the desired speed in time τ_α.

Algorithmically, the acceleration of individuals is achieved by using (i) a parallel array of the same size as that of the data table and (ii) the corresponding parameter of the CA cell. When the movement of an individual is interrupted either because she/he is trapped nor due to the presence of another individual, a flag is activated to the corresponding cell of the so-called *acceleration table*. The value of the flag depends on the maximum speed of the individual. According to the acceleration table, as the flag value is reduced the person is enabled to move with increasing speed. Moreover, in case that an individual stops moving, then in order to reach the maximum speed she/he should pass all different stages defined by the acceleration table (Fig. 2).

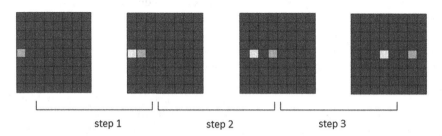

step 1   step 2   step 3

Fig. 2. Depiction of successive speed development. The lighter color shows the place occupied cell during the previous time step. (Color figure online)

Another remarkable phenomenon that is appointed in mass crowd movement is the development of huge forces during mass crowd movement. Thus, within the model an algorithm has been incorporated that detects the pressure that is exerted among individuals and is able to simulate fairly realistic the generation of accidents due to overcrowding. Thus, for each occupied cell, it is approximately calculated the pressure that is exerted on it by its neighboring cells. The calculated value depends on the current movement of the crowd. Afterwards, the corresponding possibility for an accident is calculated; as the pressure increases, the likelihood of an accident rises alike. Additionally, another factor that affects the generation of accidents is the time duration of the exerted pressure. An individual can last for a short time quite a lot of pressure, but if the same pressure is exerted for a relatively longer time, then irreparable situation could take place. Thus, when both sizes, i.e. pressure and time are increasing then the possibility of a generation of an accident approaches that of a certain event, according to the equation:

$$P = w_1 F_p(N) + w_2 F_t(T) \tag{6}$$

wherein P is the possibility for an accident, F_p is the pressure calculation function that each cell receives, w_1 is the weight contribution of F_p, F_t is the function for calculating the duration of the exerted and w_2 is the weight of F_t contribution.

Furthermore, the model incorporates the action of individuals that are called leaders and that they have the ability to guide other individuals that are called followers towards the exits. The main attribute of the leaders is that they are assigned with their own array of weights-distances, which is consistently updated by smart devices, in order to enable them to select optimum routes and/or to avoid clogged exits, barriers etc. Leaders dominantly affect the floor field values that define the movement of followers. Each leader has a field of influence that is schematically depicted as a semicircle (Fig. 3). By changing the radius of the semicircle, this field can dynamically change. This feature enables the model to increase or decrease the influence of the leaders within the crowd. For instance, the strength of the field of influence is reduced when followers reach an exit, whereas

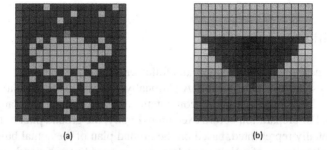

(a)   (b)

Fig. 3. (a) The upward movement of a leader (orange) and the crowd following him, (b) the weight-distance array of the followers. The gradation of colors is based on the distance from the leader; from lower (blue) to highest (red). (Color figure online)

its strength increases in order to note the impact of a significant event during the evacuation (e.g. closed door or low visibility). Furthermore, for reasons of enhanced realistic emulation, leaders differ in terms of speed and size of the sphere of influence.

The evaluation of the model is completed with the comparison of fundamental characteristics and diagrams generated from various scenarios with corresponding distributions from literature. More specifically, the overall density of the crowd is measured by counting all individuals in the area of interest and then dividing by the area of this region. The total flow is calculated from the total number of individuals who move through the exits per simulation step by dividing with the length of the this intersection. The flow of people results from experimental relations of speed with the density of people. Assuming that people move smoothly, the flow per meter of width is expressed by the equation:

$$Q(\rho) = \rho V(\rho) \tag{7}$$

Variable Q represents the flow per meter of width and variable ρ the density of individuals. Another equation that expresses the relationship between the speed and density of individuals is:

$$V(\rho) = V_o \left\{ 1 - exp\left[-\alpha \left(\frac{1}{\rho} - \frac{1}{\rho_{max}} \right) \right] \right\} \tag{8}$$

where V_o is the free speed at low densities of people and α an adjustment parameter [17]. One of the basic principles of the model is that each person can cover a minimum area of about $0.55 \times 0.55 = 0.3$ m^2. Therefore the maximum density will range from 4 to 6 people/m^2. The region of interest occupies from 170 to 330 cells of the CA, depending on the simulation scenarios, i.e. an area equal to 51 up 99 m^2. Moreover, the number of people in the building reaches up to 1500 people. For each step the number of people within the region of interest (RoI) is counted and the value of the density is calculated from the relationship:

$$\rho = \frac{num\ of\ people\ in\ RoI}{area\ of\ RoI} \tag{9}$$

3   Simulation and Results

The navigation of a number of leaders and followers in complex environments requires adequate representation of the virtual. Additionally, in order better simulation speed to be achieved, with as little as possible computational workload, the simulation program requires a kind of preparation before execution. Firstly, the ground plan of the building is computationally represented, based on the ground plan of the actual building. Then the corresponding arrays of weights and data are generated for each simulation scenario. The site chosen for the simulation are the two floors of the building B of the Department of Electrical and Computer Engineering at the Democritus University of Thrace (DUTh) in Kimmeria, Xanthi, Greece.

Simulation results are presented in the form of graphs for better understanding. It should be noted that the choice of the location of the leaders is not random and it does not change from simulation to simulation. This way, a more effective distribution of leaders is succeeded. During the experiments, ten different possible positions of leaders are assessed, by counting the number of people that enter the area of influence for each position. The experiment is performed ten times for each different location. The position with the greater impact is chosen as the initial point of the leader.

A characteristic simulation process is elaborated in this study. According to the adopted scenario, individuals are not aware of the exact location of the exits and they do not have full knowledge of their environment. Thus, a situation of low visibility due to smoke or darkness is simulated and it is examined the impact of leaders on the response of the model (Fig. 4). Below (Figs. 5, 6 and 7), there are comparative diagrams of the experiment either with or without the presence of leaders.

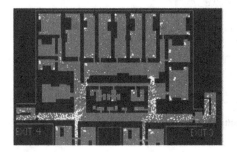 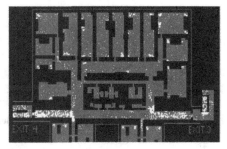

Fig. 4. Successive snapshots of simulation process. Their movement is in the direction of exits and it is influenced by the presence of leaders.

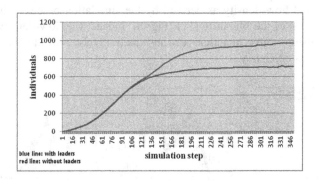

Fig. 5. The cumulative flow chart of people over time, as measured by the model

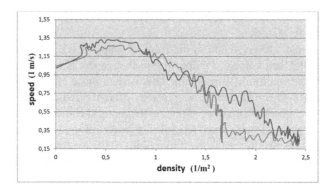

Fig. 6. Speed-density diagram of individuals.

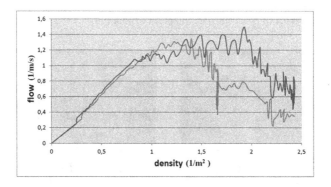

Fig. 7. Flowchart-density of people resulting from the model

The validation of the model is achieved by comparing the fundamental diagrams of speed-density and flow-density as derived by the simulation process with the corresponding diagrams of the literature [17] (Fig. 8). Indeed, the flow-density and speed-density relationships agree quantitatively and qualitatively with literature references, thus enhancing its efficiency.

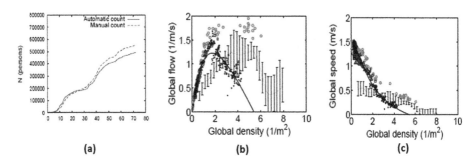

Fig. 8. [17] (a) Cumulative flow diagram (b) The total flow as a function of the total density (c) The overall speed as a function of the total density.

4   Conclusions

The proposed CA-based model could establish a fundamental part of an active crowd system that allows dynamic management of crowd evacuation. The model is characterised by a quick response and fast processing of prominent features of crowd movement, thus providing more reaction time to evacuating individuals. The evaluation process indicates particular characteristics of crowd behavior, such as clustering phenomena, bottlenecks at the exits, change of motion from accidental to coordinated, or transition to detuning due to panic. Furthermore, the model is evaluated by comparing key features of the dynamic movement of the crowd with those from charts that have resulted in similar distributions for real data. The respective diagrams show a good quantitative and qualitative approach, thus enhancing the efficiency accuracy of the model. Finally, the hardware implementation of the monitoring and guidance algorithm of leaders along with the simultaneous development of a program compatible with portable devices, e.g. based on popular platforms such as Android, IOS and Windows Mobile, could further accelerate the overall response of the system.

References

1. Henderson, L.F.: The statistics of crowd fluids. Nature **229**, 381–383 (1971)
2. Helbing, D., Farkas, I., Vicsek, T.: Simulating dynamical features of escape panic. Nature **407**(6803), 487–490 (2000)
3. Helbing, D., Farkas, I.J., Molnar, P., Vicsek, T.: Simulation of pedestrian crowds in normal and evacuation situations. Pedestrian Evacuation Dyn. **21**(2), 21–58 (2002)
4. Feynman, R.P.: Simulating physics with computers. Int. J. Theor. Phys. **21**(6/7), 467–488 (1982)
5. Marcou, O., El Yacoubi, S., Chopard, B.: A bi-fluid Lattice Boltzmann model for water flow in an irrigation channel. In: Yacoubi, S., Chopard, B., Bandini, S. (eds.) ACRI 2006. LNCS, vol. 4173, pp. 373–382. Springer, Heidelberg (2006)
6. Georgoudas, I., Sirakoulis, G.C., Andreadis, I.: An intelligent cellular automaton model for crowd evacuation in fire spreading conditions. In: Proceedings of 19th IEEE ICTAI 2007, vol. 1, pp. 36–43 (2007)
7. Bandini, S., Manzoni, S., Mauri, G., Redaelli, S.: Emergent pattern interpretation in vegetable population dynamics. J. Cellular Automata **2**(2), 103–110 (2007)
8. Georgoudas, I.G., Koltsidas, G., Sirakoulis, G.C., Andreadis, I.T.: A cellular automaton model for crowd evacuation and its auto-defined obstacle avoidance attribute. In: Bandini, S., Manzoni, S., Umeo, H., Vizzari, G. (eds.) ACRI 2010. LNCS, vol. 6350, pp. 455–464. Springer, Heidelberg (2010)
9. Boukas, E., Kostavelis, I., Gasteratos, A., Sirakoulis, G.C.: Robot guided crowd evacuation. IEEE Trans. Autom. Sci. Eng. **12**(2), 739–751 (2015)
10. Li, J., Yang, L.Z., Zhao, D.L.: Simulation of bi-direction pedestrian movement in corridor. Phys. A **354**, 619–628 (2005)
11. Kirchner, A., Klupfel, H., Nishinari, K., Schadschneider, A., Schreckenberg, M.: Simulation of competitive egress behavior: comparison with aircraft evacuation data. Phys. A **324**, 689–697 (2003)
12. Varas, A., et al.: Cellular automaton model for evacuation process with obstacles. Phys. A **382**, 631–642 (2007)

13. Wąs, J., Lubaś, R., Myśliwiec, W.: Proxemics in discrete simulation of evacuation. In: Sirakoulis, Georgios C., Bandini, S. (eds.) ACRI 2012. LNCS, vol. 7495, pp. 768–775. Springer, Heidelberg (2012)

14. Aubé, F., Shield, R.: Modeling the effect of leadership on crowd flow dynamics. In: Sloot, P.M., Chopard, B., Hoekstra, A.G. (eds.) ACRI 2004. LNCS, vol. 3305, pp. 601–611. Springer, Heidelberg (2004)

15. Vihas, C., Georgoudas, I.G., Sirakoulis, G.C.: Cellular automata incorporating follow-the-leader principles to model crowd dynamics. J. Cell. Automata **8**(5–6), 333–346 (2013)

16. Yuan, W.F., Tan, K.H.: An evacuation model using cellular automata. Phys. A **384**, 549–566 (2007)

17. Johansson, A., Helbing, D., A-Abideen, H.Z., Al-Bosta, S.: From crowd dynamics to crowd safety: a video-based analysis. Adv. Complex Syst. **11**(4), 497–527 (2008)

Heterogeneous Dynamics Through Coupling Cellular Automata Models

Stefania Bandini[1,2] and Giuseppe Vizzari[1(✉)]

[1] Complex Systems Artificial Intelligence Research Center,
University of Milano-Bicocca, Viale Sarca 336/14, 20126 Milano, Italy
{stefania.bandini,giuseppe.vizzari}@disco.unimib.it
[2] RCAST, The University of Tokyo,
4-6-1 Komaba, Meguro-ku, Tokyo 153-8904, Japan

Abstract. In certain situations the simultaneous dynamics of two systems influencing each other, for instance due to the fact that they share a portion of space, must be simulated to study the interaction among them. When a CA approach is adopted to model this kind of situation, we must consider that particular care in selecting the proper granularity level in environmental representation and time resolution must be paid. In addition to this, specific interaction rules, *"inter-rules"*, must be defined in addition to the traditional transition function, representing *"intra-rules"*. In this paper we discuss the general issues of the above general scenario and we describe in details a relevant example represented by the dynamical interplay among pedestrians and vehicles in non-signalized crossings.

Keywords: Pedestrian crossing · Model coupling · Cellular automata

1 Introduction

In certain situations the simultaneous dynamics of two systems influencing each other, for instance due to the fact that they share a portion of space or (more generally) the same *environment*, must be simulated to study the interaction among them. Examples can be found in extremely different fields, ranging from economics (e.g. in [14] actors like universities and large firms share the same environment with different actors like a National Research Agency and venture capitalists), biology (e.g. in [12] cells of the immune system interact with humors), and also the human built environment, as recent developments in autonomous vehicles testify.

When a CA approach is adopted to model and simulate this kind of situation, we must consider that particular care in selecting the proper granularity level in environmental representation and time resolution must be paid. In addition to this, specific interaction rules, *"inter-rules"*, must be defined in addition to the traditional transition function, representing *"intra-rules"*. In this paper we discuss the general issues of the above general scenario and we describe in details

© Springer International Publishing Switzerland 2016
S. El Yacoubi et al. (Eds.): ACRI 2016, LNCS 9863, pp. 387–395, 2016.
DOI: 10.1007/978-3-319-44365-2_38

a relevant example represented by the dynamical interplay among pedestrians and vehicles in non-signalized crossings.

The main aim of this work is to present the results of a modeling effort aimed at simulating heterogeneous integrated dynamics for representing the interaction of distinct entities sharing the same environment. The different kind of analyzed dynamics, taken in isolation, may have already been successfully modeled by Cellular Automata. However their interaction would imply both considering scale factors (for both space and time) but also additional interaction rules to represent the overall interactive behavior.

The main contribution of this work concerns the design of a set of cooperative rules as a solution for the management of this kind of interaction. After evaluating the plausibility of actually coupling the base CA models, an example situation was selected to experiment this approach. A relevant example of this kind of interaction situation is represented by the dynamical interplay among pedestrians and vehicles in non-signalized crossings. Pedestrians and vehicles have very different characteristics, such as size, velocity, acceleration/deceleration and degrees of freedom in their movement. Successful CA models exist for simulating separately vehicles, in particular the Nagel and Schreckemberg model for vehicular traffic [9] and the floor field model for pedestrian dynamics [1], but little attention, so far, has been paid to a joint modeling of the integrated dynamics.

The following Section will more thoroughly describe this scenario and the current state of the art, whereas Sect. 3 will introduce the adopted modeling approach; a description of the achieved results will then be given. Conclusions and future developments will end the paper.

2   Reference Scenario: Pedestrian Crossings

Microscopic simulation of vehicular traffic represents a mature research area that has led to a successful technology transfer, producing results characterized by a significant impact both on the activity of traffic engineers and planners, as well as to the creation of successful companies developing commercial simulation systems or providing consultancy on their employment. Cellular automata approaches, starting from pioneering works such as [10], have successfully tackled different aspects of vehicular traffic: see, for instance, [11] for a review of different approaches, also applied to complicated road scenarios such as roundabouts [15].

Models for the micro-simulation of pedestrian dynamics have also emerged and affirmed as instruments supporting the design of environments subject to crowding situations. Also in this case, successful researches have produced discrete approaches, like the floor-field Cellular Automata model [1], and continuous ones, like the social force model [8]; like for vehicular traffic, also for pedestrians successful commercial simulation systems can be found in the market.

Whereas separately the above micro-simulation models have produced a significant impact, efforts characterized by an integrated investigation on the simultaneous presence of vehicles and vulnerable road users (in particular pedestrians, but also bicycles) are not as frequent or advanced as isolated vehicular traffic and pedestrian models. Although observation studies of pedestrian and driver behavior in crossing can be found, both in normal conditions [6] and with respect to the presence of crossing warning systems [5], few attempts towards the modeling of this kind of scenario have been carried out. With the exception of [7], most efforts in this direction are relatively recent, such as [4], and they just analyze simple scenarios and they are not validated against real data. The most significant and recent work in this direction is represented by [17] which adapt the social force model to this kind of scenario, considering vehicles as generators of a repulsive force for pedestrians; while this work considers real world data, the analyzed scenario is not very general, being characterized by a signalized crosswalk in which only turning cars can actually interact with pedestrians and their behavior is not thoroughly analyzed.

Most relevant commercial products for traffic simulation provide the possibility to perform some kind of integration of simplified pedestrian models inside the overall simulated scenario, but the level of integration of the two represented phenomena is generally sketchy and the possibility to achieve plausible results severely increases the overall effort of the modeler.

3 Pedestrian Crossing: Modeling Approach

Unlike a previously developed hybrid CA and agent based model [2], in the present approach we essentially represent both vehicular and pedestrian dynamics by means of the CA modeling approach. Moreover, pedestrians and vehicles share the same environment, they are not represented in distinct but connected systems. To represent both types of entities within the same coupled model implies to take decisions on the scale of discretization of the environment and the turn duration: in this case, we decided to fix the size of a cell equal to the spatial occupation of the smallest modeled entity, i.e. a pedestrian. As a consequence, a vehicle will occupy more than a single cell and it will also be able to move more than one cell at a time.

The information for initializing and managing the simulation scenario is introduced by annotating the environment with *spatial markers*, that are, special portions of space that describe relevant elements for the simulation and in particular: (i) **Start areas**, for the introduction of respectively pedestrians and vehicles in the environment, which can be done by a user-defined frequency; (ii) **Target areas**, representing final targets of pedestrians and vehicles; (iii) **Obstacle**, to represent potential obstacles in the sideways; (iv) **Edge of crossing area**, the shared space between the different entities.

3.1 Pedestrians

Space annotation allows the definition of virtual grids of the environment as containers of information for agents and their movement, developing the *floor field* approach [1]. This method is based on the generation of a set of superimposed grids (similar to the grid of the environment) starting from the information derived from spatial markers. Floor field values are spread on the grid as

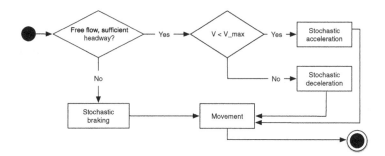

Fig. 1. Vehicular rules.

a gradient and they are used to support pedestrians in the navigation of the environment, representing their interactions with static object (i.e., destination areas and obstacles) or with other pedestrians. In this model *static floor field* is used, that indicates for every cell the distance S_{ij} from one destination area (i.e. one floor field is computed for each pedestrian destination).

Pedestrians essentially follow typical floor-field approach stochastic rules, split into three phases associated to intermediate as well as final goal areas: first, they consider the field leading them from their entrance point towards their side of the crossing area (the closer edge of the crossing area), then to the other side of the crossing area (the farther edge), then to their target area: this kind of path is exemplified in Fig. 2(b). When passing from the first to the second phase, they evaluate the interaction rules, that will be described in the following.

3.2 Vehicles

The mechanism for regulating vehicles' decisions does not require floor-fields since they are guided by simpler behavioral rules, due to the much lower degree of freedom for drivers in a simplified scenario such as the one analyzed in this work. For the basic vehicular behavior, we employed a slightly modified version of the Nagel and Schreckemberg model [9], on one hand adjusting it to fit urban traffic characteristics (e.g. speed) and, on the other, to implement a more plausible stochastic model of acceleration and deceleration (since in the basic model there was no constraint on the maximum deceleration, whereas in this case we wanted to avoid implausible hard braking situations). Moreover, we had to consider that a single vehicle occupies several cells, whereas the decision is actually taken by the transition function applied to a single one, generating effects also for all the others. Finally, due to the potentially high velocity, vehicles can generally move many cells in a single turn. The rules of the basic model assure that vehicles do not collide and that the model produces a quantitatively plausible flow of vehicles in the simulated road section (i.e. a straight section). The adopted rules are summarized and depicted in Fig. 1.

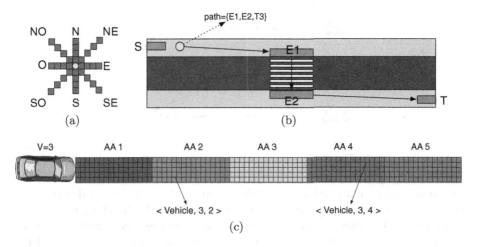

Fig. 2. (a) Pedestrian anticipation, (b) intermediate areas and overall pedestrian path, (c) vehicle anticipation.

3.3 Interaction Among Pedestrians and Vehicles

In addition to the above modeling choices, to grant vehicles and pedestrian a mutual perception we adopted the idea of anticipation, a consolidated approach already applied for simulation of pedestrian behavior [13] and robotic control [16]. Both cars and pedestrians project their movement intention on the shared grid and this allows the detection of potential conflicts. The different entities, due to their different maximum velocity and to the very different capability to reach it quickly (i.e. cars can be quite fast, but have limited acceleration and deceleration capability, whereas pedestrians do not move so quickly, but they can reach typical walking speed or stop almost instantly), have different forms of anticipation: cars must be perceivable by pedestrians even at a relatively high distance (and the overall anticipation is subdivided in different areas to allow the perception of the distance of the car from the specific cell of the anticipation), whereas the intention of movement generated by pedestrians can be limited to few cells. The different forms of anticipation are depicted in Fig. 2(a) and (b) respectively for pedestrians and vehicles.

Potential conflicts detected by means of the perception of the anticipation of another entity through an own anticipation (or by the direct perception of an entity) are solved through the application of cooperative rules allowing the involved partners, at the same time, to achieve their goals while not harming the others.

More precisely, let us consider first of all a pedestrian that has just reached the edge of the crossing area and that is about to cross the road: the pedestrian will evaluate the presence of a vehicle or the anticipation of a vehicle in the set of cells representing its own anticipation. In case of perception of a vehicle, the pedestrian will wait for its passage; should an anticipation of a vehicle be perceived, the involved pedestrian will estimate the velocity of the incoming

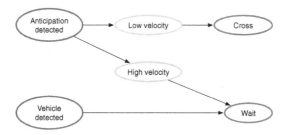

Fig. 3. Coordination rules for a pedestrian.

vehicle and its actual possibility to safely stop: in this case, the pedestrian will pass (i.e. enter the next phase and start moving towards the other edge of the crossing area) trusting that the vehicle will yield. On the other hand, should the vehicle be too fast to come to a stop, the pedestrian will instead yield and try to cross after its passage. This overall set of coordination rules, on the side of the pedestrian, is summarized in Fig. 3.

Vehicles need to carry out a similar and especially compatible form of decision making process, evaluating the perception of a pedestrian in the crossing area or even its anticipation. The principle is that, whenever this happens, the vehicle should brake whenever it is possible to safely stop and let the pedestrian pass, otherwise the vehicle should proceed assuming that the pedestrian will not cross. Different cases must be defined for the detection of a pedestrian, depicted in Fig. 4(a), and for the detection of the anticipation of a pedestrian, depicted in Fig. 4(b).

The involved entities take therefore an overall cooperative attitude to avoid collisions. Pedestrians have a form of precedence, but they are assumed not to take unreasonable choices and yield whenever crossing would put them in a risky situation.

4   Simulation Results

The model has been implemented with the Repast simulation framework and it has been tested in a non-signalized zebra crossing to evaluate the effectiveness of the interaction model (i.e. absence of collisions), but also to quantitatively show that increased arrival rates of pedestrians strongly reduce the maximum flow of vehicles in the road section.

An example situation, qualitatively showing the kind of overall simulation dynamics achieve through this modeling approach, is depicted in Fig. 5: vehicles are large entities depicted in light gray (cyan in the color version of the manuscript) in the middle of the road, pedestrians are much smaller entities depicted in dark grey (red in the color version of the manuscript) starting from the sidewalks.

In particular, the screenshots of the relevant road section between the simulation start and the first 25 s of simulated time show two pedestrians crossing from the different road sides and vehicles (cars of the same size, in this example)

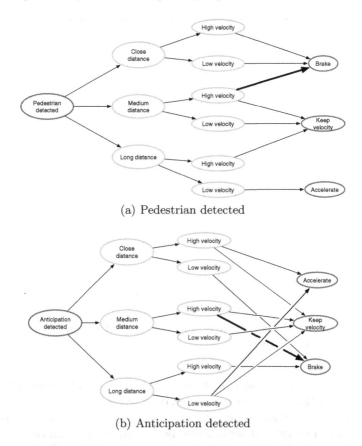

(a) Pedestrian detected

(b) Anticipation detected

Fig. 4. Coordination rules for a vehicle.

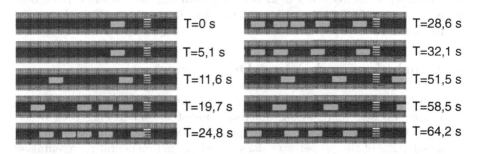

Fig. 5. Screenshots of a simulation run with two crossing episodes. (Color figure online)

accumulating, awaiting to be able to cross. It must be noted that the vehicles are not uniformly spaced, due to the stochastic braking rule. From seconds 25 to 58 the vehicles are able to pass, since the first two pedestrians have exited the

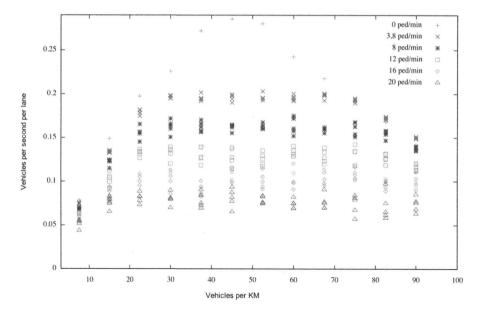

Fig. 6. Variation of vehicular flow as a function of vehicular density and frequency of pedestrian arrival at the crossing.

scenario and two new pedestrians, from the lower road side, have not reached the crossing yet; then a new crossing episode starts.

Figure 6 shows instead aggregated results of several simulation runs with a growing vehicular density, under different pedestrian traffic conditions. In particular, pedestrians were generated randomly according to a uniform distribution generating a certain frequency of arrival to the crossing site. Results are encouraging and reasonably in tune with empirical data (in particular, considering the results described in [3]).

5   Conclusions and Future Developments

This paper has presented an example of simulation model comprising two different components, representing different subsystems influencing each other. In particular, a CA approach was adopted and particular care has been paid to the selection of the proper granularity level in environmental representation and time resolution. In addition to this, specific interaction rules, *"inter-rules"*, have been defined in addition to the traditional transition function, representing *"intra-rules"*. The general issues of this general scenario have been exemplified in details through a relevant example represented by the dynamical interplay among pedestrians and vehicles in non-signalized crossings. The model has been described and results of its application have been presented. Future works are aimed at validating the presented approach and model by comparing simulation results with acquired empirical evidences on this kind of situation.

References

1. Burstedde, C., Klauck, K., Schadschneider, A., Zittartz, J.: Simulation of pedestrian dynamics using a two-dimensional cellular automaton. Physica A **295**(3–4), 507–525 (2001)
2. Crociani, L., Vizzari, G.: An integrated model for the simulation of pedestrian crossings. In: Wąs, J., Sirakoulis, G.C., Bandini, S. (eds.) ACRI 2014. LNCS, vol. 8751, pp. 670–679. Springer, Heidelberg (2014)
3. Geroliminis, N., Daganzo, C.F.: Existence of urban-scale macroscopic fundamental diagrams: some experimental findings. Transp. Res. Part B Methodological **42**(9), 759–770 (2008)
4. Godara, A., Lassarre, S., Banos, A.: Simulating pedestrian-vehicle interaction in an urban network using cellular automata and multi-agent models. In: Schadschneider, A., Pöschel, T., Kühne, R., Schreckenberg, M., Wolf, D.E. (eds.) Traffic and Granular Flow'05, pp. 411–418. Springer, Heidelberg (2007)
5. Hakkert, A., Gitelman, V., Ben-Shabat, E.: An evaluation of crosswalk warning systems: effects on pedestrian and vehicle behaviour. Transp. Res. Part F: Traffic Psychol. Behav. **5**(4), 275–292 (2002)
6. Hamed, M.M.: Analysis of pedestrians' behavior at pedestrian crossings. Saf. Sci. **38**(1), 63–82 (2001)
7. Helbing, D., Jiang, R., Treiber, M.: Analytical investigation of oscillations in intersecting flows of pedestrian and vehicle traffic. Phys. Rev. E **72**, 046130 (2005)
8. Helbing, D., Molnár, P.: Social force model for pedestrian dynamics. Phys. Rev. E **51**(5), 4282–4286 (1995)
9. Nagel, K., Schreckenberg, M.: A cellular automaton model for freeway traffic. Journal de Physique I France **2**(2221), 222–235 (1992)
10. Nagel, K., Schreckenberg, M.: A cellular automaton model for freeway traffic. Journal de Physique I **2**(12), 2221–2229 (1992)
11. Nagel, K., Wagner, P., Woesler, R.: Still flowing: approaches to traffic flow and traffic jam modeling. Oper. Res. **51**(5), 681–710 (2003)
12. Puzone, R., Kohler, B., Seiden, P., Celada, F.: A discrete models of cellular/humoral responses. In: Bandini, S., Worsch, T. (eds.) Theoretical and Practical Issues on Cellular Automata, Proceedings of the Fourth International Conference on Cellular Automata for Research and Industry, pp. 117–125. Springer, London (2000)
13. Suma, Y., Yanagisawa, D., Nishinari, K.: Anticipation effect in pedestrian dynamics: modeling and experiments. Physica A **391**(1–2), 248–263 (2012)
14. Triulzi, G., Pyka, A.: Learning-by-modeling: insights from an agent-based model of university-industry relationships. Cybern. Syst. **42**(7), 484–501 (2011)
15. Wang, R., Ruskin, H.J.: Modelling traffic flow at multi-lane urban roundabouts. Int. J. Mod. Phys. C **17**(5), 693–710 (2006)
16. Weyns, D., Holvoet, T., Schelfthout, K., Wielemans, J.: Decentralized control of automatic guided vehicles: applying multi-agent systems in practice. In: Companion to the 23rd Annual ACM SIGPLAN Conference on Object-Oriented Programming, Systems, Languages, and Applications, OOPSLA 2008, 19–13 October 2007, Nashville, TN, USA, pp. 663–674 (2008)
17. Zeng, W., Chen, P., Nakamura, H., Iryo-Asano, M.: Application of social force model to pedestrian behavior analysis at signalized crosswalk. Transp. Res. Part C Emerg. Technol. **40**, 143–159 (2014)

Advanced CA Crowd Models of Multiple Consecutive Bottlenecks

Pavel Hrabák[1](✉), Jakub Porzycki[2], Marek Bukáček[3], Robert Lubaś[2], and Jarosław Wąs[2]

[1] Brno University of Technolgy, Brno, Czech Republic
pavel.hrabak@vutbr.cz
[2] AGH University of Science and Technology, Krakow, Poland
{porzycki,rlubas,jarek}@agh.edu.pl
[3] Czech Technical University in Prague, Prague, Czech Republic
marek.bukacek@fjfi.cvut.cz

Abstract. Simulation results from two advanced CA based crowd dynamics models, namely Social Distances Model and Bonds Floor Field Model, are investigated using experimental data. Two experiments regarding pedestrian egress from simple network of rooms with multiple consecutive bottlenecks were conducted in Prague and Krakow. Simulation results comparison is the basis for discussion about models properties.

Keywords: Social Distances · Bonds Floor Field · Egress experiment

1 Introduction

Crowd dynamics models based on Cellular Automata have some significant advantages over the other kinds of pedestrian movement models. An important aspect is their simplicity - movement of occupants is modelled by set of fairly simple rules [7]. Moreover, one can easily establish sufficient balance between efficiency and accuracy, that makes CA-based models suitable e.g. to large scale data–driven simulation e.g. [10]. However, the usage of CA based models is connected with a number of issues, related mostly with coarse discretization of space and time [6].

The most popular and well-established approach in CA based crowd simulation is the family of models that utilize different floor fields(FF) [3]. Vast majority of such models use *static FF* - i.e. gradient potential field that lead occupants to points of attraction. Other types of fields models different aspects of pedestrians behaviour: *dynamic FF* - is responsible for mimicking the following others behaviour, *wall FF and proxemics FF* describes repulsive forces from obstacles and other pedestrians respectively, *anticipation FF* introduces in advance collision avoidance, while *force FF* introduce pushing behaviour for CA based models. Superposition of chosen set of mentioned fields is used as main factor that drive pedestrian movement. For details see [9] and references therein.

© Springer International Publishing Switzerland 2016
S. El Yacoubi et al. (Eds.): ACRI 2016, LNCS 9863, pp. 396–404, 2016.
DOI: 10.1007/978-3-319-44365-2_39

In recent years, one can notice growing trend of Agent Based Modelling, *on the top* of floor field, CA-based models. Occupied cells are represented by autonomous agents (e.g. Situated Cellular Automata [1]). This allows on differentiation of pedestrians' behaviour according to e.g.: their role (leader - follower), group affiliation, cognitive abilities, etc. On the other hand a lot of effort is made to overcome issues related with grid discretization. Typical grid consist of square with side equals to 40 cm, but different sizes and shapes are constantly tested. Similarly, an issue of detailed floor field generation algorithm is a subject of intensive research.

In this paper, simulation results from two advanced CA based crowd dynamics models, namely Social Distances Model [13] and Floor Field model with Bonds Principle (further referred as Bonds Floor Field Model) [5] are investigated using experimental data. Two experiments regarding pedestrian egress from simple network of rooms with multiple consecutive bottlenecks was executed in Prague and Krakow. Simulation results comparison is the basis for discussion about models properties.

2   Experiment

This study leans over data from two conducted experiments, which focus on the egress of a group of pedestrians from a small network of rooms with multiple consecutive bottlenecks. In both experiments several groups of university students were instructed to egress the classrooms and leave the monitored part of the facility using one exit. The experimental layout is schematically depicted in Fig. 1.

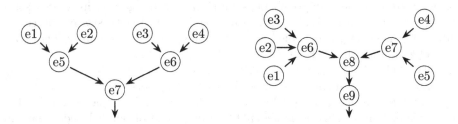

Fig. 1. Schema of the experiment PRG (left), KRK (right). Arrows indicate the direction of motion.

Important characteristic of the experiments is joining of pedestrian streams, i.e., pedestrians from more entrances walked towards one exit. Key quantity used for the comparison of the models with experiment is the cumulative flow $J_j^{cum}(t)$ through each exit denoting at each time t the number of pedestrian, who passed through the exit j until time t.

PRG experiment was conducted in Prague in the lecture hall of the Czech Technical University with help of 54 students. In the lecture hall, four staircases (exits 1–4) lead to two gathering places. Two exits 5 and 6 lead from the gathering points to the vestibule with one exit 7. The widths of the bottlenecks are 70 cm for exits 5 and 6, 75 cm for exit 7. The egress was repeated three times, the evacuation time was between 40 and 42 s.

KRK experiment was conducted in Krakow on one floor of the AGH University. Three rooms (exits 1–3) lead to a common hallway, which leads through exit 6 to the staircase hall. Similarly, two rooms (exits 4 and 5) lead to a hallway attached to the staircase hall on the opposite side. The staircase hall leads to the stairs through exit 8, the stairs go downwards one floor leading to another hall through exit 9. The widths of the bottlenecks are 75 cm for exits 6 and 7, 177 cm for exits 8 and 9. The egress was repeated two times, 54 and 51 participants took place in this runs, respectively. In the first run the streams from exits 6 and 7 did not merge - corridor before exit 6 is longer than corresponding corridor before exit 7. Therefore, in the second run the part related to exit 7 was delayed by 11 s in order to obtain the merging behaviour. The total evacuation time was 61 and 62 s.

3   Cellular Models

Two advanced CA models have been used to simulate the above mentioned experiment. In this section we provide brief information about the models with sufficient references to obtain detailed definition.

3.1   Bonds Floor-Field Model

The Bonds Floor-Field Model (BFF) introduces to the classical FF model the principle of bonds [5], adaptive time span [2], and heterogeneity in conflict solution [4]. The space is divided to rectangular lattice of cells, size of the cell is 40 cm. Each cell can be occupied by exactly one pedestrian or empty. The space discretization for the BFF model is visualised in Fig. 2.

The choice of the new target cell from the Moore neighbourhood is fully probabilistic and is mainly influenced by the static floor-field S and interaction between pedestrians. The model allows the choice of the occupied cell using the principle of bonds. This principle enables the motion of bonded pedestrians in lines and therefore supports the motion in lines within a crowd as well as the creation of unstable queues in front of the exit. This principle is related to the parameter of sensitivity to occupation k_O, which combines two strategies: to stay in line and wait for the motion of the predecessor ($k_O = 0$), or to try to run around the crowd ($k_O = 1$).

Let e be the position of the exit cell and $S(y) = \text{dist}(y, e)$ the distance of cell y to the exit e. Let $O_x(x) = 0$ and for $y \neq x$ let $O_x(y) = 1$ if y is occupied and $O_x(y) = 0$ if y is empty. Let $D_x(y) = 1$ if $(x_1 - y_1) \cdot (x_2 - y_2) \neq 0$ and $D_x(y) = 0$ otherwise be the identifier of the diagonal motion. The conditional probability of choosing next target cell y from the Moore neighbourhood $\mathcal{N}$ given the agent is occupying cell x is calculated via

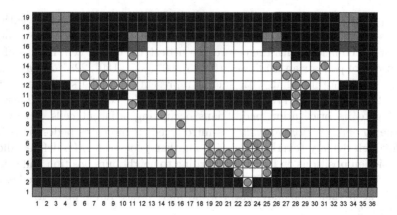

Fig. 2. Discretization of space of the PRG experiment for the Bonds Floor-Field Model. Snapshot from the simulation 10 s after the initiation.

$$P(y \mid x) = \frac{\exp\left\{-k_S S(y)\right\}\left(1 - k_O O_x(y)\right)\left(1 - k_D D_x(y)\right)}{\sum_{z \in \mathcal{N}(x)} \exp\left\{-k_S S(z)\right\}\left(1 - k_O O_x(z)\right)\left(1 - k_D D_x(z)\right)}. \tag{1}$$

The coefficients $k_S \in [0, +\infty)$, $k_O, k_D \in [0, 1]$ are coefficients of sensitivity to corresponding field.

The used update is a partially synchronized event-driven update following the concept of adaptive time span. The time line is divided to isochronous intervals of the length $h > 0$. The agent is activated (i.e. called to choose new target cell) in the k-th algorithm step if his next desired actualisation time falls to the interval $[kh, (k+1)h)$. The desired actualisation time is influenced by the own actualisation period (reflecting free-flow velocity) and diagonal movement time-penalisation.

The partially synchronized update is necessary to maintain sufficient number of conflicts (more agents willing to enter the same cell), which are key element for the concept of aggressiveness in the model. The aggressiveness is agent's free parameter determining the ability to win the conflict. The heterogeneity in this parameter leads to variances in time spent by the agent in the crowd, which is an important observed phenomenon.

The heterogeneous behaviour of agents is as well described by the heterogeneity in sensitivity to occupation, i.e., parameter k_O, influencing the probability of choosing next target cell. The heterogeneity in k_O can describe different strategies regarding the choice of proper path. More precisely, whether to stay in line and wait or whether to try to run around the crowd.

3.2   Social Distances Model

The main concept behind Social Distances Model (SDM) is incorporation of proxemics theory into CA crowd dynamics models. It is achieved by use of smaller cells - squares $25 \times 25\,\mathrm{cm}^1$, and elliptical representation of pedestrians with axis equals to 45 and 27 cm [11]. One cell can be occupied by one pedestrian and the centre of cell coincides with the centre of a pedestrian on the cell. Eight different orientations of pedestrian is allowed (0°, 45°, 90°, 135°, 180°, 225°, 270°and 315°).

It is worth noting, that with such a representation, the size of pedestrian is over 52 % bigger ($953{,}775\,\mathrm{cm}^2$) that the size of the cell ($625\,\mathrm{cm}^2$). Therefore, according to its orientation pedestrians occupying adjacent cells can overlap. Here the *compressibility parameter* is introduced. It indicates pedestrians tolerance for high density (overlapping with another pedestrian). It, defines allowed and forbidden positions on the grid according to neighbours position and orientation. Low value of *compresibility parameter* bring the situation when pedestrians wants to keep their personal space, while high values allow pedestrians to get closer (Fig. 3).

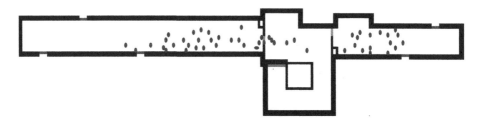

Fig. 3. Discretization of space of the KRK experiment for the Social Distances Model.

What is interesting, our recent research [8] shows that tolerance for close neighbours depend on its position according to pedestrian. Neighbours on the sides can be ignored, even if they are relatively close, while the ones in front of (behind) are strongly avoided. However, it is not yet implemented in model.

SDM is based on typical Floor Field Model. Two kinds of floor field are included into the model: static FF which defines POIs, as well as dynamic FF which take into account proxemics issues. Additional parameters are added in order to model wall avoidance and inertia effect.

Pedestrian can have the different desired speed. Desired speed is related with the number of steps that can be made in each second of simulation - from 1 to 8 steps. Thus, desired speed vary from $0.25\,\frac{m}{s}$ up to $2\,\frac{m}{s}$. The distribution of desired speed is the main calibration parameter for this model.

Detailed algorithm of floor field calculation and motion rules definition is provided in [13] Taking into account massive evacuation we proposed a dedicated version of the model [12].

4   Comparison with Experimental Data

Both models have been applied to the geometries related to the above mentioned experiments. The aim was to study, whether the models can reproduce

---

[1] Typical cells in CA models are $40 \times 40\,\mathrm{cm}$.

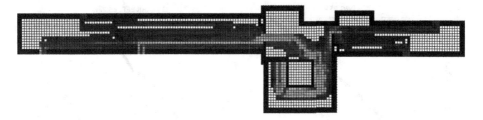

Fig. 4. Pedestrians occurrence frequency during single simulation of KRK experiment using SDM. The hotter the color the more time given cell was visited. (Color figure online)

same cumulative outflow from the main exit given that the inflow through the border/leaves exits (1–4 or 1–5) is known. Agents representing pedestrians are entering the system through the leaves exits in the same times as measured in the experiment (Fig. 4).

4.1 Bonds FF and Experiment

For the simulation by means of the FF model with Bonds Principle we have chosen the homogeneous set of parameters from the article [4], where the model was calibrated for the simulation of one room with open boundaries.

In comparison to the above mention article, the value of the friction μ has been changed from 0.9 to 0.8 in order to reflect the fact, that the widths of the bottlenecks related to exits 5 and 6 (PRG) and 6 and 7 (KRK) were higher than in the previous experiment (The exits are modelled by one cell corridors of the width 40 cm. Since it was impossible for two pedestrians to pass simultaneously in the experiment, the width is rather improved by lower friction then two cells corridor.). Secondly, in the case of KRK experiment, the own period of pedestrians τ has been changed from 0.2 s to 0.25 s, because the free flow velocity of pedestrians in the KRK experiment was lower than in the PRG experiment.

In Fig. 5 you can see the comparison of cumulative flow from the experiment with several realisations of the stochastic Bonds FF model (BFF) for the PRG experiment (left) and the KRK experiment (right). We can see good agreement of the model data with the experiment. It is worth noting that the model produces faster evacuation for the KRK experiment when considering the motion from exit 8 to exit 9, i.e., on the stairs. Here the model is not able reflect the slow-down of pedestrians while walking on stairs.

4.2 Social Distances Model and Experiment

Both experiments are modelled as non-competitive egress [13]. Moreover, since non significant clogs are present the compressibility parameter is set to 0 - ellipses that represent pedestrians can not overlap. The main parameter used for calibration is the desired maximal speed v_{max} and its standard deviation σ.

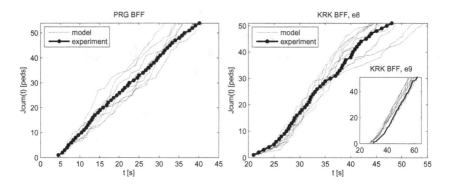

Fig. 5. Comparison of cumulative flow from the experiments (black circles) and the BFF model (red lines). Left is the PRG experiment, first run, exit 7. Right is the KRK experiment, second run, exits 8 and 9. (Color figure online)

For Prague experiment the best results was obtained for $v_{max} = 1.1$ and $\sigma = 0.25$, while for Krakow experiment we use $v_{max} = 1.25$ and $\sigma = 0.1$.

In Fig. 6 one can see comparison of experimental results with ten runs of its simulation. Good agreement between data and results can be observed. In both cases results are slightly shifted - for Prague egress in simulation is slower than in real data, while for Krakow is faster. This phenomenon can be explained mainly by discretization of pedestrians velocity.

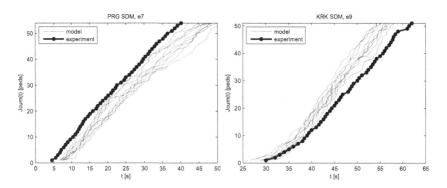

Fig. 6. Comparison of cumulative flow from the experiments (black circles) and the SDM model (red lines). Left is the PRG experiment, first run, exit 7. Right is the KRK experiment, second run, exit 9. (Color figure online)

5   Summary and Conclusions

Two advanced CA models of crowd dynamics, Social Distances Model (SDM) and Bonds Floor Field Model (BFF), have been used for the simulation of an egress of simple network of rooms. The simulations have been compared to the measured data from two original experiments organized in Prague and Krakow.

The goal is to simulate the egress from a complex facility through a common exit given that the occupation flow from primary rooms (lecture halls, class rooms) is known or can be anticipated sufficiently precise. The performed experiments were designed correspondingly to such anticipation. As the main comparison tool the cumulative outflow from the main exit has been used. By the cumulative outflow we understand the number of egressed pedestrians over time.

As shown in Sect. 4, the simulation results are in good agreement with the measured experimental data. Nevertheless, the stochastic nature of the models causes some variances in the individual trajectories of the simulation.

In Bonds Floor Field model, the stochasticity is caused mainly by the mechanism of conflict solution related to the situation when more agents are entering the same cell. This happens mostly in the cluster in front of the exit and therefore the conflict solution directly influences the exit capacity.

The stochasticity in Social Distances Model is contrarily caused by the deviation of the desired velocity related mainly to the motion in free flow. Such stochasticity can be controlled by appropriate choice of agents properties.

An important question to be answered is, whether the variance in evacuation times can be observed in reality. Such information can be helpful for appropriate choice of the model parameters. This is the goal of our further study, which requires to conduct the same experiment in various conditions, at different time, with different group of pedestrians.

Acknowledgements. This work was supported by the Czech Science Foundation under grant GA15-15049S. Further support was provided by the CTU grant SGS15/214/OHK4/ 3T/14. This work was also supported by AGH University of Science and Technology, contract No. 11.11.120.859.

References

1. Bandini, S., Federici, M.L., Vizzari, G.: Situated cellular agents approach to crowd modeling and simulation. Cybern. Syst. **38**(7), 729–753 (2007)
2. Bukáček, M., Hrabák, P., Krbálek, M.: Cellular model of pedestrian dynamics with adaptive time span. In: Wyrzykowski, R., Dongarra, J., Karczewski, K., Waśniewski, J. (eds.) PPAM 2013, Part II. LNCS, vol. 8385, pp. 669–678. Springer, Heidelberg (2014)
3. Burstedde, C., Klauck, K., Schadschneider, A., Zittartz, J.: Simulation of pedestrian dynamics using a two-dimensional cellular automaton. Phys. A Stat. Mech. Appl. **295**(3–4), 507–525 (2001)
4. Hrabák, P., Bukáček, M.: Influence of agents heterogeneity in cellular model of evacuation Submitted to Journal of Computational Science. arXiv:1604.08226 [cs.MA]
5. Hrabák, P., Bukáček, M., Krbálek, M.: Cellular model of room evacuation based on occupancy and movement prediction: comparison with experimental study. J. Cell. Automata **8**(5–6), 383–393 (2013)

6. Lubaś, R., Porzycki, J., Wąs, J., Mycek, M.: Validation and verification of CA-based pedestrian dynamics models. J. Cell. Automata **11**(4), 285–298 (2016)
7. Nishinari, K., Kirchner, A., Namazi, A., Schadschneider, A.: Extended floor field CA model for evacuation dynamics. IEICE Trans. Inf. Syst. **E87–D**, 726–732 (2004)
8. Porzycki, J., Mycek, M., Lubaś, R., Wąs, J.: Pedestrian spatial self-organization according to its nearest neighbor position. Transp. Res. Procedia **2**, 201–206 (2014). http://www.sciencedirect.com/science/article/pii/S2352146514000696. The Conference on Pedestrian and Evacuation Dynamics 2014 (PED 2014), pp. 22–24, Delft, The Netherlands (October 2014)
9. Schadschneider, A., Chowdhury, D., Nishinari, K.: Stochastic Transport in Complex Systems: From Molecules to Vehicles. Elsevier Science B.V., Amsterdam (2010)
10. Vizzari, G., Manenti, L.: An agent-based model for pedestrian and group dynamics: experimental and real-world scenarios. In: van der Hoek, W., Padgham, L., Conitzer, V., Winikoff, M. (eds.) AAMAS, pp. 1341–1342. IFAAMAS (2012)
11. Wąs, J., Gudowski, B., Matuszyk, P.J.: New cellular automata model of pedestrian representation. In: El Yacoubi, S., Chopard, B., Bandini, S. (eds.) ACRI 2006. LNCS, vol. 4173, pp. 724–727. Springer, Heidelberg (2006)
12. Wąs, J., Lubaś, R.: Adapting Social Distances model for mass evacuation simulation. J. Cell. Automata **8**, 395–405 (2013)
13. Wąs, J., Lubaś, R.: Towards realistic and effective agent-based models of crowd dynamics. Neurocomputing **146**, 199–209 (2014)

Totally Asymmetric Simple Exclusion Process on an Open Lattice with Langmuir Kinetics Depending on the Occupancy of the Forward Neighboring Site

Daichi Yanagisawa[1(✉)] and Shingo Ichiki[2]

[1] Research Center for Advanced Science and Technology,
The University of Tokyo, 4-6-1, Komaba, Meguro-ku, Tokyo 153-8904, Japan
tDaichi@mail.ecc.u-tokyo.ac.jp
[2] Department of Advanced Interdisciplinary Studies, School of Engineering,
The University of Tokyo, 4-6-1, Komaba, Meguro-ku, Tokyo 153-8904, Japan

Abstract. We have generalized the update rule of the Langmuir kinetics, which is attachment and detachment dynamics of particles, in the totally asymmetric simple exclusion process. The attachment and detachment rates in our extended model depend on the occupancy of the forward neighboring site. Although there are some extended models that consider the effect of the occupancy of the neighboring sites, our model is the first one that allows one to set the attachment and detachment rates independently without any restrictions.

We have performed a mean-field analysis and obtained phase diagrams and density profiles. It is elucidated that the attachment to vacant region and detachment from congested region extend the area of the phase that accompanies a shock, i.e., a domain wall, which divides the low and high density regime. Results of Monte Carlo simulations show good agreement with the mean-field density profiles, so that the validity of the phase diagrams are verified.

Keywords: Totally asymmetric simple exclusion process · Langmuir kinetics · Open boundary

1 Introduction

The totally asymmetric simple exclusion process (TASEP) [1], which is a fundamental model for one-dimensional stochastic transport system, has been theoretically investigated [2] and exploited as a model for self-driven particles such as vehicles, pedestrians, and molecular motors in biological systems [3]. TASEP with periodic boundary condition and deterministic parallel-update rule is equivalent to the elementary cellular automaton rule 184 [4].

In the open boundary TASEP, a particle enters the system at the one boundary, moves forward if there is no other particle in front of it, and exits the system at the other boundary. Several phases are observed by controlling the entering

© Springer International Publishing Switzerland 2016
S. El Yacoubi et al. (Eds.): ACRI 2016, LNCS 9863, pp. 405–412, 2016.
DOI: 10.1007/978-3-319-44365-2_40

and exiting rates (boundary induced phase transition), which is a characteristic of non-equilibrium system. In equilibrium systems, the effect of boundaries can be neglected in the thermodynamic limit.

From a practical view, it is difficult to apply the original TASEP to the phenomena in the real world. Thus, many extended models have been developed. One of the most important extensions is the introduction of the Langmuir kinetics (LK) [5–8], which is attachment and detachment dynamics in the bulk part of the system. This extended model of TASEP is often abbreviated as TASEP-LK. LK is practically important to model biological molecular motors because it corresponds to binding and unbinding processes of the motors to the microtubule [9]. Moreover, vehicles do not only enter and exit at the ends of highways, but also at the ramps along there. This dynamics is also considered by LK. Besides, LK is theoretically interesting. Firstly, the domain wall (DW), which divides the low and high density region in the system, stays at the same position in the stationary state. In TASEP, DW never stops, but randomly moves in the system. Secondly, much richer phase diagrams are obtained by controlling the attachment and detachment rates.

Recently, it has been reported that LK is also influenced from the occupancy of the motors on microtubule [10]. Due to this fact and the significance of LK as described in the previous paragraph, extended LK, whose attachment and detachment rates depend on the occupancy of the neighboring sites, has been investigated recently. Vuijk et al. [11] and Messelink et al. [12] consider the effect of occupancy of both back and front neighboring sites in the open system with specific case, whereas, Ichiki et al. [13] solve a more general model where the attachment and detachment rates are equivalent and show that the boundary of phases and position of DW change according to the parameters.

If one considers the occupancy of both back and front neighboring sites, there are four cases: (empty, empty), (empty, occupied), (occupied, empty), and (occupied, occupied). The model in [11,12] does not allows one to determine the four attachment and detachment rates completely independently. The model in [13] permits one to set the four rates independently; however, the attachment and detachment rates should be equivalent. These restriction enables one to perform theoretical analysis, but deteriorates applicability of the model since attachment and detachment do not always occur similarly in the real system.

Therefore, we have developed an extended model, which considers the effect of occupancy of the forward site and neglect that of the back site. We call the model TASEP with Langmuir Kinetics depending on the occupancy of the Forward neighboring site (TASEP-LKF). In this model, the attachment and detachment rates for each case can be determined independently without any restrictions. Furthermore, a mean-field analysis gives explicit results as shown in Sect. 3. Note that the model is not included in previous ones in [11–13]. The effect of occupancy of the front site is important in vehicle and pedestrian dynamics since vehicles and pedestrians change lane or route if their proceeding direction is congested. Besides, it is possible to study the effect of occupancy of the back site at the same time by considering particle-hole symmetry.

Periodic boundary version of TASEP-LKF is analyzed in [14] and the relaxation dynamics to the stationary state is studied. Hence, in this paper, we analyze the open boundary version of TASEP-LKF.

The reminder of the paper is organized as follows. In the next section, the model TASEP-LKF is introduced in detail, and it is analyzed by mean-field approximation in Sect. 3. In Sect. 4, phase diagrams and density profiles are depicted by the result of both theoretical analysis and Monte Carlo simulation, and the effect of the occupancy of the neighboring site is investigated by comparing TASEP-LKF with original TASEP-LK. The Sect. 5 is devoted to conclusion.

2   Model

We consider a system of one-dimensional lattice, which consists of L sites ($i = 1, 2, 3 \cdots L$), as in Fig. 1. The boundaries are open and the time is continuous. The states of the sites are represented by τ_i ($\tau_i = \{0, 1\}$). If the site i is empty $\tau_i = 0$, while if it is occupied by a single particle $\tau_i = 1$. Multiple particles cannot stay at the same site at the same time.

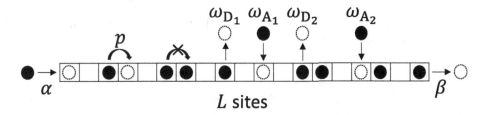

Fig. 1. Schematic view of TASEP-LKF on an open lattice.

At the left boundary a particle enters the leftest site 1 with the rate α. Particles at the site $i \in [1, L-1]$ move to the site $i+1$ if it is empty with unit rate, while a particle at the rightest site L leaves the system with the rate β.

At the bulk sites $i \in [2, L-1]$, the extended LK is applied. If the site i is empty, a particle attaches there with the rate ω_{A_1} (ω_{A_2}) if the site $i+1$ is empty (occupied). Similarly, if the site i is occupied, a particle leaves the lattice with the rate ω_{D_1} (ω_{D_2}) if the site $i+1$ is empty (occupied). In the case $\omega_{A_1} = \omega_{A_2}$ and $\omega_{D_1} = \omega_{D_2}$, our model reduces to the original TASEP-LK [5].

3   Mean-Field Analysis

In this section, we conduct a mean-field analysis in order to derive phase diagrams and density profiles.

At the bulk site $i \in [2, L-1]$, the following equation can be derived from the master equation:

$$
\frac{d\langle \tau_i \rangle}{dt} = \langle \tau_{i-1}(1 - \tau_i) \rangle - \langle \tau_i(1 - \tau_{i+1}) \rangle + \omega_{A_1}\langle (1 - \tau_i)(1 - \tau_{i+1}) \rangle
$$
$$
+ \omega_{A_2}\langle (1 - \tau_i)\tau_{i+1} \rangle - \omega_{D_1}\langle \tau_i(1 - \tau_{i+1}) \rangle - \omega_{D_2}\langle \tau_i\tau_{i+1} \rangle, \tag{1}
$$

where $\langle \cdot \rangle$ represents the expectation value of the quantity. In addition, the equations for the boundaries are described as follows:

$$
\frac{d\langle \tau_1 \rangle}{dt} = \alpha\langle 1 - \tau_1 \rangle - \langle \tau_1(1 - \tau_2) \rangle, \tag{2}
$$

$$
\frac{d\langle \tau_L \rangle}{dt} = \langle \tau_{L-1}(1 - \tau_L) \rangle - \beta\langle \tau_L \rangle. \tag{3}
$$

We perform a mean-filed approximation. In other words, we factor the correlation functions, for example, by replacing $\langle \tau_{i-1}(1 - \tau_i) \rangle$ with $\langle \tau_{i-1} \rangle(1 - \langle \tau_i \rangle)$. Moreover, we expand

$$
\langle \tau_{i\pm1} \rangle = \rho(x) \pm \frac{1}{L}\frac{\partial \rho}{\partial x}(x) + \frac{1}{2}\frac{1}{L^2}\frac{\partial^2 \rho}{\partial x^2}(x) + \mathcal{O}\left(\frac{1}{L^3}\right), \tag{4}
$$

where $x = i/L$, and take the hydrodynamic limit, i.e., $L \to \infty$ with $t = \bar{t}L$. Then, (1)–(3) become as follows:

$$
\frac{\partial \rho}{\partial \bar{t}} + (1 - 2\rho)\frac{\partial \rho}{\partial x} = a\rho^2 + b\rho + c, \tag{5}
$$
$$
(\rho(0) - \alpha)(\rho(0) - 1) = 0, \tag{6}
$$
$$
(\rho(1) - (1 - \beta))\rho(1) = 0, \tag{7}
$$

where

$$
a = \Omega_{A_1} - \Omega_{A_2} + \Omega_{D_1} - \Omega_{D_2}, \tag{8}
$$
$$
b = -2\Omega_{A_1} + \Omega_{A_2} - \Omega_{D_1}, \tag{9}
$$
$$
c = \Omega_{A_1}. \tag{10}
$$

$\Omega_X = \omega_X L$ ($X = A_1, A_2, D_1, D_2$) are kept finite, otherwise, LK dominates the dynamics in the system as $L \to \infty$. This replacement is necessary to keep the strength of the boundary effect (α and β) and LK comparable.

We are interested in the stationary state of the system, so that we substitute 0 into $\partial \rho/\partial \bar{t}$ in (5) and obtain the ordinary differential equation as follows:

$$
(1 - 2\rho)\frac{d\rho}{dx} = a\rho^2 + b\rho + c. \tag{11}
$$

Note that the discriminant $D = b^2 - 4ac = (\Omega_{A_2} - \Omega_{D_1})^2 + 4\Omega_{A_1}\Omega_{D_2} > 0$. We focus on the case $\rho \neq 1/2$. Then, (11) is solved as

$$
\ln|\rho - \rho_+|^{C_+}|\rho - \rho_-|^{C_-} = x + C, \tag{12}
$$

where ρ_+ and ρ_- are the solutions of the quadratic equation $a\rho^2 + b\rho + c = 0$, and

$$C_+ = \frac{1 - 2\rho_+}{a(\rho_+ - \rho_-)}, \tag{13}$$

$$C_- = \frac{2\rho_- - 1}{a(\rho_+ - \rho_-)}. \tag{14}$$

The integral constant C is determined from the left and right boundary conditions, i.e., $\rho(0) = \alpha$ and $\rho(1) = 1 - \beta$, obtained from (6) and (7), respectively. Then, the left (right) neighborhood solution $\rho_L(x)$ ($\rho_R(x)$) are calculated as follows:

$$x = \ln \left| \frac{\rho_L(x) - \rho_+}{\alpha - \rho_+} \right|^{C_+} \left| \frac{\rho_L(x) - \rho_-}{\alpha - \rho_-} \right|^{C_-}, \tag{15}$$

$$x = 1 + \ln \left| \frac{\rho_R(x) - \rho_+}{1 - \beta - \rho_+} \right|^{C_+} \left| \frac{\rho_R(x) - \rho_-}{1 - \beta - \rho_-} \right|^{C_-}. \tag{16}$$

Next, we consider the position of a shock, i.e., the domain wall (DW), x_{DW}, which is a discontinuity in the density profile. The velocity of DW is expressed as $1 - \rho_L - \rho_R$ [6,15], so that the position of DW is numerically computed from

$$\rho_L(x_{DW}) = 1 - \rho_R(x_{DW}). \tag{17}$$

Note that (5)–(7) are invariant under the simultaneous exchanges as follows:

$$\rho \leftrightarrow 1 - \rho, \tag{18}$$

$$x \leftrightarrow 1 - x, \tag{19}$$

$$\Omega_{A_1} \leftrightarrow \Omega_{D_2}, \tag{20}$$

$$\Omega_{A_2} \leftrightarrow \Omega_{D_1}, \tag{21}$$

$$\alpha \leftrightarrow \beta, \tag{22}$$

so that the approximated Eqs. (5)–(7) exhibit particle-hole symmetry. However, the Eq. (1) before approximation does not hold against the exchange (18)–(21). It becomes TASEP-LK depending on the occupancy of the back neighboring site as we have shortly mentioned in Sect. 1. Hydrodynamic limit diminishes the difference between the front and back site and similarly regards them as neighboring sites. Therefore, (5) shows particle-hole symmetry.

4   Phase Diagram and Density Profile

In this paper, we focus on how the new model (TASEP-LKF) is different from the original one (TASEP-LK). Therefore, we investigate the three cases (O), (A), and (B) summarized in Table 1. In the case (O), the parameters are set as $\Omega_{A_1} = \Omega_{A_2}$ and $\Omega_{D_1} = \Omega_{D_2}$, so that the effect of the occupancy of the forward site is not considered and the model reduces to TASEP-LK.

In the case (A), Ω_{A_1} and Ω_{D_2} are set large, while Ω_{A_2} and Ω_{D_1} are set small. In the case (B), the attachment and detachment rates are set in the opposite way to the case (A). Note that the sums of the attachment rates $(\Omega_{A_1} + \Omega_{A_2})$ and detachment rates $(\Omega_{D_1} + \Omega_{D_2})$ are same in all the three cases.

Table 1. Parameter sets of the attachment and detachment rates used in this paper.

Case	Ω_{A_1}	Ω_{A_2}	Ω_{D_1}	Ω_{D_2}
(O)	0.5	0.5	0.25	0.25
(A)	0.8	0.2	0.1	0.4
(B)	0.2	0.8	0.4	0.1

When we consider vehicular traffic, the case (A) seems to be qualitatively realistic since the motivation of lane change is reproduced. The large Ω_{A_1} represents strong motivation to enter to the vacant road, whereas, the small Ω_{A_2} represents the refusal of entering to the congested road. Similarly, the large Ω_{D_2} represents strong motivation to leave the congested road, whereas, the small Ω_{D_1} represents the refusal of leaving the vacant road. Hence, the result of the case (A) would give a more useful insight to vehicular traffic than that of the case (O), i.e., the original model, so that investigation on the difference between the case (O) and (A) are especially important.

Figure 2 shows the phase diagrams of the model. The boundaries of the phases in the case (O) are depicted by the dashed lines in the diagrams for comparison. We see two phases, which are the coexistence phase (LH), where the low and high density regions are divided by a shock, i.e., DW, and the high-density phase (H).

In the case (A) (Fig. 2(A)), we observe LH and H phases similar to the case (O); however, the boundary moves to the right and the LH phase area becomes larger. In contrast, the boundary moves to the left in the case (B) (Fig. 2(B)). Moreover, the low density regime, which does not appear in the case (O) because

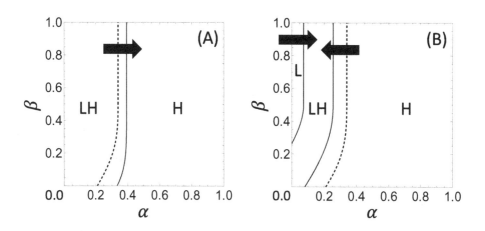

Fig. 2. Phase diagram obtained by mean-field analysis. Solid lines represent the boundaries of the phases. Dashed lines are the result in the case (O), i.e., the original model, for comparison. The attachment and detachment rates in the case (O), (A) and (B) are set as in Table 1.

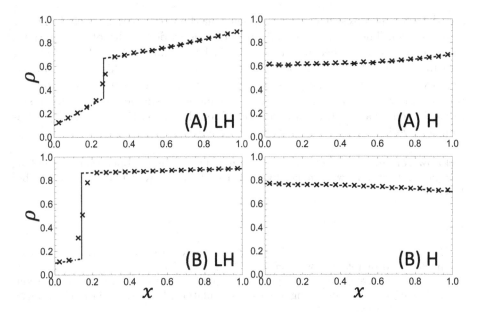

Fig. 3. Density profiles of the model. Dot-dashed and dashed lines represent the result in the low and high density regime, respectively, obtained by mean-field analysis. Vertical solid lines are the domain wall, which divide the low and high density region. Cross markers represent the result of our Monte Carlo simulation with the random-sequential update rule and $L = 1000$. The data from the time step $t = 10001$ to $t = 110000$ are used. The attachment and detachment rates in the case (A) and (B) are summarized in Table 1. The entering and exiting rates at the boundaries are set as $(\alpha, \beta) = (0.1, 0.1)$ and $(0.7, 0.3)$ in the LH phase and H phase, respectively.

of the large attachment and detachment rates, recovers from the left end of the diagram. Consequently, the LH phase area becomes smaller.

Therefore, we have revealed that the attachment in the vacant region and the detachment in the congested region (case (A)) extends the LH phase area. By contrast, the attachment in the congested region and the detachment in the vacant region (case (B)) yield opposite effect. This result implies that a shock (DW) is easier to observe in the dynamics of vehicles, which prefer moving in vacant region, than particles that are insensitive to local density.

Figure 3 are the density profiles obtained from the mean-field analysis and the Monte Carlo simulation. The results correspond well each other, so that we believe the phase diagrams in Fig. 2 are precise although they are depicted by a mean-field analysis.

5 Conclusion

In this paper, we have investigated an extended model of the totally asymmetric simple exclusion process with the Langmuir kinetics. The attachment and detachment rates at each site depend on the occupancy of their front site in our model. The mean-field analysis allows us to depict the phase diagrams, whose precision is verified by the Monte Carlo simulation. It is elucidated that attachment and detachment behavior similar to vehicles, which avoid congestion, extend the area of the phase with a shock, i.e., a domain wall that divides the low and high density region. Since our model is simple enough, this result is considered as a general characteristic of self-driven particles, which waits for empirical verification.

Acknowlgement. We are grateful to Jun Sato for kind cooperation in checking this paper. This work was financially supported by JSPS KAKENHI Grant Number 15K17583.

References

1. MacDonald, C.T., Gibbs, J.H., Pipkin, A.C.: Kinetics of biopolymerization on nucleic acid templates. Biopolymers **6**(1), 1–5 (1968)
2. Derrida, B., Evans, M.R., Hakim, V., Pasquier, V.: Exact solution of a 1D asymmetric exclusion model using a matrix formulation. J. Phys. A Math. Gen. **26**(7), 1493–1517 (1993)
3. Schadschneider, A., Chowdhury, D., Nishinari, K., Santen, L.: Stochastic Transport in Complex Systems. Elsevier, Amsterdam/Oxford (2010)
4. Wolfram, S.: Cellular Automata and Complexity: Collected Papers. Westview Press, Boulder (1994)
5. Parmeggiani, A., Franosch, T., Frey, E.: Phase coexistence in driven one-dimensional transport. Phys. Rev. Lett. **90**(8), 086601 (2003)
6. Evans, M.R., Juhász, R., Santen, L.: Shock formation in an exclusion process with creation and annihilation. Phys. Rev. E **68**(2), 026117 (2003)
7. Parmeggiani, A., Franosch, T., Frey, E.: Totally asymmetric simple exclusion process with Langmuir kinetics. Phys. Rev. E **70**(4), 046101 (2004)
8. Sato, J., Nishinari, K.: Relaxation dynamics of the asymmetric simple exclusion process with Langmuir kinetics on a ring. Phys. Rev. E **93**(4), 042113 (2016)
9. Kruse, K., Sekimoto, K.: Growth of fingerlike protrusions driven by molecular motors. Phys. Rev. E - Stat. Nonlinear, Soft Matter Phys. **66**(3), 1–5 (2002)
10. Muto, E., Sakai, H., Kaseda, K.: Long-range cooperative binding of kinesin to a microtubule in the presence of ATP. J. Cell Biol. **168**(5), 691–696 (2005)
11. Vuijk, H.D., Rens, R., Vahabi, M., MacKintosh, F.C., Sharma, A.: Driven diffusive systems with mutually interactive Langmuir kinetics. Phys. Rev. E **91**(3), 032143 (2015)
12. Messelink, J., Rens, R., Vahabi, M., MacKintosh, F.C., Sharma, A.: On-site residence time in a driven diffusive system: violation and recovery of a mean-field description. Phys. Rev. E **93**(1), 012119 (2016)
13. Ichiki, S., Sato, J., Nishinari, K.: Totally asymmetric simple exclusion process with Langmuir kinetics depending on the occupancy of the neighboring sites. J. Phys. Soc. Jpn. **85**(4), 044001 (2016)
14. Ichiki, S., Sato, J., Nishinari, K.: Totally asymmetric simple exclusion process on a periodic lattice with Langmuir kinetics depending on the occupancy of the forward neighboring site. Eur. Phys. J. B **89**(5), 135 (2016)
15. Lighthill, M.J., Whitham, G.B.: On kinematic waves. I. Flood movement in long rivers. Proc. R. Soc. A Math. Phys. Eng. Sci. **229**(1178), 281–316 (1955)

Agent-Based Simulation and Cellular Automata-ABS&CA

Multiscale Pedestrian Modeling with CA and Agent-Based Approaches: Ubiquity or Consistency?

Luca Crociani[1], Gregor Lämmel[2], and Giuseppe Vizzari[1(✉)]

[1] Complex Systems and Artificial Intelligence Research Centre,
University of Milano-Bicocca, Milano, Italy
{l.crociani,giuseppe.vizzari}@unimib.it
[2] German Aerospace Center (DLR), Institute of Transportation Systems,
Cologne, Germany
gregor.laemmel@dlr.de

Abstract. The simulation of complex system often pushes the modelers to face issues related to conflicting goals, constraints and limits of the available computational instruments: we often want to simulate large scale scenarios but with very good computational performances. A way to deal with this kind of situation is to couple simple modeling approaches with more fine grained representations of portions of the simulated system requiring higher degree of fidelity. This paper describes an approach adopting this scheme for large scale pedestrian simulation and focusing on issues related to the connection of the models representing the system at different granularities. In particular, to achieve a consistent behavior of the adopted models, in certain portions of the environment a single pedestrian needs to be represented in both models at the same time.

Keywords: Multi-scale modeling · Cellular Automata · Multi-agent systems

1 Introduction

The simulation of complex system often pushes the modelers to face issues related to conflicting goals, constraints and limits of the available computational instruments. For instance, models for the simulation of pedestrians and crowds are actually mature enough to support the everyday activities of operators and decision makers (designers, crowd managers, organizers of events implying the presence of large quantities of pedestrians in constrained areas) but they still present serious limits in terms of scalability. The growth of the number of pedestrians in the simulated area implies overall computation times for simulations that are generally incompatible with the usage of these tools for supporting decisions of heads of operations in actual case of evacuation (as discussed in [15]), and sometimes, for specific scenarios (e.g. portions of the Hajj [1]), it makes practically impossible to use certain simulation approaches and tools.

© Springer International Publishing Switzerland 2016
S. El Yacoubi et al. (Eds.): ACRI 2016, LNCS 9863, pp. 415–423, 2016.
DOI: 10.1007/978-3-319-44365-2_41

A possible way to deal with large scale scenarios is to simplify the adopted model, and in particular its fidelity in the representation of the simulated environment or in its internal mechanisms. For instance, in a biological system simulation by means of Cellular Automata, a relatively large cell of the CA could actually include a very large number of biological cells, as well as concentrations of humors, antibodies and antigens (see, e.g., [11]). Of course the transition rule will not represent precisely the interactions among the different relevant individual entities included in each cell of the CA model (whose identity is actually irrelevant), but rather manage the imprecision of the spatial representation by means of stochastic mechanisms. On the other hand, sometimes the goals of the simulation require the modeler to assure that the simulated entities preserve their identity throughout the simulation and that, at least in some portions of the simulation, they interact with other entities or elements of the environment in a precise way.

For pedestrian simulation situations in which pedestrian density is relatively low and conflicts are rare (e.g. in absence of crossing pedestrian flows, such as a large avenue) a coarse grained model, like a graph in which vertices are associated to road crossings and edges correspond to road sections, can provide sufficient information to manage pedestrian dynamics. For instance, in [14] a queue model is introduced for the management of pedestrians in this kind of environmental structure: a pedestrian is generally situated in a part of an edge and it moves with a velocity related to the current density in this road section. This approach, coupled with an iterative approach for the decision of the actual path to be followed in the graph, is adopted in the MATSIM model [9], which was originally conceived for simulating vehicular traffic but that has been successfully adapted to manage pedestrian simulation scenarios.

In situations of relatively high local density (e.g. bottlenecks, gateways in which conflicting pedestrian flows meet), however, the interactions among pedestrians are more frequent and their implications are much more significant, for instance on the actual spatial utilization of the environment, making it unreasonable to simply ignore them. In these situations, a finer grained model of the environment and a different model for the simulation of pedestrian behaviour are necessary. Cellular Automata represent a viable choice for the integrated representation of the environment and the pedestrians situated and moving throughout its spatial structure (see, e.g. [2] or [3]). The main goal of this paper is to present a multiscale approach adopted to tackle this kind of scenario and focus on issues related to the connection of the models representing the system at different granularities. In particular, to achieve a consistent behavior of the adopted models (e.g. not allowing a pedestrian to move towards a different portion of the environment, represented in a different way, when the target are is heavily congested), in certain portions of the environment a single pedestrian needs to be represented in both models at the same time. The following section will introduce the overall structure of the multiscale approach, briefly presenting the sub-models. Section 3 will instead discuss how the sub-model connection can influence the overall achieved dynamics and how to manage it in order to achieve a consistent behavior.

2 Structure of the Multiscale Approach

The approach adopted for this work is characterized by the fact that a multiscale representation of the environment is adopted to try to preserve the good computational properties of the agent based model adopting a coarse grained spatial representation, but employing a connected CA model for simulating portions of the environment requiring a higher degree of fidelity. An example of this kind of approach is described in Fig. 1: in particular, whereas the overall simulated environment is a typical portion of a urban system in the city of Milan (Italy), in which pedestrians can walk on sidewalks, a bridge is connecting two roads separated by a railway. This bridge generally does not represent a bottleneck, but in specific days in Spring a set of events involving the presence of a large number of pedestrians (over 100,000 mostly concentrated into Friday and Saturday nights) turns it into an actual bottleneck. In this kind of situation, using simulation to evaluate alternative crowd management schemes trying to reduce the congestion on the bridge requires to consider the fact that simulating all the area with a CA model would have considerable (if not unbearable) simulation costs, whereas for most of the simulated scenario the achieved degree of precision would be unnecessary. The adopted approach, instead, adopts the MATSIM model and its graph representation of the environment for most of the simulated area, employing the CA model only for the bridge and the immediate nearby

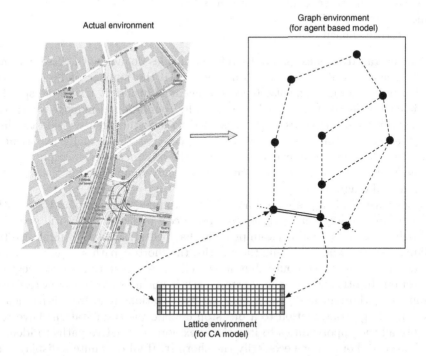

Fig. 1. Multi scale representation of the simulated environment.

area. Pedestrians choosing to cross the bridge instead of following a longer path avoiding the congested area will exit the mesoscopic graph environment and they will be appear in the CA microscopic model. The approach and example application are described more thoroughly here [6], here we will mostly focus on the interaction among the meso and micro scale model after having briefly introduced them.

2.1   Mesoscopic Model

The mesoscopic model has been implemented within the MATSim framework[1]. The standard simulation approach in MATSim employs a queuing model based on [14]. Originally, the model was designed for the simulation of vehicular traffic only, but it has also been adapted for pedestrian simulation [9].

The basic network structure of the environment, in traditional transportation scenarios, is modeled as a graph whose links describe urban streets and the nodes describe their intersections. In the pedestrian context "streets" also include side walks, ramps, corridors, and so on. Links behave like FIFO queues controlled by the following parameters:

- the length of the link l;
- the area of the link A;
- the free flow speed $\hat{v}$;
- the free speed travel time t_{min}, given by $l/\hat{v}$;
- the flow capacity FC;
- the storage capacity SC.

The overall dynamics follows therefore the rules defined with these parameters. An agent is able to enter to a link l until the number of agents inside l is below its storage capacity. Once the agent is inside, it travels at speed $\hat{v}$ and it cannot leave the link before t_{min}. The congestion is managed with the flow capacity parameter FC, which is used to lock the agents inside the link to not exceed it: this mechanism basically increases the actually experienced travel time whenever the level of density in the link increases, incorporating in the model dynamics empirical evidences, essentially summarized in the so-called fundamental diagram [13].

Considering this representation of the environment, agents plan their paths through this graph structure trying to reproduce a plausible real-world pedestrians' behavior. A reasonable assumption is that pedestrians try to minimize the walking distance when planning their paths: the shortest path among two nodes is straightforward to compute, but it is well known that this choice neglects congestion. In other words, the shortest path is not necessarily the fastest one. Commuters who repeatedly walk between two locations (e.g. from a particular track in a large train station to a bus stop outside the train station) have reasonably all the opportunities to iteratively explore alternative paths to identify the fastest, although not necessarily the shortest. If all commuters display that

[1] http://www.matsim.org.

same behavior, they might reach a state where it is no longer possible to find any faster path. If this is the case, then the system has reached a state of a Nash [10] equilibrium with respect to individual travel times. This behavior can be emulated by applying an iterative best-response dynamic [4] and has been widely applied in the context of vehicular transport simulations (see, e.g., [7,8,12]). It must be noted that the Nash equilibrium is not actually the system optimum: the latter does not minimize individual travel times but the system (or average) travel time. Like the Nash equilibrium, the system optimum can also be achieved by an iterative best response dynamic, but based on the marginal travel time instead of the individual travel time. The marginal travel time of an individual traveler corresponds to the sum of the travel time experienced by her/him (internal costs) and the delay that he/she impose to others (external costs). While it is straightforward to determine the internal costs (i.e. travel time), the external costs calculation is not so obvious. An approach for the marginal travel time estimation and its application to a microscopic simulation model has been proposed in [5].

2.2   The Discrete Microscopic Model

The model is a 2-dimensional Cellular Automaton with a square-cells grid representation of the space. The $0.4 \times 0.4\,\mathrm{m}^2$ size of the cells describes the average space occupation of a person [16] and reproduces a maximum pedestrian density of 6.25 persons/m^2, that covers the values usually observable in the real world. A cell of the environment can be basically of type *walkable* or of type *obstacle*, meaning that it will never be occupied by any pedestrians during the simulation.

Intermediate targets can also be introduced in the environment to mark the extremes of a particular region (e.g. rooms or corridors), and so decision points for the route choice of agents. Final goals of the discrete environment are its open edges, i.e., the entrances/exits of the discrete space that will be linked to roads. Since the concept of region is fuzzy and the space decomposition is a subjective task that can be tackled with different approaches, the configuration of their position in the scenario is not automatic and it is left to the user.

Employing the floor field approach [3] and spreading one field from each target, either intermediate or final, allows to build a network representing this portion of the simulated environment. In this graph, each node denotes one target and the edges identify the existence of a direct way between two targets (i.e. passing through only one region). To allow this, the floor field diffusion is limited by obstacles and cells of other targets. An example of such an environment with the overlain network is shown in Fig. 2. The open borders of the microscopic environment are the nodes that will be connected to the other network of the mesoscopic model.

To integrate the network with the one of the mesoscopic model and to allow the reasoning at the strategic level, each edge a of the graph is firstly labeled with its length l_a, describing the distance between two targets δ_i, δ_j in the discrete space. This value is computed using the floor fields as:

$$l_a(\delta_1, \delta_2) = Avg\left(FF_{\delta_1}(Center(\delta_2)),\ FF_{\delta_2}(Center(\delta_1))\right) \tag{1}$$

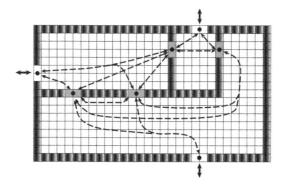

Fig. 2. Sample scenario with its network representation. While the blue cells represent intermediate targets, the outside arrows describe the links with the outside network that will be simulated with the mesoscopic model.

where $FF_\delta(x,y)$ gives the value of the floor field associated to a destination δ in position (x,y); $Center(\delta)$ describes the coordinates of the central cell of δ and Avg computes the average between the two values and provides a unique distance. Together with the average speed of pedestrians in the discrete space, l_a is used to calculate the free speed travel time of the link $T_a^{free} = \frac{l_a}{s_a}$.

3   Connecting the Models

As suggested in Sect. 2 both the mesoscopic and the microscopic model are mapped on the same global network of links and nodes; a link can either be in a congested or non congested state. Initially, all links are considered as non congested, and they switch from this state to congested once the observed travel time along the link is longer than the free speed travel time. Vice versa, a link in the congested state switches to non congested as soon as the first pedestrian is able to walk along the link in free speed travel time. Every pedestrian that leaves a given link while it is in the congested state imposes external costs to the others. The amount of the external costs corresponds to the time span from the time when the pedestrian under consideration leaves the congested link till the time when the link switches to the non congested state again.

In this work, the iterative search of equilibrium/optimum follows the logic of the iterative best response dynamic and it is described by the following tasks:

1. Compute plans for all agents
2. Execute the multi-scale simulation
3. Evaluate executed plans of the agents
4. Select a portion of the agents population and re-compute their plans
5. Jump to step 2, if the stop criterion has not been reached

The stopping criterion is implemented as a predetermined number of iterations defined by the user. This is due to the fact that the number of iterations needed for the system to reach a relaxed state depends on the complexity of the scenario and is not known a-priori. In the described scenario, one hundred iterations gives a good compromise between relaxation and runtime.

Initial plan computation is performed with a shortest path algorithm. In the subsequent iterations the agents try to find better plans based on the experienced travel costs. Depending on the cost function, the agents learn more convenient paths either for them individually (relaxation towards a Nash equilibrium) or for the overall population (relaxation towards the system optimum).

A basic requirement for this kind of multi scale modeling is a consistent transfer of travelers (e.g. pedestrians or vehicles) between the involved simulation models. Besides obvious properties, like eventual preservation of the number of pedestrians overall present in the whole environment, we must assure additional properties.

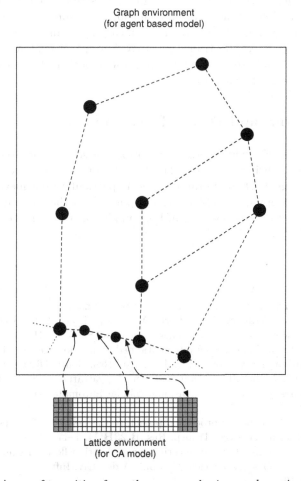

Fig. 3. Areas of transition from the meso and micro scale environments.

In particular, no link must contain a number of pedestrians exceeding its own capacity (explicitly specified for the meso level links and equal to the number of cells in the micro level environment): whenever the destination link is full, the pedestrian must be kept waiting in the source link, until space becomes available. Whenever this happens, however, the passage of a pedestrian towards the destination link should not generate immediately an effect of acceleration in the source link. In particular, this is important when the transition is from a meso level link towards a micro scale CA grid: the reduction in the density on the source link would, in fact, cause an immediate increase in the velocity of pedestrians still inside it.

In order to avoid this kind of dynamic, the connection at the borders of the pedestrian microscopic model environment are managed with so-called transition areas, that is, links characterized by a dual nature, since they are at the same time both a meso level link and a micro level CA grid. Figure 3 shows how this scheme is realized in the example scenario. Pedestrians that transit from the meso level link and enter the CA still count for the computation of the velocity in the meso level link, and they are removed, causing an increase in the velocity, only after they vacated the transition area. For a transient amount of time, therefore, pedestrians are simultaneously present both in the meso and micro level environmental representations.

4   Conclusions and Future Developments

This paper has described an approach adopting this scheme for large scale pedestrian simulation focusing on issues related to the connection of the models representing the system at different granularities. In particular, to achieve a consistent behavior of the adopted models, in certain portions of the environment a single pedestrian needs to be represented in both models at the same time.

References

1. Abdelghany, A., Abdelghany, K., Mahmassani, H.: A hybrid simulation-assignment modeling framework for crowd dynamics in large-scale pedestrian facilities. Transp. Res. Part A Policy Pract. **86**, 159–176 (2016). http://www.sciencedirect.com/science/article/pii/S0965856416000458
2. Blue, V., Adler, J.: Emergent fundamental pedestrian flows from cellular automata microsimulation. Transp. Res. Rec. J. Transp. Res. Board **1644**, 29–36 (1998)
3. Burstedde, C., Klauck, K., Schadschneider, A., Zittartz, J.: Simulation of pedestrian dynamics using a two-dimensional cellular automaton. Physica A **295**(3–4), 507–525 (2001)
4. Cascetta, E.: A stochastic process approach to the analysis of temporal dynamics in transportation networks. Transp. Res. B **23B**(1), 1–17 (1989)
5. Crociani, L., Lämmel, G.: Multidestination pedestrian flows in equilibrium: a cellular automaton-based approach. Comput. Aided Civ. Infrastruct. Eng. **31**(2016), 432–448 (2016)

6. Crociani, L., Lämmel, G., Vizzari, G.: Multi-scale simulation for crowd management: a case study in an urban scenario. In: Proceedings of the 1st Workshop on Agent Based Modelling of Urban Systems, ABMUS 2016 (2016)
7. Gawron, C.: An iterative algorithm to determine the dynamic user equilibrium in a traffic simulation model. Int. J. Mod. Phys. C **9**(3), 393–407 (1998)
8. Krajzewicz, D., Erdmann, J., Behrisch, M., Bieker, L.: Recent development and applications of SUMO - Simulation of Urban MObility. Int. J. Adv. Syst. Meas. **5**(3–4), 128–138 (2012)
9. Lämmel, G., Klüpfel, H., Nagel, K.: The MATSim network flow model for traffic simulation adapted to large-scale emergency egress and an application to the evacuation of the Indonesian city of Padang in case of a tsunami warning. In: Timmermans, H. (ed.) Pedestrian Behavior, pp. 245–265. Emerald Group Publishing Limited, Bradford (2009). Chapter 11
10. Nash, J.: Non-cooperative games. Ann. Math. **54**(2), 286–295 (1951)
11. Puzone, R., Kohler, B., Seiden, P., Celada, F.: Immsim, a flexible model for in machina experiments on immune system responses. Future Gener. Comput. Syst. **18**(7), 961–972 (2002). Selected papers from CA 2000 (6th International Workshop on Cellular Automata of IFIP working group 1.5, Osaka, Japan, 21–22 August 2000) and ACRI 2000 (4th International Conference on Cellular Automata in Research and Industry, Karlsruhe, Germany, 4–6 October 2000). http://www.sciencedirect.com/science/article/pii/S0167739X02000754
12. Raney, B., Nagel, K.: Iterative route planning for large-scale modular transportation simulations. Future Gener. Comput. Syst. **20**(7), 1101–1118 (2004)
13. Seyfried, A., Steffen, B., Klingsch, W., Boltes, M.: The fundamental diagram of pedestrian movement revisited. J. Stat. Mech Theory: Exp. **2005**(10), P10002 (2005). http://stacks.iop.org/1742-5468/2005/i=10/a=P10002
14. Simon, P., Esser, J., Nagel, K.: Simple queueing model applied to the city of Portland. Int. J. Mod. Phys. **10**(5), 941–960 (1999)
15. Wagoum, A.U.K., Steffen, B., Seyfried, A., Chraibi, M.: Parallel real time computation of large scale pedestrian evacuations. Adv. Eng. Softw. **60–61**, 98–103 (2013). cIVIL-COMP: Parallel, Distributed, Gridand Cloud Computing. http://www.sciencedirect.com/science/article/pii/S0965997812001391
16. Weidmann, U.: Transporttechnik der Fussgänger - Transporttechnische Eigenschaftendes Fussgängerverkehrs (Literaturstudie). Literature Research 90, Institut füer Verkehrsplanung, Transporttechnik, Strassen- und Eisenbahnbau IVT an der ETH Zürich (1993)

Line Patterns Formed by Cellular Automata Agents

Rolf Hoffmann[1]($\boxtimes$) and Dominique Désérable[2]

[1] Technische Universität Darmstadt, Darmstadt, Germany
hoffmann@informatik.tu-darmstadt.de
[2] Institut National des Sciences Appliquées, Rennes, France
domidese@gmail.com

Abstract. Considered is a 2D cellular automaton with moving agents. Each cell contains a particle with a certain spin/color that can be turned by an agent. Four colors are used. The objective is to align the spins in parallel along horizontal and vertical lines, in order to form long orthogonal "line patterns". The quality of a line pattern is measured by a degree of order computed by counting matching 3 x 3 patterns. Additional markers are used and signals between agents are introduced in order to improve the task efficiency. The agents' behavior is controlled by a finite state machine (FSM). An agent can perform 128 actions altogether as combinations of moving, turning, color changing, marker setting and signaling. It reacts on its own state and on the sensed colors, markers and signals. For a given set of n x n fields, near optimal FSM were evolved by a genetic algorithm. The evolved agents are capable of forming line patterns with a limited degree of order. The scalability of two FSM against a varying number of agents is studied as well as the efficiency gain through the newly introduced signals.

Keywords: Cellular automata agents · Multi-agent system · Pattern formation · Evolving FSM behavior · Spatial computing

1 Introduction

How can cellular automata agents (CAA) be configured in order to form specific structures? CAA are *agents* modeled by classical CA using relatively complex rules. There are many applications, e.g. the forming of mechanical, chemical, biological [1] or artificial structures, or the building of computational devices and communication networks. Nano-structures can be built by nano-robots, or by beaming focused energy onto certain cells in order to change their physical state [2–6]. Building special nano-polymers or functional polymers could be another application. The alignment of spins – as discussed in this paper – allows to minimize the conductivity of a thin-film structure based on the giant magnetoresistance.

The Task. Given is a field of $N = n \times n$ cells with border, n assumed to be even. A given number k of agents is moving around in the field. The agents' task

© Springer International Publishing Switzerland 2016
S. El Yacoubi et al. (Eds.): ACRI 2016, LNCS 9863, pp. 424–434, 2016.
DOI: 10.1007/978-3-319-44365-2_42

is to construct a global state where a certain spatial *line pattern* appears that belongs to a predefined line pattern class. The agents behavior is controlled by an embedded finite state machine (FSM). The main objective is to find "intelligent" agents that are able to solve this task. Each cell, except the border cells, contains a particle with a certain color/spin, $color \in \{0, 1, 2, 3\}$. The border cells' color is NIL with value -1. In addition, *markers* are available in each cell, $marker \in \{0, 1\}$. An agent can change color and marker on its site. Markers are used as a distributed global memory. A marker can later be used by the same agent or by another agent. Markers enlarge the control and data space and allow indirect communication between agents: e.g. an agent may set a marker from 0 to 1 indicating that the current site is already locally ordered. As an extension to previous works [7,8], explicit *signals* between agents are introduced. Now a further objective is to study how signals act onto system performance. Initially the color, marker and agents' position and direction are randomly distributed.

We define the aimed *line pattern class* by long horizontal lines of parallel up-or-down spins, or vertical lines of right-or-left spins. The neighboring cells of a line shall have another spin/color. The capabilities of the agents shall be constrained, i.e. the number of control states, the action set and the amount of perceived information.

Agents. What is the advantage to solve this task by agents? Generally speaking, agents can behave in a flexible, powerful and coordinated way because of their intelligence and their specific sensors and actuators. Important properties that can be achieved by agents are: (*Scalability*) The problem can usually be solved with a variable number of agents, and faster with more agents in a certain range; (*Tuneability*) The problem can be solved faster or with a higher quality by increasing the agent's intelligence; (*Flexibility*) Similar problems can be solved by the same agents, e.g. when the shape or size of the environment is changed; (*Fault-tolerance*) When obstacles are introduced or some agents are faulty, the problem can still be solved in a gracefully degraded way; (*Updating-tolerance*) Often the time-evoluted global state depends only weakly on the updating-scheme (synchronous, asynchronous). This is important if no global clock is available.

Related Work. (i) *FSM-controlled agents:* We have designed evolved FSM-controlled CAA for several tasks, like the *Creature's Exploration Problem* [9, 10], the *All-to-All Communication Task* [10–12], the *Target Searching Task* [13], the *Routing Task* [14,15]. The FSM for these tasks were evolved by genetic algorithms mainly. Other related works are a multi-agent system modeled in CA for image processing [16], and modeling the agent's behavior by an FSM with a restricted number of states [17]. An important pioneering work about FSM-controlled agents is [18]. FSM-controlled robots are also well known.

(ii) *Pattern formation:* Agent-based pattern formations in nature and physics are studied in [19,20]. A programming language is presented in [21] for pattern-formation of locally-interacting, identically-programmed agents – as an example, the layout of a CMOS inverter is formed by agents; related is a new "Global–to–Local" theory emerging in [22]. In [23] a general framework is proposed to discover rules that produce special spatial patterns based on a combination of Machine Learning strategies including Genetic Algorithms and Artificial Neural Networks.

(iii) *Modeling moving agents:* CAA used herein are modeled within the CA paradigm [7] and implemented from the *write access* CA–w concept [24–26] allowing a cell to write information onto a neighbor. Other modeling concepts related to CA are lattice-gas cellular automata [27], block substitutions [28] or partitioned CA as used in [12].

This work extends the issues presented in [7]. The class of patterns was different therein and satisfactory patterns could only be found with two colors. Now the aim is to generate patterns with four colors using explicit markers and additional communication signals. In Sect. 2 the class of target patterns and a measure for them are defined and in Sect. 3 the multi-agent system with its agent's actions, sensing features and control structure is presented. The used genetic algorithm is explained in Sect. 4, the effectiveness and efficiency of selected FSMs and signals are evaluated in Sect. 5.

2   Line Patterns and Degree of Order

How can the class of line patterns be defined? The idea is to use a set of small $m \times m$ matching patterns (or *templates*) and test them on each site (x,y) of the cell field. So each template is applied in parallel on each cell, which can be seen as a classical CA rule application. If a template fits on a site, then a hit (at most one) is stored at this site. Then the sum of all hits is computed which defines the *degree of order h*. For our problem the size of the templates is 3×3. Larger templates could be used if more sophisticated patterns should be generated. The process is illustrated in Fig. 1. In order to detect lines more easily in a pattern, small rectangles with redundant colors (b) are used in the representation instead of the spin-arrows (a). A black dot is used to display a hit (c). The used templates are depicted in (d–g): a (horizontal) row of 3 parallel up-spins (d), a (vertical)

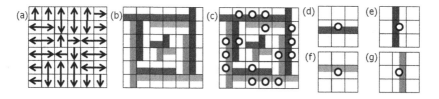

Fig. 1. (a) An optimal balanced line pattern of a 6×6 field with a maximum number of hits. A line is defined by a row or column of parallel spins. (b) Another representation of (a), each spin is represented by a specific rectangle within a square. Additional redundant colors are used in order to make the lines more distinguishably. (c) Hits are depicted as dots. (d–g) The templates defining the class of line patterns. Templates are local test patterns which are expected to appear in a target pattern. (Color figure online)

column of 3 parallel right-spins (e), a row of 3 parallel down-spins (f), a column of 3 parallel left-spins (g). The six empty sites of each template have a color different from the line's color. Thereby two or more parallel lines with the same color/spin are not allowed.

A line of length $w > 2$ has a hit count $h = w - 2$ because the beginning and ending of a line are not counted. This means also that lines of length 1 and 2 are not counted. Not counting the terminal cells of each line can be seen as a penalty reflected in the fitness function which is used during the optimization process, thereby the searching for long lines is favored. The aimed patterns consist in a maximum number of long lines. The theoretically maximum order is at least $h_{max} = (n-2)^2$ (for even side length n). The relative order is $h_{rel} = h/h_{max}$. The maximum can be reached by optimal line patterns, e.g. the one shown in Fig. 1(a–b). Patterns are *balanced* if the frequency for each color is the same, i.e. $\forall i \in \{0, 1, 2, 3\} : n^2/4 = \sum(color(x, y) = i)$ and *unbalanced* otherwise. Unbalanced patterns can be generated easier than balanced patterns and can even have higher hit counts than optimal balanced patterns.

3   Modeling the Multi-Agent-System

The cell rule has to react on several non-uniform situations, such as:an agent is actively operating on that cell, an agent is in the neighborhood, or a border cell is in front. Therefore the cell state is modeled as a record of several data items.
$CellState = (Border, Color, Marker, Agent)$, where
$Border \in \{true, false\}$, $Color\ L \in \{0, 1, 2, 3\}$, $Marker\ M \in \{0, 1\}$
$Agent = (Activity, Identifier, Direction, ControlState)$
$Activity \in \{true, false\}$, $Identifier\ ID \in \{0, 1, ..., k-1\}$
$Direction\ D \in \{0, 1, 2, 3\} \equiv \{toN, toE, toS, toW\}$
$ControlState\ S \in \{0, 1, ..., N_{states} - 1\}$.

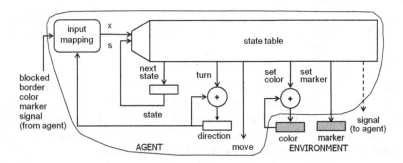

Fig. 2. An agent is controlled by a finite state machine (FSM). The state table defines the agent's next control state, its next direction, and whether to move or not. The table also defines the next color, the next marker and the signal to another agent. (Color figure online)

This means that each cell is equipped with a potential agent, which is either active or not. When an agent is moving from A to B, it is copied from A to B and the *Activity* bit on A is set to false. The agent's behavior is depicted in Fig. 2. The FSM corresponds to the "brain" or algorithm controlling the agent.It contains a *state table* (also called *next state/output table*). Outputs are the actions and the next control state. Inputs are the control state *s* and defined input situations *x*. An input mapping function is used in order to limit the size of the state table. The *input mapping* reduces all possible input combinations to an index $x \in X = \{0, 1, \ldots, N_x - 1\}$ used in combination with the control state to select the actual line of the state table. The capabilities of the agents have to be defined before designing or searching for the agents' behavior. The main capabilities are: the perceivable inputs from the environment, the outputs and actions an agent can perform, the capacity of its memory (number of possible control and data states) and its "intelligence" (useful pro- and reactive activity). Here the intelligence is limited and realized by a mapping of its state and inputs to the next state, actions and outputs. Actions and outputs that an agent is able to perform are:

- **nextstate**: $state \leftarrow nextstate \in \{0, \ldots, N_{states} - 1\}$.
- **move**: $move \in \{0, 1\} \equiv \{wait, go\}$.
- **turn**: $turn \in \{0, 1, 2, 3\}$.
  The new direction is $D(t + 1) \leftarrow (D(t) + turn) \bmod 4$.
- **setcolor**: $setcolor \in \{0, 1, 2, 3\}$.
  The new color is $L(t + 1) \leftarrow (L(t) + setcolor) \bmod 4$.
- **setmarker**: The new marker is $M(t + 1) \leftarrow setmarker \in \{0, 1\}$.
- **signal**: An agent emits a $signal \in \{0, 1\}$ that can be used by another agent.

An agent shall react on the following inputs:

- its **own control state**,
- its **own direction**,
- the **cell's color and marker** it is situated on,
- a **border cell** in front,
- a **blocked** situation/condition, caused either by a border, another agent in front, or when another prior agent can move to the front cell in case of a conflict. The inverse condition is called *free*.
- a **signal** from another agent if it stays in front.

An agent has a moving direction *D* that also selects the cell in front as the actual neighbor. What can an agent directly observe from a neighboring agent? In the used model it can only register the presence of an agent in front and the emitted signal from that agent. So only a small part of the state of that agent is revealed in the form of a *signal*, which can be used for cooperation.

All actions can be performed in parallel. There is only one constraint:when the agent's action is *go* and the situation is *blocked*, then the agent cannot move and has to wait, but still it can turn and change the cell's color and marker. In case of a moving conflict, the agent with the lowest identifier (ID = 0 .. $k - 1$) gets priority. Instead of using the identifier for prioritization, it would be possible to use other schemes, e.g. random priority, or a cyclic priority with a fixed or space-dependent base. The following input mapping was used, $x \in \{0, 1, \ldots, 12\}$:

$x = 0$, if the agent is *blocked* by a border cell in front,
$x = 1 + (L - D) mod\ 4 + 4(marker)$, if the agent is *not blocked*,
$x = 9 + 2(signal)$, if $L \in \{0, 2\}$ and the agent is *blocked* by an agent in front,
$x = 10 + 2(signal)$, if $L \in \{1, 3\}$ and the agent is *blocked* by an agent.

This mapping was designed by experience and experiments. Of course, other input mappings could be defined, with more or less x codes, or other assignments, e.g. the color or marker in front of the agent or in its neighborhood could be taken into account. Note that agent's view is very limited, it can react only the cell data (control state, direction, color, marker) where it is situated on, and sometimes on the signal from an agent in front. Therefore the agent's task is really difficult to solve. (Imagine you are the agent, moving around in a dark space where you can only observe the color and marker on the ground, and sometimes you detect a border or a signal in front!): the larger the agent's view, the easier the task can be solved.

The used updating scheme is *synchronous*; An important issue is that asynchronous updating is more natural, as studied in [29,30]; see further Sect. 5.5.

4   Evolving FSMs by a Genetic Algorithm

An ultimate aim could be to find an FSM that is optimal for all possible initial configurations on average. This aim is very difficult to reach because it needs an huge amount of computation time. Furthermore, it depends on the question whether all-rounders or specialists are favored. Therefore, in this work we searched only for *specialist* optimized for (i) a fixed field size of $N = n \times n$, $n = 8$, (ii) a fixed number of agents k and (iii) 100 initial random configurations (for training and evaluation).

The number of different FSMs which can be coded by a state table is $Z = (|s||y|)^{(|s||x|)}$ where $|s|$ is the number of control states, $|x|$ is the number of inputs and $|y|$ is the number of outputs. As the search space increases exponentially, we restricted the number of states to $|s| = N_{states} = 8$, and the number of inputs to $|x| = 13$. A relatively simple genetic algorithm similar to the one in [7] was used in order to find (sub)optimal FSMs with reasonable computational cost. A possible solution corresponds to the contents of the FSM's state table. For each input combination $(x, state) = j$, a list of actions is assigned: $actions(j) = (nextstate(j), move(j), turn(j), setcolor(j), setmarker(j), signal(j))$.

The fitness is defined as the number t of time steps which is necessary to emerge successfully a target pattern with a given degree h_{target} of order, averaged over all given initial random configurations. Successfully means that a target pattern with $h \geq h_{target}$ was found. The fitness function F is evaluated by simulating the system with a tentative FSM_i on a given initial configuration. Then the mean fitness $\overline{F}(FSM_i)$ is computed by averaging over all initial configurations of the training set. $\overline{F}$ is then used to rank and sort the FSMs.

Evolved Finite State Machines. In general it turned out that it was very time consuming to find good solutions with a high degree of order, due to the difficulty of the agent's task in relation to their capabilities. In addition the search space is very large and difficult to explore. The total computation time on a Intel Xeon QuadCore 2 GHz was around 3 weeks to find the needed FSMs.

Let the best found FSM for k agents and a reached order of h be denoted by FSM(k,h). At first the FSM($k=16$, $h=18$) was evolved and used in Sects. 5.1 and 5.2; then FSM(1,18) in Sect. 5.3 and finally FSM(16,12), FSM(32,12), FSM(48,12) in Sect. 5.4.

5   Simulations and Evaluations

5.1   Simulation

The whole multi-agent system using the evolved FSM(16, 18) was simulated (Fig. 3). The snapshots (a) show how the line patterns are being built. The communication by signals is shown in Fig. 3b. It can be seen that at the end long lines in four colors appear. The markers (depicted as green or red small squares) are random at the beginning and almost all of them are changed during the run by the agents. The information stored in the markers is used for feedback and indirect communication. Although it was not detectable in which way, experiments without markers showed that the performance is much lower, a result also found in [8,11]. Note that a formed line pattern is not stable. After having

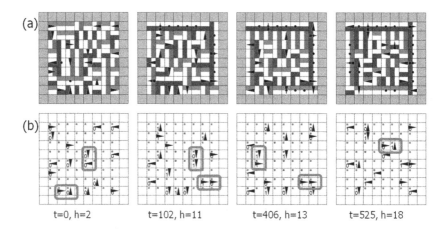

t=0, h=2   t=102, h=11   t=406, h=13   t=525, h=18

Fig. 3. (a) Snapshots showing how a line pattern is formed in a 8×8 field by 16 agents starting from a random configuration. $h =$ degree of order. Agents are represented by black triangles, spins by colors, and markers by small squares (red $= 1$, yellow $= 0$). Dots represent template hits. (b) The signals that the agents emit are shown, colors and hits are hidden. When an agent is blocked by another agent in front, it can read its signal. Some communication situations by signals are encircled in orange. (Color figure online)

reached the required degree of order the pattern is changing and the degree of order is fluctuating. Detecting a certain degree of order in a decentral way for termination is a seperate issue. It could be achieved by all-to-all communication of the hits.

5.2   Effectiveness Test

At first FSM($k = 16$, $h = 18$) was investigated. The chosen density of the agents was $\delta = 1/4$, because from [7] this density turned out to be most cost-effective in terms of $time \times agents$. The degree of order to be reached was incremented from lower levels until $h_{target} = 18$, the theoretical maximum is at least $h_{max} = (n - 2)^2 = 36$. The aimed relative degree of order was $h_{rel} = 50\,\%$, which is relatively low. The problem was that it was very difficult to reach a higher degree for this task with the given features of the agents. The found FSM was successful on all given 100 initial configurations of the test and evaluation set. The mean and extrema times to order a field were $t_{mean} = 1079 \pm 1011$, $t_{min} = 73$, $t_{max} = 5365$.

Then this FSM was simulated for another number of agents and it was expected that it is also 100\,\% successful, but that was not the case. Therefore FSM(16, 18) was tested with a lower order to be reached, $h = 12$ instead of $h = 18$. The result of this test is shown in Fig. 4a, success rate $vs.$ number of agents. The success rate is the number of fields out of 100 which were ordered with degree 12. This diagram shows that this FSM is working effectively (satisfactorily successful) for a number of agents nearby 16, the number it was evolved for. This is an argument that a specialist was evolved.

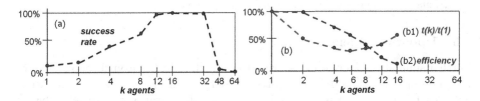

Fig. 4. (a) Effectiveness test. The top evolved FSM($k = 16$, $h = 18$) for size $= 8 \times 8$ was used. Then it was tested on how many fields it was successful for a different number k of agents, with a lower $h = 12$. This FSM is only effective for a number of agents nearby 16. (b) The top evolved FSM($k = 1$, $h = 18$) was used then tested with $h = 12$. Successful for 100 fields in the range $k = 1,..., 16$. (b1) Mean time ratio, minimal for $k = 6$. (b2) The efficiency decreases continuously with the number of agents.

5.3   FSM Evolved for One Agent

Mean and extrema times for FSM(1, 18) to order a field were $t_{mean} = 2272 \pm 1666$, $t_{min} = 260$, $t_{max} = 7828$. Now the question is, how does FSM(1, 18), evolved for one agent, behaves if the number of agents is varied. Time-scaling and efficiency were evaluated for a lowered degree of order $h = 12$; time $t(k)$ was normalized to $t(1)$. The graph (b1) in Fig. 4b shows that the minimal time is reached for $k = 6$, whence a density of agents $\delta = 6/64 = 9.4\%$. This result was not expected, because in [7] the optimal density was 25 %. An explanation could be that this task is more difficult, and therefore each agent needs a larger "personal" local memory (more markers and colors) to store intermediate ordering information. The graph (b2) shows the *efficiency*, i.e. the speedup divided by the number of agents: $(t(1)/t(k))/k$. The decreasing efficiency with the number of processors is quite common in multiprocessor systems, as we can interpret agents as moving processors.

5.4   Effect of Signals

The question is how much the communication with signals speed up the task. A scientifically sound answer goes beyond the scope of this paper. Nevertheless a partial answer can be given for some test cases. For that reason six top FSMs were evolved with order $h = 12$, for $k = 16, 32, 48$, and with (resp. without) signal. The following values were obtained:

```
no. of agents k            16    32    48
t1 = t(with signal)       111   185   1553
t2 = t(without signal)    134   237   2146
t1/t2                     .83   .78    .72
```

This evaluation shows that the time ratio t_1/t_2 is significantly lower than 1 (signals are efficient) and it increases with the number of agents when more communication is probable. Another result is that times t_1 and t_2 increase with k in this interval; this confirms the observation from the previous cases, that a high density of agents is not efficient.

5.5   Updating-Tolerance

Further simulations were done in order to show the effect of asynchronous updating. The optimal FSM(16, 18) evolved under synchronous updating was used. Then each generation was divided into $k = 16$ subgenerations. For each subgeneration one active agent was selected at random. The time counter was incremented by $1/k$ for each subgeneration, i.e. by one for one generation. 10 runs with different random seeds were performed on the given 100 initial fields. The mean and extrema times to order a field are $t_{mean} = 859.13 \pm 856.78$, $t_{min} = 34.25$, $t_{max} = 5628.94$. Compared to synchronous updating (Sect. 5.2), the t_{mean} ratio $t_{asyn}/t_{syn} = 859.13/1079 = 0.8$. This means that asynchronous updating was successful on all fields using the same synchronous rule, and the time was even 20 % lower for this test case.

6   Conclusion

The objective was to find FSM-controlled agents that can form specific line patterns. The class of path patterns was defined by a set of templates, small

3×3 local patterns. For 8×8 fields, several FSM were evolved with a different number of agents and a certain degree of order h. The agents are able to form successfully the aimed line patterns with the predefined degree of order by means of markers and signals. The FSM evolved for 16 agents is only effective for an agent number nearby 16. The FSM evolved for 1 agent is effective for up to 16 agents and most efficient for 6 agents. Signals speed-up the task significantly, especially for a higher density of agents when the communication probability is higher. The general result is that the generation of specific patterns by CA agents can be designed in a methodical way.

References

1. Deutsch, A., Dormann, S.: Cellular Automaton Modeling of Biological Pattern Formation. Birkäuser, Basel (2005)
2. Shi, D., He, P., Lian, J., Chaud, X., Bud'ko, S.L., Beaugnon, E., Wang, L.M., Ewing, R.C., Tournier, R.: Magnetic alignment of carbon nanofibers in polymer composites and anisotropy of mechanical properties. J. App. Phys. **97**, 064312 (2005)
3. Itoh, M., Takahira, M., Yatagai, T.: Spatial arrangement of small particles by imaging laser trapping system. Opt. Rev. **5**(1), 55–58 (1998)
4. Jiang, Y., Narushima, T., Okamoto, H.: Nonlinear optical effects in trapping nanoparticles with femtosecond pulses. Nat. Phys. **6**, 1005–1009 (2010)
5. Roberts, Jr., G.: X-ray laser explores how to write data with light. National Accelerator Laboratory, 19 March 2013. https://www6.slac.stanford.edu/news
6. Press, D., Ladd, T.D., Zhang, B., Yamamoto, Y.: Complete quantum control of a single quantum dot spin using ultrafast optical pulses. Nature **456**, 218–221 (2008)
7. Hoffmann, R.: How agents can form a specific pattern. In: Wçs, J., Sirakoulis, G., Bandini, S. (eds.) ACRI 2014. LNCS, vol. 8751, pp. 660–669. Springer, Heidelberg (2014)
8. Hoffmann, R.: Cellular automata agents form path patterns effectively. Acta Phys. Pol. B Proc. Suppl. **9**(1), 63–75 (2016)
9. Halbach, M., Hoffmann, R., Both, L.: Optimal 6-state algorithms for the behavior of several moving creatures. In: El Yacoubi, S., Chopard, B., Bandini, S. (eds.) ACRI 2006. LNCS, vol. 4173, pp. 571–581. Springer, Heidelberg (2006)
10. Ediger, P., Hoffmann, R.: Optimizing the creature's rule for all-to-all communication. In: Adamatzky, A., Alonso-Sanz, R., Lawniczak, A., (eds.) Automata-2008: Theory and Applications of Cellular Automata, pp. 398–412 (2008)
11. Ediger, P., Hoffmann, R.: Solving all-to-all communication with CA agents more effectively with flags. In: Malyshkin, V. (ed.) PaCT 2009. LNCS, vol. 5698, pp. 182–193. Springer, Heidelberg (2009)
12. Hoffmann, R., Désérable, D.: All-to-all communication with cellular automata agents in 2D grids. J. Supercomp. **69**(1), 70–80 (2014)
13. Ediger, P., Hoffmann, R.: CA models for target searching agents. Elec. Notes Theor. Comp. Sci. **252**, 41–54 (2009)
14. Ediger, P., Hoffmann, R., Désérable, D.: Routing in the triangular grid with evolved agents. J. Cell. Automata **7**(1), 47–65 (2012)
15. Ediger, P., Hoffmann, R., Désérable, D.: Rectangular vs triangular routing with evolved agents. J. Cell. Automata **8**(1–2), 73–89 (2013)

16. Komann, M., Mainka, A., Fey, D.: Comparison of evolving uniform, non-uniform cellular automaton, and genetic programming for centroid detection with hardware agents. In: Malyshkin, V. (ed.) PaCT 2007. LNCS, vol. 4671, pp. 432–441. Springer, Heidelberg (2007)

17. Mesot, B., Sanchez, E., Peña, C.-A., Perez-Uribe, A.: Artificial Life VIII. SOS++: Finding Smart Behaviors Using Learning and Evolution. MIT Press, Cambridge (2002)

18. Blum, M., Sakoda, W.J.: On the capability of finite automata in 2 and 3 dimensional space. In: SFCS 1977, pp. 147–161 (1977)

19. Bonabeau, E.: From classical models of morphogenesis to agent-based models of pattern formation. Artif. Life **3**(3), 191–211 (1997)

20. Hamann, H.: Pattern Formation as a Transient Phenomenon in the Nonlinear Dynamics of a Multi-agent System. MATHMOD, Vienna (2009)

21. Nagpal, R.: Programmable pattern-formation and scale-independence. In: Minai, A.A., Bar-Yam, Y. (eds.) Unifying Themes in Complex Systems IV: Proceedings of the Fourth International Conference on Complex Systems, pp. 275–282. Springer Berlin Heidelberg, Berlin, Heidelberg (2008). http://dx.doi.org/10.1007/978-3-540-73849-7_31

22. Yamins, D., Nagpal, R.: Automated global-to-local programming in 1-D spatial multi-agent systems. In: Proceedings of 7th International Conference AAMAS, pp. 615–622 (2008)

23. Bandini, S., Vanneschi, L., Wuensche, A., Shehata, A.B.: A neuro-genetic framework for pattern recognition in complex systems. Fund. Inf. **87**(2), 207–226 (2008)

24. Hoffmann, R.: The GCA-w massively parallel model. In: Malyshkin, V. (ed.) PaCT 2009. LNCS, vol. 5698, pp. 194–206. Springer, Heidelberg (2009)

25. Hoffmann, R.: Rotor-routing algorithms described by CA-w. Acta Phys. Pol. B Proc. Suppl. **5**(1), 53–67 (2012)

26. Hoffmann, R., Désérable, D.: Routing by cellular automata agents in the triangular lattice. In: Sirakoulis, G., Adamatzky, A. (eds.) Robots and Lattice Automata, Emergence, Complexity and Computation, vol. 13, pp. 117–147. Springer, Switzerland (2015)

27. Hardy, J., Pomeau, Y., de Pazzis, O.: Time evolution of a two-dimensional classical lattice system. Phys. Rev. Lett. **31**(5), 276–279 (1973)

28. Achasova, S., Bandman, O., Markova, V., Piskunov, S.: Parallel Substitution Algorithm - Theory and Application. World Scientific, Singapore (1994)

29. Bouré, O., Fatès, N., Chevrier, V.: Probing robustness of cellular automata through variations of asynchronous updating. Nat. Comp. **11**(4), 553–564 (2012)

30. Bandini, S., Bonomi, A., Vizzari, G.: An analysis of different types and effects of asynchronicity in cellular automata update schemes. Nat. Comput. **11**(2), 277–287 (2012)

On Formal Presentation of Update Rules, Density Estimate and Using Floor Fields in CA FF Pedestrian Dynamics Model SIgMA.CA

Ekaterina Kirik$^{(\boxtimes)}$ and Tat'yana Vitova

Institute of Computational Modelling SB RAS,
Krasnoyarsk, Akademgorodok 660036, Russia
{kirik,vitova}@icm.krasn.ru

Abstract. The article deals with a formal presentation of transition rules in the CA pedestrian dynamics model. The model is stochastic and supposes short-term decisions made by the pedestrians [9,11]. A possibility to move according the shortest path and the shortest time strategies are implemented to the model. This feature is reflected in update rules and transition probabilities which are presented in the paper in formal mathematical way. Computational artifacts which concern using of static floor field and people density estimate are discussed as well.

Keywords: Pedestrian dynamics · Cellular automata · Update rules · Transition probabilities · Floor field · Density estimate

1 Introduction

In the article the discrete pedestrian dynamics model SIgMA.CA is considered. The model is a stochastic floor field CA model and supposes short-term decisions made by the pedestrians [9,11]. A possibility to move according the shortest path and the shortest time strategies and peoples' patience are implemented to the model. It is reflected in update rules and transition probabilities. It was shown how to regulate movement regimes by model parameters [14]. The influencing of a space geometry on models' dynamics [10], the validation with fundamental diagrams [12] and bottleneck flows [13] were presented as well.

Mainly all previous papers were concentrated on investigations of the model. We presented more or less in details transition probabilities but update rules, only in a descriptive level. Here we are aimed to present in a formal mathematical way [2,24] update rules. One can find papers [4,8,16] where similar formalism takes place for other models. Such presentation gives evolution of the decision process during a time step and is a computational algorithm how to implement the decision-making process into programming code.

Dynamics of people movement is density dependent [19,21]. Short-term decisions in the model are based on density estimate in the nearest neighborhood. A way to estimate density is discussed in the paper.

© Springer International Publishing Switzerland 2016
S. El Yacoubi et al. (Eds.): ACRI 2016, LNCS 9863, pp. 435–445, 2016.
DOI: 10.1007/978-3-319-44365-2_43

In the models using the static floor field S the main driving force making a pedestrian move to the exit is to change S at each time step. Originally pure values of field S are used in the probability formula in FF models, e.g. [7,15,17, 22,26]. We propose to use only a value of gradient ΔS [11]. Why and how to treat with static floor field S, computational aspect and restrictions that arises using static floor field in traditional way are considered in the paper.

In the next sections a statement of the the task, update rules, transition probabilities, density estimate, computational aspects of using static floor field are presented. We conclude with a summary.

2   Statement of the Task

Let modeling area (plane) $\Omega \in R^2$ and its open border $\partial\Omega$ are known and sampled into cells $40\,cm \times 40\,cm$ in size which are either empty or occupied by the only pedestrian (particle) [17]. The cells can contain walls and other stationary obstacles. So there are two arrays: W – the array of obstacles, F^t – the array of particles.

Matrix W is constant, not changed with the time, $W = \{w_{ij} : i = \overline{1,I}, j = \overline{1,J}\}$, where

$$w_{ij} = \begin{cases} 1, & \text{if } (i,j) \text{ is wall;} \\ 2, & \text{if } (i,j) \text{ is exit;} \\ 0, & \text{if } (i,j) \text{ is empty.} \end{cases} \tag{1}$$

Matrix F^t (t is a step number) is changed with the time and depicts an evolution of a cellular automata, $F^t = \{f_{ij}^t : i = \overline{1,I}, j = \overline{1,J}\}$, where

$$f_{ij}^t = \begin{cases} 1, & \text{if } (i,j) \text{ is pedestrian \& } w_{ij} = 0; \\ 0, & \text{if } (i,j) \text{ is empty.} \end{cases} \tag{2}$$

Thus we have each cell (i,j) in a state $f_{ij}^t \in A$, alphabet $A = \{0;1\}$.

In the time $t = 0$ N elements of matrix F^0 are in state $f_{ij}^0 = 1$, $N \leq |\{w_{ij} = 0 : i = \overline{1,I}, j = \overline{1,J}\}|$. We consider this as N particles are in the modeling area Ω. New state of matrix F^t we consider as new positions of the particles.

In the model, static floor field $S = \{s_{ij} : i = \overline{1,I}, j = \overline{1,J}\}$ is used. Field S coincides with the sampled area. Each s_{ij} value stores the information on the shortest distance from cell (i,j) to the nearest exit; i.e., field S increases radially from the exit cells. Field S of the exit cells is zero. It does not change with time and is independent of the presence of the particles. Field S can be considered as a map used by the pedestrians during their movement to the nearest exit.

The starting positions of people are known and saved in the matrix F^0. A target point of each pedestrian is the nearest exit. Each particle can move to one of its four adjacent cells or stay in the present cell (the von Neumann neighborhood) at each discrete time step $t \rightarrow t+1$ – Fig. 1; i.e., $v_{max} = 1[step]$.

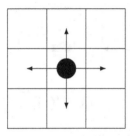 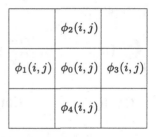

Fig. 1. Target cells for a pedestrian in the next time step.

So the neighboring template is $T(i,j) = \{\phi_k(i,j) : k = \overline{0,4}\} = \{(i,j),(i,j-1),(i-1,j),(i,j+1),(i+1,j)\}$. Below we refer to $\phi_k(i,j)$ as a candidate cell to move from position (i,j).

The direction of the movement of each particle at each time step is random and determined in accordance with the distribution of transition probabilities and transition rules.

In the next section update rules (which include transition probabilities and transition rules) for synchronous CA to simulate directed movement of the particles to the target (exit) are presented.

3   Transition Rules

New state of the CA is realized by the substitution $Transfer : F^t \to F^{t+1}$. In other words this substitution moves particles to new positions according to the array of directions R^t:

$$Transfer(i,j) : Conf(i,j) \star Conf''(i,j) \to Conf'(i,j), \text{ where} \qquad (3)$$

$Conf(i,j) = \{(f^t_{ij})\},$
$Conf'(i,j) = \{(trans,(i,j))\},$
$Conf''(i,j) = \{(r_{\phi_0(i,j)}, r_{\phi_1(i,j)}, r_{\phi_2(i,j)}, r_{\phi_3(i,j)}, r_{\phi_4(i,j)}\}.$

$$trans,(i,j) = \begin{cases} 1, & \text{if } \exists k, k = \overline{0,4} : r_k = (i,j); \\ 0, & \text{else.} \end{cases} \qquad (4)$$

Array of directions $R^t = \{r_{ij} : i = \overline{1,I}, j = \overline{1,J}\}$ is changed each time step and stores final direction to move for each particle:

$$r_{ij} = \begin{cases} \phi_{k^*}(i,j), k^* \in \{0,1,2,3,4\}, & \text{if } f^t_{ij} = 1; \\ 0, & \text{if } f^t_{ij} = 0. \end{cases} \qquad (5)$$

An example of a substitution is presented in Fig. 2.

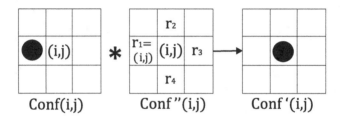

Fig. 2. An example of the substitution

3.1 A Choice of the Next Step Movement Directions Array R^t

Step 1. Transition probability distributions.

Each cell $(i, j) : f^t_{ij} = 1$, $i = \overline{1, I}$, $j = \overline{1, J}$ (it means that there is particle in the cell) each time step is assigned with transition probabilities $\{p_{\phi_k(i,j)} : k = \overline{0, 4}\}$ to move to the cells $\{\phi_k(i, j) : k = \overline{0, 4}\} = \{(i, j), (i, j - 1), (i - 1, j), (i, j + 1), (i + 1, j)\}$:

ξ	(i, j)	$(i, j - 1)$	$(i - 1, j)$	$(i, j + 1)$	$(i + 1, j)$
p_ξ	0	$p_{\phi_1(i,j)}$	$p_{\phi_2(i,j)}$	$p_{\phi_3(i,j)}$	$p_{\phi_4(i,j)}$

Function *calc_p* gives such probabilities for each particle:

$$calc\_p(i, j) = \begin{cases} \{0, p_{\phi_1(i,j)}, p_{\phi_2(i,j)}, p_{\phi_3(i,j)}, p_{\phi_4(i,j)}\}, & \text{if } f^t_{ij} = 1; \\ 0, & \text{if } f^t_{ij} = 0. \end{cases} \tag{6}$$

The probability of retaining the current position $p_{\phi_0(i,j)}$ initially is supposed to be equal zero and not calculated directly. Nevertheless, the decision rules are organized so that such opportunity could be taken; thus, peoples' patience is implemented[1].

Step 2. Choosing a direction. Patient people strategy.

Let random variable $rand \in R[0; 1]$. Function *direct* is based on Monte-Carlo [23] method and determines direction to move for the particle in the cell (i, j):

$$direct(\{p_{\phi_k(i,j)} : k = \overline{0, 4}\}) = \begin{cases} \phi_0(i, j), \text{if } rand \in [0, p_{\phi_0(i,j)}]; \\ \phi_1(i, j), \text{if } rand \in (p_{\phi_0(i,j)}; p_{\phi_0(i,j)} + p_{\phi_1(i,j)}]; \\ \phi_2(i, j), \text{if } rand \in \left(\sum_{k=0}^{1} p_{\phi_k(i,j)}; \sum_{k=0}^{2} p_{\phi_k(i,j)} \right]; \\ \phi_3(i, j), \text{if } rand \in \left(\sum_{k=0}^{2} p_{\phi_k(i,j)}; \sum_{k=0}^{3} p_{\phi_k(i,j)} \right]; \\ \phi_4(i, j), \text{if } rand \in \left(\sum_{k=0}^{3} p_{\phi_k(i,j)}; \sum_{k=0}^{4} p_{\phi_k(i,j)} \right]. \end{cases}$$

---

[1] This trick of choosing the current position is provoked by the fact that when moving directionally people usually stop only if the preferable direction is occupied. The original FF model [22] never gives zero probability to the current position, and it may be chosen independent of the environment.

Let $\phi_{k^*}(i,j)$ is a chosen direction for the particle in the cell (i,j). Preliminary version of directions array R^t is:

$$r_{ij} = \begin{cases} \phi_{k^*}(i,j) = direct(calc\_p(i,j)), & \text{if } f^t_{ij} = 1; \\ 0, & \text{if } f^t_{ij} = 0. \end{cases}$$

If $f^t_{\phi_{k^*}(i,j)} = 0$, then we fix $r_{ij} = \phi_{k^*}(i,j)$.

If $f^t_{\phi_{k^*}(i,j)} = 1$, then cell $\phi_{k^*}(i,j)$ is not available as it is occupied by a particle, and a "peoples' patience" can be implemented. For this purpose, the probabilities of cell $\phi_{k^*}(i,j)$ and all the other occupied adjacent cells are given for the current position:

$$p'_{\phi_0(i,j)} = \sum_{k:f^t_{\phi_k(i,j)}=1} p_{\phi_k(i,j)};$$

$$p'_{\phi_k(i,j)} = 0, \text{if } f^t_{\phi_k(i,j)} = 1, \ k = \overline{1,4};$$

$$p'_{\phi_k(i,j)} = p_{\phi_k(i,j)}, \text{if } f^t_{\phi_k(i,j)} = 0, \ k = \overline{1,4}.$$

For example, let $\phi_{k^*}(i,j) = (i, j-1)$ and $f^t_{i,j-1} = 1$, $f^t_{i+1,j} = 1$. In this case transition probability distribution takes the form:

ξ	(i,j)	$(i,j-1)$	$(i-1,j)$	$(i,j+1)$	$(i+1,j)$
p'_ξ	$p_{\phi_1(i,j)} + p_{\phi_4(i,j)}$	0	$p_{\phi_2(i,j)}$	$p_{\phi_3(i,j)}$	0

Again, the target direction (cell) $\phi_{k^*}(i,j)$ is chosen with function $direct(\{p'_{\phi_k(i,j)} : k = \overline{0,4}\})$. Next version of direction array R^t is:

$$r_{ij} = \begin{cases} r_{ij}, & \text{if } f^t_{ij} = 1 \& f^t_{r_{ij}} = 0; \\ direct(\{p'_{\phi_k(i,j)} : k = \overline{0,4}\}), & \text{if } f^t_{ij} = 1 \& f^t_{r_{ij}} = 1; \\ 0, & \text{if } f^t_{ij} = 0. \end{cases}$$

Step 4. Conflict resolution.

Whenever two or more pedestrians have the same target cell a conflict resolution procedure is applied. A result of the procedure is a final version of direction array R^t.

Cell (i,j) is a target for two or more pedestrians if $\exists$ at least $k_1 \neq k_2$, $k_1 = \overline{1,4}$, $k_2 = \overline{1,4}$: $r_{\phi_{k_1}(i,j)} = r_{\phi_{k_2}(i,j)} = (i,j)$.

Let us form three extra arrays. Array $Wish^1 = \{wish^1_{ij} : i = \overline{1,I}, j = \overline{1,J}\}$ contains number of candidates to take cell (i,j) next step: $wish^1_{ij} = \sum_{k=1}^{4} g^1(\phi_k(i,j))$, where

$$g^1(\phi_k(i,j)) = \begin{cases} 1, & \text{if } r_{\phi_k(i,j)} = (i,j); \\ 0, & \text{else}. \end{cases}$$

Array $Wish^2 = \{wish_{ij}^2 : i = \overline{1,I}, j = \overline{1,J}\} = \{\{wish_k^2 : k = \overline{1,4}\}_{ij} : i = \overline{1,I}, j = \overline{1,J}\}$ contains coordinates of candidates to take cell (i,j): $wish_{ij}^2 = \{wish_k^2 = g^2(\phi_k(i,j)) : k = \overline{1,4}\}_{ij}$, where

$$g^2(\phi_k(i,j)) = \begin{cases} \phi_k(i,j), & \text{if } r_{\phi_k(i,j)} = (i,j); \\ 0, & \text{else.} \end{cases}$$

In array $Wish^3$ each element from $Wish^2$ such as $(wish_k^2)_{ij} \neq 0$ is assigned with random variable $rand \in R[0,1]$ which is considered as a wish measure to move to cell (i,j): $Wish^3 = \{wish_{ij}^3 : i = \overline{1,I}, j = \overline{1,J}\} = \{\{wish_k^3 : k = \overline{1,4}\}_{ij} : i = \overline{1,I}, j = \overline{1,J}\}$. $wish_{ij}^3 = \{wish_k^3 = g^3(k,(i,j)) : k = \overline{1,4}\}_{ij}$, where

$$g^3(k,(i,j)) = \begin{cases} rand, & \text{if } (wish_k^2)_{ij} \neq 0; \\ 0, & \text{else.} \end{cases}$$

Arrays $Wish^1$, $Wish^2$, $Wish^3$ are used to chose the certain candidate for each cell (i,j) and to determine final states of the elements from direction array R^t which are in connection with conflict situation considered:

1. If $wish_{ij}^1 > 1$, then
$$max\_rand(i,j) = \max_{k=\overline{1,4}}\{wish_k^3 : k = \overline{1,4}\}_{ij}.$$
$k_{max} = k : (wish_k^3)_{ij} = max\_rand(i,j), k = \overline{1,4}.$
2. Some elements of direction array R^t take final states (Fig. 3):

$$r_{(wish_{k_{max}}^2)_{ij}} = (i,j);$$
$$r_{(wish_k^2)_{ij}} = (wish_k^2)_{ij}, k = \overline{1,4} : k \neq k_{max} \ \& \ (wish_k^2)_{ij} \neq 0.$$

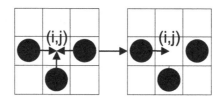

Fig. 3. An example of conflict resolution

4   Transition Probabilities Calculation

The probability of movement from cell (i,j) to next neighbor cell $\phi_k(i,j)$ is

$$p_{\phi_k(i,j)} = \frac{\tilde{p}_{\phi_k(i,j)}}{Norm_{ij}} = \frac{1}{Norm_{ij}} A_{\phi_k(i,j)}^{SFF} A_{\phi_k(i,j)}^{people} A_{\phi_k(i,j)}^{wall} |1 - w_{\phi_k(i,j)}|, k = \overline{1,4} \quad (7)$$

where

1. $Norm_{ij} = \sum_{k=1}^{4} \tilde{p}_{\phi_k(i,j)}$, $Norm_{ij} \neq 0$, $\tilde{p}_{\phi_k(i,j)} \geq 0$. $\tilde{p}_{\phi_k(i,j)} = 0$, $k = \overline{1,4}$ only if
   $w_{\phi_k(i,j)} = 1$, then $Norm_{ij} = 0$ only if $\tilde{p}_{\phi_k(i,j)} = 0$ $\forall k = \overline{1,4}$.
2. $|1 - w_{\phi_k(i,j)}| = 0$ if cell $\phi_k(i,j)$ is wall ($w_{\phi_k(i,j)} = 1$), $p_{\phi_k(i,j)} = 0$.
3. $A_{\phi_k(i,j)}^{SFF} = \exp[k_S \Delta S_{\phi_k(i,j)}]$ is the main driven force:
   (a) $k_S \geq 0$ is the (model) sensitivity parameter which can be interpreted as knowledge of the shortest way to the destination point or a wish to move to the destination point. The equality $k_S = 0$ means that the pedestrians ignore the information from field S and move randomly. The higher k_S, the better directed the movement;
   (b) $\Delta S_{\phi_k(i,j)} = s_{\phi_0(i,j)} - s_{\phi_k(i,j)} \in [-1;1]$.
4. $A_{\phi_k(i,j)}^{people} = \exp\left[-k_P D_{\phi_k(i,j)}(r^*)\right]$ is the factor taking into account people density in the given direction:
   (a) $k_P \geq 0$ is the (model) people sensitivity parameter which determines the effect of the people density. The higher parameter k_P, the more pronounced the shortest time strategy;
   (b) $0 < r^* \leq r$ is the distance to the nearest obstacle in the given direction $\phi_k(i,j)$. $r > 0$ is the visibility radius (model parameter) representing the maximum distance (number of cells) at which the people density and the presence of obstacles influence on the probability in the given direction;
   (c) the density lies within $D_{\phi_k(i,j)}(r^*) \in [0,1]$;
   We estimate density using kernel Rosenblat-Parzen density estimate [18, 20] which is presented below;
   (d) $k_P D_{\phi_k(i,j)}(r^*)$ is a factor taking into account other particles which can be interpreted as proxemis [1,5,6,25][2].
5. $A_{\phi_k(i,j)}^{wall} = \exp\left[-k_W(1 - \frac{r^*}{r})\tilde{1}'(\Delta S_{\phi_k(i,j)} - \max \Delta S_{i,j})(1 - \tilde{1}(D_{\phi_k(i,j)}(r^*)))\right]$
   is the factor taking into account walls and obstacles:
   (a) $k_W \geq 0$ is the (model) wall sensitivity parameter which determines the effect of walls and obstacles;
   (b) $1 - \frac{r^*}{r} \in [0,1]$, [16];
   (c) $\tilde{1}'(a) = \begin{cases} 1, & a \geq 0, \\ 0, & \text{else.} \end{cases}$ $\tilde{1}(a) = \begin{cases} 1, & a \neq 0, \\ 0, & a = 0. \end{cases}$
   (d) $\max \Delta S_{i,j} = \max_{k=\overline{1,4}}\{\Delta S_{\phi_k(i,j)}\}$,
   An idea of the function $\tilde{1}'(\Delta S_{\phi_k(i,j)} - \max \Delta S_{i,j})$ comes from the fact that people avoid obstacles only when moving towards the destination point. When people make detours (in this case, field S is not minimized), approaching the obstacles is not excluded.

---

[2] In contrast with original floor field models [3,17] to take in to account other people we use current local density in the direction instead of dynamical field D which store "historical" data of the flow intensivity.

4.1   A Using Floor Field S

Originally pure values of field S are used in the probability formula in FF models, e.g. [7,15,17,22,26]. We propose to use only a value of gradient $\Delta S_{\phi_k(i,j)}$ [11]. From a mathematical view point, it yields the same result.

The main driven force term is the only term which affects the inference; the rest terms in the probability formula are omitted here. Let field S increases towards the exit as in the original FF model; then, $\Delta S_{i-1,j} = s_{i-1,j} - s_{i,j}$, $\Delta S_{i,j+1} = s_{i,j+1} - s_{i,j}$, $\Delta S_{i+1,j} = s_{i+1,j} - s_{i,j}$, $\Delta S_{i,j-1} = s_{i,j-1} - s_{i,j}$, and $s_{i-1,j} = \Delta S_{i-1,j} + s_{i,j}$, $s_{i,j+1} = \Delta S_{i,j+1} + s_{i,j}$, $s_{i+1,j} = \Delta S_{i+1,j} + s_{i,j}$, $s_{i,j-1} = \Delta S_{i,j-1} + s_{i,j}$. Therefore, we have

$$\frac{e^{k_S s_{i-1,j}}}{e^{k_S s_{i-1,j}} + e^{k_S s_{i,j+1}} + e^{k_S s_{i+1,j}} + e^{k_S s_{i,j-1}}}$$

$$= \frac{e^{k_S s_{i,j}} e^{k_S \Delta S_{i-1,j}}}{e^{k_S s_{i,j}} \left(e^{k_S \Delta S_{i-1,j}} + e^{k_S \Delta S_{i,j+1}} + e^{k_S \Delta S_{i+1,j}} + e^{k_S \Delta S_{i,j-1}} \right)}$$

$$= \frac{e^{k_S \Delta S_{i-1,j}}}{e^{k_S \Delta S_{i-1,j}} + e^{k_S \Delta S_{i,j+1}} + e^{k_S \Delta S_{i+1,j}} + e^{k_S \Delta S_{i,j-1}}}.$$

If field S increases from the exit as in our model, the gradients are calculated in the opposite direction; i.e., $\Delta S_{i-1,j} = s_{i,j} - s_{i-1,j}$, $\Delta S_{i,j+1} = s_{i,j} - s_{i,j+1}$, $\Delta S_{i+1,j} = s_{i,j} - s_{i+1,j}$, $\Delta S_{i,j-1} = s_{i,j} - s_{i,j-1}$, and field S has to have negative sign.

Computationally this trick has a great advantage. The values of field S may be too high (it depends on the space size); in this case, $\exp\left[k_S s_{\phi_k(i,j)} \right]$ can appear uncomputable. For double precision we have $k_S s_{\phi_k(i,j)} \leq 710$ (a decision of the equation $e^x = 1,7 \cdot 10^{308}$ gives $x = 710$). For quadruple precision (double extended) we have $k_S s_{\phi_k(i,j)} < 11356$ (a decision of the equation $e^x = 1,1 \cdot 10^{4932}$ gives $x = 11356$). Thus a maximum distance to the exit could be $710 * 0,4 = 284$ m and $11356 * 0,4 = 4542$ m correspondingly for $k_S = 1$. If $k_S > 1$ (it is typical for directed movement [11]) maximum distance reduces. This is a significant limitation of the models. At the same time, $-1 \leq \Delta S_{\phi_k(i,j)} \leq 1$, and the computation of $A_{\phi_k(i,j)}^{SFF}$ does not make difficulties.

The other negative side of using pure values of field S is not uniform contribution of the terms in probability formula over the considered area. The farther from the exit the area, the more pronounced field S term. To get balance other components should be field S dependent, but it gives additional complication of the model.

Since field S increases radially from the exit(s) in our model, then, $\Delta S_{\phi_k(i,j)} > 0$ if cell $\phi_k(i,j)$ is closer to the exit than the current cell (i,j), $\Delta S_{\phi_k(i,j)} < 0$ if the current cell is closer, and $\Delta S_{\phi_k(i,j)} = 0$ if cells (i,j) and $\phi_k(i,j)$ are equidistant from the exit.

4.2 Density Estimation

We estimate the density using kernel Rosenblat-Parzen density estimate [18, 20]:

$$D_{\phi_k(i,j)}(r^*) = \frac{\sum\limits_{m=1}^{r^*} \Phi\left(\frac{m}{C(r^*)}\right) \cdot (f_m)_{\phi_k(i,j)}}{r^*},$$

where

$$\Phi(z) = \begin{cases} (0,335 - 0,067(z)^2)\, 4,4724, & |z| \leq \sqrt{5}; \\ 0, & |z| > \sqrt{5}, \end{cases}$$

$$C(r^*) = \frac{r^* + 1}{\sqrt{5}}.$$

$(f_m)_{\phi_k(i,j)}$ is m-th cell in direction $\phi_k(i,j)$ from cell (i,j). For example, if $\phi_k(i,j) = (i-1,j)$, then $(f_m)_{\phi_k(i,j)} = f_{i-m,j}$.

If r^* cells are empty in direction $\phi_k(i,j)$, we have $D_{\phi_k(i,j)}(r^*) = 0$; if r^* cells are occupied by people in this direction, we have $D_{\phi_k(i,j)}(r^*) = 1$. If only some cells are occupied, then Rosenblat-Parzen density estimate gives weighted value for each occupied cell depending on distance from cell (i,j), see Table 1.

Table 1. A comparison of density estimates $D_{\phi_k(i,j)}$ versus positions of other particle in direction $\phi_k(i,j)$, $r = 10$

	1	2	3	4	5	6	7	8	9	10	$D_{\phi_k(i,j)}$
(i,j)	1		1		1		1		1		0,55
(i,j)		1		1		1		1		1	0,48
(i,j)						1	1	1	1	1	0,34

In contrast to the method presented here in other papers one can find density estimate as a number of occupied cells in Moore neighborhood [15] or a number of occupied cell among r in the considered direction [4, 16].

5 Conclusion

This paper is theoretical. The discrete floor field CA model SIgMA.CA was presented in formal mathematical way to give clear description of the update rules. Persons' patience which is implemented in the model make traditional CA transition rules to be changed and it is done in the model presented. Following the shortest path and the shortest time strategies is mainly concern of transition probability and parameters k_P and k_S. Following the shortest time strategy implies that, wherever possible, the detours around high-density regions are made. Term A^{people} reduces the main driving force, which provides following the shortest path strategy, and the probability of the detours grows. The higher

$k_P \geq k_S$, the more pronounced the shortest time strategy. Of course, k_P can not increase infinitely, and we propose the following upper bound $k_P \leq 4k_S$. Note that probabilities are density adaptive; the low people density lowers the effect of A^{people}, and the probability of the shortest path strategy increases automatically.

It was shown that Rosenblat-Parsen density estimate is weighted and gives spatial-dependent evaluation of the situation in the considered direction. Using field S increasing radially from the exit(s) and its gradient ΔS in the probability formula simplify computations and remove restrictions on geometrical sizes of the modeling area Ω.

References

1. Bandini, S., Gorrini, A., Vizzari, G.: Towards an integrated approach to crowd analysis and crowd synthesis: a case study and first results. Pattern Recogn. Lett. **44**, 16–29 (2014)
2. Bandman, O.: Cellular automata composition techniques for spatial dynamics simulation. In: Kroc, J., Sloot, P.M.A., Hoekstra, A.G. (eds.) Simulating Complex Systems by Cellular Automata, pp. 81–115. Springer, Heidelberg (2010)
3. Burstedde, V., Klauck, K., Schadschneider, A., Zittartz, J.: Simulation of pedestrian dynamics using a 2-dimensional cellular automaton. Physica A **295**, 507–525 (2001)
4. Dudek-Dyduch, E., Was, J.: Knowledge representation of pedestrian dynamics in crowd: formalism of cellular automata. In: Rutkowski, L., Tadeusiewicz, R., Zadeh, L.A., Żurada, J.M. (eds.) ICAISC 2006. LNCS (LNAI), vol. 4029, pp. 1101–1110. Springer, Heidelberg (2006)
5. Gwizdałla, T.M.: Some properties of the floor field cellular automata evacuation model. Phys. A Stat. Mech. Appl. **419**, 718–728 (2015)
6. Hall, E.T.: The Hidden Dimension. Garden City, New York (1966)
7. Henein, C.M., White, T.: Macroscopic effects of microscopic forces between agents in crowd models. Physica A **373**, 694–718 (2007)
8. Kirchner, A., Schadschneider, A.: Simulation of evacuation processes using a bionics-inspired cellular automaton model for pedestrian dynamics. Physica A **312**(1), 260–276 (2002)
9. Kirik, E., Yurgel'yan, T., Krouglov, D.: The shortest time and/or the shortest path strategies in a CA FF pedestrian dynamics model. J. Sib. Fed. Univ. Math. Phys. **2**(3), 271–278 (2009)
10. Kirik, E., Yurgel'yan, T., Krouglov, D.: On influencing of a space geometry on dynamics of some CA pedestrian movement model. In: Bandini, S., Manzoni, S., Umeo, H., Vizzari, G. (eds.) ACRI 2010. LNCS, vol. 6350, pp. 474–479. Springer, Heidelberg (2010)
11. Kirik, E., Yurgel'yan, T., Krouglov, D.: On realizing the shortest time strategy in a CA FF pedestrian dynamics model. Cybern. Syst. **42**(1), 1–15 (2011)
12. Kirik, E., Yurgel'yan, T., Krouglov, D.: On time scaling and validation of a stochastic CA pedestrian dynamics model. In: Peacock, R.D., Kuligowski, E.D., Averill, J.D. (eds.) Pedestrian and Evacuation Dynamics, pp. 819–822. Springer, US (2011)
13. Kirik, E., Vitova, T.: On validation of the SIgMA.CA pedestrian dynamics model with bottleneck flow. In: Bandini, S., Sirakoulis, G. (eds.) ACRI 2012. LNCS, vol. 7495, pp. 719–727. Springer, Heidelberg (2012)

14. Kirik, E., Vitova, T.: Cellular automata pedestrian movement model SIgMA.CA: model parameters as an instrument to regulate movement regimes. In: Was, J., Sirakoulis, G., Bandini, S. (eds.) ACRI 2014. LNCS, vol. 8751, pp. 501–507. Springer, Heidelberg (2014)

15. Kretz, T., Schreckenberg, M.: F.A.S.T. - Floor field and agent-based simulation tool. In: Proceedings of International Symposium of Transport Simulation 2006, pp. 125–136 (2006)

16. Malinetski, G.G., Stepantsov, M.E.: Application of cellular automata to modeling the motion of a group of people. Comput. Math. Phys. **44**(11), 1992–1996 (2004)

17. Nishinari, K., Kirchner, A., Namazi, A., Schadschneider, A.: Extended floor field CA model for evacuation dynamics. IEICE Trans. Inf. Syst. **E87–D**(3), 726–732 (2004)

18. Parzen, E.: On estimation of probability density function. Ann. Math. Stat. **33**, 1065–1076 (1962)

19. Predtetschenski, W.M., Milinski, A.I.: Personenströme in Gebäuden - Berechnungsmethoden für die Projektierung. Verlagsgesellschaft Rudolf Müller, Köln-Braunsfeld (1971)

20. Rosenblat, M.: Remarks on some non-parametric estimates of a density function. Ann. Math. Stat. **27**, 832–837 (1956)

21. Schadschneider, A., Klingsch, W., Kluepfel, H., Kretz, T., Rogsch, C., Seyfried, A.: Evacuation dynamics: empirical results, modeling and applications. In: Meyers, R.A. (ed.) Extreme Environmental Events. Encyclopedia of Complexity and System Science, vol. 3, pp. 3142–3176. Springer, Heidelberg (2009)

22. Schadschneider, A., Seyfried, A.: Validation of CA models of pedestrian dynamics with fundamental diagrams. Cybern. Syst. **40**(5), 367–389 (2009)

23. Sobol', I.M.: Monte Carlo method. Nauka, Moscow (1972). (in Russian)

24. Toffolli, T., Margolus, N.: Cellular automata machines. Physica D **10**, 117–127 (1987)

25. Was, J., Gudowski, B., Matuszyk, P.J.: Social distances model of pedestrian dynamics. In: El Yacoubi, S., Chopard, B., Bandini, S. (eds.) ACRI 2006. LNCS, vol. 4173, pp. 492–501. Springer, Heidelberg (2006)

26. Yanagisawa, D., Nishinari, K.: Mean-field theory for pedestrian outflow through an exit. Phys. Rev. E **76**, 061117 (2007)

Effects of Agents' Fear, Desire and Knowledge on Their Success When Crossing a CA Based Highway

Anna T. Lawniczak[1]([✉]), Leslie Ly[1], Shengkun Xie[2], and Fei Yu[1]

[1] Department of Mathematics and Statistics, University of Guelph, Guelph, ON, Canada
{alawnicz,fyu03}@uoguelph.ca, lyl@alumni.uoguelph.ca
[2] Ted Rogers Management School, Ryerson University, Toronto, ON, Canada
shengkun.xie@Ryerson.ca

Abstract. We describe a model of a population of simple autonomous cognitive agents with fear and desire learning to cross a CA based highway. The agents use an "observational social learning" mechanism in their decision to cross the highway or not. We study how agents' attributes and their accumulated observational knowledge affect their success of crossing the highway under various traffic conditions. We consider the case when agents are not allowed to change their crossing point and when they are allowed to change it.

Keywords: Agents · Cognitive agents · Observational learning · Knowledge base · Cellular automata · Nagel-Schreckenberg model · Swarm robotics

1 Introduction

Swarm robotics research has shown that often it may be more efficient, reliable and economical to employ a large number (hundreds or thousands) of very simple robots to achieve various tasks than to employ a small number of sophisticated and expensive robots, [1, 2]. As swarms of robots may be required to carry out some of the tasks in unknown, dynamically changing environments they may have to learn, through observation and repetition, how to operate in such environments. Since swarms, robots may be identified with cognitive autonomous agents, [3, 4], their process of learning can be studied through modeling and simulation of cognitive agents.

We study performance of a simple learning algorithm based on an "observational social learning" mechanism, [5–7], in a model of a population of simple autonomous cognitive agents, called naïve creatures, learning to cross a highway. Through the observation and repetition, the creatures try to mimic what worked for others in the past and they try to avoid what did not. We study how creatures' propensities to risk taking and/or risk aversion, and the creatures' accumulated observational knowledge affect their success of crossing the highway under various traffic conditions. We consider the case when agents are not allowed to change their crossing point and when they are allowed to change.

The paper is structured as follows: Sect. 2 describes briefly the considered model; Sect. 3 presents simulation experiments setup of parameters; Sect. 4 discusses selected simulation results; Sect. 5 provides our conclusions and outlines the future work.

© Springer International Publishing Switzerland 2016
S. El Yacoubi et al. (Eds.): ACRI 2016, LNCS 9863, pp. 446–455, 2016.
DOI: 10.1007/978-3-319-44365-2_44

2   Model of Naïve Creatures Learning to Cross a Highway

We review here only the main features of the model introduced in [8, 9], and for its software implementation we refer the reader to [10, 11] for details.

In this work, we assume that the environment is a single lane unidirectional highway without intersections. We model the highway traffic by adopting the Nagel-Schreckenberg cellular automaton (CA) model and refer the reader to [12–15] for details. At each time step a creature is generated only at a crossing point (CP) set at initialization step, based on the value stored in the configuration file, and it is placed into the queue at this CP. Each generated creature falls with equal probability (0.25) into one of the four categories: (1) no fear nor desire; (2) only fear; (3) only desire; (4) both fear and desire. The creatures' attributes play a role in their decision making process on whether or not to cross the highway through the values of fear (aversion to risk taking) and desire (propensity to risk taking) that creature may experience. Creatures want to cross the highway without being killed by the oncoming vehicles. Each creature is "an autonomous entity" capable of: (1) evaluating distance and the velocity of an approaching car in an approximate way; (2) with exclusion of the first creature, witnessing and evaluating what had happened to the creatures that previously crossed the highway at this CP (i.e., if the crossing was successful or not); (3) imitating the creatures, which crossed successfully; (4) deciding not to cross and wait for better conditions or to look for a different CP when unsuccessful crossings outnumber the successful ones. All of these allow to build common knowledge base (KnB) at each CP that is available to all creatures at that CP during the experiment.

The creatures attempt to cross the highway having a limited horizon of vision and perceiving only fuzzy levels of distance of cars within this horizon and perceiving only fuzzy levels of their speeds. The creatures may build up in the queue as a result of not crossing at each time step. If the simulation setup permits (i.e., when parameter Horiz. Cre. = 1) after deciding not to cross the highway, a creature may move randomly, with equal probability of 1/3, to a new CP in either direction, or it may stay at the same CP. The number of horizontal cells a creature may move in one-time step is 1 and the maximum distance the creature may deviate from its original CP in both directions is 5. If the creature at the top of a queue leaves the queue, the creature that was behind moves to the top of the queue. When a creature crosses the highway at a given CP, information if the crossing was successful or not is recorded into the KnB shared by all the creatures at this CP. The KnB table's rows and columns index the different combinations of the qualitative car's distance and velocity categories, as perceived by the creatures. Each KnB table entry records the value: the number of the "*successful crossings*" minus the number of the "*unsuccessful crossings*" for that particular (distance, velocity) pair up to this time.

The KnB table is initialized as "tabula rasa", i.e. with all its entries set to 0, allowing creatures to cross the highway regardless of the observed (distance, velocity) levels until the first successful crossing of a creature, or five consecutive unsuccessful crossings, whichever comes first. If a creature successfully crossed the highway, the perceived (distance, velocity) score in the KnB table is increased by one point. If the creature was killed, it is decreased by one point.

After the initialization of simulation, each creature at the top of the queue consults the KnB table to decide if it is safe or not to cross. Its decision is based on the implemented intelligence/decision making algorithm, which for a given (distance, velocity) pair combines the *"success ratio"* of crossing the highway for this (distance, velocity) pair with the creature's fear and/or desire values, as follows. For each (distance, velocity) pair at each time step, the numerator in the *success ratio* is the current value from the KnB and the denominator is the total number of creatures that have crossed the highway successfully, regardless of the (distance, velocity) combination up to this time. If for some (distance, velocity) configuration at the simulation start, all creatures were killed, the ratio becomes "−5/0". In this case, we set the success ratio to zero since "division by zero" is undefined.

A randomly generated creature will base its decision on the formula: (1) *"success ratio + value of desire − value of fear"*, if it has both fear and desire; (2) *"success ratio − value of fear"*, if it has only fear; (3) *"success ratio + value of desire"*, if it has only desire; (4) *"success ratio"*, if it has no fear and no desire. If for a given (distance, velocity) combination observed by a creature the formula's value is less than zero, then the creature will not attempt to cross the highway under this condition and it will wait for a configuration for which the value of the formula is non-negative, or it may move to another crossing point if the simulator setup permits.

The main simulation loop of the model consists of: (1) generation of cars at each lane of the highway using the Car Prob.; (2) generation of creatures at each CP with their attributes; (3) update the car speeds according the Nagel-Schreckenberg model; (4) movement of the creatures from the CP queues into the highway (if the decision algorithm indicates this should occur); (5) update of locations of the cars on the highway and checking if any creature has been killed; (6) advancement of the current time step. After the simulation has been completed, the results are written to output files using an output function.

3   Simulation Experiments Setup of Parameters

We consider the model parameters as factors with various levels in the sense of the experimental design paradigm [16]. The parameters/factors that remain constant through our simulations are: (1) single lane highway with a length of 120 cells (900 m long, each cell represents a segment of a highway of 7.5 m in length as customary in traffic engineering literature, [12]); (2) 1511 time steps; (3) 30 repetitions; (4) random deceleration equal to 0 (there are no erratic drivers); (5) 3 by 4 KnB table with an extra entry at CPs. Each KnB table has 3 groupings of distance and 4 groupings of speed. A car is perceived as: (1) "close", if it is 0 to 3 cells away, "medium" if it is 4 or 5 cells away, "far" if it is 6 or 7 cells away and "out of range" if it is 8 or more cells away, regardless of the velocity of the car, and this is encoded in the extra entry; (2) "slow" if its perceived velocity is 0 to 3 cells per time step, "medium" if it is 4 or 5 cells per time step, "fast" if it is 6 or 7 cells per time step and "very fast" if it is 8 to 11 cells per time step. A car's max speed can be 11 cells per time step.

There are 6 parameters/factors values which vary through the main simulation loop. These parameters are: (1) car creation probability (Car Prob.); (2) crossing point (CP); (3) value of fear; (4) value of desire; (5) the KnB transfer direction (KnB Transf.), and (6) horizontal creature movement (Horiz. Cre.). The Car Prob. determines the density of the car traffic and it varies between the values: 0.1, 0.3, 0.5, 0.7, and 0.9. A car is generated with a given Car. Prob. at the beginning of the highway at each time step. The CP determines the location at which the creature will cross the highway and it varies between the values: 40, 60, and 80 (the cell number of the highway). The distance of CP from where the cars are generated is important because the traffic nature changes with this distance, e.g. there will likely be more cars travelling at max speed and in a more homogenous manner near CP 80 than at CP 40. The values of fear and desire parameters both vary between the values: 0, 0.25, 0.5, 0.75, and 1. Being a part of the decision making formula, these values influence the creatures' decision making process of whether or not to cross. If Horiz. Cre. $= 1$, the creatures can change their crossing point. If Horiz. Cre. $= 0$, they cannot.

If in each traffic environment with a given Car Prob. value, the KnB is built from "tabula rasa" each time in each repeat, i.e. if it is built by creatures without having any preexisting knowledge in each repeat, then we call this simulation setup Framework (I). If in each traffic environment with a given Car Prob. value, the KnB tables are always transferred from the current repetition to the next one within any particular configuration of the parameters' values, then we call this Framework (II). Thus, in Framework (II) the nth repeated simulation with the same Car Prob. value always starts with the KnB table accumulated over "n–1" previous simulation repeats, i.e. each population of creatures (except the first one) has preexisting knowledge when it starts building its KnB table. The distinction between these frameworks is important as the amount of learning under each framework is different and this affects the creatures' success in crossing the highway. In Framework (II), the KnB tables become much more developed as they are transferred much more. In Framework (II), for each given value of Car Prob. the KnB tables are built by several populations of creatures, depending on a number of considered repeats. The KnB Transf. parameter varies from: "none", "forward", and "backward". It determines for the initial CP whether or not the KnB table at the end of one run of the simulation with a given Car Prob. value is transferred to the beginning of the simulation with a different Car Prob. value. This applies to both frameworks. When KnB Transf. is set to "none", the KnB table is not transferred from an environment with a given Car Prob. value to the environment with immediately higher or lower Car Prob. value. When KnB Transf. is set to "forward" ("backward"), the KnB table is transferred from a traffic environment with lower (higher) Car Prob. value to the one with immediately higher (lower) Car Prob. value. In this case, the simulations start in the environment with Car Prob. 0.1 (or 0.9) and with KnB table containing all entries of 0 at the beginning of each repeat under Framework (I), and under Framework (II) only at the beginning of the first repeat. Thus, the simulations with Car Prob. equal to 0.9 (or 0.1) start with the KnB accumulated over the other four less dense (denser) traffic environments.

4   Effects of Model Parameters on Creatures Success

We present selected simulation results showing the effects of creatures' fear, desire and accumulation of knowledge on their success of crossing a single-lane unidirectional traffic highway under various car traffic density conditions, characterised by Car Prob. values. The creatures' performance is measured by the mean number of successful (the focus of this paper), queued and killed creatures at simulation end. We consider the case when creatures are not allowed to change their CP and when they are allowed to change it. Our focus is on interaction plots.

An interaction plot is a multiple line plot [16] where each line/graphs corresponds to a different level of a factor. Given two factors, it has the levels of one factor on the x-axis and the average of the response variable by the treatment combinations of the two factors on the y-axis, so the multiple lines/graphs correspond the levels of the second factor. Interaction exists between these two variables if the lines/graphs follow a different shape [16]. For example, they may intersect, or converge, or diverge.

The presented work shows selected interaction plots for the simulation data of each framework partition into groups split by the combinations of KnB Transf. and Horiz. Cre. parameters. In each figure the plots are organized by rows and columns, as follows: (1) "Horiz. Cre. = 0", the first column; (2) "Horiz. Cre. = 1", the second column; (3) "KnB Transf. = none", the first row; (4) "KnB Transf. = forward", the second row; (5) "KnB Transf. = backward", the third row. The mean number of successful creatures' interaction plots for values of Car. Prob. and fear factors, using Framework (I) data, split by KnB Transf. and Horiz. Cre. combinations, are displayed in Fig. 1 and using Framework (II) data, with the same type of split, are displayed in Fig. 2. The mean number of successful creatures' interaction plots for values of desire and fear factors, using Framework (II) data, split by KnB Transf. and Horiz. Cre. combinations, are displayed in Fig. 3. The displayed figures illustrate in a synthetic way how various factors (KnB Transf., Horiz. Cre., Car. Prob. fear, desire) and their interactions affect the numbers of successful creatures.

We observe on these figures that the non-zero value of fear drastically reduces number of successful creatures when they cannot move to a different CP, regardless of Car. Prob. value, the left columns of Figs. 1 and 2. The higher the value of fear is the less successful the creatures are. This is most likely because some fearful creature is jamming the queue for too long, preventing the other ones from crossing. When creatures are allowed to move to different CPs the non-zero values of fear factor have less negative impact on creatures' numbers of successful crossings, the right columns of Figs. 1 and 2. In the case when creatures can change the CP, with more learning and with more accumulation of the knowledge (i.e., with more transferring of KnB) the negative effect of the non-zero values of fear on creatures' numbers of successful crossings diminishes, compare the right columns of Figs. 1 and 2.

Under Framework (II), regardless of the KnB transfer type, the negative effect of the non-zero values of fear on creatures' success of crossing the highway is almost negligible when creatures are allowed to change CPs, see the right column of Fig. 2. This is not the case for both types of KnB transfers under Framework (I), see the right column of Fig. 1. This is because there is much less of KnB transferring under Framework (I), and

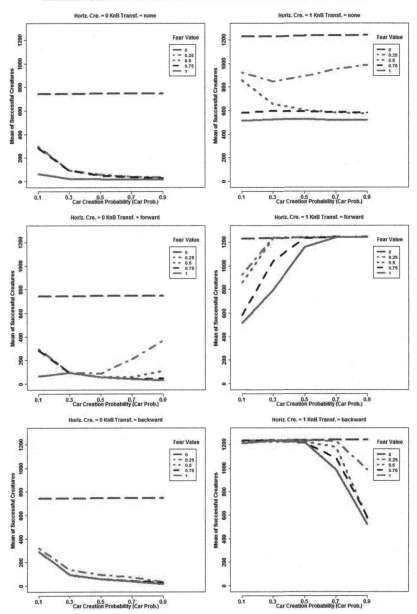

Fig. 1. Interaction plots of mean numbers of successful creatures for values of Car. Prob. and fear factors, using Framework (I) data split by KnB Transf. and Horiz. Cre. combinations

the accumulated knowledge is not strong enough to compensate fully the negative effects of the fear factor. The same phenomenon is observed in the case of the mean number of

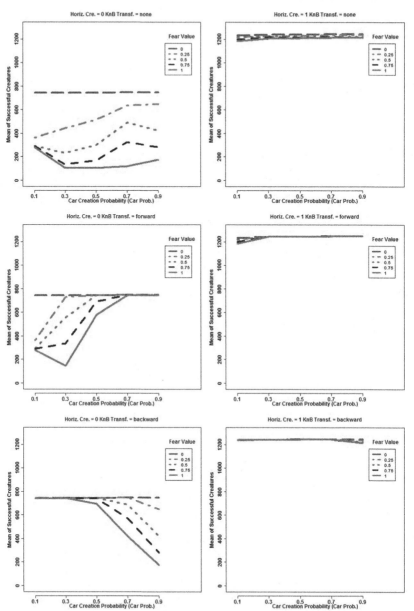

Fig. 2. Interaction plots of mean numbers of successful creatures for values of Car. Prob. and fear factors, using Framework (II) data split by KnB Transf. and Horiz. Cre. combinations

successful creatures' interaction plots for values of desire and fear factors. The interaction plots under Framework (I) are not displayed here, under Framework (II) they are displayed on Fig. 3. On this figure we observe that the fear factor has almost no negative

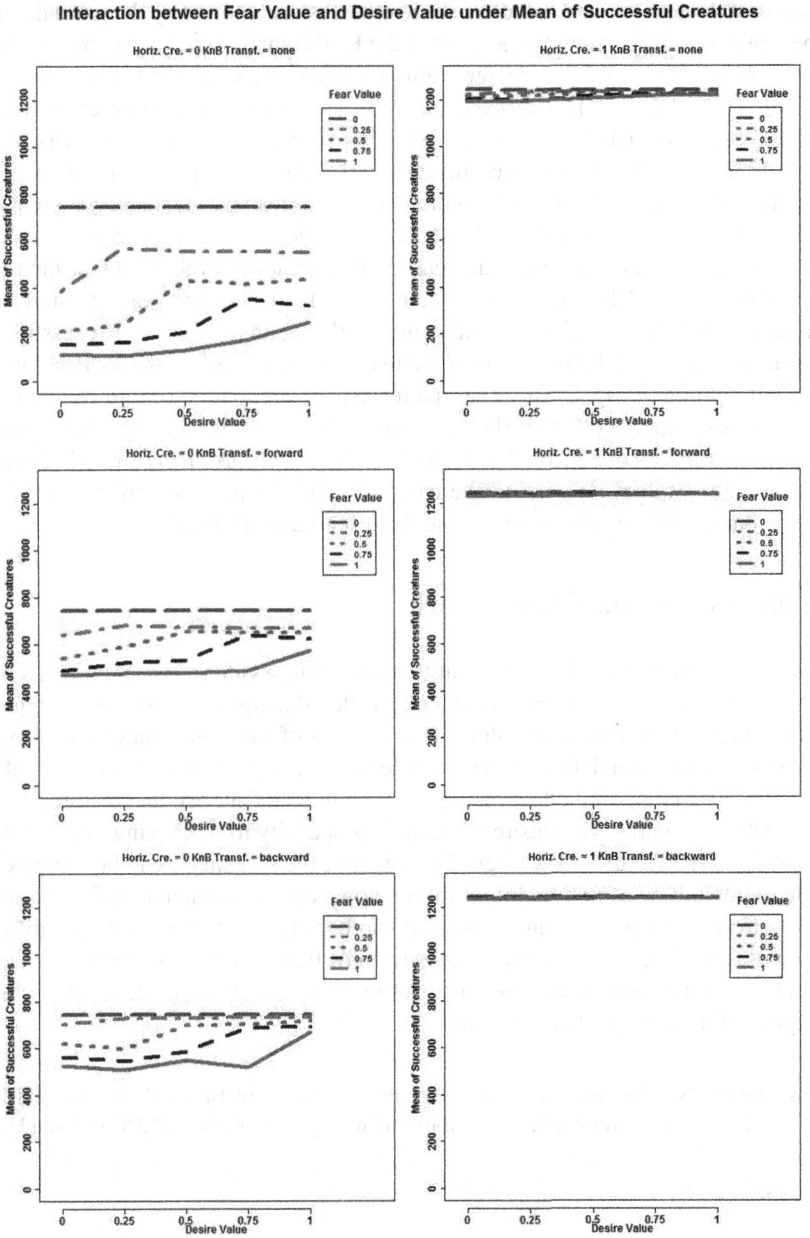

Interaction between Fear Value and Desire Value under Mean of Successful Creatures

Fig. 3. Interaction plots of mean numbers of successful creatures for values of desire and fear factors, using Framework (II) data split by KnB Transf. and Horiz. Cre. combinations

impact on the mean number of successful creatures when "Horiz. Cre. = 1", see the right column. However, this is not the case when creatures are not allowed to move to a different CP, i.e. when "Horiz. Cre. = 0", see the left column of Fig. 3. In this case, regardless of the level of desire factor, the fear values monotonically decrease the mean numbers of successful creatures and none of the KnB transfer types can compensate this negative effect of the fear factor under Framework (II). In the case of Framework (I) the degrading effect of the fear factor on the numbers of successful creatures is even stronger. The same phenomenon holds true, when creatures are not allowed to move to a different CP, for the mean number of successful creatures' interaction plots for values of Car Prob. and fear factors, see the left columns of Figs. 1 and 2. Under Framework (I), regardless of Car Prob. values and the KnB transfer types, the mean numbers of successful creatures are very much decreased by the non-zero values of fear factor, see left column of Fig. 1. This degrading effects of fear factor are less dramatic in the case of Framework (II). When "KnB Transf. = none", the mean numbers of successful creatures still decrease with the increases of the fear values, regardless of Car Prob. values, see the left column of Fig. 2. However, increase in accumulation of knowledge is able to mitigate this negative effect of the fear factor. This factor loses its degrading impact on the mean numbers of successful creatures with more transferring of KnB from one environment to another one, i.e. in the cases of "KnB Transf. = forward" and "KnB Transf. = backward", as can be seen from the left column of Fig. 2.

5   Conclusions and Future Work

The presented selected results show that there is strong evidence of interactions being present among various combinations of the considered factors, as the interaction graphs follow different shapes on many plots. The strength of these interactions will require further studies. Our simulations show that the fear factor (i.e., aversion to risk taking) has a very strong degrading effect on the mean numbers of successful creatures even in the case when creatures with desires (i.e., with propensity to risk taking) are present in the population of creatures. The degrading effect of the fear factor can be mitigated by more learning and by accumulation of more knowledge, in particular, being passed by creatures from one environment to those in another one, or by considering a different decision making formula. We plan to investigate further the effects of the model factors on agents' learning success, and the effects of knowledge accumulation and transfer for other types of decision-making formulas.

Acknowledgments. The authors acknowledge the prior work of Bruno Di Stefano and Jason Ernst. A.T. Lawniczak acknowledges partial financial support from the NSERC of Canada.

References

1. Tan, Y., Zheng, Z.-Y.: Research advance in swarm robotics. Elsevier Defence Technol. **9**, 18–39 (2013)
2. Navarro, I., Matia, F.: An introduction to swarm robotics. ISRN Robotics, **13**, Article ID 608164, 10 pages (2013). Hindawi Publishing Corporation
3. Russell, S., Norvig, P.: Artificial Intelligence, A Modern Approach. Pearson Education Limited, Upper Saddle River (2014)

4. Ferber, J.: Multi-agent Systems. An Introduction to Distributed Artificial Intelligence. Addison Wesley, London (1999)
5. Bandura, A.: Social Learning Theory. Prentice Hall, Englewood Cliffs (1977)
6. Nehavin, C.L., Dautenhahn, K.: Imitation and Social Learning in Robots, Humans and Animals. Cambridge University Press, Cambridge (2007)
7. Alonso, E., d'Inverno, M., Kudenko, D., Luck, M., Noble, J.: Learning in multi-agent systems. Knowl. Eng. Rev. **16**(3), 277–284 (2001)
8. Lawniczak, A.T., Ernst, J.B., Di Stefano, B.N.: Creature learning to cross a CA simulated road. In: Sirakoulis, G.C., Bandini, S. (eds.) ACRI 2012. LNCS, vol. 7495, pp. 425–433. Springer, Heidelberg (2012)
9. Lawniczak, A.T., Ernst, J.B., Di Stefano, B.N.: Simulated naïve creature crossing a highway. Proceedia Computer Science **18**, 2611–2614 (2013)
10. Lawniczak, A.T., Di Stefano, B.N., Ernst, J.B.: Software implementation of population of cognitive agents learning to cross a highway. In: Wąs, J., Sirakoulis, G.C., Bandini, S. (eds.) ACRI 2014. LNCS, vol. 8751, pp. 688–697. Springer, Heidelberg (2014)
11. Lawniczak, A.T., Di Stefano, B.N., Ernst, J.B.: Naïve creature learns to cross a highway in a simulated CA-like environment, 2014 IEEE Symposium on Intelligent Agents (IA), Orlando, FL, 09–12 December 2014, pp. 30–37 (2014)
12. Nagel, K., Schreckenberg, M.: A cellular automaton model for freeway traffic. J. Physique I **2**(12), 2221–2229 (1992)
13. Lawniczak, A.T., Di Stefano, B.N.: Development of CA model of highway traffic. In: Adamatzky, A., Alonso-Sanz, R., Lawniczak, A., Martinez, G.J., Morita, K., Worsch, T. (eds.) Automata-2008, Theory and Applications of Cellular Automata. Luniver Press, New York (2008)
14. Lawniczak, A.T., Di Stefano, B.N.: Multilane single GCA-w based expressway traffic model. In: Bandini, S., Manzoni, S., Umeo, H., Vizzari, G. (eds.) ACRI 2010. LNCS, vol. 6350, pp. 600–612. Springer, Heidelberg (2010)
15. Lawniczak, A.T., Di Stefano, B.N.: Digital laboratory of agent-based highway traffic model. Acta Physica Polonica B Proceedings Supplement **3**(2), 479–493 (2010)
16. Dean, A., Voss, D.: Design and Analysis of Experiments. Springer Science + Business Media, Inc., New York (1999)

Probabilistic Binary Classification with Use of 2D Cellular Automata

Miroslaw Szaban$^{(\boxtimes)}$

Institute of Computer Science,
Siedlce University of Natural Sciences and Humanities, Siedlce, Poland
mszaban@uph.edu.pl

Abstract. In this paper are presented wide known classification methods modified from almost deterministic into probabilistic forms. The rule for the classification problem designed by Fawcett, known as $n4\_V1\_nonstable$ is modified into two proposed forms partially ($n4\_V1\_nonstable\_PP$) and fully probabilistic ($n4\_V1\_nonstable\_FP$). The effectiveness of classifications of these three methods is analysed and compared. The classification methods are used as the rules in the two-dimensional three-state cellular automaton with the von Neumann and Moore neighbourhood. Preliminary experiments show that probabilistic modification of Fawcett's method can give better results in the process of reconstruction (classification) than the original algorithm.

Keywords: Cellular automaton · Binary classification · Reconstruction · Nondeterministic methods

1 Introduction

A cellular automaton (CA) is a discrete, dynamical system consisted of identical cells arranged in a regular grid, in one or more dimensions [9]. A two-dimensional CA considered in this paper is a rectangular grid of cells. Each cell can take one of a finite number of states and has an identical arrangement of local connections with other cells called a neighbourhood, which also includes the cell itself. After determining initial states of all cells (an initial configuration of a CA), states of cells are updated synchronously at discrete time steps, according to a local rule defined on a neighbourhood. In this paper is considered finite CA with the periodic boundary conditions. There are many possible variations on this basic CAs concept including other types of rules (e.g. totalistic, probabilistic), but in this paper are used rules based on methods of classification like the Fawcett's [1] $n4\_V1\_nonstable$ method, and new proposed modifications. Above rules are applied to the rectangular grid with both neighbourhood types i.e. von Neumann and Moore.

Despite the fact that CAs have the potential to efficiently perform complex computations; the main problem is a difficulty of designing CAs which would behave in the desired way. One must not only select a neighborhood type and size, but most importantly the appropriate rule (or rules). In some applications of CAs one can design an appropriate rule by hand (e.g. the GKL rule designed

© Springer International Publishing Switzerland 2016
S. El Yacoubi et al. (Eds.): ACRI 2016, LNCS 9863, pp. 456–465, 2016.
DOI: 10.1007/978-3-319-44365-2_45

in 1978 by Gacs, Kurdyumov and Levin for density classification task [2]) or can use partial differential equations describing a given phenomenon [5]. Since the number of possible rules is usually huge, this is the extremely hard task, and it is not always possible to select them by hand. Therefore, in the 90-ties of the last century Mitchell et al. proposed to use GAs to find CAs rules able to perform one-dimensional density classification task [3]. The results obtained in [3] showed that the GA was able to discover CAs rules demonstrating emergent computational strategies. The literature shows many examples concerning the concept of generating CAs rules using artificial evolution.

In a classification problem, we wish to determine to which class new observations belong, based on the training set of data containing observations whose class is known. The binary classification deals with only two classes, whereas in a multi-class classification observations belong to one of the several classes. The well-known classifiers are neural networks, support vector machines, k-NN algorithm, decision trees, and others. The idea of using CAs in the classification problem was described by Maji et al. [4], Povalej et al. [7] and recently by Fawcett [1]. Fawcett designed the heuristic rule based on the von Neumann neighborhood (so-called voting rule) moreover, tested its performance on different data sets. Recently, GA was considered as a tool to select CA rules with von Neumann neighbourhood for binary classification problem by Piwonska et al. [6].

In this paper are proposed two modifications of Fawcett's rule into a probabilistic form of such method. The effectiveness of the modified rules is compared with the effectiveness of the original Favcett's rule for two neighbourhoods von Neumann and Moore.

This paper is organized as follows. Section 2 describes two-dimensional CAs and binary classification problem. In Sect. 3 are proposed new CA-based classifier as a modification of the Favcett's rule. Experimental results are presented in Sect. 4. The last section contains conclusions and future work plans.

2 Two-Dimensional Cellular Automata and Binary Classification Problem

A two-dimensional CA consists of a rectangular grid of $N \times M$ cells, each of which can take on k possible states. After determining initial states of all cells (i.e. the initial configuration of a CA), each cell changes its state according to a rule - transition function TF which depends on states of cells in a neighborhood around it. This is usually done synchronously, although asynchronous mode is used too. Two types of the neighborhood are commonly used: the von Neumann neighborhood (the four cells orthogonally surrounding the central cell) and the Moore one (the eight cells around the central cell).

The evolution of a CA with the von Neumann neighborhood can be described by Eq. 1:

$$a_{i,j}^{(t+1)} = TF[a_{i,j-1}^{(t)}, a_{i-1,j}^{(t)}, a_{i,j}^{(t)}, a_{i+1,j}^{(t)}, a_{i,j+1}^{(t)}], \tag{1}$$

where $a_{i,j}^{(t)}$ denotes the state of a cell at position i, j in the two-dimensional cellular grid, at time step t, and with the Moore neighborhood can be described by Eq. 2:

$$a_{i,j}^{(t+1)} = TF[a_{i-1,j-1}^{(t)}, a_{i,j-1}^{(t)}, a_{i+1,j-1}^{(t)}, a_{i-1,j}^{(t)}, a_{i,j}^{(t)}, a_{i+1,j}^{(t)}, a_{i-1,j+1}^{(t)}, a_{i,j+1}^{(t)}, a_{i+1,j+1}^{(t)}].$$
(2)

The evolution of a CA is usually presented using so-called 'space-time diagrams' displaying grid of cells at subsequent time steps, with each state marked with different color.

2.1   Binary Classification Problem and Cellular Automata

The square state of the data space in classification problem should be i.e. $[0,1] \times [0,1]$. Suppose that $N \times M$ data-points $p_{(i,j)} = (x_i, y_j)$, where $i = 1, 2, ..., N$ and $j = 1, 2, ..., M$ are given as a training set from two classes: class 1 and class 2. When each of $p_{(i,j)}$ data-points is known as one of two classes then we have the classification. On the other hand, when even one of the data-points is not one of two known classes we have the classification problem. Moreover, to answer the question, what kind of class 1 or class 2 are unclassified data points it should be applied one of known the classification method or created a new one, as in this paper. In CA the data space of such problem should be mapped from $[0,1] \times [0,1]$ into the grid of $N \times M$ cells, in this paper into the grid of $N \times N$ for the simplicity. Each of cells can take one of 3 states, classified the state 1 (class 1) and state 2 (class 2) and also unclassified state (class 0). Classifier - the rule of CA will analyze the unclassified cells and changes its states into one of two known states 1 or 2.

3   Proposed CA-based Classifier

The classification problem described in [1] is the base of this paper. The rule of CA known as $n4\_V1\_nonstable$ and presented there was the starting point to create a better classifier. The classification with use of the rule $n4\_V1\_nonstable$ is defined as:

– classify as *class* 0, if *class* 1 neighbors + *class* 2 neighbors = 0,
– classify as *class* 1, if *class* 1 neighbors > *class* 2 neighbors,
– classify as *class* 2, if *class* 1 neighbors < *class* 2 neighbors,
– classify as $rand(\{class\ 1, class\ 2\})$, if *class* 1 neighbors = *class* 2 neighbors.

Maybe the Fawcett's rule is productive enough for classification problems in little CA grids. This rule was presented in [1] as better than other in particular k-NN method, but it was tested and compared for only 81×81 wide CA grid it means only 6561 cells to classify. And what for the huge problems for example 800×800 and hugest, where the 640000 cells should be recovered. It will be helpful heuristic and in particular probabilistic methods. Therefore, in this paper are proposed modifications of Fawcett's rule into two patterns: partially and fully probabilistic. A proposed modification should strengthen an original and more accurate classify binary data, specially for large CA grid. Let $p(i)$ will be the probability The partially probabilistic modification ($n4\_V1\_nonstable\_PP$) of $n4\_V1\_nonstable$ rule is proposed as follows:

- classify as *class* 0, if *class* 1 neighbors + *class* 2 neighbors = 0,
- classify as *class* 1, with probability $p(1)$,
- classify as *class* 2, with probability $p(2)$,

where probability are calculated form classified neighbours in the neighbourhood, i.e.:

$$p(i) = \frac{class\ i\ neighbors}{class\ 1\ neighbors + class\ 2\ neighbors}, \quad (3)$$

where $i = \{1, 2\}$.

And the full probabilistic modification ($n4\_V1\_nonstable\_FP$) of $n4\_V1\_nonstable$ rule is proposed as follows:

- classify as *class* 0, with probability $p(0)$,
- classify as *class* 1, with probability $p(1)$,
- classify as *class* 2, with probability $p(2)$.

where probabilities are calculated form each class of neighbours in the neighbourhood, i.e.:

$$p(i) = \frac{class\ i\ neighbors}{\sum_{j=0}^{2} class\ j\ neighbors}, \quad (4)$$

where $i = \{0, 1, 2\}$.

The $n4\_V1\_nonstable$ rule presented in [1] and newly proposed modifications: $n4\_V1\_nonstable\_PP$ and $n4\_V1\_nonstable\_FP$ will be examine on the testing sets (CA grids) shown in the Fig. 1(a).

In the Fig. 1(b, c and d) one can observe a classification process of the linear goal. In the classification was used $n4\_V1\_nonstable$ rule in CA size: 100×100. In the first step (see, Fig. 1(b)), 1 % cells of known state (classified as class 1 - cells in black state or class 2 - cells in the white state) was randomly chosen from the linear goal. This initial configuration of CA was subject to the classification and the unclassified (cells in the gray state) with the use of $n4\_V1\_nonstable$ rule. Figure 1(c) presents the temporary state of CA under classification process. After the classification, the obtained result shows Fig. 1(d). The effectiveness of classification in presented example achieved level $93, 38$ % it means that 662 CA cells was badly classified from 10000 CA cells.

Effectiveness of classification process was calculated from goal and final CA state, i.e. number of CA cells with the same states from goal and final configuration divided by number of all cells in CA (in %). Suppose, the $G_{N \times M}$ is the binary matrix of the classification goal. Also, the $F_{N \times M}$ is the binary matrix of the final configuration. The $E_{N \times M} = |G_{N \times M} - F_{N \times M}|$ is the absolute difference between two matrixes. Therefore, the Effectiveness (in %) is calculated by the formula:

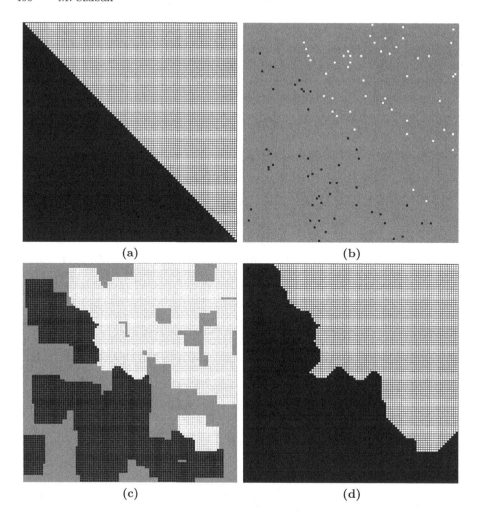

Fig. 1. Two-dimensional classification linear goal (a), and example of classification process with use of *n4_V1_nonstable* rule in CA with size 100 × 100 and linear goal: initial configuration of CA - 1 % of classified cells (b), temporary CA state - classification in progress (c), final CA state - after classification (d).

$$Effectiveness = \frac{N * M - \sum_{i=1}^{N} \sum_{j=1}^{M} e_{(i,j)}}{N * M} * 100, \qquad (5)$$

where $e_{(i,j)} \in E_{N \times M}$.

4 Experimental Results

4.1 An Analysis of the Incorrect Classifications for CA Rules

Proposed modifications of Fawcett's CA rule was tested and compared with original one. The results of analysis for the efficiency of classification are described above. During each test were used $N \times N$ CA, where $N \in \{100, 200, ..., 700, 800\}$, according to each of CA rules ($n4\_V1\_nonstable$, and newly proposed: $n4\_V1\_nonstable\_PP$, $n4\_V1\_nonstable\_FP$) with the von Neumann neighbourhood. In the goal, a 99 % random states of CA cells was changed into the unclassified. Such form of the goal was the initial configuration of CA to classification. After classification (reconstruction of goal) we obtained the finite CA state, and it was compared with the goal CA state; then the differences between both states (badly classified CA cells) and next $Effectiveness$ were calculated with the use of the upper formula.

In the Table 1 one can see the results of classification in CA with the use of the $n4\_V1\_nonstable$ (Fawcett's rule), and new proposed probabilistic modification $n4\_V1\_nonstable\_PP$, $n4\_V1\_nonstable\_FP$ with von Neumann neighbourhood for 1000 tests. Each test was started with random initial configuration with only 1 % classified CA states. We can see that the effectiveness grows with the CA size, but it only depends on the fast growing area with the same class of data where the border with the different classes is growing very slowly. The best results of classification for the different CA sizes are underlined. Also we can see marked in bold results for better from Fawcett rule and proposed probabilistic rules. We can see that the effectiveness of new proposed modifications is better than for the original Fawcett's rule. It could be observed for higher CA sizes, in particular for partially probabilistic one ($n4\_V1\_nonstable\_PP$), despite the some kind anomaly for CA size equal to 700×700. But for CA size equal to

Table 1. Classification results of goal linear set for CA rules: $n4\_V1\_nonstable$, $n4\_V1\_nonstable\_PP$, $n4\_V1\_nonstable\_FP$ with von Neumann neighbourhood. The worst effectiveness and (highest number of incorrect classified CA cells) from 1000 tests.

CA size	CA rules		
$N \times N$	$n4V1nonstable$ effect. (inc. classif.)	$n4\_V1\_nonstable\_PP$ effect. (inc. classif.)	$n4\_V1\_nonstable\_FP$ effect. (inc. classif.)
100×100	91,78 % (**822**)	91,37 % (863)	91,22 % (878)
200×200	96,58 % (**1368**)	96,48 % (1408)	96,37 % (1454)
300×300	97,72 % (2048)	97,76 % (**2017**)	97,67 % (2093)
400×400	98,38 % (2597)	98,46 % (**2466**)	98,44 % (**2500**)
500×500	98,76 % (3102)	98,78 % (**3056**)	98,77 % (**3075**)
600×600	98,99 % (3650)	99,02 % (**3546**)	98,99 % (**3645**)
700×700	99,17 % (4081)	99,14 % (4215)	99,18 % (**4040**)
800×800	99,24 % (4866)	99,27 % (**4665**)	99,26 % (**4706**)

700×700 (see, Table 1) can be observed the best result of classification for fully probabilistic classifier ($n4\_V1\_nonstable\_FP$), better than Fawcett's rule and much better than partially probabilistic one. Also in Table 1 is shown better classifications for the fully probabilistic method then the Fawcett's rule for CA size from 400 to 800.

Table 2 presents the results of classification for a linear goal in CA with the use of the $n4\_V1\_nonstable$ (Fawcett's rule), and new proposed probabilistic modification $n4\_V1\_nonstable\_PP$, $n4\_V1\_nonstable\_FP$ with Moore neighbourhood for 1000 tests. Also, only 1 % random classified CA states, in each test was an initial configuration of CA. Like for the linear goal with von Neumann neighbourhood (see, Table 1), we can see that the effectiveness grows with the CA size, but it only depends on the fast growing area with the same class of data where the border with the different classes is increasing very slowly. Almost each from presented CA sizes, for both modifications (marked in bold), in particular for partially probabilistic one ($n4\_V1\_nonstable\_PP$), characterised by better effectiveness than the original Fawcett's rule. Only for the CA size equal to 700×700 the Fawcett's rule gives better effectiveness. The underlined numbers mean the best results in general, from all analysed rules.

The observed highest effectiveness for modification of Fawcett's rule is not so spectacular, but we should interpret it from the another point of view; it means the number of incorrectly classified CA cells should be analyzed. One can see that the modifications have the lowest number of incorrectly classified CA cells than the original rule. The partially probabilistic modification ($n4\_V1\_nonstable\_PP$) for CA size 800×800 has 201 CA cells less than the original rule, it is much better because the border between two classes of data in CA is 800 cells. So, the worst effectiveness and highest number of incorrect classification presented in Table 1 shows that if the worst results for classification with use of proposed modifications are better than for the original rule, then the new classifiers are more efficient because

Table 2. Classification results of goal linear set for CA rules: $n4\_V1\_nonstable$, $n4\_V1\_nonstable\_PP$, $n4\_V1\_nonstable\_FP$ with Moore neighbourhood. The worst effectiveness and (highest number of incorrect classified CA cells) from 1000 tests.

CA size	CA rules		
$N \times N$	$n4V1nonstable$ effect. (inc. classif.)	$n4\_V1\_nonstable\_PP$ effect. (inc. classif.)	$n4\_V1\_nonstable\_FP$ effect. (inc. classif.)
100×100	90,73 % (927)	91,84 % (**816**)	91,59 % (**841**)
200×200	96,25 % (1502)	96,68 % (**1327**)	96,27 % (**1494**)
300×300	97,72 % (2052)	97,89 % (**1895**)	97,92 % (**1872**)
400×400	98,3 % (2728)	98,47 % (**2446**)	98,44 % (**2503**)
500×500	98,8 % (3012)	98,81 % (**2984**)	98,83 % (**2929**)
600×600	98,98 % (3659)	99,05 % (**3434**)	98,98 % (3669)
700×700	99,19 % (**3973**)	99,18 % (4021)	99,16 % (4108)
800×800	99,29 % (4517)	99,3 % (**4499**)	99,31 % (**4388**)

their worst classifications are much better. The same trends we can observe for the average effectiveness and average number of incorrect classifications.

4.2   An Analysis of the Scattering Ranges for Incorrect Classifications for CA Rules

The scattering range is the difference between the highest number of incorrect classifications and the lowest number of incorrect classification. The scattering

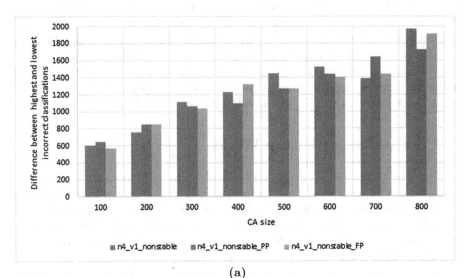

(a)

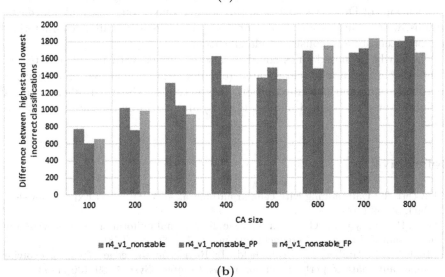

(b)

Fig. 2. Ranges of scattering for incorrect classifications for 1000 tests with a linear goal: (a) von Neumann neighbourhood, (b) Moore neighbourhood.

ranges were calculated for each analysed CA rules for linear goal with the use of both neighbourhoods von Neumann and Moore. The highest and lowest number of incorrect classifications were selected from 1000 tests for random initial configuration of CA.

We can observe in the Fig. 2 the scattering ranges for linear goal with von Neumann neighbourhood Fig. 2(a) and Moore neighbourhood Fig. 2(b). One can see in Fig. 2(a) the scattering ranges for newly proposed modified CA rules are shorter in general than for original rule, in particular for fully probabilistic modification ($n4\_V1\_nonstable\_FP$) with the use of von Neumann neighbourhood. Moreover, remembering such rule has, in general, the lowest incorrect classifications we can conclude that fully probabilistic classifier shows up the more accurate and consistent with Moore neighbourhood for the sinusoidal goal.

Similarly, in Fig. 2(b) can be observed in general the shortest scattering ranges for proposed modification in particular for partially probabilistic modification ($n4\_V1\_nonstable\_FP$) of CA rule with the use of Moore neighbourhood.

5 Conclusions an Future Works

In this paper was presented problem of classification with use of three-state two-dimensional cellular automaton. Among classifiers were analyzed the wide known Fawcett's rule and two proposed probabilistic modifications of such rule. The conducted experiments show the better effectiveness for classification applying a newly proposed classifiers (modifications). Moreover, the proposed modifications result in a much lower number of incorrectly classified CA cells.

Also, from Fig. 2 ensue in general the shortest scattering range for proposed modifications of Fawcett's rule than the original one. From that and above conclusions, we can understand that proposed probabilistic classifiers characterized by more accurate and consistent classification.

The newly proposed rules could be also examined with use of new testing goals like e.g.: parabolic, closed area (circular, square, concave boundary ...), sinusoidal (done and described in [8]), disjunctive ..., also with different initial configurations (unclassified number of cells) and it will be the subject of future works.

References

1. Fawcett, T.: Data mining with cellular automata. ACM SIGKDD Explor. Newslett. **10**(1), 32–39 (2008)
2. Gacs, P., Kurdyumov, G., Levin, L.: One dimensional uniform arrays that wash out finite islands. Problemy Peredachi Informatsii **12**, 92–98 (1978)
3. Mitchell, M., Hraber, P., Crutchfield, J.: Revisiting the edge of chaos: evolving cellular automata to perform computations. Complex Syst. **7**, 89–130 (1993)
4. Maji, P., Sikdar, B.K., Pal Chaudhuri, P.: Cellular automata evolution for pattern classification. In: Sloot, P.M.A., Chopard, B., Hoekstra, A.G. (eds.) ACRI 2004. LNCS, vol. 3305, pp. 660–669. Springer, Heidelberg (2004)

5. Omohundro, S.: Modelling cellular automata with partial differential equations. Physica D **10**(1–2), 128–134 (1984)
6. Piwonska, A., Seredynski, F., Szaban, M.: Learning cellular automata rules for binary classification problem. J. Supercomput. **63**(3), 800–815 (2013)
7. Povalej, P., Lenič, M., Kokol, P.: Improving ensembles with classificational cellular automata. In: Gallagher, M., Hogan, J.P., Maire, F. (eds.) IDEAL 2005. LNCS, vol. 3578, pp. 242–249. Springer, Heidelberg (2005)
8. Szaban, M.: Probabilistic 2D cellular automata rules for binary classification. In: 12th Federated Conference on Computer Science and Information Systems - FedCSIS, (in print) (2016)
9. Wolfram, S.: A New Kind of Science. Wolfram Media, Champaign (2002)

Author Index

Printed in the United States
By Bookmasters